PEARSON
HEALTH »

Pruitt, Allegrante, Prothrow-Stith

Master essential health skills with these new features!

Updated highlights include

- Information on school violence

- MyPlate Food Guide

- Current information on building healthy relationships, including dating and online friendships

- Health and Human Services: Healthy People 2020 Goals

- Digital Courseware, including eTexts and online resources

- Up-to-date statistics and data throughout the program

Glenview, Illinois • Boston, Massachusetts • Chandler, Arizona • Upper Saddle River, New Jersey

ALWAYS LEARNING   PEARSON

PEARSON
HEALTH »»

Print Resources
- Student Edition
- Teacher's Edition
- Reading and Note Taking Guide
- Answer Key for Reading and Note Taking Guides
- Human Sexuality
- Human Sexuality, Teacher's Edition

Technology Resources

Media Resources
- Discovery Education™ Teens Talk Video Series DVDs
- ExamView® Test Generator CD-ROM

Digital Courseware on PearsonSuccessNet.com
- Student Edition and Teacher's Edition eTexts*
- Human Sexuality Student Edition and Teacher's Edition eTexts*

  *Available for PC, Mac, iPad with iOS 5 or greater, and Android tablets with Android OS 3.1 or greater

Editable Resources
- Teaching Resources:
  - Lesson Plans
  - Letter to Parents
  - Practice and Enrichment Worksheets
  - Section Quizzes
  - Chapter Tests
  - Answer Keys

- Reading and Note Taking Guide —English and Spanish
- Adapted Reading and Note Taking Guide
- Video Viewing Guide With Worksheets—English and Spanish

Presentation Materials
- Image Bank With Editable Worksheets
- Chapter PowerPoint® Presentations, including Warm-Ups and Building Health Skills

Audio and Video Resources
- Discovery Education™ Teens Talk Videos
- Audio Section Summaries—English and Spanish

Online Activities
- Web Links
- Chapter Review Activities
- Skills for Physical Fitness Worksheets

Additional Material
- Teacher Online Access Pack

Acknowledgments appear on p. 780, which constitutes an extension of this copyright page.

ISBN-13: 978-0-13-327030-3
ISBN-10: 0-13-327030-0

3 4 5 6 7 8 9 10   V082   18 17 16 15 14

B. E. Pruitt

B. E. Pruitt, Ed.D., is Professor of Health Education at Texas A&M University. He served as executive director of the American Association for Health Education, and was the editor of the *American Journal of Health Education*. He has received numerous professional honors, including two National Professional Service Awards and the "Scholar" Award from the American Association for Health Education.

John P. Allegrante

John P. Allegrante, Ph.D., is Professor of Health Education and Deputy Provost at Teachers College and Adjunct Professor of Public Health in Sociomedical Sciences at Columbia University. A past president and Distinguished Fellow of the Society for Public Health Education, he is editor-in-chief of *Health Education & Behavior*. He received the Distinguished Career Award in Public Health Education and Health Promotion from the American Public Health Association.

Deborah Prothrow-Stith

Deborah Prothrow-Stith, M.D., is a Consultant with Spencer Stuart and Adjunct Professor of Practice at Harvard School of Public Health. As former Massachusetts Public Health Commissioner, she expanded HIV and substance abuse services. She is nationally recognized for her leadership in addressing violence as a public health problem and for her books *Murder Is No Accident* and *Sugar and Spice and No Longer Nice*.

Content Reviewers

Amanda S. Birnbaum, Ph.D., M.P.H.
Weill Medical College
Cornell University
New York, New York

Marla R. Brassard, Ph.D.
Teachers College
Columbia University
New York, New York

Loretta Brewer, M.S.W., Ph.D.
Arkansas State University
Jonesboro, Arkansas

Elizabeth Coolidge-Stolz, M.D.
North Reading, Massachusetts

Jena Curtis, Ed.D.
State Unversity of New York
    College at Cortland
Cortland, New York

Jean DeSaix, Ph.D.
Department of Biology
University of North Carolina
Chapel Hill, North Carolina

Ralph J. DiClemente, Ph.D.
Rollins School of Public Health
Emory University
Atlanta, Georgia

Joseph R. DiFranza, M.D.
Department of Family Medicine
University of Massachusetts Medical School
Worcester, Massachusetts

Theodore C. Dumas, Ph.D.
Institute of Neuroscience
University of Oregon
Eugene, Oregon

Timothy E. Fenlon, M.D.
Clemson University
Clemson, South Carolina

Carl I. Fertman, Ph.D., CHES
University of Pittsburgh
Pittsburgh, Pennsylvania

Elizabeth M. Ginexi, Ph.D.
National Institute on Drug Abuse
Bethesda, Maryland

Dawn Graff-Haight, Ph.D., CHES
Department of Health, Human
    Performance and Athletics
Linfield College
McMinnville, Oregon

**Molly Green, Kristen McCausland,
    Katherine Wunderink**
American Legacy Foundation
Washington, D.C.

Mary Fran Hazinski, R.N., M.S.N.
Vanderbilt Children's Hospital
Nashville, Tennessee

Richard A. Jenkins, Ph.D.
Centers for Disease Control and
    Prevention
Atlanta, Georgia

Jerome Kotecki, Ph.D.
Department of Physiology and
    Health Science
Ball State University
Muncie, Indiana

Lori Lange, Ph.D.
Department of Psychology
University of North Florida
Jacksonville, Florida

Christopher M. Ledingham, M.P.H., CHES
Texas A&M University
College Station, Texas

Bruce Lubotsky Levin, Ph.D., M.P.H.
Louis de la Parte Institute
College of Public Health
University of South Florida
Tampa, Florida

Marylin Lisowski, Ph.D.
Eastern Illinois University
Charleston, Illinois

Kim MacInnis, Ph.D.
Department of Sociology
Bridgewater State College
Bridgewater, Massachusetts

James P. Marshall, Ph.D.
Utah State University
Logan, Utah

Jennifer McLean, M.S.P.H., CHES
Pennsylvania College of Technology
Williamsport, Pennsylvania

Angela D. Mickalide, Ph.D., CHES
Home Safety Council
Washington, D.C.

Linda Ponder, M.A.
Department of Health Policy and
    Management
Texas A&M University
College Station, Texas

Janet F. Pope, Ph.D.
School of Human Ecology
Louisiana Tech University
Ruston, Louisiana

David L. Reid, Ph.D.
Blackburn College
Carlinville, Illinois

Glenn E. Richardson, Ph.D.
Department of Health Promotion and
    Education
University of Utah
Salt Lake City, Utah

Richard W. Robins, Ph.D.
Department of Psychology
University of California, Davis
Davis, California

Rochelle D. Schwartz-Bloom, Ph.D.
Department of Pharmacology and
    Cancer Biology
Duke University Medical Center
Durham, North Carolina

Arturo Sesma, Jr., Ph.D.
Search Institute
Minneapolis, Minnesota

David Shaffer, M.D.
Columbia University College of Physicians
    and Surgeons
New York, New York

Edward J. Zalisko, Ph.D.
Department of Biology
Blackburn College
Carlinville, Illinois

Teacher Reviewers

Mike Code
Highlands High School
Fort Thomas, Kentucky

Elizabeth J. Godwin
Cape Coral High School
Cape Coral, Florida

Diane Henson
Conway High School East
Conway, Arkansas

Margo Jones
Taylorsville High School
Taylorsville, Utah

Charles Muller
Ida Baker High School
Cape Coral, Florida

Brenda Pasek
Melbourne High School
Melbourne, Florida

Jason A. Perch
Eisenhower High School
Blue Island, Illinois

Joanne Ray
G. Ray Bodley High School
Fulton, New York

Kathleen St. Laurent, R.N., M.S.N.
Coyle and Cassidy High School
Taunton, Massachusetts

Jerry D. Styrsky
Thornwood High School
South Holland, Illinois

Cristina Thyron
Prairie High School
Vancouver, Washington

Susan L. Tutko
Riverdale High School
Fort Myers, Florida

Coleen Walsh
Springfield School Department
Springfield, Massachusetts

Melissa Diane Williamson, D.P.M.
Titusville High School
Titusville, Florida

Contents

Unit 2   Social Health

TEENS Talk
Family Matters

TEENS Talk
Choosing Abstinence

TEENS Talk
Bully-Proof

Unit 3   Nutrition

TEENS Talk

Food for Thought

TEENS Talk

Goals for Healthy Eating

TEENS Talk

Feeding the Need

Unit 4   Physical Fitness

TEENS Talk

The Risks of Steroids

TEENS Talk

Living With Asthma

TEENS Talk

Fit for Life

TEENS Talk

Taking Care of You

Unit 5   Substance Abuse

TEENS Talk
Drinking Dangers

TEENS Talk
Tackling Tobacco

TEENS Talk
The Risks of Drug Abuse

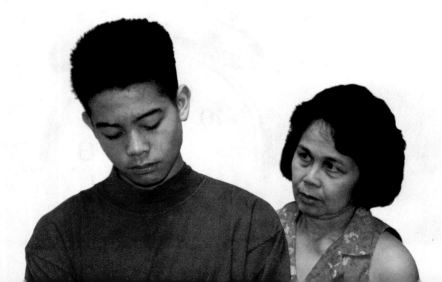

Unit 6   Human Development

TEENS Talk
Hormones in the Balance

TEENS Talk
Teen Pregnancy

TEENS Talk
Pictures of "Perfection"

Unit 7   Preventing Disease

TEENS Talk
Protection from Infection

TEENS Talk
Risks and STIs

TEENS Talk
Living With Disabilities

Unit 8   Community Health and Safety

TEENS Talk

Taking Charge
of Your Health

TEENS Talk

Making a Difference

TEENS Talk

Playing It Safe

Building Health Skills

Master essential health skills by following simple step-by-step procedures.

VIDEO

TEENS Talk

Watch and discuss how teens handle real-world issues.

Features

Media Wise

Analyze the influence of the media on the health decisions you face.

Hands-On Activity

Reinforce health concepts through hands-on experiences.

Technology & Health

Evaluate how technological advances affect personal, family, and community health.

Focus on ISSUES

Communicate your opinions about some of today's important health issues.

CAREERS

Explore a variety of health-related careers.

Online Resources

GO ONLINE PearsonSuccessNet.com

- **eText***
*(Available for PC, Mac, iPad with iOS 5 or greater, and Android tablets with Android OS 3.1 or greater)

- **Teens Talk Videos**

- **Video Viewing Guides in English and Spanish**

- **Audio Section Summaries**

- **Chapter Review Activities**

- **Web Links and Activities on Current Health Topics**

- **Focus on Issues Resources**

- **Career Resources**

- **Skills for Physical Fitness Worksheets**

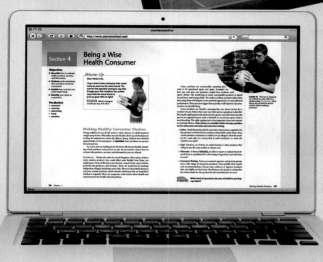

CHAPTER 1

Making Healthy Decisions

GO ONLINE PearsonSuccessNet.com

VIDEO 1

TEENS Talk

Decisions, Decisions

Preview **Activity**

How Many Decisions Do You Make?

Complete this activity before you watch the video.

1. Predict how many decisions you make in an hour during a typical day.

2. List all the decisions you made today from the time you woke up until the time you arrived at school.

3. Select one decision from your list and describe the process you used to make that decision. **WRITING**

What Is Health?

Objectives

▶ **Describe** two factors that can be used to evaluate overall health.

▶ **List** three aspects of overall health.

▶ **Explain** how the choices that people make can affect their positions on the health continuum.

Vocabulary

- health
- life expectancy
- quality of life
- goal
- physical health
- mental health
- emotional health
- social health
- continuum
- wellness

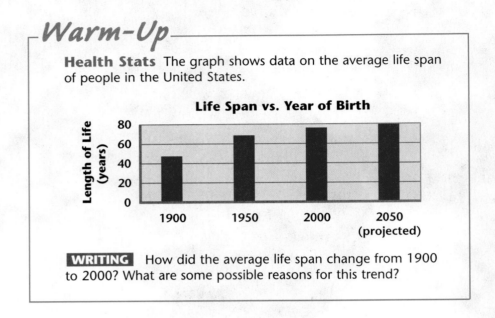

Warm-Up

Health Stats The graph shows data on the average life span of people in the United States.

Life Span vs. Year of Birth

Length of Life (years)

WRITING How did the average life span change from 1900 to 2000? What are some possible reasons for this trend?

Health Today

In the past, if you didn't have an illness, you were considered healthy. Today, the term *health* no longer means just the absence of illness. Instead, **health** refers to the overall well-being of your body, your mind, and your relationships with other people. **Two factors that can be used to evaluate health are life expectancy and quality of life.**

Life Expectancy   At the time when your great-grandparents lived, it was quite an accomplishment for a person to survive until age 50. Today, most people live well beyond age 50. The number of years a person can expect to live is called **life expectancy.** In the United States, life expectancy increased by 30 years between 1900 and 2000. Some reasons for this increase were better healthcare, nutrition, sanitation, and working conditions.

Quality of Life   Two women are born in the same year. One woman is physically active and mentally alert throughout her life. She has close relationships with family and friends. The other woman has a series of health problems during her life that reduces her ability to enjoy life. Although the women have the same life expectancy, they have a different quality of life. **Quality of life** is the degree of overall satisfaction that a person gets from life. For many people, a high quality of life is one of their goals. A **goal** is a result that a person aims for and works hard to reach.

Aspects of Health

To achieve a high quality of life, a person cannot concentrate on only one aspect of health. Instead, the person must work hard to improve all aspects of health. **The aspects of health that are important to overall well-being are physical health, mental and emotional health, and social health.**

Physical Health   Do you have enough energy to go to school, enjoy your spare time, and take care of your responsibilities at home? If so, your physical health is probably good. **Physical health** refers to how well your body functions. When you are physically healthy, you are able to carry out everyday tasks without becoming overly tired. A healthy diet, regular exercise, adequate sleep, and proper medical and dental care are all important for physical health.

Mental and Emotional Health   The state of being comfortable with yourself, with others, and with your surroundings is called **mental health.** When you are mentally healthy, your mind is alert, you can learn from your mistakes, and you recognize your achievements. **Emotional health** refers to how you react to events in your life. You are emotionally healthy when the feelings you experience are appropriate responses to events. To maintain your emotional health, you need to take the time to relax, and you need to share your feelings with others.

Social Health   Being able to make and keep friends is one sign of social health. **Social health** refers to how well you get along with others. When you are socially healthy, you have loving relationships, respect the rights of others, and give and accept help. Building healthy relationships with family and friends is important for social health. So is communicating your needs to others. But good social health doesn't just happen. You have to work at it by getting involved with others at school and in your community, and perhaps most importantly, by building strong relationships with members of your family.

FIGURE 1   All aspects of health are equally important. They "fit" together like the pieces of a puzzle. A problem in one area can affect other areas. **Evaluating** How would you rate your overall physical, emotional, and social health?

Social Health

Physical Health

Mental and Emotional Health

Hands-On *Activity*

Health in the Balance

In this activity you will create a mobile that balances the three aspects of health.

Materials
cardboard • scissors • pen or pencil
magazines • glue • string • tape

Try This

❶ Cut out a cardboard triangle that is 8 inches on each side. Label the sides of the triangle "Physical Health," "Mental and Emotional Health," and "Social Health."

❷ Carefully punch a small hole through the center of the triangle. Thread a piece of string through the hole, then tie a knot.

❸ Cut pictures from magazines that show healthy activities.

❹ Glue each picture onto cardboard. Use string and tape to attach each picture to the appropriate side of the triangle.

❺ Hang the mobile from the center string to see how well it balances.

Think and Discuss

❶ Describe each of the activities in your mobile and explain how it contributes to physical, social, or mental and emotional health.

❷ How well did the mobile balance? In your life, are your physical, social, mental, and emotional health in balance? Explain.

❸ Describe some things you could do to improve each aspect of your overall well-being.

GO ONLINE

PearsonSuccessNet.com
For: More on assessing your health

A Continuum of Health

Suppose that someone asked you this question: "Would you say that you are in perfect health or in poor health?" How would you answer? You might not feel comfortable choosing either of these options. You might wish that you had been given some choices in between the two extremes.

Defining a Continuum Try to picture a solid line that is white at one end, then light gray, gray, dark gray, and finally black at the other end. What you have just pictured is one type of continuum. A **continuum** (kun TIN yoo um) is a gradual progression through many stages between one extreme and another. In the example of the line, the extremes are white and black and the stages are the many shades of gray in between.

A Health Continuum Figure 2 shows one model of a continuum for health. One end of the continuum represents poor health, which is often referred to as "illness." The other end represents perfect, or ideal, health, and is often referred to as "wellness." **Wellness** is a state of high-level health. Look at Figure 2 to see some characteristics that describe people at either end of the continuum. Because the continuum includes the full range of health, each person's health status would be marked by a point along the continuum.

 Connect to Your Life Where do you think you are on the health continuum and why?

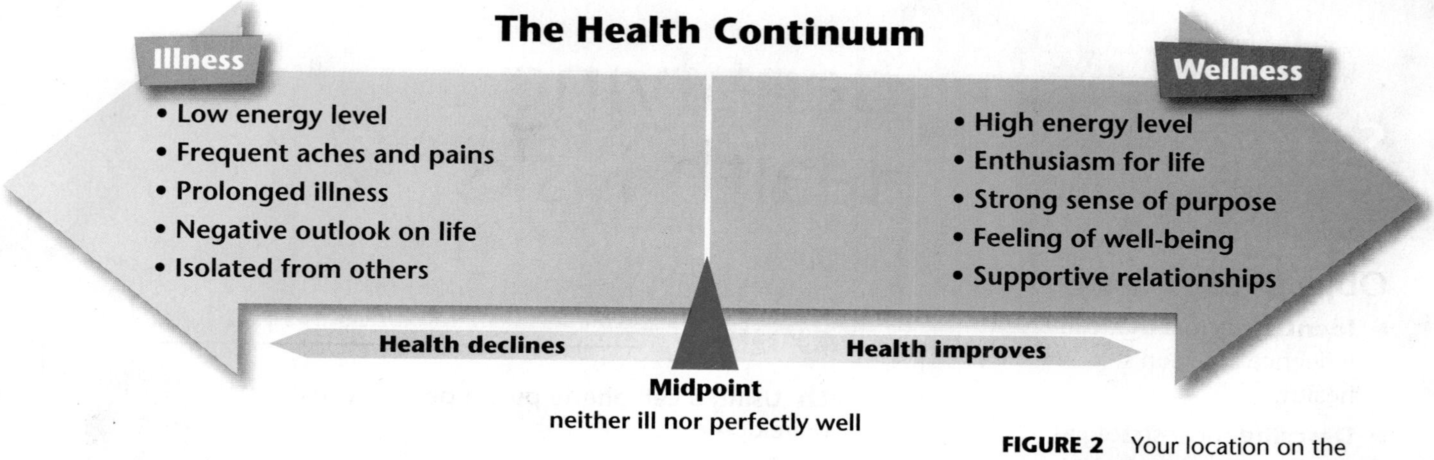

The Health Continuum

Illness

- Low energy level
- Frequent aches and pains
- Prolonged illness
- Negative outlook on life
- Isolated from others

Wellness

- High energy level
- Enthusiasm for life
- Strong sense of purpose
- Feeling of well-being
- Supportive relationships

Health declines   Health improves

Midpoint
neither ill nor perfectly well

Movement Along the Continuum   Your location on the health continuum is not constant throughout your life. You can move toward illness or you can move toward wellness.

At a point in the middle of the continuum, you are not sick, but you are not enjoying the full benefits of overall health either. At one time, many people were satisfied just to be in the middle of the continuum. They were more concerned about avoiding illness and death than about improving the quality of their lives. Today, however, achieving a higher level of health and a better quality of life is possible for most people.

Many of the choices you make on a daily basis affect your position on the health continuum. Some decisions move you closer to the illness end of the continuum. Suppose you choose to ride a bicycle without a helmet. If you are thrown from the bicycle in a crash, the result could be serious brain damage. Some decisions move you closer to the wellness end of the continuum. If you choose not to smoke, you will be less likely to develop lung cancer or heart disease later in life. You have more control over your health than you may think.

FIGURE 2   Your location on the health continuum and the direction in which you are moving are both important. **Predicting** How might deciding not to smoke affect your position on the health continuum?

Section 1 Review

Key Ideas and Vocabulary

1. Why are both life expectancy and quality of life used to evaluate overall health?

2. What are the three aspects of overall health?

3. What is a **continuum**? Describe the extremes of the health continuum.

4. How are the choices people make related to their positions on the health continuum?

Critical Thinking

5. Comparing and Contrasting What is the difference between mental health and emotional health?

Health at School

Promoting Well-Being Think of two programs that a school could offer to help improve the overall health of students and teachers. Write a paragraph explaining your ideas. **WRITING**

6. Relating Cause and Effect What are two ways you could improve your physical health? Your emotional health? Your social health?

7. Evaluating Cody eats a lot of "junk" food and doesn't get much exercise. However, he doesn't have any obvious signs of illness. Where would you place Cody on the health continuum? Explain.

Identifying Health Risks

Objectives

▶ **Identify** factors that can influence a person's health.

▶ **Describe** three strategies you can use to evaluate risk factors.

Vocabulary

- heredity
- gender
- environment
- culture
- media
- habit
- risk factor

Warm-Up

Myth Using a cell phone puts a person at risk for developing cancer.

Fact Cell phone use does not increase the risk of developing cancer. However, cell phone use while driving does greatly increase the risk of a car crash.

WRITING Where do you think people get their information about health risks? How reliable are those sources of information?

Influences on Health

Two babies are born on the same day in the same city in the United States. Which baby will live longer? Which will have a higher quality of life? To answer these questions, you would need to consider the different factors that influence a person's health. **Factors that can influence health include heredity, environment, media, technology, healthcare, and behavior.**

Heredity To some extent, your level of health is already determined at the time you are born. This is because of your **heredity,** all the traits that are passed biologically from parent to child. Traits that you inherit can affect your health. Your skin color, for example, can affect your risk of developing skin cancer. With fair skin, you have a greater likelihood of developing skin cancer than if your skin is dark. Another example is breast cancer. Some women inherit a higher risk for this disease.

Even if you inherit a risk factor, you can lower your overall risk by avoiding other risk factors. If you have fair skin, you can be sure to use sunscreen. Women who inherit a risk factor for breast cancer can choose not to smoke because smoking is another risk factor for breast cancer.

Another part of your heredity is your **gender**—whether you are male or female. Gender can influence your health because risk factors may vary between males and females.

Physical Environment The **environment** is all of the physical and social conditions that surround a person and can influence that person's health. Your physical environment includes both your outdoor and indoor surroundings. The quality of the air you breathe and the water you drink are important to your health. So is your exposure to disease-causing organisms, to loud noise, and to radiation from the sun and other sources.

Being aware of potential risks in your physical environment can help you protect your health. If you know that breathing in the smoke exhaled by a smoker increases your risk of lung cancer, you can try to avoid second-hand smoke. If you know that loud noises damage your hearing, you may be more likely to keep your music at less-than-harmful levels.

Social Environment Your social environment includes the people you spend time with—your family, friends, classmates, and other people in your community. Most people learn their first basic health lessons from their family. Wash your hands before you eat. Brush your teeth before going to bed. Look both ways before crossing the street. Family members also can have a major influence on your mental and emotional health.

Your friends can influence your health in many ways. Friends who take too many risks can put a lot of pressure on you to do the same. Your social environment is healthier when you choose friends who show concern for their own health and yours.

Culture A person's culture is part of his or her social environment. **Culture** is the beliefs and patterns of behavior that are shared by a group of people and passed from generation to generation. The group may be a nation, a region of a country, or an ethnic group. Some aspects of culture can influence your health. One example is the foods you choose to eat. In some cultures people eat little or no meat; in others, meat is the main part of the diet. Another example is the way you show your emotions. In some cultures, public displays of emotion are typical; in others, people tend to keep their emotions private.

Connect to Your Life How do your friends affect your physical, emotional, and social health?

FIGURE 3 Your physical and social environments, including culture, influence your health.
Relating Cause and Effect Use the examples in the photographs to explain how the environment could affect a person's health.

Physical Environment

Social Environment

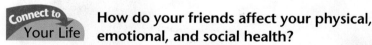

Culture

Media How much time each week do you spend watching television, listening to music, playing video games, or going to the movies? Do you read magazines or newspapers? What all these activities have in common is that they involve media. **Media** are forms of communication that provide news and entertainment. You may not realize that media can have a positive or negative influence on your health.

Think about television, for example. An average teen spends about 20 hours a week watching television. How can television have a positive influence on your health? You might receive useful information from a public service announcement or from a news report on a health topic. You might learn about a medical issue from a television series or talk show.

How can television have a negative influence on your health? The hours you spend in front of the television are hours that you are not exercising. You also are not relating to other family members or taking part in community projects. Some characters on television shows may be poor role models who indulge in risky behavior. Advertisers may present misleading claims about health products they want you to buy.

Technology Advances in technology help doctors to detect health problems sooner and improve the quality of life for patients. Many people use sites on the Internet to learn about health topics that interest them. This approach requires caution and good judgment. Some Web sites provide accurate information about health. Others are filled with misleading or self-serving information. Be sure to consider the source of the information on a Web site and the purpose of the site. What is the goal of the people posting the information, and what are their qualifications?

Spending many hours on the computer also limits the time for other activities, such as exercise. If you use the computer to meet new people, there is the risk that you will connect with someone dangerous.

FIGURE 4 The photographs show different influences on health. **Relating Cause and Effect** Use the examples in the photographs to explain how media, technology, healthcare, and behavior can affect a person's health.

Media

Technology

Healthcare Your health is influenced by the healthcare that is available to you and your family. Healthcare includes the medical services provided by doctors, nurses, dentists, and therapists. Healthcare also includes the places these people work, such as clinics and hospitals.

Some factors increase the likelihood that a person will take advantage of available healthcare. The service must be in a location that is easy to get to. The service should be open on weekends or evenings for people who can't take time off from work. Finally, people need some form of health insurance so that they can afford the costs of necessary checkups and treatments, including medicines.

Behavior Suppose that a friend came up to you and said, "A group of us are going swimming tonight at the lake after dark. Be ready at eight—I'll pick you up." What would you do? Would you go along without giving things a second thought? Or would you stop and think about the risks involved? Of all the influences on your health, the decisions you make and the actions you take often have the greatest impact on your health.

Sometimes behaviors become habits. A **habit** is a behavior that is repeated so often that it becomes almost automatic. For example, you may have a habit of brushing your teeth after meals. That is a healthy habit because it helps prevent tooth decay and gum disease. You may also have a habit of staying up late watching television. That is not a healthy habit because it reduces the number of hours available for sleep. When you lose sleep, it is difficult to concentrate the next day. A repeated lack of sleep can make it hard for your body to fight off an illness or repair an injury.

Unhealthy habits can be broken. When you find that you keep repeating a behavior that may threaten your health, you can set a goal to change your behavior. Your goal should include a plan for changing your habit. Such a plan often works best when you involve friends or family members for support.

Connect to Your Life Why do you think that teenagers tend to take more risks than any other age group?

Behavior

Healthcare

NO JUMPING, DIVING OR SWIMMING FROM DOCK

FIGURE 5 Spending time outside on a sunny day could increase a person's risk of developing skin cancer. **Observing** Which risk factor for skin cancer can this person control? Which risk factor can't he control?

GO ONLINE

PearsonSuccessNet.com
For: More on risk factors

Evaluating Health Risks

Should you try the latest fad diet to lose weight? How do you decide? One way to think about the decision is in terms of its risk factors. A **risk factor** is any action or condition that increases the likelihood of injury, disease, or other negative outcome. For example, one risk factor of a fad diet is that it may not include all the foods that your body needs.

There are three ways you can evaluate a risk factor. **Consider both short- and long-term consequences. Decide whether you can control the risk factor. Analyze the possible benefits and risks of a decision.**

Short- and Long-Term Consequences Some behaviors can have an immediate effect on your health. You take a shortcut through an unfamiliar yard and end up with a nasty case of poison ivy. You don't buckle your seatbelt and get injured in a car crash.

With some risky behaviors, the consequences are not immediate. Suppose you eat a mainly fast-food diet, which is high in fats, sugar, and salt. People tell you that your diet increases your risk of developing heart disease and diabetes later in life. But you feel healthy and energetic. So why not wait until you are older to change your behavior? First, it can be very difficult to change habits that have existed for years and, even if you do change your eating habits later in life, you may not be able to repair the damage you have done to your body.

 List three of your current habits that could have negative long-term consequences.

Risk Factors You Cannot Control A friend invites you to the beach. You are worried because you have fair skin. You can't control the color of your skin or other risk factors that are part of your heredity. Nor can you control all the risk factors in your environment. For example, you may have less emotional support if someone you are close to gets ill and dies.

Risk Factors You Can Control So what risk factors can you control? You can control risk factors that are related to your behavior. For example, you can control your exposure to ultraviolet radiation in sunlight and in tanning booths, which will reduce your risk of developing skin cancer. Or you can maintain close relationships with many people. That way, if one of your relationships ends, you will still have emotional support. These are other examples of risk factors over which you have control.

▶ Your level of physical activity

▶ Your intake of fat, sugar, or salt

▶ Your use of tobacco, alcohol, and other drugs

▶ Your use of protective gear, such as seat belts

▶ Your choice of friends

You may be able to control some risk factors in your environment. For example, you can join with others in your community to find solutions for problems such as pollution or lack of open spaces.

Analyzing Benefits and Risks There is no such thing as a risk-free life. Most of the things you do involve some degree of risk. Without taking risks and trying new things, it would be impossible to grow as a person. So how can you decide which risks are worth taking and which are not? You need to weigh the risks of an action against the possible benefits.

Suppose that a friend who only has a learner's permit offers to drive you home so you won't miss your curfew. What are the risks and benefits of accepting this offer of a ride? You can use a risk-benefit chart like the one in Figure 6 to help you decide if the benefits outweigh the risks.

Analyzing Benefits and Risks

Benefits	Risks
Home before curfew	Inexperienced driver crashes car
Avoid argument with parents	Parents are angry about decision
Show confidence in friend's skills	Friend loses permit or is arrested

FIGURE 6 A risk-benefit chart can help you decide whether to accept a ride from a friend who doesn't have a license.
Making Judgments Would you accept a ride with a driver who has only a learner's permit? Why or why not?

Section 2 Review

Key Ideas and Vocabulary

1. What does the term **heredity** mean?
2. List five factors other than heredity that can influence your health.
3. What is a **habit?** Describe one healthy habit and one unhealthy habit.
4. In relation to health, how is a **risk factor** defined?
5. List three ways to evaluate a risk factor?

Critical Thinking

6. **Applying Concepts** List the risks and benefits of swimming in a lake at night with friends.

Health at Home

Identifying Health Risks Identify three risk factors that affect the health of your family. Think about risks related to heredity, environment, and behavior. Then pick one of the risk factors and describe some ways that your family could reduce this health risk. **WRITING**

7. **Evaluating** Do you think that your physical environment or your social environment is a more important influence on your health? Explain.

8. **Predicting** How could spending a lot of time playing video games have a negative influence on someone's health?

Taking Responsibility for Your Health

Objectives

▶ **Describe** the broad goals of *Healthy People 2020*.

▶ **Identify** three steps you can take to meet your personal health goals.

Vocabulary

- prevention
- values
- action plan
- advocacy
- health literacy

Warm-Up

Quick Quiz How many of these statements accurately describe your behaviors?

① I exercise at least three times a week.

② I set aside some time each day to relax.

③ I get about eight hours of sleep each night.

④ I avoid alcohol, tobacco, and other drugs.

⑤ I always wear a seat belt when riding in a car.

WRITING Make a connection between the number of "Yes" answers and how responsible you are about your health.

Healthy People 2020

A nation wants its people to be as healthy as possible. Healthy people are more productive at school and at work. Plus, the cost of caring for people once they become ill can be a burden on families, employers, and the government. For decades, the Department of Health and Human Services has led a national effort to improve health in the United States. A major focus of this effort is on **prevention**—taking action to avoid disease, injury, and other negative health outcomes.

Healthy People 2020 has four broad goals:

▶ **Increase the quality and years of healthy life**

▶ **Eliminate differences in health based on race, ethnic group, or income**

▶ **Create social and physical environments that promote good health**

▶ **Promote healthy behaviors, health development, and quality of life across all life stages**

Healthy People 2020 includes a set of specific objectives aimed at reducing risky health behaviors. Look at the graph in Figure 7. Note that the leading causes of death for young people are related to behaviors. So, one goal of Healthy People 2020 is for 92.4% of the population to use seat belts by the year 2020, which would represent a 10 percent increase over current levels of seat belt use.

Leading Causes of Death for Young People

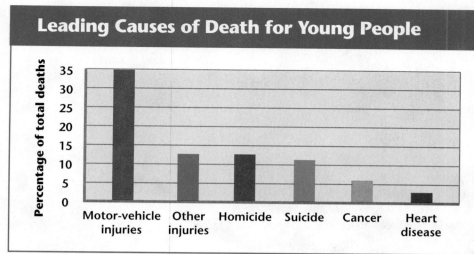

Bar graph. Y-axis: Percentage of total deaths (0, 5, 10, 15, 20, 25, 30, 35). X-axis categories: Motor-vehicle injuries, Other injuries, Homicide, Suicide, Cancer, Heart disease.

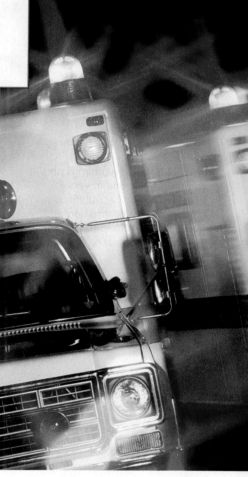

FIGURE 7 The graph shows causes of death for young people in the United States. **Interpreting Graphs** What percentage of the total deaths are due to injury or violence?

A Healthy You

You, too, can set goals to eliminate personal health risk factors. Some of your goals may match those in *Healthy People 2020.* Others may be unique to you. Some goals, such as wearing a seat belt, are easy to achieve. Others, such as cutting down on fat in your diet, may be more challenging. Whatever your target goals, your overall goal should be the same as the one set for the nation—a healthier you in 2020 and beyond. **There are three steps you can take to help you meet your personal health goals—gaining awareness, gaining knowledge, and building skills.**

Gaining Awareness You must first be able to recognize a health problem before you can do anything about it. Some problems are easy to recognize. You know, for example, when you twist your ankle or have a cold. However, other health problems, such as high blood pressure, don't have obvious signs. This is one reason why it is important to see a doctor for an annual checkup. Doctors are trained to recognize early signs of disease and to help you identify risk factors.

Gaining Knowledge Once you become aware of a health problem, the next step is to learn about the problem. This can mean learning about causes, warning signs, and possible outcomes. You also need to know how the problem can be prevented or treated. Most importantly, you need to learn about risk factors, especially those related to behavior.

Reports about new research results and health studies appear in the news all the time. Popular magazines, Web sites, and friends are some other sources of information about health. Some sources are more reliable than others. But even with reliable sources, you may see two reports on the same topic that have opposing conclusions. One goal of this book is to provide enough basic information about health so that you will be better able to evaluate new information.

Connect to Your Life What is your most common source of health information? What is your most reliable source?

FIGURE 8 This woman is on a camping trip alone in winter.
Predicting How could knowing how to access information and make decisions help to keep her safe during her trip?

GO ONLINE

PearsonSuccessNet.com
For: More on health skills

Building Health Skills Knowledge isn't very useful if you do not have the skills to apply it. What would you think of a baseball player who knew the rules of baseball but never practiced hitting a curve ball or laying down a bunt? In the same way, just knowing which behaviors are healthy isn't a guarantee of good health. You need to master the skills listed below. You will get to practice these skills throughout the year, especially in the Building Health Skills section of each chapter.

▶ **Analyzing Influences** How do you decide what foods to eat? Do you select certain foods because they are familiar from your culture? Does advertising affect your choices? Do you try foods if your friends like them? An important skill for promoting health is recognizing the influence culture, media, and friends have on your health habits.

▶ **Accessing Information** Which sources of information about health-related products and services can you trust? How do you locate a doctor or mental-health counselor in your community? To answer such questions you need to know how to find and evaluate health information.

▶ **Communicating** Being able to communicate your thoughts and feelings effectively helps you to maintain close relationships. Good communication skills allow you to resolve conflicts. They also help you express your opinions and show caring and respect for others.

▶ **Making Decisions** Making wise decisions is key to protecting your health. The DECIDE process on pages 16–17 can help you make difficult decisions. This process teaches you to identify your alternatives, think about the possible outcomes of a decision, and consider your values. Your **values** are the standards and beliefs that are most important to you.

▶ **Setting Goals** The goals you set help you translate knowledge into behavior. Once you set a goal, you can develop an **action plan**—a series of specific steps you can take to achieve the goal. The plan is like a roadmap that helps you get from where you are to where you want to go.

▶ **Practicing Healthful Behaviors** Do some of your current behaviors enhance your health? Do others place your health at risk? You need to develop strategies for maintaining healthy behaviors and reducing risky behaviors. Often, you will need to practice a new behavior repeatedly until it becomes a habit.

▶ **Advocacy** To *advocate* means to speak or write in support of a person or issue. The skill of **advocacy** involves using communication to influence and support others in making positive health decisions. For example, you can advocate for a friend who has frequent severe headaches by encouraging your friend to see a doctor. You can offer to go with your friend to the doctor's appointment. You can also advocate for changes that will make your community a healthier place to live.

Achieving Health Literacy   The term *literacy* is used to describe the ability to read and write. But the term can be applied to many areas. For example, a person with computer literacy has the knowledge and skills to use a computer. A person with **health literacy** has the ability to gather, understand, and use health information to improve his or her health.

Awareness, knowledge, and skills all contribute to health literacy. If you become aware that the amount of fat in a diet is a health concern, you can learn which foods are high in fat. Then you can apply the skills of decision making and setting goals to lower your intake of high-fat foods.

FIGURE 9 Making your community a healthier place to live is one type of advocacy. These people are growing foods in a community garden that can provide a healthier diet for their neighbors.

Section 3 Review

Key Ideas and Vocabulary

1. What does the term **prevention** mean in relation to health?

2. List the four broad goals of *Healthy People 2020*.

3. What are three steps that can help people meet their personal health goals?

4. What is an **action plan?** What health skill are you applying when you develop an action plan?

Critical Thinking

5. Relating Cause and Effect Look at the causes of death in Figure 7. For which cause of death is diving into a shallow pool a risk factor? Explain.

Health at School

Preventing Injuries One *Healthy People 2020* goal is to reduce injuries during school-sponsored sports events. The specific goal is to increase the use of protective gear for the head, face, eye, and mouth. What are the rules about using such protective gear at your school? Do these rules support the *Healthy People 2020* goal? Write a paragraph summarizing your findings. **WRITING**

6. Classifying Each day on the way to band practice, Kelsey buys a large order of French fries. Her friend Ana encourages her to buy some fruit or a low-fat energy bar instead. What health skill is Ana using? Explain your answer.

Making Decisions

The **DECIDE** Process

You just found the perfect after-school job. It's near home, it will be fun, and it will pay for the bicycle you've wanted to buy. That same day, you find out that you finally made the basketball team. Unfortunately, team practices will occur during the hours you would need to be at work. How do you choose between the team and the job?

Many of your decisions are not this complicated, but some decisions are even more difficult. Such decisions require much thought and soul-searching because they can make an important difference in your life. Do you sometimes "hide from" tough choices because they make you feel anxious? Do you ever rush headlong into decisions without really thinking? There is a process, called DECIDE, that can help you think through decisions. This process is easy to remember because each letter in the word DECIDE stands for a step in the process.

Define the problem.

Consider the decision you are facing, and state the issue clearly. Is it important or complex enough to warrant using DECIDE? Some choices are so easy that you already know what to do. In other situations, your decision won't really make much difference—a flip of a coin would do.

Explore the alternatives.

Make a list of possible alternatives for solving your problem. Include "doing nothing" if it is appropriate. If you need more information to fully understand the problem or any of the alternatives, do the research now. You may find that some of the choices are unrealistic. If so, remove them from the list.

Consider the consequences.

One by one, think through what might happen if you were to choose each alternative on your list. Be sure to do the following.

▶ Include both positive and negative results.

▶ Consider what probably would happen, not what you hope would happen.

▶ Ask yourself: How risky is each alternative? What are its chances of success? How would it affect my future? Remember to consider the effects on other people as well.

Identify your values.

Sometimes your values influence your decisions even when you are not aware of the influence. At other times, you may overlook your values because you want something badly. When you do this, however, you may feel uncomfortable with your decision later.

▶ Consider your long-term goals as well as the beliefs of your family and culture.

▶ Consider your own and others' health and safety, and your self-respect.

▶ Identify those choices that are a good match for your values.

Decide and act.

▶ Use the information you have collected to compare the alternatives. Decide which one is best for you. Remember, sometimes there is more than one "right" choice.

▶ Make a plan to act on your decision. You may need to break the plan into smaller steps. Set realistic deadlines for each step. Then follow through with your plan.

Evaluate the results.

Sometime after you have put your decision into effect, take some time to review it.

▶ How did your decision work out?

▶ How has it affected your life?

▶ How has it affected others?

▶ What did you learn?

▶ If you could do it over again, what would you do differently? If you can still change some things for the better, do it now.

Practice the Skill

1. Suppose you were facing the decision described in the introduction—to choose the job or the team. Follow the steps of DECIDE to determine what you would do in this situation. Be sure to consider all alternatives; there may be more than two. (For example, it may be possible to postpone a choice or to take another route to a goal.)

2. List some other important decisions for which DECIDE might be useful. Do they fall into categories? What categories of decisions might not be suitable for DECIDE?

3. Think about a tough decision that you have made in the past or that you are facing now. Use DECIDE to determine what you should do (or should have done).

4. Did using DECIDE help you focus on important values or choices you might otherwise have overlooked? Which ones? Did DECIDE make the decision-making process easier? Why or why not?

Being a Wise Health Consumer

Objectives

▶ **Describe** how to evaluate health products, services, and information.

▶ **Evaluate** what advertising does and does not do for a consumer.

▶ **Explain** how a person can avoid health fraud.

▶ **Identify** your rights as a consumer.

Vocabulary

- consumer
- warranty
- advertising
- fraud
- quackery

Warm-Up

Dear Advice Line,

I buy a brand-name shampoo that costs twice as much as the store brand. The ads for the expensive shampoo say that it keeps your hair healthier. My mother says that the store brand is just as good. Who is right?

WRITING Which shampoo would you buy and why?

Making Healthy Consumer Choices

Young children do not decide when to visit a doctor or which brand of cough syrup to buy. When they become ill, they don't search the Internet looking for information about the illness. Young children have limited opportunities to be consumers. A **consumer** buys products or services for personal use.

As a teen, you are making more decisions about your health, including which products and services to use. So you need to know how to evaluate the products, services, and information you are offered.

Products Picture the aisles in a local drugstore. How many of those aisles contain products that could affect your health? More than you might guess. Some of the items are obvious—snack foods, sports drinks, personal care products, and vitamins. There are medicines for treating indigestion, allergies, headaches, and colds. There are household cleansers and pest-control products, which contain substances that are harmful if inhaled or ingested. There are magazines with articles about health and advertisements for health-related products.

American teens spend more than 150 billion dollars each year.

Some products are consumable, meaning they need to be purchased again and again. Examples are hair care and skin care products, weight loss products, and sports drinks. The marketing of many consumable products is aimed toward teens and young adults. The makers of these products often claim that using them will improve your personal appearance or your physical performance. They may also suggest that a product will improve your emotional or social well-being.

Some products are durable, meaning they are meant to last for a number of years before they wear out. Most sports equipment is durable. Having the right equipment and protective gear is essential when you take part in an organized sport, such as football, or an extreme sport, such as snowboarding. The right equipment is also important when you exercise to maintain fitness. **Some factors to consider before buying a product are its safety, cost, warranty, and consumer testing.**

► **Safety** Read the product labels and other information supplied with the product to determine its contents and possible safety issues. Does a food contain a substance to which you are allergic? Must the product be used only in a room that is well ventilated, as when the windows are open?

► **Cost** Check to see if there are other brands or other products that will give you the same results at a lower cost.

► **Warranty** Is there a **warranty,** an offer to repair or replace the product if there is a problem? If so, how long is it good for and what does it cover?

► **Consumer Testing** Some government agencies and private groups test a wide range of consumer products. They publish their results and recommendations. Groups may endorse, or approve products that rate highly on their tests. By doing so, the group is saying that the claims made for the product by the manufacturer are true.

 Connect to Your Life What kind of questions do you ask before you buy a product?

FIGURE 10 This teen is shopping for a helmet to wear while he is skateboarding. **Predicting** What factors do you think he should consider before making a purchase?

FIGURE 11 A fitness center is an example of a health-related service. **Predicting** How could attending a class as a guest help you to decide whether to join a fitness center?

Services   You probably don't get to choose your doctor or dentist. But you do get to choose some services that can affect your health. For example, if you choose the wrong nail salon, you might develop an infection. If you choose the wrong health club, you might end up with an injury because of poor advice from a trainer.

When you evaluate a service, you need to find out whether the person who will perform the service is qualified. Whether you choose a service on your own or use a service chosen for you, there are questions you should ask.

▶ What kind of education and experience does the person have? Does the person have the required educational degree, license, or certification?

▶ Does the person have references? Ask for the names and telephone numbers of people who have used the service.

▶ Have any complaints been filed with your state's Attorney General?

Information   Before you purchase a product or service, you need to evaluate the information you receive about it. Is it accurate? Is it useful? You need to ask the same type of questions about any health information you receive. **To evaluate health information, you need to evaluate the source of the information.**

▶ Is the source qualified to speak on the topic?

▶ Does the source bring a bias, or slant, to the topic? For example, are they trying to sell a product or service?

▶ Are there other reliable sources that reach the same conclusion?

▶ Is the information current and up to date?

Government agencies, medical associations, and non-profit private health groups often provide reliable information. So do reporters who specialize in science and health topics.

The Effects of Advertising

Businesses spend millions of dollars each year on advertising because they want to attract customers. **Advertising** is the public promotion of a product or service. Ads appear on television and radio, in newspapers and magazines, on billboards, and in movie theaters. They also pop up on the Internet. Everyone is influenced to some extent by advertising. But as a consumer, you need to base your choices on facts, not on advertisements.

Ads can let you know what products and services are available, but they rarely provide the information you need to make wise choices. For example, an ad may say that a certain medicine contains an ingredient that most doctors recommend. The statement may be true. However, this ingredient is likely to be found in all similar medicines.

An ad may say that a certain store is selling a product at the lowest possible price. Unless you check to see what the price is at other stores, you will not know if this claim is true. An ad may mention scientific studies. But unless the ad explains how the studies were done or provides actual results, a claim based on these studies may be false or misleading. Figure 12 discusses six methods advertisers use to sell products and services. For more information on advertising, see the Building Health Skill on analyzing advertising appeal on pages 404–405.

Connect to Your Life Have you bought a product based on an ad? If so, how did the ad convince you to buy the product?

FIGURE 12 Advertising can influence people to buy certain products. **Evaluating** Which of these advertising methods do you think is most effective? Why?

Advertising Methods

Method	Message	Example
Scientific studies	Scientific tests prove the product is effective.	"Tests prove that Brand X works fast."
Bandwagon approach	Everyone is using the product. You should, too.	"Don't be left behind—use Product X."
Testimonial	The product is effective because trustworthy people recommend it.	"The medicine recommended by doctors and their families"
Comparison to other products	The product is more effective than others.	"Brand X now has 20% more painkiller than Brand Y."
Emotional appeal	The product is safest for you and your family.	"Choose Brand X—your family's health depends on it."
Price appeal	The product gives you more for your money.	"Brand X—the most for the least"

FIGURE 13 Promises of impossible cures are a sure sign of quackery. **Observing** What claim does this poster make about wizard oil?

Health Fraud

If a person tells lies to obtain money or property, the person is guilty of an illegal act called **fraud.** People who sell useless medical treatments or products are engaged in health fraud, or **quackery** (KWAK ur ee). These people are called quacks. Quacks promise that a treatment or product will bring about a miracle cure or at least greatly improve a person's health. One danger of quackery is that it can keep someone from receiving proper medical care. If a person believes that a quack remedy is working or might work, he or she might postpone seeing a doctor.

Recognizing Health Fraud Quacks depend on people's lack of knowledge and their desperate desire to find a cure. If a disease is life threatening, such as cancer, it is a likely target of quacks. So are conditions that are long lasting, such as arthritis or problems with weight control. **People can avoid health fraud by carefully evaluating the claims made about a treatment or product.** These are some warning signs of quackery.

▶ Someone claims that a product or treatment is the only possible cure for a health problem.

▶ The promised results seem too good to be true.

▶ A product or treatment is said to cure many different ailments.

▶ A product is said to contain "special" or "secret" ingredients.

Responding to Health Fraud If you have doubts about any product or treatment, ask a doctor or pharmacist. Notify your state's Office of the Attorney General about any health fraud you uncover in your state. If a local business is involved, let your local Better Business Bureau know as well. If you buy a fraudulent product that is shipped to you by mail, notify your local postmaster.

GO ONLINE
PearsonSuccessNet.com
For: More on fraud, quackery, and health

Connect to Your Life **What health claim have you seen that was too good to be true?**

Your Rights as a Consumer

Kiana bought an exercise bike so she could stay fit all year round. A week later, a pedal broke off the bike. She went back to the store and was given a new pedal. Two months later, the speedometer stopped working. She went back to the store again, but the salesperson told her the exercise bike only had a 30-day warranty, and the store was no longer responsible. Kiana was upset but was not sure what her rights were as a consumer. **As a consumer, you have the right to information, the right to consumer protection by government agencies, and the right to complain.**

The Right to Information As a consumer, you need information in order to make wise choices. You need enough information to make an informed judgment about whether a product or service will be safe and effective.

Consumer Protection Figure 14 lists some government agencies that help to protect consumers. Some agencies test products before they can be sold to consumers. Other agencies take action against quackery. Some agencies remove unsafe products from the marketplace.

The Right to Complain If you have a problem with a product, complain to both the store that sold you the product and the manufacturer. Ask for a refund. Follow these steps to make your complaint effective. Use the same approach if you have a problem with a service.

- ▶ **Identify the Problem** Be as clear and specific as possible about what is wrong.

- ▶ **Decide on Your Goal** Decide on a fair way to resolve your complaint. Do you want a refund, replacement, repair, or credit?

- ▶ **Collect Documents** Gather sales receipts, warranties, canceled checks, contracts, or repair records to back up your complaint.

- ▶ **Identify the Person in Charge** Find out who has the power to deal with your problem. It may be a customer service representative or a manager.

Government Consumer Agencies

The Federal Trade Commission (FTC)
Prevents unfair or deceptive advertising and labeling

The Food and Drug Administration (FDA)
Protects public from sale of unsafe foods, drugs, and cosmetics

The Consumer Product Safety Commission (CPSC)
Establishes safety standards for consumer goods and takes dangerous products off the market

WARNING

CHILDREN CAN FALL INTO BUCKET AND DROWN.

KEEP CHILDREN AWAY FROM BUCKET WITH EVEN A SMALL AMOUNT OF LIQUID.

FIGURE 14 These agencies help protect consumers from unsafe products and from health fraud. **Classifying** Which agency would you notify to report false advertising?

FIGURE 15 When you complain about a product, you will need documents, such as a sales receipt, to back up your claim. So you should store important documents in a place where you can easily find them.

Put Your Complaint in Writing Sometimes you will need to write a letter of complaint. It might be because you no longer live near the store where you bought a product or that you ordered from a catalog or a Web site. You might also need to write a letter if you do not get satisfactory results by complaining in person. A letter is especially important if the product has a time-limited warranty. Include the following information.

▶ the product's model and serial number

▶ the location and date of purchase

▶ your specific complaint and suggested resolution

▶ your name, address, and phone number and the best times to reach you

▶ a summary of any conversations you had in person

▶ a reasonable date by which you expect action to be taken

Be firm, calm, and respectful. Avoid writing an angry or threatening letter. Keep a copy of the letter and all the documents.

If you don't receive a response or are unhappy with the response, contact the national headquarters of the company. You can also write a letter to the Better Business Bureau or your local or state consumer protection agency. When all else fails, people may file a complaint in small claims court. These court proceedings usually do not require a lawyer and are relatively simple, quick, and inexpensive.

Section 4 Review

Key Ideas and Vocabulary

1. What is a **warranty?** What are three other factors to consider when buying a product?

2. In general what do you need to do when you evaluate a service or information?

3. What is **advertising?** What can you learn from advertising? What can't you learn?

4. How can you avoid health fraud?

5. What three rights do consumers have?

Critical Thinking

6. **Predicting** Why might a company president answer a letter from an unhappy customer?

Health and Community

Comparison Shopping Pick a consumable product that you use. Compare prices at as many stores in your area as possible. Write a paragraph discussing your results. Is there a noticeable pattern in the price differences? For example, does the size or the location of a store matter? **WRITING**

7. **Classifying** A company chooses a popular sports figure to advertise a product. Which advertising method is the company using?

8. **Making Judgments** A health club has inexpensive introductory memberships. List three questions you should ask before joining.

Chapter 1
At a Glance

VIDEO

TEENS Talk ◓

Decisions, Decisions List three ways that this video changed how you think about making decisions.

Section 1   What Is Health?

Key Ideas

▶ Two factors that can be used to evaluate health are life expectancy and quality of life.

▶ The aspects of health that are important for overall well-being are physical health, mental and emotional health, and social health.

▶ Many of the choices that you make on a daily basis affect your position on the health continuum.

Vocabulary

- health (2)
- life expectancy (2)
- quality of life (2)
- goal (2)
- physical health (3)
- mental health (3)
- emotional health (3)
- social health (3)
- continuum (4)
- wellness (4)

Section 2   Identifying Health Risks

Key Ideas

▶ Heredity, environment, media, technology, health-care, and behavior are factors that influence health.

▶ When you evaluate a risk factor, consider both the short-term and long-term consequences. Decide whether you can control the risk factor. Analyze the possible benefits and risks of a decision.

Vocabulary

- heredity (6)
- gender (6)
- environment (7)
- culture (7)
- media (8)
- habit (9)
- risk factor (10)

Section 3   Taking Responsibility for Your Health

Key Ideas

▶ The broad goals of *Healthy People 2020* are to increase the quality and years of healthy life, to eliminate differences in health based on race, ethnic group, or income, to create environments that promote good health, and to promote healthy behaviors across all life stages.

▶ There are three steps you can take to help you meet your personal health goals—gaining awareness, gaining knowledge, and building skills.

Vocabulary

- prevention (12) • values (14) • action plan (15)
- advocacy (15) • health literacy (15)

Section 4   Being a Wise Health Consumer

Key Ideas

▶ Before buying a product, consider safety, cost, the warranty, and consumer testing. Find out whether the person who will perform a service is qualified. To evaluate health information, you need to evaluate the source of the information.

▶ Ads can let you know what products and services are available, but they rarely provide the information you need to make wise choices.

▶ People can avoid health fraud by evaluating the claims made about a treatment or product.

▶ As a consumer, you have the right to information, the right to consumer protection by government agencies, and the right to complain.

Vocabulary

- consumer (18) • warranty (19) • advertising (21)
- fraud (22) • quackery (22)

Chapter 1 Review

GO ONLINE

PearsonSuccessNet.com
For: Chapter 1 review activity

Reviewing Key Ideas

Section 1

1. The number of years that a person can expect to live is called
   a. quality of life.
   b. quantity of life.
   c. life expectancy.
   d. life history.

2. Describe ways to recognize good physical health, mental health, emotional health, and social health.

3. List two behaviors that could move you toward wellness on the health continuum.

4. **Critical Thinking** How could having to deal with a physical, mental, or emotional problem affect a person's social health?

5. **Critical Thinking** What are four standards you would use to measure the quality of your life?

Section 2

6. Which of these factors is part of your social environment?
   a. heredity
   b. culture
   c. media
   d. technology

7. Do you think that you have more control over risk factors in your environment or behavioral risk factors? Explain.

8. What is one possible short-term consequence of eating a high-fat diet? What is a possible long-term consequence?

9. **Critical Thinking** Analyze the risks and benefits of going rock climbing.

Section 3

10. When you try to influence decisions others make about health, which skill are you using?
    a. setting goals
    b. making decisions
    c. advocacy
    d. analyzing influences

11. How does a focus on reducing risky health behaviors help the nation to achieve the broad goals of *Healthy People 2020?*

12. Explain what it means to gain awareness and to gain knowledge about a health problem.

13. **Critical Thinking** Use the saying "an ounce of prevention is worth a pound of cure" to explain the importance of prevention to your well-being.

Section 4

14. A flyer announcing the opening of a health food store is an example of
    a. advertising.
    b. quackery.
    c. advocacy.
    d. public service.

15. What questions could you ask to find out if a person who runs a gym is qualified?

16. List two reliable sources and one poor source of health information. Explain your choices.

17. Describe three ways that government agencies protect consumers.

18. **Critical Thinking** Which do you think makes people more vulnerable to fraud, a lack of knowledge or desperation? Explain.

 ## Building Health Skills

19. **Advocacy** Why do you think many teens smoke despite the health risks? What argument against smoking would be most effective for teens?

20. **Analyzing Influences** Do ads for healthcare products appeal more to your emotions than to your ability to reason? Explain.

21. **Making Decisions** You are thinking about using a liquid diet supplement. What steps should you take before making this decision?

22. **Setting Goals** Choose a behavior that moves you closer to the wellness end of the health continuum. Make an action plan for making this behavior a habit. Put your plan into action for a week and monitor your progress. Then adjust your plan, if necessary. **WRITING**

Health and Community

Defining Health Ask ten people of different ages to define the term *health*. Record the responses. Then write a paragraph comparing and contrasting the responses. How were the definitions alike? How were they different? **WRITING**

Standardized Test Prep

Math Practice

The graph compares data on smoking for high school students from 2009 and adults from 2008. It also shows the **Healthy People 2020** *target goals for smoking. Use the graph to answer Questions 23–26.*

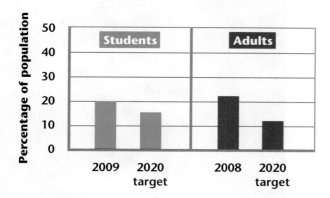

23. What percentage of high school students were cigarette smokers in 2009?
    A 12%   B 16%
    C 21%   D 20%

24. What was the difference in percentage of high school students who smoked and adults who smoked in the late 2000s?
    F 1%   G 8%
    H 12%   J 20%

25. What is the percentage decrease in high school smokers targeted by *Healthy People 2020?*
    A 0%   B 4%
    C 16%   D 20%

26. Assume the target goals for 2020 are met. Out of 500 high school students, how many would you predict would be smokers?
    F 16   G 35
    H 60   J 80

Test-Taking Tip

On test day, think positive thoughts. Tell yourself, "I will do well on this test. I am prepared."

Reading and Writing Practice

Read the passage. Then answer Questions 27–30.

People's perceptions of risk often don't match the facts. More people are afraid of flying than of car travel. Yet, the risk of a fatal car crash is much higher than the risk of a plane crash. A risk seems smaller than it actually is when you think you are in control or when you can benefit from taking the risk. New risks, especially those that are highlighted in the media, seem greater than risks that are familiar. The danger of inaccurate perception of risks is that people worry too much about low-level risks, such as shark attacks, and too little about significant risks, such as smoking.

27. What is the main idea of this passage?
    A People should worry less about risks.
    B People often misjudge the level of a given risk.
    C Car travel is more risky than air travel.
    D Your level of control affects how you view a risk.

28. Based on this passage, what does the word *perceptions* mean?
    F feelings
    G fears
    H understandings
    J observations

29. Which of the following statements is supported by this passage?
    A People are usually less concerned about risks that are discussed in the media.
    B The media only discusses risks that are new.
    C The media decides which behaviors are risky.
    D The media can affect your assessment of a risk.

Constructed Response
30. Why do you think it is dangerous for people to focus too much on low-level risks and not enough on more common risks?

CHAPTER 2

Personality, Self-Esteem, and Emotions

1 Personality

2 Self-Esteem

 Building Health Skills
- **Communicating** Expressing Anger in Healthy Ways

3 Expressing Your Emotions
- **Media Wise** News Content and Emotions

GO ONLINE PearsonSuccessNet.com

VIDEO 2

TEENS Talk

Being Yourself

Preview **Activity**

Whose Opinion of You Matters Most?

Complete this activity before you watch the video.

1. Read the quote below.
  No one can make you feel inferior without your consent.
  Eleanor Roosevelt

2. Then write a short paragraph describing what the quote means to you. **WRITING**

3. Pair up with another student to share and discuss your paragraphs.

Personality

Objectives

▶ **Name** five traits that are used to define personality.

▶ **Identify** two factors that determine how your personality develops.

▶ **Describe** what happens to personality over a lifetime.

Vocabulary

- personality
- psychologist
- modeling
- peer group
- identity

Warm-Up

Quick Quiz For each pair of adjectives, rate yourself on a scale from 1 to 5. For example, if *cautious* describes you perfectly, pick 1. If *adventurous* is perfect, pick 5. Otherwise, pick 2, 3, or 4.

	1 2 3 4 5	
Cautious	① ② ③ ④ ⑤	Adventurous
Outgoing	① ② ③ ④ ⑤	Shy
Calm	① ② ③ ④ ⑤	Anxious
Suspicious	① ② ③ ④ ⑤	Trusting
Excitable	① ② ③ ④ ⑤	Even-tempered

WRITING Use an example from your life to support the rating you chose for one of the adjective pairs.

Describing Personality

Think about how people behave at a party. One person may be the "life of the party." Another person may sit quietly on the couch. Did you ever wonder why people act so differently in the same situation? It is because each person has a unique personality. Your **personality** consists of the behaviors, attitudes, feelings, and ways of thinking that make you an individual. For example, when you are introduced to new people, you may be characteristically outgoing or you may be shy.

Being outgoing or shy are examples of personality traits. So are being reliable, organized, and forgiving. A **psychologist** (sy KAHL uh jist) studies how people think, feel, and behave. Psychologists have described hundreds of personality traits. **Many researchers use five central traits to describe how people behave, relate to others, and react to change. These traits are extroversion, agreeableness, conscientiousness, emotional stability, and openness to experiences.**

Extroversion This trait describes how much you like being with other people. The labels extrovert (EK struh vurt) and introvert are often used to describe the extremes of this personality trait. An extrovert tends to be outgoing, talkative, and sociable. An introvert tends to be shy, quiet, and reserved. Extroverts tend to seek out other people. Introverts are more comfortable spending time on their own.

Agreeableness This trait describes your tendency to relate to other people in a friendly way. People who are agreeable tend to cooperate with others. They are usually forgiving and good-natured. They assume that other people are honest and trustworthy. People who are disagreeable tend to be suspicious or hostile. They assume that other people are unreliable or ready to take advantage of them.

Conscientiousness This trait describes how responsible and self-disciplined you are. Conscientious (kahn shee EN shus) people tend to be dependable and make good decisions. They approach tasks in an organized, deliberate, and thorough manner. On the other end of the scale are people who do not think through decisions, are careless, and easily distracted. They may give up on a task or lose interest in the task before the task is complete.

Emotional Stability People who are emotionally stable tend to be relaxed, secure, and calm, even during difficult situations. They tend to focus on the positive side of things. On the other end of the scale are people who are fearful, worried, and angry. They tend to focus on the negative and to expect the worst in most situations.

Openness to Experiences People who are open to new experiences tend to be curious, imaginative, and creative. They are likely to have a wide range of interests and may be less predictable. People who are less open tend to be more predictable and less independent. They are likely to do what everyone else is doing.

Connect to Your Life How would you describe your personality, using the five central traits?

FIGURE 1 Keeping one's room clean and orderly takes self-discipline. **Evaluating** Based solely on these photographs, where would you rate these young women on the conscientiousness scale?

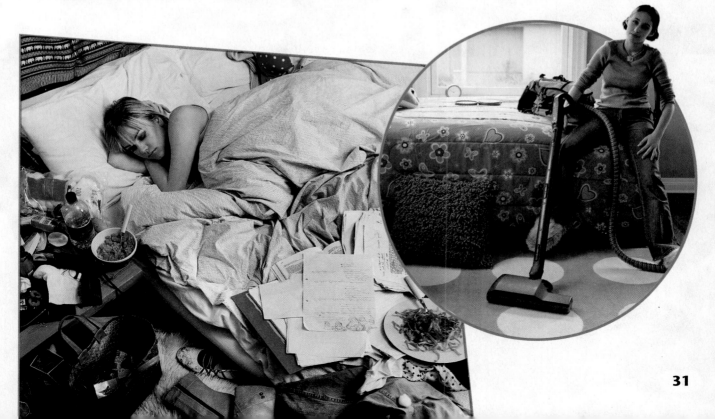

How Personality Forms

Which has the greater influence on personality—"nature" or "nurture"? Nature refers to traits you are born with, ones you inherit from your parents. Nurture refers to the environment you are raised in and the experiences you have during your life. **Personality traits are influenced by a combination of heredity and environment.**

Heredity Why are some infants calm and cheerful while others tend to cry a lot? Why do some babies seem uncomfortable in new surroundings while others seem to thrive? These early differences are evidence that infants are born with distinct tendencies to act in certain ways. In fact, some differences are evident before birth. For example, some babies kick and move around a lot inside their mothers, while others are relatively quiet. There is evidence that traits such as cheerfulness and shyness are inherited. There is also evidence that talents, such as musical and artistic abilities, can be inherited.

One way that researchers study how heredity influences personality is by studying identical twins. Identical twins come from a single fertilized egg. Thus, they inherit the same traits. The identical twins in Figure 2 were separated as infants and raised by different families. When they met as adults they were surprised to discover how many behaviors and interests they shared. Identical twins who are raised separately often have similar careers and hobbies. They even like the same type of clothing and food.

FIGURE 2 These identical twins were raised by different families and reunited as adults. They were surprised how much they had in common, including their chosen careers as firefighters.

FIGURE 3 Young people learn how to behave by observing older relatives. They can also learn skills, attitudes, and cultural traditions.

Environment Just because you inherit certain tendencies doesn't mean that your personality is set for life when you are born. Heredity is only half the picture. Environment plays an equally important role. Your family, your friends, and your cultural group are important parts of your environment. They all have an influence on your personality.

▶ **Family** Experiences you had as a child helped to shape your personality. Children learn about feelings, attitudes, and appropriate ways to behave from their families. As children develop, they copy the behavior of others. This is called **modeling.** For example, a child may learn to be respectful to older adults by observing a parent's behavior toward grandparents. Children also learn by being rewarded for desirable behaviors and punished for less desirable ones.

▶ **Friends** Starting in childhood and throughout the teenage years, friends become an increasingly important influence on personality. Most teens in the United States spend more time with other teens than with their families. These friends, who are about the same age and share similar interests, are called a **peer group.** If your peer group models healthy behaviors, such as cooperation, the group can have a positive influence on your personality.

▶ **Culture** Personality traits that are valued in one culture may not be as highly valued in another culture. Some cultures encourage people to be independent while others put a higher value on fitting in with the group. In some cultures, it is normal to show your feelings in public. In other cultures, people are expected to be more reserved. When people from different cultures meet, such differences can lead to misunderstandings.

 GO ONLINE
PearsonSuccessNet.com
For: More on personality

 In what ways have your friends influenced your personality?

2 **Learn to Be Independent**
18 months to 3 years

1 **Develop Trust**
birth to 18 months

3 **Take Initiative**
3 to 6 years

4 **Develop Skills**
6 to 12 years

FIGURE 4 According to Erikson, in each stage of life people will confront a different challenge. **Interpreting Photographs** Look at the content of each photograph. How does the content illustrate the series of challenges a person will meet throughout life?

Stages of Personality Development

By age 25, your central personality traits will be well established. But, this does not mean that you will not continue to change. **According to the psychologist Erik Erikson, personality develops throughout life as people meet a series of challenges.** Erikson divided life into the eight stages shown in Figure 4. Each stage presents a different challenge to work on. When you successfully accomplish the challenge in one stage, you are better prepared to meet the challenge of the next stage.

1 **Develop Trust**   An infant depends on other people to meet its need for food, a clean diaper, and affection. If these needs are met, the child learns to trust other people. If the needs are not met, the child learns mistrust and may withdraw from others.

2 **Learn to Be Independent**   This is the stage when young children learn to do things on their own. They start to gain control over their own bodies. They learn to walk and use the toilet. If children fail to master these tasks, they develop self-doubt. If their efforts are ridiculed, they may feel ashamed.

3 **Take Initiative**   During this stage, children start to plan their own activities. Through imitating others and through fantasy play, they begin to develop a sense of right and wrong. If children are harshly scolded for poor initiatives, they may feel unworthy, guilty, or resentful.

4 **Develop Skills**   Children learn skills they will need as adults. They learn how to help around the home, how to succeed at school, and how to get along with others. These skills make children feel competent—capable of achieving their goals. Without skills, a child may feel like a failure.

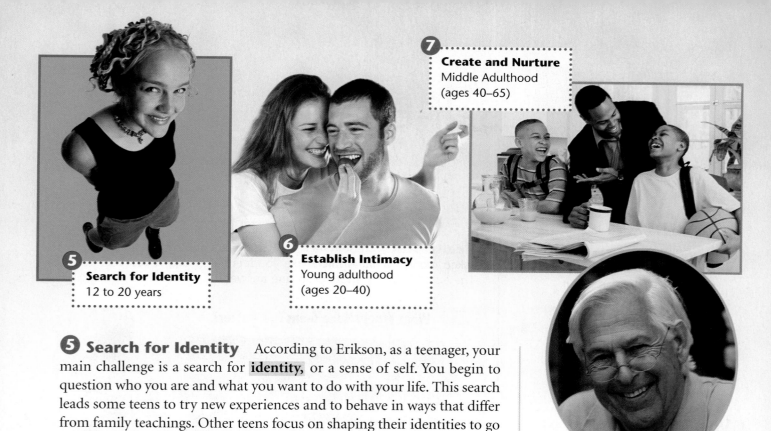

5 Search for Identity
12 to 20 years

6 Establish Intimacy
Young adulthood
(ages 20–40)

7 Create and Nurture
Middle Adulthood
(ages 40–65)

8 Look Back With Acceptance
Late Adulthood (age 65+)

5 Search for Identity According to Erikson, as a teenager, your main challenge is a search for **identity,** or a sense of self. You begin to question who you are and what you want to do with your life. This search leads some teens to try new experiences and to behave in ways that differ from family teachings. Other teens focus on shaping their identities to go along with standards set by their family or culture.

6 Establish Intimacy As a young adult, your challenge will be to establish close bonds with others. If you learn to make commitments to other people, you will have their support as you face other challenges.

7 Create and Nurture During middle adulthood, people need to stay productive and creative in all parts of their life. During this stage, adults get satisfaction from helping younger people to learn and grow.

8 Look Back With Acceptance During older adulthood, people reflect on their lives. Some accept the choices they made, while others may regret the opportunities they missed.

Section 1 Review

Key Ideas and Vocabulary

1. What five central traits can be used to define personality?

2. What two general factors combine to influence your personality?

3. What did Erickson say about how your personality develops throughout your life?

4. Define the term **identity.** At what life stage does the search for identity begin?

Health and Community

Role Models Think of a person you consider a role model. Why did you choose this person? Have you met this person or do you know the person through the media? Write a paragraph summarizing your answers. **WRITING**

Critical Thinking

5. Evaluating Do you choose friends whose personality traits are similar to or different from yours? Why do you think that is so?

Self-Esteem

Objectives

▶ **Compare** the effects of high and low self-esteem on health.

▶ **Describe** the changes in self-esteem that can occur as people age.

▶ **Identify** ways to achieve and maintain high self-esteem.

▶ **Summarize** Maslow's theory of self-actualization.

Vocabulary

• self-esteem
• self-actualization
• hierarchy of needs

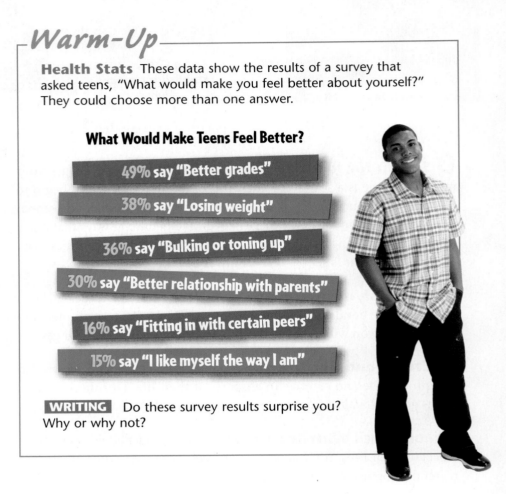

Warm-Up

Health Stats These data show the results of a survey that asked teens, "What would make you feel better about yourself?" They could choose more than one answer.

What Would Make Teens Feel Better?

49% say "Better grades"

38% say "Losing weight"

36% say "Bulking or toning up"

30% say "Better relationship with parents"

16% say "Fitting in with certain peers"

15% say "I like myself the way I am"

WRITING Do these survey results surprise you? Why or why not?

Self-Esteem and Your Health

How do you decide which movie to go to? Do you read or listen to a review of the movie? Do you notice what rating the movie has or how long the lines are at the box office? Perhaps you depend on the opinions of friends to help you decide. Everyone, including you, has opinions—about movies, music, clothing, food, and other people. You may not be aware of it, but you also have an opinion about yourself.

One term psychologists use to describe your opinion of yourself is self-esteem. **Self-esteem** refers to how much you respect yourself and like yourself. As with so many other concepts in mental health, you can think of self-esteem as a continuum, ranging from high self-esteem to low self-esteem. **Many psychologists think that high self-esteem has a positive effect on health, while low self-esteem has a negative effect on health.**

Benefits of High Self-Esteem   People with high self-esteem accept themselves for who they are. They have a realistic view of their strengths and weaknesses and maintain a positive attitude even when they fail at a task. They form close relationships with people who respect and value them because they value themselves.

Some research shows that, if you feel good about yourself, you will be more likely to eat well, to exercise regularly, and to avoid risky behaviors. You will also be more likely to set goals for yourself, ask for help when you need it, and bounce back quickly from setbacks and disappointments.

Risks of Low Self-Esteem   People with low self-esteem don't have much respect for themselves. They judge themselves harshly and worry too much about what others think of them. They may "put on an act" in public to impress others and hide their insecurities. Their fear of failure and looking bad may prevent them from trying new things. Negative thoughts such as "I can't do that" or "I'm not smart enough" make it difficult to succeed. So does thinking that success is a matter of luck rather than hard work.

Some studies show that teens with low self-esteem are more likely than their peers to use drugs, drop out of school, become pregnant, and suffer from eating disorders. They are also more likely to engage in violent or self-destructive behaviors.

 Do you have high or low self-esteem? How does your self-esteem affect the way you behave?

Boost Your Self-Esteem

▶ Maintain a positive attitude.
▶ Focus on your strengths.
▶ Form close relationships.
▶ Set goals for yourself.
▶ Avoid risky behaviors.
▶ Ask for help.
▶ Help others.

FIGURE 5   Identifying and developing your talents is one way to boost your self-esteem.

GO ONLINE

PearsonSuccessNet.com

For: More on building healthy self-esteem

How Self-Esteem Develops

Self-esteem is not a constant. It can increase or decrease as people interact with their family, their peers, and their community. Figure 6 shows the results of studies of self-esteem that were done with different age groups. **On average, self-esteem drops in early adolescence, increases gradually during adulthood, and decreases again toward the end of life.**

Childhood   Young children need support and encouragement from family members. If they have the chance to succeed at small tasks and to build skills, they are likely to become confident individuals. Most children enter school with relatively high self-esteem, but there is often a gradual decline in self-esteem during elementary school. This may be because students begin to compare themselves with other children. Or the students may receive more negative feedback from teachers, parents, or peers.

Adolescence   It is normal for teens to be critical of their appearance, their abilities, their interests, and their shortcomings. But some teens are overly self-conscious and judge themselves too harshly. They may compare themselves only to the best athletes or the most attractive celebrities. As a result, their self-esteem may suffer.

The larger world around you has an influence on your self-esteem. You receive messages about your appearance, your gender, your cultural group, and your values from the media. Messages like "only thin people have fun" or "the latest electronic gadget will make you popular" can make you feel that you are not as good as others.

Adulthood   Self-esteem generally rises during adulthood. Adults begin to accomplish their goals and take control of their lives. Also, adults are better able to keep things in the proper perspective. Researchers are not sure why self-esteem tends to decrease in older adults. The drop may be caused by health problems or limited roles for older adults in society.

FIGURE 6   The graph shows how the self-esteem of females and males changes as they age. **Comparing and Contrasting** How does the self-esteem of females and males compare?

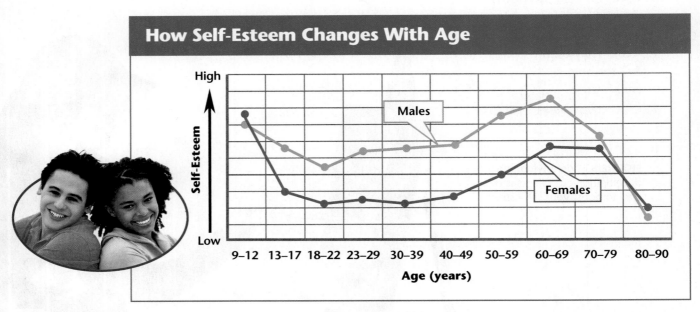

How Self-Esteem Changes With Age

Improving Your Self-Esteem

How can you achieve and maintain high self-esteem? **Don't base your self-esteem solely on other people's opinions of you. Focus on your accomplishments, your talents, and your contributions to your family and community.** If you do well in school, excel at a sport, or display other talents, your achievements and the encouragement you receive can boost your self-esteem. Below are some additional tips for boosting self-esteem. Try to incorporate some of these suggestions into your daily life. You will gain confidence in your abilities and feel better about yourself.

▶ **Make a list of your strengths and weaknesses.** Learn to focus on your strengths and build on the things you do well. Don't dwell on your weaknesses, but identify areas where you can make an effort to improve.

▶ **Set ambitious, but realistic goals for yourself.** Then develop a plan to achieve your goals. Take the time to appreciate and reward yourself when you accomplish a goal.

▶ **Do not be too hard on yourself.** When you make a mistake or experience a defeat, figure out what went wrong. Try to learn something positive from the experience and then move on.

▶ **Rely on your values.** You will feel better about yourself when you do things that match your values. Avoid doing things just to "go along with the crowd." Choose friends who share your values, support your goals, and encourage your efforts to do your best.

▶ **Learn to accept compliments.** However, try to distinguish genuine praise from insincere flattery.

▶ **Look beyond your own concerns.** Do something nice for others. Consider helping out more at home or doing volunteer work in your community.

▶ **Do not focus too much on appearance.** A focus on appearance can undermine self-esteem. Making sure that you are well groomed, however, can help build self-confidence.

FIGURE 7 You can improve your self-esteem by doing something nice for others. This teen is removing a window from the second floor of a house she helped to renovate.

Connect to Your Life
Think about the last time you made a mistake. How did you respond? Was your response helpful?

Self-Actualization

Esteem

Belonging

Safety

Physical Needs

Physical Needs

Safety

Belonging

FIGURE 8 The pyramid shows the hierarchy of human needs that Maslow proposed. Martin Luther King is an example of a self-actualized person.
Interpreting Diagrams Which needs did Maslow think must be satisfied before the need to belong can be met?

Achieving Your Potential

The psychologist Abraham Maslow thought that people have an inborn drive to be the best that they can be. The process by which people achieve their full potential is called **self-actualization.** In the 1950s, Maslow offered an explanation for why few people ever reach their full potential.

According to Maslow, before people can achieve self-actualization, their basic needs must be met. These needs are physical needs, the need to feel safe, the need to belong, and the need for esteem. Maslow arranged these needs in a pyramid, as shown in Figure 8. He called this arrangement the **hierarchy of needs** (HY ur ahr kee).

▶ **Physical Needs** A person's most basic needs are the physical needs of the body. Physical needs include the need for food, water, and sleep. If these basic needs are not met, a person has little or no energy to pursue higher needs.

▶ **Safety** The next level of need is for safety, or protection. A person needs shelter from the elements, such as heat, cold, and rain. A person needs to feel safe from violence in the home and in the community. In the modern world, safety needs also include a need for enough money to meet basic physical needs and other safety needs.

▶ **Belonging** The third level of needs is a need to connect with other people. Family, friends, and others in your community can provide the love and acceptance needed for your emotional health.

▶ **Esteem** Maslow's fourth level is a need for esteem. He divided esteem into the approval of others and self-esteem. The need for the approval of others includes the need for recognition, respect, appreciation, and attention. It can also include the need for fame, glory, and status— your position in life. Maslow regarded self-esteem as a more important need than the approval of others because, once achieved, it is more permanent.

Esteem

Self-Actualization

Personality Traits of Self-Actualized People

► Realistic and accepting
► Independent, self-sufficient
► Appreciative of life
► Concerned about humankind
► Capable of loving others
► Fair, unprejudiced
► Creative and hard-working
► Not afraid to be different

► **Self-Actualization** Once all of a person's other needs are met, he or she can go on to achieve the qualities of a self-actualized person. Maslow made a list of personality traits that people who had reached their potential share. Figure 8 lists these ideal traits.

Research has shown that Maslow correctly identified the set of human needs. However, psychologists now think that people don't have to progress through the hierarchy of needs in the way that Maslow described. It is possible to not meet some of your basic needs and still strive to meet higher needs. For example, Mozart was an extremely creative composer even though some of his basic needs were not met. Nevertheless, a well-fed person who has adequate shelter is more likely to be friendly and self-confident. This person is also more likely to perform tasks better than a person with low self-esteem.

Section 2 Review

Key Ideas and Vocabulary

1. Define **self-esteem**. Explain the effects that high and low self-esteem may have on health.

2. In general, what happens to self-esteem during adolescence? Explain why this change occurs.

3. Identify three things you should focus on if you want to improve your self-esteem.

4. Define the term **self-actualization**. What did Maslow claim must happen before a person can achieve self-actualization?

Health at School

Building Self-Esteem Make a list of events that happen in school that can increase a person's self-esteem. Make a second list of events that happen in school that can lower a person's self-esteem. Choose one event from each list and write a paragraph explaining how these events can affect self-esteem. **WRITING**

Critical Thinking

5. **Making Judgments** Describe something that you accomplished in the past year that made you feel proud and explain why. **WRITING**

6. **Classifying** Which personality traits in Figure 8 do you have?

Expressing Anger in Healthy Ways

Matt and Toni had been going out for over a year. Matt thought that things were great between them. Toni felt differently. She wanted to stop seeing Matt. When she told Matt, he was stunned at first and couldn't speak. Then, he began to yell at Toni. Now Toni was angry too. She later told friends a secret about Matt that she had promised not to tell.

How would you react if you were in this situation? Yell? Cry? Act as if you didn't care? These behaviors are possible responses to anger. Some responses can improve the situation or at least make you feel better. Other responses can make a bad situation worse. The following guidelines will help you learn to express your anger in healthy ways.

1 Accept your feelings.

Anger is a normal emotion. Denying your anger will not make it go away, and ignoring your anger can lead to more destructive behaviors later on. Once you accept your anger, you can start to work on expressing your anger in healthy ways.

2 Identify your triggers.

Before you can deal with your anger, you need to know what makes you angry. You may be angry at a specific person or situation. Thinking about events in your past might make you angry. So might thinking about your future. One way to monitor your feelings is to record them in a journal.

❸ Describe your response.

Record what you did in response to your anger and what happened after you responded. Circle those responses that led to a positive outcome.

> **Friday**
>
> 1. My sister wore my sweater. I yelled at her. She yelled back. Mom got mad.
>
> 2. Argued with Dad about the car. Went for a bike ride. Then talked to Dad.

❹ Seek constructive alternatives.

▶ **Address the Problem** After you calm down, try to discuss the problem. Make it clear how you feel without blaming the other person. Listen with respect to what the other person has to say. Even if talking doesn't fix the problem, you may feel ready to move on.

▶ **Release Excess Energy** Do some physical activity that you enjoy or do some activity that requires you to be creative. Something as simple as taking a walk can also help.

▶ **Avoid Certain Situations** If some situations act as triggers for your anger, you may be able to avoid them. Or you may decide to leave a situation if you start to feel angry.

▶ **Avoid Destructive Behaviors** Overeating or not eating, drinking, smoking, using drugs, or taking extreme physical risks may help you forget your problems for a short time. However, these behaviors can cause damage that lasts a lifetime.

▶ **Ask for Help** If you are having trouble controlling your anger, talk to a trusted adult. The adult can either help you figure out how to cope or can direct you to someone who can. There are counselors who specialize in helping people learn to manage their anger.

❺ Evaluate your progress.

Continue to keep track of your responses to anger in your journal. At first it may take a lot of self-control to change the way you respond to anger. But the more you practice constructive behaviors, the more automatic they will become.

Practice the Skill

1. Review what happened between Matt and Toni. List two positive ways they could have expressed their anger. Predict what the results might have been for each strategy.

2. Briefly describe three times in the past when you experienced anger. For each, describe what caused you to become angry, how you expressed your anger, and the result of your response. Which response worked best? Which was the least effective? Why?

3. For a week, keep a journal to record each time you felt angry. Include the cause, how you responded, and the result. Circle those responses that led to positive outcomes. At the end of the week, use your journal to evaluate your progress. Did your responses improve during the week?

4. If you are not happy with the progress you are making, set a specific goal for controlling your anger. Your goal could be walking away from certain situations or waiting to express your anger until you calm down. Write your goal in your journal and monitor your progress over the next few weeks.

Section 3

Expressing Your Emotions

Objectives

▶ **Identify** four primary emotions and three learned emotions.

▶ **Explain** why it is important to recognize your emotions.

▶ **Distinguish** helpful from harmful coping strategies.

Vocabulary

- emotion
- primary emotion
- grief
- learned emotion
- coping strategy
- defense mechanism

Warm-Up

Myth It is always healthy to "let your feelings out."

Fact Some ways of expressing your emotions are positive and constructive. Other ways of expressing emotions are negative and destructive.

WRITING Think of a time when you felt afraid and a time when you felt guilty. Describe how you behaved in response to each feeling.

Primary Emotions

One important part of a healthy personality is being able to express emotions in appropriate ways. An **emotion** is a reaction to a situation that involves your mind, body, and behavior. Research shows that people are born with a few basic, or primary, emotions. **Primary emotions** are emotions that are expressed by people in all cultures. **Happiness, sadness, anger, and fear are examples of primary emotions.**

Happiness   People feel happy for many different reasons and sometimes for no particular reason at all. Happiness is a normal response to pleasant events in one's life. Feeling happy helps you feel good about yourself. Make a list of the things you enjoy. Then, try to make room in your daily life for these experiences. If you enjoy skating with friends, for example, make plans with your friends to go skating. If you like to read books, set aside some time each day for reading. The good feelings that result will stay with you for the rest of the day.

Sadness   Sadness is a normal response to disappointing events in your life. A day when nothing goes right, a poor grade in school, or family problems can all leave you feeling sad and empty. When you are sad, you may cry, eat more or less than normal, feel tired, or withdraw from those around you. If you are sad about the death of a loved one, you will likely experience a period of deep sorrow known as **grief.**

What can you do to overcome feelings of sadness? You can share your feelings with a close relative or friend. If you are sad about a failure, it might help to make a list of your accomplishments or do something nice for yourself. It is important not to withdraw from other people or isolate yourself. If you do, your sadness can become overwhelming.

Anger   Feelings of anger can range from mild resentment to intense rage. You probably have experienced the tense muscles, racing heart, and rapid breathing associated with anger. You may even have gotten red in the face and clenched your fists. Anger is a normal response to feeling frustrated or helpless.

Anger can be either a helpful or harmful emotion. Anger is helpful when it provides you with the energy necessary to try to change things. Clayton is angry because his parents often say, "Why can't you get good grades like your brother?" After thinking about the situation, Clayton realizes that his brother puts a lot of effort into his schoolwork. He decides to ask his brother to help him improve his approach to his studies.

Anger can also be destructive. What if Clayton decides to focus his anger on his brother? He might start avoiding his brother or find reasons to fight with him. People who tend to express anger in negative ways may hurt themselves and others. They are also at greater risk for developing illnesses such as heart disease. The Building Health Skills activity on pages 42–43 offers strategies for dealing with anger in healthy ways.

Connect to Your Life   **If a close friend insulted you, how would you feel? How might you react?**

FIGURE 9   Primary emotions produce distinct facial expressions that are easy to recognize.
Observing   Which emotion is being expressed in each photo—happiness, anger, sadness, or fear?

GO ONLINE
PearsonSuccessNet.com
For: More on emotions

Fear   Fear is the emotion you feel when you recognize a threat to your safety or security. You feel fear if the car you are riding in starts to skid, someone threatens to hit you, or the smoke alarm goes off in your home. As with anger, when you are afraid, your heart races and your breathing speeds up. You may also feel cold and sweaty.

Fear can be a helpful emotion because it can lead you to run from life-threatening situations. Fear can be a harmful emotion when it is not based on a real threat or when it is an overreaction to a perceived threat. Unrealistic fears can prevent people from living a normal life and doing the things they want to do. For example, a person who is afraid of elevators may be unable to live or work in a high-rise building.

Learned Emotions

Some emotions are not expressed in the same way by all people. These emotions are called social emotions, or **learned emotions.** The expression of learned emotions depends on the social environment in which a person grows up. **Love, guilt, and shame are examples of learned emotions.**

Love   What do love between family members, love between friends, and romantic love have in common? All are marked by deep feelings of affection and concern. These feelings can be expressed in many different ways—through caring words, loving touches, thoughtful actions, and more.

In many cultures, women tend to express love differently than men. Women are often more comfortable expressing their love in words. Many men are more comfortable expressing their love through actions such as shared activities. These different tendencies reflect what women and men learn about expressing emotions from their culture.

You can feel love toward places and things, as well as toward people. You may love your country. You may love a certain style of music. You may feel love and concern for your fellow humans. Love is one of the most positive emotions people are capable of feeling. The capacity to give and receive love is essential for mental health.

FIGURE 10   You can express love by showing affection and concern for others. You may also express love for your country.

Media Wise

News Content and Emotions

What stories appear on the evening news and why? To attract viewers, news directors may select stories that are highly emotional. Can watching the news increase your level of fear or anxiety? Evaluate the evening news using this checklist.

Were two or more stories about a crime or a trial?	Yes	No
Did you see a car crash, train wreck, or plane crash?	Yes	No
Were there reports about fires, floods, or other disasters?	Yes	No
Did most of the people who were interviewed express sadness, fear, or anger?	Yes	No
Did a majority of the reports show events with negative outcomes?	Yes	No

Two or more "Yes" answers indicate a program that could increase your level of fear or anxiety.

Activity Watch a local news program and record the content of each story. Don't include weather or sports. Use the checklist to evaluate the program. Write a paragraph summarizing what you learned. Also describe how the news affected you. **WRITING**

Guilt and Shame Leah's dad lost his job. Leah is angry because there isn't enough money and she can't find a part-time job to help out. Today she spotted a twenty-dollar bill in her friend Rosa's locker. When Rosa looked away, Leah grabbed the money and stuffed it into her pocket. Because Leah knows that what she did was wrong, she feels guilty.

Guilt can be a helpful emotion. Guilt can stop you from doing something you know is wrong, or it can make you take action to correct something you've done. The best way to deal with feelings of guilt is to correct the situation, if possible, and to talk about your feelings. Sometimes people feel guilty when they haven't done anything wrong. For example, when parents divorce, children often blame themselves.

Leah might also feel shame for stealing the money. Shame is different from guilt because it focuses on the person rather than the action. When you feel guilty you think, "I did a bad thing." When you feel ashamed, you think, "I am a bad person." Shame can be harmful because it lowers self-esteem. Shame also makes it less likely that a person will try to correct the bad situation.

Connect to Your Life

What advice would you give Leah to help her correct the situation with Rosa?

Recognizing Your Emotions

Have you ever been overwhelmed by emotion without knowing what emotions you were feeling? If this experience sounds familiar, then you know how difficult it can sometimes be to understand what you are feeling. **Yet, recognizing your emotions is the important first step toward dealing with them in healthful ways.** The next time you experience a strong emotion, pause briefly to reflect on your feelings. Then, follow these steps.

▶ Name the emotion you are feeling. Be aware, however, that some emotions, such as anger, can mask other emotions, such as fear, guilt, and shame.

▶ Determine what triggered the emotion. Try to pinpoint the exact source of your feeling. It may be difficult to isolate the cause from everything else that is happening at the time.

▶ Think back to past times that you felt the same way. What similarities do you notice about the situations? Are there any important differences?

By pausing to reflect on your feelings, you will learn a lot about yourself and your emotions. With practice, recognizing your emotions will become more automatic. Over time, you will begin to see patterns in your reactions and emotional responses. Still, there will always be times when intense feelings cloud your ability to sort things out. When this happens, use the steps listed above to make your feelings clearer. The end result will be a deeper understanding of the situation and of yourself.

Which is more difficult to do, name the emotion you're feeling or pinpoint its source? Why?

Coping With Your Emotions

Sometimes emotions can become too much to handle. In such cases, you may use coping strategies. A **coping strategy** is a way of dealing with an uncomfortable or unbearable feeling or situation. **Coping strategies are helpful when they improve a situation or allow a person to handle a situation in a better way. Coping strategies are harmful when they make a situation worse or a person is less able to handle a situation.**

Defense Mechanisms   You use some coping strategies without being aware that you are using them. **Defense mechanisms** are coping strategies that help you to protect yourself from difficult feelings. You may recognize some of the defense mechanisms described in Figure 12. Notice that they all involve a bit of mental juggling. By twisting the reality of a situation a bit in your mind, the situation becomes easier to accept. Fooling yourself in this way allows you to put off dealing with the problem and the emotions it causes.

FIGURE 11   When a player is arguing with an umpire, you do not need to hear the words to recognize the emotion. You only need to look at the gestures and body language.

Common Defense Mechanisms

Denial	Refusing to recognize an emotion or problem	Your parents are getting divorced, but you act as though nothing is wrong. When friends express their concern, you laugh and tell them it does not bother you.
Compensation	Making up for weaknesses in one area by excelling in another area	You are failing two classes in school. You compensate by becoming the lead saxophone player in the school band.
Rationalization	Making excuses for actions or feelings	You work in a convenience store. When no one is watching, you take some magazines. You figure it's a large store and they can afford it.
Reaction Formation	Behaving in a way opposite to the way you feel	You feel guilty for bullying a kid at school. You cover up your feelings by bragging to friends about your actions.
Projection	Putting your own faults onto another person	At your after-school job you do not complete your tasks. When you get fired, you blame your boss, saying she did not take the time to explain the tasks to you.
Regression	Returning to immature behaviors to express emotions	You are angry at your brother for reading your diary. You scream at him and your parents, run into your room, and sulk.

FIGURE 12 Defense mechanisms can be helpful if they are not overused. However, if you become too dependent on defense mechanisms, you may not learn to express your true feelings. You may not develop skills that are important for your mental and emotional health.

FIGURE 13 One helpful way of coping with your emotions is to write about them.

Helpful Ways of Coping Think back to the last time you experienced a strong emotion. How did you react? Internally, you may have used a defense mechanism, such as rationalization, to make the situation easier to accept. But how did you react outwardly? People react in many different ways to their own strong feelings. Some helpful ways of coping are listed below. What are some other helpful coping strategies that have worked for you?

- ▶ Confront the situation head-on. If possible, take action to improve the situation.

- ▶ Release your built-up energy by exercising, cleaning your room, or being active in some other way.

- ▶ Take a break by reading a book, listening to music, taking a walk, writing in your journal, or otherwise relaxing.

- ▶ Talk through your feelings with a family member, friend, counselor, or other trusted person. Sometimes, just talking about your feelings will help you see things more clearly.

Harmful Ways of Coping People may respond in unhealthy ways to intense emotions. They may use coping strategies that make their problems worse. Using alcohol or other drugs is an example of a harmful coping strategy. Withdrawing from friends and family is another.

Learning to express your emotions in positive ways is not an easy skill to master. Most people need help dealing with their emotions from time to time. If you find that you resort to harmful coping strategies, it may be time to ask for help.

Section 3 Review

Key Ideas and Vocabulary

1. Define the term **emotion**. What is the difference between primary emotions and learned emotions?
2. Explain the importance of being able to recognize your emotions.
3. How do healthful and harmful coping strategies differ? Give an example of each.
4. Define the term **defense mechanism**. When do defense mechanisms stop being helpful?

Critical Thinking

5. Classifying Students often pick on Tito, but he says that this behavior is a sign that the other students like him. What defense mechanism is Tito displaying? Explain.

Health at Home

Expressing Emotion Discuss with your family how you typically express emotions such as sadness or joy. Are there "rules" in your culture about when it is appropriate to express emotions and when it is not? Write a summary of what you learn. **WRITING**

6. Predicting People who design ad campaigns want you to react to their ads by buying their products. Think about ads you have seen for products. Based on these ads, do you think that advertisers are more likely to design ads that appeal to your mind or your emotions? Explain your answer.

Chapter 2
At a Glance

VIDEO

TEENS Talk ◉

Being Yourself What did you learn from the video about ways to build self-esteem?

Section 1   Personality

Key Ideas

▶ Many researchers use five central traits to describe how people behave, relate to others, and react to change. These traits are extroversion, agreeableness, conscientiousness, emotional stability, and openness to experiences.

▶ Personality traits are influenced by a combination of heredity and environment.

▶ According to the psychologist Erik Erikson, personality develops throughout life as people meet a series of challenges.

Vocabulary
- personality (30)
- psychologist (30)
- modeling (33)
- peer group (33)
- identity (35)

Section 2   Self-Esteem

Key Ideas

▶ Many psychologists think that high self-esteem has a positive effect on health, while low self-esteem has a negative effect on health.

▶ On average, self-esteem drops in early adolescence. It increases gradually during adulthood and decreases again toward the end of life.

▶ Don't base your self-esteem solely on other people's opinions of you. Focus on your accomplishments, your talents, and your contributions to your family and community.

▶ According to Maslow, before people can achieve self-actualization, their basic needs must be met. These needs are physical needs, the need to feel safe, the need to belong, and the need for esteem.

Vocabulary
- self-esteem (36)
- self-actualization (40)
- hierarchy of needs (40)

Section 3   Expressing Your Emotions

Key Ideas

▶ Happiness, sadness, anger, and fear are examples of primary emotions.

▶ Love, guilt, and shame are examples of learned emotions.

▶ Recognizing your emotions is the important first step toward dealing with them in healthful ways.

▶ Coping strategies are helpful when they improve a situation or allow a person to handle a situation in a better way. Coping strategies are harmful when they make a situation worse or a person is less able to handle a situation.

Vocabulary
- emotion (44)
- primary emotion (44)
- grief (44)
- learned emotion (46)
- coping strategy (48)
- defense mechanism (48)

Chapter 2 Review

Reviewing Key Ideas

GO ONLINE
PearsonSuccessNet.com
For: Chapter 2 review activity

Section 1

1. A person who is very talkative and sociable is demonstrating a high degree of
   a. conscientiousness.
   b. agreeableness.
   c. extroversion.
   d. emotional stability.

2. According to Erikson, the main challenge people face during adolescence is to
   a. develop competence.
   b. search for identity.
   c. develop trust.
   d. look back with acceptance.

3. Why is it important how adults behave in front of children?

4. Describe how young children begin to gain independence.

5. **Critical Thinking** Review the five central personality traits. Which traits would help elect someone as class president? Which traits would help the elected president do a good job?

6. **Critical Thinking** Would your friends and your family describe your personality in the same way? Explain your answer.

Section 2

7. Which of the following describes people with low self-esteem?
   a. They judge themselves harshly.
   b. They have a positive attitude.
   c. They accept themselves for who they are.
   d. They have a realistic view of their abilities.

8. Self-actualization is the process by which people can
   a. improve self-esteem.
   b. reach their full potential.
   c. establish an identity.
   d. develop trust.

9. How can helping others have a positive effect on your self-esteem?

10. **Critical Thinking** Describe a person who has achieved self-actualization. Use someone you know, someone you admire, or a character in a book you have read.

Section 3

11. An example of a learned emotion is
    a. fear.   b. anger.
    c. sadness.   d. guilt.

12. A child who had been toilet-trained starts to wet the bed again when a new baby arrives. This behavior is an example of
    a. regression.   b. denial.
    c. projection.   d. compensation.

13. How can anger and fear be both helpful and harmful emotions?

14. Explain why love is such an important emotion.

15. **Critical Thinking** Why is withdrawing from family and friends a harmful way to cope with strong emotions?

Building Health Skills

16. **Advocacy** Design a poster to teach young children healthful ways to cope with anger.

17. **Analyzing Influences** Design a survey to help you determine the major influences on the self-esteem of teens. Include questions about factors such as parents, friends, teachers, religion, culture, and media.

18. **Setting Goals** Identify a defense mechanism from Figure 12 that you overuse. Then make an action plan to limit your overuse of the defense mechanism. Decide on a series of steps you can use to break this habit. Monitor your progress and adjust your action plan, if necessary. **WRITING**

Health and Community

Shared Emotions Sometimes an emotion is felt throughout a community in response to an event. Find two newspaper articles that include words such as *anger, grief, joy, fear, guilt,* or *pride.* For each article, write a paragraph explaining the source of the emotion and the response to the emotion. **WRITING**

Standardized Test Prep

Math Practice

The graph shows how two central personality traits—emotional stability and conscientiousness—change as people age. The scores are based on studies of thousands of people. Use the graph to answer Questions 19–22.

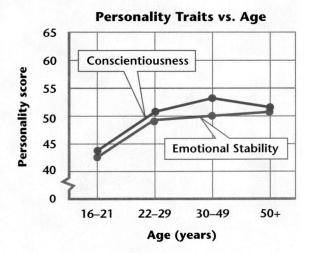

Personality Traits vs. Age

19. What was the score for emotional stability for people ages 16–21?
    A 40   B 43
    C 44   D 50

20. At what age are the scores for conscientiousness highest?
    F 16–21   G 22–29
    H 30–49   J 50+

21. At what ages are the conscientiousness and emotional stability scores most similar?
    A 16–21 and 22–29
    B 16–21 and 30–49
    C 16–21 and 50+
    D 30–49 and 50+

22. According to the graph, which of the following statements is true?
    F Adults are less conscientious and more emotionally stable than teenagers.
    G Adults are more conscientious and less emotionally stable than teenagers.
    H Adults are less conscientious and less emotionally stable than teenagers.
    J Adults are more conscientious and more emotionally stable than teenagers.

Reading and Writing Practice

Read the passage. Then answer Questions 23–26.

There is no scientific basis for personality profiles based on birth dates, palm readings, or handwriting analysis. However, people who read or hear these profiles often say, "That sounds just like me." People react this way because the descriptions are usually so general that they could apply to anyone. The statements also tend to use flattering words, such as *smart* or *honest* or *kind*. People usually pay attention to statements that they either think are true or want to be true and ignore the incorrect statements.

23. What is the main idea of this passage?
    A Personality profiles are never accurate.
    B Personality profiles have a scientific basis.
    C Everyone has the same general personality.
    D People believe personality profiles that have no scientific basis.

24. According to this passage, flattering descriptions are
    F accurate.   G used to please people.
    H often untrue.   J general and vague.

25. Which of the following statements is supported by this passage?
    A Handwriting can tell you a lot about your personality.
    B People tend to ignore statements they agree with.
    C People are likely to accept positive descriptions of themselves and reject negative ones.
    D People born on the same day have similar personalities.

Constructed Response
26. In a paragraph, write a personality profile that might appear in a magazine. Try to make it so general that it could apply to almost anyone.

Test-Taking Tip

When taking a test, have confidence in the first answer you choose. Change an answer only if you are sure your first choice is wrong.

Managing Stress

GO ONLINE PearsonSuccessNet.com

VIDEO 3

TEENS Talk

Stressed Out

Preview **Activity**

Have Sources of Stress Changed Over the Years?

Complete this activity before you watch the video.

1. Make a list of the top five everyday problems that cause stress in your daily life.

2. Interview one or two adults and ask them to recall the top five everyday problems they faced in high school.

3. Write a paragraph that compares the problems you listed with the problems the adults listed. Based on this comparison, would you say that sources of everyday stress have changed, or stayed the same? Explain. **WRITING**

What Causes Stress?

Objectives

▶ **Describe** what causes a person to experience stress.

▶ **Identify** four general types of stressors.

Vocabulary

- stress
- eustress
- distress
- stressor
- catastrophe

Warm-Up

Myth People should try to avoid all situations that can lead to stress.

Fact Stress is a normal part of life that you cannot avoid. Sometimes stress can have a positive outcome.

WRITING You are invited to a friend's birthday party. What about this situation could cause you to experience stress?

What Is Stress?

It is early morning and you are fast asleep. Suddenly, your alarm clock sounds. You sit up quickly, open your eyes, and jump out of bed. As you react to the ringing alarm, you experience stress. **Stress** is the response of your body and mind to being challenged or threatened. **You experience stress when situations, events, or people make demands on your body and mind.** Most people think of stress as a negative experience, but stress can be positive as well. Stress is positive when it helps you escape from a dangerous situation, promotes your personal growth, or helps you accomplish your goals. Positive stress is sometimes called **eustress.** Negative stress is sometimes called **distress.**

Think about something you have accomplished lately—perhaps you did well on a test or your team defeated a tough opponent in soccer. You may remember the feelings you experienced before and during the event. Do you think you performed better as a result of the stress?

At moderate levels, stress can actually improve your ability to concentrate and perform at your best. Beyond that level, however, it begins to take a negative toll on performance. Suppose that you were scheduled to take your driver's test next week. Feelings of stress might assure that you practice during the week. On the day of the test, your nervousness might make you more alert behind the wheel. But what if you experience overwhelming stress during the test? You might find it difficult to concentrate and you might make mistakes that cause you to fail the test.

The Many Causes of Stress

An event or situation that causes stress is called a **stressor.** A ringing alarm clock is one example of a stressor. Other stressors in your life may be a difficult homework assignment or an argument with a friend. These events make demands on your body and mind. **Four general types of stressors are major life changes, catastrophes, everyday problems, and environmental problems.**

Major Life Changes Do you remember how you felt on your first day of high school? Were you excited? Were you nervous? Perhaps you experienced both emotions at the same time. You had to adjust to new surroundings, new people, and increased expectations. Starting high school is an example of a major life change. So is graduating from high school. Major life changes are stressful because it takes energy to adjust to a new situation. A major life change may also threaten your sense of security or your self-esteem. The more major life changes you experience in a year, the more stress you are likely to feel.

Figure 1 lists some major life changes. Notice that the list includes positive changes as well as negative ones. While being accepted to the college of your choice is indeed a positive event, it can be just as stressful as a negative event, such as having a parent lose a job. It is important to realize that change, both positive and negative, is in itself stressful.

Connect to Your Life List three major life changes you experienced during the past five years.

Major Life Changes

- Graduating from high school
- Experiencing death of a parent
- Going through parents' divorce
- Experiencing remarriage of parent
- Having a newborn sister or brother
- Having a serious illness
- Moving to a new school district
- Failing a grade
- Being accepted to college
- Breaking up with boyfriend or girlfriend
- Having parent lose his or her job
- Learning you were adopted
- Not making the team
- Being elected to student government
- Being recognized for an achievement
- Leaving home for college or a job

FIGURE 1 A major life change may be related to health, family, employment, friendships, or education.
Classifying Which of the life changes listed would you classify as positive?

GO ONLINE

PearsonSuccessNet.com
For: More on stress

Catastrophes   Major life changes are an expected part of life; other highly stressful events are unexpected. A **catastrophe** (kuh TAS truh fee) is an event that threatens lives and may destroy property. Natural disasters such as hurricanes, floods, and tornadoes are catastrophes. So are violent crimes, terrorism, and war. A person who experiences a catastrophe may deal with the psychological effects for years after the event. Reading about a catastrophe or seeing images on television can also cause stress.

Everyday Problems   Some of the most common stressors are minor, but frequent, everyday events. These common stressors are sometimes called "hassles." Hassles include misplacing your keys, missing your bus, or having too many homework assignments on the same day. While such problems seem minor, they contribute greatly to your overall feeling of stress. This is because hassles occur day in and day out. Can you remember a day in the past month that was free of hassles?

Conflict—disagreements with family members, friends, or others—is another common source of stress. Some high school students experience more conflict than they did when they were younger or disagree over issues that are more serious. How you dress, what music you listen to, what friends you see—these are all possible sources of conflict and stress.

For many people, the pressure to succeed is a major source of stress. They don't want to fail and they don't want to disappoint their families, their friends, or themselves. You can feel this pressure any time there is competition—in class, at a swim meet, playing chess, or in a debate. Not knowing what you will do once you leave school can also be stressful.

Connect to Your Life **What everyday problems did you experience today that were stressful for you?**

FIGURE 2   For some people, waiting in line to buy a ticket can be stressful.

Avoid Waiting in Line
- **Purchase tickets in advance.**
- **Pick a different time of day.**
- **Wait a while to see a new release.**

Environmental Problems Conditions in your immediate surroundings affect your level of stress each day. Suppose, for example, that you commute to school on an overcrowded subway or bus. Your level of stress might be quite high by the time you arrive at school. If you then have to hunt for a book in a messy locker, your level of stress will continue to rise.

A major stressor that occurs all around you but is often overlooked is noise. People who live near airports show signs of high stress levels due to the noise of airplanes taking off and landing. Living near an elevated commuter rail or a busy highway can have a similar effect.

Living in unsafe or crowded conditions also tends to increase feelings of stress. So does living where the air quality is poor or where litter collects on sidewalks. Weather conditions can also contribute to stress. During a heat wave or a long spell of freezing temperatures, people may feel increased stress. This may be because they feel cooped up indoors. Or they may be stressed because they cannot afford to keep the temperature indoors as cool or as warm as they might like it to be.

FIGURE 3 Adding something attractive to the neighborhood can help to reduce stress. These teens are painting a mural.

Section 1 Review

Key Ideas and Vocabulary

1. What is **stress**? Explain how stress can be both positive and negative.
2. When do people experience stress?
3. What is meant by the term **stressor**?
4. List the four general types of stressors and give an example of each type.

Critical Thinking

5. **Applying Concepts** List five stressful experiences that you have faced in the past two weeks. Next to each, note whether it was a positive or a negative experience for you.

Health and Community

Noise Pollution Does your community have any regulations related to noise? If so, do the regulations vary with time of day or location? Sources of noise that might be regulated are radios, car exhausts, power lawnmowers, and blasting for construction. Write a paragraph summarizing your findings. **WRITING**

6. **Classifying** Explain why getting your driver's license could be classified as a major life change.
7. **Comparing and Contrasting** How is a catastrophe similar to a major life change? How is it different?

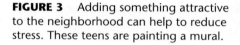

How Stress Affects Your Body

Objectives

▶ **List** in order the three stages of the body's response to stress.

▶ **Identify** four types of early warning signs for stress.

▶ **Describe** the relationship between stress and illness.

Vocabulary

• fight-or-flight response

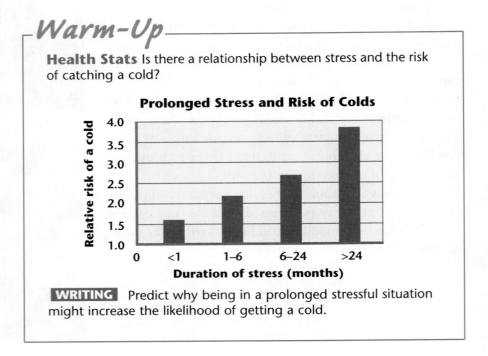

Warm-Up

Health Stats Is there a relationship between stress and the risk of catching a cold?

Prolonged Stress and Risk of Colds

(y-axis) Relative risk of a cold: 4.0, 3.5, 3.0, 2.5, 2.0, 1.5, 1.0

(x-axis) Duration of stress (months): 0, <1, 1–6, 6–24, >24

WRITING Predict why being in a prolonged stressful situation might increase the likelihood of getting a cold.

Stages of Stress

You are walking in a park. Suddenly, you see a large dog that isn't on a leash. The dog is growling. How do you react? Instantly, your mind sizes up the situation. You recognize that the dog could be a threat to your safety. When you perceive something to be a threat, your body springs into action. Your body's response isn't under your control—it's automatic.

All stressors trigger the same stress response. However, the intensity of the response will vary. **The body's response to stress occurs in three stages—the alarm stage, the resistance stage, and the exhaustion stage.**

Alarm Stage During the alarm stage, your body releases a substance called adrenaline (uh DREN uh lin) into your blood. Adrenaline causes many immediate changes in your body, as shown in Figure 4. Your heart beats faster, your breathing speeds up, and your muscles tense. Your attention narrows as you focus on the stressor.

These changes prepare you to either "fight" the stressor or "take flight" and escape. Thus, this initial reaction of the body to stress is called the **fight-or-flight response.** This response probably helped early humans survive. Today, your body still reacts to any stressor with the same set of changes even when fight-or-flight is not a useful response.

Fight-or-Flight Response

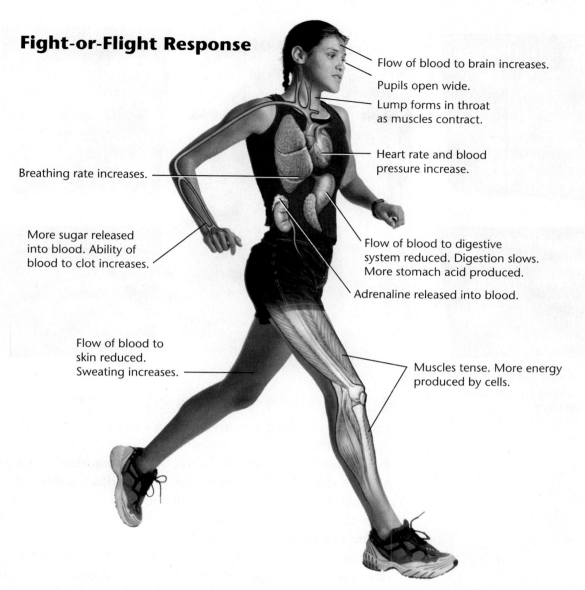

Flow of blood to brain increases.

Pupils open wide.

Lump forms in throat as muscles contract.

Heart rate and blood pressure increase.

Breathing rate increases.

More sugar released into blood. Ability of blood to clot increases.

Flow of blood to digestive system reduced. Digestion slows. More stomach acid produced.

Adrenaline released into blood.

Flow of blood to skin reduced. Sweating increases.

Muscles tense. More energy produced by cells.

Resistance Stage   Sometimes you can deal with a stressor quickly. You find the keys you thought were lost or you know the answers to the questions on a quiz. If, however, you are unable to successfully respond to a stressor during the alarm stage, your body moves into the resistance stage. During this stage, your body adapts to the continued presence of the stressor. You may think you are no longer stressed because the symptoms from the alarm stage disappear. However, the work that your body does during the resistance stage uses up a lot of energy. As a result, you may become tired, irritable, and less able to handle any added stress.

Exhaustion Stage   The third stage of the stress response is the exhaustion stage. Your body can no longer keep up with the demands placed on it. Your physical and emotional resources are depleted.

The exhaustion stage does not occur with each stress response. If it did, your body would wear out. Exhaustion occurs only if a stressor continues for a long time—usually weeks, months, or even years. People may reach the exhaustion stage when they experience extreme stress that is beyond their control—such as a death of a family member.

FIGURE 4   During the alarm stage, adrenaline triggers many changes in the body. For example, extra sugar released into your blood combines with oxygen in body cells to give you a burst of energy. **Interpreting Diagrams** List two body functions that speed up during the alarm stage. List two that slow down.

Warning Signs of Stress

Behaviorial Changes
- Overeating or hardly eating at all
- Sleep problems
- Hurrying; talking fast
- Withdrawing from relationships
- Reckless behavior

Physical Changes
- Muscle tension
- Headache
- Upset stomach
- Pounding heart
- Shortness of breath
- Increased sweating
- Skin rash

Changes in Thinking
- Unable to concentrate
- Negative thinking
- Excessive worrying
- Self-criticism
- Critical of others

Emotional Changes
- Irritable
- Angry
- Impatient
- Nervous
- Increased crying

FIGURE 5 These are some common warning signs of stress. They include physical changes, emotions, thoughts, and behaviors.

Recognizing Signs of Stress

If you have ever tried to concentrate on a task after a stressful day, then you know that stress can interfere with your ability to focus and think clearly. When people are distracted, they risk injuring themselves and others. A driver may not notice that a pedestrian has stepped into the crosswalk. Or the pedestrian may not notice the car. Reducing the risk of injury is one reason to reduce your level of stress. Another reason is to prevent the effects of prolonged stress on your body.

Before you can deal with stress, you must recognize the warning signs. **The warning signs of stress include changes in how your body functions and changes in emotions, thoughts, and behaviors.** As you look over the list of warning signs in Figure 5, think about how you act and feel when under stress. Begin your own personal list of warning signs by selecting items from Figure 5 that apply to you. Add other changes you associate with being stressed. The next time you experience some of the warning signs on your list, you will know that you are under stress.

The next step is to try to identify the stressor you are facing. Sometimes this task is easy because the source of the stress is obvious; for example, a close friend is moving away. Noticing patterns can help you identify a stressor. Perhaps you always show signs of stress when you haven't had enough sleep. When it is difficult to pin down the source of your stress, try recording your activities and responses in a journal. Don't get discouraged. It may take time for a pattern to emerge. By recognizing the warning signs as early as possible and by identifying stressors, you may be able to prevent some of the more serious effects of stress.

 What warning signs of stress do you routinely experience?

 GO ONLINE
PearsonSuccessNet.com
For: More on how to recognize stress

Stress and Illness

Severe or prolonged stress can affect your health. **Stress can trigger certain illnesses, reduce the body's ability to fight an illness, and make some diseases harder to control.**

Stomachaches A "stomachache" can occur in your stomach, small intestine, or large intestine. Stress disrupts the movement of food through the digestive system. The food may move too quickly or too slowly. You might experience gas, cramps, diarrhea (dy uh REE uh), or constipation.

Stress also increases the amount of stomach acid. Doctors used to think that excess acid attacked the lining of the stomach and caused open sores, called ulcers, to form. Then researchers found bacteria in the stomach that could cause ulcers. When medicine was used to kill the bacteria, the ulcer healed. Current thinking is that excess acid makes it more likely that an ulcer will form and makes it more difficult for an ulcer to heal.

Asthma Asthma (AZ muh) is another illness for which stress can be a trigger. An asthmatic attack happens when the air passages of the respiratory system narrow, making it difficult to breathe. During an attack, the person coughs, wheezes, and gasps for air. These symptoms usually can be controlled by medication that is inhaled. But it helps if people with asthma recognize which stressors can trigger an attack.

Headaches Stress can trigger headaches. Tension in the muscles around your scalp, face, and neck may produce an aching or pounding sensation in your head. A type of headache called a migraine (MY grayn) begins when blood vessels in the brain and scalp narrow, which limits the supply of oxygen to the brain. The blood vessels must then open wide to increase the flow of oxygen. This stretching of the blood vessels causes the painful throbbing of a migraine. If you suffer from frequent headaches, you may want to keep a diary to determine what factors trigger the onset of a headache. In addition to stress, certain foods, such as chocolate or large amounts of caffeine, can trigger headaches.

37.6% of female teens and 21.3% of male teens report having a least one headache each week.

FIGURE 6 This image illustrates the pain associated with a migraine headache.

Lowered Resistance to Disease   The immune system protects your body from disease through a complex process involving many specialized cells. When you speak of fighting off the flu or a cold, your immune system does the fighting. When your immune system functions well, you are better able to resist some of the illnesses to which you have been exposed.

Scientific research has shown that, during the alarm stage, some parts of your immune system may function better than usual. However, prolonged stress can prevent the immune system from functioning well. If your immune system is weakened, you may develop minor illnesses, such as colds, more often. For people with diseases such as cancer, a weakened immune system makes it harder to control the disease.

Heart Disease   Some effects of frequent or prolonged stress don't show up until later in life. Remember that during the alarm stage, your heart beats faster. Your blood vessels narrow and your blood pressure rises. Your heart must work harder to keep blood flowing through your body. Stress that is frequent or prolonged can cause damage to the muscle fibers in the heart. Prolonged stress can also damage the linings of blood vessels, which are under increased pressure. Because high blood pressure has no obvious symptoms and often goes undetected, it is sometimes called the "silent killer." Reducing stress is one of the ways that people can lower their blood pressure and reduce the risk of heart disease and stroke.

FIGURE 7   Prolonged stress can weaken your immune system, which makes it harder to fight off a cold or flu.

Section 2 Review

Key Ideas and Vocabulary

1. What are the three stages of the stress response? In what order do they occur?

2. Why is the body's response during the first stage of stress called the **fight-or-flight response?**

3. Describe four ways that you can recognize when you are under stress.

4. What is the relationship between stress and illness?

Critical Thinking

5. Relating Cause and Effect Why is it important to identify signs of stress early?

Health at Home

Warning Signs of Stress Ask a few friends and trusted adults if they can tell when you are under stress. Ask them to describe the warning signs that you exhibit. Write a paragraph about what you find out. **WRITING**

6. Applying Concepts Explain how changes that occur during the alarm stage could help you escape from a threatening situation.

7. Making Judgments A doctor with a patient who complains about stomach pains is likely to do a series of tests to determine the cause. Why might the doctor also ask about the patient's mental and emotional health?

Stress and Individuals

Objectives
► **Explain** how individuals can have different responses to the same stressor.
► **Describe** two ways that personality affects stress.
► **Identify** the key factor in resilience.

Vocabulary
• optimism
• pessimism
• perfectionist
• resilience

Warm-Up

Quick Quiz How many of the following statements accurately describe how you think or behave?

1. **I need to be the best at everything I do.**

2. **If something doesn't go as planned, I feel like a failure.**

3. **I tend to expect the worst in most situations.**

4. **I want to be liked by everyone.**

5. **I really enjoy competition.**

WRITING Review your responses. Then explain why you might be more or less likely to be under stress than others.

Responses to Stress Vary

Your teacher walks into class and says, "Okay, everyone, put away your books. We are going to have a surprise quiz now." How would you react? Now look around the classroom and imagine your classmates' reactions. Would their reactions be the same as yours? Your teacher's announcement might bring on a wide range of reactions—mild stress, extreme stress, confidence, and indifference are just some reactions you could predict.

Why does one person remain calm when faced with a stressor while another becomes anxious and tense? The answer to this question points out an important fact about stress—it is a highly personal experience. **How you react to a stressor depends on how you assess the situation.** As you assess the situation, you are answering two important questions:

► Is this situation a threat to my well-being?

► Do I have the necessary resources to meet the challenge?

Time, energy, skills, and experience are resources. Situations that cause the most distress are those in which you answer *no* to the second question.

You might see a surprise quiz as a threat if you need to maintain a certain grade to be eligible to play on a team. If you did poorly on previous quizzes, you might not be confident of doing well on this one. Your past experiences have a lot to do with how you respond to new situations.

Player A is...
- Confident
- Eager
- Calm
- Focused
- Optimistic

Player B is...
- Uncertain
- Hesitant
- Nervous
- Distracted
- Pessimistic

Figure 8 Personality can affect how two people respond to the same situation. **Predicting** How could these players' thoughts and feelings affect their ability to perform?

Stress and Personality

Your personality also has a lot to do with how you respond to stressors. For example, a friend invites you to a party. The only person that you will know at the party is your friend. How you respond to the situation will depend on your personality. If you are outgoing and confident, you might look forward to the opportunity to meet new people. However, if you are shy, you might feel threatened by the thought of meeting so many strangers. **Your personality influences your assessment of a situation.**

Optimism and Pessimism Carla and Joan play on a softball team. Their team is about to face the best team in the league. Carla is looking forward to the challenge. She likes competing against the best opponents. Her response reflects her optimism. **Optimism** is the tendency to focus on the positive aspects of a situation. Joan is threatened by the situation. She assumes that she will play poorly and that the other team will win by a wide margin. Her response reflects her pessimism. **Pessimism** is the tendency to focus on the negative and expect the worst.

Aiming for Perfection A **perfectionist** is a person who accepts nothing less than excellence. If you are a perfectionist about your appearance, for example, you may spend hours getting ready to go to school. If you are a perfectionist about your work, you may spend hours agonizing over each sentence in a paper and still not be satisfied.

Because perfectionists set goals that are impossible to attain, they are never satisfied with what they have accomplished. This can lead to a vicious cycle of trying harder, not being satisfied, and trying harder still. There are ways to break the cycle and reduce your stress.

▶ Accept that you cannot be perfect.

▶ Take pride in the things you do well.

▶ Don't focus on your mistakes.

GO ONLINE

PearsonSuccessNet.com

For: More on stress and personality

Connect to Your Life

Are the goals that you set for yourself easy to reach, difficult to reach, or impossible to reach?

Resilience

Some people seem to tolerate high levels of stress. They tend to view stressful events as challenges rather than as threats. For example, they might view the loss of a job as an opportunity to pursue a new career. Also, they believe that they are in control—that they can influence the outcome of a stressful event.

Even stress-hardy people will face a catastrophe or major life change that they are unable to control. They need to find a way to adapt to an extremely distressful situation. The ability to recover, or "bounce back," from extreme or prolonged stress is called **resilience.** Many factors contribute to resilience. **The key factor in resilience is having the support of family and friends.** These relationships offer encouragement, reassurance, and love. People with resilience share other characteristics.

▶ They know their strengths and have confidence in their abilities.

▶ They make realistic plans and take the steps to carry out those plans.

▶ They have good communication and problem-solving skills.

▶ They are able to recognize and control their feelings.

▶ They recognize that change is a normal part of life. They are able to put life changes in perspective.

In the next section, as you study ways to cope with stress, you will learn how to build your resilience.

FIGURE 9 People may use a "group huddle" to encourage one member of the group or the group as a whole.

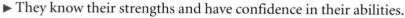

Section 3 Review

Key Ideas and Vocabulary

1. Why might two individuals have different responses to the same stressor?

2. How does personality affect a person's response to stress?

3. Define the term **resilience.**

4. What is the key factor in determining whether a person has resilience?

Critical Thinking

5. Applying Concepts The weather report says there is a 50 percent chance of rain. How might your optimism or pessimism affect how you interpret this report?

Health at School

Resilience Interview a guidance counselor, school nurse, or social worker. Ask the person you interview to describe those factors that make it easier for a student to recover from an extremely stressful situation. Summarize what you learn in a paragraph. **WRITING**

6. Predicting Impatience is a common personality trait. Predict how impatience could affect a person's level of stress.

7. Classifying After Kenny completes his math homework, he checks his answers to see if they make sense. Based solely on this behavior, do you think Kenny is a perfectionist? Explain.

Managing Your Time

Last night, José stayed up late to write a report that was assigned two weeks ago. He planned to do his math homework in the morning, but then slept through his alarm. In his haste this morning, José left his gym clothes at home. Running toward the school as the bell rang, José felt anxious and tense.

José needs to manage his time better. A good time manager completes daily tasks and still finds time to relax. Follow these steps to better manage your time.

① Track how you spend your time.

► Use a sheet from a daily planner that is divided into 15-minute blocks or make your own version on ruled paper. Prepare a sheet for each day of the week.

► Mark all your scheduled activities on the grid, beginning with your classes at school. Include other activities that you attend on a regular schedule, such as religious classes or team practice.

► Use the grids to track how you currently spend your "free" time.

Monday	
8:00	Algebra I
9:00	English
10:00	American History
11:00	Earth Science
12:00	Lunch
1:00	Studio Art I
2:00	Basketball Practice

② Make a daily "To Do" list.

► Before you go to bed, make a list of the tasks you need to do the next day.

► Include tasks that you know you have to do, such as homework and chores, along with tasks that you would like to do.

► Break long-range tasks, such as term papers and projects, into smaller, more manageable tasks. This makes it easier to fit these tasks into your schedule.

❸ Prioritize your tasks.

Rate each task according to this scale.
A = very important
B = somewhat important
C = not very important

To Do List	
Do math homework	A
Do laundry	B
Outline history paper	A
Organize CDs	C
Call grandmother	B
Watch TV	C
Practice jump shots	B
Get permission slip signed	A

❹ Plan your day.

▶ Assign an amount of time for each task. Make a practice of allowing more time for a task than you think it will require.

▶ Use copies of the grids you made in Step 1 to schedule your tasks.

▶ Do not schedule too many tasks each day. Allow some time for unplanned events.

▶ Try to do "A" tasks before you do "B" tasks, and "B" tasks before you do "C" tasks, even if a "C" task is easier.

❺ Monitor your progress.

At different points during the day, ask yourself, "Is this the best use of my time?" If your answer is *no,* consider these questions:

▶ *Am I doing a "C" task because an "A" task seems overwhelming?* If so, break the "A" task into smaller steps that can be done in less than fifteen minutes.

▶ *Am I avoiding a task because I am afraid to fail or make a mistake?* You can waste a lot of time worrying about a task. If you just begin doing the task, you may realize that it is not as difficult as you thought.

▶ *Is this the right time to do this task?* For example, if your math homework is challenging, don't leave it until late at night when you are tired.

▶ *Am I being distracted by phone calls or instant messages?* Tell your friends when it is okay to contact you and when you need time to concentrate on homework or chores.

Practice the Skill

1. For one week, keep track of how you spend your time each day. Decide whether or not you are spending your time wisely. Are there tasks that you can eliminate? Are there tasks that you can do more quickly?

2. During the second week, make a "To Do" list each day. Break down complex activities into a set of simpler tasks. Assign a specific, realistic amount of time for each task.

3. Use the A-B-C scale to prioritize your tasks and then decide which tasks you will do in each of the available time periods. Do your "A" tasks first each day, followed by "B" and "C" tasks.

4. If you are having trouble finishing your tasks, ask yourself the questions from Step 5.

5. At the end of the week, report to your class on how helpful the time management process has been for you. What can you do to improve your time-management skills?

Section 4

Coping With Stress

Objectives

▶ **Identify** ways to control stress, reduce tension, and change the way you think about stressors.

▶ **Explain** why building resilience is important.

▶ **Describe** the value of seeking support from others when you are under stress.

Vocabulary

• mental rehearsal

Warm-Up

Dear Advice Line,

When I have to speak in front of a group, I panic. I begin to sweat and my heart pounds. My mouth gets so dry that it's hard to speak. Is there anything I can do about this problem?

WRITING What advice would you offer to someone who is afraid of speaking in public?

Take Control of Stress

Many people tend to think that all stress is out of their control. This is not true. You can do many things to keep stress under control. In a sense, everything you do to maintain your health is a way to manage stress.

It is important to distinguish between stressors that you can control and those that you cannot. You cannot control natural disasters or major life changes such as the death of a grandparent. The adults in your family control your physical environment. They decide where you live and who lives with you.

There are, however, many stressors in your life that you can work to change. These stressors tend to be the everyday problems. For example, suppose you were in danger of failing math. What could you do? You could ignore the problem and pretend not to be worried or you could confront the problem and devise a plan to improve your grade. Your plan might include asking a friend for help, cutting down on other activities to focus more on math, and paying closer attention in class.

If you direct your energy toward those things that are within your power to change, you may be surprised to see what a difference you can make. **Two techniques that can help you keep stress under control are time management and mental rehearsal.**

70 *Chapter 3*

Time Management   Do you often wish there were more hours in the day? Do you tend to put things off until the last minute? If you answered *yes* to these questions, you may not be managing your time effectively. Poor time management is one of the biggest contributors to stress. The Building Health Skills on pages 68–69 can help you learn to use time more productively. Not only will you get more done each day, but you will also feel more in control of your life. As a bonus, you might also end up with more time for fun and relaxation.

Mental Rehearsal   Suppose you have a big event coming up, such as a solo in a concert. If you are worried about your performance, you might use a technique known as a mental rehearsal to help you prepare. In a **mental rehearsal,** you practice an event without actually doing the event. The event takes place in your mind as you imagine yourself performing at your best. You might rehearse every aspect of the event a few times over until you feel confident that you can perform it as imagined. Of course, a mental rehearsal doesn't replace the need to actually practice for an event.

Athletes often use mental rehearsal while preparing for a competition. This technique helps athletes stay focused on their performances during highly stressful times. You also can use mental rehearsal to prepare for a difficult conversation with a family member or a friend.

When you first try this technique, it may be difficult to keep your mind focused on your rehearsal. You might find that you are easily distracted by outside events. With practice, though, you will improve your ability to focus and put all distractions aside.

Have you used mental rehearsal before an event? If so, did it help your performance?

FIGURE 10   Time wasters keep you from making the best use of the time you have to study. **Evaluating** Which example do you think costs you the most time? What other examples would you add to the list?

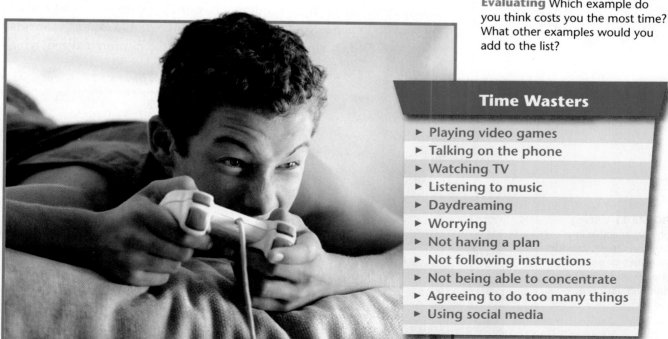

Time Wasters

- ▶ Playing video games
- ▶ Talking on the phone
- ▶ Watching TV
- ▶ Listening to music
- ▶ Daydreaming
- ▶ Worrying
- ▶ Not having a plan
- ▶ Not following instructions
- ▶ Not being able to concentrate
- ▶ Agreeing to do too many things
- ▶ Using social media

Reduce Tension

Even when a stressor isn't under your control, there are things you can do to reduce the stress. When you recognize warning signs of stress, such as muscle tension or restlessness, you need to find a way to relieve the tension. **Two strategies that can help you relieve tension are physical activity and relaxation.** These methods work by altering the physical state of your body.

Physical Activity   Bicycling, taking a walk, playing the drums—these are some ways to release tension when you are under stress. By doing something physically active, you provide your body with a healthy outlet for built-up energy. At the same time, you shift your focus from your problems to the task at hand. This gives your mind a chance to relax, too.

You do not have to be an athlete to use physical activity to manage stress. The activities you choose don't have to be competitive sports, and you don't have to be the best at them. Instead, select activities that you enjoy. If you enjoy an activity, you are more likely to do it on a regular basis. Try to incorporate physical activity into your daily routine. That way, you will always have a way to work off the day's tension.

Relaxation   The goal of relaxation techniques is to give your mind and body a rest. When you are relaxed, you may be awake and alert, but you are not responding actively to stressors. You may relax your mind by reading a book, taking a nap, listening to music, or doing something creative, such as playing the guitar. You can relax tense muscles by taking a hot shower or bath, stretching, or having someone massage your neck.

Deep breathing is a relaxation method that offers quick relief from stress. Take a few deep breaths in a row. Slowly breathe in as much air as you can through your nose. Hold the air in for a few seconds and then slowly exhale through your mouth. Place one hand on your chest and one on your abdomen as you inhale. Your abdomen should expand more than your chest. When you breathe deeply, you take in more oxygen, which helps your body to function better.

FIGURE 11   Being physically active improves physical fitness, provides an outlet for excess energy, and takes your mind off your problems.

Hands-On *Activity*

Progressive Relaxation

You can use progressive relaxation to release the tension that builds up in your muscles.

Try This

1. Sit quietly in a comfortable chair or lie down and close your eyes. Make sure that your arms and legs are uncrossed.
2. Tighten each muscle group in your body, hold for 10 seconds, and relax. Follow the order in the bulleted lists.
3. Finally, tense all the muscles in your whole body. Hold for 10 seconds and relax.

Think and Discuss

1. Compare how you felt before doing this activity to how you felt after doing the progressive relaxation.
2. Think back to what you learned about the alarm stage of your body's response to stress. Why do you think progressive relaxation is an effective stress-reduction technique?
3. List some times during a typical week when it would be helpful to use progressive relaxation.

- Wrinkle your forehead. Try to make your eyebrows touch your hairline.
- Close your eyes as tightly as you can.
- Form a frown with the corners of your mouth.

- Raise your shoulders up to your ears.
- Bend your elbows and tense your upper arms.
- Tightly clench your fists.
- Gently arch your back.

- Tighten your stomach muscles.
- Tighten your hip and buttock muscles.
- Squeeze your legs together.
- Curl your toes under as tightly as you can.

The Importance of Happiness   Recall that happiness is one of the primary emotions that are expressed by people in all cultures. Yet happiness is more than just a pleasant universal emotion—it may be one of the keys to a healthy life. What is happiness? It is the perception of your own well-being and the belief that your own life is worthwhile. There is growing scientific evidence that happiness can actually make you healthier and may even help you live longer.

If happiness can make you healthier, you need to know what makes you happy. Scientists have shown that a positive attitude and being involved with activities that you find rewarding can result in happiness. What probably won't make you happy, according to current studies, are money and material things.

Sometimes happiness results from activities you do by yourself, such as going for a walk or volunteering for a good cause, or from activities you do with other people, such as dancing, singing, or playing games.

Connect to Your Life

What makes you happy? Did you identify things that you do by yourself or with other people?

GO ONLINE

PearsonSuccessNet.com
For: More on coping with stress

Change Your Thinking

Do you tend to overreact to unexpected events or worry a lot about the future? Sometimes you can reduce your level of stress by changing the way you think about stressors. **One way to change your thinking is to replace negative thoughts with positive ones. You can also use humor in some stressful situations.**

Avoiding Negative Thinking   Think back to the last time you were in a stressful situation. What thoughts were going through your mind? Were you thinking things like "I'll never be able to do this," or "Everyone will think I'm stupid," or "I'm not as good as the others"? For many people, negative thoughts like these accompany stressful situations. Of course, such negative thinking only increases a person's stress level. With negative messages running through the person's mind, it becomes almost impossible to succeed.

How can you stop yourself from thinking negative thoughts when you are under stress? One way is to monitor your internal conversations closely and substitute positive or realistic thoughts for negative thoughts. For example, instead of thinking "I'll never be able to do this," you might think, more positively, "I've done things like this before." Another way to eliminate negative thinking is to act as a "coach" while you think about an upcoming stressful event. As you do a mental rehearsal of the event, give yourself positive messages such as "You can do it." This will boost your self-confidence, which will help you during the actual event.

Humor   Finding humor in a situation can be an effective way to deal with stress. Have you ever laughed at yourself after doing something that was not really funny, such as slipping on a wet floor or saying something embarrassing in front of a group of people? If so, you probably realized that your laughter helped to relieve your feelings of stress.

If you use humor carefully, it can be an effective tool for managing stress. Humor allows you to deal quickly with a stressor and keep it in the proper perspective. But don't use humor to cover up your true feelings. Also avoid laughing at serious situations. Remember that making fun of yourself is different than making fun of other people's problems.

FIGURE 12 Humor can be an effective way to ease tension and provide relief from stress.

Build Resilience

The strategies discussed so far for coping with stress may not be sufficient for dealing with all types of stressors. **You need to build your resilience to help you deal with extreme or prolonged stress.** The strategies listed below can help you increase your resilience. Pick the approaches that you think will work best for you.

Even the most resilient person in the world will be unhappy or worried some of the time. However, knowing these strategies can help you "bounce back" from setbacks in your life.

FIGURE 13   A library can provide a quiet place to get away from the everyday hassles of school and home.

▶ **Take Care of Yourself** Exercise, eat well, and get enough sleep. Find time for activities you enjoy. When your general health is good, you are better able to deal with stressful situations.

▶ **Build a Support System** Develop good relationships with family, friends, and other people who will care for and listen to you.

▶ **Take Action** Decide what needs to be done and act on your decision. Set short-term goals that you know you can accomplish.

▶ **Help Somebody** Volunteer to work on a project in your community or help a friend with a problem.

▶ **Confide in Yourself** Sometimes it is too difficult to talk with others about your feelings. You can confide in yourself by writing about stressful events in a journal.

▶ **Go Easy on Yourself** When something bad happens, your response to other stressors may be more intense. So cut yourself a little slack.

▶ **Put Things in Perspective** Look beyond a difficult situation to a time when things will be better. When you talk about bad times, remember to talk about the good times in your life, too.

▶ **Find a Hassle-Free Zone** Find someplace where you can feel free from stress—your home, a relative's house, a community center, or the library.

▶ **Stick to Your Routines** During a major life change, keep to daily routines, such as a nightly conversation with a friend.

Connect to Your Life **Where are some places you can go to feel free from stress?**

Reach Out for Support

What if you try many of the stress-management techniques described in this chapter and nothing seems to work? Sometimes the stress in your life becomes too overwhelming for you to handle on your own. At those times, you may want to ask someone to help you with your problems. Sometimes all you need is someone to talk to. **Sharing your problems can help you see them more clearly. Just describing your concerns to someone else often helps you to understand the problem better.** Many people are willing to listen and lend support if you ask.

- ▶ a parent or other adult relative
- ▶ a teacher or a coach or a religious leader
- ▶ a school counselor or nurse
- ▶ a sibling or friend

The person you choose to talk to may not be able to help you with your specific concerns. But he or she may be able to refer you to someone who can.

At some time in your life, you may want or need some kind of counseling. Many specialists are available to work with people who need help coping with stress. Some specialists are trained to help you identify the stressors in your life and learn constructive strategies for coping with them.

FIGURE 14 Sharing a problem with someone you trust can help you to better understand the problem. Just talking about your problems can often help reduce your stress.

Section 4 Review

Key Ideas and Vocabulary

1. List seven techniques you can use to cope with stress:
   a. two techniques that help you take control
   b. three strategies to help relieve tension
   c. two ways to change your thinking
2. What are some ways you can relax?
3. Why is it important to build resilience?
4. How can seeking the support of others help when you are under stress?

Critical Thinking

5. **Relating Cause and Effect** Explain how relaxation techniques help to reduce stress.

Health at Home

Building Resilience Look at the list of strategies for building resilience on page 75. Describe specific ways that you could use four of the strategies to help manage your stress. **WRITING**

6. **Making Judgments** Do you think the saying "Don't sweat the small stuff" is good advice for coping with stress? Why or why not?
7. **Applying Concepts** Your best friend's father just lost his job. Your friend is worried that his family might have to move to a different city. How could you help your friend through this stressful time?

Chapter 3
At a Glance

VIDEO **TEENS** Talk ⊙
Stressed Out What did you learn from the video about dealing with the stress in your life?

Section 1   What Causes Stress?

Key Ideas

▶ You experience stress when situations, events, or people make demands on your body and mind.

▶ Four general types of stressors are major life changes, catastrophes, everyday problems, and environmental problems.

Vocabulary
- stress (56)
- eustress (56)
- distress (56)
- stressor (57)
- catastrophe (58)

Section 2   How Stress Affects Your Body

Key Ideas

▶ The body's response to stress occurs in three stages—the alarm stage, the resistance stage, and the exhaustion stage.

▶ The warning signs of stress include changes in how your body functions and changes in emotions, thoughts, and behaviors.

▶ Stress can trigger certain illnesses, reduce the body's ability to fight an illness, and make some diseases harder to control.

Vocabulary
- fight-or-flight response (60)

Section 3   Stress and Individuals

Key Ideas

▶ How you react to a stressor depends on your assessment of the situation.

▶ Your personality influences your assessment of a situation.

▶ The key factor in resilience is having the support of family and friends.

Vocabulary
- optimism (66)
- pessimism (66)
- perfectionist (66)
- resilience (67)

Section 4   Coping With Stress

Key Ideas

▶ Two techniques that can help you keep stress under control are time management and mental rehearsal.

▶ Two strategies that can help you relieve tension when you are stressed are physical activity and relaxation.

▶ One way to change your thinking is to replace negative thoughts with positive ones. You can also use humor in some stressful situations.

▶ You need to build your resilience to deal with extreme or prolonged stress.

▶ Sharing your problems can help you see them more clearly. Just describing your concerns to someone often helps you to understand the problem better.

Vocabulary
- mental rehearsal (71)

Chapter 3 Review

Reviewing Key Ideas

GO ONLINE

PearsonSuccessNet.com
For: Chapter 3 review activity

Section 1

1. A good friend is in the hospital with a serious illness. This stressor can be classified as
   a. an everyday problem.
   b. a major life change.
   c. a catastrophe.
   d. an environmental problem.

2. Explain how stress can be a positive experience.

3. Why are major life changes stressful?

4. **Critical Thinking** Do you think that adolescence is an especially stressful time? Explain.

Section 2

5. The stage when your body adapts to the continued presence of a stressor is the
   a. alarm stage.   b. resistance stage.
   c. exhaustion stage.   d. adaptation stage.

6. List six things that happen to your body during the fight-or-flight response.

7. Explain the relationship between stress and the onset of an asthmatic attack.

8. What effect can prolonged stress have on your immune system?

9. **Critical Thinking** Why do you think that sleep problems are a useful warning sign of stress?

Section 3

10. What is the statement "I'll never be able to do this" an example of?
    a. aiming for perfection
    b. negative thinking
    c. optimism
    d. resilience

11. As you assess a stressful situation, what two general questions are you answering?

12. How does having the support of family and friends contribute to resilience?

13. **Critical Thinking** Researchers have compared the level of stress in different sports. They found that individual sports, such as gymnastics, can cause more stress than team sports, such as basketball. Why do you think this difference exists?

Section 4

14. Stressors that you can control tend to be
    a. catastrophes.
    b. major life changes.
    c. everyday hassles.
    d. environmental problems.

15. Explain how the process of mental rehearsal can help you manage stress.

16. When is it important for a person who is stressed to reach out for support?

17. **Critical Thinking** A lie detector measures changes in a person's heart rate and breathing rate. How might changes in these body functions indicate that a person is lying?

Building Health Skills

18. **Advocacy** You have a friend who is involved in so many activities that he no longer has time for you. Lately, he complains that he "can't think straight anymore." Use an e-mail to offer some advice to your friend. **WRITING**

19. **Making Decisions** A product called "Stress Vitamins" claims to "replace essential vitamins that are lost during times of stress." How would you decide whether or not to buy the vitamins?

20. **Setting Goals** Make an action plan to help you reduce the stress of test-taking. Apply strategies you learned for coping with stress. Put your plan into action a week before your next test and monitor your progress. After the test, adjust your action plan, if necessary. **WRITING**

Health and Community

Volunteering Helping others is one way to build resilience. Describe something you could do for one hour each week to help younger students learn to deal with stress. **WRITING**

Standardized Test Prep

Math Practice

The graph shows how listening to music affects the heart rates of surgery patients. Group A listened to the music of their choice during and after surgery. Group B did not. Use the graph to answer Questions 21–24.

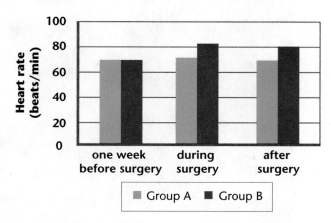

21. What was the average heart rate for both groups a week before surgery?
  A 65 beats per minute
  B 70 beats per minute
  C 75 beats per minute
  D 80 beats per minute

22. What happened to the average heart rate of Group B during surgery?
  F The heart rate increased.
  G The heart rate decreased.
  H The heart rate stayed the same.
  J The heart rate was equal to the average heart rate of Group A.

23. What happened to the average heart rate of Group A during surgery?
  A The heart rate increased.
  B The heart rate decreased.
  C The heart rate stayed the same.
  D The heart rate increased and then decreased.

24. Based on the graph, which of the following statements is true?
  F Listening to music has no effect on stress.
  G Listening to music can increase stress.
  H Listening to music can decrease stress.
  J Average heart rate is not a good measure of stress.

Reading and Writing Practice

Read the passage. Then answer Questions 25–28.

When people rely heavily on technology, they may become victims of *technostress*. With cell phones and instant messaging, people expect to be able to reach someone at any time and at any place—at work, in the car, at home. This constant stimulation and interruption can be stressful. So can having a computer crash when you are facing a deadline. This situation is ironic. Technology is designed to make people more productive—able to accomplish more in the same amount of time. But technostress can make people less productive because they become forgetful or cannot concentrate.

25. What is the main idea of the passage?
  A People should not use technology.
  B Technology makes people less productive.
  C Relying on technology can cause stress.
  D Stress makes it harder to concentrate.

26. Based on this passage, the word *ironic* means
  F stressful.
  G predictable.
  H unexpected.
  J funny.

27. Technology is designed to
  A reduce the time a person spends at work.
  B increase the time a person spends at work.
  C increase the time needed to do a given task.
  D decrease the time needed to do a given task.

Constructed Response
28. In a paragraph, explain how technology can cause stress. Give at least two examples of technostress.

> ### Test-Taking Tip
> **When taking a test, be aware of how much time you have and the total number of questions. Wear a watch to keep track of your progress.**

CHAPTER 4

Mental Disorders and Suicide

GO ONLINE PearsonSuccessNet.com

TEENS Talk

VIDEO 4

Starving for Control

Preview **Activity**

How Do You Relate to Food?

Complete this activity before you watch the video.

1. How many of the following statements describe ways you behave or think about food?
   a. I keep eating even when I no longer feel hungry.
   b. Feeling sad or angry affects the amount of food I eat.
   c. I prefer to eat when I am alone rather than with others.
   d. I often feel guilty after I eat.
2. Review your responses. Would you say that your eating habits and thoughts about food are healthy or unhealthy? Write a paragraph explaining your answer. **WRITING**

Mental Disorders

Section 1

Objectives

▶ **Explain** how mental disorders are recognized.

▶ **Identify** four causes of mental disorders.

▶ **Describe** five types of anxiety disorders and four other types of mental disorders.

Vocabulary

- mental disorder
- anxiety
- anxiety disorder
- phobia
- obsession
- compulsion
- mood disorder
- depression
- schizophrenia
- personality disorder

Warm-Up

Quick Quiz Which of the following statements are always true? Which are sometimes true? Which are always false?

① It is easy to identify a person with a mental disorder.

② Mental disorders are caused by emotional problems.

③ Mental disorders affect a person's ability to function.

④ People who have a mental disorder are dangerous.

WRITING For each of your responses, explain why you gave the answer you did.

What Are Mental Disorders?

A **mental disorder** is an illness that affects the mind and reduces a person's ability to function, to adjust to change, or to get along with others. For example, a mental disorder could affect a person's ability to study, keep a job, or make friends.

Recognizing Mental Disorders   Some behaviors fall outside the broad range of normal behaviors. For example, it is normal to wash your hands before eating. But it isn't normal to keep washing your hands when they are already clean. If behaviors, feelings, or thoughts are highly unusual and not appropriate to a situation, they are considered abnormal. **Mental health experts see abnormal thoughts, feelings, or behaviors as signs, or symptoms, of a mental disorder.** The distress that people who have mental disorders experience affects their ability to function.

Figure 1 lists symptoms of attention-deficit/hyperactivity disorder or ADHD. ADHD usually appears in childhood. A person with ADHD often has difficulty in school, at home, and in social settings. When ADHD is treated with medication, the results may be immediate and dramatic.

Remember, just because someone has trouble sitting still or paying attention from time to time, it doesn't mean that person has ADHD. The symptoms must be frequent and affect the person's ability to function.

Signs of Attention Deficit
- Doesn't pay attention to details
- Makes careless mistakes
- Does not seem to listen
- Is disorganized
- Forgets to do daily activities
- Is easily distracted
- Has difficulty following instructions

Signs of Hyperactivity
- Fidgets or squirms while seated
- Has trouble staying in seat
- Frequently runs about or climbs
- Has trouble working quietly
- Talks excessively
- Has trouble waiting or taking turns
- Interrupts others

FIGURE 1 Some people with ADHD display the entire range of symptoms. Others mainly show signs of attention deficit or hyperactivity.

Causes of Mental Disorders   Researchers have made progress on figuring out what causes mental disorders, but there is still much to learn. Sometimes a mental disorder has a single cause. But more often a combination of factors are involved. **Physical factors, heredity, early experiences, and recent experiences can cause mental disorders.**

▶ **Physical Factors** Damage to the brain may cause a mental disorder. The damage could be caused by a growth, or tumor, in the brain; an injury to the brain; or an infection that destroys brain cells. Exposure to a poison such as lead, or prolonged use of alcohol or other drugs can also damage the brain.

▶ **Heredity** A person may inherit a tendency toward a mental disorder. This doesn't mean the person will necessarily have the disorder. It only means that the person is at greater risk if events in his or her life act as a trigger for the disorder.

▶ **Early Experiences** Extremely negative experiences that occur early in life can lead to mental illness. For example, a child who is neglected or a child who is abused may develop a mental disorder.

▶ **Recent Experiences** Some mental health experts think that recent experiences are more likely than early experiences to trigger a mental disorder. An example would be the death of a loved one.

Connect to Your Life

How would having ADHD affect someone's ability to study?

FIGURE 2 About 19 million Americans are affected by phobias at some point in their lives. **Predicting** Which of these phobias might interfere with normal, everyday activities?

Common Phobias

Arachnophobia	fear of spiders
Aviophobia	fear of flying
Acrophobia	fear of high places
Agoraphobia	fear of open or public places
Claustrophobia	fear of small, closed-in places
Ophidiophobia	fear of snakes

Anxiety Disorders

Have you ever been extremely afraid in a situation even though you knew the actual threat did not justify such an intense response? Have you ever been fearful without knowing why? If so, you have experienced anxiety. **Anxiety** (ang ZY ih tee) is fear caused by a source you cannot identify or a source that doesn't pose as much threat as you think.

Everyone experiences anxiety now and then. For example, you may feel anxious before a final exam, a school dance, or tryouts for the wrestling team. These feelings are normal and usually short-lived. When the anxiety persists for a long time and interferes with daily living, this is a sign of an **anxiety disorder.** About 13 percent of children and teens age 9 to 17 will have an anxiety disorder. **Examples of these disorders are generalized anxiety disorder, phobias, panic attacks, obsessive-compulsive disorders, and post-traumatic stress disorder.**

Generalized Anxiety Disorder A person with this disorder displays intense worry, fears, or anxiety most days for at least six months. These thoughts and emotions do not have a single specific source. They occur in many different situations. Many of the warning signs of stress can also be signs of this disorder, including irritability, muscle tension, trouble falling asleep, and trouble concentrating.

Phobias Martin was on his way to visit his grandparents. As he walked toward the elevator in their building, he began to feel dizzy and nauseous. His heart began to pound, and he had trouble catching his breath. He knew he could not face getting into the elevator, so he climbed three flights of stairs instead. Martin has a fear of small, closed-in places, such as an elevator. Anxiety that is related to a specific situation or object is called a **phobia** (FOH bee uh). Martin's phobia is called claustrophobia. Figure 2 lists some common phobias.

Connect to Your Life

Do you have a phobia that you are aware of? If so, how do you deal with your phobia?

Panic Attacks   Brianna was standing in line at the movies. Suddenly, for no apparent reason, she felt intense fear and a strong desire to leave the theater. Brianna was having a panic attack. During a panic attack, a person will experience some of the following symptoms.

- ▶ fast heart rate
- ▶ rapid breathing
- ▶ fear of suffocation
- ▶ believes he or she is dying
- ▶ sweating
- ▶ trembling or shaking

- ▶ choking sensation
- ▶ chest discomfort or pain
- ▶ nausea or stomach distress
- ▶ dizziness or lightheadedness
- ▶ fear of losing control
- ▶ an "out of body" sensation

People who have repeated panic attacks tend to worry about having another. To avoid another attack, they may change their behavior. If, for example, they have attacks in restaurants, they may stop going out to eat.

Obsessive-Compulsive Disorder   An unwanted thought or image that takes control of the mind is an **obsession** (ub SESH un). An obsession may lead to a **compulsion** (kum PUHL shun), an unreasonable need to behave in a certain way to prevent a feared outcome. Repeatedly checking that the stove isn't on or that a door is locked is a compulsion. A person who thinks and acts in such ways has an obsessive-compulsive disorder (OCD).

Post-Traumatic Stress Disorder   People who survive a life-threatening event may develop post-traumatic stress disorder. They may have flashbacks or nightmares that produce intense fear or horror. They may be unable to sleep or to concentrate. Because situations that remind them of the event can produce intense anxiety, they begin to avoid those situations. They may feel guilty because they survived and others did not.

FIGURE 3   People who witness traumatic events as part of their jobs are at risk for post-traumatic stress disorder. This firefighter witnessed the September 11th attacks in New York City.

Other Mental Disorders

Young people can have mental disorders other than anxiety disorders. **Some teens and young adults have mood disorders or schizophrenia. Others have impulse-control disorders or personality disorders.**

Mood Disorders People who have a ==mood disorder== experience extreme emotions that make it difficult to function well in their daily lives. Bipolar disorder is an example of a mood disorder. Normally, people have moods that shift from happy to sad, based on what is happening in their lives. People who suffer from bipolar disorder shift from one emotional extreme to another for no apparent reason.

Bipolar disorder is also called manic-depressive disorder. During a manic episode, people are usually overly excited and restless. They may talk so rapidly that it is impossible to follow what they are trying to say. They may have difficulty concentrating for long on any one thing. They often show poor judgment. Manic episodes alternate with periods of deep depression. ==Depression== is an emotional state in which a person feels extremely sad and hopeless. In between manic episodes and periods of depression, a person with bipolar disorder may behave normally.

Schizophrenia One of the most serious mental disorders is called ==schizophrenia== (skit suh FREE nee uh). It can be identified by severe disturbances in thinking, mood, awareness, and behavior. *Schizophrenia* means "split mind." People with this disorder have minds that are "split off" or separated from reality.

People who have schizophrenia are rarely harmful to others. At times they may even appear normal. At other times, they may talk to themselves, display inappropriate emotional responses, dress and act strangely, and withdraw from others. Sometimes they develop fears that are not supported by reality. They may believe that someone or something controls their thoughts or wants to harm them.

GO ONLINE

PearsonSuccessNet.com

For: More on bipolar disorder

FIGURE 4 The English artist Louis Wain had schizophrenia. His cat drawings alternated between those that were more realistic and those that were less realistic, or abstract.

FIGURE 5 Some teens spend hours playing poker online or with their friends. A person who cannot resist the urge to gamble has an impulse-control disorder.

Impulse-Control Disorders   People with an impulse-control disorder cannot resist the impulse, or drive, to act in a way that is harmful to themselves or to others. You may have heard of people who cannot resist the impulse to take items that they don't need or want. These people have an impulse-control disorder called kleptomania.

About 4% of people in the United States cannot control the urge to gamble. Their need to gamble is so great that they will go into debt or even steal in order to continue to gamble. This impulse-control disorder is most common among males. Being able to place a bet on the Internet has contributed to the problem. Plus, poker tournaments on television have made poker more popular among younger people. Uncontrolled gambling among male teens is on the rise. One teen became so addicted to playing poker online that he lost $5000 of his parents' money. He then stole another $3500 from a friend's house.

Mental health experts may add uncontrolled shopping to the list of impulse-control disorders. For shopping to be classified as uncontrolled, the shoppers must buy many things that they do not need and must know that they don't need these things. The shopping must also interfere with work, school, or family obligations, or cause financial problems. About 85 percent of uncontrolled shoppers are female.

Do you know someone with an impulse-control disorder? How does this affect his or her life?

Personality Disorders Recall that your personality determines how you tend to relate to other people. Most people can get along with a variety of people in different situations. Other people are not as flexible. People who have a **personality disorder** display rigid patterns of behavior that make it difficult for them to get along with others. The many different types of personality disorders fall into three broad groups.

▶ **Group A:** People with personality disorders in this group tend to be cold and distant. They cannot form close relationships. Some may be so absorbed in their own thoughts that they withdraw from reality. Paranoid personality disorder is a Group A disorder. The term *paranoid* is used to describe someone who is overly suspicious of other people.

▶ **Group B:** People with personality disorders in this group are often overly emotional or unstable. They can be selfish and demanding. They may place a high value on themselves and no value on others. Antisocial personality disorder is a Group B disorder. A person with this disorder may commit violent acts without any sense of guilt.

▶ **Group C:** People with personality disorders in this group often cannot make decisions. They may have a strong need for the approval of others. They may avoid people for fear of rejection. Dependent personality disorder is a Group C disorder. People with this disorder often need help from others to properly care for themselves.

FIGURE 6 Just looking at a crowd of people usually won't tell you who has a personality disorder.

Section 1 Review

Key Ideas and Vocabulary

1. What is a **mental disorder**? How are mental disorders recognized?

2. List four possible causes of mental disorders.

3. What is an **anxiety disorder**? What is the key difference between a phobia and generalized anxiety disorder?

4. What is a **compulsion**? How does a compulsion differ from an **obsession**?

5. What are some symptoms of a **mood disorder**?

Critical Thinking

6. **Relating Cause and Effect** Explain how someone who has frequent unexpected panic attacks might develop a phobia.

Health at School

Dealing With ADHD Interview a teacher or guidance counselor at your school. Ask what strategies can help a student with ADHD to succeed in school. How can students help a classmate with ADHD? Write a paragraph summarizing your findings. **WRITING**

---

7. **Classifying** Eric spends about six hours a day playing video games. He resents being called away from the computer for supper. He has lost interest in most other activities and his grades are dropping. What type of mental disorder might Eric have? Explain.

GO ONLINE PearsonSuccessNet.com Audio Summary Section 4.1

Technology & Health

Virtual Reality and Phobias

Today, virtual reality technology can help people overcome their phobias. Typically, therapists treat people with phobias by having them slowly confront the actual object or situation they fear. With virtual reality, a similar process can occur without leaving the therapist's office. A person who is afraid of heights, for example, might be placed in a series of "virtual situations" with increasing heights. At each stage, the person learns to relax and control the anxiety.

WRITING Pick another phobia from Figure 2 on page 84. Describe the images you would include in a virtual reality program to help a person deal with this phobia.

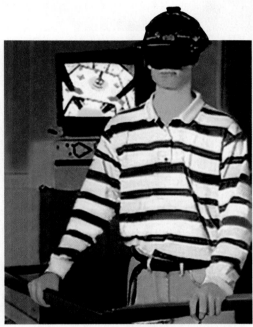

▲ **A Virtual Reality Session**

With the visor, a person can see 3D computer-generated images. The images change when the person moves his or her head or uses a joystick.

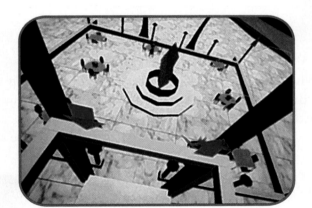

▲ **Riding a Virtual Elevator**

This is a virtual view from a glass elevator in a 46-story hotel. When a person feels comfortable at this height, he or she can move the elevator to a higher floor.

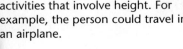

◄ **A Real-World Test**

If the therapy is successful, the person will be able to do actual activities that involve height. For example, the person could travel in an airplane.

Eating Disorders

Objectives

▶ **Identify** health risks associated with anorexia.

▶ **Explain** the relationship between bulimia and dieting.

▶ **List** the main health risks of binge eating disorder.

Vocabulary

• eating disorder
• anorexia nervosa
• bulimia
• binge eating disorder

Warm-Up

Myth Eating disorders affect only females.

Fact Eating disorders affect females more than males, but males do develop eating disorders. Because of this myth males are even less likely than females to seek help for an eating disorder.

WRITING What factors other than gender might keep someone from seeking help for an eating disorder?

Anorexia Nervosa

What image comes to mind when you hear the word *Thanksgiving?* Do you think of a turkey dinner with all the trimmings? In most cultures, people celebrate holidays and other important occasions by preparing traditional foods. But for some people food can be a source of anxiety.

An **eating disorder** is a mental disorder that reveals itself through abnormal behaviors related to food. Eating disorders are about more than just food. They are about emotions, thoughts, and attitudes. A person with **anorexia nervosa** (an uh REK see uh nur VOH suh) doesn't eat enough food to maintain a healthy body weight. The main symptom is extreme weight loss. Other symptoms include slowed heart and breathing rates, dry skin, lowered body temperature, and growth of fine body hair. In females, another symptom is loss of menstrual periods.

FIGURE 7 People with anorexia think they are fat even when they are thin. Anorexia affects about one out of every one hundred teenaged girls.

Media Wise

Body Image and Magazines

Many teens are not satisfied with the size or shape of their bodies. This dissatisfaction can sometimes lead to an eating disorder. Images in magazines can contribute to the problem. Use this checklist to evaluate the messages that teen magazines send about your body and appearance.

Do the images show a narrow range of body shapes and sizes?	Yes No
Are the females in the images taller and thinner than typical teenage girls?	Yes No
Are the males in the images taller and more muscular than typical teenage boys?	Yes No
Are there stories about people who are dieting, bulking up, or getting a makeover?	Yes No
Does the magazine make you feel dissatisfied with your body?	Yes No

Two or more "Yes" answers reveal how magazines influence readers' feelings about their own bodies.

Activity Look at a magazine that is aimed at teens. Use the checklist to evaluate the images in the magazine. Then write a paragraph summarizing what you learned. Also describe how looking at the images affected you. **WRITING**

Health Risks Even when they are extremely thin, people with anorexia see themselves as fat and work hard to lose more weight. They may use exercise or diet pills to help lose weight. **A person with anorexia can starve to death. In some cases, a lack of essential minerals causes the heart to stop suddenly, leading to death.**

Possible Causes The lack of a chemical that regulates mood is one possible cause of anorexia. Other possible causes are low self-esteem and a strong desire to please others. A person with anorexia may have a history of troubled relationships. By controlling what they eat, or more accurately what they don't eat, people with anorexia may be attempting to take control of their lives. Instead, the disorder begins to control them.

Treatment People with anorexia usually deny that there is a problem. They need to be encouraged to get help. Because of their extreme weight loss, they are often first treated in a hospital. Doctors, nurses, and dietitians work together to stop the weight loss and change a person's eating habits. At the same time, mental health experts work with the patient and family members to address the underlying emotional problems.

What factors might influence a person's decision to gain or lose weight?

GO ONLINE

PearsonSuccessNet.com

For: More on eating disorders

Bulimia

Another eating disorder that is seen mainly in young women is bulimia. People who have **bulimia** (byoo LIM ee uh) go on uncontrolled eating binges followed by purging, or removing, the food from their bodies. They purge the food by making themselves vomit or by using laxatives.

Health Risks   Most people with bulimia maintain a weight within their normal range. However, the cycle of bingeing and purging has a negative effect on their health. They may suffer from dehydration, kidney damage, and a lack of necessary vitamins and minerals. The stomach acid in vomit irritates the throat and erodes the enamel from teeth. People with bulimia often become depressed and may even think about suicide.

Possible Causes   Many of the causes listed for anorexia also apply to bulimia. In addition, people who binge may use food as a way to feel better emotionally. Then they purge because they are concerned about gaining weight. **Bulimia may begin in connection with a diet, but the person soon becomes unable to stop the cycle of bingeing and purging.**

Treatment   People who have bulimia are aware of what they are doing, but they are unable to control their behavior. They often are too ashamed of their behavior to seek help. If you know someone with the signs listed in Figure 8, offer your support in private. Then gently encourage the person to seek the help of a mental-health professional. There are many effective treatments for bulimia.

Connect to Your Life

If you suspected that a friend was bingeing and purging, what would you say to your friend?

FIGURE 8 Some athletes are at risk for an eating disorder because their sport has rules about weight. For example, a wrestler must be within a set weight range to qualify for a given weight class.

Possible Signs of Bulimia

- Unable to control eating binges
- Eating too much food too quickly
- Eating in private
- Cycles of weight gain and loss
- Bathroom visits right after eating
- Hoarding or storing food

Binge Eating Disorder

Have you ever eaten so much at a holiday dinner that you couldn't eat dessert? Or perhaps you ate all of your Halloween candy in a single evening. Everyone overeats once in awhile. But some people cannot control their compulsion to overeat. People with **binge eating disorder** regularly have an uncontrollable urge to eat large amounts of food. They usually do not purge after a binge. People with binge eating disorder cannot stop eating even when they are full. They may intend to eat two slices of bread and end up eating the entire loaf.

Health Risks   Someone with binge eating disorder isn't going to starve to death or suffer the consequences of repeated purging. But there are health risks with binge eating. **The main physical risks of binge eating disorder are excess weight gain and unhealthy dieting.** When people gain an unhealthy amount of weight, they are at greater risk for illnesses such as diabetes, and physical disorders such as high blood pressure. To deal with the weight gain from binges, some people try extreme diets that promise rapid weight loss. The hunger caused by such diets can trigger more binges, which can trigger more dieting—a yo-yo effect.

Possible Causes   Some people use binge eating to avoid dealing with difficult emotions, such as anger, or with stressful situations. The food may provide some temporary relief, but it can lead to other difficult emotions, such as guilt or depression.

Treatment   People with binge eating disorder need help in learning how to control their eating. They may need to eat more slowly and deliberately. They often need to address underlying emotional problems.

FIGURE 9   Someone with a binge eating disorder eats a large amount of food in a short amount of time. **Evaluating** Based on the containers, do you think the amount of food eaten qualifies as a binge? Explain.

Section 2 Review

Key Ideas and Vocabulary

1. What is an **eating disorder**?
2. What health risks are associated with anorexia? Why are people with anorexia unlikely to ask for help?
3. What is **bulimia**? Explain the connection between bulimia and dieting.
4. What health risks are possible for someone with binge eating disorder?

Critical Thinking

5. **Comparing and Contrasting** How are bulimia and anorexia alike? How are they different?

Health at School

Eating Disorders and Athletes Interview a coach or trainer about the role athletics may play in some eating disorders. Ask in which sports eating disorders are most often seen. Ask what a coach or trainer can do to help prevent eating disorders. Write a paragraph summarizing what you find out. **WRITING**

6. **Evaluating** When Brittany visits her aunt, her aunt insists that she take second helpings at dinner. To please her aunt, Brittany eats beyond the point that she feels full. Is this a sign that Brittany has an eating disorder? Explain your answer.

Depression and Suicide

Objectives

▶ **Explain** why it is important to identify and treat clinical depression.

▶ **Explain** why individuals might deliberately injure themselves.

▶ **Describe** one major risk factor for suicide.

Vocabulary

• clinical depression
• cutting
• suicide
• cluster suicides

Warm-Up

Health Stats What relationship is there between risk of depression and how connected teens feel to their school?

Connection to School	Risk of Depression
Very connected	Very low
Quite a bit	Low
Somewhat	Low to moderate
Very little	Moderate
Not at all connected	High

WRITING What could make someone feel very connected to school? What could make someone feel disconnected?

Clinical Depression

Everyone feels depressed now and then. It is normal to feel depressed if you experience a significant loss or failure. For example, you would expect to feel depressed if someone you loved moved away or if you didn't make a team you tried out for. Usually, however, the feeling of depression lifts after a few days or weeks, and you get on with your life. Sometimes, however, feelings of depression linger.

Defining Depression   Maria used to be energetic and happy. She had good grades and loved playing in the school band. But recently her grades have dropped and she quit the band. She cannot sleep and feels tired all the time. Feelings of despair have taken over Maria's life.

Maria has a mood disorder known as clinical depression. People with **clinical depression** may feel sad and hopeless for months. They are unable to enjoy activities that were once a source of pleasure. As the depression deepens, people often are unable to accomplish their daily tasks. **Depression can cause problems at school, at home, and in one's social life. If untreated, depression can also lead to substance abuse, serious behavior problems, and even suicide.**

Recognizing Depression For a teen to be moody, irritable, or tired at times is not unusual. So how do mental health experts distinguish the signs of depression from typical teenage moods and behaviors? Mental health experts use the symptoms listed in Figure 10 to diagnose depression. A person who has clinical depression will experience four or more of the symptoms nearly every day for at least two weeks.

About one out of 10 teens will experience clinical depression before they are 18. After age 15, females are twice as likely as males to suffer from depression. Some teens may have a single episode of clinical depression; others experience more than one episode of depression.

Risk Factors Depression sometimes seems to arrive "out of the blue," but there are often explanations. The following risk factors have been identified for depression. It is important to know that having one or more risk factors doesn't mean that you will become depressed.

► A parent or other close biological relative with a mood disorder

► A major life change or a prolonged stressful situation

► Being the victim of a violent crime or witnessing violence

► A previous bout of depression

► A sense of hopelessness

Treatment for Depression Medication is an effective treatment for clinical depression. Normally, chemicals in the brain control how signals pass from one nerve cell to another. When someone is depressed, the brain does not use these chemicals properly. Medication helps to restore normal brain function. Mental health experts can also help people who are depressed to learn new strategies for coping with their problems.

Connect to Your Life **Do you have any of the signs of depression? Do you have any of the risk factors for depression?**

GO ONLINE
PearsonSuccessNet.com
For: More on depression

FIGURE 10 People who are depressed often avoid being with others. However, doing things you enjoy on your own is not a sign of depression.

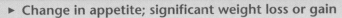
Signs of Clinical Depression

► Change in appetite; significant weight loss or gain
► Change in sleep patterns; difficulty sleeping or sleeping too much
► Change in activity level; sluggish (slow) or frantic (fast-paced)
► Loss of interest in usual activities
► Loss of energy; always tired
► Hopelessness; boredom; guilt; worthlessness
► Unexplained crying; easily annoyed
► Repeated thoughts of death and suicide
► Body pains; headaches; digestive problems
► Difficulty remembering details, concentrating on tasks, and making decisions

FIGURE 11 Some people with a mental disorder use cutting to cope with their emotions or anxiety.

Self-Injury

When Nicole's mother asked about the cuts on Nicole's arms, Nicole said that her friend's cat scratched her. But the truth is that Nicole cut her arms with a razor blade. **Cutting** is the use of a sharp object to intentionally cut or scratch one's body deep enough to bleed. Cutting is one example of self-injury. Burning the skin on purpose with a lighted match or cigarette is another. Although cutting and burning leave scars, people often hide these signs of their behavior. For example, they may wear long-sleeved shirts even in warm weather. Self-injury occurs most often in young women, but it can occur in young men, too.

Self-injury is an unhealthy way to cope with emotions, stress, or traumatic events. People who self-injure are not usually trying to kill themselves. They are trying to feel better. They say that the behavior provides temporary relief from painful feelings. But self-injury doesn't address any of their underlying problems. Self-injury can be a symptom of a mood disorder, anxiety disorder, or eating disorder.

Self-injury isn't common, but it is a serious problem. The behavior may begin as an unplanned impulsive act, but it often turns into a compulsion. Someone who relies on cutting or burning to cope with emotions should tell a trusted adult. With the help of a mental health professional, they can learn better ways to cope with their problems.

Suicide Prevention

Suicide is the intentional killing of oneself. Suicide affects all kinds of people: young, old, bright, average, rich, poor, female, male. In the United States, suicide is the tenth-leading cause of death among young people ages 15–24. Between 1950 and 1990, the teen suicide rate quadrupled. But since 1990, the rate has declined.

Is there any way to tell whether or not someone is going to attempt suicide? Mental health experts have identified factors that put people at risk for suicide. They have identified other factors that protect people from suicide. If people understand these risk factors and protective factors, they can take steps to further reduce the suicide rate.

Risk Factors   Is there a connection between depression and suicide? **Mood disorders, such as depression, are a major risk factor for suicide.** Other factors that may put a person at risk for suicidal behavior include:

▶ A previous suicide attempt or a family history of suicide

▶ Having both a mental disorder and a substance abuse disorder

▶ Feelings of hopelessness or isolation

▶ Lack of access to mental health treatment

▶ Being influenced by the suicide of family members, peers, or celebrities

Protective Factors   If a person is at risk for suicide, there are some factors that can help reduce the risk. The first is treating a person's mental disorders, especially depression. Getting treatment for the abuse of alcohol or other drugs is important. So is feeling connected to school and having close relationships with family, friends, and others in the community.

Another protective factor is having personal beliefs that discourage suicide. Knowing how to resolve conflicts in non-violent ways also lowers a person's risk for suicide.

Cluster Suicides   Sometimes a suicide or an attempted suicide triggers other suicides, especially among teens. **Cluster suicides** are a series of suicides that occur within a short period of time in the same peer group or community. Some cluster suicides involve a pact between friends. Others occur in response to an initial suicide. Immediate counseling of peers after a suicide or a suicide attempt can help to prevent cluster suicides.

FIGURE 12 Feeling connected to school helps protect teens from suicide.

Connect to Your Life   **What other factors do you think are protective factors for suicide?**

When a Friend Is Thinking About Suicide

Do . . .

- trust your feelings.
- take the threats seriously.
- say how concerned you are.
- listen carefully.
- talk calmly.
- involve a trusted adult.
- stay until help arrives.

Do Not . . .

- dare the person to go ahead with the suicide attempt.
- judge the person.
- analyze the person's motives.
- argue or offer reasons not to attempt suicide.
- leave the person alone.

FIGURE 13 These lists identify things you can do and things you should avoid doing when a person is thinking about suicide. **Evaluating** Which of the items on the list of things to do would you feel most able to do and why?

Warning Signs It would be very helpful if someone who was about to attempt suicide showed unmistakable warning signs. Unfortunately, most suicides occur without warning. Teens who attempt suicide usually don't talk about it in advance, write about it in school essays, or give away their possessions. A sudden drop in grades or an increase in drug abuse are warning signs of a problem, but that problem isn't always suicide.

So should you ignore radical changes in behavior that you observe in a friend? No, but you should proceed with caution. Don't assume you know what problem the person is dealing with. Offer your support and encourage the friend to talk to a trusted adult.

Helping Others A friend makes comments like "They'll be sorry when I'm gone" or "I have nothing to live for." What would you do? If you know that your friend has tried suicide before or if your friend describes a detailed plan of action, this is cause for serious concern. Your friend may make you promise not to tell anyone about his or her plan. Whether or not your friend realizes it, by confiding in you, your friend is asking you for help. To help your friend, you must break the promise and notify an adult that your friend is in danger. You should also notify an adult if you become aware of a suicide pact among a group of teens.

An important thing to remember is that suicidal behavior is a cry for help in dealing with problems that seem overwhelming. Suicidal people often feel that they have looked to others for support and have received no response. It is important that you show care and concern for the person. You can help by listening to and providing support for friends or family members who are feeling depressed, hopeless, or overwhelmed by stress. When the support you offer is backed by professional intervention, a life may be saved. Figure 13 offers suggestions about what to do and what not to do if you are faced with this situation.

What would you do if someone told you about a plan to commit suicide?

Helping Yourself If you have been feeling depressed, remember that no matter how overwhelming the problems in your life may seem, suicide is never a solution. It is vital that you talk about your feelings with a trusted adult or mental health professional. Together, you will be able to find solutions that you may not have thought of on your own. No matter how isolated you may feel, you do not have to deal with your problems alone. No matter how hopeless you feel your situation is, there are positive steps that you can take.

Perhaps you are unable or unwilling to talk with an adult you live with. If so, consider talking with a family member who lives nearby, an adult friend of the family, or an adult in your faith community. There are also resources at your school that you can turn to—a school nurse, a social worker, a counselor, or a psychologist. These people are trained to screen for depression and suicide. If you are asked whether you have thought about or attempted suicide, tell the truth. That way, the person you are talking with will be able to get you the help you need.

Crisis centers and suicide-prevention hotlines are other resources you can use. These resources are staffed 24 hours a day. Look in the front of your local telephone directory or online for a listing of these hotlines. You can also get telephone numbers for crisis centers and hotlines in your area from the information operator, or directory assistance.

FIGURE 14 People have jumped from the Golden Gate Bridge in San Francisco. So the city placed a phone on the bridge that connects people to a crisis center.

Section 3 Review

Key Ideas and Vocabulary

1. How do mental health experts diagnose **clinical depression**?

2. Why is it important to identify and treat clinical depression?

3. Describe the self-injury behavior known as **cutting**. Explain why individuals might injure themselves on purpose.

4. What is a major risk factor for suicide? What protective factor can help to reduce the effect of this risk factor?

5. What are **cluster suicides**? What can be done to prevent them?

Health and Community

Suicide Hotlines Find out whether there are suicide hotlines in your community. Are the people who answer the phones employees or volunteers? What kind of training do people have before they are allowed to answer the phone? Are teens allowed to be volunteers? If so, what kind of role can they play? Write a paragraph summarizing what you find out. **WRITING**

Critical Thinking

6. **Evaluating** Why do you think cluster suicides occur most frequently among teenagers?

7. **Applying Concepts** Your friend Bryan has shown some signs of clinical depression for a month. You are very worried about Bryan, but he refuses to talk to you about his feelings. What could you do to help Bryan?

Dealing With Setbacks

Sarah stared at her coach with disbelief—she was no longer a starter on her soccer team! All of the friends she's played soccer with for years would be on the field at the start of the game, but not her. "I'm such a failure. I can't do anything right," Sarah said to herself. "Why do bad things always happen to me?"

Like Sarah, everyone experiences setbacks in their lives. And, like Sarah, most people are discouraged by a setback, at least at first. But, what do you do next? Do you think of yourself as a failure or a victim? Or are you able to bounce back and move on? Here are some tips that can help you handle setbacks in positive ways.

1 Think of a setback as an isolated event.

If you experience a setback, remind yourself of its limits. In other words, don't think of a setback as evidence that you're a failure overall. Instead, tell yourself that you did not succeed at one thing at one particular time. By thinking this way, you keep the setback in the proper perspective. Otherwise, the setback can begin to affect other things you do.

2 Recognize that a setback is temporary.

Some setbacks have long-term effects, but many setbacks do not. Although a setback will probably alter your immediate plans and goals, you can view a setback as an opportunity. For example, Sarah could ask her coach for advice on how she could work toward becoming a starter again.

Also, remember that a setback doesn't mean that you need to abandon your original goal. Ask yourself these questions, which may help you discover a new path to pursue.

▶ Is there a different path I can take to reach my goal?

▶ Can I arrange for a second opportunity to try and reach my goal, either now or in the near future?

▶ Can I modify my goal somewhat?

3 Become aware of your "self-talk."

Pay attention to what you are thinking and saying to yourself about the setback. One way to monitor your thoughts is by jotting them down. Then, dispute each negative thought ("I can't do anything right") with a response ("I play guitar really well."). This will help you turn off the negative thinking.

4 Take action.

One key to bouncing back from a setback is to focus your energy in productive ways. For example, do you now have time to pursue a new interest? Can you view the setback as a challenge to work even harder at improving your skills? By looking ahead and focusing your efforts toward a new goal, you can put the setback behind you.

BUILDING HEALTH SKILLS

Practice the Skill

1. Your friend, Sarah, just told you that she is no longer a starter on her soccer team. What could you say to help her view the setback as an isolated and temporary event?

2. For each of the negative thoughts below, write a response to yourself that disputes it.
   a. "I never do anything right."
   b. "Nobody likes me."
   c. "I'm the stupidest person in the class."

3. Recall a setback you experienced recently. In a paragraph, describe how you handled the setback. Include details about what you were feeling and thinking, and what actions you took. In a second paragraph, describe other, more positive steps you could have taken to deal with the setback.

Section 4

Treating Mental Disorders

Objectives

▶ **List** reasons that might prevent a person from seeking help for a mental disorder.

▶ **Identify** four types of mental health professionals.

▶ **Describe** some general types of treatment for mental disorders.

Vocabulary

- psychiatrist
- neurologist
- clinical psychologist
- psychiatric social worker
- therapy

Warm-Up

Dear Advice Line,

Lately, I spend a lot of time just staring at the ceiling or crying for no reason at all. I haven't told anyone about my problems. I don't want to be labeled as "a mental case."

WRITING What advice would you give to this person? What would you say about the person's fear of being labeled?

Locating Community Resources

Each year, about 20 percent of Americans experience the symptoms of a mental disorder. However, the majority of these people do not seek help. What could keep a person with a mental disorder from getting the help he or she needs? **Sometimes people don't recognize the signs of a mental disorder. Or they may have been told that, with willpower alone, they can overcome the problem. Or they may not know where to go for help.**

The first step toward recovery is recognizing the need for help. Do not ignore the warning signs of mental disorders. But don't rely too much on your own diagnosis. Treat a mental disorder the same way you would treat a physical illness. If you have a physical illness, you should see a doctor to receive appropriate treatment. If you have a mental disorder, you should see a mental health professional for treatment.

Although it may be difficult, try to share your problems with an adult that you trust. This could be a parent, guardian, teacher, counselor, doctor, or religious leader. The adult can help you find mental health services in your community. A local hospital may have a mental health center. Some communities have mental health clinics or counseling centers. Others have drop-in centers for teens, where counselors provide help and guidance. For some types of treatment, you will need the consent of a parent or guardian. See the Building Health Skill on locating community resources in Chapter 25 for additional information.

Types of Mental Health Professionals

Mental health professionals are trained to recognize mental disorders and to treat them. The type of treatment they offer depends upon their training. **Psychiatrists, clinical psychologists, social workers, and mental health counselors are four types of mental health professionals.**

Psychiatrists After medical school, doctors may get advanced training in the treatment of mental disorders. Their goal is to become a **psychiatrist** (sy KY uh trist), a physician who can diagnose and treat mental disorders. A psychiatrist will do a medical exam to rule out physical causes. Then, he or she will talk with a patient to find out what symptoms the patient has.

Psychiatrists use a variety of treatment methods. As physicians, they are able to prescribe medications. If they suspect that a patient's symptoms may have a physical cause, they may ask the patient to see a neurologist (noo RAHL uh jist). A **neurologist** is a physician who treats physical disorders of the nervous system.

Clinical Psychologists A **clinical psychologist** is trained to recognize and treat behavior that is not normal. Clinical psychologists have a doctoral degree in psychology and at least two years of practical training in clinics or hospitals. A psychologist may help a psychiatrist to diagnose a patient's disorder. The psychologist may interview the patient or use a diagnostic test. In some states, clinical psychologists can prescribe medications.

Social Workers Social workers listen to and advise people. Often, they act as a link between people who need help and community resources that provide help. A **psychiatric social worker** helps people with mental disorders and their families to accept and adjust to an illness.

Mental Health Counselors Some mental health counselors focus on specific problems or work with specific groups of people. Substance abuse counselors, for example, work with people who have problems with alcohol or other drugs. School counselors work with students. Youth counselors work with teenagers. Members of faith communities often have practical training as counselors.

FIGURE 15 Talking about a problem can help a person identify the source of the problem. **Predicting** What kinds of questions might a mental health professional ask?

Connect to Your Life Are there mental health counselors at your school? If so, what type of problems do they deal with?

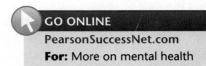
GO ONLINE
PearsonSuccessNet.com
For: More on mental health

Kinds of Treatments

How does a mental health professional decide which treatment method, or therapy, to use? Some disorders and some patients respond better to some treatments than to others. **Psychotherapy, drug therapy, and hospitalization are three methods used to treat mental disorders.**

Psychotherapy   During psychotherapy (sy koh THEHR uh pee), a person talks with a therapist. These talks help people understand and overcome their mental disorders. Three types of psychotherapy are:

▶ **Insight Therapy** This type of therapy helps people better understand the reasons for their behavior. The hope is that, with this insight, they will be able to change some of their behaviors.

▶ **Cognitive and Behavioral Therapy** This type of therapy helps a person to identify situations, objects, or thoughts that trigger abnormal behaviors. The goal is for the patient to learn new ways to behave.

▶ **Group Therapy** In group therapy, people meet with other people who have similar disorders. A mental health professional leads the group. Group members work together to develop coping skills.

Drug Therapy   Doctors prescribe drugs to treat many mental disorders. The drugs can relieve symptoms and allow patients to function normally. Drug therapy and psychotherapy may be used together.

Hospitalization   Sometimes people with mental disorders need constant attention or are in danger of harming themselves or others. These people may have to be treated in a hospital. In the hospital, patients receive therapy. The staff helps patients prepare to leave the hospital. When patients return home, social workers often help them adjust to the change.

FIGURE 16   One type of therapy is group therapy. The counselor works with a group of people who have similar mental disorders.

Section 4 Review

Key Ideas and Vocabulary

1. State three reasons why someone might not seek help for a mental disorder.

2. Briefly describe four types of mental health professionals.

3. What three general methods are used to treat mental disorders?

Critical Thinking

4. **Relating Cause and Effect** Why might a person with a mental disorder end up in a hospital?

Health at Home

Views on Mental Illness Talk with some adults in your family about their attitudes toward mental illness. Do they think of mental disorders in the same way that they think of other illnesses? Have their attitudes about mental illness changed over the years? Write a paragraph summarizing what you find out. **WRITING**

5. **Classifying** In what type of therapy are people most likely to discuss their childhood experiences? Explain.

Chapter 4
At a Glance

VIDEO **TEENS** Talk
Starving for Control What three things did you learn from the video about dealing with eating disorders?

Section 1   Mental Disorders

Key Ideas

▶ Mental health experts see abnormal thoughts, feelings, or behaviors as signs of a mental disorder.

▶ Physical factors, heredity, early experiences, and recent experiences can cause mental disorders.

▶ Anxiety disorders include generalized anxiety disorder, phobias, panic attacks, obsessive-compulsive disorders, and post-traumatic stress disorder.

▶ Some teens have mood disorders, schizophrenia, impulse-control disorders, or personality disorders.

Vocabulary
- mental disorder (82)
- anxiety (84)
- anxiety disorder (84)
- phobia (84)
- obsession (85)
- compulsion (85)
- mood disorder (86)
- depression (86)
- schizophrenia (86)
- personality disorder (88)

Section 2   Eating Disorders

Key Ideas

▶ A person with anorexia can starve to death or die from a lack of essential minerals.

▶ Bulimia may begin in connection to a diet, but the person soon becomes unable to stop the cycle of bingeing and purging.

▶ The main physical risks of binge eating disorder are excess weight gain and unhealthy dieting.

Vocabulary
- eating disorder (90) • anorexia nervosa (90)
- bulimia (92) • binge eating disorder (93)

Section 3   Depression and Suicide

Key Ideas

▶ Depression can cause problems at school, at home, and with one's social life. If untreated, depression can also lead to substance abuse, serious behavior problems, and even suicide.

▶ Self-injury is an unhealthy way to cope with emotions, stress, or traumatic events.

▶ Mood disorders are a major risk factor for suicide.

Vocabulary
- clinical depression (94)
- cutting (96) • suicide (96)
- cluster suicides (97)

Section 4   Treating Mental Disorders

Key Ideas

▶ Sometimes people don't recognize the signs of a mental disorder. Or they may not know where to go for help.

▶ Psychiatrists, clinical psychologists, social workers, and mental health counselors are four types of mental health professionals.

▶ Psychotherapy, drug therapy, and hospitalization are three methods used to treat mental disorders.

Vocabulary
- psychiatrist (103) • neurologist (103)
- clinical psychologist (103)
- psychiatric social worker (103) • therapy (104)

Chapter 4 Review

Reviewing Key Ideas

GO ONLINE
PearsonSuccessNet.com
For: Chapter 4 review activity

Section 1

1. Claustrophobia is an example of a(n)
   a. mood disorder.
   b. anxiety disorder.
   c. personality disorder.
   d. impulse-control disorder.

2. An unreasonable need to behave in a certain way is called a(n)
   a. obsession.
   b. phobia.
   c. compulsion.
   d. panic attack.

3. Give an example of how an experience in a person's life could trigger a mental disorder.

4. What is the common factor in all personality disorders?

5. **Critical Thinking** Use the definition of a mental disorder to explain why schizophrenia is a serious mental disorder.

Section 2

6. An eating disorder marked by bingeing and purging is
   a. anorexia nervosa.
   b. binge eating disorder.
   c. bulimia.
   d. yo-yo dieting.

7. What are some possible causes of anorexia?

8. How are bulimia and binge eating disorder similar? How are they different?

9. **Critical Thinking** Why do you think that eating disorders are classified as mental disorders? Do you agree with this classification? Explain.

Section 3

10. A person with clinical depression
    a. feels sad now and then.
    b. feels extremely sad for a week.
    c. feels sad or hopeless for months.
    d. still tends to find enjoyment in life.

11. What is the link between depression and suicide?

12. How can having close relationships help you stay mentally healthy?

13. **Critical Thinking** You feel depressed at times, but always snap out of it quickly. Should you seek help? Why or why not?

Section 4

14. Which mental health professional acts as a link between a patient and community resources?
    a. psychologist
    b. psychiatrist
    c. social worker
    d. neurologist

15. How are mental and physical disorders similar?

16. How are psychotherapy and drug therapy similar? How are they different?

17. **Critical Thinking** Families of people with mental disorders often need support and counseling. Why do you think this is so?

Building Health Skills

18. **Analyzing Influences** Many works of fiction focus on characters with mental disorders. What positive or negative effects could reading about these characters have on readers?

19. **Communicating** People who are hospitalized for mental disorders may be released to "halfway houses." At the halfway house, they learn to readjust to life in the community. What would you say if someone objected to having a halfway house in your neighborhood?

20. **Setting Goals** Make a list of qualities that are important in someone you could confide in. Then use the list to evaluate yourself. Make an action plan to be a better confidant. Decide on steps you can take to improve your communication and listening skills. Monitor your progress and adjust your action plan, if necessary. **WRITING**

Health and Community

Suicide and Older Adults The suicide rate is high among adults over age 65. One of the risk factors for older adults is a sense of isolation. What does your community do to reduce feelings of isolation among older adults? Are there ways you can help? Write a paragraph summarizing what you find out. **WRITING**

Standardized Test Prep

Math Practice

The risk of developing schizophrenia changes when different family members have the disorder. Use the graph to answer Questions 21–23.

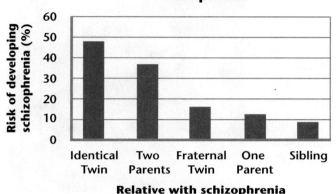

Heredity as a Risk Factor for Schizophrenia

21. What is the risk of developing schizophrenia if one parent has the disorder?
    - **A** 9%
    - **B** 12%
    - **C** 16%
    - **D** 45%

22. When is a person at greatest risk for developing schizophrenia?
    - **F** when one parent has the disorder
    - **G** when two parents have the disorder
    - **H** when any sibling has the disorder
    - **J** when an identical twin has the disorder

23. How does the risk of having an identical twin with schizophrenia compare to the risk of having a fraternal twin with schizophrenia?
    - **A** The risk is the same.
    - **B** The risk is twice as great.
    - **C** The risk is three times as great.
    - **D** The risk is four times as great.

Test-Taking Tip

When taking a test, answer the easy questions first. This approach can boost your confidence.

Reading and Writing Practice

Read the passage. Then answer Questions 24–27.

A lack of natural light can cause seasonal affective disorder (SAD). As the supply of natural light decreases in winter, people with SAD become depressed. Unlike some depressed people, who have trouble eating and sleeping, SAD patients may sleep up to 18 hours a day, crave starchy foods, and gain weight. Treatment for SAD involves phototherapy, exposure to a full range of bright lights, for 10–30 minutes a day. For up to 70 percent of SAD sufferers, the treatment restores the balance of chemicals in the body, which relieves the symptoms of SAD.

24. What is the main idea of this passage?
    - **A** Depression is caused by a lack of natural light.
    - **B** A lack of natural light causes one kind of depression.
    - **C** Phototherapy can cure all types of depression.
    - **D** Phototherapy can cure all cases of SAD.

25. From this passage, you can infer that a lack of natural light
    - **F** decreases certain chemicals in the body.
    - **G** increases certain chemicals in the body.
    - **H** restores the balance of chemicals in the body.
    - **J** upsets the balance of chemicals in the body.

26. Which statement is supported by this passage?
    - **A** Some symptoms of SAD are not typical of depression.
    - **B** Most depressed people crave starchy foods.
    - **C** Sleeping for 18 hours is a typical sign of depression.
    - **D** SAD and clinical depression are similar disorders.

Constructed Response
27. There is a type of SAD that occurs in the summer when the hours of daylight increase. Write a paragraph predicting what the symptoms of summer SAD might be.

CAREERS

Mental Health

Some mental health workers help treat people with mental disorders. Others help people deal with stress and anxiety.

Recreational Therapist

Recreational therapists use activities as therapy. Activities can include art, dance, music, or sports. The goal may be to reduce anxiety, build confidence, and develop social skills. Recreational therapists help patients express themselves. For example, they may teach people to communicate their feelings through dance movements. This career usually requires a bachelor's degree, but some jobs require only an associate degree.

Social Worker

Some social workers assist people with mental disorders by providing counseling for patients and their families. They may help people who have been in a hospital adjust to life back in the community. For example, a social worker may help a person find a job or enroll in school. Many social workers have a master's degree in social work and are licensed and certified by their states.

Psychiatric Aide

A psychiatric aide helps care for people who have mental disorders. The aide helps patients with basic functions such as eating, dressing, and personal grooming. An important part of the job is to socialize with patients during activities and to observe their behavior. Entry into this career requires a high school degree.

Sport Psychologist

Sport psychologists work with athletes to improve their performance. They teach athletes to use relaxation and mental rehearsal to cope with the stress of competition. They help athletes increase their motivation, confidence, and focus. A sport psychologist must know about both the mind and the body. This career requires at least a master's degree. Certification by the Association for the Advancement of Applied Sport Psychology (AAASP) is recommended.

Career Focus

Kirsten Peterson, Sport Psychologist for the U.S. Olympic Committee

How did you get interested in sport psychology?

"In high school I was a softball pitcher. In college, I suddenly could not throw a strike. It was a very difficult experience and there was no one available to help me. I was studying psychology then when I learned about the field of sport psychology. I realized this was a way for me to help athletes deal with difficult sport experiences like mine."

Where do you work and which athletes do you work with?

"I work for the U.S. Olympic Training Committee in Colorado Springs. In the summer, I work with the wrestling teams. In the winter, I work with the bobsled and skeleton teams. I attend my teams' practices and I travel with the teams quite a lot."

What do you do as a sport psychologist?

"I help Olympic athletes develop their mental skills so they can perform at a higher level. I help them to recognize and manage their anxiety in competition. I teach athletes how to quickly refocus when difficult situations happen; this can save critical time in a competition. I also counsel them on their regular life issues so that they can focus and do their job."

Health and Careers

Careers in Mental Health Research other careers in mental health. Choose a career that interests you and explain why your personality would be a good match for this career. **WRITING**

Family Relationships

1 Families Today
- **Technology & Health** *How's Your Driving?*

2 Family Problems

 Building Health Skills
- **Communicating** Using Win-Win Negotiation

3 Keeping the Family Healthy
- **Hands-On Activity** Group Juggling

GO ONLINE PearsonSuccessNet.com

VIDEO 5

TEENS Talk

Family Matters

Preview **Activity**

What Causes Tension in a Family?

Complete this activity before you watch the video.

1. Parents and teens may disagree about a number of things. Rank the following areas of possible disagreement from 1 (most likely) to 8 (least likely) to be a source of tension between parents and teens.
   ___ privacy   ___ appearance
   ___ chores   ___ friends
   ___ grades   ___ music
   ___ money   ___ curfew

2. Are there other areas of disagreement that should be added to the list? If so, what are they and where would you rank them?

3. Are you sometimes the cause of tension in your family? If so, how? **WRITING**

Families Today

Objectives

▶ **Explain** why healthy family relationships are important.

▶ **Identify** three main factors that have changed the form of families.

▶ **Describe** some family forms that exist today.

▶ **Summarize** the division of responsibilities within a family.

Vocabulary

- divorce
- nuclear family
- adoption
- single-parent family
- extended family
- blended family
- foster family
- socialization

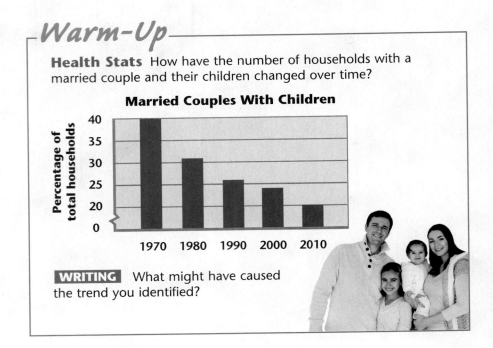

Warm-Up

Health Stats How have the number of households with a married couple and their children changed over time?

Married Couples With Children

WRITING What might have caused the trend you identified?

The Family and Social Health

The family is often called the "basic unit of society." It is the structure within which children are raised, and values and customs are passed from generation to generation. The family is also the basic unit of social health because it is where a person first learns to relate to other people. **If the relationships with family members are healthy, a child learns to love, respect, and get along with others, and to function as part of a group.**

In a family, a child can see that each person depends on the others in the group. One person's actions can affect everyone else in the family. Ideally, the child learns that lasting relationships must be based on mutual caring, trust, and support. People often use the relationships they observe and participate in at home as a model for relationships outside the home.

Families are part of larger social units that influence what happens within families. For example, a family often shares many of the traditions, values, and views on relationships of its cultural group. The neighborhood a family lives in can affect how much freedom children are given to explore the area beyond their home. Where a parent works can affect how much time the parent has to spend with his or her children.

Connect to Your Life Do you agree that the family is the basic unit of society? Why or why not?

Today, fathers account for over 3% of all stay-at-home parents.

The Changing Family

Until the mid-1800s, parents both stayed home, farming or working at trades, and both shared in raising the children. The Industrial Revolution changed things—men went to work in factories and offices while most women stayed home. Today, fewer than 10 percent of families in the United States fit this model. **Three main factors account for changes in the American family: more women in the work force, a high divorce rate, and an increase in the age at which people marry.**

More Women in the Work Force Today, more than half of all mothers with preschool children are in the work force. Women work outside the home for different reasons. Some are single parents, others want to continue a career, or the family needs two incomes to pay the bills. When parents work outside the home, families spend less time together. The parents have to trust other people to care for their children.

High Divorce Rate Each year, many children experience their parents' divorce. A **divorce** is a legal agreement to end a marriage. In most states, it is easier to get a divorce now than in the past because of "no-fault" divorce. With this type of divorce, neither person is blamed for the divorce. There is some positive news. Since 1990, the divorce rate has gradually decreased.

Divorce affects a family's structure, finances, and health—emotional and physical. Family members have to adjust to new roles, relationships, and living arrangements. If a parent remarries, the adjustments continue.

Postponing Marriage Today many young people delay marriage and parenthood until later in life. As a result, families tend to be smaller. Most women have two children, and a growing number have none. In contrast, in the 1950s women had three or four children, on average.

Single-Parent Family

Nuclear Family

Family Forms

The word that best describes families today is *diversity*. Families reflect the diverse circumstances, needs, values, and cultures of the people in them. **Children can live in nuclear, single-parent, extended, blended, or foster families.** As you read about these family forms, think about the important qualities that all families share.

Nuclear Family   A **nuclear family** consists of a couple and their child or children living together in one household. The children may be the parents' biological children, or they may have been adopted. **Adoption** is the legal process by which parents take another person's child into their family to be raised as their own.

Single-Parent Family   About half of all children today will live, at least for a time, in single-parent families. A **single-parent family** is a family in which only one parent lives with the child or children. Some single-parent families are the result of divorce. Other single-parent families form when one parent dies, when parents never marry, or when a single person adopts a child.

Mothers head about 85 percent of single-parent families. However, a growing number of fathers are raising children on their own. Caring for the family alone can be difficult for single parents. They must earn a living, care for children, and perform all the other tasks needed to keep the family functioning. Financial worries are often a major problem in single-parent families.

Extended Family   A nuclear or single-parent family may be part of a larger family unit. An **extended family** is a group of close relatives living together or near each other. The extended family often includes grandparents, aunts, uncles, or cousins.

Extended Family

Blended Family

In extended families, family responsibilities are shared among all members. Children might be raised by their grandparents, aunts, and uncles as well as by their parents. Extended families provide a strong system of support for family members. For single parents, especially, this extra support helps strengthen the family.

Blended Family   When parents remarry, they form a blended family. A **blended family** consists of a biological parent, a stepparent, and the children of one or both parents. A stepparent is a parent related by marriage. Today, at least five million children under the age of 18 live in blended families.

In blended families, the usual problems of families may become more complex. Children may feel that a stepparent is an intruder and not really part of the family. Children may have trouble getting along with stepbrothers and stepsisters. Successful blended families say that it is important to be flexible. Parents need to spend time with their biological children, their stepchildren, and the entire family group.

Foster Family   In a **foster family,** an adult or couple cares for children whose biological parents are unable to care for them. The foster family provides a temporary home for the children. Some children remain in a foster family for an extended time. Sometimes foster parents are able to adopt the children in their care.

Other Families   Other groups of people also are considered families. One example is a married couple without any children. Another is a group of unrelated people who choose to live together and support and care for one another.

GO ONLINE
PearsonSuccessNet.com
For: More on families

Connect to Your Life

Which family forms most closely match your family and those of your friends?

Typical Household Rules

- No watching television or playing video games before homework is done or after bedtime.
- Be home by 10 P.M. on weekdays and by midnight on weekends.
- Keep your room clean, take out the trash, and do other chores.
- Only use the internet for school work before homework is done.
- No friends over when an adult isn't home, without permission.

FIGURE 3 In a family, children are often responsible for assigned chores. One of the responsibilities of adults is to set rules for children. **Evaluating** Do you think the rules in this list are fair? Why or why not?

Responsibilities Within the Family

For a family to function effectively, each member of the family must do his or her part. Each family divides up responsibilities in its own way. **Often there are some responsibilities that clearly belong to the adults, some that clearly belong to the children, and some that can be shared.**

Adults' Responsibilities The heads of families are expected to provide for their children's basic needs. These needs include food, clothing, shelter, education, health care, security, and love. When children's basic needs are met, they feel loved and secure, and they gain self-esteem.

Adult family members are also responsible for teaching children to behave in a way that is acceptable to the family and to society. This process is called **socialization** (soh shuh lih ZAY shun). Through this process, children develop into responsible adults. They learn to respect the rights of others and to give and receive love. They also absorb the values, beliefs, and customs that are important to their families.

Adult family members set rules to protect their children's safety and to maintain order within the family. Figure 3 lists some typical rules that parents may set for teenage children.

Connect to Your Life **What kinds of tasks are the adults in your family responsible for doing?**

Children's Responsibilities As a young child, you may have been responsible for dressing yourself, tidying up your room, and doing your homework. Today, you may have to do household chores or care for younger brothers and sisters. You may even add to the family income with earnings from a part-time job. You are also responsible for following family rules and for showing respect for all family members.

At times, young people may disagree with some of the rules set by their parents. For example, teens may want to stay out later on weeknights or weekends. Disagreements may also arise between brothers and sisters. They may argue about items that must be shared, such as a computer.

When such conflicts arise, family members need to discuss their problems in a calm, respectful manner. If each member recognizes the need for rules and limits that are satisfactory to all, it will be easier to work together to resolve the conflict. The Building Health Skills on pages 124–125 teaches a method for resolving conflicts.

Shared Responsibilities In most families, there never seems to be enough time for chores. Many families divide up the responsibilities. For example, each person may prepare dinner one night a week. Children may take turns doing the laundry or grocery shopping. All family members may help care for elderly or disabled family members.

There are other benefits to sharing household chores. Children can master skills such as cooking that will be vital to them as adults. Children who are trusted with important tasks develop a sense of responsibility and higher self-esteem. Most importantly, family members learn that the family is stronger when they work as a team and depend on each other.

FIGURE 4 When family members share chores they learn to depend on one another and work as a team.

Section 1 Review

Key Ideas and Vocabulary

1. Explain why the family is called the basic unit of social health.

2. What are the three main factors that account for changes in the American family? Give an example of the impact of each factor.

3. What is a **blended family?** What other types of families exist?

4. What is **socialization?** Which family members are responsible for this process?

Critical Thinking

5. Evaluating List three tasks that you are responsible for in your family. How do these tasks help prepare you for adulthood?

Health at School

Responsibilities In some ways, a school is like a family. The responsibilities are divided between students and teachers. Make a list of things you think teachers are responsible for at school. Make a second list of things that students are responsible for. Do students and teachers have any shared responsibilities? **WRITING**

6. Predicting Sankong lives with his father, who is divorced. The father is about to marry a woman with two teenage sons. They will all live in Sankong's apartment. List the possible advantages and disadvantages of this change for Sankong. How could focusing on the advantages help Sankong cope with the change? **WRITING**

Technology & Health

How's Your Driving?

The leading cause of death for teens is car crashes. So when teens begin to drive without adult supervision, parents worry. A new device can reassure parents and help teens improve their driving skills. The device is installed in the car to monitor speed and aggressive behaviors, such as tailgating. Some devices even provide feedback on the use of direction signals and seat belts.

WRITING How could using a monitoring device help a family to build trust? How could it lead to more freedom for a teen driver?

Vehicle Trip Report	
Report Date	08-21
Ending Odometer	7215
Total Miles	23
Overforce Count	20
Overspeed count	5
Highest Overspeed (mph)	80
Unsafe reverses	0
Seatbelt violations	2

▲ **The Monitoring Device**

The device monitors and captures driving behavior. It collects data and video. Parents can see a report that lists all the violations.

▼ **Location of Vehicle**

Some devices can record the route taken by a driver and any stops made along the way. Some systems can notify a parent if a driver leaves an agreed-upon area.

Seat Belts ▶

When the device detects an unsafe behavior, such as an unbuckled seat belt, it beeps or a light goes on.

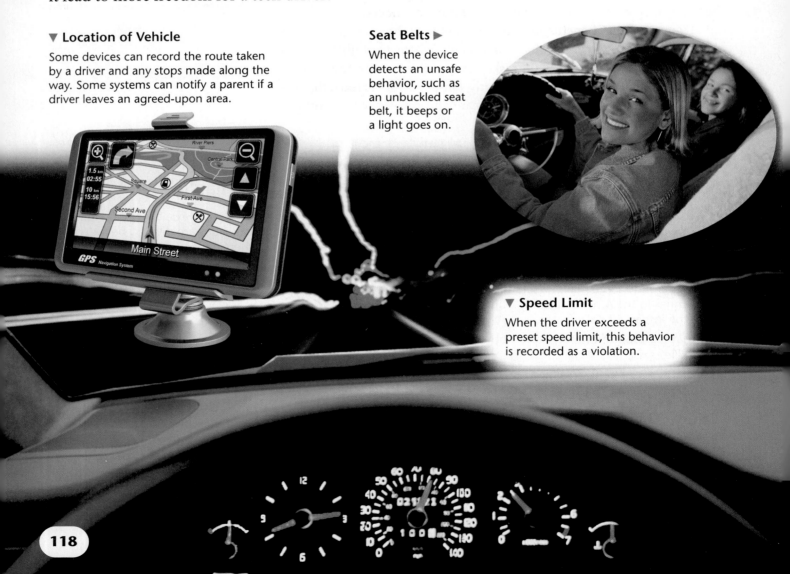

▼ **Speed Limit**

When the driver exceeds a preset speed limit, this behavior is recorded as a violation.

Family Problems

Objectives
▶ **List** some causes of stress in families.
▶ **Describe** three types of abuse that can happen in families.
▶ **Explain** what problems runaways are likely to have.

Vocabulary
- separation
- domestic abuse
- physical abuse
- sexual abuse
- emotional abuse
- neglect
- runaway

Warm-Up

Dear Advice Line,

My parents are getting a divorce. My father complains to me about my mother and my mother does the same about my father. It feels like they want me to pick a side.

WRITING What advice would you give to someone whose parents are getting a divorce?

Causes of Family Stress

The families shown in television shows seem to solve their problems quickly and easily. In real families, however, problems are not resolved so easily. **Some sources of family stress are illness, financial problems, divorce, and drug abuse.**

Illness When one family member has a serious illness, it affects everyone in the family. Everyone worries about the outcome of the illness. Will the person recover? Will the family change? The family's focus is on the person who is sick. Other family members may feel ignored, and then they may feel guilty for thinking about themselves.

Financial Problems A serious illness can lead to financial problems in the family. So can a divorce or the loss of a job. Financial problems can have serious emotional effects on all family members. Adults may feel guilty that they are unable to provide for their families. Children may feel angry that they must go without things that friends have. Both adults and children may worry about the future.

Financial problems can be less stressful if family members work together to improve the situation. Teenagers can try to find part-time work to help out. Younger children can find ways to cut back on their spending. Other relatives may offer help as well.

FIGURE 5 When parents divorce, children need to deal with their anger and sadness. Talking with other teens who are in a similar situation may help.

Advice for Dealing With Divorce

What to Do	What Not to Do
▶ Concentrate on things you enjoy.	▶ Don't feel responsible for the divorce.
▶ Read a book or articles about divorce.	▶ Don't get drawn into arguments between your parents or act as a messenger.
▶ Talk with relatives about your feelings.	▶ Don't feel forced to choose sides.
▶ Meet with other teens who are dealing with divorce.	▶ Don't feel guilty about being angry. You can feel anger and love at the same time.
▶ Talk with a mental health counselor, especially if you are depressed.	▶ Don't isolate yourself from your friends.

Separation and Divorce   It is normal for couples to experience conflict and tension. But sometimes the conflicts are so serious or frequent that a couple may try a separation. A **separation** is an arrangement in which spouses live apart and try to work out their problems. If a couple is not able to work out their differences, a separation may lead to divorce. For many, divorce is a devastating experience. People who divorce sometimes think of themselves as failures, and suffer from grief and loss.

A separation or divorce is often painful for children in the family. They may feel helpless because they are unable to solve their parents' problems. They may feel a range of emotions—resentment, guilt, sadness, anger, or embarrassment. Children may think that the separation or divorce is their fault. They need to be reassured that they are not to blame for their parents' problems. Figure 5 lists things that you should do and things you should avoid doing if your parents are getting a divorce.

Drug Abuse   When a family member has a problem with alcohol or another drug, the whole family is affected. Some effects are subtle. Family members may be embarrassed or worried about their loved one. Some effects are serious. Family members may be afraid to go home or to bring friends home for fear that the person who is abusing drugs will be violent.

There are groups that can help families deal with a drug or alcohol problem. Al-Anon, for example, helps people cope with a family member who has an alcohol problem. Alateen provides help for teenagers who have an alcoholic in the family. These groups hold meetings that are open to anyone who wants to share experiences about living with an alcoholic. To find groups in your area that help family members of drug abusers, look under "Drug Abuse" in your telephone book or search online.

GO ONLINE
PearsonSuccessNet.com
For: More on family stress

Who can you turn to for help if you are experiencing a family problem?

Family Violence

Violence in families may be the most destructive problem that a society must deal with. Violence can occur in all kinds of families—rich or poor, urban or rural, uneducated or educated. The heart of the problem is one person's desire to have power or control over others. **The violence, or abuse, may be physical, sexual, or emotional.** Any family member can be a victim of abuse—a spouse, a child, or an elderly parent. The abuse of one spouse by the other is sometimes called **domestic abuse.** This discussion of abuse will focus on the abuse of children by adults.

Physical Abuse   When an adult punishes a child and leaves a mark that can be seen the next day, this act is considered physical abuse. **Physical abuse** is intentionally causing physical harm to another person. A child who is physically abused may avoid going home. Some victims start to think that they are responsible for the beatings. They think, that if they could figure out the right way to behave, the abuse would stop. But victims are not responsible for the abuse. Only the abuser is responsible.

Children who are physically abused often hide the signs of abuse. They may be ashamed or they may be afraid that, if they tell, their family will be destroyed. They may also be afraid that the abuser might retaliate for revealing the secret.

It is far more damaging, however, for a child to keep silent than to seek help. Web sites and phone books list toll-free numbers for child abuse hotlines. If children cannot find an appropriate group to call, they should talk with a trusted adult. Speaking up is the first step toward putting an end to a dangerous situation.

KEEP OUT OF REACH OF CHILDREN.

REPORT CHILD ABUSE.

Over 700,000 cases of child abuse or neglect are confirmed each year in the United States.

FIGURE 6   Posters like this one are used to advocate against physical abuse of children. **Predicting** What people do you think this poster is aimed at? Explain.

FIGURE 7 A volunteer removes shoes from the steps of the statehouse in Boston, Massachusetts. Hundreds of pairs of shoes were used as symbols of child abuse and neglect cases in the state. The display was organized as part of a news conference to proclaim April as Child Abuse Prevention Month.

Sexual Abuse When an adult uses a child or adolescent for sexual purposes, he or she commits a criminal offense known as **sexual abuse.** Both boys and girls can be victims of sexual abuse. Typically, the adult is someone the child knows well. The adult may be a parent, stepparent, older brother or sister, other relative, or a family friend.

Even a single instance of sexual abuse can have a devastating effect. The child often feels guilty and ashamed. In the victim's mind, he or she assumes all the responsibility or blame for the event. Later in life, it may be difficult for the child to trust others and develop caring relationships.

Victims of sexual abuse should talk with a trusted adult or call the Child Abuse Hotline. Deciding to seek help may be difficult. Victims risk angering, hurting, or betraying the abuser. Sometimes other relatives don't want to believe what is going on and may accuse the victim of lying. The abuser may threaten the child to keep the child from telling. But it is more dangerous to believe the abuser's threats than to report the abuse. Remember, no one has the right to touch you without your consent.

Emotional Abuse "You rotten, no-good punk, you never do anything right." "I wish you had never been born." A child who constantly hears negative statements like these is likely to suffer from emotional abuse. **Emotional abuse** is the nonphysical mistreatment of a person. Emotional abuse doesn't leave visible scars. But it does leave victims feeling helpless, inadequate, or worthless. Children who are emotionally abused need help just as much as children who are physically or sexually abused.

Neglect When adults fail to provide for the basic needs of children, it is called **neglect.** These needs include food, security, socialization, and love. When parents fail to give their children love and emotional support, the children can feel that they do not belong. Victims of emotional neglect often have trouble developing a healthy personality. The state may remove children from a home if they suffer from neglect.

What would you do if you knew that a friend was being abused?

Runaways

A **runaway** is a child who leaves home without permission and stays away for at least one night, or two nights for teens 15 or older. Some leave home because of violence in their families. Others run away because of emotional problems or school failure. Some are angry about family rules that they think are too strict.

Some runaways go to safe locations such as the home of a relative or friend. But many runaways end up with no place to live and no means of support. **They may become ill or turn to crime. They become easy targets for people who are involved with prostitution, pornography, and drugs.**

Many communities have shelters for homeless youth. Some hotlines for runaways, such as the National Runaway Switchboard, arrange for free bus rides home. They supply more than a free ticket. They arrange a call with the family and negotiate a course of action before the runaway returns home. They help the family find resources in the community to help rebuild the family relationships.

If you are thinking of running away, you owe it to yourself to call your local runaway hotline. Call directory assistance, look in the self-help pages at the front of your telephone book, or search online. The counselors can advise you about where to get help for family or other problems.

FIGURE 8 Running away might seem to be a solution to problems. In reality, most runaways encounter serious problems while on their own.

Section 2 Review

Key Ideas and Vocabulary

1. List four general types of problems that can cause stress in families.
2. How is a **separation** different from a divorce?
3. Briefly describe physical abuse, sexual abuse, and emotional abuse.
4. What is **neglect**?
5. What kinds of problems might running away from home lead to?

Critical Thinking

6. Relating Cause and Effect Explain why a serious illness affects all members of a family.

Health and Community

Managing Money Some financial problems in families are caused by major life crises such as a serious illness or job loss. But sometimes, people just don't know how to manage money wisely. Ask someone at a local bank or credit union about programs in your community that help teens to learn about managing money. Write a paragraph summarizing what you learn. **WRITING**

7. Predicting How might meeting with other teens whose parents are getting divorced help a teen cope with a family breakup?
8. Relating Cause and Effect More children run away in summer than in winter. What factors could help explain this difference?

Using Win-Win Negotiation

"Dad, there's no good reason why I shouldn't be able to stay out late on weekends. I'm tired of being treated like a baby!"

"You're only fifteen, Rosa. You can't just come and go as you please. Midnight is late enough."

Rosa and her father have been having this "discussion" for weeks. They just go around and around, getting more and more annoyed and stubborn. Often at the heart of a disagreement is a breakdown in communication.

When communication is poor, conflict can tear a relationship apart. But with good communication, conflict can lead to a solution and to greater understanding and growth as well.

The key to resolving conflicts is to find common goals that both people share. By using "win-win" negotiation, you can turn a no-win situation into one where everyone comes out a winner.

1 Describe the problem.

When you have a conflict, take the time to really understand the problem. Write out answers to the following questions.

▶ What do you think the problem is?

▶ How does it make you feel?

▶ What don't you like about the situation?

▶ What do you want out of the situation?

Dad makes me come in so early. It makes me angry that he doesn't trust me, but I hate fighting with him. I'd like to have more freedom and to get along with him.

Rosa's not old enough to stay out late. I worry about her safety. I don't want to fight with her, but I don't want her to get hurt.

② See the other point of view.

Now describe the problem as you think the other person sees it. What do you think are the other person's thoughts, feelings, and goals?

Dad thinks he's protecting me. He worries when I'm out late, but he wants to get along with me and keep me out of trouble.

Rosa thinks I don't trust her. She's angry because she can't spend enough time with her friends. She wants me to trust her.

③ Involve the other person.

Explain the "win-win" process and ask the other person to try Steps 1 and 2. If the person isn't willing to try the process, ask another adult to play the role of the other person. Even if you don't have a partner, go through the steps yourself. Your willingness to see the other person's point of view may help the situation.

④ Share and discuss.

Discuss the situation with the other person.

► Listen closely and don't interrupt while the other person is talking.

► Say something that shows that you understand the other person's point of view. Understanding isn't the same as agreeing.

► Talk about and acknowledge each other's feelings. Unexpressed feelings often get in the way of resolving conflicts.

► Attack the problem, not the person. Seek solutions, and do not blame.

► Look for shared goals. Avoid taking specific positions at first.

► Focus on what you want to happen in the future. Look forward, not back.

Dad, I understand that you worry when. . . .

Rosa, I realize that time with your friends is important. . . .

⑤ Invent solutions.

Make a list of solutions that meet at least some of the needs that both of you have expressed. Invent solutions first; judge them later.

Dad, what if I call you if I'm out after 11 and have late hours twice a month?

Why don't you invite your friends over to our house sometimes, Rosa?

⑥ Agree on a solution.

Select the solution that best meets the most important goals that you both expressed. The two of you must agree on the solution.

So, Dad, I'll call you at 11 to let you know where I am and when I will be home.

OK, Rosa. That way I won't have to worry as much about where you are and whether you're all right.

Practice the Skill

1. Omar and Ty are having a disagreement. In writing, describe their problem and use win-win negotiation to find a solution.

   Omar: "How could you go to a baseball game tonight, Ty? You promised to help me study for tomorrow's math test!"

   Ty: "How could you expect me to turn down free tickets to the most important game of the season?"

2. List five conflicts people your age may have with friends, family members, or teachers.

3. Think of a conflict you are now (or recently have been) involved in. Ask the other person to work through the win-win method with you. Then evaluate how successful the process was in resolving the conflict.

Keeping the Family Healthy

Objectives

▶ **List** some characteristics of healthy families.

▶ **Describe** four skills families need to stay healthy.

▶ **Identify** places where families can go for help with their problems.

Vocabulary

• empathy
• sibling
• support group

Warm-Up

Quick Quiz Which of the following statements accurately describe your family relationships?

① I enjoy spending time with my family.

② We find it easy to say "I love you."

③ When I have a problem, I can confide in a parent or guardian.

④ My parents support my goals.

WRITING Using these statements as a starting point, describe the qualities of a healthy family.

Healthy Families

Most people in the United States are satisfied with the way their families function—even teenagers. **Healthy families share certain characteristics: caring, commitment, respect, appreciation, empathy, communication, and cooperation.**

▶ **Caring and Commitment** People in healthy families really care about each other. They are committed to staying together through good times and bad times. When one family member makes a mistake, the others offer their support, even if they are angry or disappointed.

▶ **Respect and Appreciation** Family members make each other feel important. They show that they appreciate what other family members do by thanking them and praising them.

▶ **Empathy** The ability to understand another person's thoughts or feelings is called **empathy** (EM puh thee). Empathy allows family members to look at situations from the other person's viewpoint.

▶ **Communication** Family members can tell each other what they honestly think and feel. They listen with respect to what others have to say.

▶ **Cooperation** Responsibilities are divided fairly among family members. Each person does what he or she has promised to do.

Reducing Sibling Rivalry
- Don't compare yourself to a sibling.
- Focus on your own achievements.
- Try to spend time alone with a parent.
- Try to resolve conflicts fairly.

Useful Skills for Families

Even healthy families have problems from time to time. For a family to remain healthy, family members must develop skills to work through their problems. **Healthy families know how to resolve conflicts, express emotions, make decisions, and manage their time.**

Resolving Conflicts   Have you ever argued with your parent over household chores? What do you do if your parent dislikes your friends? Does your sister complain about the time you spend on the computer?

These conflict situations often involve a struggle for power. Teens want control over their lives, while parents want family life to function in ways they believe are best. **Siblings,** or brothers and sisters, compete for their parent's attention, for possessions, and for recognition.

When trying to resolve conflicts, family members need to talk openly, honestly, and lovingly. The goal is to learn from one another. Good communication skills are key to conflict resolution. Saying what you mean, listening to others, and voicing disagreement respectfully are important.

Expressing Emotions   When you are trying to resolve a conflict, it is important to express your emotions in constructive ways. Suppose you attack the other person in an angry outburst such as "All you ever do is criticize me!" The other person is likely to attack you in return or to stop talking to you. Either way, the outburst will make the problem worse. It is better to focus on your own feelings by saying things like "I get upset when people criticize me." Then listen to the other person's concerns.

Being able to say "I'm sorry," "I love you," and "Thank you" also helps. If family members feel loved and appreciated, they are often more willing to help solve problems. The problem-solving process should not be seen as an opportunity to judge or place blame. If the process is a loving one, it can be easier and quicker to reach a solution.

When you have an argument, how does the other person's actions affect how you respond?

FIGURE 9   Even when siblings are close, they can sometimes have conflicts. There are steps you can take to reduce sibling rivalry. **Evaluating** Which of the steps listed do you think is most important and why?

GO ONLINE
PearsonSuccessNet.com
For: More on useful skills

Making Decisions Suppose that a friend asks you to go to the movies on Saturday night. However, you promised your mother weeks ago that you would baby-sit your younger brother. What would you do? You could keep your promise to your mother and tell your friend that you are busy. But what if you haven't seen this friend in a long time?

Families often use decision-making skills to resolve conflicts. These skills involve choosing between two or more alternatives. If you and your mother discuss the problem, you may be able to think of alternatives and reach a solution that works for both of you. Perhaps you can find another baby sitter, or maybe you can take your brother to the movies with you. By using decision-making skills, you can avoid an argument. Plus you can show your mother that you are a mature and responsible person.

Making decisions as a family can be difficult. Each person has different needs or opinions. Some may find it difficult to communicate their opinions in a respectful way. A family member may disrupt the process or people outside of the family may try to influence the decision. In these cases, families may seek outside help to solve their problems.

Managing Time Between work, school, and chores, most families don't have much time to spend together. So the time that families do spend together is valuable. Figure 10 lists a few simple ways that families can spend their time together wisely and improve their relationships.

Healthy families tend to have strong ties with other relatives. These relatives often join the family for holidays and other important events. These events provide a sense of belonging and security. If problems arise, members of the extended family can offer their advice and support.

 When you spend time with your family, what kinds of things do you do?

FIGURE 10 The time this family spends together can help to strengthen the ties between family members.

Making the Most of Family Time
- Develop family traditions. Celebrate occasions in special ways.
- Make mealtimes special. Try to eat together and share the day's events.
- Hold family meetings. Discuss important issues or problems; make plans to do things together.
- Show that you care. Do an unassigned chore; give a sincere compliment.

Hands-On *Activity*

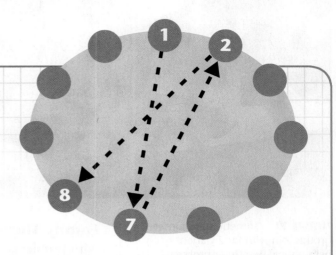

Group Juggling

In this activity you will work with others to accomplish a difficult task.

Materials (per group)

3 lightweight balls, volleyball size

Try This

1. Form a large circle with 10 other people.
2. Starting with one person and going clockwise, count off from 1 to 11. Then decide how you will pass the ball around the circle. It is best to pass the ball across the circle to the opposite side (for example, from 1 to 7, 7 to 2, 2 to 8, and so on).
3. Person 1 throws the ball across the circle to the next person according to the decided order. That person throws the ball to the next person, and so on across the circle.
4. Continue passing the ball until it has gone around the circle five times. If the ball drops, just pick it up and continue passing it around.
5. Repeat Steps 3 and 4, but with two balls instead of one. Start one ball with person 1 and the other with person 3.
6. When you have mastered "juggling" the two balls, add a third ball, starting it with person 5.

Think and Discuss

1. How were cooperation and teamwork important in this activity? How are those same skills important for living in a family?
2. How is group juggling easier than juggling alone? How is it more difficult? Relate this to living in a family.
3. Suppose that, while juggling three balls, the group suddenly decided to reverse the direction of one ball. What do you think would happen? How is this similar to what happens when unexpected problems arise in families?

Getting Help for the Family

Even when a family is healthy, there may be times when the family is faced with a problem that seems overwhelming. The problem may be too difficult for the family to solve by itself. In this situation, asking for help is a sign of strength rather than a sign of weakness.

Where can families go for help in solving problems? Many families depend on relatives or trusted friends for help and support. Relatives and friends may offer useful advice because they know the family well. But they will not be qualified to deal with every problem. Some families may turn to members of the clergy or mental health professionals for advice.

When faced with a problem that needs immediate attention, a family may use a crisis hotline or contact a crisis center. People who work in crisis centers can serve as sympathetic listeners. They also can refer people to other sources of help. **Some sources of help for families are family agencies, family therapists, and support groups.**

FIGURE 11 Sometimes volunteer groups join with family agencies to help people with their problems. These young women are helping to build a home for a family.

Family Agencies Public and private agencies offer help to families in most communities. Some agencies offer counseling for families. Others may offer parenting classes. Mental-health agencies help meet the needs of people with mental disorders. Child-welfare agencies offer services for the protection of children. These services include arranging for foster care or dealing with child abuse. Other agencies help families with financial aid, food, housing, employment, healthcare, and other basic needs.

Family Therapy Some family agencies provide therapy for families with problems. If not, they can refer families to a therapist. Therapists work with family members to find better ways to solve problems. In most cases, family therapists encourage all family members to take part in the process. This helps the family learn how to resolve conflicts and improve family relationships.

Support Groups A **support group** is a network of people who help each other cope with a particular problem. Group members learn from one another rather than from a group leader. They share information about the problem and discuss their experiences. This process helps members of the group learn to deal effectively with their problems.

One well-known support group is Alcoholics Anonymous (AA). There are AA meetings in communities across the country for those who abuse alcohol. Some support groups help people cope with serious illness or death. Other groups deal with relationship problems in families related to divorce, family violence, gambling, or teens who commit crimes.

Section 3 Review

Key Ideas and Vocabulary

1. What characteristics do healthy families share?
2. What is **empathy?** How can empathy contribute to healthy family relationships?
3. Identify four skills that families need to stay healthy.
4. Define the term **siblings.** How can siblings cause conflicts in families?
5. What type of help is available for families from outside the family?

Critical Thinking

6. Evaluating Is this statement a constructive way to express your emotions? "You never listen when I talk." Why or why not?

Health at Home

Family Rules Ask other family members to work with you to develop rules for family discussions. The goal is to develop a set of rules that make it easier to resolve conflicts and communicate effectively. Also discuss some polite ways to deal with someone who breaks the rules. **WRITING**

7. Predicting If you were the parent of a teenager, how would you handle conflicts about curfews?
8. Applying Concepts Your sister borrowed your bike without asking again. Now you have no way to get to your friend's house to work on a project. How could you handle this situation in a positive manner? **WRITING**

GO ONLINE PearsonSuccessNet.com   Audio Summary Section 5.3

Chapter 5
At a Glance

VIDEO **TEENS** Talk ⊙
Family Matters What did you learn from the video about how to cope with changes within a family?

Section 1   Families Today

Key Ideas

▶ If the relationships with family members are healthy, a child learns to love, respect, and get along with others, and to function as part of a group.

▶ Three main factors account for changes in the American family: more women in the work force, a high divorce rate, and an increase in the age at which people marry.

▶ Children can live in nuclear, single-parent, extended, blended, or foster families.

▶ In families some responsibilities clearly belong to the adults, some clearly belong to the children, and some can be shared.

Vocabulary

- divorce (113)
- nuclear family (114)
- adoption (114)
- single-parent family (114)
- extended family (114)
- blended family (115)
- foster family (115)
- socialization (116)

Section 2   Family Problems

Key Ideas

▶ Some sources of family stress are illness, financial problems, divorce, and drug abuse.

▶ The violence, or abuse, that occurs in families may be physical, sexual, or emotional.

▶ Runaways may become ill or turn to crime. They become easy targets for people who are involved with prostitution, pornography, and drugs.

Vocabulary

- separation (120)
- domestic abuse (121)
- physical abuse (121)
- sexual abuse (122)
- emotional abuse (122)
- neglect (122)
- runaway (123)

Section 3   Keeping the Family Healthy

Key Ideas

▶ Healthy families share certain characteristics: caring, commitment, respect, admiration, empathy, communication, and cooperation.

▶ Healthy families know how to resolve conflicts, express emotions, make decisions, and manage their time.

▶ Family agencies, family therapists, and support groups offer help to families.

Vocabulary

- empathy (126)
- siblings (127)
- support group (130)

Chapter 5 Review

Reviewing Key Ideas

GO ONLINE

PearsonSuccessNet.com

For: Chapter 5 review activity

Section 1

1. A group of close relatives living together or near each other is called a(an)
   a. nuclear family.   b. extended family.
   c. blended family.   d. foster family.

2. When a couple adopts a child, the unit that results is a(an)
   a. nuclear family.   b. blended family.
   c. foster family.   d. extended family.

3. Explain why it is important that children observe healthy relationships in the family.

4. What are some benefits of living in an extended family?

5. **Critical Thinking** How are the adoption of a child and the addition of a child to a foster family similar? How are they different?

6. **Critical Thinking** Which kinds of adjustments might the formation of a blended family require? Explain your answer.

Section 2

7. Domestic abuse is the abuse of
   a. a child by an adult.
   b. one spouse by the other.
   c. an elderly parent by a child.
   d. one family member by another.

8. The nonphysical mistreatment of a person is
   a. physical abuse.
   b. sexual abuse.
   c. emotional abuse.
   d. neglect.

9. Why is it as important to address emotional abuse as it is to deal with physical abuse?

10. Explain the possible relationship between family violence and runaways.

11. **Critical Thinking** Explain how a serious illness, divorce, and drug abuse can all lead to financial problems.

12. **Critical Thinking** Why do you think that a child who is abused by an adult might feel responsible for the abuse?

Section 3

13. The ability to understand another person's thoughts or feelings is called
    a. appreciation.   b. empathy.
    c. respect.   d. caring.

14. A network of people who help each other deal with a particular problem is called a(an)
    a. support group.   b. family agency.
    c. crisis center.   d. crisis hotline.

15. How can good communication skills and expressing emotions in constructive ways help families resolve conflicts?

16. Describe four types of services that a family agency might provide.

17. **Critical Thinking** Describe one advantage that a small family might have over a larger family in keeping the family healthy. Describe one advantage the larger family might have.

Building Health Skills

18. **Advocacy** Should companies be required to give parents a leave of absence upon the birth of a child? Should this benefit apply to fathers as well as mothers? Explain your answers. **WRITING**

19. **Setting Goals** Make an action plan to spend more time with a busy parent or other family member. Are there things this person must do that you can do together? Are there things you can do for this person so he or she has more free time? Put your plan into action for a week and monitor your progress. Then adjust your action plan, if necessary. **WRITING**

Health and Community

Help for Families Work with your classmates to produce a booklet listing resources in your community for families. Use Web sites, brochures, or telephone interviews to find out what services each resource provides. Include a summary of these services for each agency. **WRITING**

Standardized Test Prep

Math Practice

The graph shows how household size changed in the United States from 1970 to 2011. Use the graph to answer Questions 20–23.

Households by Size

1970	
20.9%	5 or more
15.8%	4 people
17.3%	3 people
28.9%	2 people
17.1%	1 person

2011	
10.5%	5 or more
10.5%	4 people
16.1%	3 people
34.6%	2 people
28.3%	1 person

20. What percentage of households had 4 or more people in 1970?
A 14.6%
B 15.8%
C 25.0%
D 36.7%

21. What was the change in percent for households with one person between 1970 and 2011?
F an increase of 17.1%
G an increase of 28.3%
H an increase of 11.2%
J a decrease of 11.2%

22. In which of these households was there the greatest change between 1970 and 2011?
A households with 1 person
B households with 2 people
C households with 4 people
D households with 5 or more people

23. Based on the graph, which of the following statements is true?
F The total number of families increased from 1970 to 2011.
G Household size was constant from 1970 to 2011.
H Household size decreased from 1970 to 2011.
J Household size increased from 1970 to 2011.

Reading and Writing Practice

Read these first two stanzas from a poem by Edgar Guest. Then answer Questions 24–26.

Gettin' together to smile an' rejoice,
An' eatin an' laughter with folks of your choice.
An' kissin' the girls an' declaring that they
Are growing more beautiful day after day;
Chattin' an' braggin' a bit with the men,
Buildin' the old family circle again;
Livin' the wholesome an' old-fashioned cheer,
Just for awhile at the end of the year.

Greetings fly fast as we crowd through the door
And under the old roof we gather once more
Just as we did when the youngsters were small;
Mother's a bit grayer, that's all.
Father's a little bit older, but still
Ready to romp an' to laugh with a will.
Here we are back at the table again
Tellin' our stories as women an' men.

24. What is the main emotion that the author is expressing in this poem?
A empathy   B guilt
C joy   D jealousy

25. Based on the poem, which of the following statements is true about the author?
F He has always lived with his parents.
G He has not seen his parents for a while.
H He has come home to live with his parents.
J He is making a visit to his childhood home.

Constructed Response
26. Choose an appropriate title for this poem. Then, in a paragraph, give reasons for your choice.

Building Healthy Peer Relationships

GO ONLINE PearsonSuccessNet.com

VIDEO 6

TEENS Talk

Choosing Abstinence

Preview **Activity**

What Do Your Choices Say About You?

Complete this activity before you watch the video

1. Think about this quote.
It is our choices that show what we truly are, far more than our abilities.

2. Then write a short paragraph describing what the quote means to you. **WRITING**

3. Pair up with another student to share and discuss your paragraphs.

Skills for Healthy Relationships

Objectives

▶ **Describe** four skills that contribute to effective communication.

▶ **Explain** how cooperation and compromise help build healthy relationships.

Vocabulary

- communication
- "I" message
- active listening
- passive
- aggressive
- assertive
- body language
- eye contact
- cooperation
- compromise

Warm-Up

Dear Advice Line,

A friend of mine makes plans for the two of us without checking with me first. He assumes that I will want to do whatever he wants, and I don't speak up to avoid problems. How can I get my friend to see that my opinion matters?

WRITING What advice would you give this person? How can he stand up for himself?

Effective Communication

When you laugh at a joke, hug a parent, or ask a friend for advice, you are communicating. **Communication** is the process of sharing information, thoughts, or feelings. Learning to communicate effectively takes practice, like learning to ride a bicycle. The more you practice, the less you have to think about what you are doing. With practice, you can master the skills of effective communication. **These skills include using "I" messages, active listening, assertiveness, and using appropriate body language.**

"I" Messages   To express your feelings accurately, it helps to use "I" messages. An **"I" message** is a statement that expresses your feelings, but does not blame or judge the other person.

Suppose you are upset with a friend who forgot to call you. When you speak to your friend the next day, you shout, "Can't you remember anything?" This approach could put your friend on the defensive and cause a serious disagreement. Instead of yelling at your friend, it would be better to focus on how the situation made *you* feel. By saying something like, "I am upset because we didn't talk last night," you open the lines of communication between you and your friend.

Active Listening   Many people think of communication as nothing more than talking. But for communication to be effective, it must be a two-way process. There must be a listener as well as a speaker. The listener must do more than simply hear what is said—he or she must be actively involved in the conversation.

Active listening is focusing your full attention on what the other person is saying and letting that person know you understand and care. An active listener responds to what is being said. The listener makes the speaker feel comfortable about opening up and expressing personal feelings. To become an active listener, try the following.

► Show your interest by looking at the person, nodding your head, and showing concern on your face.

► Encourage the speaker to begin speaking by saying "Do you want to talk about …" or "You seem upset about…."

► When the speaker pauses, show your interest by offering comments such as "Then what happened?" or "What did you do then?"

► Avoid passing judgment on what the speaker says.

► Show you have been listening by summarizing the speaker's ideas with phrases such as "It sounds like you were angry when…" or "I heard you say…."

► Help the speaker explore things further with phrases such as "Tell me more about…" or "I guess you felt…."

► Do not steer the conversation away from the speaker's problem and onto a problem of your own.

Connect to Your Life   **How would you rate yourself as an active listener? In what ways could you improve?**

FIGURE 1   Using active listening in the classroom can help you to learn. **Evaluating** How do the questions that a teacher asks students contribute to the process of active listening?

Passive, Aggressive, and Assertive Communication

Passive Behaviors	Aggressive Behaviors	Assertive Behaviors
▶ Hoping the other person will guess your feelings	▶ Using "you" messages to blame the other person	▶ Using "I" messages to explain your feelings
▶ Always listening; rarely talking	▶ Interrupting; being sarcastic	▶ Actively listening to the other person
▶ Denying your own feelings; making excuses	▶ Making fun of the other person's feelings	▶ Trying to understand the other person's feelings
▶ Criticizing yourself; always apologizing	▶ Criticizing the other person; never giving a compliment	▶ Expressing appreciation; being respectful
▶ Always giving in to the other person	▶ Always wanting your own way	▶ Seeking a compromise that does not go against either person's values
▶ Mumbling; looking away; fidgeting nervously	▶ Yelling; refusing to talk; finger pointing; glaring; using physical force	▶ Speaking confidently and clearly; making eye contact; showing interest

FIGURE 2 People provide both verbal clues and nonverbal clues when they communicate. **Classifying** Suppose a person mumbles and fidgets during a conversation. How would you describe that person's communication style?

Assertiveness How do you express your opinions and feelings when they differ from those of another person?

▶ Are you **passive,** holding back your true feelings and going along with the other person?

▶ Are you **aggressive?** Do you communicate opinions and feelings in a way that may seem threatening or disrespectful to other people?

▶ Are you assertive? When you are **assertive** (uh SUR tiv), you are able to stand up for yourself while expressing your feelings in a way that does not threaten the other person.

Figure 2 compares passive, aggressive, and assertive behaviors.

Assertiveness involves more than just what you say. How you say something, or the tone of your voice, also communicates your message. To understand how your tone of voice affects a message, try saying "Open your book to page 70" three different ways. First use a loud, demanding voice, then whisper the sentence, and then say it in a direct, assertive tone. The message changes with your tone of voice. The loud, demanding tone carries the implied threat "or else." The whisper suggests that you aren't sure the direction will be followed. The assertive tone shows that you expect the direction to be followed, without any implied threat.

People who are assertive tend to have healthier relationships than those who are passive or aggressive. Assertive behavior communicates respect both for yourself and for others. Passive behavior shows lack of respect for yourself. Aggressive behavior shows lack of respect for others.

Body Language You can also communicate information or feelings through body language. **Body language** includes posture, gestures, facial expressions, and body movements. People are often unaware of the silent messages sent by their body language. For example, if you slouch in your chair during class, the teacher may think you are bored or unprepared.

Sometimes a person's body language matches their spoken words, as when a person gestures to emphasize a point. Other times, the messages you send with your body language may contradict what you are saying. People may smile while saying something cruel or show little warmth with their face while saying something nice. In fact, people who lie sometimes give themselves away through their body language.

Like spoken language, body language varies from culture to culture. For example, most Americans expect you to make **eye contact,** or meet their gaze, when you talk with them. They may interpret a failure to make eye contact as shyness, indifference, embarrassment, or even sneakiness. But in Japanese and Native American cultures, making eye contact in some situations is a sign of disrespect.

 Which term describes your communication style, passive, aggressive, or assertive? Explain why.

 GO ONLINE
PearsonSuccessNet.com
For: More on being assertive

Cooperation

Have you ever worked with classmates to complete a project? If so, then you know the importance of **cooperation,** or working together toward a common goal. To successfully meet the goal, people must work together as a team. Everybody on the team must meet their responsibilities and trust others to meet theirs.

Cooperation is important in all relationships. Suppose your aunt is coming to visit and your family needs to clean the house. If everyone works together to complete this chore, things will get done more easily than if one person has to do it alone. When friends study together, each can help the others master difficult material. **Cooperation builds strong relationships that are based on mutual trust, caring, and responsibility.**

FIGURE 3 These teens were asked to find a way to rise from a seated position while keeping their arms linked. This task demonstrates the need to cooperate to achieve a goal.

"Let's go to the mall tonight!"

"Let's go to a movie tonight!"

"Let's go to the mall first, then to a movie!"

FIGURE 4 For a compromise to work, both people must be satisfied with the solution

Compromise

Imagine that you and a friend are having a disagreement. You would like to go to the mall tonight, but your friend would rather go to the movies. How would you handle this problem? Because disagreements arise from time to time in all close relationships, it is important to be willing to compromise. **Compromise** (KAHM pruh myz) is the willingness of each person to give up something in order to reach agreement. Compromising is a skill of give-and-take. Both people must be willing to sacrifice something to get something in return. Both people also must feel comfortable with the solution reached.

Possible Solutions You and your friend could compromise in a number of ways. You could agree to go to the mall tonight and to a movie tomorrow. Or you could go to the mall first and then to a movie. Or you could even decide to do a totally different activity. Whatever agreement you arrive at, the ability to compromise will strengthen your relationship. **When you are willing to compromise, you let the other person know how important the relationship is to you.**

When Not to Compromise Of course, there are some situations in which it is important not to compromise. A friend might ask you to do something that is dangerous or that goes against your values. Instead of compromising with your friend, you need to use assertive communication. Let your friend know how you feel, and make it clear that there is no room for compromise on the issue.

Section 1 Review

Key Ideas and Vocabulary

1. What are four important communication skills?
2. Give an example of an "I" **message.**
3. How does **active listening** differ from just listening?
4. How can a willingness to cooperate or compromise strengthen a relationship?

Critical Thinking

5. Evaluating Can a person's body language affect a listener more than his or her words? Give an example to support your answer.

Health at School

Working in Groups With four of your classmates, write a short skit that illustrates the importance of good communication. After you have completed the skit, discuss how well the members of your group worked together to get the task done. Write a paragraph summarizing your discussion. **WRITING**

6. Comparing and Contrasting How does being aggressive differ from being assertive?
7. Predicting Which communication skills would be most helpful when you use e-mail or instant messaging? Which would be more difficult to apply? Use examples to support your answer.

GO ONLINE PearsonSuccessNet.com Audio Summary Section 6.1

Friendships

Objectives
▶ **Explain** the importance of having friends.
▶ **Distinguish** different types of friendships.
▶ **Describe** some problems that occur in friendships.

Vocabulary
• friendship
• gender roles
• clique
• peer pressure

Warm-Up

Quick Quiz Which of these do you value most in a friend?

1. Someone who offers to help when you have a problem

2. Someone who makes you laugh even when you are sad

3. Someone who expresses emotions without hurting others

4. Someone who is honest and reliable

5. Someone who is a good listener

WRITING Explain why you selected the answer that you did.

The Importance of Friendships

Do you have a close friend whom you have known since early childhood? Perhaps, as preschoolers, you spent hours together building whole cities with wooden blocks. Later, you may have discussed sports or favorite television programs. Now, as teenagers, you may talk about problems you face at home and school and give each other advice and encouragement.

The bond that you two have established is one kind of friendship. **Friendship** is a relationship based on mutual trust, acceptance, and common interests or values. **People look to their friends for honest reactions, encouragement during bad times, and understanding when they make mistakes.** Friends offer a sense of belonging. They are a handy reminder that there are other people who understand and care about you.

Most teens think that it is important to be part of one or more groups of friends. Interacting with others helps you to build self-esteem and to learn about yourself. You can experiment with different roles: leader, helper, advice-seeker, or supporter. Also, activities such as exercising, washing a car, or studying for a test can be more enjoyable when you do them with friends. Something that may seem silly to do alone, like dressing up in a costume, can be fun to do with friends.

GO ONLINE

PearsonSuccessNet.com
For: More on friendships

Types of Friendships

Friendships range from the casual acquaintances you find through social media, to the friends you greet in the halls at school, to the friends who share your most personal thoughts. **Some friendships are casual, and some are close. Some are with friends of the opposite sex.** Each type of friend is valuable for different reasons.

Casual Friends Casual friendships can occur because people go to the same school, live in the same neighborhood, or have interests in common. Many casual friendships do not actually meet the definition of friendship. They are the so-called "friends" you make through social media. These electronic acquaintances provide an avenue to chat about food, or movies, or sports, but rarely involve communicating about highly personal or private matters. These "friends," however, provide a comforting sense of fitting in during this electronic age.

Short-term, casual friendships offer the chance to have fun, to try new things, and to learn to get along with a variety of people. Casual friends enjoy each other's company, and enjoy communicating through texts or telephone conversations. These friendships may remain casual, or they may develop into deeper, long-lasting friendships over time. Figure 5 offers some tips on making new friends.

Close Friends People tend to form close friendships with others who share similar goals, values, or interests. Sometimes people are drawn to each other because their personalities just seem to match.

No matter how a friendship forms, most people agree on four qualities that are important in a close friend.

▶ **Loyalty** A close friend sticks by you in both good times and bad.

▶ **Honesty** You can trust a close friend to be truthful, even when the truth is painful. You know that your friend isn't trying to hurt you.

▶ **Empathy** A close friend is caring and sensitive to your feelings.

▶ **Reliability** A close friend can always be counted on. You know your friend will try hard not to let you down.

FIGURE 5 Close friendships provide some security, while allowing you the chance to act independently.

Tips for Making Friends

▶ Be yourself; don't put on an act.
▶ Join groups that share your values or offer activities you like.
▶ Treat everyone with respect.
▶ Take a little time to talk with people you know casually.
▶ Ask questions that require more than just a *yes* or *no* answer.

Media Wise

Gender Roles and Movies

People learn about gender roles by observing how other people behave. Family members, friends, and other adults may serve as roles models. People also receive messages about gender roles from movies. Use this checklist to evaluate how gender roles are shown in a movie.

Do the females tend to be less assertive than the males?	Yes No
Are the male roles more action-oriented than the female roles?	Yes No
Do the females share their feelings more easily than the males?	Yes No
When there is a problem to solve, is the problem solver usually male?	Yes No
Do the men tend to work outside the home and the women inside the home?	Yes No

Two or more "Yes" answers indicate a movie that supports traditional gender roles.

Activity Use the checklist to evaluate gender roles in two movies. Then write a paragraph about what you observed. How do you think these movies affect people's opinions about gender roles? **WRITING**

Friends of the Opposite Sex When you were in elementary school, boys may have formed friendships with other boys with whom they had common interests. Girls may have formed close friendships with other girls. Today, you probably have both male and female friends.

Opposite-sex friendships may develop more easily now than in earlier generations because of changes in gender roles. **Gender roles** are the behaviors and attitudes that are socially accepted as either masculine or feminine. Gender roles vary from culture to culture. In the United States, gender roles are less rigid today than they have been in the past. Many people now choose activities and behave in ways that traditionally were reserved for members of the other gender. Both males and females learn to express various emotions, including tenderness and assertiveness. They let the event or situation dictate which emotion is appropriate.

In choosing friends today, most people look for males and females with interests and goals similar to their own. Friendships between males and females can be satisfying and close, but not involve romance. These friendships help you to feel comfortable with members of the opposite sex and allow you to develop fully as a person. A friendship with the opposite sex may develop into a romantic relationship. Often, it does not.

Connect to Your Life Are you comfortable having close friendships with both males and females? Why or why not?

FIGURE 6 A cartoon often uses humor to make a serious point. **Interpreting Illustrations** How would you classify the problem illustrated in this cartoon? Explain.

Problems in Friendships

In all friendships, even close ones, problems arise from time to time. For a friendship to be a lasting one, it is important that friends face problems that arise and work together to resolve them. **Some possible problems in friendships are envy and jealousy, cruelty and manipulation, and cliques.**

Envy and Jealousy   Envy can occur in a friendship when one person has something that the other person desires. The source of the envy can be appearance, talent, possessions, or popularity. Jealousy can occur when a "best" friend wants to develop other close friendships and the first friend feels left out.

It is normal at times to feel envy or jealousy, but if these feelings linger they can cause problems in a friendship. If you feel envy or jealousy, use your communication skills to discuss the problem. First, use "I" messages to get your feelings out in the open. It is best to do this in person, but if this is too difficult, write to your friend explaining your feelings. Be sure to listen to your friend's point of view and try to understand his or her feelings. Through active listening, you can gain a better understanding of your friendship and of ways to work things out.

Cruelty and Manipulation   Sometimes a friend may be cruel or try to manipulate you even though you have done nothing to deserve such treatment. Your friend's behavior may have nothing to do with you. Your friend may be facing problems at home, at school, or elsewhere. Your friend may believe that controlling you, or being mean to you, will result in a stronger friendship. But cruelty and manipulation only lead to problems in a friendship. Unfortunately, people sometimes transfer the pain or anxiety they are feeling onto their close friends.

If a friend is cruel or tries to manipulate you, confront your friend to find out what the real problem is. Communicate that you are not willing to be mistreated. Also show your concern and desire to help your friend work things out.

 Have you ever felt envy or jealousy toward a friend? If so, how did you deal with the feeling?

Cliques Do you know a small, closed circle of friends that does not accept people who are different? If so, then you know a **clique** (klik), a narrow, exclusive group of people with similar backgrounds or interests.

Being a member of a clique can give a person a sense of belonging, but it also can deprive a person of forming friendships with a variety of people. A clique often discourages its members from thinking and acting independently. Clique members may experience **peer pressure,** a need to conform to the expectations of the tight circle of friends. Peer pressure can be a positive force when friends encourage each other to study hard, avoid drugs, or work hard toward a goal. It can be a negative force when friends feel pressured to do things that go against their values.

Peer pressure doesn't magically go away when you become an adult. Peer pressure is an issue that people deal with throughout their lives. However, peer pressure is an important issue during adolescence because this is the stage of life where you are searching for your identity. Health skills that you learn—making good decisions, refusing bad behaviors, setting goals, being assertive—will help you resist negative peer pressure. You will be less likely to encounter negative peer pressure if you choose your friends wisely. Choose people who care about you, share your values, and support your goals.

FIGURE 7 Members of a clique may feel pressured to dress and act in certain ways to go along with the group.

Section 2 Review

Key Ideas and Vocabulary

1. What is **friendship?** Why are friendships important?

2. Briefly describe three different types of friendships.

3. What are **gender roles?** How have changes in gender roles affected friendship patterns?

4. What kinds of problems can arise in friendships?

5. Explain how **peer pressure** can be both positive and negative.

Critical Thinking

6. Comparing and Contrasting How are casual friendships and close friendships similar? How are they different?

Health at School

Welcoming New Classmates Work in small groups to figure out ways to make teens who move to your school feel welcome. Make a list of possible things you could do. Then evaluate your list and decide which idea you think would work best. Finally, draft a proposal explaining how your idea would work. **WRITING**

---

7. Applying Concepts You and Cal have been friends for years, but recently he has been avoiding you. You're angry and hurt. What can you do to address the situation?

8. Evaluating What do you see as the most important problem that can arise within a social media friendship? Use an example to support your answer. How would you handle the problem?

Supporting a Friend

Ricardo has a part-time job after school working in a hardware store. He just heard of an opening at work and immediately called his friend Luis to tell him about it. Ricardo told Luis the questions he was asked in his interview so that Luis could be prepared when he met the manager. Ricardo also put in a good word for Luis with his boss. Ricardo knows that Luis really needs a job to help support his family because Luis' father just lost his job.

What are ways you can support a friend? The guidelines that follow offer helpful suggestions.

1 Identify ways you already support your friends.

There are many different kinds of support—a phone call, a visit, a hug, a ride to school, help with a project, advice, a sympathetic ear.

▶ Think of the important friends in your life. List the ways you think you support each of them.

▶ Ask yourself what else you could do to support them.

2 Offer support that empowers.

Make sure that the kind of support you offer doesn't take power or responsibility away from your friend. You don't want to make your friend feel helpless or incompetent. Support that empowers helps a friend to develop his or her own strengths and self-confidence.

▶ Help your friend improve at a skill you may be good at. But also let your friend teach or help you with something in return. Empowering support is a two-way street.

▶ Encourage your friend when he or she tries something new. Compliment your friend on doing well.

❸ Be an active listener.

▶ Show that you understand and care about your friend's problems. Be empathetic, not judgmental.

▶ Don't offer advice unless your friend asks for feedback. Then be constructive by helping your friend look beyond his or her current feelings or situation for possible solutions.

▶ If your friend is going through a difficult time, be especially sensitive. Make time to talk or do things with your friend. Sometimes just being there is helpful when a friend feels sad or angry.

▶ If your friend is doing something you think is dangerous or destructive, express your concern using "I" messages: "I feel … when you do.…" Offer to go with your friend if you think he or she needs professional help.

❹ Ask your friends for support.

Friends are not mind readers. If you need or want support, ask for it. Asking for support will make it easier for your friends to ask you for support when they need it.

▶ Make a list of the ways you would like to be supported by your friends.

▶ Be specific about what kind of support you would like.

▶ Show your appreciation when a friend does something nice for you.

❺ Encourage friends to ask you for support.

▶ Ask your friends if you can help them. Offer suggestions for how you might help.

▶ Follow through on what you say you will do.

Practice the Skill

1. For a few days, do what you normally would do, but keep a "support" journal. Record each time you offer support to a friend and each time a friend offers support to you. Write a brief description of the situation, the type of support offered, and the outcome.

Support Journal	
Incident 1	**Incident 2**
Description	Description
I noticed that Marcus seemed dejected.	Olivia realized that I was having trouble keeping up in Social Studies.
Type of support	Type of support
When we had a moment alone, I told him what I had noticed and asked if he wanted to talk.	She offered to show me her system for taking notes in class.
Outcome	Outcome
Marcus told me about a problem he was having with his parents and I actively listened.	We reviewed my notes and Olivia showed me ways to improve them.

2. Review your journal entries. How often did you offer support to a friend? How often did a friend offer support to you? Were there any kinds of support offered that took away power? If so, how could these offers of support have been more empowering?

3. During the next week, look for at least three opportunities to support a friend. Also ask for support from one friend.

Section 3

Responsible Relationships

Objectives

▶ **List** some things you can learn about a person by dating.

▶ **Describe** the cycle of violence.

Vocabulary

• infatuation
• dating violence
• date rape

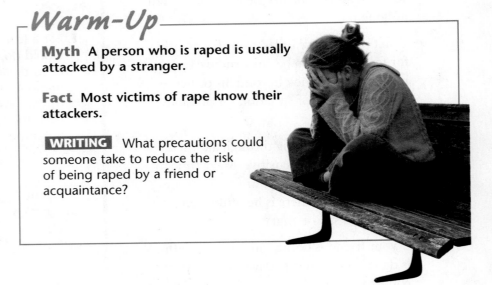

Warm-Up

Myth A person who is raped is usually attacked by a stranger.

Fact Most victims of rape know their attackers.

WRITING What precautions could someone take to reduce the risk of being raped by a friend or acquaintance?

Physical Attraction and Dating

The teenage years are a time when most young people begin to experience feelings of physical attraction. Have you ever had a "crush" on a movie star, athlete, teacher, or other person you admire? Most teenagers have. Another name for these feelings of intense attraction to another person is **infatuation.** Although these feelings can sometimes be overwhelming, they are normal and healthy for teenagers. From these feelings, you develop the ability to form close attachments later in your adult life.

When you are attracted to someone, you want to spend time with that person. Some people use the term *dating* to describe the time you spend together. **By dating someone, you can learn about his or her interests, personality, abilities, and values.** You can also learn how the other person views the gender roles that he or she learned as a child. You may even discover what qualities you want in a future marriage partner.

Dating practices vary with individuals, families, and cultures. Some teens don't date at all during high school because they don't want to or because dating is not permitted in their culture. When teens do date, some stick to traditional practices. For example, females may wait for males to ask them out, or expect the males to pay for the date. Today, however, many dating arrangements are more informal than in the past.

Hanging Out and Talking   People who are physically attracted to each other often begin to recognize that attraction when they hang out together for lengthy periods of time. Talking (and listening) can be a great way to get to know someone. Hanging out and talking can also occur in groups. There are advantages to hanging out as a group. It gives you an opportunity to see how people behave when they are with others. In return, the person you are attracted to can get to know more about you.

Going Out as Couples   You may discover that you especially enjoy being with a certain friend. The person may be someone who shares your interests or has a similar sense of humor. You also may be physically attracted to this person. It is natural and healthy to feel physical attraction and to want to get to know the person better. This may lead to dating, either on your own or with other couples.

Dating   After a few dates, a couple may decide not to go out with other people and to see each other on a regular basis. Dating a person exclusively can be a form of security—partners are assured of having someone to hang out with.

Exclusive dating has some drawbacks. You limit your chances of meeting other people you might like. You may feel pressured to make decisions about sexual intimacy before you are ready. If conflicts arise, it may be difficult to break off the relationship.

For some couples, exclusive dating leads to marriage. For couples who marry as teens, there are challenges beyond those faced by most married couples. These challenges may include a lack of emotional maturity, loss of freedom, and loss of shared activities with friends.

FIGURE 8   If you go out as a group or as couples, you get to know many different people. You also get to observe how a person you are attracted to interacts with others.

Connect to Your Life   **Do you think exclusive dating during high school is a good idea? Why or why not?**

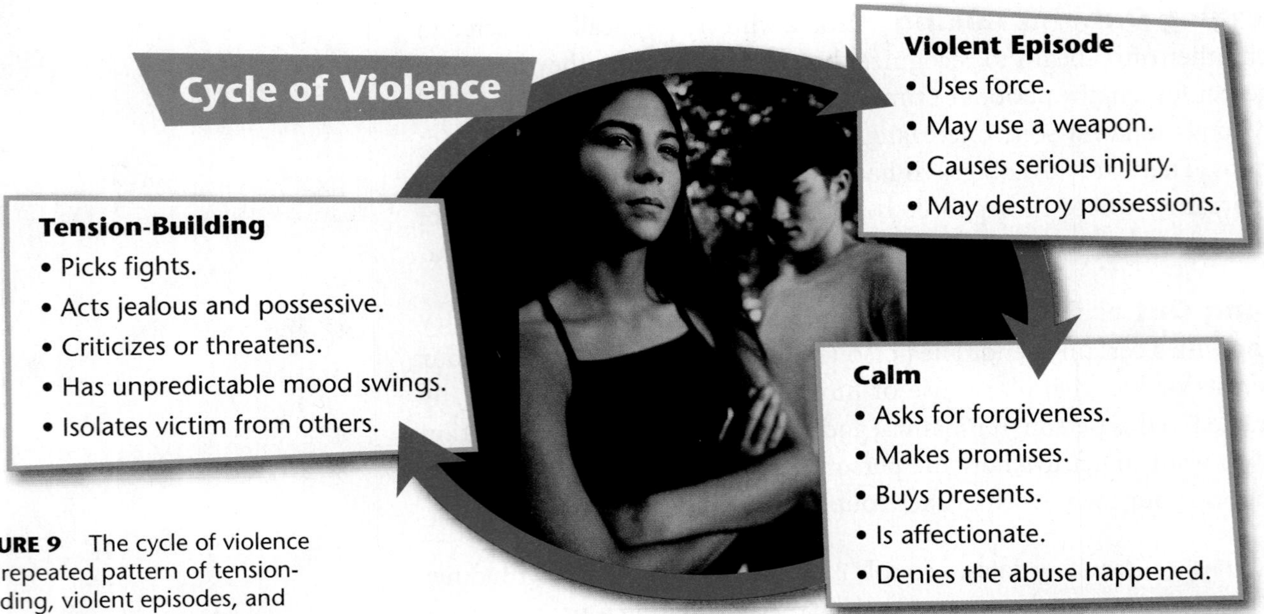

Cycle of Violence

Violent Episode
- Uses force.
- May use a weapon.
- Causes serious injury.
- May destroy possessions.

Tension-Building
- Picks fights.
- Acts jealous and possessive.
- Criticizes or threatens.
- Has unpredictable mood swings.
- Isolates victim from others.

Calm
- Asks for forgiveness.
- Makes promises.
- Buys presents.
- Is affectionate.
- Denies the abuse happened.

FIGURE 9 The cycle of violence is a repeated pattern of tension-building, violent episodes, and calm. Over time, the cycle may shorten. The tension-building and calm stages may disappear, leaving only a series of violent episodes. **Predicting** What control does the victim have over the cycle of violence?

Violence in Dating Relationships

Unfortunately, some teen relationships turn violent. One partner may slap the other when he or she is angry. Or make fun of the other's looks or abilities. Or constantly check up to find out what the person is doing. These are examples of dating violence. **Dating violence** is a pattern of emotional, physical, or sexual abuse that occurs in a dating relationship. One partner uses the abuse to gain control of the other partner.

The Cycle of Violence Often abuse occurs as part of the three-stage cycle in Figure 9. **The cycle of violence consists of a tension-building stage, a violent episode, and a calm or "honeymoon" stage.** During the tension-building stage, the victim may try to please the abuser or reason with the abuser in order to prevent violence. Sometimes victims describe this stage as "walking on eggshells." The tension is broken by a violent episode. During the calm stage, the abuser may apologize and promise to never abuse the victim again. The abuser may also blame the victim for the abuse. The calm is followed by another tension-building stage.

Warning Signs of Abuse A good way to avoid the cycle of violence is to recognize the warning signs that can lead to abuse.

▶ Your date is jealous when you talk to others. Your date makes fun of you in front of others.

▶ Your date makes all the decisions and tries to control what you do.

▶ Your date has a history of bad relationships.

▶ You feel isolated from your friends and family.

▶ You feel less self-confident. You worry about doing or saying the right thing. You change how you behave to avoid an argument.

GO ONLINE

PearsonSuccessNet.com

For: More on violence in dating relationships

Date Rape   More than half of young women who are raped know the person who raped them. The person may have been a steady date, a casual date, or an acquaintance. When the rape occurs during a date, the abuse is often referred to as **date rape.**

The rapist may have used a "date rape drug." These fast-acting drugs are hard to detect in food or a drink because they are colorless, tasteless, and odorless. Later, the victim will feel "hung over" and be unable to recall the rape. Friends will say that the victim acted drunk.

Rape and other forms of abuse are not just a problem for women. Men can be victims too. The emotional effects of rape can be long lasting. Thus, it is important to do what you can to decrease your chances of being attacked. Figure 10 lists some tips to reduce the possibility of date rape.

Ending the Abuse   Why would a teen remain in an abusive relationship or hide the abuse from others? Some teens may view a possessive or jealous partner as romantic. Or they may think the behavior is normal because friends are in similar relationships. Females may think that males are supposed to act in a controlling manner or that physical aggression is a sign of masculinity. Males may be ashamed to admit that they are being abused for fear of being seen as weak. Sadly, some teens may think that they deserve to be abused. Others may fear being alone.

The first step to ending an abusive relationship is to admit that the abuse exists. The second step is to realize that you are not to blame for the abuse and that you cannot change how your abuser behaves. Finally, you don't have to deal with the problem on your own. Seek the support of friends and family. Call an abuse hotline if you want anonymous advice. Talk to a counselor, teacher, doctor, or social worker, but be aware that these adults are legally required to report abuse.

Tips for Dating Safely

- Go out as a group.
- Let someone know where you are going.
- Avoid alcohol or other drugs.
- Have money to get home.
- In an emergency, call 911.

FIGURE 10   These tips can help decrease the chances of date rape.

Section 3 Review

Key Ideas and Vocabulary

1. What does the term **infatuation** mean?

2. List three things people can learn by dating.

3. What is **dating violence?**

4. Describe the cycle of violence that can occur in a relationship.

Critical Thinking

5. Comparing and Contrasting What are some differences between infatuation and dating?

6. Applying Concepts Jordan has been your steady date for six months. You like Jordan, but want to start seeing others. What would be a caring way to tell Jordan how you feel?

Health and Community

Help Combat Dating Violence Find out about volunteer organizations in your community that deal with dating violence. For example, you could baby-sit for children at a local women's shelter. Or invite a police officer to talk about dating violence at a school assembly. Then write a paragraph summarizing what you learned. **WRITING**

7. Evaluating When Tamara's friends complain about how Dillon treats Tamara, she usually makes excuses for him. She says that he is under a lot of pressure and that her behavior often angers him. What advice would you give Tamara about her relationship with Dillon? **WRITING**

Choosing Abstinence

Objectives

▶ **Identify** some risks of sexual intimacy.

▶ **Explain** why emotional intimacy is important in close relationships.

▶ **List** some skills that can help you choose abstinence.

Vocabulary

• emotional intimacy
• abstinence

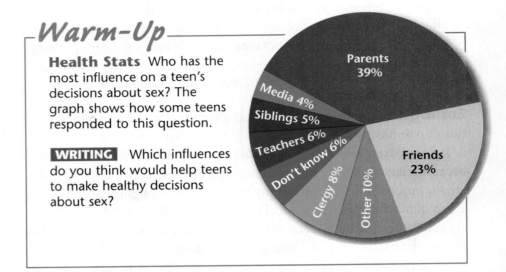

Warm-Up

Health Stats Who has the most influence on a teen's decisions about sex? The graph shows how some teens responded to this question.

WRITING Which influences do you think would help teens to make healthy decisions about sex?

Parents 39%
Media 4%
Siblings 5%
Teachers 6%
Don't know 6%
Clergy 8%
Other 10%
Friends 23%

Risks of Sexual Intimacy

As teenagers become aware of their sexuality, some tough questions arise: How can I show affection without things going too far? Are my partner and I emotionally ready for a sexual relationship? There are no easy answers for such questions. It is important, however, to think about these questions before you have to make decisions that can affect the rest of your life.

As you think about sexual intimacy, there are some important issues for you to consider. **Sexual intimacy is not risk free. The risks include the effect on your emotional health, the effect on your relationship, the risk of pregnancy, and the risk of sexually transmitted infections.**

Effect on Your Emotional Health Decisions about sexual intimacy should be based on the values that you hold. Your family, friends, religion, culture, experiences, and the media help shape your values. Often the messages you receive from different sources will be contradictory. This makes it more difficult to sort out how you truly feel.

A decision to become sexually involved may go against a person's values. If the person makes the decision anyway, the person may feel guilty or ashamed. The person may feel that he or she has let down parents, friends, and others as well as himself or herself. The result of making snap decisions about sex is often a loss of self-respect. Using sex to prove something to oneself and others can also lower self-esteem.

Effect on Your Relationship   A decision to become sexually intimate alters the way couples spend their time together. It also changes the way a couple relates to friends. Sexual intimacy can affect each person's expectations. One person may expect to have sex whenever the couple is together, while the other person may not. One person may become more possessive and put more demands on the other's time. One person may decide to end the relationship.

Often couples are not prepared for the complications that sexual intimacy adds to their relationship. Most couples find that these changes to their relationship are permanent. Although they may try, it is almost impossible to go back to the way things were before they had sex.

Risk of Pregnancy   A teenage pregnancy can pose serious health problems for the baby and the mother. Babies born to young mothers are often smaller and less healthy than those born to older women. Teenage mothers are more likely to have health problems during pregnancy than women in their twenties. This is because pregnant teens do not always eat well or get adequate medical care during pregnancy, especially in the early months.

Besides health problems, what effect does a baby have on a teenage couple? Parents are legally responsible to care for their children. Teenage parents often report feeling overwhelmed and trapped. Many teenage mothers drop out of school. Some fathers don't help support or care for the child; others drop out of school and work at low-paying jobs.

Young people are aware of the problems teenage parents face, but they often don't think that pregnancy can happen to them. Few teens want to become pregnant. But almost one third of young women become pregnant before age 20. Sexual intimacy is a high-risk behavior for anyone who isn't ready to accept the responsibility of children.

What effect might a pregnancy have on a teenage couple's relationship?

FIGURE 11   After caring for a baby, a teenage mother may not have enough energy left for school. **Predicting** How could dropping out of school affect the mother? How could it affect the baby?

About 25% of teen mothers have a second baby before age 20.

Risk of Sexually Transmitted Infections   Some infections can be passed, or transmitted, from one person to another during sexual activity. These are called sexually transmitted infections, or STIs. If left untreated, many STIs cause serious health problems. For example, some STIs can cause infertility, or the inability to have children. Others shorten a person's life or require medical treatment throughout a person's life.

Emotional Intimacy

Contrary to what you may think, every teen is not sexually experienced. Millions of young people today choose to postpone sexual activity. On a television show, a young man spoke of his relationship with his girlfriend. "We're not ready for sex, but we share lots of other intimate experiences."

How can two people be intimate without being sexually involved? They can trust each other with personal feelings or dreams that they haven't told anyone else. They can exchange "inside" jokes. They can do kind things for each other and be best friends.

Emotional intimacy refers to the openness, sharing, affection, and trust that can develop in a close relationship. Two things can help a couple develop emotional intimacy. They must be honest with one another. They must be accepting and supportive of each other. **A couple can have a close relationship without being sexually intimate. But it is hard for them to keep a relationship close if there is no emotional intimacy.**

Abstinence Skills

Sergio and Selena met in class and became good friends. Soon, they started to date. As they spent more time together, they began to express their feelings of affection by hugging, kissing, and holding hands. Over time, the pressure to become more physically intimate grew stronger. But Sergio and Selena felt that abstinence was the best choice at this point in their lives.

Abstinence is the act of refraining from, or not having, sex. There are skills you can learn to help you choose abstinence when you are faced with the pressure to become more physically intimate. **These abstinence skills include setting clear limits, communicating your limits, avoiding high-pressure situations, and asserting yourself.**

FIGURE 12   Sharing and affection are two signs of strong emotional bonds. These bonds form when couples are honest and supportive of one another.

FIGURE 13 It is important to discuss your limits on sexual intimacy as early as possible in a relationship. **Evaluating** Which communication skills are most important when you want to clearly state your limits?

Set Clear Limits It is natural to feel sexual attraction to someone you are dating. It is also natural to be unsure of how to handle these feelings. Most teenagers try to think ahead and set limits for expressing their sexual feelings. If you set limits before a situation arises, it will be easier to stick to the standards you set. Take some time now to set limits that you feel comfortable with. It is important to know your limits before you go out so you can avoid having to make a hasty decision.

To help yourself set limits, be sure to consider the important values that you hold and the possible consequences of your actions. Use the DECIDE process on pages 16–17 to help you make decisions with which you feel comfortable. Do not allow the expectations of friends, the media, and others to influence you to make decisions that may not be right for you.

Communicate Your Limits Once you have decided on your limits, it is important to communicate your feelings to your partner. Of course, it is best to discuss things as early as possible in a relationship. Do not wait until a situation arises in which your partner's expectations may be different from yours. It may be difficult to have an open, constructive discussion if you wait until that point to talk.

Try to talk honestly to your partner about your feelings and values. You may be surprised at how relieved your partner may be to hear how you feel. He or she may have been anxious about your expectations.

If you have been sexually involved, it doesn't mean that you have to continue to be sexually involved. You may decide that a relationship built around emotional intimacy makes more sense and choose abstinence. If your partner tries to make you feel guilty, you may need to rethink your relationship. Do you really want to be with a person who does not respect your feelings or who does not value emotional intimacy?

 GO ONLINE
PearsonSuccessNet.com
For: More on abstinence

 Are you comfortable talking with friends about your values? Why or why not?

FIGURE 14 One way for couples to avoid high-pressure situations is to go out as a group.

Avoid High-Pressure Situations Sticking to the limits you set can be difficult. You can make it easier for yourself by avoiding certain situations. For example, if you are at an unsupervised party, you might feel pressured to have sex. But if you are in a public place, the temptation to engage in sexual activities is not as great. It is also important to avoid alcohol and other drugs, as they can blur your ability to think clearly.

Spend time with friends that share your values. You might want to include your date in family outings. Not only will you not be tempted to have sex, you will see how your date interacts with different people.

Assert Yourself If you find yourself in a situation where you are not comfortable with the level of physical intimacy, don't feel guilty about saying no. State clearly and directly that you want to stop. You may want to offer a reason, such as "I'm just not ready," so that the other person won't feel hurt or rejected.

At times, however, simply saying no once may not be effective. You may need to be firm and say something like "No! I said I don't want to do that." You may need to repeat yourself a few times before your partner realizes that you are serious. If necessary, get up and walk away.

One person may try to pressure another by saying that, at some levels of intimacy, it is impossible to stop without causing physical harm. This isn't true. The person might also say things like "If you loved me, you would do it," or "Everybody does it." Remember that you will respect yourself more for sticking to your limits than for giving in to pressure.

If your partner does not respect the limits you set, the relationship may not be worth continuing. Try to meet people who understand the importance of dealing responsibly with sexual feelings. Look for people who value emotional intimacy.

Section 4 Review

Key Ideas and Vocabulary

1. What are four possible risks of sexual intimacy?

2. Define **emotional intimacy.**

3. How can emotional intimacy help a relationship to grow?

4. What is **abstinence?** What skills can help you to choose abstinence?

Critical Thinking

5. Making Judgments Review the risks of sexual intimacy. Which risk would be most likely to keep you from being sexually intimate? Give a reason for your choice.

Health at Home

Comparing Viewpoints Work with a parent or another trusted adult. Select two letters about teenage sexual choices from an advice column in a newspaper. Separately, the two of you should write responses to the letters. Then compare your responses to each other's and to the actual advice offered in the newspaper. **WRITING**

6. Applying Concepts How could a person who doesn't want to be sexually involved respond to each of these "pressure" lines?

a. "If you loved me, you would have sex with me."

b. "Everyone else is having sex. What's wrong with you?"

c. "You know you want to. Everyone wants to."

Chapter 6
At a Glance

VIDEO **TEENS** Talk ⊙
Choosing Abstinence Describe three things you learned from the video about the benefits of choosing abstinence.

Section 1   Skills for Healthy Relationships

Key Ideas

▶ Skills for effective communication include using "I messages," active listening, assertiveness, and using appropriate body language.

▶ Cooperation builds strong relationships that are based on mutual trust, caring, and responsibility.

▶ Being willing to compromise tells the other person how important the relationship is to you.

Vocabulary
- communication (136)
- "I" message (136)
- active listening (137)
- passive (138)
- aggressive (138)
- assertive (138)
- body language (139)
- eye contact (139)
- cooperation (139)
- compromise (140)

Section 2   Friendships

Key Ideas

▶ People look to their friends for honest reactions, encouragement, and understanding.

▶ Some friendships are casual and some are close. Some are with friends of the opposite sex.

▶ Some possible problems in friendships are envy, jealousy, cruelty, and cliques.

Vocabulary
- friendship (141)
- gender roles (143)
- clique (145)
- peer pressure (145)

Section 3   Dating Relationships

Key Ideas

▶ By dating someone, you can learn about his or her personality, interests, abilities, and values.

▶ The cycle of violence consists of a tension-building stage, a violent episode, and a calm stage.

Vocabulary
- infatuation (148)
- dating violence (150)
- date rape (151)

Section 4   Choosing Abstinence

Key Ideas

▶ The risks of sexual intimacy include the effect on your emotional health and your relationship; and the risk of pregnancy and sexually-transmitted infections.

▶ A relationship can be close without being sexually intimate. But it is hard to keep a relationship close without emotional intimacy.

▶ Abstinence skills include setting clear limits, communicating your limits, avoiding high-pressure situations, and asserting yourself.

Vocabulary
- emotional intimacy (154)
- abstinence (154)

Chapter 6 Review

Reviewing Key Ideas

GO ONLINE
PearsonSuccessNet.com
For: Chapter 6 review activity

Section 1

1. A person who communicates feelings in a way that is disrespectful to another person is being
   a. passive.
   b. aggressive.
   c. assertive.
   d. an active listener.

2. If you use body language to communicate in another culture, what problem might arise?

3. When is it not a good idea to compromise?

4. **Critical Thinking** Person A says, "I'm angry because you are late." Person B says, "Did you think that I was being rude?" Which communication skill does each statement represent? Explain your answer.

Section 2

5. A clique is a small group of people
   a. who are part of an extended family.
   b. with similar backgrounds and interests.
   c. who value each other's differences.
   d. who are all the same age.

6. What qualities are important in a close friend?

7. Explain how envy or jealousy can cause problems in a friendship.

8. **Critical Thinking** Why do you think some people have trouble making or keeping friends?

Section 3

9. An infatuation is characterized by
   a. intense physical attraction.
   b. loyalty and empathy.
   c. shared interests and values.
   d. mutual trust and acceptance.

10. What are some benefits of steady dating? What are some drawbacks?

11. List at least four reasons why a teen might remain in an abusive relationship.

12. **Critical Thinking** Often people are first attracted to other people based on looks and personality. What other qualities might attract you to a person as you get to know him or her?

Section 4

13. The act of refraining from sex is called
    a. sexual intimacy.
    b. emotional intimacy.
    c. abstinence.
    d. sexual involvement.

14. In what ways does having a baby change the lives of teenage parents?

15. Describe two things a couple could do to increase their emotional intimacy.

16. Explain why it is important to think about your limits before you are faced with a decision about sexual intimacy.

17. **Critical Thinking** Jada's communication style is passive. How could this style lead to misunderstandings about sexual intimacy?

Building Health Skills

18. **Communicating** You sit next to a teen you don't know at a club meeting. What would you say about yourself? What would you ask in return?

19. **Making Decisions** Develop a list of rules to follow in a dating relationship. Make sure your rules emphasize respect for yourself and others.

20. **Setting Goals** Choose one of the abstinence skills you studied in Section 4. Make an action plan to apply this skill to situations other than choosing abstinence. For example, you could set clear limits not to be interrupted when you are doing your homework. Monitor your progress and adjust your action plan, if necessary. **WRITING**

Health and Community

Community Guide for Teens Design a guide for teens who are new to your community. Describe things they can do to meet people. Include all the necessary details such as times, dress codes, and costs for activities. You may want to include a map with locations marked. **WRITING**

Standardized Test Prep

Math Practice

The graph compares yes responses from teens in four countries to the following question: Do you often feel lonely? Use the graph to answer Questions 21–24.

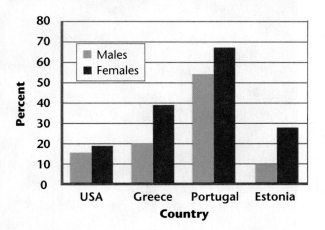

21. What percentage of male teens in the United States often feel lonely?
    A 10%   B 15%
    C 20%   D 25%

22. In which country are 19 percent of female teens often lonely?
    F United States   G Greece
    H Portugal   J Estonia

23. In which country is the difference between males and females greatest?
    A United States   B Greece
    C Portugal   D Estonia

24. In which country is the percent of lonely females almost double that of males?
    F United States
    G Greece
    H Portugal
    J Estonia

Test-Taking Tip

It may help to work with a friend while studying for a test. You can ask each other questions to see what you remember.

Reading and Writing Practice

Read the passage. Then answer Questions 25–28.

A communication device can give people who cannot speak the ability to communicate. A speech synthesizer in the device produces a voice. Some devices have a typical keyboard. The computer simply speaks the words typed in. Other keyboards have pictures instead of letters. This makes typing easier because each picture stands for an entire word. These systems are for people who have limited use of their hands. Many devices are small enough to be portable so that users are never without their "speech."

25. What is the main idea of this passage?
    A Communication devices are designed for people with limited use of their hands.
    B Some computer keyboards have pictures.
    C Computers can synthesize speech.
    D People who cannot speak can use technology to communicate.

26. Based on this passage, what does the word portable mean?
    F battery-operated
    G easily carried or moved
    H extremely small
    J easy to use

27. Which of the following statements is supported by this passage?
    A A speech synthesizer is used to speak words that are typed.
    B A speech synthesizer is used to translate typed words into pictures.
    C A speech synthesizer is used to increase the volume of spoken words.
    D A speech synthesizer is used to translate one language into another.

Constructed Response

28. A company asks you to design a machine that will improve people's ability to communicate. What kind of machine would you design? What would its purpose be and what features would it have?

CHAPTER 7

Preventing Violence

GO ONLINE PearsonSuccessNet.com

VIDEO 7

TEENS Talk

Bully-Proof

Preview **Activity**

What Do You Think About People Who Are Bullies?

Complete this activity before you watch the video.

1. Think about people you know who are bullies. Make a list of 5–10 words that describe a typical bully. For example, do you think a typical bully is strong or weak?

2. Do you think that bullying is a choice? If so, why would someone choose to be a bully? **WRITING**

Section 1 — What Is Violence?

Objectives

▶ **Describe** all of the costs related to violence.

▶ **Identify** five risk factors for violence.

Vocabulary

- violence
- homicide
- victim
- assailant
- territorial gang

Warm-Up

Myth Most acts of violence are committed by strangers, often as part of robberies or other crimes.

Fact In the United States, most acts of violence are done by people who know their victims.

WRITING Why do you think that many people believe strangers commit most violent acts?

Violence and Health

What does the word *violence* mean to you? **Violence** is the threat of or actual use of physical force against oneself or another person. Violence often results in injury or death. Homicide is a type of violence that gets a lot of attention from the media. **Homicide** (HAHM ih syd) is the intentional killing of one person by another. It is the second leading cause of death for people age 15 to 24. Other examples of violence are suicide and rape. So is threatening to harm another person.

Violence is a huge problem in the United States. Consider this data from one recent year.

▶ There were 16,259 deaths by homicide—one every 32.5 minutes.

▶ There were 38,364 deaths by suicide—one every 13.5 minutes.

▶ There were 81,280 reported rapes of women—one every 6.5 minutes.

Figure 1 compares the homicide rates for selected countries.

Violence is of major concern to health professionals. Doctors and nurses treat people who are injured by violence. Mental health counselors deal with the emotional harm. People who work in the area of public health look for ways to reduce the level of violence. These health professionals are aware of the costs of violence. **With violence, there are costs to the victim, costs to the assailant, and costs to society as a whole.**

162 *Chapter 7*

Costs to the Victim The **victim** is the person who is attacked. Death is the most serious outcome of a violent act, but it is not the only possible result. Victims who survive may suffer serious permanent injuries. Injuries to the head can lead to the loss of brain function. Other injuries can cause a permanent loss of feeling and movement in some part of the body. But even when injuries are less serious, they still may cause pain, require medical treatment, take time to heal, and leave scars.

There may also be emotional scars. Victims often experience anger, fear, and depression. It is also common for victims to replay the event over and over in their minds. This may make it difficult for them to focus on the future instead of the past. Family members and friends have to deal with feelings of loss or the burden of caring for an injured person.

Costs to the Assailant Another person who pays a price for violence is the assailant. An **assailant** (uh SAY lunt) is a person who attacks another person. The assailant may be seriously injured in a fight. The assailant may feel guilt or shame, and live in fear of an act of revenge.

The assailant also may face criminal charges, court costs, lawyer's fees, and possible jail time. Having a criminal record can seriously affect a person for the rest of his or her life. For example, it can limit a person's chances of finding a job or prevent a person from voting in some states.

Homicide Rates by Country

	Country	Rate
	Australia	1.2
	Brazil	22.7
	Costa Rica	11.3
	Denmark	0.9
	Japan	0.5
	Philippines	5.4
	Portugal	1.2
	Spain	0.9
	Thailand	5.3
	United Kingdom	1.2
	United States	5.0

FIGURE 1 The United Nations collected this data. The rates are given as deaths per every 100,000 people.
Reading Tables Which country listed has the highest homicide rate? Which countries have the lowest?

Costs to Society There are financial costs associated with violence. It costs the healthcare system over 2 trillion dollars a year to treat injuries that result from violence. Taxpayers also must pay for law enforcement, courts, and prisons. If schools spend money for metal detectors or guards, there may not be money left in the budget to pay for music, art, or sports.

There are emotional costs to society as well. Violent acts affect people even when they don't know the victims or assailants. In communities where violent acts are common, a fear of violence controls many day-to-day decisions. People avoid certain neighborhoods or are afraid to go out at night. They install security locks or alarms, and are suspicious of strangers.

 Connect to Your Life **Do you know a survivor of a violent attack? If so, how did the attack affect the person?**

GO ONLINE

PearsonSuccessNet.com

For: More on media violence

Risk Factors for Violence

Researchers have identified some risk factors for violence. **These risk factors are poverty, family violence, exposure to media violence, availability of weapons, drug abuse, and membership in gangs.**

Poverty   Most people who are poor are not violent. But when people don't have jobs, adequate food, healthcare, or respect from others, they may feel hopeless. They also may have a high level of frustration and anger because they are unable to improve their lives. A minor event may cause people who are already frustrated and angry to react more violently than normal. This helps to explain why the rate of violence is highest in poor urban communities where unemployment rates are high.

Movies and television shows can leave the impression that certain racial groups are more violent than others. Some racial groups are represented in higher numbers in violence statistics. But the reason is that some racial groups are poorer, on average, than others. When poor communities with different racial groups are compared, the homicide rates are similar.

Family Violence   Children who grow up in violent homes—who witness violence or are victims of violence—are more apt to use violence to solve their own problems. Violence may be the only strategy they have been taught for solving problems. Children who are neglected are also more likely than other children to respond to conflict with violence.

Children can learn to avoid violence if adults don't use violence to solve their own problems or to discipline children. Parents reveal their values about violence by the toys they buy and the television shows they allow their children to watch. They also pass along their values by sharing how they feel about violence.

Connect to Your Life   **What kinds of children's toys do you think might promote violence?**

FIGURE 2   In poor communities, the buildings and streets are often in need of repair. These conditions can add to a person's frustration and anger.

Media Wise

Violence in Video Games

People who play violent video games often take on the role of assailant. What effect might identifying with an assailant have on a player or group of players? Studies have linked violent video games to an increase in a player's level of aggression. Use this checklist to evaluate the content of a video game.

Is performing violent acts necessary to win the game?	Yes	No
Is the effect of the violence on the victim ignored?	Yes	No
Are women depicted as sexual objects?	Yes	No
Does the video game package use violence to make the game look exciting?	Yes	No
Does the video game have a *mature* or *adults only* rating?	Yes	No

Two or more "Yes" answers may indicate a video game with a high level of violent content.

Activity Look at the packaging for a few video games that have a *mature* rating. Is violence used to sell these games? Provide some examples to support your answer. Do the text and visuals make you want to play the game? **WRITING**

Media Violence In the first cartoons you watched, the characters may have attacked each other and lived to fight another day. These cartoons were likely your first example of media violence. The media uses the excitement provided by violence to keep you glued to the screen. An action hero may use violence to kill or capture a villain. Or an expert in self-defense may take on 10 villains and beat them all. Viewers may be left with the impression that violence is a reasonable response to many situations. But violence in the world beyond television and the movies creates more problems than it solves.

People's attitudes and behavior can be shaped by the violence they see in the media. This is especially true of young children because their actual life experience is limited. Children may think what they see on television or in the movies is really happening. Children who witness a lot of media violence may grow up with an exaggerated sense of the amount of violence in the world. They also may tend to react with violence when they face a threatening situation in their own lives.

The way women are portrayed and treated in the media is also an issue. Some types of music and music videos can make people think that violence toward women is acceptable. There may be a link between these media portrayals and the rise in dating violence, rape, and other forms of violence toward women.

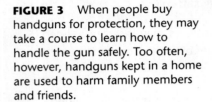
A gun kept in the home is more likely to kill a family member or friend than an intruder.

FIGURE 3 When people buy handguns for protection, they may take a course to learn how to handle the gun safely. Too often, however, handguns kept in a home are used to harm family members and friends.

Availability of Weapons The relationship between weapons and violence is controversial. Most people agree that when weapons are used in fights, fights are more deadly. But some people don't think that the availability of weapons is an important risk factor for violence. They point to countries such as Switzerland, where guns are found in nearly every household. Yet homicide rates in Switzerland are very low.

In the United States, handguns are used in the majority of homicides and suicides. Every 18 minutes someone in the United States dies from a gunshot wound. If firearms were not available, could these deaths be prevented? Experts do not know the answer.

The cycle of violence related to firearms seems difficult to break. When the homicide rate rises, fear of violence increases. More people purchase handguns for protection. But having a gun in the home can be more dangerous than not having one. The risk is even greater when the gun and the ammunition are not stored in separate locked locations.

Drug Abuse Would it surprise you to learn that at least 30 percent of homicide victims have alcohol in their blood? Would you expect the percentage to be the same or higher for assailants?

The reasons why alcohol use increases the risk of violence are not entirely clear. Researchers do know that alcohol affects the brain, clouding a person's judgment. This lack of judgment may lead people to say or do things that they ordinarily would not. This behavior may lead to a fight. In some cases, however, alcohol is used as an excuse or "to get up the nerve" to carry out preplanned acts of violence.

Drugs other than alcohol are also linked to violence. Like alcohol, illegal drugs, such as crack cocaine, can affect a person's judgment. In addition, people who are addicted to drugs may resort to robbery or other crimes to get money for drugs. Also, because many illegal drugs are sold for a large profit, the people who sell drugs often carry weapons.

Connect to Your Life

From what you have observed, how does alcohol or other drugs affect a person's behavior?

Membership in Gangs The term *gang* is used to describe a variety of groups, from loose bands of rowdy teens to criminal organizations. You can think of a gang as a type of clique. Gang members have similar backgrounds or interests. They are often subject to significant peer pressure. Because gangs don't readily associate with people who are perceived as different, their members are often isolated from the rest of the community.

Territorial gangs are groups that are organized to control a specific neighborhood or "turf." They are also referred to as "fighting" gangs because they will fight those who intrude on their turf. Most territorial gangs sell drugs and many are involved in other criminal behaviors. About two-thirds of territorial gang members are adults. They recruit students from poor or troubled families. The recruits may know of no way, other than gang membership, to gain a sense of belonging and protection.

Members of a gang may wear certain colors and jewelry, and use "secret" hand signs to identify themselves as gang members. A gang may hold elaborate initiation ceremonies. To join a gang, new members may undergo a beating. Or gang leaders may order them to commit a crime, such as robbery, kidnapping, rape, or murder. Quitting a gang can be much harder than joining one.

In many communities gang violence is a serious and growing problem. This is true for communities in urban, suburban, and rural areas.

FIGURE 4 One way to reduce violence is to offer choices for gang members. This bakery in Los Angeles was part of a community-based effort to provide jobs for former gang members.

Section 1 Review

Key Ideas and Vocabulary

1. How are **victim** and **assailant** defined?

2. List two possible costs of violence for a victim, an assailant, and society as a whole.

3. What are six risk factors for violence?

4. What is a **territorial gang**?

Critical Thinking

5. Predicting What is the possible cost to a victim of repeated threats of violence?

Health and Community

Survivors of Violence Sometimes survivors of violent acts or the families of victims who did not survive find positive ways to deal with their pain and grief. They may form groups to advocate against violence. Find out what anti-violence groups there are in your community. Then write a paragraph summarizing your findings. **WRITING**

6. Evaluating Which of the risk factors for violence do you think is most important? Give a reason for your answer.

Violence in Schools

Objectives

▶ **Explain** the relationship between harassment and the use of weapons at school.

▶ **Describe** effective ways to reduce bullying, hazing, sexual harassment, and hate violence in schools.

Vocabulary

- harassment
- bullying
- cyber bullying
- hazing
- sexual harassment
- hate violence
- prejudice
- stereotype
- intolerance
- discrimination
- vandalism

Warm-Up

Health Stats These data show the results of a recent survey of teens.

In one year...

20.1% reported being bullied on school property

12% of teens reported being in a physical fight on school property

7.4% reported being threatened or injured with a weapon on school property

WRITING   Do these numbers surprise you? What do you think could be done to decrease school violence?

Weapons in School

On December 14, 2012, a 20-year-old man carried three guns into Sandy Hook Elementary School in Newtown, Connecticut. The man killed 20 students and 6 adults before killing himself.

Despite tragic events such as the murders at Sandy Hook, schools remain a safe place when compared to other places in society. In terms of weapons, most schools are safer now than they were 30 years ago. Between 1983 and 2011, the number of males who reported carrying a weapon to school dropped from 18 percent to 8 percent. The number of females carrying weapons dropped from 5 percent to about 2 percent.

Even though most school violence does not end in murder, schools still need to worry about violence. Tragic episodes, such as the one at Sandy Hook, are called random acts of violence because the assailant doesn't target specific people. But the episodes themselves often are predictable. Many are a result of harassment. **Harassment** is unwanted remarks or actions that cause a person emotional or physical harm. **Students who use weapons at school often are acting on the rage they feel as victims of harassment.**

Bullying

Robert hates going to school because almost every day, Amber and her friends pick on him. They call him names like "pimple boy" and "tiny." They make fun of the way he stutters. Sometimes their jock friends join in and literally toss him around or stuff him in his locker. He hates himself for not being able to stop them.

Bullying is the use of threats or physical force to intimidate and control another person. The bully chooses a victim who is less powerful in terms of physical strength or social connections. The bully may use name-calling and put-downs. He or she may shove or trip the victim. The bully may pressure friends to exclude or isolate the victim. The goal may be to steal money or other property from the victim. But sometimes the bully simply takes pleasure from the victim's embarrassment or humiliation.

Cyber Bullying Bullying that takes place by e-mail, instant messaging, text messaging, or at Web sites is called **cyber bullying** (SY bur). This form of bullying is especially cruel because the bullies can harass their victims at home at all hours of the day. The cyber bullies make threats or spread rumors about the victim. A bully may even enter a chat room, pretend to be the victim, and post messages that make the victim appear silly or offensive to others. This leaves the victim open to ridicule and may place the victim in danger.

Causes and Effects As a child, a bully may have learned to feel good at the expense of others. Bullies take out their frustrations and insecurities on others. A bully may seem extremely confident. But displays of bravado often hide a lack of self-confidence.

Bullying produces a climate of fear and disrespect at schools. The victims have increased levels of anxiety and depression. They may think about suicide. Most victims suffer in silence, but a few strike back. **The most effective way to stop bullying is to get bystanders involved.** Figure 5 lists some specific ways you can help stop bullying.

Connect to Your Life **Were you ever a target of bullying? How did you feel? How did you respond?**

GO ONLINE
PearsonSuccessNet.com
For: More on bullying

FIGURE 5 Bullies often look to bystanders for approval. So bystanders can play a key role in stopping bullying. **Predicting** Which strategy listed do you think would be most effective for stopping bullying?

Ways to Help Stop Bullying

- ▶ Don't make jokes at others' expense or single out a person for exclusion.
- ▶ Don't reward a bully with laughter or other positive attention.
- ▶ Speak up. Silence is seen as approval.
- ▶ Don't believe rumors and don't spread rumors.
- ▶ Reach out to students who seem isolated.

FIGURE 6 Students who join the cheerleading squad or other teams expect to work hard. They shouldn't have to worry about possible hazing from older members of the team.

Hazing

When Zoe auditioned for the cheerleading squad, she was excited to make the cut. Then she heard disturbing news. There would be a member-led initiation for new members. She was concerned about what might happen, but she didn't tell her parents. She was afraid they would make her quit cheerleading.

Hazing is requiring a person to do degrading, risky, or illegal acts in order to join a group. Sadly, hazing is a fairly common practice in school clubs and athletic teams. A person may be yelled at, forced to do personal chores, or asked to wear a ridiculous costume in public. Physical abuse and sexual abuse are part of some initiations.

Gender and Hazing Almost half of all high school students on school teams or clubs report being hazed. Male teens are more likely to report being beaten, being required to steal, or being forced to destroy property. Males also report being tied up and confined to small places.

Female teens report less physical abuse than do males, although the number of female athletes who report being beaten is surprisingly large. Females are more likely to report emotional abuse. This can take the form of put downs or being required to perform demeaning acts in public.

Preventing Hazing Hazing isn't an issue that students can easily deal with as individuals. Some students are confident and assertive enough to refuse to haze or be hazed. But most feel uncomfortable challenging older students. They also fear being rejected or being called a wimp.

In most states, hazing is illegal at both high schools and colleges. A school could also be sued if a student is injured during hazing. **School administrators and teachers need to take the lead in the prevention of hazing.** They must establish strict rules against hazing and make sure that students understand the rules. Coaches and other adults should be alert for signs of hazing. When a student reports an incident, the school should support the student and address the issue quickly and fairly.

Connect to Your Life **Do you agree that all types of hazing should be banned at school? Why or why not?**

Sexual Harassment

Mariah's friend, Eduardo, told her that there were some explicit sexual comments about her in the boy's bathroom. She didn't pay much attention until a student she didn't know asked her for a sexual favor. Humiliated and angry, Mariah talked with a teacher and then with the principal. She was told not to let the remarks get to her. The guys were just fooling around.

Sexual harassment is any uninvited and unwelcome sexual remark or sexual advance. Making comments about a person's body parts is an example. So is unwanted touching or spreading rumors about someone's sexual behavior. Telling crude jokes in study hall is also an example. The jokes may make some students uncomfortable and distract them from their studies. Sometimes sexual harassment is a part of hazing. A group may make sexual demands in exchange for admission into the group.

Sadly, sometimes the person doing the harassing is an adult. The difference in power between the adult and the student makes the behavior even less acceptable. **If school administrations, teachers, and students work together, they can stop sexual harassment.**

What Schools Must Do   Sexual harassment in schools is illegal. The administration at a school is required by law to respond quickly and forcefully when students complain about sexual harassment. If the school doesn't act, and the harassment continues, the victim has grounds to sue the assailant and the school.

What You Can Do   Here are ways you can stop sexual harassment.

► Speak up assertively when you feel disrespected.

► Use your refusal skills to reject unwanted sexual advances.

► Avoid having to be alone with someone you don't trust.

► Report behavior that you think is sexual harassment to an adult.

FIGURE 7   These young men are admiring two young women who are passing by. **Classifying** Do you think staring at a person's body is an example of sexual harassment? Why or why not?

Hate Violence

After a basketball game at a rival school, 16-year-old Troy was badly beaten by three youths. The violent act seemed to be racially motivated. According to Troy, the youths shouted racial slurs as they repeatedly kicked and punched him.

Hate violence is speech or behavior that is aimed at a person or group based on personal characteristics. Behaviors range from gestures to physical attacks. Hate speech may be spoken or written. A person might be targeted because of race, ethnicity, gender, or religion. If the violence that takes place is against the law, the action is classified as a hate crime.

Prejudice and Intolerance Hate violence often stems from prejudice and intolerance. **Prejudice** is negative feelings about a group based on stereotypes. A **stereotype** is an exaggerated belief or overgeneralization about an entire group of people. A person who is prejudiced will prejudge people based solely on their connection to a group. He or she fails to see people as individuals.

Prejudice can lead to intolerance. **Intolerance** is a lack of acceptance of another person's opinions, beliefs, or actions. Too often, people who are intolerant are looking for an excuse to attack someone. They may try to justify their actions by saying things like, "She was asking for it," or "It was him or me," or "I wasn't the only one."

Discrimination Frequently, intolerance leads to discrimination. **Discrimination** is the unfair treatment of a person or group based on prejudice. People who are discriminated against may be unable to find jobs that fit their talents and education. They often cannot rent an apartment or buy a house in certain areas. They may receive poor service in restaurants or stores.

Psychologists use the term *microinsults* to describe a series of small but frequent acts of discrimination. For example, a person may be made to feel like an outsider or be treated impolitely. Or a person may have his or her talents underestimated. The anger brought on by microinsults can build over time and may eventually lead to violence.

FIGURE 8 When people have a wide variety of friends, they often are more tolerant of differences.

Have you ever experienced prejudice? If so, how did you feel?

Reducing Intolerance Many people believe that prejudice and intolerance are rooted in a fear of the unknown. When people see behaviors that are unfamiliar, they may think, "That's strange." They may even feel threatened and afraid. When people understand unfamiliar behaviors, they are less likely to be fearful. **The most effective way to deal with violence based on hate is through education.** When people learn about different cultures and get to know individuals from other groups, they are often more tolerant of differences.

Vandalism Sometimes hate is expressed through acts of vandalism. **Vandalism** is intentionally damaging or destroying another person's property. Not all acts of vandalism are motivated by hate. When teens break windows at school, they are not targeting a specific group. But when teens damage gravestones at a cemetery or scrawl offensive words on a school wall, they are usually targeting a group. Their intention is to humiliate and degrade.

Research shows that students who feel a strong positive connection to school are less likely to take part in vandalism of school property. How can schools strengthen students' feelings of connection to school? They can foster a climate in which students feel supported and better able to achieve their goals. Students feel supported when they have positive interactions with teachers and other school staff. They also feel supported when the school encourages teamwork among students.

> **36% of high school students report seeing hate-filled graffiti at school.**

FIGURE 9 These students are painting over hate-filled graffiti at their school. This action helps remove the graffiti and shows that the students disapprove of hate violence.

Section 2 Review

Key Ideas and Vocabulary

1. What does the term **harassment** mean?

2. What is the connection between harassment and the use of weapons at school?

3. What is **cyber bullying?** What is the most effective way to stop bullying?

4. How can school administrators help prevent hazing and sexual harassment?

5. What is **hate violence?** What is the most effective way to deal with hate violence?

Critical Thinking

6. Comparing and Contrasting How are bullying and sexual harassment alike? How are they different?

Health at School

Role Playing Work with a group of students to prepare a skit about bullying. Include roles for a bully, a victim, and bystanders. Write a few different endings to show how the way that the bystanders respond can affect the outcome. **WRITING**

7. Evaluating Older students often feel that hazing is justified because they were hazed when they were freshman or sophomores. Do you think that these older students are right? Give reasons for your answer. **WRITING**

8. Predicting Yasmeen is the only person at her school who practices a particular religion. How might this fact affect her experiences at school?

How Fights Start

Objectives

▶ **Explain** how anger and a desire for revenge can lead to fights.

▶ **Describe** the role that friends and bystanders play in fights.

▶ **Explain** the relationship between a need for control and violence.

Vocabulary

• escalate
• instigator

Warm-Up

Dear Advice Line,

There's a guy at school who whispers "loser" every time he sees me in the hall. I know this guy is a jerk, so I ignore him. My friends think I should insult him back.

WRITING Do you agree with this student's response? Why or why not? What if the insults were shouted, not whispered?

Arguments

Hey, what did you call me?
You heard what I said. What are you going to do about it?

Too often, a simple exchange like this one—on the basketball court, in a school hallway, on the streets—leads to tragic results. What starts as a disagreement may end up as a fight, leading to injury or even death. In fact, about 40 percent of all homicides stem directly from arguments. **Anger is at the root of most arguments and of many fights.**

Anger The body reacts to anger the same way it does to stress. Recall the fight-or-flight response from Chapter 3. The physical changes that occur in this first stage of the stress response include tensed muscles, and increased heart and breathing rates. These changes prepare the body to fight or run.

Fighting or running away are not your only options for dealing with anger. Although the body's reaction to anger is automatic, you can control your overall reaction to anger. If you resort to fighting when someone makes you angry, you give the other person control over you. The person knows that, by provoking you, he or she can force you to fight. This means that the person can cause you to be kicked out of a game, suspended from school, or suffer other negative consequences of fighting. By choosing not to fight, you do not let the other person control you.

FIGURE 10 A fight may start because of verbal insults or aggressive body language. **Observing** What aspects of this teen's body language might help to provoke a fight?

Hurt Pride and Embarrassment Think of a time when your pride was hurt or someone embarrassed you in public. Perhaps a classmate made negative remarks about your family or culture. Or students from a rival school chanted insults as your football team suffered a bad defeat. Maybe a friend revealed a secret that you had shared in confidence. Or you walked into a room and heard someone doing an unflattering imitation of you.

You may have been surprised at just how angry you felt when your pride was hurt or you were embarrassed. It is not surprising that hurt pride and embarrassment often lead to fighting.

Revenge

There's the guy who beat up your brother. What are you going to do?

He's going to pay for what he did. But this time I'll choose the time and place. He'll never know what hit him.

Some people mistakenly believe that fighting can settle an argument. But more often than not, this approach does not work. The person who loses the fight is usually left feeling angry and embarrassed. He or she may enlist the help of friends or family members to get revenge, or "even the score." **The desire for revenge leads to a dangerous cycle of fighting.**

In cases where revenge is the motive for a fight, the fighting can quickly **escalate,** or grow more intense. Where the first fight may have been a fistfight, the second fight may involve knives or guns. Where the first fight may have involved only two people, the second fight may involve many more. Plus, chances are good that the second fight will not settle the argument, which will only lead to more fights.

Revenge is a common motive in fights between territorial gangs. Gang members feel responsible for protecting one another and defending their turf. When one gang member is wronged, other members come to his or her aid. A cycle of revenge between gangs may last for years.

 GO ONLINE
PearsonSuccessNet.com
For: More on anger management

 Connect to Your Life Have you ever had a fight to settle an argument? If so, did the fight settle things? Why or why not?

Peer Pressure

You're not going to let her get away with that, are you?
Girl, I wouldn't take that from anyone.
Why do you carry a knife if you're afraid to use it?

One aspect of fights that is often overlooked is the role of friends and bystanders. When you hear the term *peer pressure* in relation to violence, you may immediately think of the influence that gang members have on each other to fight. But peer pressure can be an important factor in non-gang violence as well. **It is often more difficult for a person to avoid a fight when friends or bystanders are present.**

The Role of Friends   You just had a loud disagreement with someone and your friends make comments like those above. How might these comments affect you? Chances are they would increase your feelings of anger and embarrassment, and add to the pressure you might already feel to fight. You might feel trapped—you don't want to fight but you may worry that your friends would lose respect for you if you walk away.

Friends who urge you to fight are acting as instigators. **Instigators** are people who encourage fighting between others while staying out of the fight themselves. Sometimes an instigator acts directly. He or she may exaggerate a conflict or embarrass a person into fighting. At other times, instigators act indirectly. For example, they may spread rumors about one person to another to create a conflict between them.

The Role of Bystanders   Another form of instigation occurs when a crowd gathers at the scene of a potential fight. The people who gather do so hoping to see a fight. They may yell things or in other ways urge the people to fight. It can be very difficult to settle a dispute peacefully once a crowd has gathered. If a fight does break out, the person who loses may face an additional problem—dealing with the embarrassment of having had so many people witness the defeat.

Connect to Your Life   **Have you ever been an instigator in a fight? If so, why did you encourage the other person to fight?**

FIGURE 11   When a fight is about to occur, bystanders can make a difference. **Observing** What role are the bystanders playing in the situation shown?

Control

Did you see her black eye and bruises?

Yes, and all because another guy gave her a ride home. How can a guy beat up on his girlfriend like that?

Girlfriend? He treats her more like a piece of property.

Domestic violence and dating violence are a growing problem in this country. **One person's desire to have control over another is the main reason for domestic violence and dating violence.** Although the victims can be men, they are most often women.

Men generally have greater physical strength than women. So a fight between a man and a woman is often quite one-sided. Plus the woman may not fight back for fear that the violence will escalate. Or she may begin to believe that she deserves to be hit. She is caught in a trap—too afraid to stay and challenge the abuser and too afraid to leave. The victim learns to follow the abuser's orders and to even anticipate his wishes to avoid further attacks.

There are laws that protect women in abusive relationships. The police can arrest the abuser or a judge can issue a restraining order telling the man to keep away from the woman. But a restraining order won't help unless the woman has a safe place to go. Doctors, counselors, or members of the clergy can help women find the support they need. In most areas, there are shelters for abused women where they can also get help for their legal, financial, and emotional needs. There are also groups that try to help abusers learn to control their violent behavior.

FIGURE 12 Often victims of violence try to hide their bruises. They might use makeup, dark glasses, or long-sleeved shirts. **Predicting** Why might a victim of violence try to hide her bruises?

Section 3 Review

Key Ideas and Vocabulary

1. How can anger and revenge lead to fights?

2. What does it mean to **escalate** a fight?

3. What effect can friends and bystanders have on fights?

4. What does the term **instigator** mean?

5. How does a desire for control contribute to violence toward women?

Critical Thinking

6. Evaluating Fighting between teenage girls has increased greatly in recent years. What reasons can you think of to explain this trend?

Health at Home

Attitudes Toward Fighting Interview three adults that you know well. Ask them how they feel about fighting as a way to resolve conflicts. Do all the adults have the same attitude? How do their attitudes compare with yours? Write a paragraph summarizing what you find out. **WRITING**

7. Predicting Do think that an insult based on characteristics such as race or religion is more likely to lead to a fight than an insult based on behavior? Why or why not? **WRITING**

8. Comparing and Contrasting Why would some of the strategies used for reducing stress also help a person control anger?

Advocacy

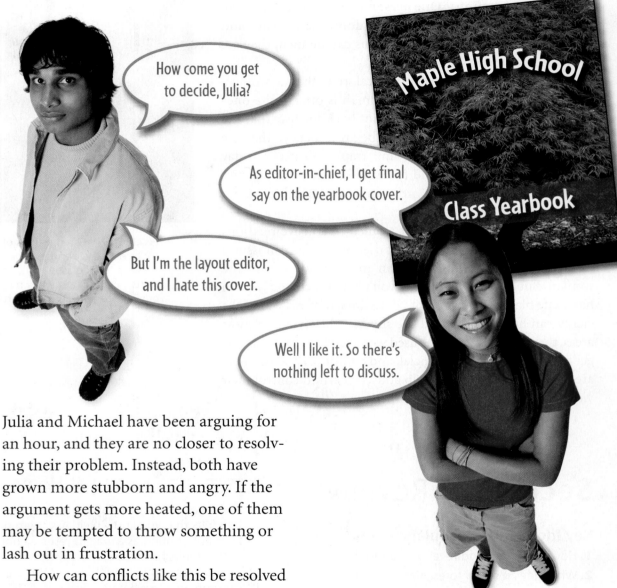

How come you get to decide, Julia?

As editor-in-chief, I get final say on the yearbook cover.

Maple High School

Class Yearbook

But I'm the layout editor, and I hate this cover.

Well I like it. So there's nothing left to discuss.

Julia and Michael have been arguing for an hour, and they are no closer to resolving their problem. Instead, both have grown more stubborn and angry. If the argument gets more heated, one of them may be tempted to throw something or lash out in frustration.

How can conflicts like this be resolved peacefully? One effective method, known as mediation, involves a third party in the negotiation process. The mediator explores the problem with the people to help them find a "win-win" solution—a solution that meets some of the important needs of both people. These steps outline the mediation process.

❶ Emphasize your neutrality.
Begin the mediation session by making it clear to both parties that you do not have a personal interest in the outcome. Explain that you will not take sides or decide who is right or wrong. Your role is to help find a solution that is acceptable to both parties.

> You both need to agree on some rules before we begin.

② Establish guidelines.

Ask the parties to agree upon the following rules before you begin.

- ▶ Keep everything that is said confidential.
- ▶ Be as honest as possible.
- ▶ Don't name-call or swear.
- ▶ Don't interrupt the other person.
- ▶ Take an active part in finding a solution.
- ▶ Follow through on any agreed-upon solution.

③ Ask each person to state his or her view.

- ▶ Allow each person to speak without interruption.
- ▶ Listen actively. If something that is said isn't clear, ask a question. Or restate the point and ask, "Is that what you mean?"
- ▶ Don't go on to the next person until you really understand the first person's position.

④ Identify each person's goal.

Try to figure out what principle, or goal, is driving each person's position. What a person truly cares about may not be what that person *says* he or she cares about.

⑤ Explore possible solutions.

If the participants seem relaxed, ask them to work together to brainstorm a list of possible solutions. During brainstorming, they should not judge any proposed solutions. Encourage the participants to use each other's suggestions to spark their own ideas.

If the participants are tense or hostile, help them explore solutions one at a time. Start by asking one person to propose a solution. Then, get the other person's reaction and ask for a counterproposal. Continue until you find a solution that satisfies both people.

⑥ Don't give up.

It isn't easy to find a win-win solution for every conflict, but it can be done.

- ▶ Focus on what the parties agree on. Use that common ground to help them bridge their different positions.
- ▶ Keep the participants involved in the process. The more involved they are, the more interest they will have in resolving the conflict.
- ▶ If you are unable to find an agreeable solution, ask for help from an adult who has the respect and trust of both participants.

BUILDING HEALTH SKILLS — Practice the Skill

1. Review the disagreement described in the introduction. What questions would you ask Julia and Michael to get at the principle behind each person's position?

2. With two of your classmates, role-play the mediation session. Take turns playing the roles of mediator, Julia, and Michael. What solution, if any, did you reach in each role-play session? What difficulties did you encounter in mediating the conflict?

3. Think about a recent conflict that you had with a friend or family member. Would a mediator have been able to help you resolve the conflict? Why or why not?

4. Make a list of the types of conflicts that occur among teens. Which of the conflicts on your list would be appropriate for mediation? Which would not? Explain.

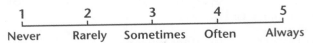

Section 4

Preventing Fights

Objectives

▶ **Describe** two general approaches for resolving conflicts.

▶ **Explain** why safety should be a person's first concern in any conflict.

▶ **Summarize** how to confront a person wisely.

▶ **Identify** ways to help others avoid fighting.

Vocabulary

• mediation

Warm-Up

Quick Quiz For each statement, rate yourself on this scale.

1	2	3	4	5
Never	Rarely	Sometimes	Often	Always

(1) When I am upset with someone, I talk to the person in private where we cannot be overheard.

(2) When I am angry, I avoid using insults or name-calling.

(3) I apologize when I do or say something hurtful.

(4) When I know a fight is brewing, I don't go to watch.

(5) I avoid spreading rumors.

WRITING The higher your total score, the better your skills as a peacemaker. In which area would you most want to improve? Explain.

Choosing Not to Fight

It isn't always easy to avoid a fight, but it can be done. You need to learn peaceful alternatives to fighting, and how to pursue those alternatives even when the other person really wants to fight. As you read, think of ways you can adapt these strategies to situations in your life. You may come up with strategies of your own that you can share with friends, siblings, and others that you care about.

When people who know each other fight, there is usually a history of events leading up to the fight. For example, the spreading of rumors or name-calling may go on for days or weeks before a fight breaks out. If a conflict grows to the point where others know about it, friends may put pressure on one or both of the participants to do something. By the time a crowd has gathered for the showdown, it's almost too late.

It is best to deal with a conflict early on when people are less angry. Also, it is more difficult to resolve a problem after someone has been embarrassed in public or when instigators start to play a role. **Once you recognize that a conflict exists, there are two general approaches you can take. You can ignore the conflict or you can confront the person.**

Ignoring a Conflict

▶ A stranger bumps into you as you pass on the sidewalk.

▶ You are angry that some friends didn't ask you to go with them to the movies, even though you really didn't want to go.

▶ According to a friend of a friend of a friend, your boyfriend was flirting with a bridesmaid at his brother's wedding.

None of these situations seem worth fighting over. In some situations it may be smartest to walk away and do nothing at all. Figure 13 lists some tips to help you decide when it is best to ignore a situation.

Some people think that ignoring a conflict is a sign of cowardice. It is actually a sign of maturity and self-control. The act of cowardice may be to fight out of pride, or to "save face," or to impress your friends. But when you decide to ignore a conflict rather than fight, you may need to be flexible and you will need to control your own anger.

Be Flexible   When you ignore a conflict, you need to proceed carefully. It is important to trust your judgment and be prepared to try a new tactic if your first choice doesn't defuse the situation. Suppose, for example, that you suspect the other person will become angrier if you ignore the situation. Then it may be better *not* to ignore the situation, even if you want to. **In deciding how to deal with any conflict, your safety should always be your first concern.**

Learn to Control Your Anger   Learning to control your anger is an important skill to master if you want to avoid conflicts. If you cannot control your anger, you may overreact to a situation. You also leave yourself vulnerable to people who want to provoke you into a fight.

If you are not satisfied with the way you now deal with anger, many people can help you. Parents, teachers, coaches, school counselors, and members of the clergy are just some of the people you can turn to for help. If these people cannot help you themselves, they may be able to refer you to trained counselors who can. By asking for help, you take an important first step toward gaining control over your behavior and your future.

FIGURE 13   Rumors are not a reliable source of information. So it is often wise to ignore conflicts based on rumors.

Ignore a Situation If...

▶ you will probably never see the person again.

▶ the person or issue isn't very important to you.

▶ the conflict is based on rumors that can be overlooked.

▶ the conflict is about something trivial or silly.

▶ a person tries to get you in trouble by provoking a fight.

Connect to Your Life   **Which conflicts are easiest to ignore—conflicts with strangers or conflicts with friends? Explain.**

Choose a Safe Place

Stay Calm

FIGURE 14 Three general steps for confronting a person wisely are choosing the correct time and place, staying calm, and negotiating a solution.
Predicting How could being unable to stay calm affect your ability to negotiate a solution?

Confronting a Person Wisely

Sometimes it may not be possible to ignore a conflict. The person may be someone with whom you are in frequent contact, or the issue may be too important to ignore. In these cases, you may decide to confront the person. The way in which you handle the confrontation, however, is critical to its success. **To confront a person wisely, you need to choose the right time and place, stay calm, and negotiate a solution.**

Choose the Time and Place Carefully When you need to confront a person, pick a time when you can talk face-to-face. Make sure that you don't have an audience. If people you know, especially friends, are around, the person may think that you want to embarrass him or her in front of the friends. The person may feel pressured to start a fight to avoid embarrassment.

It is best to meet in a public area, such as the food court in a mall or on a bench in a public park. Don't choose an isolated spot where there are no other people within shouting distance. That way you can get help if things don't go as you planned.

It is also important to avoid a confrontation when a person has been using alcohol or other drugs. Recall that alcohol and other drugs impair judgment and are a risk factor for violence. If you suspect the other person is under the influence of drugs, postpone your discussion.

Stay Calm It can be difficult to remain calm when you are upset, but it is important to try. Focus on keeping your voice low. By avoiding screaming or name-calling, you can remain in control of the situation.

People have different techniques for keeping calm under pressure. Some people find it helpful to rehearse the confrontation beforehand with an uninvolved person. Other people use deep breathing or count to 20 when they feel their temper begin to rise. Despite all your efforts, however, you may find yourself unable to stay calm and control your temper. If that happens, you may have to postpone your discussion.

 GO ONLINE

PearsonSuccessNet.com

For: More on handling conflicts

Why did you let me take all the blame for the cartoon on the board?

I was afraid of what my mom would say if I got another detention.

Negotiate a Solution

Negotiate a Solution When you want to resolve a conflict peacefully, your communication style can affect the outcome. It is important to use skills such as "I" messages, assertiveness, and seeing the other person's point of view. When you say things like "I know this issue is important to both of us…," the other person is likely to be less defensive. Here are other strategies that may be useful during a negotiation.

▶ **Do the Unexpected** If, instead of being hostile, you are friendly, confident, and caring, the other person may relax his or her guard. Try to make the situation seem as if it is not serious enough to fight about.

▶ **Provide a Way Out** Sometimes fighting breaks out simply because people see no other way to resolve things without losing pride. To avoid fighting, present the other person with compromise solutions that you both can live with. By saying something like, "Let's try this for a week and see how it goes," you give the person an easy way out.

▶ **Be Willing to Apologize** In some situations, be willing to say "I'm sorry" or "I didn't mean to embarrass you." Sometimes a sincere apology can be the quickest way to defuse the situation.

Helping Others to Avoid Fights

When you are not personally involved in a conflict, you can still play an important role. **You can help prevent fighting through mediation, through your role as a bystander, and by involving an adult.**

Mediation A process for resolving conflicts that involves a neutral third party is called **mediation** (mee dee AY shun). The Building Health Skills activity on pages 178–179 describes this process. As with all conflicts, mediators need to think about their own safety first. They should never get involved in heated conflicts that could turn violent at any moment.

What strategies do you use to help others avoid fights?

FIGURE 15 Discouraging others from fighting is an important part of preventing violence.

Tips for Peacemakers
- Listen to people who are hurt.
- Help to correct unfair situations.
- Praise helps.
- Put-downs don't help.

Your Role as a Bystander You learned how friends and acquaintances often put pressure on people to fight. These same people, however, can play a key role in preventing fights. As a bystander, you can use the following strategies to show your disapproval of fighting as a way to resolve conflicts.

▶ Ignore those people who make negative remarks about other people.

▶ Refuse to spread rumors.

▶ Do not relay a threat or insult from one person to another.

▶ Stay away from any area where you expect a fight could take place.

As a friend, you can use your influence to support positive behaviors. You can show respect for people who apologize to others, ignore insults, and otherwise avoid fights. If you advise your friends to ignore someone's insults or not to hold grudges, you do them a very important service. You help keep them safe from the potential of deadly violence.

When to Involve an Adult If a friend reveals plans of violence to you, it is important to ask for help. Such plans should always be taken seriously, especially if your friend talks about using a weapon. Although it is never easy to break a friend's confidence, it is critical for you to share your friend's plans with a trusted adult. Doing so is a true act of caring. It shows that you care too much to let your friend be lost to violence.

Section 4 Review

Key Ideas and Vocabulary

1. What are two possible approaches when you are faced with a conflict?
2. What should your first concern be in any conflict?
3. Describe three steps you should take when you confront a person.
4. What does the term **mediation** mean?
5. How can you help others avoid a fight?

Critical Thinking

6. **Comparing and Contrasting** Why should you use "I" messages when you negotiate a solution for yourself? Why should a mediator not use "I" messages?

Health at School

Peer Mediation Interview a few students who have taken mediation training. Ask them what they learned and how they have used what they learned to resolve conflicts. Then write a paragraph discussing why you would or would not want to be trained as a mediator. **WRITING**

7. **Making Judgments** You hear that a fight is brewing between two students. A friend tells you that one of the students has a knife and intends to use it. What would you do? Why?

8. **Evaluating** Why do you think that it is difficult for some people to apologize even when they know they are wrong?

GO ONLINE PearsonSuccessNet.com   Audio Summary Section 7.4

Chapter 7
At a Glance

VIDEO **TEENS** Talk ⊙
Bully-Proof What did you learn from the video about how you can help to reduce violence at school?

Section 1 What Is Violence?

Key Ideas

▶ With violence, there are costs to the victim, costs to the assailant, and costs to society as a whole.

▶ Risk factors for violence include poverty, family violence, exposure to media violence, availability of weapons, drug abuse, and membership in gangs.

Vocabulary
- violence (162)
- homicide (162)
- victim (163)
- assailant (163)
- territorial gang (167)

Section 2 Violence in Schools

Key Ideas

▶ Students who use weapons at school often are acting on the rage they feel as victims of harassment.

▶ The most effective way to stop bullying is to get bystanders involved.

▶ School administrators and teachers need to take the lead in the prevention of hazing. If school administrations, teachers, and students work together, they can stop sexual harassment.

▶ The most effective way to deal with violence based on hate is through education.

Vocabulary
- harassment (168)
- bullying (169)
- cyber bullying (169)
- hazing (170)
- sexual harassment (171)

- hate violence (172)
- prejudice (172)
- stereotype (172)
- intolerance (172)
- discrimination (172)
- vandalism (173)

Section 3 How Fights Start

Key Ideas

▶ Anger is at the root of most arguments and of many fights. The desire for revenge leads to a dangerous cycle of fighting.

▶ It is often more difficult for a person to avoid a fight when friends or bystanders are present.

▶ One person's desire to have control over another is the main reason for domestic violence and dating violence.

Vocabulary
- escalate (175)
- instigator (176)

Section 4 Preventing Fights

Key Ideas

▶ Once you recognize that a conflict exists, you can ignore the conflict or confront the person. In deciding how to deal with any conflict, your safety should always be your first concern.

▶ To confront a person wisely, choose the right time and place, stay calm, and negotiate a solution.

▶ You can help prevent fighting through mediation, through your role as a bystander, and by involving an adult.

Vocabulary
- mediation (183)

Chapter 7 Review

Reviewing Key Ideas

GO ONLINE
PearsonSuccessNet.com
For: Chapter 7 review activity

Section 1

1. For an action to be classified as violence, the action must
   a. result in death.
   b. result in physical injury.
   c. involve physical force.
   d. involve a threat or actual use of physical force.

2. Describe the emotional costs of violence to victims, assailants, and society as a whole.

3. Explain why poverty and family violence are risk factors for violence.

4. **Critical Thinking** Why do you think that the homicide rate in the United States is so high? What could be done to lower the rate?

Section 2

5. A lack of acceptance of another person's opinions, beliefs, or actions is
   a. prejudice.   b. stereotyping.
   c. intolerance.   d. discrimination.

6. Explain how bullying might lead to the use of weapons at school.

7. What should a student do when faced with sexual harassment at school?

8. **Critical Thinking** Do you think that school courses in managing anger could help students learn to handle anger better? Why or why not?

Section 3

9. People who encourage fighting between others are called
   a. bystanders.   b. instigators.
   c. assailants.   d. peers.

10. How can the presence of acquaintances and friends make it more difficult to avoid a fight?

11. What is the main cause of domestic violence and dating violence? Explain how a woman may get trapped in an abusive relationship.

12. **Critical Thinking** Use the saying "an eye for an eye and a tooth for a tooth" to explain the role that revenge can play in fighting.

Section 4

13. Ignoring a conflict is
    a. never a good approach.
    b. an act of cowardice.
    c. one approach to handling conflicts.
    d. the best approach to all conflicts.

14. Explain how your safety could be at risk when you ignore a conflict, when you confront a person, and when you mediate a conflict.

15. What can bystanders do to help prevent fights?

16. **Critical Thinking** A person sitting next to you on a crowded subway is smoking, despite the *No Smoking* sign. Make a list of the potential risks and benefits of confronting this person. Then state what you would do. **WRITING**

Building Health Skills

17. **Advocacy** Your friend has been spreading untrue rumors about a new student at school. The new student is very angry. How could you prevent this situation from becoming violent?

18. **Analyzing Influences** Why do you think a teen might videotape an act of violence by other teens instead of trying to stop the violence?

19. **Setting Goals** Make an action plan to reduce the number of times you say negative things about other people. Put your plan into action for a week and monitor your progress. Then adjust your plan, if necessary. **WRITING**

Health and Community

Teens in the News Look through your local newspaper each day for a week. Record a brief summary of each story about teens. What percentage of the stories are about violence? What impression do you think an adult reading this newspaper would have of today's youth? **WRITING**

Standardized Test Prep

Math Practice

The table compares the number of homicides in eight states in 2011. Use the table to answer Questions 20–23.

State	Population	Homicides	Rate*
California	37,254,000	1,790	4.8
Florida	18,801,000	984	5.2
Iowa	3,046,000	44	1.5
Missouri	5,989,000	364	6.1
Nevada	2,701,000	129	5.2
New Jersey	8,792,000	379	4.3
Rhode Island	1,053,000	14	1.3
Utah	2,764,000	51	1.9

* Homicides per 100,000 people

20. Of the states listed, which state had the most homicides?
    A Florida   B California
    C Nevada   D Missouri

21. Of the states listed, which state had the largest population?
    F Florida   G California
    H Nevada   J Missouri

22. Of the states listed, which state had the highest homicide rate?
    A Florida   B California
    C Missouri   D Nevada

23. Based on the data, which of the following statements is true?
    F The smaller the population of a state, the lower its homicide rate.
    G There is no relationship between population and number of homicides.
    H States with larger populations have higher homicide rates.
    J When comparing homicide data for states, you should compare rates, not number of homicides.

Test-Taking Tip

If you are frustrated by the questions on a test, don't disturb others. Try to calm down so you can think clearly.

Reading and Writing Practice

Read the passage. Then answer Questions 24–27.

Police and health professionals have different roles when they deal with violence. Police respond to a violent event to find out what happened. Their goal is to gather enough evidence to make an arrest and help convict the person who committed the violent act. Police are charged with assigning blame and punishment after an episode of violence. Health professionals use what is known about violent events to try to understand what causes violence. Health professionals are charged with identifying the risk factors that can lead to violence.

24. What is the main idea of this passage?
    A Police are not interested in preventing violence.
    B Police and health professionals have different approaches to violence.
    C Health professionals are not concerned about placing blame for violent acts.
    D Health professionals try to identify risk factors for violence.

25. Based on this passage, what does the phrase "charged with" mean?
    F in favor of
    G trained to
    H responsible for
    J obsessed with

26. Which statement is implied—not said, but understood—by the passage?
    A The causes of violence are easy to understand.
    B All violent acts have the same cause.
    C Police and health professionals don't agree on how to prevent violence.
    D Identifying risk factors can help prevent violence.

Constructed Response

27. Which approach to reducing violence do you think is more effective, the one used by police or the one used by health professionals? Give some specific reasons for your answer.

Focus on ISSUES

How Has Technology Affected Teens' Communication Skills?

Every day, teens use e-mail, cell phones, instant messaging, and text messaging to communicate with family and friends. In fact, over 90 percent of teens in the United States have Internet access and at least 75 percent have cell phones.

Can you communicate as well electronically as you can when you are face to face? Does electronic communication have an effect on your communication skills and other social skills? Is the effect positive or negative?

The Case for Electronic Communication

Electronic communication has broadened teens' communication skills. The wide range of communication options allows teens to choose the best method for a particular situation. Also, teens can now stay in close touch with a larger circle of people—even friends and relatives around the world. With electronic communication, teens have mastered the communication skills they will need for careers in a "wired" world.

❝ **I used to be nervous about going up to someone at school that I didn't know that well. But if you send the person an instant message and chat that way, then you know you can go up to them in person. So now I feel much more comfortable talking to people and I've made a lot of new friends.** ❞

The Case Against Electronic Communication

When teens rely on electronic communication, their face-to-face communication skills suffer. They don't develop the ability to interpret clues such as body language and tone of voice. They also might favor e-mail and other less personal forms of communication when problems need to be resolved. In doing so, teens might not learn how to confront people directly—an important communication skill that people need throughout their lives.

❝ **I have friends who spend all their time on their cell phones, even when we're out together. They don't know how rude it is when they ignore you and keep talking really loudly. I go to a summer camp where no electronic stuff is allowed, and I love it. I think my communication skills are much better than those of kids who are wired all the time.** ❞

What do **YOU** think?

Use these steps to analyze and express your opinion about technology and communication skills.

1. Analyze the Issue Carefully consider both sides of the issue. Make a table listing the positive and negative effects of electronic communication on teens' communication skills.

2. Consider Your Values Look at your list of pros and cons. Which items are most important to you? Which are least important? Explain how these choices reflect your values.

3. Take a Stand Write a paragraph expressing your opinion on the effect of electronic communication on teens. State your opinion clearly and give several reasons to support your opinion. **WRITING**

189

Food and Nutrition

GO ONLINE PearsonSuccessNet.com

VIDEO 8

TEENS Talk

Food for Thought

Preview **Activity**

How Do Food Ads Influence You?

Complete this activity before you watch the video.

1. Predict how many food ads you are exposed to in a typical day.
2. Keep a log for a day. For each food ad you see, note the type of ad, where you saw it, and its message.
3. Did the actual number of food ads you saw surprise you? Was the number higher than you predicted?
4. In a paragraph, discuss some of the ways that food ads influence the food choices that you and other teens make. **WRITING**

Carbohydrates, Fats, and Proteins

Objectives

▶ **Name** the three classes of nutrients that supply your body with energy.

▶ **Explain** how the body obtains energy from foods.

▶ **Describe** the roles that carbohydrates, fats, and proteins play in your body.

Vocabulary

- nutrient
- metabolism
- calorie
- carbohydrate
- fiber
- fat
- unsaturated fat
- saturated fat
- cholesterol
- trans fat
- protein
- amino acid

Warm-Up

Quick Quiz Which of these statements are always true? Which are sometimes true? Which are always false?

1. Foods that are high in calories are unhealthy.
2. You should avoid foods with sugars in them.
3. You should avoid fats in your diet.
4. Vegetarian diets are low in protein.
5. Snacking is bad for you.

WRITING For each of your responses, explain why you gave the answer you did.

Foods Supply Nutrients

What do you think of when you hear the word *food?* You probably recall your favorite foods. Maybe you imagine the smell of fresh-baked bread or the spicy taste of curry. You might also think of occasions when food is especially important, such as family celebrations and meals with friends. Food is more than something that satisfies your hunger. It is a source of enjoyment, and it is an important aspect of your social life as well.

Your body needs food, and the food that you eat affects your health in many ways—how you look and feel, how well you resist disease, and even how well you perform mentally and physically. It does all those things by providing your body with **nutrients** (NOO tree unts), substances that the body needs to regulate bodily functions, promote growth, repair body tissues, and obtain energy. Your body requires more than 40 different nutrients for these tasks. The process by which the body takes in and uses these nutrients is called nutrition.

There are six classes of nutrients: carbohydrates, fats, proteins, vitamins, minerals, and water. Each class of nutrient is necessary for good health. **Carbohydrates, fats, and proteins can all be used by the body as sources of energy.** Vitamins, minerals, and water perform other essential functions that will be discussed in the next section.

Foods Supply Energy

The foods you eat are your body's energy source. You rely on the energy from food for everything you do—running, playing a musical instrument, and even sleeping. You need energy to maintain your body temperature, keep your heart beating, and enable you to understand what you read.

Fuel for Your Body **When your body uses the nutrients in foods, a series of chemical reactions occurs inside your cells. As a result, energy is released.** Metabolism (muh TAB uh liz um) is the chemical process by which your body breaks down food to release this energy. Metabolism also involves the use of this energy for the growth and repair of body tissues.

What Are Calories? The amount of energy released when nutrients are broken down is measured in units called **calories.** The more calories a food has, the more energy it contains. You can see in Figure 1 that the calorie content of different foods varies greatly. Contrast the energy that you get from a slice of pizza with the energy that you get from an apple, an orange, or a salad.

For good health, the number of calories in the food that you eat should match the calorie needs of your body. But when planning what to eat, you need to think about more than just the calorie content of foods. You also need to consider whether or not the foods you choose contain all the nutrients your body needs.

How many calories are in a serving of your favorite snack food?

FIGURE 1 These two meals contain the same amount of energy but different nutrients. **Calculating** About how many salads would it take to equal the calories found in one slice of pizza? **MATH**

Which Lunch Would You Eat?

A **B**

375 calories

375 calories

TOTAL:
750 calories

110 calories

85 calories

180 calories

375 calories

TOTAL:
750 calories

Food and Nutrition **193**

Watermelon (1 slice)
Total Carbs 22 g

Sugars	18 g
Starches	3 g
Fiber	1 g

Wheat Bread (1 slice)
Total Carbs 15 g

Sugars	1.5 g
Starches	12.0 g
Fiber	1.5 g

Pasta (1 cup)
Total Carbs 40 g

Sugars	1 g
Starches	37 g
Fiber	2 g

FIGURE 2 Whole-grain breads, fruits, and pasta are good sources of carbohydrates.

Carbohydrates

Carbohydrates (kahr boh HY drayts) are nutrients made of carbon, hydrogen, and oxygen. **Carbohydrates supply energy for your body's functions.** There are two general types of carbohydrates—simple carbohydrates and complex carbohydrates.

Simple Carbohydrates   Simple carbohydrates are also known as sugars. Sugars occur naturally in fruits, vegetables, and milk. They are added to many manufactured foods, such as cookies, candies, and soft drinks. There are several types of sugars, but glucose (GLOO kohs) is the most important because it is the major provider of energy for your body's cells. All other types of sugar are converted to glucose once they are inside your body.

Complex Carbohydrates   Complex carbohydrates are made up of sugars that are linked together chemically to form long chains, something like beads in a necklace.

Starches are one of the main types of complex carbohydrates. They are found in many plant foods, including potatoes and grains. Rice, oats, corn, and wheat are grains. Foods such as tortillas, whole-wheat rolls, and Chinese moo shu pancakes are excellent sources of starch. When you eat foods containing starch, your digestive system breaks the starch into simple sugars that can be absorbed into your bloodstream.

Fiber Fiber is a type of complex carbohydrate that is found in plants. Strictly speaking, fiber is not really a nutrient because it cannot be broken down and then absorbed into your bloodstream. Instead, fiber passes out of your body without being digested. However, it is still necessary for the proper functioning of your digestive system. A high-fiber diet

▶ helps prevent constipation

▶ may reduce the risk of colon cancer

▶ may help prevent heart disease

Whole-grain breads and cereals, vegetables, fruits, nuts, beans, and seeds provide fiber in your diet.

Your Body's Energy Reserves At a meal, you usually eat more carbohydrates than your body can immediately use. The extra glucose is converted into a type of starch called glycogen (GLY kuh jun), which is stored in your body. When your body needs more glucose, the glycogen is converted back to glucose. If you eat so many carbohydrates that the body's glycogen stores are full, then the excess carbohydrates are stored as fat instead.

Daily Carbohydrate Intake Nutritionists recommend that 45 to 65 percent of a person's daily calorie intake come from carbohydrates. It is better to eat foods rich in complex carbohydrates rather than simple carbohydrates. One reason is that while simple carbohydrates give quick bursts of energy, complex carbohydrates provide better long-term, sustained energy.

When you choose foods containing complex carbohydrates, try to choose whole grains. Whole grains are better than processed grains because they contain more fiber and nutrients. Whole-wheat breads and pastas and brown rice are examples of whole-grain foods. In contrast, foods high in sugars, such as candy and soft drinks, may have few valuable nutrients. If you have a craving for sweets, eat naturally sweet foods, such as fruits. Those foods provide vitamins and trace amounts of some minerals, too.

 List some carbohydrates you typically eat. Are they sugars or starches?

FIGURE 3 Beans and vegetables with edible skins and seeds are good sources of fiber.

Fats

Like carbohydrates, **fats** are made of carbon, hydrogen, and oxygen, but in different proportions. **Fats supply your body with energy, form your cells, maintain body temperature, and protect your nerves.** Ounce for ounce, fat has twice as many calories as carbohydrates.

Unsaturated Fats   Fats come in different forms. **Unsaturated fats** have at least one unsaturated bond in a place where hydrogen can be added to the molecule. Unsaturated fats are usually liquid at room temperature. These fats are found in vegetable oils, nuts, and seeds.

Unsaturated fats are classified as either monounsaturated fats or polyunsaturated fats. Foods that contain monounsaturated fats include olive oil, peanuts, and canola oil. Foods that contain polyunsaturated fats include safflower, corn, and soybean oil, as well as seafood. A balance between monounsaturated and polyunsaturated fats in the diet is important for cardiovascular health. Unsaturated fats can actually help fight heart disease.

Saturated Fats   Fats that have all the hydrogen the carbon atoms can hold are called **saturated fats.** Saturated fats are usually solid at room temperature. Animal fats, such as lard, and dairy products contain saturated fats. Too much saturated fat in your diet can lead to heart disease.

Daily Fat Intake   Nutritionists recommend that 20 to 35 percent of your calories come from fat, primarily unsaturated fat. To reduce your intake of saturated fat, you can substitute low-fat foods for the meats and dairy products that are high in saturated fats.

FIGURE 4   Eating foods containing unsaturated fats, such as olive oil, is more healthful than eating foods containing saturated fats.
Reading Graphs Which of the fat sources in the graph is lowest in saturated fat?

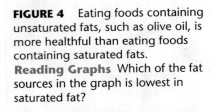

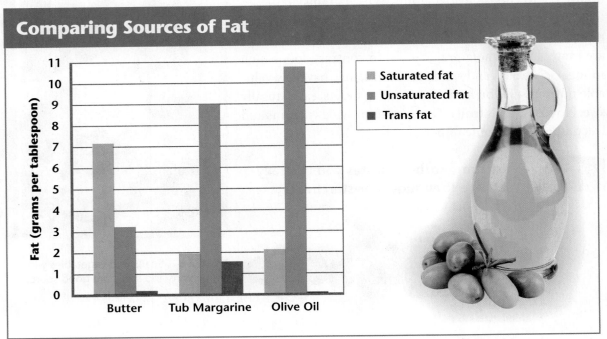

Comparing Sources of Fat

Fat (grams per tablespoon)

- Saturated fat
- Unsaturated fat
- Trans fat

Butter   Tub Margarine   Olive Oil

Hands-On *Activity*

Which Foods Contain Fats?

Materials
brown paper bag
scissors
marker
dropper
potato chip
milk chocolate
carrot
whole milk
skim milk
apple juice
ground beef

Try This

❶ Cut a brown paper bag into squares about 3 inches on each side. Write the name of each food on a square.

❷ Rub each food on the square with its name. If the food is a liquid, place a few drops on the square.

❸ Let the squares dry. Then hold each square up to a light.

Think and Discuss

❶ Which squares had a spot when you held them up to the light? Those foods contain fat. Which squares did not have a spot?

❷ Does your daily diet include many foods that are high in fat? (To be sure, try testing some foods that you commonly eat.) How could you reduce the amount of fat that you consume each day?

Cholesterol   **Cholesterol** (kuh LES tuh rawl) is a waxy, fatlike substance that is found only in animal products. Your body needs a certain amount of cholesterol to make cell membranes and nerve tissue, certain hormones, and substances that aid in the digestion of fat. Your liver can make all of the cholesterol your body needs. Therefore, cholesterol is not a necessary part of the diet.

A diet high in fat and cholesterol can increase the amount of cholesterol in the blood. When the level of cholesterol circulating in the blood gets too high, deposits called plaque form on the walls of blood vessels. Heavy plaque buildup may block blood flow to the heart, depriving the heart of oxygen and leading to a heart attack.

Some research suggests that high blood cholesterol is hereditary. Cholesterol levels also tend to rise as a person ages. These are risk factors you can't change, but there is one you can control: your diet. You can reduce your risk of heart disease by reducing the amount of meat and dairy fat in your diet.

Trans Fats   You may have heard about trans fats. **Trans fats** are made when manufacturers add hydrogen to the fat molecules in vegetable oils. Foods that contain trans fats stay fresh longer than foods that contain unsaturated fats. But, trans fat seems to have few of the benefits of unsaturated fat and many of the risks of saturated fat. Trans fats are found in margarine, chips, and commercially baked goods. The stick forms of margarine tend to contain more trans fats than the softer, tub margarines.

GO ONLINE
PearsonSuccessNet.com
For: More on healthy eating

What high-fat foods do you eat? How can you cut down on these foods?

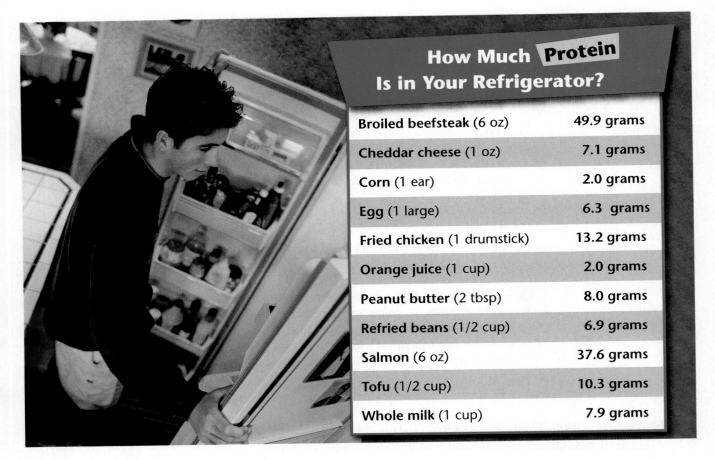

How Much Protein Is in Your Refrigerator?	
Broiled beefsteak (6 oz)	49.9 grams
Cheddar cheese (1 oz)	7.1 grams
Corn (1 ear)	2.0 grams
Egg (1 large)	6.3 grams
Fried chicken (1 drumstick)	13.2 grams
Orange juice (1 cup)	2.0 grams
Peanut butter (2 tbsp)	8.0 grams
Refried beans (1/2 cup)	6.9 grams
Salmon (6 oz)	37.6 grams
Tofu (1/2 cup)	10.3 grams
Whole milk (1 cup)	7.9 grams

FIGURE 5 Meats, fish, eggs, and dairy products are excellent sources of protein. **Calculating** Which has more protein per ounce: beefsteak or cheddar cheese? **MATH**

Proteins

Nutrients that contain nitrogen as well as carbon, hydrogen, and oxygen are called **proteins.** Like carbohydrates and fats, proteins can serve as a source of energy. **The most important function of proteins, however, is their role in the growth and repair of your body's tissues.** A good portion of your body is made up of protein. High-protein foods include meats, eggs, poultry, milk, and milk products. Nuts, dried beans, dried peas, and lentils also contain a lot of protein.

Amino Acids Like carbohydrates, proteins are long chains of smaller "links" that are bound together chemically. These smaller substances are known as **amino acids** (uh MEE noh). When you eat protein, your digestive system breaks it down into individual amino acids. These amino acids are then absorbed into your bloodstream and reassembled by cells to form the kinds of proteins you need.

Essential Amino Acids The proteins in your body are made up of 20 different amino acids. Your diet has to supply nine of these amino acids; your body can manufacture the rest. The nine amino acids that the body cannot manufacture are called essential amino acids. You can remember this by thinking of them as an essential part of your diet.

Connect to Your Life

What are the main sources of protein in your diet?

Complete and Incomplete Proteins Protein from animal sources—meats, fish, and so forth—is said to be complete protein because it contains all nine essential amino acids in the proportions needed by your body. In contrast, most protein from plant sources, such as beans, is incomplete, because it lacks one or more essential amino acids.

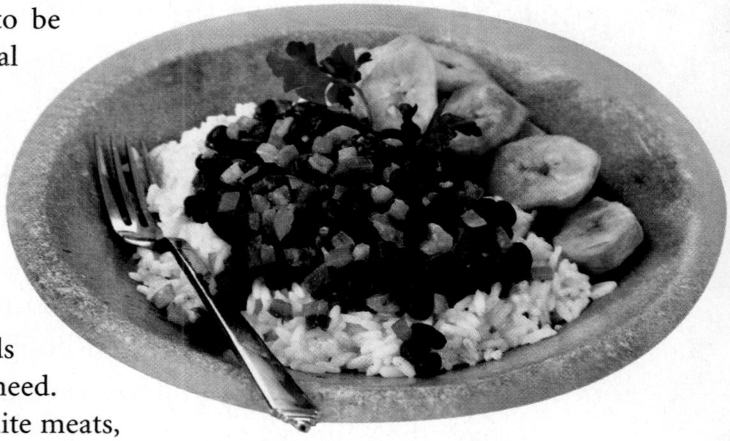

FIGURE 6 Together, rice and beans form a complementary protein combination that contains all of the essential amino acids.

Daily Protein Intake Nutritionists recommend that 10 to 35 percent of your calories come from proteins. A diet that contains both plant and animals foods can easily supply all of the essential amino acids you need. Simply eat a wide variety of foods, such as red and white meats, fish, dairy products, legumes, nuts, and grains.

Proteins for Vegetarians People who don't eat meat can combine two or more plant protein sources that, taken together, provide all the essential amino acids. Suppose, for example, you prepare a casserole that contains both rice and beans. The protein found individually in the rice and beans is incomplete. When the rice and beans are combined, however, they supply all the essential amino acids needed by your body. When you combine incomplete protein foods in such a way that you obtain all nine of the essential amino acids, you form a complementary protein combination.

Section 1 Review

Key Ideas and Vocabulary

1. Which three classes of nutrients supply the body with energy?
2. Define the term **metabolism.** How is metabolism related to the nutrients in food?
3. What roles do the following nutrients play in the body?
   a. carbohydrates **b.** fats **c.** proteins
4. What is **cholesterol?** How does diet affect cholesterol levels in the blood?

Critical Thinking

5. Predicting Name some circumstances during which you might use your body's stores of glycogen.
6. Comparing and Contrasting How do saturated fats differ from unsaturated fats? Name two sources of each type of fat.
7. Calculating Suppose that you ate 2,500 calories in a day. Of those calories, 1,200 calories were from carbohydrates, 875 from fats, and the rest from protein. What percentage of your total day's calories came from carbohydrates? From fats? From protein? MATH

Health at School

Promoting Well-Being Evaluate your school's lunch menu over a three-day period. To do this, list each lunch item and the classes of nutrients it provides. Then, write a paragraph about the influence of school lunches on health. WRITING

Breaking a Bad Habit

Sam has developed a poor nutritional habit—snacking on high-fat foods, such as potato chips. Although he wants to cut down on the amount of fatty foods he eats each day, he thinks that he doesn't have the willpower to do it.

The key to changing a habit you don't like is to replace it with a new, positive habit. The process works best in small steps and by putting everything in writing in a behavior contract. The steps given here will help you change almost any habit.

❶ Define the habit you want to change.

Describe your habit in a specific way. For example, instead of saying, "I don't eat very well," you might say, "I eat too many potato chips."

❷ Set your goal.

A goal describes the behavior you would like to substitute for the habit.

▶ Your goal should be specific. If a goal is too broad, break it into sub-goals.

▶ The goal should emphasize what you will do, not what you won't do—"For snacks, I will choose foods low in fat, such as fruits and low-fat cheeses."

▶ Set a realistic deadline.

▶ Write a behavior contract like the one shown, and fill in your goal.

Behavior Contract

Habit: *eating too many chips*

I *Sam Brown* plan to *substitute fruit or low-fat cheese* by *May 4th*.

I will reach this goal by doing the following target behavior: *substituting fruit/cheese once a day at first and gradually increasing to three times a day*

To create a supportive change environment, I will get help from the following role models: *Mom and Loretta*, reward myself by *going to the movies with friends after successful weeks* along the way, and by *buying myself a new baseball glove* when I reach my goal.

Signed *Sam Brown*   Date *March 6th*

❸ Design an action plan.

▶ Monitor your habit. Spend a week carefully observing and recording your habit. Use a chart like the one shown. This will help you understand what triggers and reinforces the habit.

Habit Record

Beforehand		Behavior	Afterward
Scene	Feelings	Details	Results
Monday lunch at school	tired and bored	1 oz. bag of potato chips	less energetic

▶ Write your plan. Describe in detail the day-to-day changes you will make to reach your goal. Your plan should be a gradual, step-by-step process.

▶ Keep a log. Log your new behavior daily, including any setbacks.

Behavior Log

Action Plan	M	T	W	Th	F	Sa	Su
	← substitute fruit or cheese for chips →						
Behavior	✓	ate potato chips	✓	ate corn chips	✓	✓	✓

❹ Build a supportive environment.

▶ Reward yourself for accomplishments along the way. Ask family and friends to keep an eye on your progress.

▶ Keep a list handy of the benefits of your new behavior.

▶ Structure your surroundings to support your efforts. If you are trying to break a potato-chip habit, try not to keep any potato chips in your house.

BUILDING HEALTH SKILLS
Practice the Skill

1. List three habits you would like to break.

2. Of the three habits, choose the one you would most like to change. Clearly define what the habit is. Set a specific goal for eliminating the habit. Write the goal on a behavior contract like the one shown.

3. Monitor your habit for one week. Every time you exhibit the habit, record where and when it occurred. Record your thoughts and feelings before and after. Can you detect any patterns in your behavior?

4. Use your behavior patterns to devise a detailed plan for breaking the habit. Record the plan on your contract. Also, fill in ways you can build a supportive environment.

5. Log your behavior for three weeks.

6. After three weeks, evaluate your performance. What made it hard for you to stick to the plan? What aspects of your plan worked for you? **WRITING**

Vitamins, Minerals, and Water

Objectives

▶ **Identify** the two main classes of vitamins.

▶ **List** seven minerals your body needs in significant amounts.

▶ **Explain** why water is so important to your body.

Vocabulary

- vitamin
- antioxidant
- mineral
- anemia
- homeostasis
- electrolyte
- dehydration

Warm-Up

Myth As part of a healthy diet, people need to take dietary supplements.

Fact A diet that contains a variety of healthful foods usually supplies all the vitamins and minerals that your body needs.

WRITING Where do you think most teens get their information about nutrition? How factual do you think their information is?

Vitamins

You're probably aware that vitamins are important for your body and health, but where do they come from? What do they do? And how many different kinds do you need?

One of the first discoveries of the importance of vitamins came in the 1700s. Sailors on long voyages survived on hard, dry biscuits, salted meat, and not much else. Because of their limited diet, many sailors developed a serious disease called scurvy. People with scurvy suffer from bleeding gums, stiff joints, and sores that do not heal.

A Scottish doctor, James Lind, discovered that sailors who were fed citrus fruits recovered from scurvy. Today, health scientists know that scurvy is caused by a lack of vitamin C, which is found in abundance in citrus fruits. After Lind made his discovery, sailors were provided with oranges, lemons, and limes. The word *limey*, a British slang term for sailor, comes from the limes that sailors ate to ward off scurvy.

What Are Vitamins? Nutrients that are made by living things, are required only in small amounts, and that assist many chemical reactions in the body are **vitamins.** Unlike carbohydrates, fats, and proteins, vitamins do not directly provide you with energy or the raw materials of which your cells are made. Instead, vitamins help the body with various processes, including the use of other nutrients. Vitamins also play roles in various chemical reactions in the body. For example, vitamin K helps your blood clot when you get a cut or a scrape.

Your body is able to make some vitamins. For example, your skin manufactures vitamin D when it is exposed to sunlight. However, most vitamins must be supplied in the food you eat. **There are two classes of vitamins: fat-soluble vitamins, which dissolve in fatty materials, and water-soluble vitamins, which dissolve in water.**

Fat-Soluble Vitamins Fat-soluble vitamins—vitamins A, D, E, and K—occur in vegetable oils, liver, eggs, and certain vegetables. Figure 7 outlines the food sources and functions of each fat-soluble vitamin.

Fat-soluble vitamins can be stored by the body. The absorption of fat-soluble vitamins by the digestive system is enhanced by dietary fat. Some indigestible fat substitutes that are used in low-fat or low-calorie products can prevent absorption of these vitamins. To prevent this from happening, extra vitamins, particularly vitamins A and D, are often added to foods prepared with fat substitutes.

Name three foods you eat regularly that supply vitamin A.

GO ONLINE
PearsonSuccessNet.com
For: More on nutrients

FIGURE 7 Fat-soluble vitamins are found in many dietary sources and have important functions.

Fat-Soluble Vitamins

Vitamin	Good Sources	Main Functions
A	Liver; eggs; cheese; milk; yellow, orange, and dark green vegetables and fruit	Maintains healthy skin, bones, teeth, and hair; aids vision in dim light
D	Milk; eggs; liver; exposure of skin to sunlight	Maintains bones and teeth; helps in the use of calcium and phosphorus
E	Margarine; vegetable oils; wheat germ; whole grains; legumes; green, leafy vegetables	Aids in maintenance of red blood cells, vitamin A, and fats
K	Green, leafy vegetables; potatoes; liver; made by intestinal bacteria	Aids in blood clotting

Water-Soluble Vitamins Water-soluble vitamins—including vitamin C and all of the B vitamins—are found in fruits, vegetables, and other sources. Unlike the fat-soluble vitamins, water-soluble vitamins cannot be stored by the body. Therefore, it is important to eat foods that supply them every day. Figure 8 outlines the food sources and functions of the water-soluble vitamins.

Water-Soluble Vitamins

Vitamin	Good Sources	Main Functions
B1 (Thiamin)	Pork products; liver; whole-grain foods; legumes	Aids in carbohydrate use and nervous system function
B2 (Riboflavin)	Milk; eggs; meat; whole grains; dark green vegetables	Aids in metabolism of carbohydrates, proteins, and fats
B3 (Niacin)	Poultry; meat; fish; whole grains; nuts	Aids in metabolism
B6 (Pyridoxine)	Meat; poultry; fish; whole-grain foods; green vegetables	Aids in metabolism of carbohydrates, proteins, and fats
B12 (Cobalamin)	Meat; fish; poultry; eggs; milk; cheese	Maintains healthy nervous system and red blood cells
Pantothenic acid	Organ meats; poultry; fish; eggs; grains	Aids in metabolism
Folate (Folic acid)	Green, leafy vegetables; legumes	Aids in formation of red blood cells and protein
Biotin	Organ meats; poultry; fish; eggs; peas; bananas; melons	Aids in metabolism
C (Ascorbic acid)	Citrus fruits; green vegetables; melons; potatoes; tomatoes	Aids in bone, teeth, and skin formation; resistance to infection; iron uptake

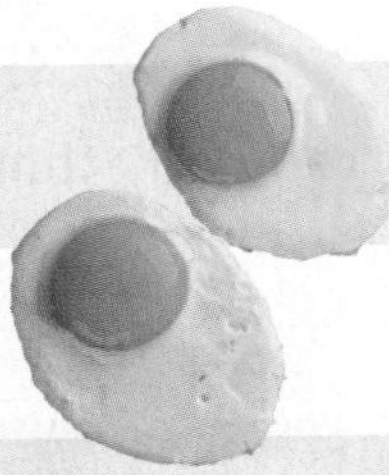

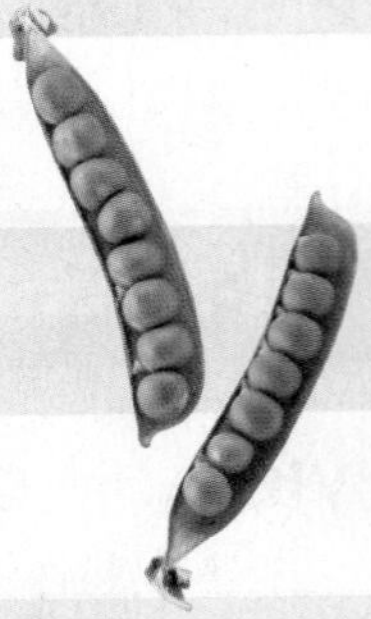

FIGURE 8 Water-soluble vitamins are found in many food sources. **Reading Tables** Which vitamins aid in metabolism?

Antioxidants   Vitamins called **antioxidants** help protect healthy cells from the damage caused by the normal aging process as well as from certain types of cancer. Vitamins C and E are two of the most powerful antioxidants. Sources of vitamin C include citrus fruits, strawberries, broccoli, tomatoes, and potatoes. Sources of vitamin E include vegetable oils, whole grains, seeds, nuts, and peanut butter.

Minerals

Your body requires only small amounts of **minerals,** which are nutrients that occur naturally in rocks and soil. Plants absorb minerals from rocks and soil through their roots. Animals obtain these nutrients by either eating the plants or eating animals that have eaten the plants.

Twenty-four different minerals have been shown to be essential for good health. **You need seven minerals—calcium, sodium, potassium, magnesium, phosphorus, chlorine, and sulfur—in significant amounts.** You need only trace amounts of others, such as iron, fluorine, iodine, copper, and zinc. Minerals perform a wide variety of functions in the body.

Calcium   Some minerals are of special nutritional concern. For example, many people's diets do not include enough calcium. Calcium is important in blood clotting and the functioning of your nervous system. It is an essential ingredient in the formation and maintenance of bones and teeth. Milk and other dairy products are good sources of calcium, but many people cannot digest dairy products. Beet greens, collard greens, broccoli, and tofu are also good sources of calcium.

A lack of calcium can sometimes lead to osteoporosis, a condition in which the bones gradually weaken. Osteoporosis is usually a disease of older people, but your calcium intake during adolescence can help you build stronger bones now to avoid osteoporosis later in life. Osteoporosis will be discussed in Chapter 11.

What are you doing now to prevent osteoporosis in the future?

85% of teenage girls do not get enough calcium in their diets.

FIGURE 9   Calcium is essential for building the strong bones you need to play sports now and to maintain bone strength as you age.

Potassium Potassium and sodium work together to maintain water balance in the body. In addition, people who consume enough potassium each day generally have lower blood pressure than people who do not. The problem is that most Americans do not consume enough potassium. Foods that are rich in potassium include baked potatoes, spinach, bananas, dried fruits, oranges, soybeans, and tomato products.

Iron Iron is necessary for healthy red blood cells. These cells have an iron-containing substance called hemoglobin, which carries oxygen from your lungs to all parts of your body. Adolescent girls and adult women need extra iron, because they lose iron during menstruation. Both adolescent girls and boys also need iron to build muscle mass.

There are many good sources of iron. During one day, for example, you might fulfill your iron requirements by eating an iron-fortified breakfast cereal, a salad containing garbanzo beans, a serving of cooked spinach, several dried apricots, and a serving of lean beef. If a person's diet does not include enough iron, he or she may develop **anemia** (uh NEE me uh), a condition in which the red blood cells do not contain enough hemoglobin. People suffering from anemia are often weak and tired, and they may become sick easily.

FIGURE 10 You can limit sodium by making your own snacks instead of eating processed foods or fast foods.

Sodium In contrast to calcium, most people consume far more sodium than they need. Table salt, or sodium chloride, is a major source of this mineral. So are some processed, or manufactured, foods, such as canned soups and frozen pizza. Salty snack foods, including chips and salted nuts, are also high in sodium.

Sodium is important in several body processes, including the functioning of the heart and water balance. However, too much sodium can cause a problem with blood pressure. People who have high blood pressure should reduce their salt intake because an excess of sodium can raise their blood pressure levels.

Connect to Your Life

Find out the sodium content of a snack that you ate today.

To Limit Sodium in Snacks
- Focus on fresh fruits and vegetables.
- Eat unsalted pretzels and popcorn.
- Choose low-fat yogurt or fruit smoothies.

FIGURE 11 Minerals are found in a variety of foods and perform many essential functions in the body. **Reading Tables** Which minerals aid in the function of the nervous system?

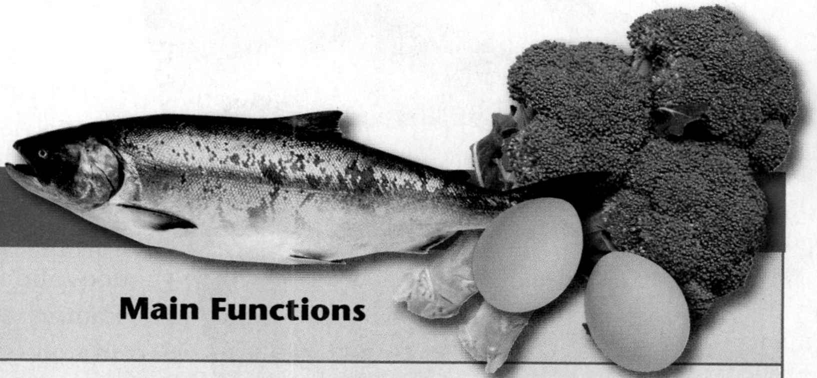

Minerals

Mineral	Good Sources	Main Functions
Calcium	Milk and milk products; dark green, leafy vegetables; tofu; legumes	Helps build and maintain bones and teeth; nerve and muscle function; blood clotting
Phosphorus	Meat; eggs; poultry; fish; legumes; milk and milk products	Helps build and maintain bones and teeth; energy metabolism
Magnesium	Leafy green vegetables; legumes; nuts; whole-grain food	Helps build bones and protein; energy metabolism; muscle contraction
Sodium	Table salt; processed food; soy sauce	Helps maintain water balance; nerve function
Chlorine	Table salt; soy sauce; processed foods	Helps maintain water balance; digestion
Potassium	Vegetables, fruits, meat, poultry, fish	Helps maintain water balance and make protein; functioning of heart and nervous system
Sulfur	Milk and milk products; meat; poultry; fish; legumes; nuts	Forms part of some amino acids and B vitamins
Iodine	Seafood; iodized salt	Helps in metabolism as part of thyroid hormone
Selenium	Seafoods; meats; organ meat	Helps break down harmful substances
Iron	Red meats; seafood; legumes; green, leafy vegetables; fortified cereals; dried fruits	Part of red blood cells; helps in energy metabolism
Zinc	Meats; poultry; seafood; milk; whole-grain foods	Part of many substances that help carry out body processes
Fluorine	Fish; fluoridated water	Helps form strong teeth and bones

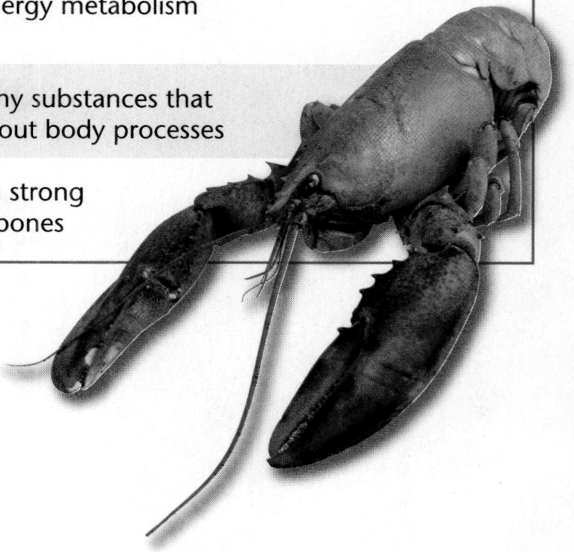

Vitamin and Mineral Supplements

If a person does not get enough of a specific nutrient, a nutrient deficiency can occur. People who eat a wide variety of healthy foods, however, seldom suffer from nutrient deficiencies. Vitamin and mineral supplements, therefore, are not usually necessary if your diet is nutritious and well-balanced. In fact, an excess, or overdose, of vitamins or minerals may damage your health. Some common symptoms of overdose include nausea, vomiting, diarrhea, and rash.

If you want to boost your intake of a particular vitamin or mineral, first consider how to meet your needs by making small adjustments to your daily diet. For example, if you need to increase your calcium intake, consider eating yogurt as a snack, or drinking milk with dinner instead of a soft drink.

If you do take a vitamin or mineral supplement, take one that meets, but does not exceed, your needs. A health care provider can advise you about how much is the right amount. Beware of megadosing, or taking in larger amounts of a nutrient than your body needs. For fat-soluble vitamins, the excess amounts would be stored in body fat and can cause vitamin poisoning. Symptoms of vitamin poisoning include nausea, vomiting, joint pain, severe headaches, and hair loss. For water-soluble vitamins, on the other hand, the excess amount would be excreted by your body. Therefore, taking megadoses of these vitamins may not be a wise investment.

FIGURE 12 Salad bars loaded with fresh vegetables are a great way to get all the vitamins and minerals you need without taking supplements.

Water

About 65 percent of your body weight is water. You do not get energy from this nutrient directly. Nevertheless, water is essential for all life processes, including the production of energy. **Nearly all of the body's chemical reactions, including those that produce energy and build new tissues, take place in a water solution.** Water is the primary component of blood and tissue. It carries dissolved waste products out of the body and helps digest food.

Water and Homeostasis Homeostasis (ho mee oh STAY sis) is the process of maintaining a steady state inside your body. What roles does water play in homeostasis?

▶ When you become overheated, your body excretes perspiration, which cools your body. Thus, water regulates body temperature.

▶ Water contains dissolved substances called electrolytes that regulate many processes in your cells. For example, your nervous and muscular systems depend on electrolytes, such as sodium and potassium.

Preventing Dehydration   Very heavy perspiring or severe diarrhea can result in **dehydration** (dee hy DRAY shun), a serious reduction in the body's water content. When the body becomes dehydrated, it loses important electrolytes along with the water. Symptoms of dehydration can include weakness, rapid breathing, and a weak heartbeat. Whenever your body loses a lot of water, you need to be careful to increase your intake of water and electrolytes to prevent dehydration.

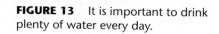

You can lose 4 cups of water during every hour of heavy exercise.

How Much Water?   Every day, you need at least ten 8-ounce cups of water if you are a female 14 to 18 years old. Males in the same age group need 14 cups of water per day. This water can be in the form of foods that contain a lot of water, such as fruits and vegetables, or juices. Drinks that contain caffeine—coffee, tea, and some sodas—may not be good sources of water for your body. This is because caffeine increases the amount of water your body excretes. It is probably better to obtain water from foods that do not contain caffeine.

FIGURE 13   It is important to drink plenty of water every day.

Water Versus Sports Drinks   Experts in the field of sports medicine recommend that you drink about 2 cups of fluid 2 hours before exercise. During exercise, take a drink about every 15 minutes. Are sports drinks a better choice than water? A sports drink is not necessary if you exercise for 60 minutes or less. If you exercise longer, a sports drink that contains carbohydrates may be beneficial. However, sports drinks with electrolytes are not necessary unless you exercise for 5 hours or more.

Section 2 Review

Key Ideas and Vocabulary

1. What are **vitamins**? How do they differ from **minerals**?
2. What are the two classes of vitamins? Which vitamins fall into each class?
3. Which seven minerals are needed by the body in significant amounts?
4. What roles does water play in the body?
5. Define **homeostasis**.

Critical Thinking

6. Classifying What vitamins are supplied by green, leafy vegetables? By citrus fruits?

Health and Community

Fluoride and the Water Supply Find out whether your community adds fluoride to its water supply. If possible, talk to a town official, dentist, or other knowledgeable adult in your community. Write a paragraph summarizing your findings. **WRITING**

7. Applying Concepts What are some ways that people with high blood pressure can reduce their sodium intake?
8. Relating Cause and Effect Explain how feelings of thirst can help a person maintain homeostasis on a hot day.

Guidelines for Healthful Eating

Warm-Up

Dear Advice Line,

My family is really busy, and we don't have a lot of time to cook. It seems like we eat an awful lot of take-out, packaged meals, and frozen dinners. I wonder if we are getting too much sodium, sugar, and fat. I also don't think we get enough fresh vegetables and whole grains. What can we do?

WRITING Write a response to this teen to help solve the problem.

The Dietary Guidelines

How can you make sure you get enough nutrients while consuming the number of calories that is right for you? The United States Department of Agriculture (USDA) and the U.S. Department of Health and Human services have published the *Dietary Guidelines for Americans* to help you figure out the answer to this question. The **Dietary Guidelines for Americans** is a document developed by nutrition experts to promote health and help people reduce their risk for heart disease, cancer, and diabetes through diet and physical activity. **The *Dietary Guidelines* provide information on how to make smart food choices, balance food intake with physical activity, get the most nutrition out of the calories you consume, and handle food safely.**

Make Smart Food Choices To obtain all the nutrients you need, choose a wide variety of foods. Include plenty of whole-grain foods, vegetables, and fruits. These foods are rich in complex carbohydrates and fiber. Milk and milk products are an important part of a healthful diet, especially for adolescents who are still growing. Milk products provide the calcium needed to prevent bone loss. Choose low-fat or nonfat milk and milk products to keep cholesterol down and thus reduce your risk of heart disease.

Hungry for a snack? Try these nutrient-dense foods:
- Fresh fruit
- Low-fat yogurt
- Nuts and raisins
- Raw veggies

Balance Food and Physical Activity   Regular physical activity is important for your overall health and fitness. Maintaining a healthy weight is a matter of balancing the calories you take in with how active you are. Health problems can develop if you are overweight or underweight. The *Dietary Guidelines* recommend that teenagers be active for 60 minutes most days.

Get the Most Nutrition Out of Your Calories   Choose foods that are nutrient-dense. **Nutrient-dense foods** contain lots of vitamins and minerals relative to the number of calories. At the same time, nutrient-dense foods are low in saturated fat, trans fat, added sugar, and salt. Lean meats, fish, poultry, and legumes are nutrient-dense foods. If you are hungry for a snack, some good nutrient-dense choices are shown in Figure 14. Limit your intake of sweet snacks and soft drinks. These foods contain lots of sugar but few other useful nutrients.

Most people consume too much sodium but not enough potassium. Eating more fruits and vegetables can boost your potassium intake. To reduce your sodium intake, limit salty snacks, pickled foods, luncheon meats, and canned soups.

Handle Food Safely   Part of good nutrition is using safe procedures to prepare, handle, and store the food you eat. Food borne illnesses can be prevented if you follow a few simple steps.

▶ Keep your hands and surfaces that come into contact with food clean.

▶ Separate raw and cooked foods while preparing or storing them.

▶ Cook meat, poultry, and fish to safe internal temperatures.

▶ If food is perishable, chill it right away.

▶ Thaw foods in the refrigerator, not on the counter.

FIGURE 14   If you're hungry for a snack, it is still possible to make healthy food choices.

 Connect to Your Life   **What kinds of things could you do to be more active each day?**

MyPlate

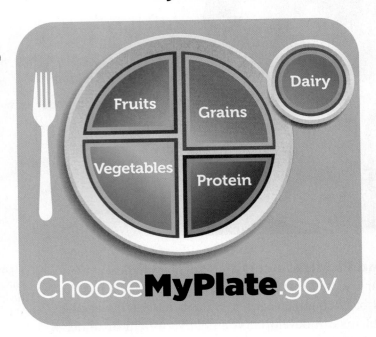

FIGURE 15 The MyPlate plan emphasizes a balance between the various groups of foods that you eat.
Interpreting Diagrams Which two groups should you consume in the largest amounts?

Grains

Make half the grains you eat whole grains. Look for the word *whole* before the name of the grain. Good choices are
- breads: whole-wheat or rye, pita, rolls, tortillas
- pasta: macaroni, spaghetti, rice noodles
- other grains: rice, crackers, couscous, bulgur, breakfast cereals

Vegetables

Vary your vegetables. Include in your diet
- dark green vegetables: spinach, kale, mustard or collard greens
- orange vegetables: carrots, squash, sweet potatoes
- dry beans and peas
- starchy vegetables: potatoes, corn, lima beans

Fruits

- Eat a variety of fruits, such as apples, bananas, mangoes, oranges, papayas, grapes, and pineapples.
- Limit your fruit juices.

Dairy

- Get plenty of calcium- rich foods.
- Choose low-fat or fat-free when you consume milk, yogurt, or cheese.

Protein

Choose low-fat or lean meats and poultry. Vary your protein by choosing
- fish, nuts, seeds
- beans or peas, such as kidney, garbanzo, fava, navy, lentils

MyPlate

You now know that you need to eat a variety of foods. To help you remember this advice, the USDA has designed a visual based on a familiar mealtime object—a plate. The **MyPlate** diagram illustrates the five food groups that you need to eat regularly, and provides a visual indication of how much of each group you need. Figure 15 shows the basic parts of the MyPlate diagram.

Balancing Calories   The MyPlate diagram reminds you to balance your calories. You can enjoy your food, but often you should eat less of some food groups and more of others. It is always a good idea to avoid oversized portions.

Foods to Increase and Foods to Reduce   The MyPlate diagram suggests that half of your plate at each meal needs to be made up of fruits and vegetables. The USDA also suggests that at least half of your grains should be whole grains, and that you switch to fat-free or low-fat (1%) milk. Other foods that you should reduce include those that are high in sodium (salt). You should also drink water instead of sugary drinks to reduce the sugar in your diet.

Creating Your Own MyPlate Plan   You can create your own personalized MyPlate plan by visiting the USDA's Web site. It contains details about the foods in each group, suggestions for planning menus, and calorie counts.

 Connect to Your Life   How could you include more whole grains in your diet?

 GO ONLINE
PearsonSuccessNet.com
For: More on MyPlate

Recommended Servings Per Day for 16-Year-Olds

Activity Level	Grains	Vegetables	Fruits	Dairy	Protein
Sedentary Male	8 ounces	3 cups	2 cups	3 cups	$6\frac{1}{2}$ ounces
Female	6 ounces	$2\frac{1}{2}$ cups	$1\frac{1}{2}$ cups	3 cups	5 ounces
Moderate Male	10 ounces	$3\frac{1}{2}$ cups	$2\frac{1}{2}$ cups	3 cups	7 ounces
Female	6 ounces	$2\frac{1}{2}$ cups	2 cups	3 cups	$5\frac{1}{2}$ ounces
Active Male	10 ounces	4 cups	$2\frac{1}{2}$ cups	3 cups	7 ounces
Female	8 ounces	3 cups	2 cups	3 cups	$6\frac{1}{2}$ ounces

Using the Food Guidelines

Planning a nutritious diet does not mean you must forego all the foods you love. You can still have a dab of margarine on your toast and your favorite chocolate bar as a rare treat. Here are some tips for following the *Dietary Guidelines* and the MyPlate plan.

Meals You don't need to consume every food group at every meal. But you should try to vary your diet at each meal.

- ► **Breakfast** Don't skip breakfast. Choose whole-grain cereals, low-fat milk or yogurt, and fruit. Limit pastries, eggs, and bacon.
- ► **Lunch** Focus on whole grains, fruits, and vegetables. Use mustard or ketchup instead of mayonnaise. Try low-fat cheese on pizza.
- ► **Dinner** Trim excess fat from meats. Instead of fried meats or fish, try them grilled. Choose low-fat dressings, and limit butter.

Snacks When snacking, choose foods with high nutrient density.

- ► Try satisfying your sweet tooth with fruit instead of cookies.
- ► Make a whole-wheat bagel, not a donut, your after-school treat.
- ► When you go to the movies, choose unbuttered popcorn.

Eating Out When you eat at fast-food restaurants, follow these tips.

- ► Substitute low-fat milk, water, or fruit juice for shakes and soft drinks.
- ► Select the salad bar in place of fries or onion rings. But go easy on dressings, cheese, bacon bits, and croutons.
- ► Choose a grilled chicken sandwich instead of a burger.

FIGURE 16 Eating a healthy breakfast will help you to resist unhealthy foods later in the day.

Section 3 Review

Key Ideas and Vocabulary

1. What are the four main recommendations contained in the *Dietary Guidelines for Americans?*
2. What does it mean to say that food is **nutrient-dense?** Give an example of a nutrient-dense food.
3. What is indicated by the different colors in the MyPlate plan?

Critical Thinking

4. Evaluating Choose the row in the chart on page 213 that best applies to you. Evaluate whether your diet is in line with the recommended number of servings from each food group.

Health at Home

Improving Your Diet Keep track of how many fats and sweets you eat over the next three days. Then, come up with a plan to substitute nutrient-dense foods for the fats and sweets you eat. Monitor your diet for a week and evaluate how well you stuck to your plan. **WRITING**

5. Classifying You eat a meal that contains beans and peas. Using the MyPlate diagram, how would you classify this meal?

GO ONLINE PearsonSuccessNet.com   Audio Summary Section 8.3

Chapter 8
At a Glance

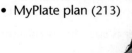

TEENS Talk ▶

Food for Thought List three ways the video helped you become a smarter consumer.

Section 1   Carbohydrates, Fats, and Proteins

Key Ideas

▶ Carbohydrates, fats, and proteins can all be used by the body as sources of energy.

▶ When your body uses the nutrients in foods, a series of chemical reactions occurs inside your cells. As a result, energy is released.

▶ Carbohydrates supply energy for your body's functions.

▶ Fats supply your body with energy, form your cells, maintain body temperature, and protect your nerves.

▶ The most important function of proteins is their role in the growth and repair of your body's tissues.

Vocabulary
- nutrient (192)
- metabolism (193)
- calorie (193)
- carbohydrate (194)
- fiber (195)
- fat (196)
- unsaturated fat (196)
- saturated fat (196)
- cholesterol (197)
- trans fat (197)
- protein (198)
- amino acid (198)

Section 2   Vitamins, Minerals, and Water

Key Ideas

▶ There are two classes of vitamins: fat-soluble vitamins, which dissolve in fatty materials, and water-soluble vitamins, which dissolve in water.

▶ You need seven minerals—calcium, sodium, potassium, magnesium, phosphorus, chlorine, and sulfur—in significant amounts.

▶ Nearly all of the body's chemical reactions, including those that produce energy and build new tissues, take place in a water solution.

Vocabulary
- vitamin (203)
- antioxidant (205)
- mineral (205)
- anemia (206)
- homeostasis (208)
- electrolyte (208)
- dehydration (209)

Section 3   Guidelines for Healthful Eating

Key Ideas

▶ The *Dietary Guidelines* provide information on how to make smart food choices, balance food intake with physical activity, get the most nutrition out of the calories you consume, and handle food safely.

▶ The MyPlate plan illustrates the five food groups that you need to eat regularly, and provides a visual indication of how much of each group you need.

Vocabulary
- *Dietary Guidelines for Americans* (210)
- nutrient-dense food (211)
- MyPlate plan (213)

Chapter 8 Review

Reviewing Key Ideas

 **GO ONLINE**
PearsonSuccessNet.com
For: Chapter 8 review activity

Section 1

1. Complex carbohydrates are
   a. composed of sugars linked together.
   b. found in grain products.
   c. good sources of energy.
   d. all of the above.

2. Which of the following foods is high in protein?
   a. an apple
   b. lettuce
   c. candy
   d. chicken

3. What is the role of glucose in the body?

4. Why is fiber necessary for the proper functioning of the digestive system?

5. How can you limit your intake of fats and cholesterol?

6. What are amino acids? Why are some of them called "essential"?

7. **Critical Thinking** In many cultures, people get very little protein from animal sources. How might these people obtain the protein they need?

Section 2

8. Which of these nutrients is sometimes associated with high blood pressure?
   a. sodium
   b. calcium
   c. iron
   d. carbohydrate

9. Loss of water through heavy perspiring can result in
   a. homeostasis.
   b. dehydration.
   c. anemia.
   d. metabolism.

10. Explain how antioxidants are important to your health. Which foods are good sources of antioxidants?

11. Which mineral can help build strong bones and teeth? Name one nondairy source of this mineral.

12. Give three reasons why water is such an important nutrient.

13. **Critical Thinking** If a person's diet does not contain enough iron, his or her tissues may not get all the oxygen they need. Explain why this is so.

14. **Critical Thinking** How can your diet today affect your future health? Explain.

Section 3

15. Which of the following is *not* used to determine the amounts you should consume from each food group in the MyPlate plan?
    a. age
    b. sex
    c. weight
    d. activity level

16. The *Dietary Guidelines* recommend that you make smart food choices. Explain what this recommendation means.

17. Which two groups in the MyPlate diagram are the largest? Explain what this means.

18. **Critical Thinking** Several friends are planning a week-long backpacking trip in the mountains. They must carry all of their food in backpacks, so amounts must be limited. What kind of foods could they take to meet their nutritional needs?

 ## Building Health Skills

19. **Analyzing Influences** Many American teenagers have diets high in fats. Write a letter to the editor of your local newspaper explaining why. Suggest steps that can be taken to improve teen diets. **WRITING**

20. **Accessing Information** Laurie dislikes dairy products. Research and plan three meals that include calcium-rich foods.

21. **Setting Goals** Write down everything you eat for a week. Classify the foods into the groups in the MyPlate plan. Then, come up with a plan to align your diet with the amounts recommended for your age, sex, and activity level. See how you do for the next week.

Health and Community

Food Pantry Visit Volunteer at a local food pantry or soup kitchen for a day. You may be involved in preparing food, chatting with patrons, or cleaning up afterward. What did you find out that you didn't know before? Write an editorial describing your experience. **WRITING**

Standardized Test Prep

Math Practice

The graphic below compares the typical American diet to the diet recommended by nutritionists. Use the graphic to answer Questions 22–24.

Typical Diet   **Recommended Diet**

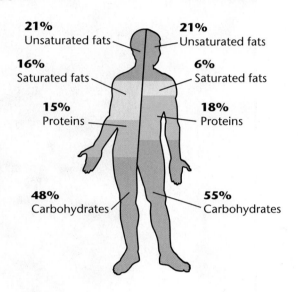

21%
Unsaturated fats

21%
Unsaturated fats

16%
Saturated fats

6%
Saturated fats

15%
Proteins

18%
Proteins

48%
Carbohydrates

55%
Carbohydrates

22. Which nutrient do Americans typically eat more than double the recommended amount?
 A unsaturated fats
 B proteins
 C carbohydrates
 D saturated fats

23. In the typical diet, if a person consumed a total of 2,000 calories in a day, how many of those calories would be from fats?
 F 420 calories
 G 620 calories
 H 740 calories
 J 940 calories

24. To bring the typical diet more in line with the recommended diet, people should
 A cut their intake of unsaturated fats by one half.
 B cut their intake of saturated fats by two thirds.
 C cut their protein intake in half.
 D double their carbohydrate intake.

Reading and Writing Practice

Read the passage. Then answer Questions 25–28.

Trans fats are produced in a laboratory by heating vegetable oil and bubbling hydrogen through it. How then do animal products, such as beef or milk, contain small amounts of trans fats? In cows, the digestive process produces hydrogen. The hydrogen then mixes with unsaturated fats from the cow's diet to produce a small amount of trans fats. However, foods such as donuts, cookies, and other baked goods contain trans fats in much greater amounts. Thus, avoiding these processed foods is the most effective way to limit trans fats in your diet.

25. In a cow, trans fats are produced when hydrogen
 A mixes with saturated fats from the cow's diet.
 B mixes with vegetable oil.
 C is given off during respiration.
 D mixes with unsaturated fats during digestion.

26. Trans fats can best be limited in the diet by
 F eating chicken instead of beef.
 G limiting baked goods.
 H drinking low-fat milk.
 J eliminating milk.

27. Which of the following does *not* contain trans fats?
 A donuts
 B a cow's diet
 C milk
 D low-fat yogurt

Constructed Response

28. In a paragraph, compare how trans fats are formed in the lab versus in an animal.

Test-Taking Tip

Be sure to eat a good breakfast the morning of your test. The brain works better when it has fuel.

Making Healthy Food Choices

GO ONLINE PearsonSuccessNet.com

VIDEO 9

TEENS Talk

Goals for Healthy Eating

Preview **Activity**

Why Are Goals Hard to Reach?

Complete this activity before you watch the video.

1. Read the quote below.

A goal without a plan is just a wish.

Antoine de Saint-Exupéry

2. In a paragraph, discuss whether or not you agree with this quote. Cite specific examples from your life to support your view. **WRITING**

Choosing Food Wisely

Objectives

▶ **Summarize** three main reasons why you eat.

▶ **Analyze** the information contained on food labels.

Vocabulary

- hunger
- appetite
- basal metabolic rate (BMR)
- Daily Values

Why You Eat

If asked why you eat, you might say, "Because I get hungry." But, is this always true? **You eat for several reasons: to meet your nutritional needs, to satisfy your appetite, and to supply your body with energy.**

Hunger is a feeling of physical discomfort that is caused by your body's need for nutrients. By contrast, **appetite** is a desire for food that is based on emotions and other factors rather than nutritional need. Unlike hunger, which is an inborn response, appetite is learned. For example, your appetite may make you want to eat popcorn because you have learned to associate its aroma with a delicious taste. Your appetite can make you eat even when you are not hungry.

Basal Metabolic Rate One factor that affects your calorie needs is your basal metabolic rate. Your **basal metabolic rate (BMR)** is the rate at which you use energy when your body is at rest. The higher your BMR, the more calories you burn. Various factors affect BMR. Younger people tend to have a higher BMR than older ones. People who have more muscle mass tend to have a higher BMR than those with less muscle mass because muscle burns calories.

Your level of activity also affects your calorie needs. The more active you are, the more calories you need. Figure 1 compares the number of calories burned per hour for various activities.

The Foods You Choose   Do you eat breakfast? What's your favorite snack? Your answers to questions like these depend on many factors.

▶ **Personal Preferences** Of course, you choose many of the foods you eat simply because they taste good. You might love the taste of peanut butter, for example, while your sister might not. You might dislike fish, or choose not to eat red meat. Whatever your personal preferences are, they have a huge impact on your food choices every day.

▶ **Cultural Background** Your cultural background, or heritage, may also influence your eating habits. For example, one family might eat a traditional Korean breakfast of soybean soup and rice. Another family might eat a typical Mexican meal of tortillas with beans and rice.

▶ **Time and Convenience** Do you sometimes eat on the run? A busy schedule might lead you to choose foods that can be prepared quickly or that can be easily carried in your backpack. Alternatively, you might choose to eat at a fast-food restaurant rather than prepare a meal at home.

▶ **Friends** When you eat a meal with friends, you may choose different foods than when you are by yourself or with your family. Friends might influence you to try new foods or to change your eating habits.

▶ **The Media** Every day, you are bombarded with information about food—in advertisements, news articles, diet books, and more. All of these messages can influence your decisions about what foods to eat or to avoid.

Connect to Your Life   Think about a food choice you made today. What factors influenced that choice?

GO ONLINE
PearsonSuccessNet.com
For: More on appetite and eating

FIGURE 1   The number of calories you burn depends on how active you are. More intense exercise burns more calories than less intense exercise or sitting.
Calculating In terms of calories burned, about how many hours of talking on the phone would it take to equal one hour of karate? **MATH**

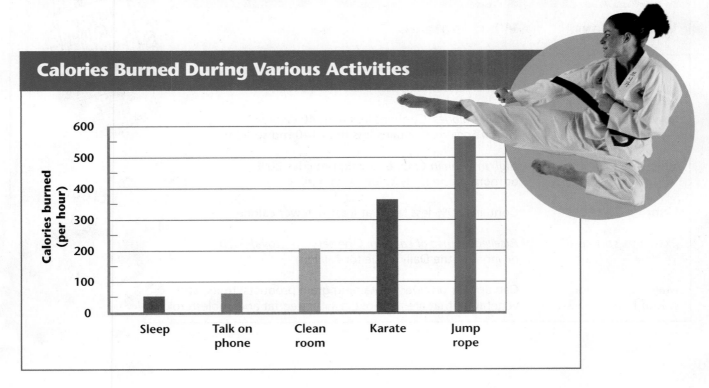

Calories Burned During Various Activities

(Bar graph: Calories burned (per hour) vs. activity)

Activity	Calories burned (per hour)
Sleep	~50
Talk on phone	~60
Clean room	~210
Karate	~370
Jump rope	~570

Evaluating Food Choices

Planning a sensible diet involves choosing nutritionally balanced meals and snacks. Your food choices may seem overwhelming, but tools are available to help you make good decisions. **When choosing foods, it is important to read and evaluate the information on the food label. The information includes nutrition facts, nutrient and health claims, Daily Values, and freshness dates.**

Food Labels The United States Food and Drug Administration (FDA) requires manufacturers to include food labels on most prepared foods, such as canned and frozen foods, breads, cereals, and drinks. Food labels must list specific nutrition facts about the food, including calorie and nutrient content, and the ingredients. The label is usually printed on the back or side of the package. You can practice reading food labels as you study the Building Health Skills on pages 224–225.

Nutrient and Health Claims Have you ever seen a label on a food that said "fat free"? Did you wonder what that claim meant? The FDA also sets standards regarding the nutrient claims that can be printed on a food label.

In addition, the FDA has approved the use of some health claims on food labels. Health claims are statements that link use of the food to certain health risks or benefits. Figure 2 explains some common nutrient and health claims you might see on food labels.

FIGURE 2 Claims about a food's nutrient or health benefits must follow standards set by the FDA. **Evaluating** How can foods that bear the claim "light" help you have a healthier diet?

Nutrient and Health Claims

What It Says	What It Means
...Free	*Fat Free:* Contains less than 0.5 g fat *Sugar Free:* Contains less than 0.5 g sugars
Low in...	*Low in Calories:* Contains less than 40 calories *Low in Sodium:* Contains less than 140 mg sodium
High in...	*High in Vitamin C:* One serving provides 20% or more of the Daily Value for vitamin C.
Light	Contains 50% less fat or at least $\frac{1}{3}$ fewer calories
Excellent source of...	*Excellent source of calcium:* One serving provides 20% or more of the Daily Value for calcium.
May reduce your risk of heart disease	Can appear on fiber-containing grain products, fruits, and vegetables that are also low in saturated fat and cholesterol.

Daily Values How much protein do you eat each day? Do you eat too much saturated fat? To help you answer these questions, nutritionists have developed a tool called Daily Values. **Daily Values** are recommendations that specify the amounts of certain nutrients that the average person should obtain each day. Daily Values are only a general guide because they are calculated for the average person who consumes a total of 2,000 calories a day. Rapidly growing adolescents, for example, may need more nutrients than the Daily Values indicate. Other factors that affect nutrient needs include age, sex, heredity, and activity level.

When you buy a food, the food label lists the percent Daily Value for each nutrient in that food. For example, the food label on a package of crackers might indicate a percent Daily Value for iron of 12 percent. This means that one serving of the crackers provides 12 percent of the iron that the average person needs each day.

Open Dates The labels on prepared foods also include open dates. These dates give you an idea of how long the food will be fresh and safe to eat.

▶ The "sell-by" date tells you the last date the product can be sold. You can still use a product after the sell-by date.

▶ The "best-if-used-by" date tells you how long the product will be at peak quality.

▶ The "do-not-use-after" date is the expiration date. This is the last date you should consume the product.

FIGURE 3 This container of milk lists both a sell-by and a use-by date.

Section 1 Review

Key Ideas and Vocabulary

1. List three main reasons why people eat.
2. What is **hunger**? Distinguish hunger from **appetite**.
3. What is **basal metabolic rate**? How does your basal metabolic rate affect your calorie needs?
4. List three types of information included on a food label to help you evaluate the food.
5. What is meant by percent **Daily Value?** How are Daily Values useful as a guide to eating?

Critical Thinking

6. **Evaluating** How do time and convenience affect the food choices you make? Give two examples.

Health and Community

Natural and Organic Foods Some food manufacturers use the terms "natural foods" and "organically grown" to describe food products. Find out what these claims mean. In a paragraph, offer your opinion about whether these products are healthier than similar products that do not make those claims. **WRITING**

7. **Predicting** How do you think Daily Values for children would differ from Daily Values for the average person? How do you think Daily Values for professional athletes would differ from Daily Values for the average person? Explain.

Reading a Food Label

Before you even enter a supermarket, advertisements in magazines, newspapers, and television try to convince you to buy certain foods.

To judge the nutritional value of a food, do not rely on advertisements or nice-looking packages. Instead, read the food label carefully. The FDA requires packaged foods to be labeled with nutrition information. For foods with more than one ingredient, the FDA also requires that ingredients be listed.

Nutrition Facts

Serving Size 2.5 oz.
(70 g/about 1/3 Box)
(Makes about 1 cup)
Servings Per Container about 3

Amount Per Serving	In Box	Prepared
Calories	260	380
Calories from Fat	25	140

		% Daily Value**
Total Fat 2.5g*	4%	23%
Saturated Fat 1.5g	8%	20%
Trans Fat 0.5g		
Cholesterol 10mg	3%	3%
Sodium 600mg	25%	32%
Total Carbohydrate 48g	16%	16%
Dietary Fiber 1g	4%	4%
Sugars 7g		
Protein 9g		

Vitamin A	0%	15%
Vitamin C	0%	0%
Calcium	20%	25%
Iron	10%	10%

*Amount in unprepared product

**Percent Daily Values are based on a 2,000 calorie diet. Your daily values may be higher or lower depending on your calorie needs:

	Calories	2,000	2,500
Total Fat	Less than	65g	80g
Sat Fat	Less than	20g	25g
Cholesterol	Less than	300mg	300mg
Sodium	Less than	2,400mg	2,400mg
Total Carbohydrate		300g	375g
Fiber		25g	30g

INGREDIENTS: ENRICHED MACARONI PRODUCT (WHEAT FLOUR, NIACIN, FERROUS SULFATE [IRON], THIAMIN MONONITRATE [VITAMIN B1], RIBOFLAVIN [VITAMIN B2], FOLIC ACID); CHEESE SAUCE MIX (WHEY, MILKFAT, MILK PROTEIN CONCENTRATE, SALT, CALCIUM CARBONATE, SODIUM TRIPOLYPHOSPHATE, CONTAINS LESS THAN 2% OF CITRIC ACID, SODIUM PHOSPHATE, LACTIC ACID, MILK, YELLOW 5, YELLOW 6, ENZYMES, CHEESE CULTURE)

1 Read the ingredients list.

▶ Notice that ingredients are listed in order by weight, from most to least.

▶ Become familiar with terms for different kinds of ingredients. For example, words ending in –ose are often names of sugars.

▶ Check for food additives, such as artificial sweeteners (aspartame, sucralose) and preservatives (BHA, BHT, sulfites). Also check for other additives, such as food dyes.

▶ Note if the food is enriched (lost nutrients have been restored) or fortified (nutrients have been added).

▶ If you have dietary restrictions or allergies, look for those foods on the ingredients list.

2 Note the number of servings per container.

Serving sizes are standardized for more than 100 different food categories. This allows you to compare similar food products by the number of servings they provide.

3 Note the number of calories in one serving.

Keep in mind that daily calorie intake depends on a person's age, sex, weight, basal metabolic rate, and activity level.

4 Look at the percentages of the Daily Values.

▶ Note the percentage Daily Values for nutrients that you should limit, such as saturated fat, cholesterol, and sodium. If a food is high in those nutrients, you may want to avoid it.

▶ Check the percentage Daily Values for fiber and valuable vitamins and minerals, such as iron and calcium.

Excellent source of calcium

5 Look for any health or nutrient claims.

Because these claims are regulated by the FDA, they reveal useful information about the product.

BUILDING HEALTH SKILLS

Practice the Skill

1. Use the information on the macaroni and cheese label to answer these questions.
   a. What ingredients are contained in the cheese sauce part of the mix? Which of those ingredients is present in the largest amount?
   b. What percentage of the Daily Values for saturated fat does one serving contain? If you wanted to eat this macaroni and cheese as part of a balanced meal, should the other foods be high in fat? Explain.
   c. Do you think that this food would be a good choice for someone on a low-sodium diet? Why or why not?
   d. Is this food a good source of vitamin C?

2. Compare the food labels for several different breakfast cereals.
   a. How many different sugars are found in each cereal?
   b. Which cereal is highest in iron? What percentage of the Daily Value for iron does that cereal provide?
   c. Which cereal is the most nutritious overall? Explain your choice.

Safely Managing Your Weight

Objectives

▶ **Examine** how heredity, activity level, and body composition influence a person's weight.

▶ **Calculate** your body mass index.

▶ **Identify** health problems associated with being overweight and underweight.

▶ **Summarize** strategies for losing or gaining weight.

Vocabulary

- body composition
- body mass index (BMI)
- overweight
- obesity
- underweight
- fad diet

Warm-Up

Health Stats What health trend do these statistics reveal?

In 1965, 4.6 % of teens were overweight.

1980, 5.0 % of teens were overweight.

Today, 18.4 % of teens are overweight.

WRITING What changes might help reverse this trend? How successful do you think the changes would be?

What Weight Is Right for You?

Cassie and her best friend, Ramona, are the same height. Although Cassie weighs 20 pounds more than Ramona, both girls have a weight that is appropriate for them. Ramona is small-boned, while Cassie has a larger bone structure. In addition, Cassie is more athletic than Ramona.

A person's weight is determined by various factors, including heredity, level of activity, and body composition. The weight that is right for you is the weight that does not present any health risks. A doctor or nutritionist can help you determine what weight is right for you.

Heredity You may have heard the expression, "it runs in the family." This expression means that certain traits are inherited and, therefore, appear regularly among family members. In the case of body weight, there is a link between body weight and heredity. This does not mean that you are "stuck with" a certain weight just because of your family history. It just means that you may have a natural tendency toward a certain weight.

Connect to Your Life What kinds of weight trends have you noticed in families you know?

Activity Level More important than family history in determining your weight is your activity level. The more active you are, the more calories you burn. If you are less active, you need fewer calories. Maintaining a healthy weight requires an energy balance. The number of calories consumed must equal the number of calories burned.

Tipping the energy balance can result in weight gain or weight loss. One pound of body weight is equivalent to 3,500 calories. If you take in 3,500 calories more than you burn, you gain a pound. You can gain a pound in two weeks by consuming only 250 extra calories a day. That's the number of calories in a small order of fast-food French fries.

Body Composition Another factor that affects weight is body composition. **Body composition** is a measure of how much body fat you have, as compared to muscle and bone. Remember Cassie and Ramona? Their body compositions were different—Cassie had more muscle mass than Ramona. One reason Cassie weighed more is that a given amount of muscle weighs more than an equal amount of fat. Strengthening exercises, such as lifting weights, can actually increase your weight as you build muscle.

Body composition is also affected by sex and age. Women tend to have more body fat and lower muscle mass than men. Body fat increases with age, while muscle mass decreases.

Body Mass Index

One simple way to assess whether your weight falls within a healthy range is to calculate your body mass index. **Body mass index (BMI)** is a ratio of your weight to your height. The following equation expresses this ratio.

$$\text{BMI} = \left(\frac{\text{Weight (in pounds)}}{[\text{Height (in inches)}]^2} \right) \times 703$$

Follow these steps to calculate your BMI.

1. Multiply your height (in inches) by your height (in inches).

2. Divide your weight (in pounds) by the number from Step 1.

3. Multiply the number from Step 2 by 703.

Although your BMI may be very different from your friend's, both of you may fall within a healthy range. You can use Figure 4 to assess your BMI. Notice that the BMI charts for teens take into account both age and sex. This is because teens are still growing. Also, males and females grow at different rates.

FIGURE 4 Your BMI is one way to assess whether your weight falls within a healthy range. **Calculating** Calculate your BMI, and compare it to the chart for your sex and age. MATH

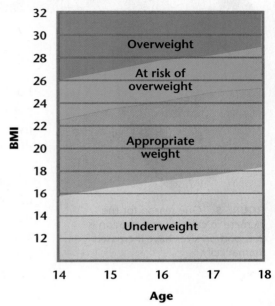

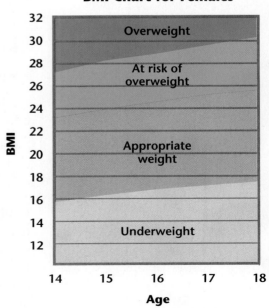

A value meal is not a bargain if you cannot afford the extra calories.

FIGURE 5 One reason for the increase in calorie consumption is that portion sizes have increased dramatically.

Overweight and Obesity

Look back at Figure 4, and notice the label "overweight." **The number of people in the United States who are overweight is increasing. Being overweight can lead to serious health problems, including heart disease and diabetes.**

A Growing Problem From the 1960s until today, the percentage of overweight teens has quadrupled. **Overweight** is a term used to describe a person who is heavier than the standard for the person's height. You may have heard the term *obesity* used interchangeably with *overweight*. This is not accurate. **Obesity** (oh BEE sih tee) refers specifically to adults who have a BMI of 30 or higher.

More people are overweight today because calorie consumption has increased at the same time that calorie use has decreased. More calories are being consumed by people today because

▶ grocery stores offer more food choices, including many prepared foods

▶ more meals are eaten outside the home

▶ portion sizes have increased

Recall that calorie use is related to activity level. People today burn fewer calories because they

▶ are less active at school, work, and in their leisure activities

▶ rely more on technological devices, such as cars and computers

Health Risks Overweight people tend to develop several conditions that can lead to health problems. Two conditions are high blood pressure and excess cholesterol in the blood. A third condition, excess glucose in the blood, is associated with type 2 diabetes. Type 2 diabetes is a disease in which the body does not properly use insulin, a substance that controls blood glucose levels. Other health problems associated with being overweight include heart disease, stroke, and certain cancers.

What You Can Do Prevention is the key to avoiding the health problems associated with being overweight. It is easier to prevent weight gain than it is to take off excess pounds. Healthy eating and regular exercise can help you avoid becoming overweight in the first place.

If you are overweight, don't be discouraged. You are still growing, and your BMI may decrease as your height increases. Remember also that changing your habits can be easier when you are in your teens than when you are older. Setting goals to improve your diet, reducing portion sizes, and increasing your activity level can help you lose weight.

Underweight

The BMI charts in Figure 4 also identify people who are "underweight." **Underweight** is a term used to describe a person who is lighter than the standard for the person's height. Remember that some people are naturally thinner than others. In addition, some teens are very thin as they are growing. Eventually, as their growth rate slows, they start to put on weight.

Health Risks Thinness in itself is not a health problem unless it is excessive. However, underweight people should be checked by a doctor. **Being underweight can be linked to health problems, such as anemia, heart irregularities, and trouble regulating body temperature.**

What You Can Do First of all, be patient. As you mature, there probably will come a time when your weight will start to increase. Remember, too, that healthy eating and exercise are as important for putting on weight as they are for taking off weight.

List five things you did this week to help manage your weight.

GO ONLINE
PearsonSuccessNet.com
For: More on food and diet

FIGURE 6 No matter if you are underweight, overweight, or at an appropriate weight, exercise is important for staying fit and healthy.

Media Wise

Evaluating Diet Plans

New diets seem to be everywhere—in magazines, on the Internet, in TV infomercials, and in best-selling books. Do these diets live up to their claims? Are they good for your health? Use this checklist to evaluate a diet.

Does the diet provide fewer than 1,200 calories a day?	Yes No
Does the diet cut out fats, carbohydrates, or proteins?	Yes No
Does the diet promise rapid weight loss in a short amount of time (more than 1 or 2 pounds per week)?	Yes No
Does the diet ignore the need for long-term changes in eating habits?	Yes No
Does the diet ignore the need for regular exercise?	Yes No

"Yes" answers to one or more questions may indicate a diet that is unlikely to work. What's worse, the diet could harm your health in the long term.

Activity Choose a diet plan that you have seen advertised or have read about. Use the checklist to evaluate the diet. Then write a paragraph evaluating the diet plan. **WRITING**

Healthy Weight Management

There is no magic method for keeping your weight within a healthy range. Whatever your weight is, weight management should be part of your daily habits. **Sensible weight management involves avoiding dangerous diet plans, choosing nutritionally balanced meals and snacks, and getting regular exercise.**

Dangerous Diet Plans   Most people who want to lose or gain weight want to do so very quickly. They may rely on strategies that promise quick results in a short period of time. Many of these approaches are unrealistic and can be unsafe.

▶ **Fad Diets** A **fad diet** is a popular diet that may help a person lose or gain weight but without proper regard for nutrition and other health issues. One example of a fad diet is a "high-protein, low-carbohydrate diet." Another example is a diet that includes a specific product that is supposed to burn fat.

Because fad diets often exclude important nutrients, they can put a dieter's health at risk. In addition, the weight loss achieved with a fad diet is usually temporary. Because fad diets often severely restrict food choices, people become bored with the diet's limitations. As a result, they stop dieting and return to their original eating habits.

▶ **Diet Aids** Diet aids include pills and candies that are supposed to suppress appetite. These diet aids are usually not effective, especially for long-term weight control. Also, diet aids can be habit-forming and cause unwanted side effects. For example, the main ingredient in many diet pills is caffeine, which may cause nervousness, sleeplessness, and high blood pressure.

▶ **Fasting** Some people fast, or refrain from eating, as a way to lose weight. Fasting for more than a brief period can lead to health problems. The body begins to break down muscle tissue to obtain the nutrients it needs. Long-term fasting may stunt your growth, put a strain on your kidneys, and cause hair loss. Fasting has also been linked with irregular menstrual periods in girls and women.

Sensible Weight Loss   Losing weight sensibly and safely requires thought, planning, and patience.

▶ **Recognize Eating Patterns** Before you start a weight-loss program, keep a diary of your current eating habits. Record the foods that you eat and when you eat them. Also record any thoughts or feelings you have just before eating. As you review your diary, you may discover eating patterns you were not aware of. You may even identify triggers for overeating, such as boredom or stress.

▶ **Plan Helpful Strategies** Do not try to lose weight too fast. Remember that it took awhile to put on the weight. Change your eating habits gradually— your weight-loss program will be more successful in the long run. Figure 7 suggests some strategies to help you eat sensibly while losing weight.

▶ **Exercise** Your weight-loss program will be far more effective if you exercise. If you decrease your calorie intake but do not exercise, your basal metabolic rate goes down. As a result, your body will not burn calories as efficiently as it did before. Weight loss may slow down or stop even though you are still consuming fewer calories.

Connect to Your Life   **What emotions and behaviors trigger your desire to eat?**

Weight-Loss Strategies
- Eat smaller portions.
- Eat your food slowly to enjoy its taste.
- Try not to eat while watching TV or reading.
- Take a walk instead of eating when you are bored.
- If you overeat occasionally, do not become upset. Just return to your sensible eating habits.

FIGURE 7   A successful weight-loss program combines sensible eating with regular exercise. Exercise helps your body burn calories more efficiently.

Frozen yogurt

Cheddar cheese on crackers

Trail mix

FIGURE 8 If you are trying to gain weight, snack on nutrient-dense foods such as the ones shown here. **Applying Concepts** List some other healthy nutrient-dense snacks.

Sensible Weight Gain A sensible plan for gaining weight is not unlike that for losing weight. The difference is that you need to *increase* your calorie intake while making sure to eat a balanced diet and to exercise. Here are some tips for changing habits that may be preventing you from gaining weight.

▶ Avoid snacks right before mealtimes because they could spoil your appetite.

▶ When you do snack, choose nutrient-dense foods that are high in calories. Figure 8 shows some good snack choices.

▶ Don't increase your fat intake over what is recommended in the MyPlate plan. Doing so can lead to other health problems.

▶ Try not to skip meals.

▶ At mealtimes, take bigger helpings of food than usual.

▶ While you are increasing your caloric intake, do not neglect exercise. Exercising will help you maintain fitness and gain healthy muscle mass.

Section 2 Review

Key Ideas and Vocabulary

1. Briefly describe how heredity, activity level, and body composition can affect a person's weight.

2. What is the formula for calculating body mass index? What does it mean for someone to have a healthy body mass index?

3. What are two diseases associated with being overweight? What health risks are associated with being underweight?

4. What is a **fad diet?** Describe two problems associated with fad diets.

5. Why is exercise an important part of a weight-loss program? Why is exercise also important for gaining weight?

Health at Home

Lunch-Time Options List some healthy lunch-time foods and snacks that students who are trying to lose weight can bring to school from home. Be creative—include some nontraditional foods on your list. Then design a poster that illustrates your suggestions.

Critical Thinking

6. **Applying Concepts** Many people have an unrealistic expectation of what their appropriate weight should be. What factors might contribute to their misconception?

7. **Evaluating** Being overweight is more common in the United States than in many other countries. Why do you think this is the case?

Nutrition for Individual Needs

Objectives
▶ **Examine** how diabetics, vegetarians, people with food sensitivities, and athletes can meet their nutritional needs.

Vocabulary
• vegetarian
• vegan
• food allergy
• food intolerance
• carbohydrate loading

Warm-Up

Dear Advice Line,

I've recently become a vegetarian, and it has my parents worried. They think I'm not getting enough nutrients, and they keep telling me that I have to eat meat to be healthy. How can I explain to them that a vegetarian diet can be healthy?

WRITING Write a response to this teen to help solve the problem.

Diets for Diabetics

People's circumstances may call for special diets. **Diabetes is a disease with dietary requirements that can help people manage their condition.**

Recall that one of the risks of being overweight is type 2 diabetes, a condition in which the blood contains high levels of glucose. Type 2 diabetes was once thought of as an adult disease. However, it is becoming more common in adolescents because of poor nutritional habits, such as eating too much sugar and fat.

Diabetes can be a life-threatening condition, so it is important for people to keep their diabetes under control. In addition to other treatments, diabetics can help control their disease by making changes in their diets. Here are some eating tips for diabetics.

▶ Eat balanced meals and snacks on a regular schedule.

▶ Keep track of your carbohydrate intake. You can replace some carbohydrates with foods that are high in unsaturated fats, such as peanut butter and almonds. If you have a sugary treat, avoid other carbohydrates that day.

▶ Control your weight. In addition to dietary changes, be sure to get regular exercise.

Connect to Your Life How could you help a diabetic friend make the necessary changes in his or her diet?

GO ONLINE

PearsonSuccessNet.com

For: More on meals for
individual needs

Vegetarian Diets

A person who does not eat meat is called a **vegetarian.** Some vegetarians, called **vegans,** eat no food from any animal source. Other vegetarians, however, include eggs and dairy products in their diets. **Because vegetarians exclude certain foods from their diets, they need to plan their food choices carefully to avoid potential health risks.**

Benefits of a Vegetarian Diet   More people are turning to vegetarian diets because of the health benefits. Vegetarians tend to have a lower BMI than other people. In addition, vegetarians may have a lower risk of heart disease, which can result from eating too much animal fat. Vegetarians also tend to have lower blood pressure and a lower risk of type 2 diabetes.

Risks of a Vegetarian Diet   As you learned in Chapter 8, animal products such as milk, eggs, and meat are complete proteins because they contain all the essential amino acids. Plant products, however, are incomplete proteins. Vegetarians who eat no food from animal sources must make sure that their diets contain all the essential amino acids. Vegetarians must also make sure to obtain adequate supplies of vitamins and minerals.

There are some risks associated with a vegetarian diet.

► A vegetarian diet may not have sufficient vitamin B12, which is found primarily in animal products. Lack of vitamin B12 can result in nerve damage.

► Vegetarians may not consume adequate calcium, which can lead to bone loss.

► Vegetarians may experience a protein deficiency, which can result in hair and muscle loss.

Vegetarians can reduce their risk of health problems by eating a varied diet. Foods should be rich in vitamins and minerals or have those nutrients added. When eaten daily, foods such as brown rice, beans, corn, nuts, seeds, and whole grains help ensure that a vegetarian gets all the essential amino acids. Tofu and dark, green leafy vegetables are good sources of calcium for vegetarians.

FIGURE 9   Protein combinations such as tofu with pasta or rice are good choices for vegetarian meals. Vegetarians who eat foods from animal sources can also get protein from milk products and eggs.

Some Complete Protein Combinations
- Peanut butter on a whole-wheat bagel
- Refried beans on a corn tortilla
- Split pea soup with rice cakes

Food Sensitivities

Sensitivity	Symptoms	Common Causes
Food allergy	Coughing, sneezing, vomiting, headache, rash, swelling, breathing difficulty, drop in blood pressure	Peanuts and other nuts, eggs, milk, soy, fish, shellfish, wheat and other grains, fruits, vegetables
Food intolerance	Rash, stuffy or runny nose, headache, anxiety, tiredness, inability to concentrate, digestive problems (cramping, diarrhea, vomiting), weight loss or gain, malnutrition	Milk products, chocolate, wheat, food additives, eggs, strawberries, citrus fruits, tomatoes

Food Sensitivities

Do you know people who itch after eating strawberries or get a stomach ache from ice cream? Reactions like these may be due to food sensitivities. **People with food sensitivities, which include food allergies and food intolerances, may require special diets.**

Food Allergies A **food allergy** is a response by your immune system to the proteins in certain foods. Some common foods associated with food allergies are listed in Figure 10. An allergic reaction is usually fast and intense. In severe cases, the tongue swells, breathing becomes difficult, and blood pressure drops. This type of reaction requires emergency treatment.

Food labels sometimes contain statements, such as "may contain traces of peanuts." If you are allergic to peanuts, be careful to avoid such foods. Fortunately, food allergies are rare. In children, the frequency ranges from 6 to 8 percent. In adults, it is about 4 percent.

Food Intolerances Food intolerances are more common than food allergies. A **food intolerance** is an inability to digest a particular food or food additive. Symptoms of food intolerance may be slower to appear and harder to recognize than those of a food allergy. Figure 10 lists symptoms and foods associated with food intolerance.

Figuring out which food is causing a food intolerance reaction can take months. The person must eliminate foods from the diet one at a time until symptoms disappear.

FIGURE 10 Food allergies are quick responses by the immune system to certain foods. Allergic reactions may require medical treatment. Food intolerances may not be as serious, but can make a person ill.
Reading Tables Which foods can cause both food allergies and food intolerances?

Connect to Your Life What are some ways you could help a family member deal with a food intolerance?

Healthy Diets for Athletes

A lot of conflicting information has been written about the dietary needs of athletes. **However, nutritionists in the field of sports medicine agree on one thing: athletes need a well-balanced diet with the recommended amounts of carbohydrates, fats, and proteins.**

Calorie Intake   Athletes need to consume extra calories to fuel their higher level of physical activity. Where these calories should come from is a subject of controversy. Many nutritionists state that most of the extra calories should come from an increase in complex carbohydrates. The extra calories should not come from high-fat foods, otherwise athletes risk developing the health problems associated with them. However, athletes should not restrict fat intake to less than that recommended in the MyPlate plan.

Fluid Intake   During competition, athletes should drink plenty of fluids, preferably water, to replace the fluid lost in perspiration. Just how much water athletes need depends on the duration and intensity of the competition. It also depends on weather factors, such as how hot and humid it is. Excessive heat and humidity require higher fluid intake.

Carbohydrate Loading   You may have heard about endurance athletes, such as runners, loading up on carbohydrates before a long race. **Carbohydrate loading** is the practice of greatly increasing carbohydrate intake and decreasing exercise on the days immediately before a competition. By doing this, athletes hope to make extra energy available to the muscles during the competition. For marathon runners or other endurance athletes, carbohydrate loading may help supply needed energy. For the average athlete, however, it probably is unnecessary.

FIGURE 11   Athletes need a balanced diet with larger portions of food for additional calories.

Section 3 Review

Key Ideas and Vocabulary

1. How can diabetics control the amount of carbohydrates in their diets?

2. What recommendation would you make to a vegetarian about his or her diet?

3. Why is it important to identify any food sensitivities that you may have?

4. List three diet-related recommendations that athletes should follow.

5. What is **carbohydrate loading?** What do athletes hope to gain from this practice?

Health at School

Vending Machine Snacks Suppose you were choosing snacks to be included in a vending machine at school. What would be some good choices for diabetics? Vegetarians? Student athletes? List your choices and note the reason for each choice. **WRITING**

Critical Thinking

6. **Comparing and Contrasting** How do food allergies differ from food intolerances? Why might it be difficult to distinguish the two?

7. **Evaluating** Suppose an athlete decides to limit his caloric intake to keep his weight down. How could you convince him of the dangers of his decision?

Chapter 9
At a Glance

VIDEO

TEENS Talk 🔘

Goals for Healthy Eating List three things you learned about goal-setting from this video.

Section 1 Choosing Food Wisely

Key Ideas

▶ You eat for several reasons: to meet your nutritional needs, to satisfy your appetite, and to supply your body with energy.

▶ When choosing foods, it is important to read and evaluate the information on the food label. The information includes nutrition facts, nutrient and health claims, Daily Values, and freshness dates.

Vocabulary
- hunger (220)
- appetite (220)
- basal metabolic rate (220)
- Daily Values (223)

Section 2 Safely Managing Your Weight

Key Ideas

▶ A person's weight is determined by heredity, level of activity, and body composition.

▶ One simple way to assess whether your weight falls within a healthy range is to calculate your body mass index.

▶ Being overweight can lead to serious health problems, including heart disease and diabetes.

▶ Being underweight can been linked to anemia, heart irregularities, and trouble regulating body temperature.

▶ Sensible weight management involves avoiding dangerous diet plans, choosing nutritionally balanced meals and snacks, and getting regular exercise.

Vocabulary
- body composition (227)
- body mass index (227)
- overweight (228)
- obesity (228)
- underweight (229)
- fad diet (230)

Section 3 Nutrition for Individual Needs

Key Ideas

▶ Diabetes is a disease with dietary requirements that can help people manage their condition.

▶ Because vegetarians exclude certain foods from their diets, they need to plan their food choices carefully to avoid potential health risks.

▶ People with food sensitivities, which include food allergies and food intolerances, may require special diets.

▶ Athletes need a well-balanced diet with the recommended amounts of carbohydrates, fats, and proteins.

Vocabulary
- vegetarian (234)
- vegan (234)
- food allergy (235)
- food intolerance (235)
- carbohydrate loading (236)

Chapter 9 Review

Reviewing Key Ideas

GO ONLINE

PearsonSuccessNet.com

For: Chapter 9 review activity

Section 1

1. Basal metabolic rate (BMR) can be affected by
   a. Daily Values.
   b. age.
   c. hunger.
   d. appetite.

2. A Daily Value of 10 percent means that
   a. a food consists of 10 percent of a particular nutrient.
   b. 10 percent of your calories should come from a particular nutrient.
   c. one serving provides 10 percent of the daily amount for a particular nutrient.
   d. a food package can bear the nutrient claim "light."

3. How might a person's muscle mass affect BMR?

4. How does BMR change as a person ages?

5. How can a person's cultural background influence his or her diet?

6. **Critical Thinking** How do you think friends can influence your appetite?

7. **Critical Thinking** How can reading food labels help you choose between two similar foods?

Section 2

8. Body mass index (BMI) is a ratio of a person's weight to his or her
   a. age.
   b. activity level.
   c. height.
   d. basal metabolic rate.

9. People who are considered overweight
   a. are generally healthier than people who are not overweight.
   b. are decreasing in number.
   c. have a BMI of more than 30.
   d. are heavier than the standard for their height.

10. Joel has a BMI of 30. Explain how this number was determined and what it means.

11. Why aren't fad diets effective for long-term weight loss?

12. Why should a person use a diet diary when attempting to gain or lose weight?

13. **Critical Thinking** Explain why skipping meals is not an effective way to manage your weight.

Section 3

14. A food intolerance is
    a. a response by the immune system to certain proteins in foods.
    b. present in one percent of the population.
    c. the inability to digest a particular food.
    d. a fast and intense reaction to food.

15. How is type 2 diabetes related to diet?

16. How can vegetarians make sure they get all the amino acids they need?

17. Why is it important for an athlete to increase calorie intake?

18. **Critical Thinking** How could diabetics benefit from reading food labels? What information should they look for?

Building Health Skills

19. **Accessing Information** Make a chart in which you compare different types and brands of yogurt. How do they compare for total fat, saturated fat, cholesterol, vitamins, and minerals?

20. **Advocacy** Tim, who is thin, has started eating a lot of potato chips and other high-fat foods in an attempt to gain weight. What advice would you give him? **WRITING**

21. **Setting Goals** Calculate your BMI. Determine if you have an appropriate weight, are overweight, or underweight. Plan meals that will increase, decrease, or keep your BMI the same. Try the meals for several weeks, and see if there is any change in your BMI.

Health and Community

Fast-Food Pamphlet Use the Internet to collect the nutrition information supplied by many fast-food restaurants. Use this data to analyze the fat and calorie content of different food items. Then, create a pamphlet comparing two meals: one that is low in fat and calories, and one that is high in fat and calories. **WRITING**

Standardized Test Prep

Math Practice

The food label below is from a box of breakfast cereal. Use the label to answer Questions 22–24.

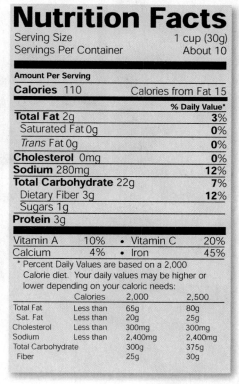

Nutrition Facts

Serving Size .... 1 cup (30g)
Servings Per Container .... About 10

Amount Per Serving

Calories 110	Calories from Fat 15

	% Daily Value*
Total Fat 2g	3%
Saturated Fat 0g	0%
Trans Fat 0g	0%
Cholesterol 0mg	0%
Sodium 280mg	12%
Total Carbohydrate 22g	7%
Dietary Fiber 3g	12%
Sugars 1g	
Protein 3g	

Vitamin A	10%	•	Vitamin C	20%
Calcium	4%	•	Iron	45%

* Percent Daily Values are based on a 2,000 Calorie diet. Your daily values may be higher or lower depending on your caloric needs:

	Calories	2,000	2,500
Total Fat	Less than	65g	80g
Sat. Fat	Less than	20g	25g
Cholesterol	Less than	300mg	300mg
Sodium	Less than	2,400mg	2,400mg
Total Carbohydrate		300g	375g
Fiber		25g	30g

22. How many servings would an average person need to consume to get the total amount of vitamin C needed in a day?
A 2   B 5
C 10   D 25

23. What percentage of the calories in one serving comes from fat?
F about 3 percent
G about 6 percent
H about 14 percent
J about 20 percent

24. If you consume a diet of 2,500 calories per day, what percentage of your Daily Value for fiber would one serving provide?
A 8 percent
B 10 percent
C 12 percent
D 15 percent

Reading and Writing Practice

Read the passage. Then answer Questions 25–28.

Could a protein called leptin help explain why people gain or lose weight? Working with a genetically obese strain of mice, scientists found that these mice made very little leptin compared to normal mice. Perhaps leptin serves as a signal to the brain to suppress appetite, the scientists hypothesized. But, unlike the obese mice, over-weight humans have plenty of leptin in their bodies. Nonetheless, the findings about leptin have opened the door for more research into weight control.

25. Leptin is a
A protein found only in mice.
B protein found only in humans.
C protein found in both mice and humans.
D medication that increases one's appetite.

26. In this passage, the word *suppress* means
F increase.
G reduce.
H stimulate.
J maintain.

27. According to the passage, which of these statements is true?
A Genetically obese mice produce high amounts of leptin.
B Normal mice produce very little leptin.
C Thin people produce very little leptin.
D Overweight people produce plenty of leptin.

Constructed Response

28. In a paragraph, explain the scientists' findings about leptin in mice and in humans.

Test-Taking Tip

Before taking a test, become familiar with its format, including the different question types. One way to do this is to complete practice tests.

CHAPTER 10

Digestion and Excretion

GO ONLINE PearsonSuccessNet.com

VIDEO 10

TEENS Talk

Feeding the Need

Preview **Activity**

Why Volunteer?

Complete this activity before you watch the video.

1. In a paragraph, discuss what "volunteering" means to you.
   WRITING

2. Interview five teens to find out how they have volunteered their time in the community. Describe the types of volunteer activities they perform. What have they gained from their experiences?

Your Digestive System

Objectives

▶ **Describe** the three main functions of the digestive system.

▶ **Identify** the organs of the digestive system and their functions.

Vocabulary

- digestion
- enzyme
- absorption
- pharynx
- epiglottis
- peristalsis
- chyme
- bile
- gallbladder
- villi

Warm-Up

Myth Food is digested in the stomach.

Fact Although protein digestion does begin in the stomach, most digestion occurs in the small intestine.

WRITING List three questions you have about how the digestive system functions. Look for the answers in the chapter.

Functions of the Digestive System

You've learned that your cells require nutrients for energy, growth, and repair. How do the nutrients from the apple you ate at lunch get to your cells? Before your body can use nutrients from your food, the food must be processed by your digestive system. **Your digestive system has three main functions—digestion, absorption, and elimination.**

Digestion The process by which the digestive system breaks down food into molecules that the body can use is called **digestion.** There are two kinds of digestion.

▶ During mechanical digestion, foods are physically broken apart into smaller pieces.

▶ During chemical digestion, chemicals produced by your body break large molecules into smaller ones that your body can use.

Because mechanical digestion breaks food into small pieces, chemicals can digest the food faster. Most of the chemicals involved in digestion are **enzymes,** substances that speed up chemical reactions.

Absorption and Elimination **Absorption** is the process by which nutrients pass through the lining of your digestive system into your blood. The blood then transports the nutrients throughout your body. Materials that are not absorbed are eliminated from the body as wastes.

Connect to Your Life **What foods are being digested and absorbed by your body right now?**

Structures of the Digestive System

The organs of the digestive system include the mouth, pharynx, esophagus, stomach, small intestine, and large intestine. The liver, gallbladder, and pancreas also are involved in digestion. Figure 1 shows the organs of the digestive system.

Mouth Mechanical digestion occurs in your mouth as your teeth tear, crush, and grind your food and your tongue pushes the food around. Chemical digestion occurs as an enzyme in saliva begins to break down starches in your food. Saliva also moistens the bites of food into a slippery mass that can be easily swallowed.

Pharynx The tongue pushes chewed food into the upper portion of the throat called the pharynx. The **pharynx** is the junction between the digestive tract and the respiratory system. As you swallow, a flap of tissue called the **epiglottis** seals off the trachea, or windpipe, preventing food and liquid from entering your lungs.

Esophagus After passing through the pharynx, the food enters the esophagus, a muscular tube that connects the pharynx to the stomach. Muscle contractions push the food through the esophagus and toward the stomach. These waves of muscle contractions, called **peristalsis,** continue to push food through the rest of the digestive system.

 GO ONLINE

PearsonSuccessNet.com
For: More on the digestive system

The Digestive System

FIGURE 1 As food moves through the digestive system, digestion, absorption, and elimination occur in a continuous process.
Interpreting Diagrams Which structure prevents food and liquid from entering the trachea?

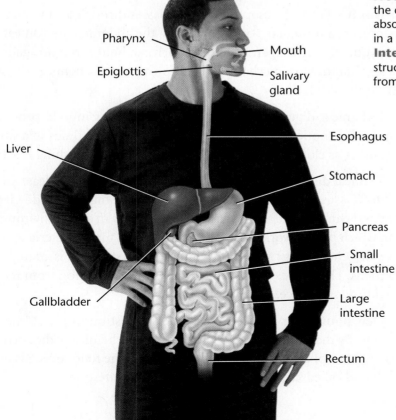

Pharynx
Epiglottis
Mouth
Salivary gland
Liver
Esophagus
Stomach
Pancreas
Small intestine
Large intestine
Gallbladder
Rectum

Hands-On *Activity*

Enzymes in Action

In this activity, you will observe the effect of enzymes on foods.

Materials
crackers • meat tenderizer • milk
orange juice • 2 clear glasses • 2 stirrers

Try This

1. Chew a cracker for 5 seconds. Do not swallow it. Note how the cracker tastes.
2. Continue chewing the cracker for 5 minutes. Note how the taste of the cracker changes before swallowing it.
3. Place 2 tablespoons of milk into one glass. Place 2 tablespoons of orange juice into another glass.
4. Add 1 tablespoon of meat tenderizer to each glass. Stir well with separate stirrers.
5. After 30 minutes, look closely at the contents of the two glasses. Record your observations.

Think and Discuss

1. How did the taste of the cracker change during the five minutes it was in your mouth?
2. Why do you think the taste of the cracker changed the longer it was in your mouth?
3. After 30 minutes, how did the appearance of the milk solution compare to that of the orange juice solution?
4. Meat tenderizer contains an enzyme called papain. Based on your observations, what nutrient does papain act on?
5. Why do you think meat tenderizer makes cooked meat tender?

Stomach From the esophagus, food passes through a valve and into the stomach, a muscular pouch located in the abdomen. As you eat and drink, your stomach expands. The stomach can hold about one gallon of food and liquid. Most mechanical digestion and some chemical digestion occur in the stomach.

▶ Mechanical digestion occurs as three layers of muscle produce a churning motion. This action mixes the food with fluids in a similar manner as clothes and soapy water are mixed in a washing machine.

▶ Chemical digestion occurs as cells lining the stomach release gastric juice. Gastric juice contains pepsin, an enzyme that breaks down proteins. Hydrochloric acid in gastric juice creates an acidic environment in which pepsin works best. The acid also kills many bacteria that you swallow with your food. The lining of the stomach is coated with mucus. The mucus gives the stomach some protection from its own acidic gastric juice.

A few hours after you eat, mechanical digestion in the stomach is complete. By that time, most proteins have been chemically digested into shorter chains of amino acids. Peristalsis moves the food, which is now a thick liquid called **chyme** (kym), into the small intestine.

Small Intestine The small intestine is where most chemical digestion and absorption of nutrients takes place. This 20-foot long tube gets its name from its small one-inch diameter. Three other organs play a role in the chemical digestion that takes place in the small intestine.

▶ **Liver** The liver plays a role in many body processes. The role of the liver in the digestive system is to produce bile. **Bile** is a substance that physically breaks up large fat droplets that clump together.

▶ **Gallbladder** Bile flows from the liver into the **gallbladder,** the organ that stores bile. As food leaves your stomach, the gallbladder releases bile through a tube into the small intestine.

▶ **Pancreas** The pancreas is a triangular organ that lies between the stomach and the first part of the small intestine. Like the liver, the pancreas plays a role in many body processes. In the digestive system, the pancreas secretes enzymes into the small intestine that complete the breakdown of carbohydrates, proteins, and fats.

Once pancreatic enzymes have broken down the food, the nutrients can be absorbed. The lining of the small intestine is covered with millions of tiny fingerlike projections called **villi** (singular, *villus*). The villi absorb nutrient molecules. As you can see in Figure 2, each villus contains tiny blood vessels. Most nutrients pass from cells on a villus into the blood vessels. Once in the blood, the nutrients are transported throughout the body.

Choose one food that you ate today. Where did digestion and absorption occur?

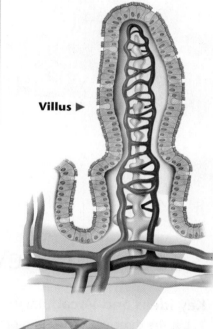
Villus ▶

FIGURE 2 The lining of the small intestine is covered with tiny projections called villi. Nutrients pass through the thin surface of villi and into blood vessels for transport.

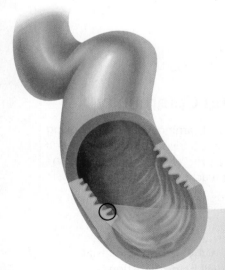
▲ **Small intestine**

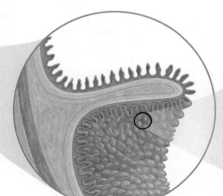
▲ **Fold covered with villi**

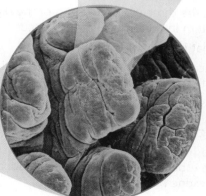
▲ **Close-up of villi**

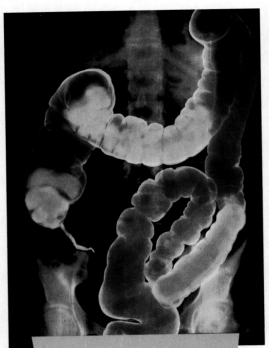

Waste materials are pushed slowly through the large intestine for about 12 to 24 hours.

The Large Intestine By the time material reaches the end of the small intestine, most nutrients have been absorbed. The remaining undigested material and unabsorbed water is pushed into the large intestine. The large intestine, also called the colon, is about 5 feet long and 3 inches wide. It runs up the right side of the abdomen, across the upper abdomen, and then down the left side. As the material moves through the large intestine, most of the remaining water is absorbed into the blood.

The large intestine ends in a short tube called the rectum. In the rectum, waste material is compressed into solid form. This waste material, called feces or stool, is eliminated from the body through the anus, a muscular opening at the end of the rectum.

Did you know that your large intestine is also a site of vitamin production? Billions of bacteria thrive in the warm and nutrient-rich environment of your large intestine. The bacteria produce several vitamins, including most of your daily requirement for vitamin K. The vitamin K is absorbed through the lining of your large intestine into your blood.

FIGURE 3 As waste materials pass through the large intestine, most of the remaining water is absorbed. The wastes are then eliminated from the body.

Section 1 Review

Key Ideas and Vocabulary

1. List the three main functions of the digestive system in the order that they occur.
2. What is **peristalsis**?
3. Trace the path of food through the digestive system. When does the food become chyme?
4. Describe the role of **bile**.

Critical Thinking

5. Predicting How would digestion be affected if the tube leading from the gallbladder to the small intestine became blocked?

Health and Community

First Aid for Choking Learning first aid for choking victims can help you save a friend, family member, or even a stranger. Find a program at your school or in your community that teaches first aid for choking. After taking the class, create a poster that summarizes what you learned. **WRITING**

6. Applying Concepts Why do you think that chewing your food well helps digestion?
7. Classifying Which three organs that participate in digestion are most likely known as accessory organs? Explain why.

GO ONLINE PearsonSuccessNet.com | Audio Summary Section 10.1

Technology & Health

Lights, Pill Camera, Action!

Disorders of the digestive system can be difficult to diagnose. The symptoms of many disorders are very similiar, and some parts of the digestive system are too deep within the body to examine. Today, however, a tiny new tool can provide doctors with clear color images of the small intestine. Patients simply swallow a pill-sized camera. During its journey, the camera transmits thousands of images to a recorder worn around the patient's waist.

WRITING The tiny parts of the pill camera are products of miniaturization. Think of another technology that has been changed by miniaturization. In a paragraph, describe how its small size impacted its use.

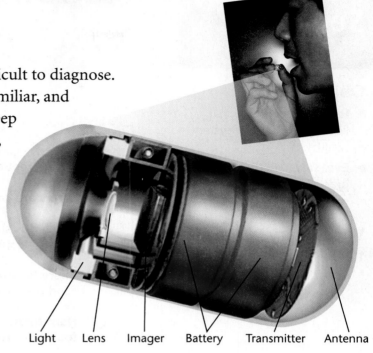

Light   Lens   Imager   Battery   Transmitter   Antenna

▲ The Pill Camera

After fasting overnight, the patient swallows the pill camera with water. As it tumbles through the small intestine, the camera captures about two images per second. About 24 hours later, the disposable pill camera is eliminated from the digestive tract.

▼ Reviewing the Images

A technician downloads the images from the recorder. A doctor examines the images for signs of bleeding, tumors, blockages, ulcers, or other disorders.

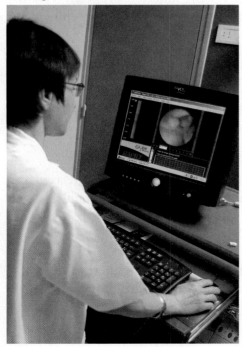

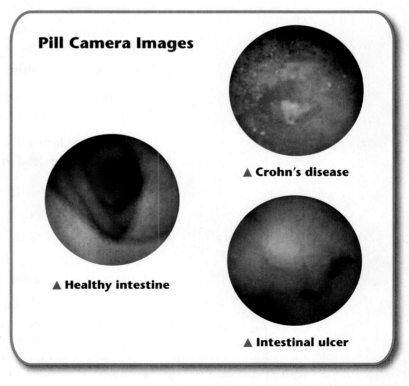

Pill Camera Images

▲ **Crohn's disease**

▲ **Healthy intestine**

▲ **Intestinal ulcer**

Keeping Your Digestive System Healthy

Objectives

▶ **Identify** behaviors that keep your digestive system healthy.

▶ **Evaluate** whether you practice proper food safety methods.

Vocabulary

• foodborne illness
• cross-contamination

Warm-Up

Quick Quiz Only one of the following statements is true. Which statement do you think it is?

(1) Ulcers are caused by eating too much spicy food.

(2) Hot foods should be cooled completely before putting them in the refrigerator.

(3) There is nothing you can do to avoid food poisoning.

(4) Harmful microorganisms can be found on fruits and vegetables.

(5) Heartburn is a sign of heart disease.

WRITING Explain why you gave the answer that you did.

Avoiding Digestive Disorders

How can you help your digestive system function properly? **Healthy eating habits and regular exercise are important for keeping your digestive system healthy.**

▶ **Consume plenty of fiber.** High-fiber foods such as vegetables, fruits, and whole-grain products help food move through the intestines.

▶ **Limit fatty foods.** Fat is digested slowly. Eating a lot of fatty food in one sitting can lead to digestive problems such as heartburn.

▶ **Eat moderately**. Overeating can strain the digestive system.

▶ **Plan meals for a time when you can relax.** When you are relaxed, you are more likely to eat slowly and chew your food thoroughly.

▶ **Drink water.** Make sure to drink water during meals and at other times during the day.

▶ **Get regular exercise.** Regular exercise stimulates peristalsis, which can prevent constipation. If you exercise, you are also more likely to maintain a healthy weight. Excess weight is a risk factor for some digestive disorders.

Disorders of the Digestive System

Condition	Cause	Symptoms	Treatments
Appendicitis	Microorganisms infect the appendix—a small pouch that projects from the colon.	Pain near the navel that spreads, nausea, diarrhea, and fever	Surgery to remove the appendix
Colon cancer	Uncontrolled cell division that leads to a cancerous tumor; risk factors include family history, high-fat diet, and lack of exercise.	Change in bowel habits, narrow stools, persistent gas or pain, unexplained weight loss	Surgery, radiation, and chemotherapy
Heartburn	Acid from the stomach irritates the esophagus; risk factors include obesity, asthma, pregnancy, ulcers, and overeating.	Burning sensation in chest, sour taste	Over-the-counter or prescription medications; rarely surgery
Hemorrhoids	Veins in the anus or rectum swell due to constipation, pregnancy and childbirth, sitting for long periods, or heavy lifting.	Bleeding, itching, pain	Over-the-counter treatments, warm baths, outpatient surgery
Inflammatory bowel disease (colitis and Crohn's disease)	Chronic inflammation of digestive tract; influenced by immune system, genetics, and environment.	Diarrhea, cramping, bleeding, loss of appetite, weight loss, fever; symptoms may come and go	Anti-inflammatory drugs, immune system suppressors, surgery to remove damaged sections of intestines
Irritable bowel syndrome	Abnormal peristalsis in the small intestine leads to bouts of diarrhea and constipation.	Diarrhea, constipation, gas, bloating; stress may worsen symptoms	Managing stress, diet changes, fiber supplements, drugs that affect nervous system activities
Lactose intolerance	Lack of the enzyme lactase in the small intestine leads to an inability to digest lactose, a sugar in milk.	Within 30 minutes to 2 hours after consuming milk products: nausea, cramps, gas, diarrhea	Drinking less milk, trying yogurt or hard cheeses, taking lactase drops or tablets, drinking lactose-free milk
Peptic ulcer (of esophagus, stomach, or small intestine)	Irritation caused by *H. pylori* infection leads to open sores.	Burning pain between the breastbone and the navel, especially at night or when the stomach is empty	Antibiotics, antacids, medications that protect the digestive tract lining

H. pylori ▶

FIGURE 5 Protect yourself and your family from foodborne illnesses by cooking and storing foods properly.

Storing Food Safely
- Quickly refrigerate leftovers and cold food items.
- Keep your refrigerator set at a temperature of 40°F or below.
- Separate raw meat, poultry, and seafood from other foods in the refrigerator.

Grilling Foods Properly

Steak (medium)	160°F
Ground beef	160°F
Pork chops	160°F
Chicken breasts	170°F
Most fish	145°F

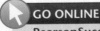
GO ONLINE
PearsonSuccessNet.com
For: More on food safety

Food Safety

Each year in the United States, about 76 million people become sick from contaminated food or beverages. **To avoid foodborne illnesses, it is very important to prepare and store food properly.**

Foodborne Illness   **Foodborne illnesses** result from consuming a food or drink that contains either a poison or a disease-causing microorganism. Some mushrooms and fish, for example, contain poisons that can cause serious illness or even death.

Bacteria and viruses cause the most common foodborne illnesses. You may have heard about people becoming sick from consuming foods that were contaminated with the bacteria *E. coli* or *Salmonella*. Microorganisms are typically spread in one of three ways.

▶ When food is undercooked

▶ When raw food touches cooked food

▶ When people preparing food transfer the organisms onto their hands, countertops, or utensils

Typical symptoms of foodborne illnesses are diarrhea, vomiting, abdominal cramps, and fever. If you contract a foodborne illness, be sure to drink plenty of fluids to replace the fluids you lose. Seek medical care if symptoms include any of the following.

▶ Fever over 101.5°F

▶ Blood in stool or diarrhea for more than three days

▶ Prolonged vomiting or signs of dehydration, such as dry mouth and dizziness

Connect to Your Life   **What steps do you take at home to avoid foodborne illness?**

Food Preparation and Storage How can you avoid becoming infected with microorganisms in foods? A few simple precautions can reduce your risk.

▶ **Cook** Cook meat, seafood, poultry, and eggs thoroughly. Eggs should be cooked until the whites and the yolks are firm. Fish should be cooked until it is opaque and flakes easily with a fork.

▶ **Separate** Keep uncooked food separated to prevent **cross-contamination,** the spread of microorganisms from one food to another food. For example, do not cut vegetables on the same cutting board you used to cut raw meat. Use plastic cutting boards for meat and poultry. Also, do not place cooked food on a platter that held uncooked food.

▶ **Chill** Quickly refrigerate leftovers, including cut-up fruits and vegetables, to slow the growth of bacteria. Do not defrost foods at room temperature.

▶ **Clean** Wash your hands with soap before preparing food and again after handling raw meat, poultry, or fish. Use paper towels, rather than sponges, to clean kitchen surfaces with a disinfectant cleaner. Rinse fruits and vegetables in running water.

FIGURE 6 Many microorganisms thrive in the moist environment of a kitchen sponge. The inset photo is a micrograph that shows bacteria (blue) and fungi (white) on the surface of a sponge.

Section 2 Review

Key Ideas and Vocabulary

1. List three eating habits that can help keep your digestive system healthy. Why is exercise important for digestive health?
2. What are two possible contaminants in food that can lead to **foodborne illness?**
3. List four tips for preparing and storing foods safely.
4. Explain how **cross-contamination** can lead to foodborne illnesses.

Critical Thinking

5. **Evaluating** List three changes you can make to your daily eating habits to keep your digestive system healthy.

Health at Home

Food Safety at Home For one week, evaluate the food safety methods practiced in your home. At the end of the week create a food-safety checklist for your family. The list could include items such as quickly putting milk back into the refrigerator and washing hands before preparing a snack.

6. **Predicting** A food worker wears plastic gloves while he works with raw chicken. Later, he chops vegetables for the salad bar while wearing the same gloves. What could be a consequence of his actions? Explain.

Thinking Critically About Health News

Every day, newspapers and magazines report the latest scientific findings on health topics. Sometimes, it may seem that this information changes from day to day. For example, one day you might read that a certain food is good for you. The next day, you may read that the same food can lead to health problems.

How can you sort out all the information? When reviewing new health information, keep a critical, but open, mind. Use the following questions to evaluate health reports.

❶ Who conducted the research?

Find out the credentials of the person or group who conducted the research. Usually, health professionals are the best-qualified researchers.

❷ Is the source trustworthy?

Always consider the type of source where the information appears.

► The most reliable sources are medical or scientific journals. These journals only accept articles that have been thoroughly reviewed by experts.

► Articles written by trained health or science writers also are generally reliable. These people have been trained in how to report scientific findings accurately.

► The least reliable sources are ads or publications funded by people with a financial interest in the information.

❸ Is the evidence convincing?

Assess the quality of the evidence upon which the news is based. Look for signs of weak evidence.

► Vague statements that lack supporting information, such as "doctors recommend."

► Statements based on opinions rather than experimental results.

► Phrases such as "in animals," "of that age group," or "in laboratory tests," indicate that the findings may not be applicable to all groups.

❹ Has the information been verified?

The best way to assess new health information is to compare findings in more than one reliable source. When a number of researchers report similar findings, the results are more likely to be accurate. However, this is not always easy. Experts often disagree about conclusions drawn from the same information. But becoming familiar with all the views on an issue can help you make decisions based on the best available information.

Practice the Skill

1. Find an article from a local newspaper or a popular magazine that discusses health information related to nutrition.

2. Evaluate the article by asking the following questions.
   ► Who conducted the research?
   ► Is the source of the information trustworthy? Explain.
   ► Is the evidence convincing? Why or why not?

3. Find out whether the information has been supported by other studies. Summarize your findings.

4. Based on your evaluation, do you think you can trust the information in the article? Explain your viewpoint. **WRITING**

Your Excretory System

Objectives

▶ **Identify** the organs of excretion in the body and their functions.

▶ **Explain** how the kidneys remove wastes from the blood and produce urine.

▶ **Describe** behaviors that can keep your excretory system healthy.

Vocabulary

- excretion
- urea
- kidney
- urine
- nephron
- glomerulus
- dialysis

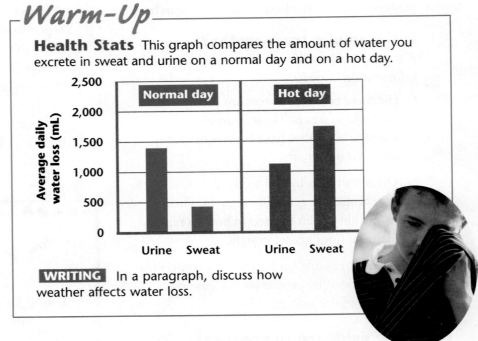

Warm-Up

Health Stats This graph compares the amount of water you excrete in sweat and urine on a normal day and on a hot day.

Average daily water loss (mL)

Normal day — Urine, Sweat
Hot day — Urine, Sweat

WRITING In a paragraph, discuss how weather affects water loss.

Organs of Excretion

Every cell in your body produces waste products that must be removed before they build up and make you sick. **Excretion** is the process by which the body collects and removes wastes. **Several organs in the body are involved in waste collection and removal, including the liver, lungs, and skin. The major organs of excretion, however, are the kidneys, which are part of the body's excretory system.**

Liver   The liver converts impurities and poisons in the body to less harmful substances. For example, the liver forms **urea** from a harmful waste product of protein breakdown. Urea can be safely transported via blood to the kidneys. Some substances processed by the liver become a part of bile. After aiding fat digestion in the small intestine, bile is eliminated from the body in stool.

Lungs and Skin   When you exhale, the lungs remove carbon dioxide and some water from the body. Sweat glands in the skin also serve an excretory function because water and urea are excreted in perspiration.

Connect to Your Life   **When you exhale on a cold day, what waste product can you see? What excretory organ is at work?**

Kidneys You have two kidneys, each about the size of a fist. The **kidneys,** which are the major organs of the excretory system, filter urea and other wastes from the blood. Figure 7 shows where the kidneys and other organs of the excretory system are located.

The wastes are eliminated in **urine,** a watery fluid produced by the kidneys that contains urea and other wastes. Urine flows from the kidneys, through the other organs of the excretory system, and out of the body.

In addition to cleansing your body of wastes, the kidneys are also the main organs involved in water balance. Hormones sent from the brain signal the kidneys to release more or less water in urine depending on the amount of water in your body. For example, on a hot day you might sweat a lot but drink little water. If so, your kidneys will not release much water. On a cool day, you might not sweat much and drink plenty of water. If so, your kidneys will release more water.

The Excretory System

FIGURE 7 The main structures of the excretory system include the kidneys, ureters, bladder, and urethra. Together they remove wastes from your body.

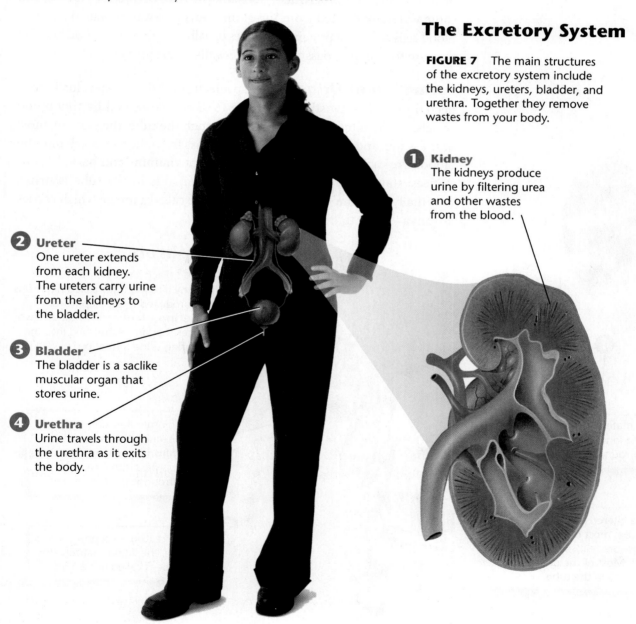

1 Kidney
The kidneys produce urine by filtering urea and other wastes from the blood.

2 Ureter
One ureter extends from each kidney. The ureters carry urine from the kidneys to the bladder.

3 Bladder
The bladder is a saclike muscular organ that stores urine.

4 Urethra
Urine travels through the urethra as it exits the body.

Filtration of Wastes

How do your kidneys remove wastes from your body, but not substances that your body needs? To answer this question, you need to understand how the kidneys filter wastes. Each kidney contains about a million **nephrons,** tiny filtering units that remove wastes and produce urine.

The nephrons filter wastes in stages. **First, both needed materials and wastes are filtered from the blood. Then, most needed materials are returned to the blood, and the wastes are eliminated from the body.** Follow the process of waste filtration and urine formation in Figure 8.

Filtering Out Wastes During the first stage of waste removal, blood enters the kidneys. Here, the blood flows through smaller and smaller blood vessels until it reaches a cluster of tiny blood vessels in a nephron called a **glomerulus** (gloh MUR yoo lus). Urea, salts, glucose, and some water are filtered from the glomerulus into a thin-walled capsule. Blood cells and most protein molecules usually remain in the blood because they are too large to pass through the walls of the glomerulus.

Formation of Urine The capsule around the glomerulus is connected to a long, twisting tube. The tube is surrounded by tiny blood vessels. As the filtered material flows through the tube, the glucose, most of the water, and other needed materials pass from the tube back into the blood. Urea and other wastes, such as excess vitamins and harmful substances, stay in the tube. The fluid that remains in the tube is urine. Eventually, the urine drains into a larger tube called a ureter, which carries it from a kidney to the bladder.

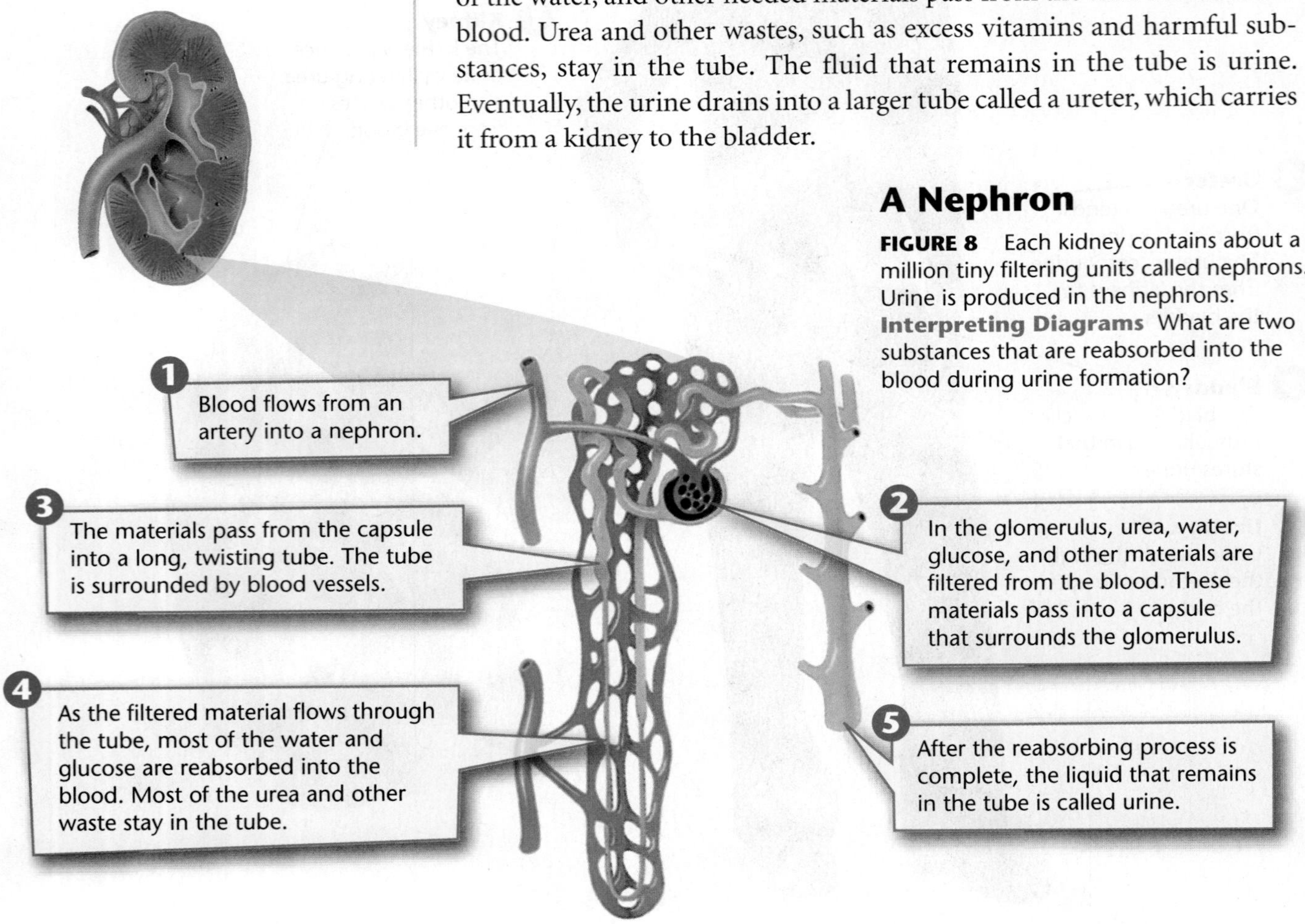

A Nephron

FIGURE 8 Each kidney contains about a million tiny filtering units called nephrons. Urine is produced in the nephrons.
Interpreting Diagrams What are two substances that are reabsorbed into the blood during urine formation?

1 Blood flows from an artery into a nephron.

2 In the glomerulus, urea, water, glucose, and other materials are filtered from the blood. These materials pass into a capsule that surrounds the glomerulus.

3 The materials pass from the capsule into a long, twisting tube. The tube is surrounded by blood vessels.

4 As the filtered material flows through the tube, most of the water and glucose are reabsorbed into the blood. Most of the urea and other waste stay in the tube.

5 After the reabsorbing process is complete, the liquid that remains in the tube is called urine.

Tips for Increasing Fluid Intake
- Eat more fruit.
- Add a splash of fruit juice to water.
- Add lemon or lime to your water.

FIGURE 9 If you find drinking plain water boring, you can increase your fluid intake in other healthful ways.

Keeping Healthy

Because the kidneys remove harmful wastes from your body, proper functioning of your kidneys is essential for your overall health. **To help your kidneys function at their best, it is important to drink plenty of water and to see a doctor if you have symptoms of an infection.**

Routine medical checkups often include a urine test, which can reveal a lot about a person's health. For example, if glucose is present in the urine, it may be a sign that a person has diabetes. Protein in urine can be a sign of high blood pressure or of poorly functioning kidneys.

Drinking Water Because many of the waste products filtered by your kidneys are harmful, it is best if they are diluted as much as possible. Drinking plenty of water is the best way to dilute these substances. In Chapter 8, you learned about the importance of drinking water. How much you should drink depends on various factors such as your health status, activity level, and the weather. In general, if you are not thirsty and your urine is only slightly yellow, you are consuming enough fluid.

Treating Infections Urinary tract infections, which are bacterial infections of the urethra or bladder, are common disorders. Most cases occur when bacteria from the digestive system come in contact with the urethra. Symptoms of urinary tract infections include frequent, painful urination and blood in the urine. Prompt treatment with antibiotics is important to prevent the infection from spreading to the kidneys. Infections of the kidneys can lead to kidney damage.

 GO ONLINE

PearsonSuccessNet.com
For: More on the excretory system

 Connect to Your Life

How much water do you consume in a typical day? Do you think that you consume enough?

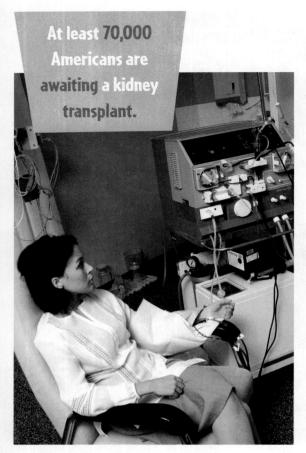

At least 70,000 Americans are awaiting a kidney transplant.

FIGURE 10 Dialysis is a treatment for kidney failure. During dialysis, a machine removes wastes from a patient's blood. Eventually, some of these patients will undergo a kidney transplant.

Preventing Kidney Stones Kidney stones are pebble-like masses that form in the kidneys. The most common stones contain calcium. When kidney stones become stuck, they are very painful. Many kidney stones eventually pass out of the excretory system in urine on their own. If a large stone blocks urine flow or damages the kidney, a procedure may be performed to shatter the stone. Drinking plenty of water and eating a low-sodium diet will reduce your risk of developing kidney stones.

Treating Kidney Failure Kidneys that are damaged from an injury, diabetes, uncontrolled high blood pressure, or other diseases may fail. When kidney failure occurs, the kidneys are unable to remove wastes and excess fluid. Kidney failure can be treated with dialysis or a kidney transplant.

▶ **Dialysis** During dialysis, a machine is used to filter wastes from the blood. Tubes carry blood from the body through the machine. The machine removes wastes and excess water. Then the blood is returned to the body. Dialysis must be performed three times a week for three to five hours. Many complications can arise from dialysis.

▶ **Kidney transplant** A transplant is a better option for some patients. During a kidney transplant, a patient's damaged kidney is replaced with a healthy kidney from another person. The kidneys often come from people who sign organ donation forms while they are alive.

Section 3 Review

Key Ideas and Vocabulary

1. What is the body's main organ of excretion? What are other organs in the excretory system?

2. Briefly describe the process of filtration and urine production that occurs in the nephrons.

3. What are two ways that you can help keep your excretory system healthy?

4. How is **dialysis** used to treat kidney failure?

Critical Thinking

5. Predicting Suppose you went for a long walk on a hot day and did not drink very much water. How might this affect urine formation?

Health at School

Water at School Does your school have working water fountains? Can you choose water with lunch? Do school vending machines sell water? Create a poster reminding students of the importance of drinking water.

6. Relating Cause and Effect Why is protein in the urine a sign that something could be wrong with the kidneys?

7. Calculating The kidneys filter about 50 gallons of fluid from the blood each day. Only 1 percent of this fluid is excreted from the body as urine. About how many gallons of urine do the kidneys produce in a day? **MATH**

Chapter 10
At a Glance

Section 1 Your Digestive System

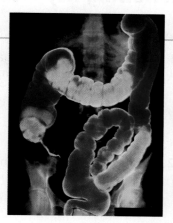

Key Ideas

▶ Your digestive system has three main functions—digestion, absorption, and elimination.

▶ The organs of the digestive system include the mouth, pharynx, esophagus, stomach, small intestine, and large intestine. The liver, gallbladder, and pancreas also are involved in digestion.

Vocabulary
- digestion (242)
- enzyme (242)
- absorption (242)
- pharynx (243)
- epiglottis (243)
- peristalsis (243)
- chyme (244)
- bile (245)
- gallbladder (245)
- villi (245)

Section 2 Keeping Your Digestive System Healthy

Key Ideas

▶ Healthy eating habits and regular exercise are important for keeping your digestive system functioning properly.

▶ To avoid foodborne illnesses, it is very important to prepare and store food properly.

Vocabulary
- foodborne illness (250)
- cross-contamination (251)

Section 3 Your Excretory System

Key Ideas

▶ Several organs in the body are involved in waste collection and removal, including the liver, lungs, and skin. The major organs of excretion, however, are the kidneys, which are part of the body's excretory system.

▶ First, both needed materials and wastes are filtered from the blood. Then, most needed materials are returned to the blood, and the wastes are eliminated from the body.

▶ To help your kidneys function at their best, it is important to drink plenty of water and to see a doctor if you have symptoms of an infection.

Vocabulary
- excretion (254)
- urea (254)
- kidney (255)
- urine (255)
- nephron (256)
- glomerulus (256)
- dialysis (258)

Chapter 10 Review

Reviewing Key Ideas

GO ONLINE
PearsonSuccessNet.com
For: Chapter 10 review activity

Section 1

1. The mixture of food and gastric juice that passes from your stomach to your small intestine is called
   a. peristalsis.
   b. chyme.
   c. bile.
   d. absorption.

2. Most mechanical digestion takes place in the
   a. epiglottis.
   b. gallbladder.
   c. stomach.
   d. large intestine.

3. What are enzymes? What is their role in digestion?

4. Describe how nutrients move from your digestive system into your blood.

5. How is the pancreas involved in digestion?

6. **Critical Thinking** Why is mechanical digestion important for chemical digestion?

7. **Critical Thinking** Some antibiotics used to fight disease also kill harmless bacteria in your body. How might this affect vitamin levels in your body?

Section 2

8. Exercise and consuming plenty of fiber may help you avoid
   a. constipation.
   b. foodborne illness.
   c. lactose intolerance.
   d. inflammatory bowel disease.

9. Cross-contamination is most likely to occur when foods are not properly
   a. cooked.
   b. separated.
   c. chilled.
   d. cleaned.

10. Describe two ways in which exercise benefits your digestive system.

11. List three ways that microorganisms that cause foodborne illnesses can be spread.

12. **Critical Thinking** Why do you think that weight loss is a symptom of several different digestive disorders?

Section 3

13. In which organ is urea produced?
    a. the kidney   b. the skin
    c. the liver   d. the bladder

14. The filtering unit of the kidney is the
    a. bladder.   b. nephron.
    c. ureter.   d. urethra.

15. List the organs in the order through which urine travels from the kidney out of the body.

16. Why is drinking plenty of water a benefit to your excretory system?

17. **Critical Thinking** How could a large kidney stone block urine flow?

Building Health Skills

18. **Making Decisions** A food worker at a take-out restaurant does several things that make you question the safety of the food you ordered. In a paragraph, describe how you would handle this situation. **WRITING**

19. **Communicating** For several weeks, a family member has had abdominal cramps and diarrhea. In an e-mail, explain to your family member why he or she should seek medical care. **WRITING**

20. **Setting Goals** Track the amount of water you consume each day over a three-day period. Also note when you drink water—with every meal or only when you are thirsty? Then develop and follow a plan to consume more water for one week. At the end of the week, evaluate how you did.

Health and Community

Organ Donors In many states, when people apply for a driver's license, they can sign a form indicating a desire to be an organ donor. Contact your state's department of motor vehicles to find out what a person needs to do to indicate a willingness to donate organs. Write a fact sheet summarizing what you learned. **WRITING**

Standardized Test Prep

Math Practice

A scientist wanted to find out the amount of time needed for the stomach to digest protein. He placed pieces of hard-boiled egg white in a solution of hydrochloric acid, water, and pepsin. Use the graph of his data to answer Questions 21–23.

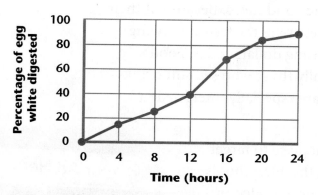

21. After how many hours would you estimate that half of the protein was digested?
   A 12
   B 14
   C 16
   D 20

22. During which four-hour period did the most digestion occur?
   F 0 to 4 hours
   G 8 to 12 hours
   H 12 to 16 hours
   J 20 to 24 hours

23. What was the average rate of egg-white digestion in this experiment?
   A 4% an hour
   B 40% a day
   C 50% an hour
   D 60% a day

Test-Taking Tip

Bring water with you the day of the test so that you will not be distracted by thirst.

Reading and Writing Practice

Read the passage. Then answer Questions 24–27.

Pasteurization is the partial sterilization of foods by heat treatment to destroy disease-causing and food-spoiling microorganisms. The process is named for the French scientist Louis Pasteur, who developed it in the 1860s. Before pasteurization, people boiled many foods. Unlike boiling, however, pasteurization doesn't significantly change a food's flavor. Pasteurization can be performed on liquids such as milk, juice, and cider, and on foods such as spices and cheese. The temperature and length of exposure vary based on the food being treated.

24. What did Louis Pasteur develop?
   A a pasteurization process that works only on milk
   B a way to kill all microorganisms
   C a way to change the flavor of foods
   D a method to prevent foodborne illness and slow food spoilage

25. Based on the information in this passage, which statement is most likely true?
   F Milk is boiled to preserve its flavor.
   G Pasteurization is only used on dairy products.
   H The pasteurization process is not the same for all foods.
   J Pasteurization can involve either heating or freezing.

26. Why do you think pasteurized milk still spoils eventually?
   A Pasteurization only partially sterilizes milk.
   B The milk was probably not treated at the right temperature.
   C Pasteurization doesn't kill any of the microorganisms that cause milk to spoil.
   D The heat used during pasteurization contributes to the spoiling of milk.

Constructed Response
27. In a paragraph, describe some of the benefits of pasteurization.

Focus on ISSUES

Should Food Ads Be Allowed in Schools?

Teens spend 140 billion dollars each year on products ranging from food and beverages to clothing, electronics, and more. Because of their spending power, teens are the fastest growing market for advertising dollars today. Food marketers, especially those who sell soft drinks and snack foods, are especially interested in reaching teens.

Food marketers see schools as the ideal place to target teens with ads. In exchange for displaying the ads, schools may receive free equipment or money to fund needed programs. Are food ads on scoreboards, school buses, vending machines, and other places in schools a good idea?

The Case for In-School Food Ads

With schools facing budget cuts for athletics, arts, and other programs, advertising provides a needed source of money for schools. How can schools prepare students for the real world if they don't have money to buy computers and other equipment? As long as the ads are approved by the school administration, they seem like a reasonable trade-off. Teens live in such a media-rich world anyway. It's unlikely that in-school ads would have an additional effect on their purchasing behavior.

"**A few years ago, we could barely afford to have a football team or a marching band. Now we have new uniforms and a really cool scoreboard. Sure, we have a few vending machines and some posters around the school now. But I don't really pay attention to them anyway. My coaches, parents, and teachers have taught me about the importance of healthy eating. No logo on a scoreboard can convince me otherwise.**"

The Case Against In-School Food Ads

Schools have a responsibility to present factual information and to help students make wise decisions. If schools teach healthy eating habits, but allow the placement of ads for unhealthy foods, they are sending mixed messages to students. On what basis would someone decide which ads are acceptable and which are not? Schools should remain "ad-free zones"—places where students know they can trust the messages they see and hear.

"**I don't think that schools should look and feel like malls. Some of my friends think that the ads wouldn't affect them, but that's not true. If ads didn't work, companies wouldn't spend so much money on them. I'm sure the ads would influence students much more than what they learn in health class. Schools should be a place for learning. Teachers shouldn't have to compete with a bunch of slick ads for students' attention.**"

What do **YOU** think?

Use these steps to analyze and express your opinion about in-school food ads.

1. Analyze the Issue Carefully consider both sides of the argument. Make a table listing the pros and cons of in-school food ads.

2. Consider Your Values Would in-school ads be a reasonable way to save programs that would otherwise be lost due to budget cuts? Why or why not?

3. Take a Stand Write a paragraph expressing your opinion about in-school food ads. Provide several reasons to support your opinion. **WRITING**

263

Movement and Coordination

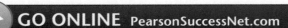

GO ONLINE PearsonSuccessNet.com

VIDEO 11

TEENS Talk

The Risks of Steroids

Preview **Activity**

What Do You Know About Steroids?

Complete this activity before you watch the video.

1. List three statements about steroids that you think are true.
2. Get together with a partner to discuss the statements you each wrote. Try to come to an agreement about whether each statement is true or false.
3. In a paragraph discuss what you learned from this activity. **WRITING**

Your Skeletal System

Objectives

▶ **Identify** the five main roles of the skeletal system.

▶ **Describe** the functions of bones and joints.

▶ **Explain** how you can keep your skeletal system healthy.

Vocabulary

- joint
- cartilage
- ossification
- marrow
- ligament
- osteoporosis
- fracture
- sprain
- dislocation
- scoliosis

Warm-Up

Quick Quiz Complete each of these statements with *always, sometimes,* or *never.*

① I __?__ warm up before exercising.

② When I ride a bicycle or play contact sports, I __?__ wear a helmet and other protective gear.

③ When I ride in a vehicle, I __?__ fasten my seat belt.

④ My backpack for school is __?__ less than 15% of my body weight.

⑤ I __?__ make an effort to exercise on a regular basis.

WRITING Why do you think that teens might not always practice these healthful behaviors?

Functions of the Skeletal System

Have you ever seen a new building under construction? Before the roof or walls can take shape, the building's frame must be built. Like a building, your body needs a frame to give it shape and support. Your body's framework is your skeletal system. **Your skeletal system has five main roles. It provides support, protects internal organs, allows your body to move, and stores and produces materials that your body needs.**

Support and Protection As you can see in Figure 1, your skeleton is made up of all the bones in your body. Your skeleton gives your body its basic shape and provides the support that you need as you move through your day. The center of your skeleton is your backbone, or vertebral column. The backbone consists of 33 bones called vertebrae (VUR tuh bray). The vertebrae support your head and give flexibility to your neck and back.

Many bones of the skeletal system protect internal organs. Your ribs and breastbone, for example, form a protective cage around your heart and lungs. Your backbone protects the spinal cord, which runs through holes in the vertebrae. The hard, thick skull protects your brain.

Movement   In coordination with your muscular and nervous systems, your skeletal system allows you to move. The range of movements can be as simple as striking a key on a keyboard, or as spectacular as pushing your body off the ground to spike a volleyball.

Storage and Production of Materials   Your bones store essential substances, such as phosphorus and calcium, which are released when other parts of the body need them. Some bones, such as the breastbone and part of the thighbone, also produce blood cells.

If you run your fingers down the center of your back, which bones can you feel?

The Skeletal System

FIGURE 1   Your skeleton provides a framework that supports and protects many other body parts.

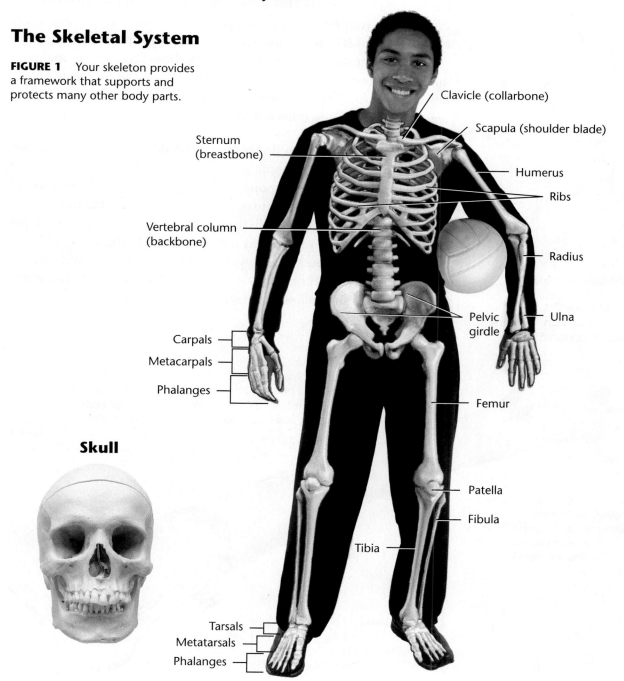

Clavicle (collarbone)

Scapula (shoulder blade)

Sternum (breastbone)

Humerus

Ribs

Vertebral column (backbone)

Radius

Pelvic girdle

Ulna

Carpals

Metacarpals

Phalanges

Femur

Skull

Patella

Fibula

Tibia

Tarsals

Metatarsals

Phalanges

GO ONLINE

PearsonSuccessNet.com
For: More on movable joints

Bones and Joints

Did you know that your skeletal system is made up of just over 200 bones? A place in your body where two or more of your bones come together is called a **joint.** Your bones and joints work together every time you move.

Development of Bones **Your bones are living structures that undergo change throughout your life.** A newborn's skeleton is made mostly of **cartilage,** a tough supportive tissue that is softer and more flexible than bone. By young adulthood, most of this cartilage is replaced by bone in a process called **ossification** (ahs uh fih KAY shun). During this process, minerals, such as calcium and phosphorus, are deposited within the developing bone, making it hard. By young adulthood, the only cartilage left in your body will be in the outer part of your ears and nose, covering the ends of some bones, and cushioning some joints.

After ossification is complete, cells in the bones continue to maintain and repair the tissue. If you were to break a bone, the cells would form new tissue to fill the gap between the broken ends. Eventually, the healed region containing new bone might be stronger than the original bone.

Structure of Bones Bones are remarkably strong, although they are light in weight. This is because bone consists of two different types of tissue—compact bone and spongy bone. Figure 2 shows the location of these tissues and other structures in the thighbone, or femur. Another type of tissue called **marrow** fills the spaces in bones. There are two types of marrow—red and yellow. Red marrow, found in the spaces of some spongy bone, produces many types of blood cells. On average, red marrow produces 100 billion blood cells every day. Yellow marrow, which can be found in the hollow centers of long bones, stores fat.

FIGURE 2 Bones are intricate living structures that contain several types of tissue. **Interpreting Diagrams** In which part of a bone is fat stored?

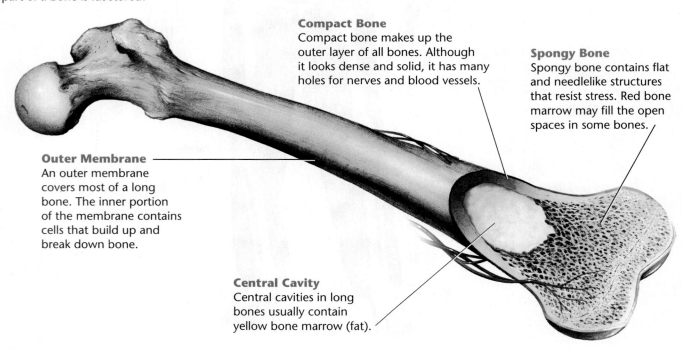

Compact Bone
Compact bone makes up the outer layer of all bones. Although it looks dense and solid, it has many holes for nerves and blood vessels.

Spongy Bone
Spongy bone contains flat and needlelike structures that resist stress. Red bone marrow may fill the open spaces in some bones.

Outer Membrane
An outer membrane covers most of a long bone. The inner portion of the membrane contains cells that build up and break down bone.

Central Cavity
Central cavities in long bones usually contain yellow bone marrow (fat).

FIGURE 3 The different kinds of joints allow you to move and position your body in a variety of ways.

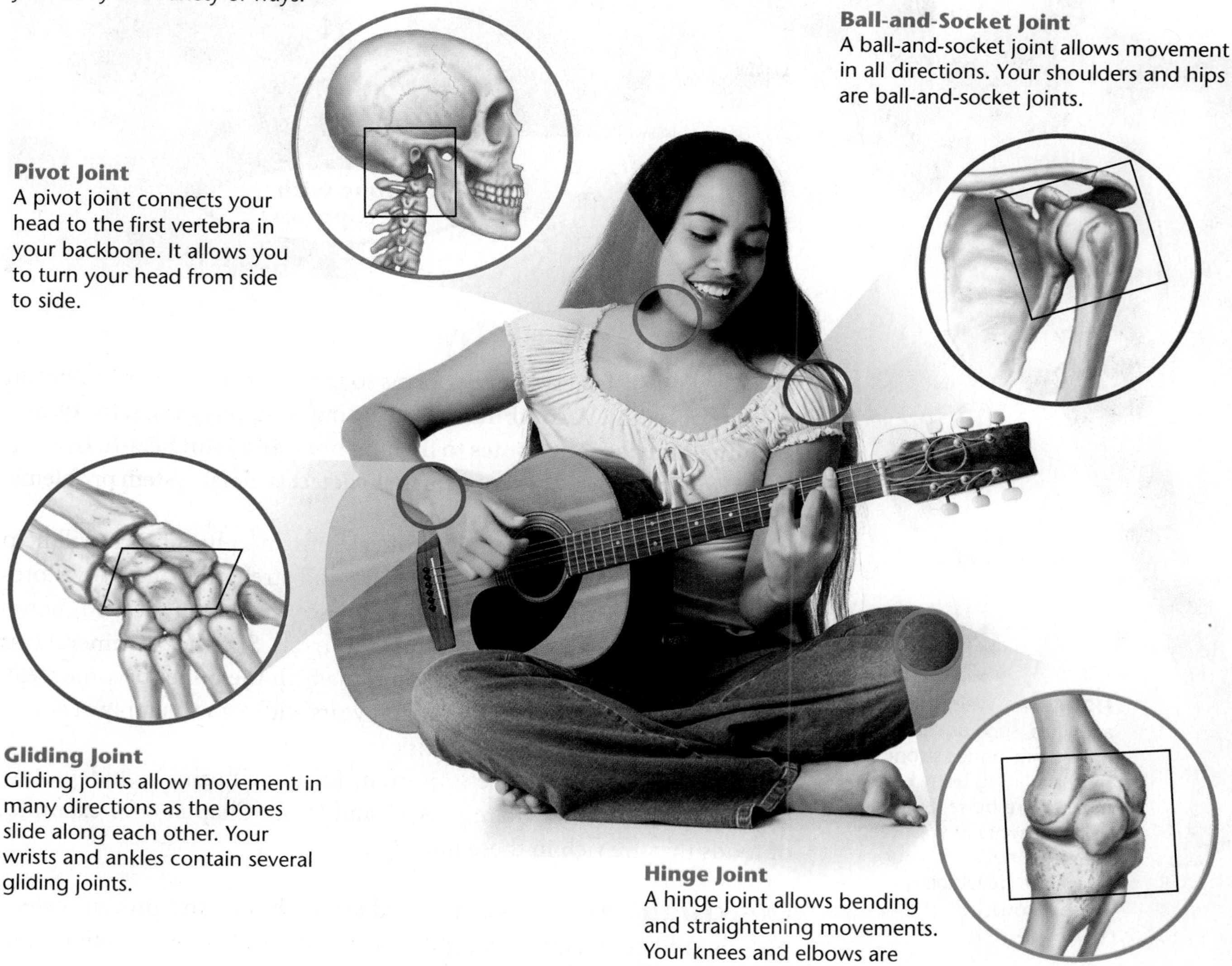

Pivot Joint
A pivot joint connects your head to the first vertebra in your backbone. It allows you to turn your head from side to side.

Ball-and-Socket Joint
A ball-and-socket joint allows movement in all directions. Your shoulders and hips are ball-and-socket joints.

Gliding Joint
Gliding joints allow movement in many directions as the bones slide along each other. Your wrists and ankles contain several gliding joints.

Hinge Joint
A hinge joint allows bending and straightening movements. Your knees and elbows are hinge joints.

Joints Without joints, your body would be like a chair with arms and legs that cannot move. **Joints allow for movement and protect bones from friction and force.** Some joints, such as those in your skull are immovable—they allow no motion. Other joints, such as those in your elbows, knees, and shoulders are movable. Four different types of movable joints are shown in Figure 3.

Bones are held together at joints by strong, fibrous bands called **ligaments.** A smooth layer of tough cartilage cushions and protects the ends of bones where they meet. Membranes around some joints secrete a fluid that lubricates the joint and reduces friction between the bones.

Connect to Your Life

What joint allows you to wave hello to a friend? What type of joint is it?

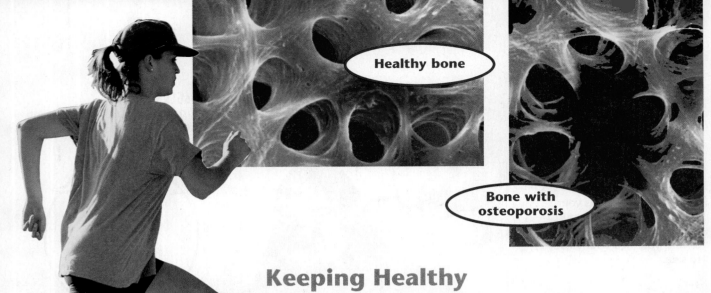

Healthy bone

Bone with osteoporosis

FIGURE 4 Weight-bearing activities, such as running, make your bones stronger by stimulating bone cells to make more bone. Building up bone mass in your teen years can decrease your chance of developing osteoporosis.

Keeping Healthy

Because your skeletal system performs so many functions, it is important to keep it healthy. **A combination of eating well, physical activity, and avoiding injuries contributes to lifelong bone and joint health. In addition, regular medical checkups can help detect skeletal system problems.**

Eating Well   Adequate intake of calcium and phosphorus will help your bones grow to their maximum size and strength. Your body stores these minerals during childhood and adolescence. As you age, your bones will begin to lose some of these stored minerals. Significant mineral loss can lead to **osteoporosis,** a condition in which the bones become weak and break easily. If you enter your adult years with a good supply of stored minerals, you can decrease your risk for osteoporosis.

Other nutrients that are important for bone health include potassium, magnesium, and vitamins A, C, and D. See Chapter 8 for examples of foods that are rich in these nutrients.

Exercising   Another way to build strong bones and prevent osteoporosis is to get plenty of weight-bearing physical activity. Activities in which the bones support the entire weight of your body help your bones grow strong and dense. Some examples of weight-bearing activities are dancing, running, racquet sports, soccer, basketball, and lacrosse.

Avoiding Bone Injuries   One common injury of the skeletal system is a **fracture,** or a break in a bone. In a simple fracture, the bone may be cracked or completely broken in two or more pieces. In a compound fracture, the broken ends of the bone pierce the skin. Fractures are treated by putting the broken ends of the bone back together. Splints or casts are used to prevent movement of the bone until the bone tissue can repair itself. In some cases, surgery is required.

You can protect your bones from fractures. When participating in a physical activity, wear appropriate safety equipment, such as helmets and pads. Always wear a seat belt when traveling in a vehicle.

Connect to Your Life

What are three weight-bearing activities that you enjoy?

Avoiding Joint Injuries As you participate in physical activities, keep in mind that your bones and joints are still developing. Some injuries can lead to permanent damage. Proper warm-up and stretching exercises are important to help prevent joint injuries.

▶ **Sprains** Most likely you or someone you know has experienced a **sprain,** an overstretched or torn ligament. Treatment for mild sprains can include ice to reduce swelling and pain relievers. Severe sprains may require a brace or surgery.

▶ **Dislocations** In a **dislocation,** the ends of the bones in a joint are forced out of their normal positions. To treat a dislocation, the bones are typically put back into their proper positions and held in place by a cast or bandage until the joint heals.

▶ **Torn Cartilage** Serious damage to the cartilage between the bones in a joint is known as torn cartilage. The knees are particularly susceptible to this injury. Surgery, such as arthroscopic surgery, is often necessary to repair or remove torn cartilage.

▶ **Overuse Injuries** When an activity is performed too often or too strenuously, joints may become irritated and inflamed. In teens, overuse injuries most commonly occur to the shoulders or knees. Teens who play the same sport year-round are susceptible to overuse injuries. Also, carrying a heavy backpack improperly may cause overuse injuries to the back and shoulders.

Medical Checkups If you experience bone or joint pain it is a good idea to see a doctor. He or she can advise you on how to prevent serious injury or recommend other professionals who can help you.

During yearly physical examinations, a nurse or doctor may check your spine for **scoliosis** (skoh lee OH sis), an abnormal curvature of the spine. Scoliosis usually develops during childhood, but it may not be detected until the teen years. Your doctor will also monitor your height and weight to make sure you are growing properly.

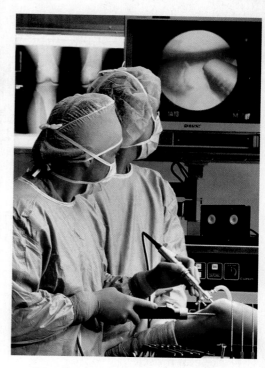

FIGURE 5 During arthroscopic surgery, doctors insert an instrument called an arthroscope into the joint. A camera attached to the arthroscope projects an image onto a monitor. Tiny instruments are then used to make repairs.

Section 1 Review

Key Ideas and Vocabulary

1. List the five main roles of the skeletal system.
2. Explain the function of bones.
3. Describe the two types of bone **marrow**.
4. What is a **joint**? Describe the function of movable joints in the body.
5. Identify four ways you can help your skeletal system stay healthy.

Health and Community

Safety Poster Create a poster aimed at young children that explains how to prevent bone, joint, and muscle injuries. With permission, display the poster in an elementary school, library, or other public place.

Critical Thinking

6. **Comparing and Contrasting** How is a newborn's skeleton different from your own?
7. **Classifying** Which type of joint allows you to kneel down? To move your arm in a circle?

Your Muscular System

Objectives

▶ **Describe** the functions of the three types of muscles.

▶ **Explain** how you can keep your muscular system healthy.

Vocabulary

- smooth muscle
- cardiac muscle
- skeletal muscle
- tendon
- muscle tone
- atrophy
- anabolic steroid
- strain
- tendonitis

Warm-Up

Myth No pain, no gain.

Fact Pain is not a sign of a good workout. Rather, pain is a signal from your body that you are working too hard or you have an injury. Continuing to exercise through the pain could lead to a more serious injury.

WRITING Where do you think most teens get their information about muscles? How factual do you think their information is?

The Muscles in Your Body

To open this book and turn its pages, you use muscles in your arms and hands. Muscles move your eyes as you read the printed words. Muscles in your chest allow you to breathe, and muscles in your heart pump your blood. Every time your body moves, muscles are at work.

Types of Muscle Your body has three types of muscle tissue that perform different functions—smooth muscle, cardiac muscle, and skeletal muscle. Some of these muscle tissues are involuntary muscle, which means they are not consciously controlled. Other muscles are voluntary muscle, which means they can be consciously controlled.

▶ **Smooth muscle** is involuntary muscle that causes movements within your body. Smooth muscles in the walls of your esophagus and intestines push food through your digestive system. Other smooth muscles in your blood vessels help circulate your blood.

▶ **Cardiac muscle** is involuntary muscle that is found only in the heart. Throughout your life, cardiac muscle allows your heart to beat and pump blood throughout your body.

▶ **Skeletal muscles** are the muscles that you control to do activities, such as walk or play a musical instrument. As the name indicates, skeletal muscles are attached to the bones of your skeleton. A thick strand of tissue called a **tendon** attaches a muscle to a bone.

 Connect to Your Life **Which type of muscle helps you move your jaw to chew your food?**

How Muscles Work   All muscles do work by contracting, or becoming shorter and thicker. Muscle cells, which are often called fibers, contract when they receive a nerve message to do so. As you can see in Figure 6, many skeletal muscles work in pairs. One muscle in the pair contracts to move the bone in one direction. Then, the other muscle in the pair contracts to move the bone back.

Muscle Tone   Even when a skeletal muscle is not contracting to cause movement, a few of its individual muscle fibers are still contracting. These contractions are not strong enough to cause movement, but they do tense and firm the muscle. This slight tension is called **muscle tone.** For example, at any given moment the muscles in your neck contract just enough to keep your head upright, even when you are not moving your head. Muscle tone also keeps your muscles healthy and ready for action. Muscles that cannot contract due to injury, or are not used often, will weaken and shrink, a condition known as **atrophy.**

FIGURE 6   Skeletal muscles are attached to bones and participate in movement. Your biceps and triceps are an example of a muscle pair. When a biceps contracts and a triceps relaxes, your arm bends. Your arm straightens when a biceps relaxes and a triceps contracts.
Relating Cause and Effect Which muscle contracts when you wrinkle your forehead?

The Muscular System

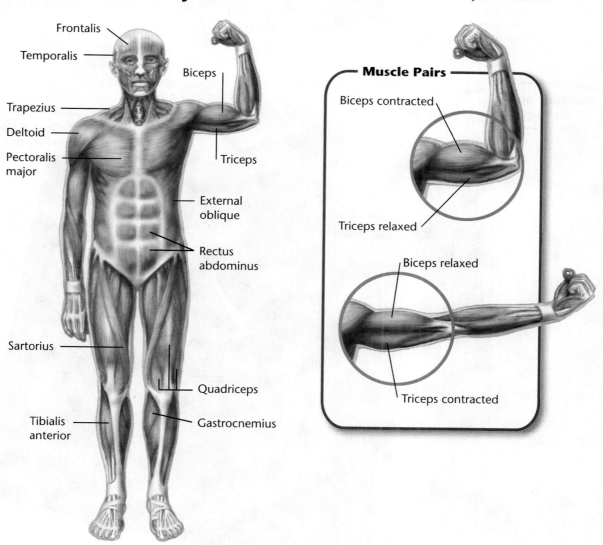

Muscle Pairs

Biceps contracted

Triceps relaxed

Biceps relaxed

Triceps contracted

Frontalis
Temporalis
Biceps
Trapezius
Deltoid
Pectoralis major
Triceps
External oblique
Rectus abdominus
Sartorius
Quadriceps
Tibialis anterior
Gastrocnemius

GO ONLINE

PearsonSuccessNet.com

For: More on keeping
muscles healthy

Keeping Healthy

Like your bones, your muscles get stronger when you use them often. But you must take care to avoid overuse and injury. **You can maintain a healthy muscular system by regularly participating in different types of exercise. To help prevent injuries, exercise sessions should include a warm-up and cool-down period.**

Working Your Muscles   Some types of exercise, such as running, increase a muscle's endurance—how long it can contract without tiring. Other exercises, such as lifting weights, make individual fibers grow, which causes the muscles to thicken and increase in strength.

To increase muscle size and strength, some athletes are tempted to use **anabolic steroids,** artificial forms of the male hormone testosterone. Doctors prescribe these drugs to treat people with certain muscle disorders. When used illegally, anabolic steroids are dangerous and can cause serious damage to many body systems. You will read more about the dangers of steroid use in Chapter 13.

 Connect to Your Life   **How many different types of exercise do you participate in?**

FIGURE 7 Muscular strength and endurance are important in sports and in everyday activities.

Building muscle strength

Building muscle endurance

Avoiding Muscle Injuries You likely have felt muscle soreness immediately after exercise or in the days that followed. Some muscle soreness is normal, but pain can be a sign of a more serious injury.

▶ **Strains** A muscle **strain,** or a pulled muscle, is a painful injury that may happen when muscles are overworked or stretched too much or too quickly. Sometimes muscle fibers rip, resulting in a torn muscle.

▶ **Tendonitis** Overuse of tendons may lead to painful swelling and irritation called **tendonitis** (ten duh NY tis). Tennis elbow, which consists of pain in the forearm, is one example of tendonitis. Excessive use of a hand-held control while playing video games can also lead to tendonitis. You should not play video games for more than one hour without taking a break.

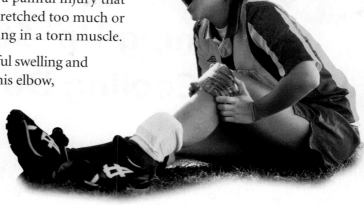

Treatment for muscle injuries usually includes rest, over-the-counter pain medication, and ice packs. If the injury is severe, surgery may be required.

Regular strengthening and stretching exercises can help you prevent injuries. Vary your exercise routine so that you are not always using the same muscles. Warm up before vigorous exercise, and include a cool-down period of mild exercise. Also, stop exercising if you feel sharp or sudden pain.

FIGURE 8 To help prevent muscle and tendon injuries, you should warm up properly and rest from exercise if you feel pain.

Preventing Muscle Cramps Have you ever felt a sudden, sharp pain in your leg or arm? If so, you may have experienced a muscle cramp, which is a strong, uncontrolled muscle contraction. To relieve a cramp, try massaging the affected area and exercising the limb gently. Stretching and drinking plenty of water before and during exercise can help you avoid muscle cramps.

Section 2 Review

Key Ideas and Vocabulary

1. Identify the three types of muscles and describe the location and function of each.
2. What is a **tendon**?
3. Explain what causes **muscle tone**. What causes the condition known as **atrophy**?
4. What can you do to prevent muscle injuries?
5. What is the cause of a muscle **strain**?

Critical Thinking

6. Evaluating Why is it an advantage that you do not have control over all of your muscles?

Health at School

Martial Arts Class Find out whether classes in martial arts such as judo, kendo, or tae kwon do are offered in your community. If so, observe a class. Then in a paragraph, describe to your classmates how the activity can help build muscular strength and endurance. **WRITING**

7. Applying Concepts Describe how a muscle pair in your thigh would work to bend and straighten your knee.

Warming Up, Stretching, and Cooling Down

Suppose that you are about to go on a ten-mile bicycle ride or play your favorite sport. These are strenuous activities that put stress on your bones, muscles, and tendons. How should you prepare your body for these activities? And after the activity, what should you do to minimize the effects of the stress your body has just experienced?

❶ Warming up

Before a workout, use slow movements to warm up the muscles that you will use. You should walk, jog slowly, or do the activity that you are about to participate in at a reduced pace. This warms up your muscles, preparing them for the more intense activity of the workout itself.

❷ Stretching

▶ Once your muscles are warmed up, stretch them. Stretching "cold" muscles is not effective and can cause injury.

▶ Although no single stretching routine is appropriate for every activity, the stretching exercises shown here provide a base for you to build on. It is important not to rush when you perform these movements. A pulled muscle can hold you up much longer than the few minutes of warming up/stretching and cooling down/stretching needed with each workout.

▶ When you perform stretching exercises, do not bounce. Bouncing can tear muscle fibers. Scar tissue can form as a result limiting how much the muscle can stretch in the future.

❸ Cooling down

After your workout, cool down by slowly moving the muscles you used at a reduced pace, much as you did to warm up. Do this for about five to ten minutes. Then stretch your muscles as you did before the work-out. This cool-down period helps ease your body back to normal levels of muscular activity.

Practice the Skill

1. After warming up, take five to ten minutes to practice these stretching exercises.

2. Each day for a week, do the stretching routine and record how you felt before and after the routine, including any soreness or stiffness. At the end of the week, evaluate the stretching routine and your reactions to it. What are its benefits?

3. Select a favorite sport or other physical activity. Ask your physical education teacher or coach to suggest an appropriate warm-up, stretching, and cool-down routine for that activity. Then perform the activity along with the routine. Record how your muscles feel before, during, and after the activity.

Lower Back Curl

Lie on your back with legs extended. Draw your knees toward your chest. Grasp your legs just below your knees and gently pull your legs into your chest. Hold for 15 seconds.

Side Stretch

Stand with feet apart, knees slightly bent, and one hand on your hip. Extend the opposite arm overhead and stretch to the side. Hold for 15 seconds. Repeat in the other direction. Do five times in each direction.

Hamstring Stretch

Sit on the floor and extend one leg, toes facing up. Tuck your other foot against your extended thigh. Reach forward over your extended leg and slide your hands down your leg until you feel a stretch. Bend from your waist, not from your neck and shoulders. Hold for 15 seconds. Switch to the other leg. Repeat with each leg twice.

Calf Stretch

Stand in a stride position with your left leg forward and hands on your hips. Lean your upper body forward. At the same time, bend your left leg and extend your right leg back in a continuous line with your upper body. Push your right heel to the ground. Hold for 15 seconds. Switch legs and repeat. Do this five times on each side.

Triceps Stretch

Raise your right arm over your head. Bend at the elbow and place the hand at the center of your back. Place your left hand on your right elbow and pull gently. Hold for 15 seconds. Repeat with other arm.

Section 3

Your Nervous System

Objectives

▶ **Explain** the functions of the nervous system and the role of neurons.

▶ **Describe** the roles of the central nervous system and the peripheral nervous system.

▶ **Identify** the most important thing you can do to keep your nervous system healthy.

Vocabulary

- neuron
- cerebrum
- cerebellum
- brain stem
- spinal cord
- reflex
- concussion
- coma
- paralysis
- meningitis
- seizure
- epilepsy

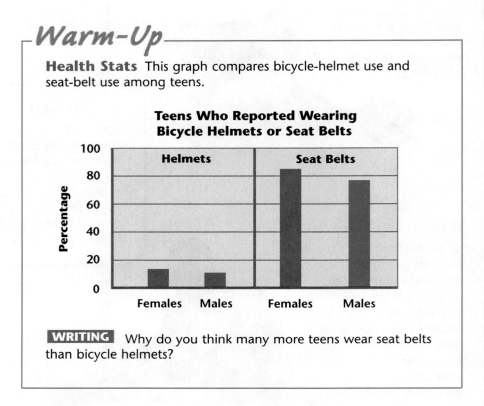

Warm-Up

Health Stats This graph compares bicycle-helmet use and seat-belt use among teens.

Teens Who Reported Wearing Bicycle Helmets or Seat Belts

WRITING Why do you think many more teens wear seat belts than bicycle helmets?

What Is the Nervous System?

Many of the actions you perform each day seem simple, but in reality, they are quite complex. For example, as you walk to class, the movement of your legs must be coordinated and your balance maintained. Also, your speed must be continually adjusted. Amazingly, your nervous system allows you to perform all of these actions while you think about your upcoming math test. **Your nervous system receives information about what is going on inside and outside of your body. Then it processes the information and forms a response to it.** These functions are accomplished with the help of the basic unit of the nervous system—a type of cell called a **neuron** (NOOR ahn).

Neuron Structure You can examine the structure of a neuron in Figure 9. **Neurons carry messages, or impulses, from one part of your body to another.** Notice that a neuron has three basic parts: dendrites, a cell body, and an axon. The junction where one neuron sends impulses to another neuron or another type of cell is called a synapse.

Types of Neurons Three types of neurons are found in your nervous system. Each type of neuron has a specific role.

▶ **Sensory Neurons** Information about your external and internal environment is gathered by sensory neurons through your sense organs or other parts of your body. For example, when your phone rings, sensory neurons carry information about the noise from your ears to your brain.

▶ **Interneurons** Located only in the brain and spinal cord, interneurons pass impulses from one neuron to another. When your phone rings, interneurons receive the messages from your sensory neurons about the ringing noise. Your brain determines that the noise is coming from your phone and you make the decision to answer it.

▶ **Motor Neurons** By command of other neurons, motor neurons send nerve impulses to muscles and glands. In the example of your ringing phone, interneurons signaled thousands of motor neurons. The motor neurons then signaled your muscles to pick up the phone.

Which type of neuron signals your eyes to move across this page?

FIGURE 9 Neurons relay impulses to other neurons, or they may send commands, in the form of chemical signals, to muscles or glands. **Interpreting Diagrams** Which part of a neuron receives impulses from another neuron?

Neuron Structure

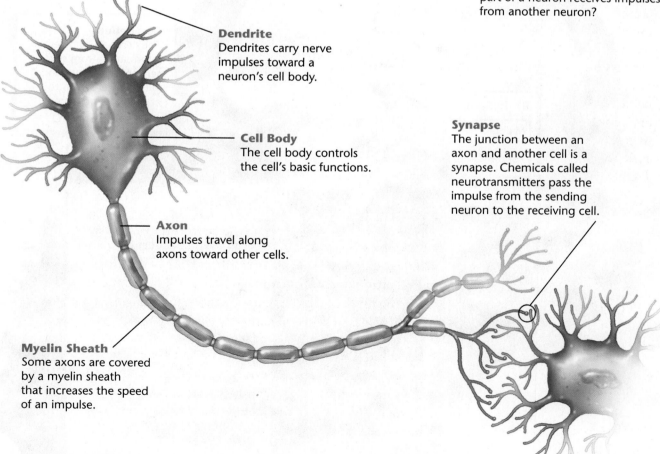

Dendrite
Dendrites carry nerve impulses toward a neuron's cell body.

Cell Body
The cell body controls the cell's basic functions.

Axon
Impulses travel along axons toward other cells.

Myelin Sheath
Some axons are covered by a myelin sheath that increases the speed of an impulse.

Synapse
The junction between an axon and another cell is a synapse. Chemicals called neurotransmitters pass the impulse from the sending neuron to the receiving cell.

Central Nervous System

The nervous system consists of two major divisions—the central nervous system and the peripheral nervous system. **The central nervous system is the control center of the body. It includes the brain and spinal cord.** The peripheral nervous system (puh RIF ur ul) includes all the other parts of the nervous system, except for the brain and spinal cord.

The Brain   The brain is a moist, spongy organ that weighs about 3 pounds. It is made up of about 100 billion neurons that control almost everything you do, feel, and remember. Within the skull, your brain is protected and cushioned by layers of membranes and fluid. The three major regions of the brain—the cerebrum, the cerebellum, and the brain stem—are shown in Figure 10.

FIGURE 10   Each of the three main regions of the brain—the cerebrum, the cerebellum, and the brain stem—carries out specific functions. **Predicting** Which region of the brain most likely controls blinking?

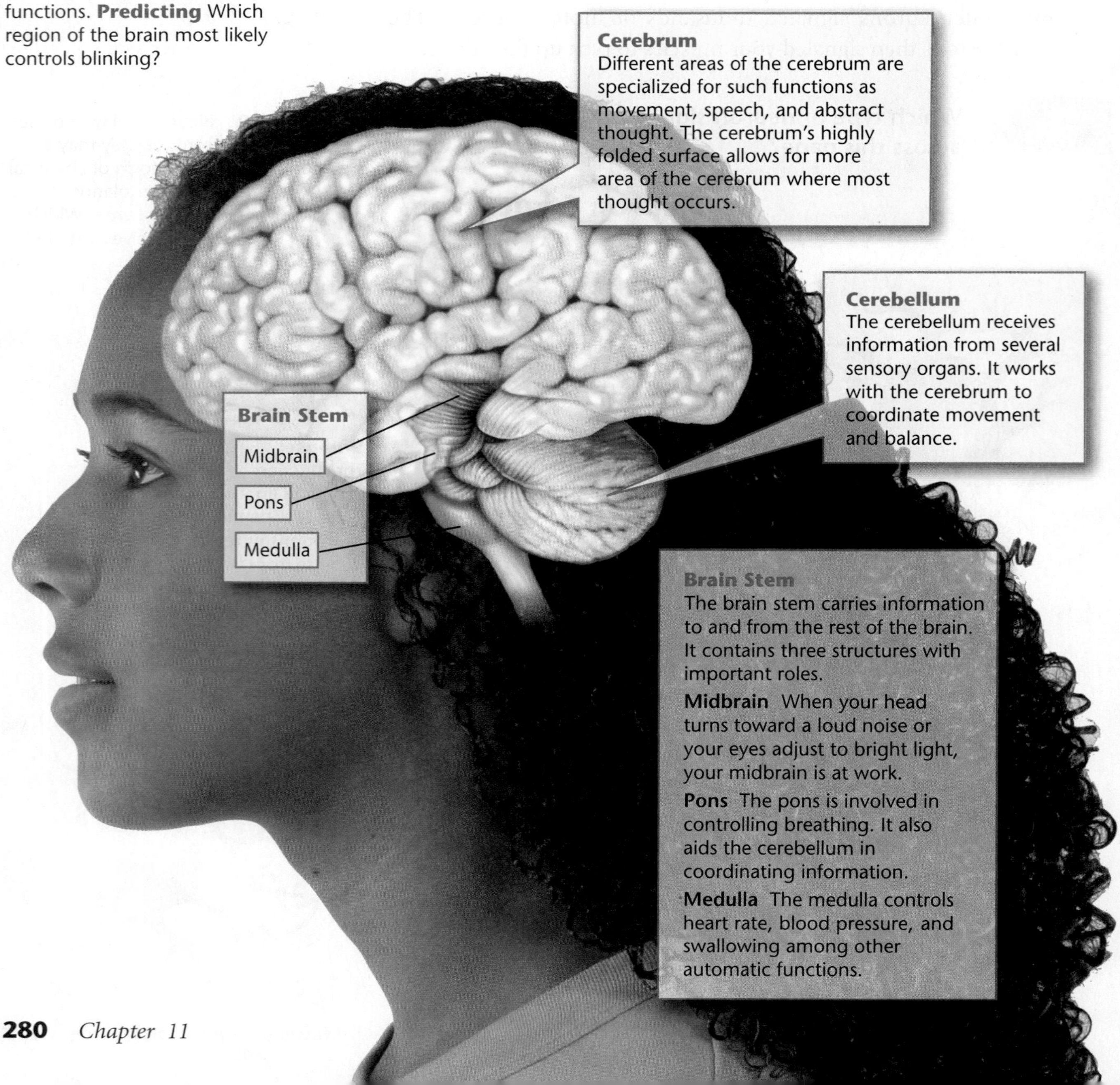

Cerebrum
Different areas of the cerebrum are specialized for such functions as movement, speech, and abstract thought. The cerebrum's highly folded surface allows for more area of the cerebrum where most thought occurs.

Cerebellum
The cerebellum receives information from several sensory organs. It works with the cerebrum to coordinate movement and balance.

Brain Stem
Midbrain
Pons
Medulla

Brain Stem
The brain stem carries information to and from the rest of the brain. It contains three structures with important roles.
Midbrain When your head turns toward a loud noise or your eyes adjust to bright light, your midbrain is at work.
Pons The pons is involved in controlling breathing. It also aids the cerebellum in coordinating information.
Medulla The medulla controls heart rate, blood pressure, and swallowing among other automatic functions.

Hands-On Activity

Mixed Messages

Test how well your brain can handle conflicting messages.

green   blue   yellow
red   green   blue
blue   yellow   green
yellow   red   red
red   green   blue

Material
watch or clock with second hand

Try This
❶ Read the list of words while your partner times how long it takes you.
❷ Notice that the words in the list are written in different colors. This time you should say the color of each word as your partner times you. Do not read the words, rather, identify their colors.

Think and Discuss
❶ Did it take you more time to read the words or say the colors? Describe the experience of saying the colors.

❷ Which part of your brain most likely works hardest during this activity? Which task is your brain better at—reading the words or identifying their colors?
❸ Once people master basic skills such as tying shoes or reading, they perform them with little thought. How do you think this fact affected your results in this activity?
❹ What do you think would happen if you asked a young child who has just learned to read to do this activity? Explain.

▶ The **cerebrum** makes up about 85 percent of the brain's weight. It consists of several specialized regions that receive messages from sense organs, and control movement, memory, communication, and reasoning. A deep groove divides the cerebrum into left and right hemispheres. The right hemisphere generally controls the muscles on the left side of your body and the left hemisphere generally controls the muscles on the right side of your body. The right hemisphere is associated with creativity and artistic ability. The left hemisphere is associated with mathematical and logical thinking.

▶ The **cerebellum** (sehr uh BEL um) coordinates your body's movements and helps you keep your balance. Without the cerebellum, simple movements, such as picking up a glass of water without spilling it, would be impossible.

▶ The **brain stem** lies between the cerebrum and the spinal cord. The brain stem consists of three structures—the midbrain, pons, and medulla. These structures control many of your body's involuntary actions, such as breathing, sneezing, and your eyes' reaction to light.

Which of the three main parts of your brain is most likely involved in yawning?

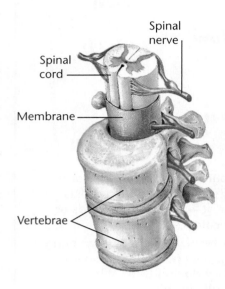

Spinal nerve

Spinal cord

Membrane

Vertebrae

The Spinal Cord

The **spinal cord** is a thick column of nerve tissue that links the brain to most of the nerves in the peripheral nervous system. The spinal cord extends from the brain down the back. As you can see in Figure 11, the vertebrae of the backbone surround and protect the spinal cord. In addition, like the brain, the spinal cord is covered with protective membranes and bathed in fluid.

Nerve impulses travel from the brain, through the spinal cord, and then out to the rest of the body via spinal nerves. In the opposite direction, impulses travel from parts of your body via spinal nerves to the spinal cord, and then to the brain. Spinal nerves are part of the peripheral nervous system.

Reflexes

What happens when you accidentally touch something hot, such as a flame? Most likely you have noticed that your hand automatically jerks away. This type of automatic response to your environment is called a **reflex.** A reflex action is shown in Figure 12.

In some reflex actions, the actions of the skeletal muscles are controlled by the spinal cord only—not the brain. These reflexes help protect your body from harm because they enable you to react very quickly. The brain receives separate signals but they take longer to arrive there. By the time the brain interprets the signals and you feel pain, the reflex action has already occurred.

A Reflex Action

FIGURE 12   Reflex actions allow you to react quickly in potentially harmful situations.

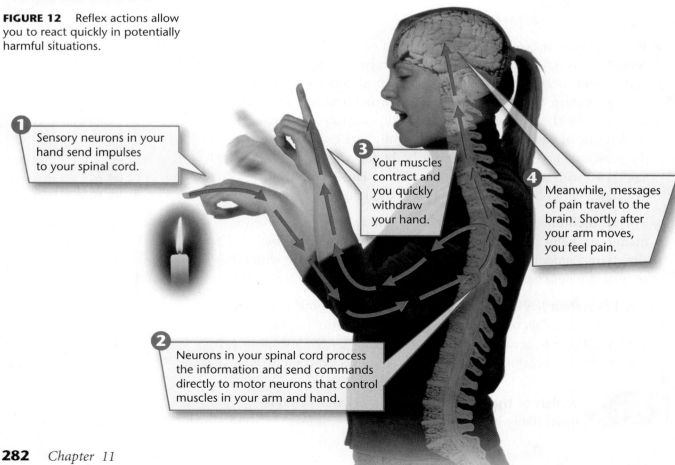

1 Sensory neurons in your hand send impulses to your spinal cord.

2 Neurons in your spinal cord process the information and send commands directly to motor neurons that control muscles in your arm and hand.

3 Your muscles contract and you quickly withdraw your hand.

4 Meanwhile, messages of pain travel to the brain. Shortly after your arm moves, you feel pain.

Peripheral Nervous System

The peripheral nervous system includes the network of nerves that links the rest of your body to your brain and spinal cord. A nerve is a bundle or bundles of axons packaged with connective tissue. Notice in Figure 13 that the nerves of the peripheral nervous system branch from the central nervous system. The peripheral nervous system carries information to the central nervous system, and then carries responses from the central nervous system to the rest of the body. Based on these two functions, the peripheral nervous system is divided into a sensory division and a motor division.

Sensory Division Some nerves in the sensory division carry information about your outside environment from your ears, eyes, and other sense organs. Other sensory nerves carry information about internal body conditions such as blood pressure and heart rate. Both sets of sensory nerves deliver this information to the central nervous system.

Motor Division Once the central nervous system has processed the information from the sensory nerves, the motor division carries the responses back to your muscles and glands. The nerves of the motor division are divided into two groups based on the functions they control.

▶ **Somatic Nervous System** Motor nerves in the somatic nervous system carry signals that control voluntary actions such as chewing food or putting on a sock. For example, these motor neurons might signal skeletal muscles in your arm to raise your hand in class.

▶ **Autonomic Nervous System** Motor nerves in the autonomic nervous system regulate actions that happen automatically. These actions include such things as your breathing rate and digestion. For example, these motor neurons might carry signals to your heart to speed it up or glands in your eyes to release tears.

 How does your brain receive information about the smell of cookies baking?

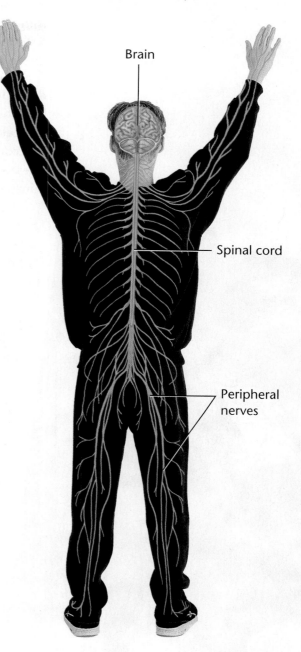

FIGURE 13 The peripheral nervous system includes all the nerves that branch out from the brain and spinal cord.

Brain

Spinal cord

Peripheral nerves

Keeping Healthy

Rest, good nutrition, and daily exercise can help keep your nervous system functioning properly. **The most important step you can take to care for your nervous system is to protect it from injury.** Because your nervous system interacts with all your body systems, damage due to trauma, disease, or drugs can have a significant impact on your health.

Avoiding Head Injuries   A severe bump to the head could cause brain tissue to hit the skull. This bruiselike injury to the brain is known as a **concussion.** Seek medical attention if, following a blow to the head, you lose consciousness, vomit, feel drowsy or confused, or your nose bleeds. These symptoms can indicate a concussion or an even more serious head injury, such as a cracked skull or bleeding within the brain.

Certain diseases or drugs that damage or kill nerve cells can also lead to impaired brain function. A severe brain injury from trauma, disease, or drugs could possibly result in a **coma,** which is a prolonged period of deep unconsciousness.

Helmets greatly lower the risk of head injuries. Wear a helmet when you play contact sports, ski or snowboard, or ride a bicycle or skateboard. Always fasten your seat belt when traveling in a vehicle. Before diving, be sure the water is deep enough and that there are no underwater hazards. Avoid drugs and alcohol. Many head injuries occur when people are under the influence of drugs and alcohol.

Avoiding Spinal Cord Injuries   Spinal cord injuries can result in **paralysis,** or the loss of the ability to move and feel some part of the body. Paralysis to the legs or to the arms and legs occurs when some nerves are so damaged that they can no longer signal the muscles they control. The extent of the paralysis is often related to the location of the spinal cord injury. Spinal cord injuries can be avoided in much the same way as head injuries—fasten your seat belt in a moving vehicle, take care when diving, and avoid drugs and alcohol.

What activities do you participate in that carry a risk of head or spinal cord injury?

FIGURE 14   In a sport such as soccer the risk of concussions is high. Teens who have had several concussions may have impaired memory and learning abilities. A doctor should decide when it is safe for a person who has had a concussion to play again.

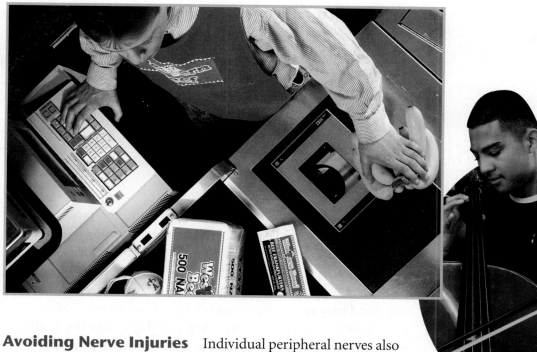

Avoiding Nerve Injuries   Individual peripheral nerves also can be injured. For example, people with jobs that include hours of cash register or keyboard use, or who play some musical instruments are prone to a nerve injury called carpal tunnel syndrome. The "carpal tunnel" is a passageway through which a nerve and many tendons travel from the forearm to the hand. Repeated movements of the wrist and fingers can cause the tendons to swell and squeeze the nerve. Other risk factors for this injury include obesity and diabetes.

Symptoms include weakness and numbness in the fingers and pain that travels from the wrist to the upper arm. Treatments include wrist splints, medications to control the swelling, or surgery. To help prevent carpal tunnel syndrome and similar nerve injuries, it is important to take breaks from repetitive motions and to maintain good posture.

FIGURE 15   Repetitive movements of the fingers and wrists can lead to a painful condition called carpal tunnel syndrome.

Preventing Infections   Nervous system infections are rare because its tissues are well protected. When infections do occur, however, they are often serious. For example, **meningitis** (men in JY tis) causes inflammation of the membranes surrounding the brain and spinal cord.

Meningitis symptoms are very similar to flu symptoms, but also include a stiff neck and severe headache. If you have not been vaccinated and have been exposed to a person with meningitis, talk to your doctor about preventive treatments. The most serious form of meningitis can be prevented with a vaccine. The vaccine is recommended for high school students and for college students living in dormitories.

A bite from an infected animal can transmit rabies, an infection of the central nervous system. Rabies is almost always fatal if not treated. Avoid contact with animals that act sick or behave strangely. If an animal bites you, seek medical attention.

 GO ONLINE
PearsonSuccessNet.com
For: More on injuries

Living With Epilepsy Under certain conditions, a person's brain may experience sudden, uncontrolled nerve impulses. This flood of brain activity can lead to a **seizure.** Anyone can experience a seizure due to an injury or a bad reaction to a medication. However, people with a disorder called **epilepsy** are prone to seizures. Epileptic seizures vary widely in type and intensity, but include facial twitching, loss of awareness, and muscle spasms. Epilepsy has many causes including genetics, problems during prenatal development, diseases, and head injuries. Medication can reduce seizures in most people with epilepsy.

Preventing Headaches The most common problem of the nervous system that people experience are headaches. Tension headaches may be brought on by physical or emotional stress. Migraine (MY grayn) headaches are especially severe, long-lasting headaches. A person with a migraine is usually sensitive to light and noise and may experience nausea and blurred vision. The cause of migraines is not clear. Some scientists think that the brains of migraine sufferers may overreact to environmental signals.

In general, proper diet, exercise, and sleep can help prevent headaches. If you can identify certain foods or odors that trigger headaches, you may be able to avoid those triggers.

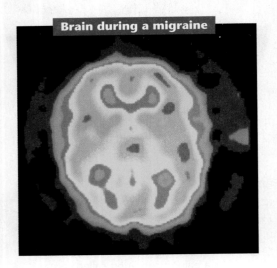

Brain during a migraine

FIGURE 16 One feature of a migraine is a change in blood flow in the brain. Researchers use imaging technology to learn more about brain activity during a migraine.

Section 3 Review

Key Ideas and Vocabulary

1. What functions does the nervous system perform?
2. What is a **neuron**? Name the three types of neurons and describe the function of each.
3. What is the role of the central nervous system? List the three main areas of the brain.
4. What is a **reflex**? How do reflexes protect the body?
5. How does the peripheral nervous system connect the central nervous system to the rest of the body?
6. Why is it so important to protect your nervous system from injury?

Health at Home

Memories Consider some of your early memories such as learning to ride a bike or a particular family vacation. Ask family members to describe their memories of the same event. In a paragraph, discuss how the memories of the same event differ from person to person. **WRITING**

Critical Thinking

7. Evaluating Suppose that after an accident, a person cannot feel or move his or her legs. What type of injury would you suspect? Explain.
8. Classifying After falling and hitting the back of her head, Lynn notices that she is having trouble catching her breath. Which part of her brain may have suffered damage in the fall?

GO ONLINE PearsonSuccessNet.com Audio Summary Section 11.3

Chapter 11
At a Glance

VIDEO **TEENS** Talk ⬤
The Risks of Steroids List three things you learned about steroids from this video.

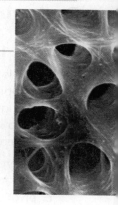

Section 1   Your Skeletal System

Key Ideas

▶ Your skeletal system provides support, protects organs, allows your body to move, and stores and produces materials that your body needs.

▶ Bones are living structures that undergo change throughout your life.

▶ Joints allow for movement and protect bones from friction and force.

▶ A combination of eating well, exercising, and avoiding injuries contributes to lifelong bone and joint health. Regular medical checkups can help detect skeletal system problems.

Vocabulary
- joint (268) • cartilage (268)
- ossification (268) • marrow (268)
- ligament (269) • osteoporosis (270) • fracture (270)
- sprain (271) • dislocation (271) • scoliosis (271)

Section 2   Your Muscular System

Key Ideas

▶ The three types of muscle tissue are smooth muscle, cardiac muscle, and skeletal muscle.

▶ You can maintain a healthy muscular system by regularly participating in different types of exercise. To help prevent injuries, exercise sessions should include a warm-up and cool-down period.

Vocabulary
- smooth muscle (272)
- cardiac muscle (272)
- skeletal muscle (272)
- tendon (272)
- muscle tone (273)
- atrophy (273)
- anabolic steroid (274)
- strain (275)
- tendonitis (275)

Section 3   Your Nervous System

Key Ideas

▶ Your nervous system receives information about what is going on inside and outside of your body. Then it processes the information and forms a response to it.

▶ Neurons carry messages, or impulses, from one part of your body to another.

▶ The central nervous system, which is made up of the brain and spinal cord, is the control center of the body.

▶ The peripheral nervous system includes the network of nerves that links the rest of your body to your brain and spinal cord.

▶ The most important step you can take to care for your nervous system is to protect it from injury.

Vocabulary
- neuron (278) • cerebrum (281)
- cerebellum (281) • brain stem (281)
- spinal cord (282) • reflex (282)
- concussion (284) • coma (284) • paralysis (284)
- meningitis (285) • seizure (286) • epilepsy (286)

Chapter 11 Review

GO ONLINE
PearsonSuccessNet.com
For: Chapter 11 review activity

Reviewing Key Ideas

Section 1

1. Where is red bone marrow found?
   a. compact bone
   b. spongy bone
   c. hollow center of bones
   d. the ends of bones

2. What type of joint allows you to turn your head?
   a. ball-and-socket   b. hinge
   c. pivot   d. gliding

3. What is ossification and when during a person's life does it occur?

4. Describe the structure of a typical bone.

5. What is the difference between a simple and a compound fracture?

6. Describe two things you can do now to help avoid osteoporosis later in life.

7. **Critical Thinking** Compare and contrast fractures and dislocations.

Section 2

8. Where is cardiac muscle found?
   a. digestive system   b. arms and legs
   c. heart   d. blood vessels

9. Which type of muscle works by shortening and thickening?
   a. smooth muscle
   b. cardiac muscle
   c. skeletal muscles
   d. all of the above

10. Explain the difference between a tendon and a ligament.

11. Why is good muscle tone important?

12. Explain the difference between muscular strength and muscular endurance.

13. **Critical Thinking** What is the difference between muscle tone and atrophy?

14. **Critical Thinking** Why could it be harmful to your muscles to suddenly start exercising intensely and for long periods of time?

Section 3

15. The part of the central nervous system that controls memory and reasoning is the
    a. cerebrum.   b. cerebellum.
    c. brain stem.   d. spinal cord.

16. What is the function of sensory neurons?

17. Describe the relationship between the central and the peripheral nervous systems.

18. **Critical Thinking** Blinking your eye whenever something touches your eyelashes is a reflex action. Explain the protective funtion of this reflex.

Building Health Skills

19. **Making Decisions** At swim practice, you hit your head while attempting a flip turn. Later that day, you feel nauseated and a little confused. If you go to a doctor, you will miss an important swim meet. In a paragraph, describe how you will make your decision. **WRITING**

20. **Communicating** Your friend is supposed to wear a brace to help correct her scoliosis. She wears it at home, but takes it off at school because she is embarrassed. Write an email to convince her she should wear her brace. **WRITING**

21. **Setting Goals** Track the amount of calcium you consume each day over a three-day period. List each food item you eat and use food labels to identify the amount of calcium in each food. Then develop and follow a plan to consume 1,300 mg of calcium a day for one week. At the end of the week evaluate how you did. **WRITING**

Health and Community

Rehabilitation Center Visit Volunteer at a local rehabilitation center for people with skeletal or nervous system injuries. Duties could include helping at mealtime, greeting patients and visitors, and assisting at special events. Write an editorial describing your experience. **WRITING**

Standardized Test Prep

Math Practice

The graph shows the average amount of bone mass in men and women through most of the life span. Use the graph to answer Questions 22–24.

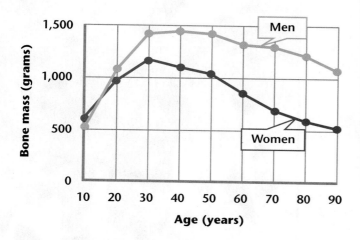

22. Between which ages do both men and women gain bone mass at the highest rate?
    - A 10–20 years
    - B 20–30 years
    - C 30–40 years
    - D 50–60 years

23. At what age does bone mass reach its peak in women?
    - F age 20
    - G age 30
    - H age 40
    - J age 50

24. Which conclusion *cannot* be drawn from this graph?
    - A As men age, they lose less bone mass than women do.
    - B During adolescence and early adulthood, women accumulate less bone mass than men do.
    - C Men accumulate more bone mass because they consume more calcium.
    - D Bone mass does not change much in men from 30 to 40 years of age.

Reading and Writing Practice

Read the passage. Then answer Questions 25–28.

Why are people apt to recall false memories? In a study, subjects were read lists of related words such as candy, cake, sugar, and taste. Later, they were shown written lists that contained these words and other similar words, such as sweet and sticky. Often, the subjects claimed that the similar words had been read aloud to them. Tests of their brain activity during the study revealed that the brain's memory center may prompt people to find memories that aren't really there, but are similar to ones that are.

25. In this study, what were the scientists studying?
    - A where people store memories
    - B how long certain memories can be stored
    - C factors that affect memory loss
    - D how the brain recalls memories

26. Which of the following words would the subjects most likely have falsely recalled?
    - F sour
    - G fork
    - H frosting
    - J table

27. According to the passage, which of these statements is true?
    - A Human memory is flawless.
    - B People are apt to remember what they see more than what they hear.
    - C When processing information, the brain searches for similar experiences.
    - D The brain cannot categorize information.

Constructed Response

28. In a paragraph, summarize what scientists learned about memory from this study.

> ### Test-Taking Tip
>
> When you take a test, remember to change your body position now and then. Otherwise, neck or back cramps might distract you from the test.

Cardiovascular and Respiratory Health

1 Your Cardiovascular System

2 Cardiovascular Health
- **MediaWise** Fast Foods and In-Store Ads

 Building Health Skills
- **Practicing Healthful Behaviors** Improving Your Cardiorespiratory Fitness

3 Respiratory Health

GO ONLINE PearsonSuccessNet.com

VIDEO 12

TEENS Talk

Living With Asthma

Preview **Activity**

What Is It Like To Live With Asthma?

Complete this activity before you watch the video.

1. Complete the following sentences.
  a. Having asthma means ___?___.
  b. People have asthma attacks when ___?___.
  c. I think an asthma attack feels like ___?___.
2. Get together with a partner to compare how you completed each of the sentences.
3. In a paragraph, discuss what you learned from this activity.
  WRITING

Your Cardiovascular System

Objectives

▶ **Describe** the main functions of the cardiovascular system.

▶ **Trace** the pathway of blood through the heart.

▶ **Identify** three types of blood vessels and the four components of blood.

Vocabulary

- atrium
- ventricle
- pacemaker
- artery
- capillary
- vein
- blood pressure
- hypertension
- plasma
- red blood cell
- white blood cell
- platelet

Warm-Up

Myth Blood is blue in color when it is not carrying oxygen.

Fact Blood is bright red when it is carrying oxygen and dark red when it is not. Veins appear blue in some people because of the way light reflects from their skin.

WRITING What other knowledge about the cardiovascular system do you hope to gain from this chapter?

Functions of the Cardiovascular System

Whenever you feel the thumping of your heart or the steady pulse in your wrist, you are experiencing your cardiovascular system in action. Your cardiovascular system, or the circulatory system, consists of your heart, blood vessels, and blood. **The main functions of the cardiovascular system include delivering materials to cells and carrying wastes away. In addition, blood contains cells that fight disease.**

Delivering Materials Your heart continually pumps the blood in your blood vessels throughout your body. Many substances that your body needs dissolve in the blood. For example, blood picks up glucose from your digestive system and brings it to cells where it is used for energy.

Removing Wastes Your cardiovascular system also transports wastes from your cells. For example, when your cells break down glucose for energy, carbon dioxide is released as a waste product. Your blood picks up carbon dioxide and transports it to the lungs, where it is exhaled.

Fighting Disease Your blood contains cells that attack microorganisms that cause disease. It also contains substances that seal cuts, preventing blood loss and the entry of microorganisms.

Connect to Your Life Why do you think you breathe harder when you exercise?

The Heart

Your cardiovascular system contains a network of blood vessels with two major loops. The first loop leads from your heart to your lungs, where the blood releases carbon dioxide, picks up oxygen, and then returns to your heart. The second loop circles through to the rest of your body, where the blood delivers oxygen and nutrients and picks up wastes. The two loops cross paths at your heart. Each time the heart beats, strong cardiac muscles push blood through the blood vessels.

Structure of the Heart   Figure 1 shows the structure of the heart. Notice that the heart has a right side and a left side, separated by a thick wall. Each side has two chambers: an upper chamber called an **atrium** (plural, *atria*) and a lower chamber, or **ventricle.** **The atria receive blood entering the heart. Blood flows from the atria to the ventricles, which pump blood out of the heart.** Between each atrium and ventricle, and between each ventricle and large blood vessel, is a flap of tissue called a valve. The valves allow blood to flow in only one direction.

FIGURE 1   Your heart is about the size of your fist. Blood travels from the right side of your heart to your lungs. The blood then returns to your heart's left side and is pumped throughout the body.
Interpreting Diagrams Which heart chamber receives blood from the lungs?

The Heart

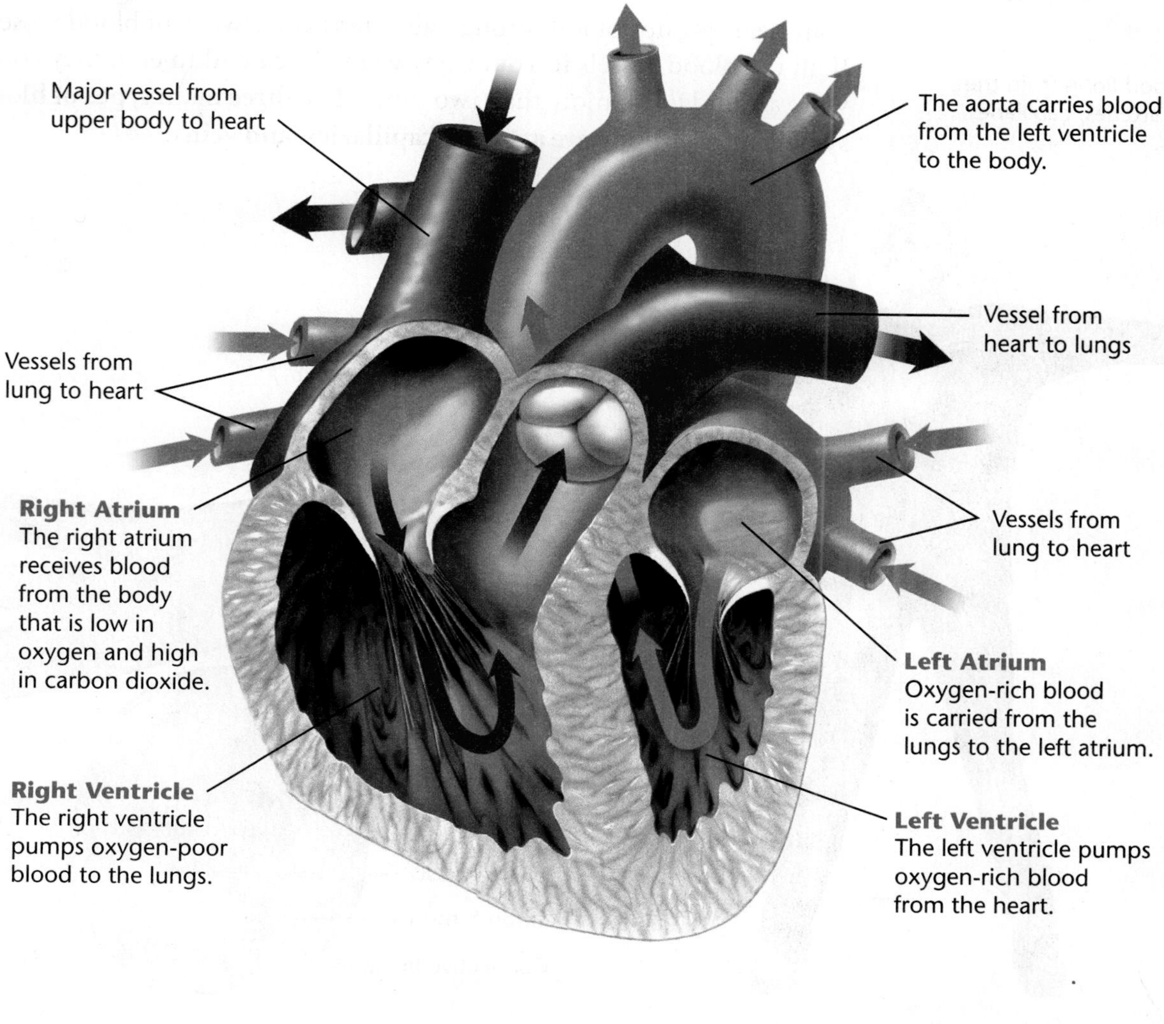

Major vessel from upper body to heart

The aorta carries blood from the left ventricle to the body.

Vessel from heart to lungs

Vessels from lung to heart

Vessels from lung to heart

Right Atrium
The right atrium receives blood from the body that is low in oxygen and high in carbon dioxide.

Left Atrium
Oxygen-rich blood is carried from the lungs to the left atrium.

Right Ventricle
The right ventricle pumps oxygen-poor blood to the lungs.

Left Ventricle
The left ventricle pumps oxygen-rich blood from the heart.

GO ONLINE

PearsonSuccessNet.com
For: More on the heart

Your Heartbeat   The action of the heart has two main phases. In the first phase, the heart relaxes and the atria fill with blood. In the second phase, the heart contracts and pumps blood. First the atria contract, pumping blood into the ventricles. Then the ventricles contract, pumping blood into the large blood vessels going toward the lungs or toward the rest of the body. The familiar *lub-dub* sound of a heartbeat occurs during the pumping phase. As the valves between the atria and ventricles close, the *lub* sound is made. The *dub* sound is heard when the valves between the ventricles and large blood vessels close.

The rate at which your heart muscles contract is regulated by the **pacemaker,** a small group of cells in the wall of the right atrium. The pacemaker receives messages from your brain to increase or decrease your heart rate.

Average heart rate varies from one person to the next and from one situation to the next. Your heart most likely beats about 70 to 80 times per minute when you are inactive. When you exercise, your heart speeds up in response to the body's need for more oxygen and nutrients and to remove excess carbon dioxide.

Blood Vessels

Your heart pumps blood through an extensive network of blood vessels. If all the blood vessels in your body were placed end to end, they could wrap around Earth more than two times. **The three main types of blood vessels in your body are arteries, capillaries, and veins.**

FIGURE 2   Blood flows from the heart through arteries, capillaries, and then veins.

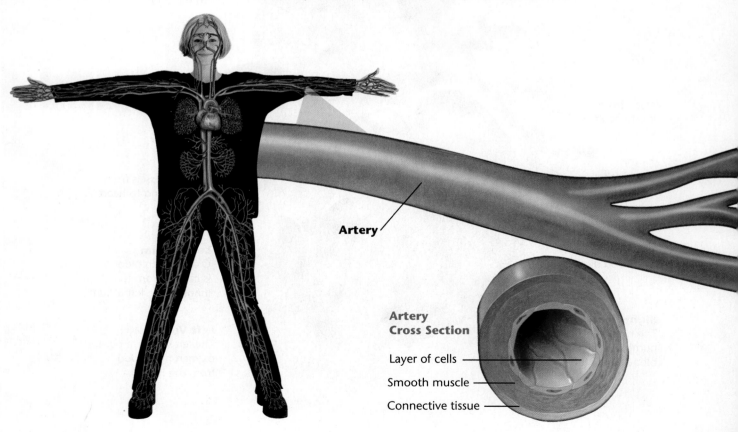

Artery

Artery
Cross Section

Layer of cells

Smooth muscle

Connective tissue

Arteries Blood vessels that carry blood away from the heart are called **arteries.** Most arteries carry oxygen-rich blood. The exceptions are the arteries that carry oxygen-poor blood from the heart to the lungs.

The largest artery in the body is the aorta (ay AWR tuh). Blood leaves the left ventricle through the aorta, which branches into many smaller arteries that carry blood to your organs, muscles, and bones.

As you can see in Figure 2, arteries have thick walls that are both strong and flexible. When your ventricles contract, blood surges through your arteries, causing their elastic walls to expand and then relax. The pulse you feel in your wrist occurs when an artery expands.

Capillaries Branching from the smallest arteries are **capillaries,** the smallest blood vessels in your body. As blood flows through the capillaries, oxygen and dissolved nutrients diffuse through the capillary walls and into your body's cells. At the same time, wastes from body cells, such as carbon dioxide, diffuse into the blood. Capillaries also are involved in temperature regulation. When you are cold, the capillaries near the surface of your skin narrow and keep heat in your body. When you are warm, they expand and allow excess heat to escape your body.

Veins From the capillaries, blood flows into small blood vessels that join together to form veins. **Veins** are large, thin-walled blood vessels that carry blood to the heart. By the time blood reaches veins, the pumping force of the heart has little effect. Skeletal muscle contractions help to squeeze blood back toward the heart. Valves inside the veins prevent blood from flowing backward.

Connect to Your Life Locate the pulse in your wrist. How many times does your pulse beat in one minute?

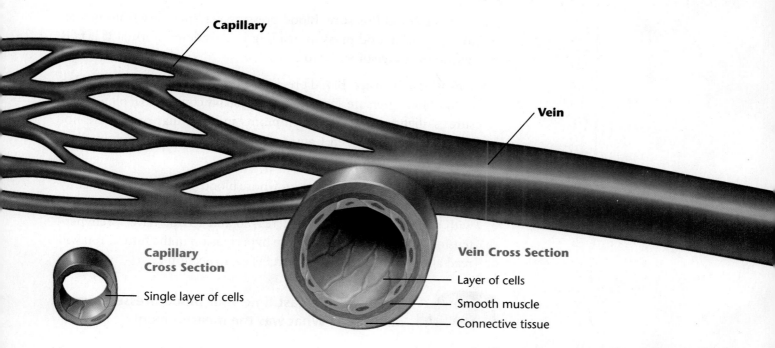

Capillary

Vein

Capillary Cross Section

Single layer of cells

Vein Cross Section

Layer of cells

Smooth muscle

Connective tissue

Blood Pressure Readings

Reading (in millimeters of mercury)	Condition
Less than 90/60	Low blood pressure
90/60 to 119/79	Normal
120/80 to 139/89	Prehypertension
140/90 or greater	Hypertension

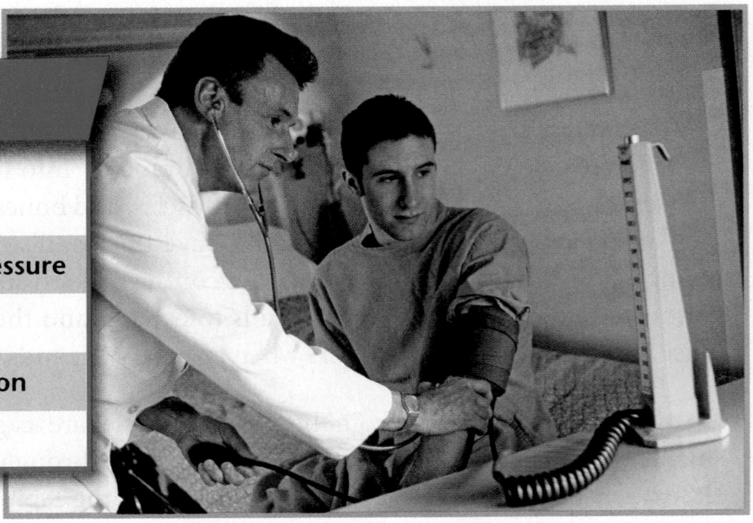

FIGURE 3 Blood pressure varies from person to person. Factors such as age, weight, fitness, and mood affect blood pressure.

Measuring Blood Pressure Visits to a doctor usually include having your blood pressure measured. **Blood pressure** is the force with which blood pushes against the walls of your blood vessels.

Figure 3 shows a sphygmomanometer (sfig moh muh NAHM uh tur), an instrument used to measure blood pressure. The healthcare provider pumps air into the cuff around the patient's upper arm until a large artery presses closed. As air is released from the cuff, the provider listens for the sound of flowing blood and records the reading from the sphygmomanometer. This first reading represents the *systolic pressure*—the pressure caused when the heart's ventricles contract. When the sound stops, the provider records the second reading. This second reading is the *diastolic pressure*—the pressure when the ventricles are relaxed.

Blood pressure readings are recorded as the systolic pressure over the diastolic pressure. For example, a person with a reading of 120/80 has a systolic pressure of 120 and a diastolic pressure of 80.

▶ **Normal Blood Pressure** Blood pressure readings vary from person to person. A blood pressure reading is considered normal if it falls within the range of 90/60 to 119/79.

▶ **Low Blood Pressure** Blood pressure lower than 90/60 is considered to be low blood pressure. Doctors are not usually concerned if blood pressure is slightly low, unless symptoms indicate that organs are not receiving enough oxygen. Causes of low blood pressure include medications, dehydration, and allergic reactions.

▶ **High Blood Pressure** A person whose blood pressure is consistently 140/90 or greater has high blood pressure, or **hypertension.** People with a blood pressure between 120/80 and 139/89 have "prehypertension," and are likely to develop hypertension in the future. You will read about the dangers of hypertension in Section 2.

When was the last time your blood pressure was measured? What was the measurement?

Blood

The average adult has about 4 to 6 quarts of blood circulating through his or her blood vessels. Blood is a complex tissue that consists of cells and cell pieces in a watery solution. **The four components of blood are plasma, red blood cells, white blood cells, and platelets.**

Plasma   The liquid component of the blood is called plasma. This straw-colored liquid makes up about 55 percent of the blood. Plasma is mostly water, with substances such as nutrients, hormones, and salts dissolved in it. These substances are necessary for many processes that occur in cells. Plasma also carries waste products such as urea to the kidneys for removal from the body.

Red Blood Cells   The cells that carry oxygen from the lungs to all the parts of your body are red blood cells. Red blood cells contain hemoglobin, which is an iron-containing substance to which oxygen binds. The reaction between oxygen and the iron in hemoglobin gives blood its bright red color. Once oxygen has diffused to tissues, blood becomes a dull red.

White Blood Cells   Your body's white blood cells help protect you against diseases and foreign substances. They are larger than red blood cells, but far less numerous. There are several kinds of white blood cells. Some white blood cells make chemicals that help your body resist diseases such as cancer. Others destroy invading microorganisms by surrounding and consuming them.

Platelets   Platelets (PLAYT lits) are cell fragments that play an important role in the blood clotting process. When you get a cut, platelets stick to the edges of the cut and release proteins called clotting factors. Clotting factors and other plasma proteins form a net of fibers across the cut. The fibers trap more platelets and blood cells until a plug forms to seal the cut. When the plug dries, it forms a scab.

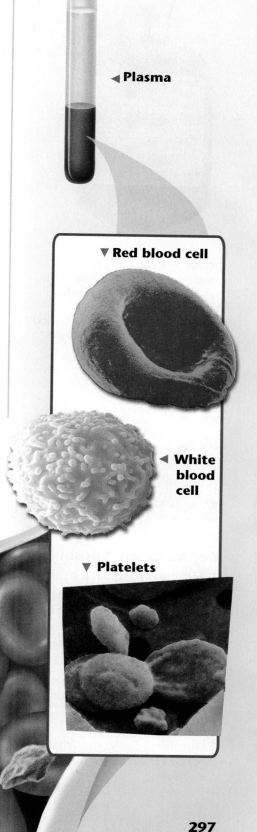

FIGURE 4   Blood consists of liquid plasma, red blood cells, white blood cells, and platelets.

◄ **Plasma**

▼ **Red blood cell**

◄ **White blood cell**

▼ **Platelets**

Safe Blood Transfusions

If You Have Blood Type	A	B	AB	O
You Can Receive Blood Type(s)	A and O	B and O	A, B, AB, and O	O

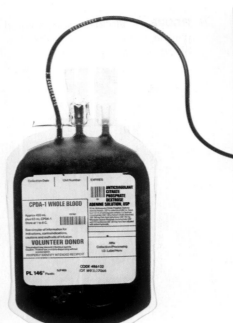

FIGURE 5 If you ever need a transfusion, your blood type will be checked to make sure you receive the correct blood.

Reading Tables If you have blood type A, what blood type(s) could you safely receive?

Blood Types   A person's blood type is determined by the proteins present on the surface of the red blood cells. Depending on which proteins are present, a person's blood type can be type A, B, AB, or O.

A second blood type is determined by the presence or absence of the Rh factor protein. If your red blood cells have the Rh factor, your blood is said to be Rh positive. If your red blood cells lack the Rh factor, your blood is Rh negative. About 85 percent of people are Rh positive.

Transfusions   After an injury, surgery, or some illnesses, a person may require a blood transfusion. During a transfusion, blood from a donor is transferred to the patient's bloodstream. Donated blood is tested to identify the blood type. It is also screened for the presence of some microorganisms such as those that cause hepatitis or AIDS.

Why is blood type important? If a patient is given the wrong blood type during a transfusion, the blood will clump together in the patient's blood vessels. This is a life-threatening reaction. Figure 5 shows which blood types can be given safely during a transfusion.

Section 1 Review

Key Ideas and Vocabulary

1. List the three main functions of the cardiovascular system.

2. Describe the pathway of blood through your heart starting at the right **atrium.**

3. List the three types of blood vessels in the order in which they receive blood from the heart.

4. Name the four components of blood and their role in the body.

Critical Thinking

5. Applying Concepts What is the function of a closed heart valve?

Health and Community

Blood Drive Contact your local chapter of the American Red Cross to find out about upcoming blood drives in your community. With their guidance, prepare a fact sheet describing the requirements for and the importance of donating blood. Get permission to display the fact sheet and a list of local blood drives in a community building or your school.

6. Predicting How might low levels of iron affect the blood's ability to transport oxygen?

7. Evaluating Why are people with blood type O called "universal donors"? Why are people with blood type AB called "universal recipients"?

Cardiovascular Health

Objectives

► **Identify** two factors that contribute to cardiovascular disease.

► **Describe** behaviors that can reduce your risk of cardiovascular disease.

Vocabulary

• low-density lipoprotein
• plaque
• atherosclerosis
• high-density lipoprotein
• arrhythmia

Warm-Up

Quick Quiz Only one of the following statements is true. Which statement do you think it is?

1. Heart attacks and strokes can't be prevented.

2. Teens do not need to be concerned about cardiovascular disease.

3. Smokers are more likely to have a heart attack than are nonsmokers.

4. To be healthy, you need to exercise intensely every day.

5. You do not need to be concerned about what you eat if you exercise regularly.

WRITING Explain why you gave the answer that you did.

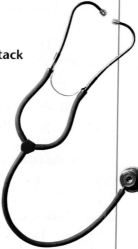

Cardiovascular Diseases

Cardiovascular diseases are the leading causes of death in the United States. These diseases develop over many decades, often without symptoms. **Hypertension and high blood cholesterol are two factors that increase your risk of heart attack and stroke. Both factors may begin in your teens.**

Hypertension   As you read in Section 1, a person whose blood pressure is consistently 140/90 or greater has hypertension. Hypertension damages blood vessel walls due to the increased force of the blood. Also, the heart must work extra hard to pump blood through the body. The heart muscle may weaken and eventually fail to pump blood adequately.

Hypertension is known as the "silent killer" because most people have no symptoms. The only way to know if your blood pressure is high is to have it measured. Hypertension can sometimes be controlled with weight loss, exercise, and a low-sodium diet. In many cases, medication is necessary.

Connect to Your Life   **Do any members of your family have high blood pressure? How do they control it?**

Blood Cholesterol Your body produces cholesterol to be used as a component of cells, hormones, and nerve tissue. You take in additional cholesterol when you eat animal products. Cholesterol is transported in your blood by carriers known as lipoproteins.

▶ **Low-density lipoproteins** (LDL) carry cholesterol to body tissues for use or storage. LDL is called "bad cholesterol" because it may become a component of **plaque,** a substance that builds up in artery walls. If the level of LDL cholesterol in your blood is continually high, you could develop atherosclerosis (ath uh roh skluh ROH sis). **Atherosclerosis** is a condition in which an artery wall hardens and thickens due to plaque buildup. Figure 6 gives you tips on how you can reduce your risk of atherosclerosis.

▶ **High-density lipoproteins** (HDL) pick up excess cholesterol from body tissues and artery walls and carry it to the liver. HDL is called "good cholesterol" because it cleans your arteries of excess cholesterol. The liver excretes the excess cholesterol in bile, which is eventually eliminated from the body. If your HDL levels are low, you could be at increased risk for atherosclerosis.

Your LDL level should be lower than 129 mg/dL (milligrams per deciliter of blood). Your HDL cholesterol level should be 40 mg/dL or higher.

Heart Attack and Stroke Why is it so important to reduce your risk of atherosclerosis? As artery walls thicken, blood flow is constricted. Eventually, some cells may not receive adequate oxygen or a blood clot could block the narrowed artery. If the artery carries blood to your heart muscles, a heart attack may result. If the artery carries blood to your brain, a stroke may result. In Chapter 23 you will learn more about heart attacks and strokes.

FIGURE 6 Your diet affects your blood cholesterol levels. Foods that are rich in fiber, certain vitamins, and monounsaturated fats may help prevent atherosclerosis.

To Prevent Atherosclerosis
- Choose fruits, vegetables, nuts, fish, and grains.
- Limit red meats, fried foods, and whole milk products.

Media Wise

Fast Foods and In-Store Ads

Have you ever entered a fast food restaurant intending to order something healthy or to eat light? Once inside, though, did you change your mind? These questions can help you understand how restaurants influence your food choices.

Do photos of tempting foods entice you to order them? **Yes** **No**

Is it difficult to find nutrition information about the foods? **Yes** **No**

Does the restaurant offer large servings at "bargain" prices? **Yes** **No**

Are there more high-fat foods and high-sugar options than healthy foods? **Yes** **No**

Does the person taking your order suggest additional foods for you to try? **Yes** **No**

"Yes" answers reveal some of the techniques restaurants use to get you to order different foods or more food than you originally planned.

Activity On the Internet, look for nutrition information for the fast food restaurants you visit. Record the information about foods you commonly order. Keep the information in your backpack or another place where you can easily access it.

Other Cardiovascular Disorders Structural problems in the heart may also prevent it from functioning properly. Some of these problems are present at birth, whereas others develop over time.

▶ **Heart Murmur** Almost half of all children are diagnosed with a heart murmur. The "murmur" is an extra sound, in addition to the lub-dub, a doctor hears when listening to a heartbeat. Often murmurs disappear over time without treatment. Occasionally, a murmur is a sign of a problem in the heart, such as a valve not closing properly.

▶ **Opening in Heart Wall** Before birth, all babies have a hole in the wall separating the two atria. If the hole does not seal after birth, oxygen-rich and oxygen-poor blood will mix in the heart, reducing its efficiency. Some people may live their entire lives with such a hole and never know it. Others may have complications and require surgery to close it.

▶ **Arrhythmia** Have you ever felt a strange fluttering in your chest? If so, you may have experienced an **arrhythmia,** or irregular heartbeat. It is normal to experience this from time to time. However, some arrhythmias are signs of serious heart conditions, such as the inability of the pacemaker to regulate the heartbeat.

GO ONLINE

PearsonSuccessNet.com
For: More on preventing heart disease

Keeping Healthy

Although few young people have heart attacks or strokes, signs of atherosclerosis can be seen in people in their late teens. And cases of teens with hypertension and high cholesterol are on the rise.

What is your risk for cardiovascular disease? One risk factor that you cannot control is heredity. Heredity plays a significant factor in the amount of LDL and HDL cholesterol your body produces. Having a family history of heart disease also puts you at higher risk for cardiovascular disease. But, many risk factors are within your control. Establishing healthy habits now will decrease your risk of serious health problems in the future. **To help maintain cardiovascular health, you should exercise regularly; eat a nutrient-rich, balanced diet; and avoid smoking.**

Exercise Teens should spend 60 minutes performing physical activity every day, or at least most days. Regular exercise has many benefits for your cardiovascular system.

▶ Heart muscles strengthen, allowing more blood to be pumped with each beat.

▶ Blood pressure may decrease.

▶ HDL levels may increase.

▶ Stress levels may lower.

Everyday activities can also help keep your cardiovascular system healthy. Anytime you walk to a friend's house instead of getting a ride, take the stairs instead of the escalator, or turn off a video game and take out the trash, you are contributing to your 60 minutes of physical activity.

 How many minutes of physical activity have you performed today?

FIGURE 7 With a little planning, you can achieve 60 minutes of physical activity a day.
Evaluating What three activities would you add to this list?

Ways to Be Active

▶ Walk the dog.
▶ Ride your bike to school.
▶ Rake the lawn.
▶ Sweep the sidewalk.
▶ Jump rope during TV commercials.
▶ Walk briskly around the mall.

Healthy Food Swaps

Instead of...	Try...
Mayonnaise	Mustard or low-fat mayonnaise
Whole milk	Low-fat or skim milk
Ice cream	Frozen yogurt
Cookies	Fruit
Hamburgers	Turkey burgers

FIGURE 8 Cardiovascular disease can start to develop during your teen years. Now is the time to begin heart-healthy eating habits.

Diet   No matter how much you exercise, you still need to pay attention to what and how much you eat. To reduce your risk of cardiovascular disease, limit your intake of fried or processed foods and of foods made from animal products. The cholesterol, saturated fat, and trans fat in these foods increase the levels of LDL in your blood. Eating high-fiber foods such as oatmeal, beans, fresh fruits, and fresh vegetables may help keep your blood cholesterol levels low. Also, limiting your salt intake may help to keep your blood pressure in a normal range.

Avoid Smoking   Tobacco products damage blood vessels and contribute to the development of atherosclerosis and hypertension. Some of the cardiovascular damage heals in the years after a smoker quits. However, your chances of living a long and healthy life are better if you never start smoking. In fact, smokers are two to three times more likely to have a heart attack than nonsmokers.

Section 2 Review

Key Ideas and Vocabulary

1. What are two factors that contribute to cardiovascular disease that may begin in your teens?
2. What is **low-density lipoprotein?** What is **high-density lipoprotein?**
3. What is one symptom of an **arrhythmia?**
4. Describe three ways you can help keep your cardiovascular system healthy.

Critical Thinking

5. Relating Cause and Effect How can atherosclerosis and hypertension affect the heart and brain?

Health at Home

Monitoring Saturated Fat Intake For one week, read food labels to track how much saturated fat you consume each day. Remember to keep track of snacks as well as meals. Less than 10 percent of your total calories should come from saturated fats. In a paragraph, discuss ways you can reduce your saturated fat intake. **WRITING**

6. Predicting Why do you think cardiovascular diseases are more common in the United States than in some other countries?

Improving Your Cardiorespiratory Fitness

How can you improve your cardiorespiratory fitness—the ability of your heart, blood vessels, and lungs to deliver nutrients and oxygen to your muscles? When you are active, your heart and lungs must be able to supply your body with the oxygen it needs. In fact, when you exercise, your heart needs to pump up to five times more blood each minute than when you are resting. Here is a simple test for assessing your cardiorespiratory fitness and guidelines for improving it. *CAUTION: Before you do this test or start an exercise program, have a physical exam to make sure you are healthy enough for vigorous exercise. Do not attempt this test if you are ill or if you have a history of health problems.*

① **Test your cardiorespiratory fitness.**

▶ To prepare for the test, do the warm-up and stretching exercises described on pages 276–277.

▶ Run or walk for one mile as fast as you can. You can alternate running with walking. A partner should time how long it takes you.

▶ Compare your time to the times listed in the table. For an average fitness level, your time should be less than those listed in the table.

Mile Walk/Run Times (min)

Age	Females	Males
14	10:30	7:45
15–18	10:30	7:30

➋ Calculate your target heart rate.

How will you know if you are exercising hard enough to improve your cardiorespiratory health, but not too hard? Your target heart rate is the heart rate you should maintain during exercise to improve your fitness. Follow these steps to calculate your target heart rate.

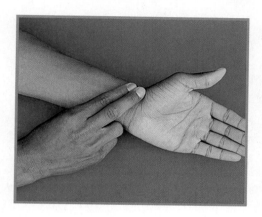

Step 1: Subtract your age from 220 if you are male; from 226 if you are female. This is an estimate of your maximum heart rate.

Step 2: Determine your resting heart rate. Use your index and middle finger to find your pulse in your wrist. Count the number of pulse beats in one minute.

Step 3: Subtract your resting heart rate from your maximum heart rate.

Step 4: Multiply the number from Step 3 by 0.6. Round to the nearest whole number. Then multiply the number from Step 3 by 0.8 and round to the nearest whole number.

Step 5: Add your resting heart rate to each of the two numbers from Step 4. The two sums give you the range in which your heart rate should be during exercise, or your target heart rate.

➌ Choose an exercise program.

▶ Ask your physical education teacher to help you select appropriate activities for building cardiorespiratory fitness. Select moderate intensity activities at first, such as walking, tennis, and volleyball. Then, as your fitness improves, include activities of higher intensity such as basketball, jogging, or jumping rope. Try to do these activities for 60 minutes a day at least 5 days a week.

▶ To check that you are exercising in your target heart rate range, take your pulse immediately after you stop exercising. Count the beats for 10 seconds. Multiply by 6 for the number of beats in one minute.

▶ After you've been exercising regularly for several weeks, repeat the walk/run fitness test to check your progress.

Practice the Skill

1. After a physical exam by a healthcare professional, complete the one-mile walk/run test to determine your cardiorespiratory fitness level. Be sure to do warm-up and stretching exercises before you begin the test. Record your results.

2. Calculate your target heart rate range. Remember to check your heart rate while you exercise.

3. Work with your physical education teacher or another trained professional to design a cardiorespiratory fitness program that will improve your fitness level.

4. Perform the one-mile walk/run every few weeks. Keep a log of your progress.

Respiratory Health

Objectives

► **List** the functions of the respiratory system.

► **Describe** how air travels through your respiratory system, and how you breathe.

► **Identify** ways to keep the respiratory system healthy.

Vocabulary

- alveoli
- diaphragm
- asthma
- bronchitis

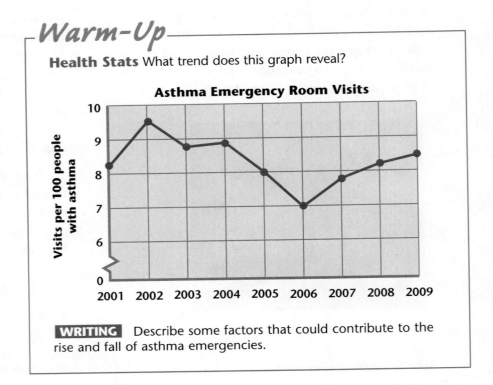

Warm-Up

Health Stats What trend does this graph reveal?

Asthma Emergency Room Visits

(y-axis: Visits per 100 people with asthma; values 0, 6, 7, 8, 9, 10)

(x-axis: 2001, 2002, 2003, 2004, 2005, 2006, 2007, 2008, 2009)

WRITING Describe some factors that could contribute to the rise and fall of asthma emergencies.

The Respiratory System

A person can survive weeks without food and days without water, but only minutes without oxygen. Your respiratory system brings a continuous supply of oxygen from the air into your body. As you have read, your cardiovascular system transports this oxygen to all of your body cells. After the cells use the oxygen to break down glucose for energy, they are left with carbon dioxide that must be expelled from the body. **The respiratory system is responsible for bringing oxygen from the outside environment into the body. It also removes carbon dioxide from the body.**

The Pathway of Air When you breathe in, or inhale, much more than just air enters your body. With every breath, you also take in such things as dust, pollen, and microorganisms that can cause disease. Most of these substances never reach your lungs. Cells lining your nasal cavities release mucus, which traps particles. Mucus also warms and moistens the air as it passes through your nasal cavities. **On its way to the lungs, air passes through the nose, pharynx, larynx, trachea, and bronchi.** Follow the pathway of air from the environment to your lungs in Figure 9.

The Respiratory System

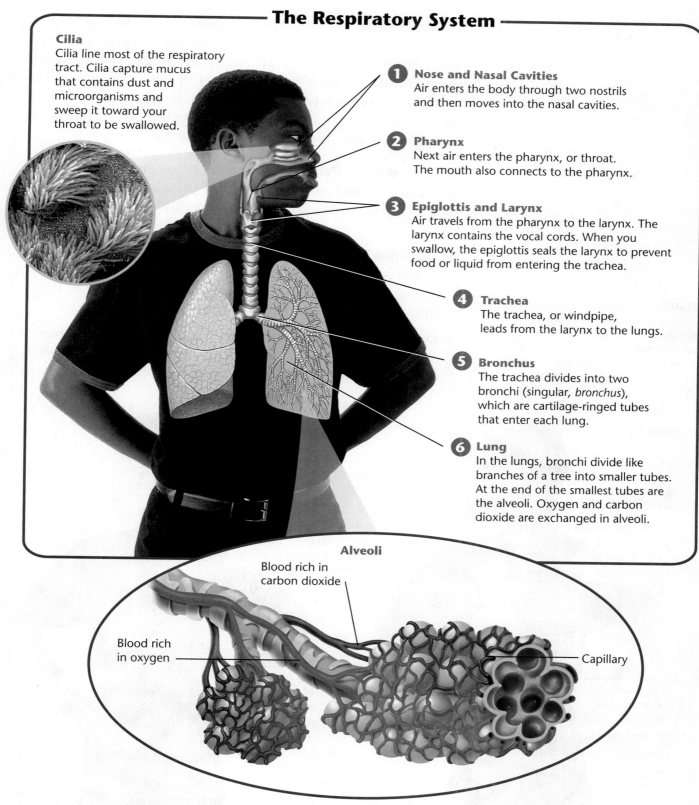

Cilia
Cilia line most of the respiratory tract. Cilia capture mucus that contains dust and microorganisms and sweep it toward your throat to be swallowed.

1 Nose and Nasal Cavities
Air enters the body through two nostrils and then moves into the nasal cavities.

2 Pharynx
Next air enters the pharynx, or throat. The mouth also connects to the pharynx.

3 Epiglottis and Larynx
Air travels from the pharynx to the larynx. The larynx contains the vocal cords. When you swallow, the epiglottis seals the larynx to prevent food or liquid from entering the trachea.

4 Trachea
The trachea, or windpipe, leads from the larynx to the lungs.

5 Bronchus
The trachea divides into two bronchi (singular, *bronchus*), which are cartilage-ringed tubes that enter each lung.

6 Lung
In the lungs, bronchi divide like branches of a tree into smaller tubes. At the end of the smallest tubes are the alveoli. Oxygen and carbon dioxide are exchanged in alveoli.

Alveoli

Blood rich in carbon dioxide

Blood rich in oxygen

Capillary

FIGURE 9 On its path to the lungs, air passes through several structures where it is filtered, warmed, and moistened.
Predicting What path does carbon dioxide take on its way out of the body?

Cardiovascular and Respiratory Health **307**

Gas Exchange   At the end of the smallest tubes in the lungs are millions of tiny sacs that look like bunches of grapes. These sacs, called **alveoli** (al VEE uh ly) (singular, *alveolus*), are where gases are exchanged between the air and the blood. You can see an illustration of alveoli in Figure 9 on the previous page. Oxygen passes through the thin walls of an alveolus and through a thin capillary wall into the blood. At the same time, carbon dioxide passes from the blood into the alveoli.

The Breathing Process   How does air get into and out of your body? **The breathing process is controlled by the actions of muscles in your ribs and chest.** As you can see in Figure 10, breathing takes place in two stages.

▶ **Inhalation** When you inhale, or breathe in, rib muscles pull the ribs up and out. At the same time the **diaphragm** (DY uh fram), a dome-shaped muscle that lies below the lungs, flattens. The chest cavity enlarges, the volume of the lungs increases, and air flows in.

▶ **Exhalation** When you exhale, or breathe out, the diaphragm moves upward. The rib muscles relax and the ribs drop. These movements make the chest cavity smaller and squeeze air from the lungs.

FIGURE 10 When you inhale, the diaphragm flattens. Pressure in the expanded lungs decreases, causing air to flow in. When you exhale, the diaphragm curves upward. Pressure in the lungs increases, pushing air out of your lungs.

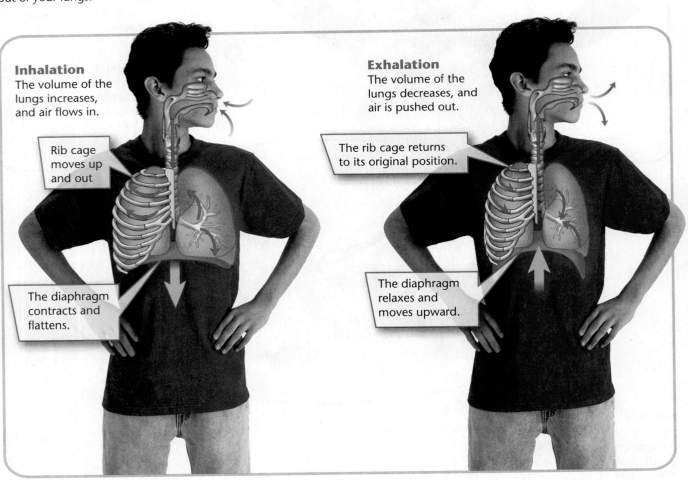

Inhalation
The volume of the lungs increases, and air flows in.

Rib cage moves up and out

The diaphragm contracts and flattens.

Exhalation
The volume of the lungs decreases, and air is pushed out.

The rib cage returns to its original position.

The diaphragm relaxes and moves upward.

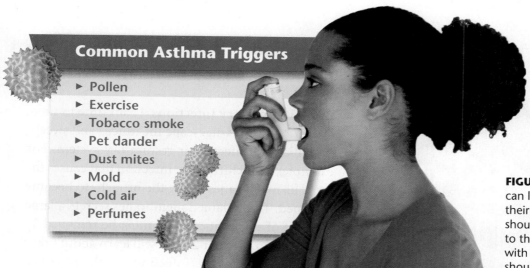

Common Asthma Triggers

▶ Pollen
▶ Exercise
▶ Tobacco smoke
▶ Pet dander
▶ Dust mites
▶ Mold
▶ Cold air
▶ Perfumes

FIGURE 11 People with asthma can lead active lives if they follow their treatment program. They should also avoid or limit exposure to their particular triggers. People with exercise-induced asthma should work with a doctor to find ways to exercise safely.

Keeping Healthy

What can you do to keep your respiratory system healthy? **You can keep your respiratory system healthy by avoiding tobacco smoke and air pollution and treating asthma if you have it. In addition, avoid respiratory infections, get regular exercise, and maintain a healthy weight.**

Avoiding Smoking and Air Pollution The most important thing you can do to protect your respiratory system is not to smoke. Over time, exposure to tobacco smoke and other air pollutants can seriously harm your respiratory health. In Chapter 16 you will learn how smoking can lead to serious respiratory system disorders such as chronic bronchitis and emphysema.

It is also important to avoid exposure to air pollutants whenever possible. If you do work that generates fumes or dust, such as sweeping a garage, wear a mask. Work in a well-ventilated area when you paint or use other chemicals that produce fumes. Before exercising outdoors on a hot, sunny day, check local news reports for warnings about air quality.

Living With Asthma About 19 million adults and 7 million children in the United States have asthma. **Asthma** (AZ muh) is a disorder in which respiratory passageways become inflamed. During an asthma attack, the passageways narrow until air can barely pass through. As a result, the person wheezes, coughs, and has difficulty breathing. Attacks can range from irritating to life threatening. Substances or behaviors that cause asthma attacks are called triggers. Common asthma triggers are exercise, allergic reactions, and stress.

Asthma is usually first diagnosed in childhood. Sometimes children outgrow the condition. Many people with asthma take medications daily to control their symptoms and avoid attacks. If an attack does occur, other medications are taken for immediate relief.

 GO ONLINE
PearsonSuccessNet.com
For: More on respiratory health

Connect to Your Life
What things do you do to keep your respiratory system healthy?

Other Healthful Behaviors You can practice other important behaviors to protect the health of your respiratory system.

▶ **Avoid Respiratory Infections** From time to time, microorganisms will escape the mucus and sweeping cilia and infect your respiratory system. For example, **bronchitis** is an infection that causes the mucous membranes lining the bronchi to become inflamed. The inflamed membranes secrete a large amount of thick mucus that must be removed by coughing. In Chapter 21 you will learn about other common respiratory infections such as colds, influenza, and pneumonia. You will also learn ways to prevent and treat these infections.

▶ **Get Regular Exercise** A regular exercise program that involves several minutes of repetitive, non-stop physical activity is extremely important for maintaining respiratory health. Exercise helps your lungs become more efficient at taking in oxygen and eliminating carbon dioxide.

▶ **Maintain a Healthy Weight** Regular exercise will also help you maintain an ideal weight. The respiratory system of an overweight person must work harder to deliver adequate oxygen than the system of a normal weight person. Maintaining a reasonable weight will help you avoid straining your respiratory system.

FIGURE 12 Protect your respiratory system by wearing a mask when you do work that generates dust or fumes.

Section 3 Review

Key Ideas and Vocabulary

1. What two functions does your respiratory system perform?
2. List the structures that air flows through on its way to the lungs.
3. Explain the action of the **diaphragm** when you inhale and exhale.
4. Identify five ways you can help your respiratory system stay healthy.

Critical Thinking

5. **Relating Cause and Effect** In a healthy person, how might coughing and sneezing protect the respiratory system?

Health at School

Asthma Attacks Talk to your school nurse, physical education teacher, or other students about asthma. What are the most common triggers for asthma attacks at school? Are attacks more common at certain times of day or times of year? How are asthma attacks treated? Summarize your findings in a paragraph. **WRITING**

6. **Comparing and Contrasting** Explain the difference between the movement of oxygen and carbon dioxide in the alveoli.
7. **Evaluating** Why is it important for someone with exercise-induced asthma to find ways to participate in physical activity?

Chapter 12
At a Glance

VIDEO **TEENS Talk**

Living With Asthma What are three things you learned about asthma from watching the video?

Section 1   Your Cardiovascular System

Key Ideas

▶ The main functions of the cardiovascular system include delivering materials to cells and carrying wastes away. In addition, blood contains cells that fight disease.

▶ The atria receive blood entering the heart. Blood flows from the atria to the ventricles, which pump the blood out of the heart.

▶ The three main types of blood vessels in your body are arteries, capillaries, and veins.

▶ The four components of blood are plasma, red blood cells, white blood cells, and platelets.

Vocabulary
• atrium (293)
• ventricle (293)
• pacemaker (294)
• artery (295)
• capillary (295)
• vein (295)
• blood pressure (296)
• hypertension (296)
• plasma (297)
• red blood cell (297)
• white blood cell (297)
• platelet (297)

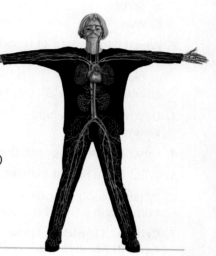

Section 2   Cardiovascular Health

Key Ideas

▶ Hypertension and high blood cholesterol are two factors that increase your risk of heart attack and stroke. Both factors may begin in your teens.

▶ To help maintain cardiovascular health, you should exercise regularly; eat a nutrient-rich, balanced diet; and avoid smoking.

Vocabulary
• low-density lipoprotein (300)
• plaque (300)
• atherosclerosis (300)
• high-density lipoprotein (300)
• arrhythmia (301)

Section 3   Respiratory Health

Key Ideas

▶ The respiratory system is responsible for bringing oxygen from the outside environment into the body. The respiratory system also removes carbon dioxide from the body.

▶ On its way to the lungs, air passes through the nose, pharynx, larynx, trachea, and bronchi.

▶ The breathing process is controlled by the actions of muscles in your ribs and chest.

▶ You can keep your respiratory system healthy by avoiding tobacco smoke and air pollution and treating asthma if you have it. In addition, avoid respiratory infections, get regular exercise, and maintain a healthy weight.

Vocabulary
• alveoli (308)
• diaphragm (308)
• asthma (309)
• bronchitis (310)

Chapter 12 Review

Reviewing Key Ideas

GO ONLINE
PearsonSuccessNet.com
For: Chapter 12 review activity

Section 1

1. In which kind of blood vessel are materials exchanged between the blood and body cells?
   a. aorta
   b. capillary
   c. vein
   d. artery

2. Which component of blood is responsible for the transport of oxygen?
   a. plasma
   b. red blood cells
   c. white blood cells
   d. platelets

3. Describe the two loops of the cardiovascular system.

4. Describe what happens during a heartbeat.

5. What is the role of platelets?

6. What is blood pressure? What do the two numbers in a blood pressure reading indicate?

7. **Critical Thinking** Three patients with blood types B, AB, and O are waiting for blood transfusions. The hospital's blood bank only contains blood types A and O. Which patient should receive which type of blood? Explain.

Section 2

8. Cholesterol is a fatty substance most closely associated with
   a. white blood cells.
   b. atherosclerosis.
   c. hemoglobin.
   d. blood pressure.

9. Which of the following foods are healthy for your cardiovascular system?
   a. butter and cheese
   b. beef and whole milk
   c. ice cream and potato chips
   d. fruits and fish

10. What is atherosclerosis and how is it related to LDL and HDL?

11. Why is hypertension called the "silent killer"?

12. Explain how exercise is beneficial to your cardiovascular health.

13. **Critical Thinking** Why is it important to know your family's history of cardiovascular disease?

Section 3

14. In which structure does gas exchange take place?
    a. alveolus
    b. bronchus
    c. trachea
    d. pharynx

15. Which of the following is *not* a respiratory infection?
    a. bronchitis
    b. influenza
    c. asthma
    d. pneumonia

16. Describe the path oxygen takes as it moves from the air outside your body into your blood.

17. How does the movement of the diaphragm affect the size of the chest cavity?

18. **Critical Thinking** Some respiratory diseases reduce the ability of the lungs to take in oxygen. How could this lead to damage of the cardiovascular system as well?

Building Health Skills

19. **Communicating** Develop an analogy to explain hypertension to a younger sibling.

20. **Analyzing Influences** Each day you make decisions about which foods you eat. Most likely there are many factors that influence your choices. Choose three of these influences and describe their effects on your decisions. **WRITING**

21. **Setting Goals** Between school, homework, and an after-school job, you have no time for school sports or other exercise. But, you want to stay fit. In a paragraph, describe how you can incorporate exercise into your busy schedule. **WRITING**

Health and Community

Blood Pressure Screenings Contact local medical centers, doctors' offices, and pharmacies to find out where people can have their blood pressure checked. Ask about free or low-cost blood-pressure screening programs. Write a letter to your local newspaper providing information about these screening programs. **WRITING**

Standardized Test Prep

Math Practice

The graph below compares lung function in smokers and in people who have never smoked. Use the graph to answer Questions 22–24.

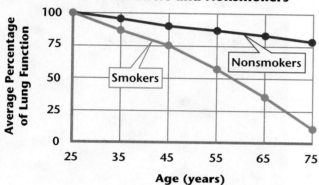

Comparing Lung Function in Smokers and Nonsmokers

22. At about what age are a smoker's lungs functioning at only 50% of their capacity?
    A 40   B 50
    C 60   D 70

23. At approximately what age do a smoker's lungs have the same capacity as the lungs of a 75-year-old nonsmoker?
    F 25   G 45
    H 65   J 75

24. What general conclusion about lung function and smoking can you draw from this graph?
    A Smoking does not affect lung function.
    B Smokers have greater lung function than people who do not smoke.
    C By the age of 50, a smoker will likely have 50 percent lung function.
    D Smoking significantly reduces a person's lung function.

Test-Taking Tip

When you take a test, try to stay relaxed. If you start to feel nervous, sit back and take a few deep breaths to calm yourself down.

Reading and Writing Practice

Read the passage. Then answer Questions 25–28.

The larynx contains two elastic folds of tissue called the vocal cords. As muscles pull on the vocal cords, air moves between them, causing them to vibrate. The vibrations produce the sounds you make when you speak, shout, or sing.

High-pitched sounds are produced when muscles shorten the vocal cords. Low-pitched sounds are produced when the muscles lengthen the vocal cords. Controlled pitch, a requirement for quality singing, can be improved by exercising the vocal cord muscles.

25. In this passage, the term *pitch* is most closely related to
    A high or low sounds.
    B the quality of one's voice.
    C the shortening of the vocal cords.
    D the lengthening of the vocal cords.

26. Children's voices are usually higher-pitched than adult's voices. This is most likely because
    F their vocal cord muscles are weak.
    G they cannot control the movement of their vocal cords.
    H they cannot control the volume of their voices.
    J their vocal cords are shorter than the vocal cords of adults.

27. The ability to control pitch while singing depends on
    A the singer's age.
    B the strength of the vocal cord muscles.
    C the arrangement of the vocal cords.
    D the amount of air passing through the vocal cords.

Constructed Response
28. In a paragraph, summarize how the vocal cord muscles control the pitch of your voice.

Exercise and Lifelong Fitness

GO ONLINE PearsonSuccessNet.com

TEENS Talk

VIDEO 13

Fit for Life

Preview **Activity**

How Has Physical Activity Changed?

Complete this activity before you watch the video.

1. Make a list of the sports or recreational activities you do with friends.
2. Interview one or two adults and ask them to describe the types of sports or recreational activities they did with friends when they were your age.
3. Write a paragraph comparing the activities you listed with the activities that the adults listed. Based on this comparison, would you say that activity levels have increased, decreased, or stayed the same? **WRITING**

The Importance of Physical Activity

Objectives

▶ **Explain** some of the physical, psychological, and social benefits of physical activity.

▶ **Define** the five components of fitness.

▶ **Describe** five types of physical activity.

Vocabulary

- physical activity
- endorphins
- physical fitness
- body composition
- aerobic exercise
- anaerobic exercise
- isometric exercise
- isotonic exercise
- isokinetic exercise

Warm-Up

Myth Being thin is a sign of fitness.

Fact Appearance is not a good indicator of overall fitness. Thin people who do not exercise are likely to have poor heart, lung, and muscular fitness.

WRITING Identify another fitness misconception that teens may hold. Why do you think they have that misconception?

The Benefits of Physical Activity

How physically active are you? To answer this question, you first need to know that physical activity includes more than just sports. Any movement that requires your large muscle groups to work is considered **physical activity.** Thus, physical activity includes actions such as walking briskly around the mall or doing household chores. Teens should spend 60 minutes or more each day performing some form of physical activity.

What happens inside your body when you rake leaves, swim, or dance? The most obvious changes affect your heart, lungs, and muscles. But did you also know that chemical changes occur in your brain that influence your mood? **The changes that occur due to physical activity are beneficial to your body, your mind, and your social interactions.**

Physical Benefits   The physical benefits of exercise extend to many of the systems in your body.

▶ **Cardiovascular System** Your heart and blood vessels receive the most benefits from regular physical activity. As your heart becomes stronger, it can pump more blood with less effort. The number of capillaries in your muscles increases, which may reduce blood pressure. Exercise also lowers blood cholesterol levels.

▶ **Weight Maintenance** Regular physical activity increases your basal metabolic rate—the amount of energy your body uses when you are at rest. An active metabolism makes it easier to remain at a healthy weight. Staying at a healthy weight can reduce your risk for developing diseases such as diabetes, heart disease, and certain cancers.

▶ **Bone Strength** Your physical activities should include some weight-bearing exercises such as jumping rope or walking. These activities make your bones stronger and denser. Having strong, dense bones may reduce your chances of developing osteoporosis later in life.

▶ **Balance and Coordination** Physical activity improves your balance and coordination, which may, in turn, improve your athletic ability. In addition, good balance and coordination can also reduce your risk of injury while performing chores such as climbing ladders or carrying packages down stairs.

Psychological Benefits During continuous exercise, your brain releases **endorphins,** chemicals that block pain messages from reaching your brain cells. Endorphins are also responsible for the feelings of satisfaction and pleasure you feel after a good workout.

People who exercise regularly are likely to be more self-confident and focused, and have reduced stress levels. Simple stretching exercises, for example, can relax tense muscles and help you sleep better. If you are upset or depressed, physical activity can help improve your mood. In fact, many health professionals consider physical activity an important part of treatment for depression.

Social Benefits Exercise is also an opportunity to have fun. Whether you play on a sports team or join an aerobics class, physical activity can be a way to bond with family and friends or build new relationships.

What benefits do you think you gain from regular physical activity?

GO ONLINE

PearsonSuccessNet.com
For: More on physical activity

FIGURE 1 Physical activity can be an opportunity to bond with friends or meet new people.

Studies show that regular physical activity also improves academic achievement.

The Components of Fitness

Most people do not have the ability to become an Olympic swimmer or a professional football player. But, with dedication, just about everyone can be physically fit. **Physical fitness** means that you have the energy and strength to participate in a variety of activities. **There are five components of fitness: cardiorespiratory endurance, muscular strength, muscular endurance, flexibility, and body composition.**

Cardiorespiratory Endurance   Cardiorespiratory endurance means that your heart, blood vessels, and lungs are able to distribute nutrients and oxygen and remove wastes efficiently during prolonged exercise. People with poor cardiorespiratory endurance become short of breath and have a very high heart rate after even light exercise. Regular exercise improves cardiorespiratory endurance.

▶ As the heart muscles become stronger, more blood is pumped with each beat.

▶ The lungs become more efficient at delivering oxygen to the blood and removing carbon dioxide.

Muscular Strength   The ability of a muscle to produce force is called muscular strength. The amount of weight you can lift is one measure of your muscular strength. Developing muscular strength requires exerting your muscles for short periods of time, such as doing push-ups.

Muscular Endurance   Muscular endurance is the ability of your muscles to work for an extended time. How long you can hold a barbell—or how many times you can lift it—is a measure of your muscular endurance. Developing muscular endurance requires repeated actions over an extended period of time, such as raking leaves, rowing, or walking.

Flexibility   The ability to move a joint through its entire range of motion is called flexibility. This means that you can bend, stretch, and twist your body easily. Flexibility can vary in different joints. For example, some people can't lean over and touch their toes. But their shoulders are flexible enough to help them throw a javelin a great distance. Stretching exercises, if done correctly, can increase flexibility and may reduce the risk of injury during exercise.

Body Composition   Your weight is not the best indicator of your fitness. In fact, when you begin an exercise program, you may gain some weight as you gain muscle. A better fitness indicator is your body composition. **Body composition** is the amount of fat tissue in your body compared to the amount of lean tissue, such as muscles and bones. Having too much, or too little, body fat can lead to health problems.

FIGURE 2   A skinfold test is one way to estimate body composition. A caliper is used to measure the top layer of skin and underlying layer of fat in different areas of the body. Then the measurements are used to estimate body fat percentage.

Connect to Your Life

In which components of fitness are you the strongest? In which do you need to improve?

A Physical Activity Pyramid

Sedentary Activities
- gaming
- watching TV
- "IM-ing"

FIGURE 3 This pyramid can guide you as you divide your time among activities to improve your fitness. **Applying Concepts** List three activities that you would add to the everyday activities list.

Occasionally

Flexibility
- stretching exercises
- ballet
- martial arts

Muscular Training
- weightlifting
- sit-ups
- push-ups

2 to 5 times a week

Cardiorespiratory
- swimming
- jogging
- dancing
- brisk walking
- rowing

3 to 5 times a week

Everyday Activities
- washing the car
- walking the dog
- cleaning your room
- sweeping the garage
- biking to school

Every day

Exercise and Lifelong Fitness **319**

Aerobic Exercise

Anaerobic Exercise

FIGURE 4 To be truly physically fit, you should participate in a variety of activities so that your muscles are worked in different ways. **Classifying** Which components of fitness do each of these activities improve?

Types of Physical Activity

No single activity can improve or maintain all five components of fitness. Instead, it is important to participate in a variety of physical activities. **Physical activities can be classified as aerobic exercise or anaerobic exercise. Strengthening and endurance activities can be further classified as isometric exercise, isotonic exercise, or isokinetic exercise.**

Aerobic Exercise Ongoing physical activity that raises your breathing rate and heart rate is called **aerobic exercise** (ehr OH bik). Aerobic exercises increase the amount of oxygen that your body takes in and uses. Swimming, running, brisk walking, and cross-country skiing are all forms of aerobic exercise.

By performing aerobic exercise for at least 20 minutes at a time on a regular basis, you can improve your cardiorespiratory endurance. Many aerobic activities also improve muscular endurance.

Anaerobic Exercise Intense physical activity that lasts for a few seconds to a few minutes is called **anaerobic exercise** (an uh ROH bik). Because anaerobic exercise is so intense and quick, your cardiovascular system cannot supply muscles with enough oxygen to produce energy. Unlike your other body cells, muscle cells do not need oxygen to meet this rapid demand for energy.

Lifting weights, doing push-ups, and sprinting are examples of anaerobic activities. Most anaerobic exercises develop muscular strength, muscular endurance, or flexibility.

Isometric Exercise Place your palms together and push them against each other. This is an **isometric exercise** (eye suh MET rik), an exercise in which muscles contract but very little body movement takes place. If you do isometric exercises on a regular basis, the muscles you use will become stronger.

Isometric Exercise

Isotonic Exercise

Isokinetic Exercise

Isotonic Exercise   Isotonic exercise (eye suh TAHN ik) involves contracting and relaxing your muscles through the full range of a joint's motion. Pull-ups are an example of isotonic exercise. Exercises with free weights, such as barbells, are also isotonic. Through repetition of isotonic exercises, you can develop muscular strength and endurance.

Isokinetic Exercise   In isokinetic exercise (eye soh ki NET ik) muscles contract at a constant rate. Isokinetic exercises require fitness machines that provide resistance to muscle movement. These exercises are often used as therapy to rebuild muscle strength after an injury.

Section 1 Review

Key Ideas and Vocabulary

1. Define the term **physical activity**. List three physical activities that are not sports.

2. List four physical benefits of regular physical activity. Then list three psychological benefits and two social benefits.

3. Briefly explain the five components of fitness.

4. List the five types of physical activity and give an example of each.

5. Explain why muscles do not use oxygen to produce energy during **anaerobic exercise**.

Critical Thinking

6. Comparing and Contrasting Explain how aerobic exercise differs from anaerobic exercise.

Health and Community

Exercise Classes Contact local community groups, fitness centers, or universities to find free or low-cost exercise classes that are open to the public. Summarize the information in a chart or poster to display at your school. **WRITING**

7. Sequencing Put the following activities in order from the one that would contribute the most to cardiorespiratory endurance to the one that would contribute the least: golf, basketball, tennis, volleyball. Explain your order.

8. Applying Concepts How would you convince a friend to start an exercise program?

Practicing Healthful Behaviors

Assessing Flexibility, Muscular Strength, and Endurance

Do you know how you rate in the areas of flexibility, muscular strength, and muscular endurance? It is important to know your current level of fitness before planning a fitness program. Although the tests described here do not evaluate all your muscles, they are good indicators of your fitness. Before you perform any of these tests, get a medical checkup by a doctor or other healthcare professional.

1 Assess your flexibility.

▶ Tape a yardstick to the floor. Place the tape across the 18-inch mark.

▶ Sit on the floor so that the 18-inch mark of the yardstick lines up with the bottom of your feet. Your legs should be straight in front of you. Your feet should be about 8 to 12 inches apart.

▶ Clasp your thumbs. With your palms down and your knees straight, slowly stretch forward and rest your fingertips on the yardstick.

▶ Repeat four times. On the fourth try, hold the stretch while your partner counts the inches above or below the 18-inch mark. For example, if you reach the 21-inch mark, your score is +3. If you reach the 15-inch mark, your score is -3.

Flexibility: Average Fitness Level

Age	Males	Females
13	+0.5 in.	+3.5 in.
14	+1.0 in.	+4.5 in.
15	+2.0 in.	+5.0 in.
16–17	+3.0 in.	+5.5 in.

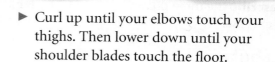

Curl-ups: Average Fitness Level		
Age	Males	Females
13–17	45/min	37/min

② Assess your abdominal muscular strength and endurance.

▶ Lie on your back with your knees flexed and feet about 12 inches from your bottom. Cross your arms. Your hands should be on your shoulders and your elbows against your chest. Your partner should hold your feet.

▶ Curl up until your elbows touch your thighs. Then lower down until your shoulder blades touch the floor.

▶ Your partner should count how many curl-ups you complete in one minute.

③ Assess your upper body muscular strength and endurance.

▶ Lie face down. Your hands should be flat on the ground under your shoulders. Your legs should be straight back and slightly apart, with toes tucked.

▶ Push up with your hands until your arms are straight. Keep your legs and back straight.

▶ Lower your body until your elbows are at a 90-degree angle and your upper arms are parallel to the floor. An entire push-up should take 3 seconds.

▶ Repeat until you cannot do a push-up every 3 seconds.

Push-ups: Average Fitness Level		
Age	Males	Females
13–14	24	11
15–16	30	15
17	37	16

Practice the Skill

1. Pair off with a partner and perform the flexibility test. Warm up before performing this test. Compare your results with the average fitness levels noted in the chart.

2. With your partner, perform the curl-ups and push-ups tests. Compare your results with the average fitness levels in the charts.

3. Evaluate your results for the three tests. Do you feel that you need to improve in one or more of these areas? If so, work with your physical education teacher to plan an appropriate fitness program.

Setting Goals for Lifelong Fitness

Objectives

▶ **Develop** a plan for achieving lifelong fitness.

▶ **Describe** the three phases of exercise.

Vocabulary

- lifelong fitness
- FITT formula
- target heart rate
- cross-training

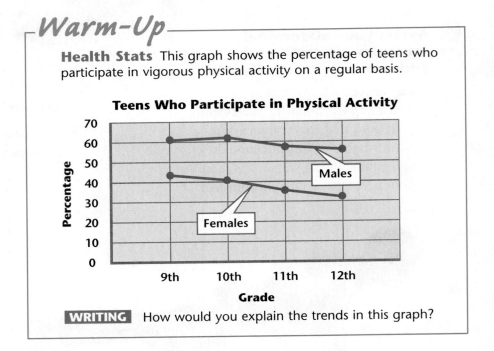

Warm-Up

Health Stats This graph shows the percentage of teens who participate in vigorous physical activity on a regular basis.

Teens Who Participate in Physical Activity

(Graph: Percentage vs. Grade (9th, 10th, 11th, 12th), showing lines for Males and Females)

WRITING How would you explain the trends in this graph?

Planning a Fitness Program

One of the most important things you can do for your health is to start exercising now. If you get into the habit of exercising, it will help you maintain **lifelong fitness**—the ability to stay healthy and fit as you age. **To plan a successful fitness program you should define your goals, develop your program, and monitor your progress.**

Define Long-Term Goals An important long-term goal of any fitness program should be lifelong fitness.

▶ Choose activities that you enjoy and can continue as you age.

▶ Vary your activities from day to day. This can lower your risk of injury, allow you to meet your schedule needs, and reduce boredom.

▶ Combine exercise with social activities whenever possible. For example, go for a hike with friends or rake leaves with your family.

Connect to Your Life

What activities do you enjoy now that could become lifelong activities?

Define Short-Term Goals In planning a fitness program, you also need to know your more immediate, or short-term goals. For example, do you want to increase your cardiorespiratory endurance? If so, your exercise program could include basketball, brisk walking, or other aerobic activities. If you want to gain more muscle mass, your program should include anaerobic exercises such as lifting weights. Or, you may have a combination of goals in mind.

Your goals should be specific to help you measure your progress. For example, "I want to be able to run an eight-minute mile" is more specific than "I want to run faster." Your time frame for reaching your goals also needs to be realistic. Otherwise, you may become discouraged and give up.

Develop Your Fitness Plan Once you have decided on your goals, think about your current schedule and fitness level. Then develop a fitness plan by marking a calendar with your typical weekly schedule. Decide what days and times are best for you to exercise. Each week, plan what activities you will do and when you will do them. Figure 5 shows an example of a weekly exercise plan.

Besides your interests and goals, there are several other things to consider when forming your plan.

▶ **Your Health** If you have health concerns, such as diabetes or asthma, work with your doctor to devise an appropriate fitness plan.

▶ **Your Budget** Do the activities require special equipment or fees?

▶ **Where You Live** What activities are appropriate for the area where you live? Will you have to alter your plans when the seasons change?

GO ONLINE

PearsonSuccessNet.com
For: More on physical fitness

FIGURE 5 Here is an example of a weekly exercise plan to improve cardiorespiratory endurance. For help in developing an exercise plan, talk to your physical education teacher or a fitness coach.

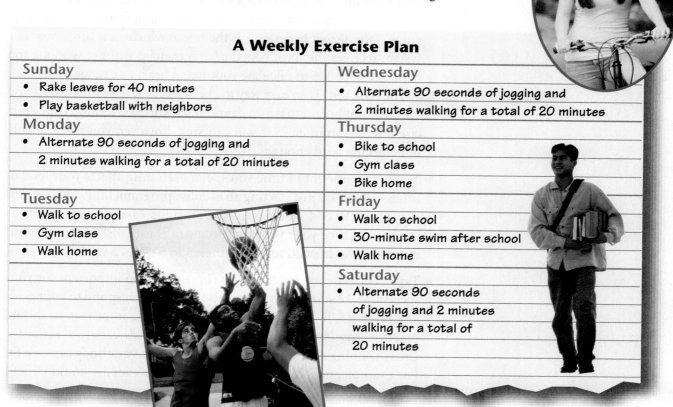

A Weekly Exercise Plan

Sunday	Wednesday
• Rake leaves for 40 minutes • Play basketball with neighbors	• Alternate 90 seconds of jogging and 2 minutes walking for a total of 20 minutes
Monday	**Thursday**
• Alternate 90 seconds of jogging and 2 minutes walking for a total of 20 minutes	• Bike to school • Gym class • Bike home
Tuesday	**Friday**
• Walk to school • Gym class • Walk home	• Walk to school • 30-minute swim after school • Walk home
	Saturday
	• Alternate 90 seconds of jogging and 2 minutes walking for a total of 20 minutes

Exercise and Lifelong Fitness **325**

The FITT Formula and Muscular Strengthening

▶ **Frequency**	3 days a week (nonconsecutive days)
▶ **Intensity**	Do as many pull-ups as possible without resting.
▶ **Time**	Include pull-ups as part of a 15-minute strengthening session.
▶ **Type**	Isotonic exercise that strengthens the biceps.

FIGURE 6 You can use the FITT formula to improve any of the components of fitness.
Applying Concepts How would you apply the FITT formula to your own fitness goals?

The FITT Formula The success of your fitness plan depends on four factors: how often you exercise, how hard you exercise, how long you exercise, and the types of exercise you choose. These factors make up the **FITT formula,** which stands for **f**requency, **i**ntensity, **t**ime, and **t**ype. Figure 6 includes an example of applying the FITT formula.

▶ **Frequency** To become or stay physically fit, you should exercise at least 3 to 5 times a week. Spread out your exercise over the week. Being inactive during the week does not prepare your body for an intense weekend workout and can lead to injury.

▶ **Intensity** The only way to improve your physical fitness is to make your body do more than it normally does. To increase cardiorespiratory endurance, for example, you must exercise within your target heart rate range. Your **target heart rate** is the rate at which your cardiovascular system receives the most benefits from exercise without working too hard. See page 305 to calculate your target heart rate range.

The "talk test" is an easy way to check your exercise intensity. If you are so out of breath that you cannot talk while exercising, your exercise level is too intense. If you can sing, however, you are probably not working hard enough.

▶ **Time** The amount of time you spend exercising affects your level of fitness. If you are just starting an exercise program, limit your time to only about 10 or 15 minutes a day. Then increase your exercise time gradually. Once your workout program is established, you should exercise for at least 20 to 30 minutes, 3 to 5 times a week.

▶ **Type** The types of activities you choose are also important for your success. Make sure that your exercise choices correspond to your goals and interests. To prevent boredom and overuse injuries, you should practice **cross-training** by participating in a wide variety of activities. Cross-training also ensures that more areas of your body become fit. For example, people who primarily walk for exercise could benefit from biking, which works different muscle groups in the legs.

FIGURE 7 It is important to monitor your progress. Create a chart, such as this one, that reflects your goals.

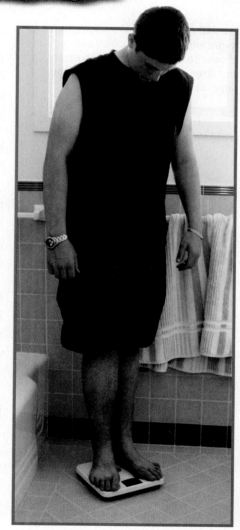

Week	Weight	Resting Heart Rate	Appetite	Sleep Pattern
0				
3				
6				
9				
12				
15				
18				

Monitor Your Progress   One of the most gratifying aspects of sticking with a fitness program is noticing progress. It is a good idea to track your overall progress using a chart like the one in Figure 7.

With most exercise programs, you will begin to notice significant changes within 12 weeks. You may find that you look better, sleep better, and feel more alert. You might also notice that you have gained muscle strength or lost weight. As you track your progress, keep in mind that monitoring your weight alone is not a good idea. Because muscle tissue is heavier than fat tissue, you may actually gain some weight as you become more fit.

One good indicator of improved fitness is a drop in your resting heart rate. Your resting heart rate is the number of times your heart beats each minute when you are at rest. A resting heart rate that is below 72 beats per minute usually indicates a good level of fitness. To find your resting heart rate, take your pulse for one minute when you first wake up in the morning.

Alter Your Fitness Plan   As your fitness improves, your workouts may become too easy. You may become frustrated because you do not notice any further progress. This may be a sign that your body has adjusted to your fitness routine. By slightly increasing the intensity or time of your workout, you should continue to see positive results.

Remember that, no matter what your fitness goals are, you need to combine your exercise program with healthy eating habits. Chapter 9 includes suggestions for what to eat and how much to eat when you are physically active.

Connect to Your Life   **How would your chart differ from the sample in Figure 7?**

Warm-up

Slowly move muscles to be used in workout.

5–10 minutes

Stretch

Stretch muscles to be used in workout.

5–10 minutes

Cardiorespiratory workout

Exercise in target heart rate range.

20–30 minutes

FIGURE 8 This is just a suggestion for an exercise session. You can choose to do both cardiorespiratory and strengthening workouts on the same day or on different days.

Phases of Exercise

The safest workouts begin with a warm-up period and end with a cool-down period. Stretching exercises should be part of both the warm-up and cool-down periods. You can find suggestions for warming up, stretching, and cooling down on pages 276–277.

Warming Up and Stretching A warm-up is a five- to ten-minute period of mild exercise that prepares your body for a vigorous workout. During the warm-up, your body temperature rises, your heart rate speeds up, and your muscles become more flexible. A warm-up should include some of the same motions as your planned activity, but at a slower pace. If you are planning to run, for example, start out by walking. Then gradually increase your speed until you reach your running pace.

Your warm-up should also include five to ten minutes of stretching. It is very important to pay attention to your body's limits when stretching. Do not bounce when you stretch, because bouncing can tear muscle fibers. You should feel tension while you stretch, but not pain. Hold stretches for 15 seconds.

The Workout The workout is when you perform an activity at its peak level. To be effective, your workout should follow the FITT formula you just read about.

Some people choose to do cardiorespiratory and muscular training during the same workout session. Others do cardiorespiratory training one day and muscular training another day. It is important that you do not do muscular training exercises with the same muscle groups two days in a row. Your muscles need an entire day of rest between strengthening workouts to repair and rebuild.

Connect to Your Life

What activities do you perform to warm up before exercise?

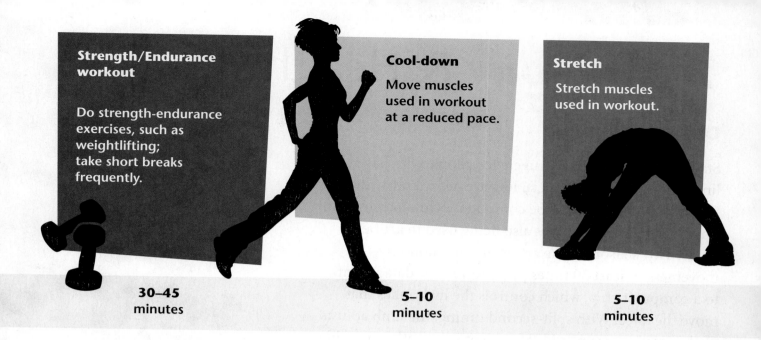

Strength/Endurance workout	Cool-down	Stretch
Do strength-endurance exercises, such as weightlifting; take short breaks frequently.	Move muscles used in workout at a reduced pace.	Stretch muscles used in workout.
30–45 minutes	**5–10 minutes**	**5–10 minutes**

Cooling Down and Stretching The cool-down is a period of mild exercise, such as walking, performed after a workout. Your cool-down should be at least as long as your warm-up. During the cool-down period, your body and your heart rate return slowly to their resting states. If you were to stop exercising abruptly, blood could collect in your muscles and not return quickly enough to your heart and brain. As a result, you could become dizzy and faint.

Stretching after your cool-down loosens muscles that may have tightened during exercise. Stretching can prevent muscle and joint soreness. Spend at least five minutes repeating the stretches you did during your warm-up period.

Section 2 Review

Key Ideas and Vocabulary

1. List the steps involved in developing a successful fitness program.
2. Name the four factors of an exercise program that are included in the **FITT formula**.
3. Describe the benefits of **cross-training**.
4. List the phases of an exercise session.

Critical Thinking

5. **Evaluating** Maria considers herself to be physically fit because she runs and swims almost every day in the summer. In the winter, however, she exercises very little. Do you agree or disagree with Maria's self-assessment? Explain.

Health at Home

Family Activity Day Plan a day of physical activity with your family. Some possibilities include a hike, a bicycle trip, or a softball game with other neighborhood families. At the end of the day, write a paragraph describing what you did and how you felt. **WRITING**

6. **Relating Cause and Effect** Why do you think that people's resting heart rates decrease as they become more fit?

7. **Comparing and Contrasting** How might a fitness program to improve muscular strength differ from one to improve flexibility?

Technology & Health

Out on a Limb

Staying active is often a struggle for people who have lost a limb. Many types of artificial legs are heavy and awkward. Recently, however, the same computer technology used to improve aircraft stability is also being used in artificial limbs. Tiny sensors in the artificial limb monitor movement at least 50 times per second. The data is sent to a computer chip, which controls the hydraulics that move the knee. With split-second timing, the limb adjusts to changes in terrain, and movement is smooth and stable.

WRITING Create an ad for this new artificial limb that highlights its benefits.

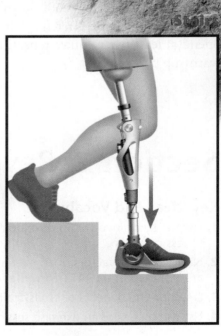

Walking

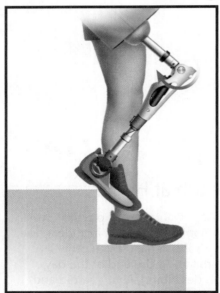

▲ Knee Bends

Sensors in the artificial leg detect when weight is being placed on the natural leg. The computer chip reduces the pressure on the artificial knee, and the knee bends.

Down

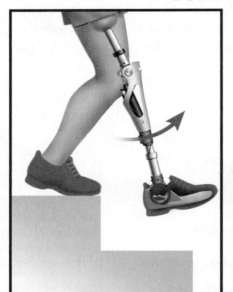

▲ Leg Swings

Sensors in the knee detect both the decrease in pressure and the knee movement. The computer chip reduces the pressure even more, allowing the leg to swing forward.

▲ Knee Straightens

As the person puts weight on the artificial leg, sensors detect the extra weight. The computer chip increases the pressure to support the person's weight.

Physical Activity and Safety

Objectives
▶ **List** five safety considerations related to physical activity.
▶ **Evaluate** the risks of using substances to enhance performance.
▶ **Identify** ways to avoid overtraining and prevent sports-related injuries.

Vocabulary
• dehydration
• dietary supplement
• overtraining

Warm-Up

Quick Quiz Complete each of these statements with *always, sometimes,* or *never.*

1. I ___?___ wear proper safety equipment when I am physically active.

2. I ___?___ follow the rules and regulations of the site where I participate in physical activity.

3. I ___?___ make sure I am properly hydrated during physical activity.

4. I ___?___ allow my body adequate time to recover from physical activity.

5. I ___?___ see a doctor if I experience an injury while exercising.

WRITING Why do you think that teens might not always practice these healthful behaviors?

Exercising Safely

Anyone who exercises faces the risk of injury. But there are many things you can do to stay healthy and safe while exercising. **Most injuries can be avoided if you get proper medical care, wear safety equipment, and pay attention to your surroundings and the weather. Proper water and food intake is also important.**

Medical Care   A safe fitness plan starts with a visit to your doctor. Even if you think you are perfectly healthy, it makes good sense to get a checkup before beginning an exercise program. If you have any conditions that limit your activity level, your doctor can offer advice about your fitness plan. You should also see your doctor whenever you experience any injuries or pain that doesn't go away.

Safety Equipment   You do not necessarily need expensive equipment to exercise safely. The key is to choose the right equipment for your particular activity.

Shopping for Athletic Shoes

▶ **Fit**	Shop late in the day when your feet are a bit swollen. Wear the same socks you wear for exercise.
▶ **Size**	Be sure your toes do not slide forward or feel pinched. Your heels should not rise as you walk.
▶ **Shoe Type**	Consider buying sport-specific shoes if you perform the same activity more than 3 times a week.
▶ **Price**	Unless you have a specific medical problem, moderately priced shoes will do the trick.
▶ **Style**	Just because your friends like a certain type of shoe doesn't mean it is the right one for you.

FIGURE 9 Choosing the right athletic shoes will not make you a state champion, but they can protect you from discomfort and injury.

GO ONLINE

PearsonSuccessNet.com
For: More on exercise safety

▶ **Clothing** Clothing should be comfortable and allow unrestricted movement. Avoid any clothing that could cause you to trip or get caught on equipment. For example, do not wear loose-fitting pants when bicycling. Wear light-colored, reflective clothing if you must exercise at night.

▶ **Footwear** To protect your feet from injury, footwear must fit properly, be in good condition, and provide support and protection. Be sure to buy footwear that fits your particular needs. For example, do not buy running shoes if your main activities are walking and bicycling. Figure 9 gives some tips for purchasing footwear.

▶ **Protective Gear** Shoulder pads, helmets, mouthguards, and other protective gear are designed to prevent injuries during contact sports. Hard-shell helmets worn by football, hockey, and baseball players protect the head from a direct blow. A helmet also should be worn any time you use wheeled sports equipment such as a bicycle, a skateboard, or inline skates. Kneepads, elbow pads, and wrist guards are also important to prevent injuries while skateboarding or skating.

Your Surroundings In planning your exercise program take into account where you live and where it is safe for you to exercise. For example, if walking to school would involve traveling along busy roads with no sidewalks, this is not a safe plan. Other safety issues to consider include whether an area is well-lit and whether there are other people around. If you listen to music while exercising, keep the earphone volumes low enough so that you can hear what is happening around you.

Weather Considerations Make sure your clothing is appropriate for the weather. Regardless of the air temperature, you should feel slightly cool at the beginning of your workout. When you exercise outdoors on warm, sunny days, wear light-colored clothing to reflect the sun's rays, and dress lightly to prevent overheating. Always wear sunscreen to protect your skin.

In cold weather, wear gloves or mittens and a hat to prevent heat loss. If you wear layers of clothing, you can regulate your temperature by taking off layers as you warm up. See the First Aid Appendix, pages 730–731, for ways to recognize and treat emergencies caused by extreme weather conditions.

Proper Water and Food Intake Proper hydration, or fluid intake, is important while exercising. You should drink about 16 ounces of water one to two hours before you exercise. Replacing the water you lose in sweat will prevent **dehydration,** or excessive water loss. Dehydration can lead to a dangerous rise in body temperature, muscle cramps, and unnecessary strain on your heart.

You have probably seen many sports drinks and foods advertised for athletes. How do you know if these products are necessary? Sports drinks replace sodium and other important substances you lose in sweat. But they also contain calories and sugar, whereas water does not. Unless you exercise for more than an hour, you only need to drink water.

Products such as sports-nutrition bars and gels also may have the most benefits for athletes who exercise for long periods of time. Your body needs nutrients for energy, maintenance, and repair, but nutritionists agree that fruits, vegetables, and whole-grain products provide the best nutrients. Chapter 9 offers examples of good foods for physical activity.

Connect to Your Life What steps do you take to ensure your safety during physical activity?

During exercise, drink water every 15 to 20 minutes.

FIGURE 10 Plan ahead to make sure you have enough water to drink while you exercise.

Avoiding Harmful Substances

When developing a fitness plan, it can be easy to get caught up in the here and now. Although your immediate goals are important, you also need to think about the future. **To achieve and maintain lifelong fitness, you need to avoid substances that can harm you.**

Dietary Supplements A **dietary supplement** is any product that contains one or more vitamins, minerals, herbs, or other dietary substances that may be lacking in the diet. Many supplement products promise short-cuts to greater fitness, such as increased muscle strength or extra energy. Keep in mind that supplements do not undergo the same strict testing as medications do. Therefore, some harmful side effects might not be discovered until after the supplement has been widely used. Also, there is no guarantee that the supplement will provide the benefits it claims.

In some situations, a doctor may recommend that you take a multi-vitamin or a similar supplement. But for most teens, a proper diet is the best way to provide your body with all the materials it needs to be healthy and physically active.

FIGURE 11 Anabolic steroids have serious effects on many body systems. Short-term goals are not worth the long-term risks. **Classifying** What effect could steroids have on mental health?

Anabolic Steroids Anabolic steroids are artificial forms of the hormone testosterone, a hormone that is involved in muscle development. Doctors may prescribe anabolic steroids for patients with muscular disorders. Some people take steroids without a prescription, which is illegal. They want to improve their athletic performance or change their appearance. This illegal use of steroids presents serious health risks. Steroids can damage organs, increase the risk of cancer, and cause depression. Some athletes inject artificial growth hormone (HGH) to increase muscle mass. But HGH also has health risks, such as organ damage.

When people illegally use steroids or HGH they risk more than their health. They risk being banned from sports and other punishments.

Effects of Steroids on the Body

In Males and Females
- Cardiovascular disease
- Liver and kidney cancer
- Stunted growth
- Mood swings
- Liver problems
- Hair loss
- Acne

In Males Only
- Enlarged breasts
- Infertility

In Females Only
- Facial hair growth
- Deepening of voice

Media Wise

Evaluating Exercise Devices

The Internet, magazines, and TV infomercials are used to sell exercise devices to help reshape your body. The ads often show impressive before and after photographs. How can you know whether the products being sold are safe and effective? Use this checklist to evaluate the products.

Work out while you work!

Does the ad guarantee you will see major changes in a week or a month? **Yes** **No**

Does the ad say that you can use the device to get fit in just a few minutes a day? **Yes** **No**

Does the ad say that the device can "spot reduce" specific parts on the body? **Yes** **No**

Does the ad promise a total body workout? **Yes** **No**

"Yes" answers may reveal that you should think carefully about your purchase. Instead, choose exercises that require little or no equipment.

Activity Find an ad for an exercise device. Use the checklist to evaluate the product. Would you buy the product? Would you recommend it to a friend? Why or why not? **WRITING**

Preventing Sports-Related Injuries

Practice is important in order to improve at any sport or activity. However, sometimes teens feel pressure to be too competitive. Pushing your body too hard can lead to injury. **An important part of achieving lifelong fitness is avoiding overtraining and preventing injuries.**

Overtraining If you exercise too intensely or for too long without allowing enough time for rest, you may be **overtraining.** The first sign of overtraining is fatigue during exercise or a few hours after a workout. Fatigue is a signal that you are overworking your body. Other signs of overtraining include nausea or vomiting during or after a workout, loss of appetite, and irritability. If you experience any of these symptoms, reduce the intensity and length of your workout. If the symptoms do not subside, seek medical care.

You can avoid overtraining by sticking to a consistent exercise schedule that includes days of rest. In addition, always exercise within your comfort level. Pushing yourself to achieve fitness goals too quickly can lead to injuries.

Connect to Your Life **Have you ever experienced signs of overtraining? What were the signs?**

FIGURE 12 The small break in this leg bone is a stress fracture. Exercise places stress on bones. If the bones do not have time to heal before repeated, intense exercise, a stress fracture could develop.

Sports-Related Injuries   Using the same joints repetitively during your workouts can lead to overuse injuries. Tendonitis, a painful swelling of a tendon, is an injury that can result from overuse. Overuse of a bone can lead to a stress fracture, like the one shown in Figure 12. Participating in a variety of activities and allowing your body to recover between workouts can help prevent overuse injuries.

In Chapter 11, you learned about two common sports-related injuries—sprains, the tearing of ligaments, and strains, the tearing of tendons. Treatment for sprains and strains usually involves controlling the swelling with rest, ice, compression, and elevation. These treatment steps are often referred to by the initials R.I.C.E. See the First Aid Appendix for more information on R.I.C.E.

Allowing injuries to heal properly is extremely important for lifelong fitness. Reinjuring bones, tendons, ligaments, or muscles before they heal can lead to ongoing problems and limit your ability to stay active. If you have an injury, work with a doctor to find ways to exercise while allowing the injured area to heal.

Section 3 Review

Key Ideas and Vocabulary

1. What are five safety considerations to keep in mind when planning a fitness program?

2. What is **dehydration?** What physical problems can dehydration cause?

3. Describe the health risks associated with dietary supplements and anabolic steroids.

4. Why is the prevention of injuries important to lifelong fitness?

Critical Thinking

5. **Comparing and Contrasting** How might the safety concerns of a physically active person living in a large city differ from those of a person living in a small town?

Health at School

Improving School Fitness With permission from school administrators, interview students to identify ways to encourage physical activity at school. For example, would more students exercise if the gym were open for a few hours after school? Choose one practical idea. In a paper, present your idea to school administrators. **WRITING**

6. **Making Judgments** Do you think that exercising with a partner would increase or decrease your risk of overtraining? Explain your reasoning.

7. **Evaluating** Felicia has never exercised regularly, but has decided to start a fitness program. She has committed to running for one hour every day regardless of the weather or the time of day. Critique her fitness plan from a safety perspective.

Chapter 13
At a Glance

VIDEO

TEENS Talk ⊙

Fit for Life Describe how watching this video affected your motivation to be physically active.

Section 1   The Importance of Physical Activity

Key Ideas

▶ The changes that occur due to physical activity are beneficial to your body, your mind, and your social interactions.

▶ There are five components of fitness: cardio-respiratory endurance, muscular strength, muscular endurance, flexibility, and body composition.

▶ Physical activities can be classified as aerobic exercise or anaerobic exercise. Muscular strengthening and endurance activities can be further classified as isometric exercise, isotonic exercise, or isokinetic exercise.

Vocabulary

• physical activity (316)
• endorphins (317)
• physical fitness (318)
• body composition (318)
• aerobic exercise (320)
• anaerobic exercise (320)
• isometric exercise (320)
• isotonic exercise (321)
• isokinetic exercise (321)

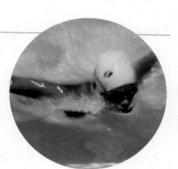

Section 2   Setting Goals for Lifelong Fitness

Key Ideas

▶ To plan a successful fitness program you should define your goals, develop your program, and monitor your progress.

▶ The safest workouts begin with a warm-up period and end with a cool-down period. Stretching exercises should be part of both the warm-up and cool-down periods.

Vocabulary

• lifelong fitness (324)
• FITT formula (326)
• target heart rate (326)
• cross-training (326)

Section 3   Physical Activity and Safety

Key Ideas

▶ Most injuries can be avoided if you get proper medical care, wear safety equipment, and pay attention to your surroundings and the weather. Proper water and food intake is also important.

▶ To achieve and maintain lifelong fitness, you need to avoid substances that can harm you.

▶ An important part of achieving lifelong fitness is avoiding overtraining and preventing injuries.

Vocabulary

• dehydration (333)
• dietary supplement (334)
• overtraining (335)

Chapter 13 Review

Reviewing Key Ideas

GO ONLINE

PearsonSuccessNet.com

For: Chapter 13 review activity

Section 1

1. Which component of fitness receives the greatest benefit from jogging?
   a. muscular strength
   b. flexibility
   c. cardiorespiratory endurance
   d. body composition

2. Pushing your palms against a wall is an example of
   a. isometric exercise.
   b. isokinetic exercise.
   c. isotonic exercise.
   d. aerobic exercise.

3. Describe the benefits of physical activity for three different body systems.

4. What are endorphins? How do they contribute to the psychological benefits of physical activity?

5. Explain the difference between muscular strength and muscular endurance.

6. **Critical Thinking** Jane and Maria are the same height and the same weight. Does this mean that they have the same body composition? Why or why not?

Section 2

7. Which types of activities should you try to perform every day?
   a. vigorous exercise such as soccer
   b. recreational activities such as walking, throwing a frisbee, or riding a bike to school
   c. watching television and playing video games
   d. strengthening exercises such as lifting weights

8. How can you determine if your cardiovascular system is becoming more fit as a result of your fitness program?

9. List the three stages of a workout session. What is the goal of each stage?

10. **Critical Thinking** You are trying out for the basketball team in a few months. Your friend is trying out for the volleyball team. He asked you to train with him. What types of activities would be beneficial to both of you? What types of activities would be more beneficial to you?

Section 3

11. Which is the best way to avoid dehydration?
    a. Avoid exercise when it is warm outside.
    b. Drink as much water as you lose in sweat.
    c. Do not wear a helmet so that heat can escape from your head.
    d. Wear dark clothing so that sweat can evaporate.

12. What factors should you consider when choosing safety equipment for physical activity?

13. Why are the claims made by supplement manufacturers less trustworthy than the claims made by prescription drug manufacturers?

14. **Critical Thinking** Your friend plays soccer for several teams. He has practice or a game every day. Lately, he cannot finish his homework without falling asleep. What advice would you give him?

Building Health Skills

15. **Communicating** Your uncle has always said that he does not need to exercise because he eats well and is not overweight. In a letter, explain to your uncle why this is not true. **WRITING**

16. **Analyzing Influences** In a paragraph, describe how your family and friends have influenced your activity choices and level of activity. **WRITING**

17. **Setting Goals** Choose two or three fitness goals you want to achieve. Rank your goals by highest priority. Explain why you placed the goals in that order. Plan an exercise program that will help you achieve your first goal. **WRITING**

Health and Community

Endurance Event Find out about local charity events, such as walk-a-thons or bike-a-thons, that will require you to train. Develop a schedule to train for the event. Write a regular column for your school newspaper describing your experiences with training and fundraising. **WRITING**

Standardized Test Prep

Math Practice

The box below gives the formula for calculating a target heart rate range. Use the formula to answer Questions 18–20.

Calculating Target Heart Rate

1. 220 − person's age = maximum heart rate

2. Maximum heart rate − resting heart rate = ___?___

3. Answer from Step 2 × 0.6 = ___?___ (Round to the nearest whole number.)

4. Answer from Step 2 × 0.8 = ___?___ (Round to the nearest whole number.)

5. Resting heart rate + answer from Step 3 = ___?___
Resting heart rate + answer from Step 4 = ___?___

The two sums from Step 5 are the target heart rate range.

18. Randy is 20 years old. He has a resting heart rate of 70 beats per minute (bpm). What is his target heart rate range?
    A 148–174 bpm
    B 78–104 bpm
    C 90–120 bpm
    D 168–198 bpm

19. After ten years, Randy's resting heart rate stays the same. What will happen to his target heart rate?
    F It will stay the same.
    G It will increase.
    H It will decrease.
    J It depends on his fitness level.

20. Ken's target heart rate range is 122–139 bpm. His resting heart rate is 73 bpm. What is his age?
    A 82
    B 73
    C 65
    D 59

Reading and Writing Practice

Read the passage. Then answer Questions 21–24.

In 1713, Italian physician Bernardino Ramazzini wrote about the association between inactivity and poor health. Ramazzini, who is considered the father of occupational medicine, noted that "those who sit at their work and are therefore called 'chairworkers,' suffer from their own particular diseases." He urged these workers to at least exercise on their days off to counteract the harm done by many days of sedentary life.

21. When Ramazzini refers to "chairworkers," he is most likely referring to people such as
    A farmers and railroad workers.
    B cobblers and tailors.
    C miners and blacksmiths.
    D furniture makers and carpenters.

22. What factor does Ramazzini blame for the poor health of "chairworkers"?
    F their poor diet
    G rare diseases
    H being overworked
    J lack of physical activity

23. Someone who practices occupational medicine is most likely concerned with
    A diseases or hazards related to the workplace.
    B helping those with sedentary lifestyles become more active.
    C treating diseases related to sedentary lifestyles.
    D diagnosing and treating rare diseases.

Constructed Response

24. In a paragraph, summarize Ramazzini's observations of inactive workers in the 18th century.

Test-Taking Tip

On the days before a test, keep to a regular physical activity routine. Because physical activity improves your mood and your focus, it may help your performance on the test.

Personal Care

GO ONLINE PearsonSuccessNet.com

VIDEO 14

TEENS Talk

Taking Care of You

Preview **Activity**

When Do You Follow Instructions?

1. Instructions with your new suede jacket tell you to treat it with a water-repellent spray, and to avoid wearing it in bad weather.
   a. Will you follow these instructions? Explain.
   b. What could happen if you don't follow the instructions? How would you feel?
2. Throughout your life, you have been told to wear sunscreen and to avoid the sun during the hottest time of the day.
   a. Do you follow these instructions? Explain.
   b. What could happen if you don't follow these instructions? How would you feel?
3. What did you learn about yourself from your answers to these questions? **WRITING**

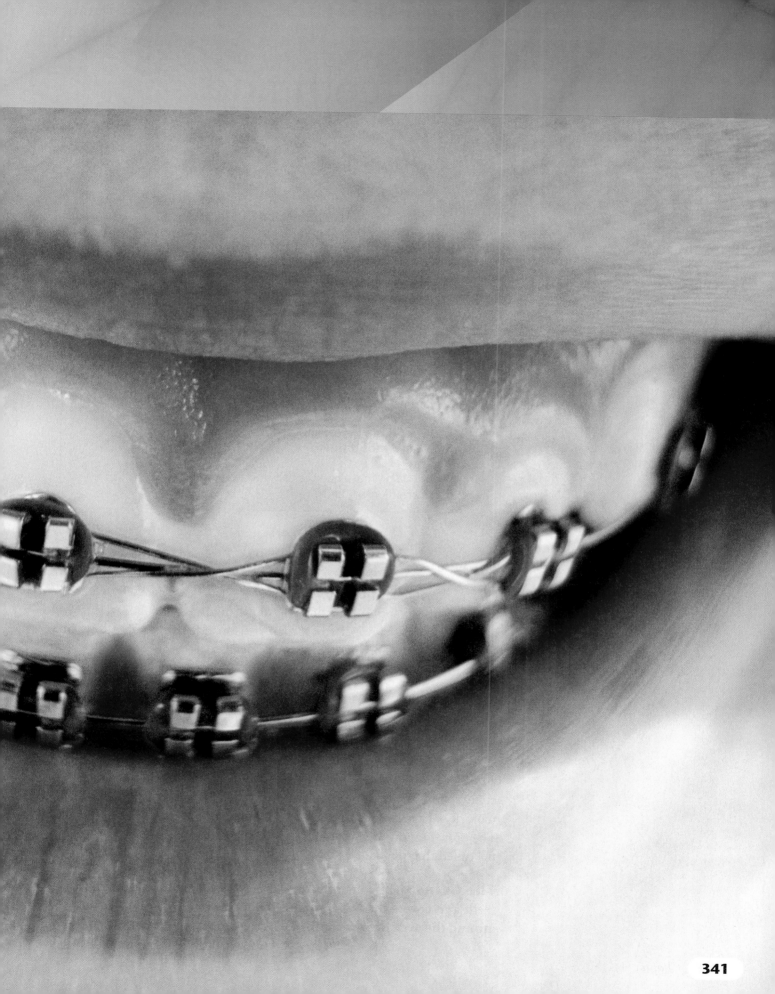

Your Teeth and Gums

Objectives

► **List** the functions of teeth and gums.

► **Identify** two structural problems of the teeth and mouth.

► **Describe** ways to prevent teeth and gum problems.

Vocabulary

- enamel
- cementum
- dentin
- pulp
- malocclusion
- orthodontist
- halitosis
- plaque
- tartar
- periodontal disease

Warm-Up

Quick Quiz How many of these questions can you answer *yes* to?

1. I brush my teeth at least twice a day.

2. I floss my teeth every day.

3. I go to the dentist at least once a year.

4. I limit my intake of sugary foods.

5. When I play a contact sport, I always wear a mouthguard.

WRITING What changes can you make to take better care of your teeth?

The Teeth and Gums

Do you remember when you lost your baby teeth? Normal activities such as biting into an apple or making an *s* sound became difficult. You learned that your teeth are important for many reasons. **Healthy teeth allow you to chew your food properly and speak clearly.**

Structure of Teeth You have four types of teeth. Figure 1 shows where they are located and describes their functions. It also shows the three basic parts of a tooth—the crown, the neck, and the root.

Each tooth is made of three types of bonelike material. **Enamel,** the hardest material in your body, covers a tooth's crown. **Cementum** covers a tooth's root and helps to anchor the tooth to the jawbone. Under the enamel and cementum is **dentin,** a living material that makes up the majority of a tooth. A soft tissue called **pulp** fills the center of each tooth. The pulp contains nerves and blood vessels, which pass through a channel called the root canal.

The Gums The gum is the pink tissue that surrounds the base of your teeth and covers the bone around the teeth. **Healthy gums fit tightly around the neck of each tooth like a collar, holding it firmly in place.**

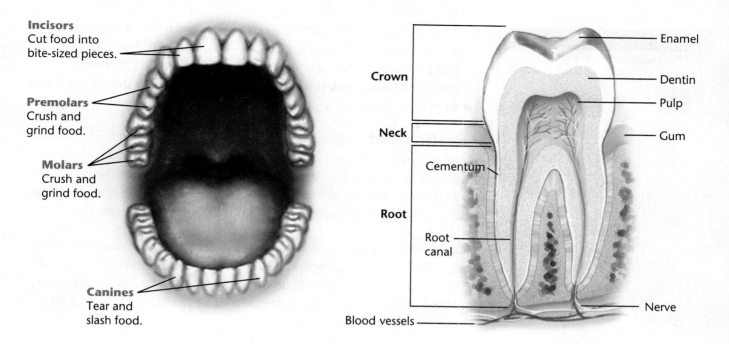

Incisors
Cut food into bite-sized pieces.

Premolars
Crush and grind food.

Molars
Crush and grind food.

Canines
Tear and slash food.

Crown

Neck

Root

Enamel

Dentin

Pulp

Gum

Cementum

Root canal

Blood vessels

Nerve

FIGURE 1 All of your teeth are made up of three parts—the crown, the neck, and at least one root.
Interpreting Diagrams What material covers a tooth's crown?

Structural Problems

By the age of 3, most children have all of their first teeth, or primary teeth. Around the age of 5 or 6, the primary teeth begin to fall out. Over the next few years, the primary teeth are replaced by 28 permanent teeth. An additional four teeth, called wisdom teeth, usually grow in between the ages of 17 and 21. **The changes that occur in the jaws throughout the growing years can lead to structural problems.**

Malocclusion   When the upper and lower teeth do not meet properly, the condition is known as a **malocclusion** (mal uh KLOO zhun), or improper bite. When the upper teeth stick out too far, the condition is called an overbite. When the lower teeth stick out beyond the upper teeth, the condition is called an underbite. A severe malocclusion can make chewing difficult or cause the teeth to wear down unevenly.

People with malocclusions, or people with crooked teeth, may seek the help of an **orthodontist** (awr thuh DAHN tist). Orthodontists are specialists who correct the position of jaws and teeth. They use braces and other devices to move teeth into their proper positions.

Impacted Wisdom Teeth   Some teens have their wisdom teeth surgically removed before they grow in because the teeth are impacted. Impacted wisdom teeth either do not have the space to emerge through the gum line or are positioned at an awkward angle. If impacted wisdom teeth are not removed, they may crowd the other teeth and cause serious gum infections.

Connect to Your Life

Have you worn braces? If so, how did they change your appearance?

GO ONLINE

PearsonSuccessNet.com
For: More on caring for your teeth

Caring for Your Teeth and Gums

If your teeth and gums are in poor condition, you may have trouble eating and speaking. Failing to properly maintain your teeth and gums can also cause mouth pain and an embarrassing condition called **halitosis,** or bad breath. **A healthy diet, proper tooth care, and regular dental checkups can prevent tooth decay and gum disease.**

Healthy Diet   You should eat a well-balanced diet that is low in sugar. Bacteria in your mouth feed on sugar and produce acids that can damage your teeth. Limit your intake of sports drinks, which contain acids that can destroy your teeth's enamel. Your diet should include foods that contain calcium and phosphorus—two minerals that help strengthen teeth.

Brushing   Your mouth is full of bacteria that adhere to your teeth in a sticky film called **plaque.** Brushing your teeth removes plaque. You should also brush your tongue to remove food particles. Brush at least twice a day, preferably after every meal. If you cannot brush after eating, rinse your mouth with water.

Flossing   Dental floss removes food and plaque from areas that a toothbrush cannot reach, such as between your teeth. You should floss your teeth once a day, preferably before bedtime. Instructions for proper brushing and flossing are given in Figure 2.

Wearing a Mouthguard   Although teeth are made of strong material, collisions can lead to broken or cracked teeth. To prevent damage to your teeth during contact sports, such as basketball or lacrosse, wear a mouthguard.

Connect to Your Life   **How many times a day do you brush your teeth? How often do you floss?**

FIGURE 2   You should spend about two minutes brushing your teeth, twice a day. You should also floss every day to remove plaque from areas where a toothbrush does not reach.

Brushing
- Use a toothbrush with soft bristles.
- Brush all surfaces of your teeth—outer, inner, and top.
- Hold the toothbrush at a 45-degree angle.
- Brush away from your gums.
- Brush your tongue.

Flossing
- Use 18 inches of dental floss—waxed or unwaxed.
- Gently move the floss up and down between your teeth.
- At the gum line, curve the floss around each tooth and glide it up and down.
- Unwind, and use a clean section of floss for each tooth.

Hands-On *Activity*

Sports Drinks, Soft Drinks, and Your Teeth

In this activity, you will observe how various drinks affect eggshells, which are composed of some of the same materials as your teeth.

Materials

three plastic cups
tape for labeling
three large pieces
    of eggshell
sports drink
soft drink
water

Try This

❶ Label the first cup "sports drink," the second cup "soft drink," and the third cup "water." Place a piece of eggshell in each cup.

❷ Pour some of the sports drink into the appropriate cup. Pour the same amount of soft drink into the second cup and water into the third.

❸ After three days, discard the liquids and examine each eggshell.

Think and Discuss

❶ Describe the appearance of each eggshell after three days.

❷ Compare the effects of the sports drink and soft drink. Was there any difference?

❸ What did you learn from this experiment about the effects of water, sports drinks, and soft drinks on teeth?

Dental Checkups Having regular dental checkups, about twice a year, can identify problems before they become painful or hard to treat. Because of checkups and other preventive care, young people today generally have fewer cavities than their parents did at the same age. An example of preventive care is the addition of fluoride to toothpastes and drinking water. Fluoride binds with enamel, making it stronger and more resistant to decay.

Some people also visit their dentist to discuss teeth whitening. Some beverages, foods, and medicines can stain teeth. The stains sometimes can be removed at the dentist's office or with products that can be used at home. Talk to your dentist before buying any teeth-whitening products.

Treating Tooth Decay When plaque is not removed often enough or well enough, the bacteria in your mouth grow and multiply. The acid that they produce eats away at enamel. When the enamel is broken down, a tiny hole, or cavity, forms.

To repair a cavity, a dentist uses a drill to remove the decay and bacteria and then fills the hole. The type of filling used depends on the area being filled. If not treated, the decay can spread through all the layers of the tooth and eventually into the root. If this happens, the dentist must either remove the tooth or perform root canal therapy. During root canal therapy, the dentist removes the infected pulp and replaces it with a rubber-like material.

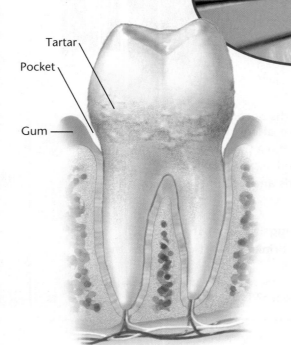

FIGURE 3 During cleanings, dental hygienists scrape away plaque and tartar buildup. If plaque and tartar are not removed, the gums may pull away from the teeth and form pockets.

Tartar

Pocket

Gum

Treating Gum Disease Plaque can also damage the gums. If plaque is not removed within 48 hours, it begins to harden into a material called **tartar,** which irritates the gums. The gum irritation caused by plaque and tartar eventually can lead to **periodontal disease,** or gum disease. During the first stage of periodontal disease, called gingivitis (jin juh VYT is), the gums become red and swollen and bleed easily.

In later stages of periodontal disease, the buildup of plaque and tartar causes the gums to pull away from the teeth and form pockets, as shown in Figure 3. Plaque, tartar, and food collect in the pockets, and the gums become inflamed and infected. Without treatment, the structures that hold teeth in place may be destroyed. The teeth may become loose and eventually fall out.

Periodontal disease can be treated surgically by dentists who specialize in gum disease. However, the need for these painful and expensive procedures can be prevented with good oral care including brushing, flossing, and regular visits to the dentist.

Section 1 Review

Key Ideas and Vocabulary

1. What are the functions of your teeth and gums?

2. What is **pulp?**

3. Describe two structural problems in the mouth and how they can be corrected.

4. What are three ways that you can prevent problems with your teeth and gums?

Critical Thinking

5. Relating Cause and Effect People with periodontal disease sometimes stop brushing their teeth because their gums hurt. What effect do you think this will have on their oral health? Explain.

Health at Home

Improving Dental Care Create a checklist of things you can do to improve your dental care. Your checklist can include brushing more often, flossing every day, and replacing your toothbrush every four months. Post your checklist on your bathroom mirror or somewhere else where you will see it.

6. Predicting Why do you think malocclusions are typically corrected during the teen years?

7. Evaluating Why do you think that some people ignore simple steps, such as brushing and flossing, that can help keep their teeth and gums healthy?

GO ONLINE PearsonSuccessNet.com   Audio Summary Section 14.1

Your Skin, Hair, and Nails

Objectives

► **Identify** the functions of the skin.

► **Describe** behaviors that can keep your skin healthy.

► **Explain** the functions of your hair and nails and how to care for them.

Vocabulary

• epidermis
• keratin
• melanin
• dermis
• pore
• follicle
• sebaceous gland
• melanoma
• acne
• dermatologist
• eczema

Warm-Up

Myth Spending time in the sun can clear up acne.

Fact Tanned skin may temporarily camouflage the redness of acne, but it does not treat the condition. Also, many acne medications make skin more sensitive to the sun.

WRITING Identify another skin-care misconception that teens may hold. Why do you think they have that misconception?

Your Skin

You may think that your skin is just a covering that separates the inside of your body from the outside environment. However, your skin is actually your body's largest organ and it plays several major roles in keeping you healthy. **The skin covers and protects the body from injury, infection, and water loss. The skin also helps to regulate body temperature and gathers information from the environment.**

► **Protection** The skin shields and protects the organs and tissues beneath it. The skin also keeps harmful substances and microorganisms out of the body. In addition, it keeps important fluids, such as water, in the body.

► **Temperature Regulation** When you are warm, sweat glands in the skin produce perspiration, which cools your body as it evaporates. In addition, blood vessels in your skin widen allowing more heat to be given off at the skin's surface. When you are cold, the blood vessels narrow, keeping more heat within your body.

► **Information Gathering** Nerves in the skin provide information to your central nervous system about outside factors such as pressure, pain, and temperature.

Connect to Your Life **What information has your skin provided to your nervous system today?**

The Epidermis Your skin consists of two major layers. The outermost layer is the **epidermis** (ep uh DUR mis). The part of the epidermis that comes into contact with the environment is made up of dead cells. These dead cells contain a protein called **keratin** that makes the skin tough and waterproof. You shed dead cells when you brush against objects, bathe, or rub your skin.

Underneath the dead cells are living cells that continually produce new cells. The new cells push older cells toward the skin's surface. Eventually the older cells die and become part of the dead surface layer.

Cells deep in the epidermis produce the protein **melanin,** a dark pigment that gives skin some of its color. The more melanin produced by your skin, the darker it is. Sunlight can stimulate melanin production, which causes the skin to tan.

The Dermis The **dermis** (DUR mis) is the tough, elastic layer of skin that lies below the epidermis. In most areas of your body, the dermis is much thicker than the epidermis. Notice in Figure 4 that the dermis contains the nerves that send information to the central nervous system. The dermis also contains blood vessels that bring nutrients to the skin and carry wastes away.

Sweat glands in the dermis produce perspiration that helps keep your body cool. Sweat travels through a narrow channel, or duct, to the surface of the skin. There, it is excreted through a tiny opening called a **pore.** Strands of hair grow within the dermis in structures called **follicles.** Oil is secreted into follicles by **sebaceous glands.** The oil softens hair and skin and keeps both from becoming too dry and brittle.

FIGURE 4 The skin is made of two main layers. The top layer is called the epidermis. The bottom layer is called the dermis.
Interpreting Diagrams Which layer of skin is thinner?

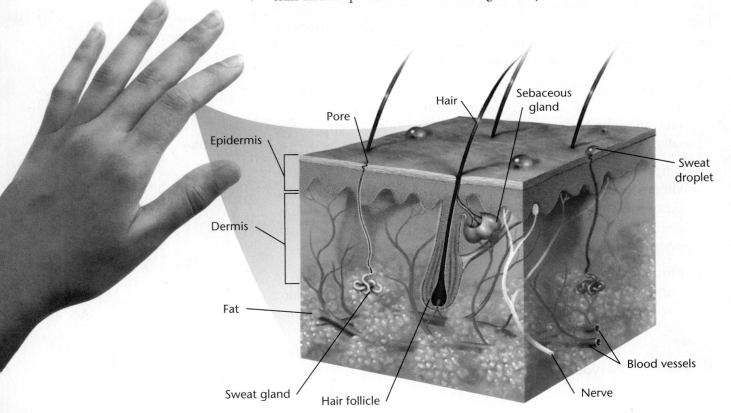

Pore Hair Sebaceous gland
Epidermis
Sweat droplet
Dermis
Fat
Sweat gland Hair follicle Nerve Blood vessels

Tips for Avoiding UV-Ray Damage
- Do not use tanning beds.
- Limit sun exposure from 10 A.M. to 4 P.M.
- Use sunscreen of SPF 15 or higher.
- Wear a hat with a brim.
- Wear long sleeves and pants when possible.
- Do not use products to help you tan.

FIGURE 5 You can enjoy the outdoors and still protect your skin from the sun.

Caring for Your Skin

Most of the time, the skin requires only basic care such as regular washing with mild soap. Eating a balanced, healthy diet; drinking plenty of water; and sleeping enough will also keep your skin healthy. **The most important things you can do for your skin, however, are to avoid damage from the sun and tanning lamps and to monitor moles.** Treating acne and other skin problems can also help you feel and look your best.

Preventing Skin Damage Overexposure to ultraviolet (UV) radiation emitted from the sun and tanning lamps causes skin to become leathery, wrinkled, and discolored. It can also lead to skin cancer, including a sometimes deadly form called **melanoma.** Melanoma is the least common form of skin cancer. Yet it causes more deaths each year than other forms of skin cancer.

When you are outside, it is important to wear sunscreen that blocks UVA and UVB rays—two types of ultraviolet radiation that reach Earth. Sunscreens are numbered with a sun protection factor (SPF). The higher the SPF, the more protection a sunscreen provides. Sunscreen should be reapplied frequently, especially if you have been swimming or sweating. See Figure 5 for other ways to protect your skin from the sun.

Monitoring Moles The first sign of melanoma is usually an irregularly shaped mole, or brown spot, that increases in size. The mole may become blue-black or have blackish spots. Without early treatment, melanoma will spread to other organs. If you notice any change in a wart, birthmark, or mole—or any skin growth that appears abnormal—you should consult a doctor.

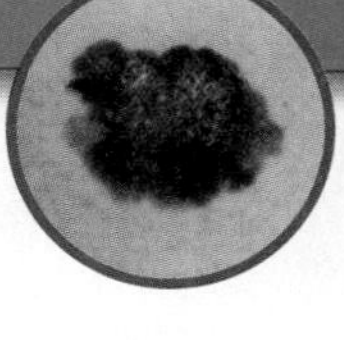

Connect to Your Life How do you protect your skin from ultraviolet radiation damage?

FIGURE 6 The ABCD rule is a guide for detecting melanoma. Note the irregularities of the mole shown below.

The ABCD Rule

ASYMMETRY One half of a mole does not match the other half.

BORDER The edges are uneven, notched, or blurred.

COLOR The color is not consistent throughout the mole.

DIAMETER The diameter is greater than 1/4 inch or has been growing.

FIGURE 7 If a follicle becomes blocked, bacteria can infect it. Your body's reaction to the infection leads to a pimple. Keeping your face clean can help prevent pimples.

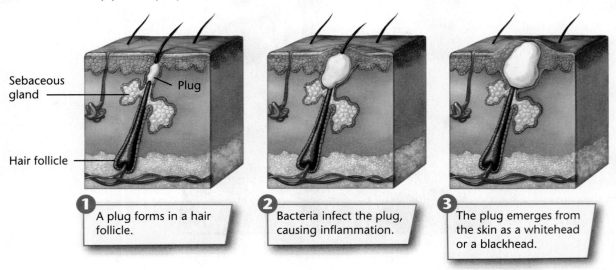

Sebaceous gland

Plug

Hair follicle

1 A plug forms in a hair follicle.

2 Bacteria infect the plug, causing inflammation.

3 The plug emerges from the skin as a whitehead or a blackhead.

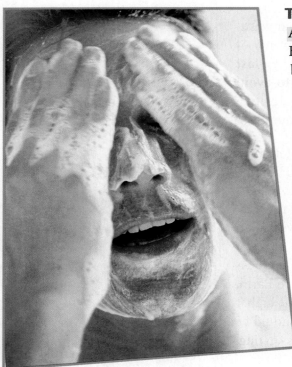

Treating Acne One common skin problem in teens is acne. **Acne** forms when excess oil and dead cells plug a hair follicle. Bacteria from the skin's surface multiply within the plug. The bacteria attract white blood cells, which cause the hair follicle to become inflamed and an acne lesion, or pimple, to form. Lesions that stay beneath the skin's surface are called whiteheads. Blackheads are lesions that open at the skin's surface.

Hormones, heredity, and stress are some factors that influence acne outbreaks. Greasy foods and chocolate do not cause acne. The best defense against acne is keeping your skin clean. If you have oily skin, wash with mild soap two or three times a day. More frequent washing may worsen acne because it will stimulate your oil glands to produce more oil.

Because your fingers and nails carry bacteria, do not scratch or squeeze acne. Products that contain benzoyl peroxide, a chemical that dries out pimples and kills bacteria, can help mild cases of acne. For a more severe case of acne, you should see a **dermatologist,** a doctor who specializes in treating skin problems.

Treating Eczema Another skin disorder is **eczema** (EK suh muh), a condition in which an area of skin becomes red, swollen, hot, and itchy. Sometimes the skin blisters and oozes. Eczema is not contagious.

Substances that irritate the skin, including chemicals, soaps, or poison ivy, can cause eczema. Certain medicines and foods may also cause this skin irritation. Some people inherit a tendency to develop eczema. In most cases, eczema can be treated with a medication applied to the skin. To prevent eczema from recurring, a person should try to identify and avoid substances that irritate the skin.

Treating Skin Infections Several types of microorganisms can infect the skin. Although the majority of these infections are not serious, they can be painful or embarrassing.

GO ONLINE

PearsonSuccessNet.com

For: More on acne

▶ **Boils** Boils are swollen, painful infections of hair follicles caused by bacteria. They start as red, tender lumps that fill with pus. Eventually they rupture and drain. Boils can occur anywhere on the body, but are most common on the face, neck, armpits, and thighs. If a boil does not heal after two weeks or is accompanied by a fever, you should see a doctor.

▶ **Cold Sores** Cold sores are clusters of watery blisters caused by a virus. These sores usually occur around the outside of the mouth and last about a week. To prevent the virus from spreading to other parts of the body, wash your hands after touching the affected area.

▶ **Warts** Warts are hardened growths on the skin that are also caused by a virus. Over-the-counter medication is available to treat warts. See a doctor if a wart persists or spreads after treatment.

▶ **Ringworm** Skin infections caused by fungi usually occur in warm, moist areas of the skin. The ringworm fungus, which is highly contagious, produces red, scaly, ring-shaped patches on the skin. Ringworm is treated with prescription medication.

▶ **Athlete's Foot** Another common fungal infection is athlete's foot. It causes burning, itching, cracking, and peeling of the skin on the feet and between the toes. Over-the-counter medication is available for athlete's foot. However, for a severe infection that does not respond to over-the-counter medication, you should see a doctor. Figure 8 lists some tips for preventing athlete's foot.

Connect to Your Life Identify a problem that you have had with your skin. How did you care for it?

FIGURE 8 The fungus that causes athlete's foot thrives in the damp and warm environment of a shoe.

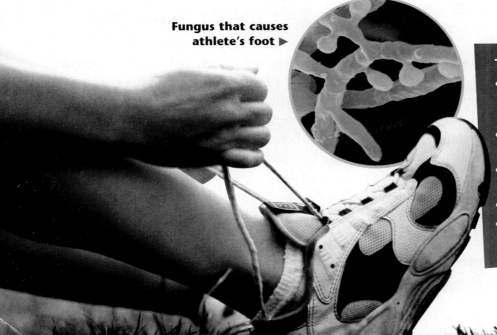
Fungus that causes athlete's foot ▶

To Prevent Athlete's Foot
• Wear flip-flops or shower shoes in locker rooms and shared showers.
• Wash your feet more than once a day.
• Dry your feet thoroughly, especially between the toes.
• Powder your feet.
• If your feet perspire, change your socks during the day.

FIGURE 9 Healthy hair requires only basic care.

Hair Care Tips
- Wash your hair every two days.
- Have your hair trimmed regularly.
- When detangling your hair, start at the ends.
- Do not brush wet hair.
- Allow hair to air dry whenever possible.
- Avoid overuse of styling products.

Your Hair

Almost every exposed surface of the body is covered with hair, except the palms of the hands and soles of the feet. **Hair protects the scalp from sunlight and provides insulation from the cold. Hairs in the nostrils and ears and your eyelashes prevent debris from entering the body.**

Caring for Your Hair Keeping your hair clean and well-groomed enhances your appearance. Frequent brushing of your hair will remove excess dirt and make your hair shine. Shampooing removes dirt and oil buildup from sebaceous gland secretions. However, your hair may become dry and brittle if you wash it too frequently or use a shampoo made with harsh chemicals. In addition, dyeing or highlighting your hair may also cause dryness and brittleness.

Hair Problems Head lice are small insects that live on the scalp and lay their eggs on hair. Head-lice infection is not a sign of poor hygiene. Anyone who comes in contact with lice can be infected. The best way to prevent infections is to avoid sharing combs, brushes, or hats. Several shampoos are available to kill lice.

Another common hair problem is dandruff. Dandruff occurs when the epidermal cells of the scalp are shed at a faster than normal rate. Some factors that may contribute to dandruff are fungal infections, overactive oil glands, stress, and heredity. Regular hairwashing with dandruff shampoo should help control this problem.

Connect to Your Life How does the appearance of your hair affect your mood? Why do you think this is so?

Your Nails

Nails grow from an area of rapidly dividing cells near the tips of the fingers and toes. **The tough, platelike nails cover and protect the tips of your fingers and toes, which come in frequent contact with objects in your environment.** During cell division, the cells fill with keratin and become nails.

Caring for Your Nails   Keeping your nails clean will help prevent the spread of infectious microorganisms to other parts of your body and to other people. Clip and file your nails so that their edges are smooth. Jagged edges may dig into your skin and cause infections. Avoid biting your nails. Nail biting can lead to breaks in your skin that allow microorganisms to enter.

Nail Problems   An ingrown toenail results when the sides of a toenail grow into the skin. If not treated properly, ingrown nails can become infected. To prevent ingrown toenails, clip your toenails straight across.

Fungal infections of the nails are common in people who often have wet hands or feet. Infected nails appear thick and discolored with white markings. If you suspect that you have a fungal infection, see a doctor.

Nail Care Tips
- Keep your nails clean and dry.
- Do not rip hangnails, cut them with a nail clipper.
- Apply lotion daily to prevent nails from cracking.
- Seek treatment for infections.
- Use nail polish remover as infrequently as possible.
- If you go to a salon, ask how they prevent the spread of infections.

FIGURE 10   Proper nail care, which includes filing, clipping, and cleaning helps to prevent minor cuts and the spread of disease.

Section 2 Review

Key Ideas and Vocabulary

1. What are the three major functions of the skin?

2. What is a **sebaceous gland?** What is its function?

3. Besides basic care, identify four other ways to keep your skin healthy.

4. What is thought to be the cause of most cases of **melanoma?**

5. What are the functions of your hair and nails?

Critical Thinking

6. Relating Cause and Effect Victims of serious burns often suffer from infection and loss of body fluids. Explain why this happens.

Health at School

Sun Safety Poster Create a poster that alerts teens to the skin damage caused by ultraviolet radiation. Use a slogan and visuals to make your point in a compelling manner. With permission, hang the poster at school.

7. Evaluating Although most people know the dangers of tanning, some people still consider a tan to be a sign of good health. Why do you think this is the case?

8. Making Judgments You are hiring people as servers in a restaurant. A person that you interview has dirty nails. How might this fact affect your decision to hire the person?

Analyzing Influences

Recognizing Misleading Claims

Each year millions of people spend billions of dollars on fraudulent health products, such as weight-loss aids, supplements, and "miracle" skin products. Many of these consumers fall victim to the persuasive product claims found in advertisements. In some situations, the loss is just monetary. But sometimes, people put their health at risk too. For example, people might not seek needed treatment from a healthcare professional if they think they have found their own "cure." These guidelines can help you avoid being a victim of misleading product claims.

Fight acne with

Acne B-Gone

"If you use Acne B-Gone, you will have perfect, blemish-free skin!"

Have clear, glowing beautiful skin!

Guaranteed—or your money back!

Acne B-Gone has a special, secret ingredient that prevents pimples from forming. Scientists have proven that Acne B-Gone works better than any other product.

1 **Examine the product's claims for misleading information.**

Ask yourself these questions.

▶ **Do any of the claims contradict common knowledge?** For example, a diet supplement that promises weight loss without the need to change eating and exercise habits should not be taken seriously.

▶ **What wording is used in the claim?** Be wary of words and phrases such as miracle, secret ingredient, ancient remedy, or scientific breakthrough.

▶ **Is the claim based on a testimonial?** An endorsement from a famous person or a "happy customer" may convince people that a product works.

▶ **Can scientific studies be verified?** A claim may state that the product has proven effective in scientific studies. However, the claim will probably offer little information about the actual studies.

▶ **Does the ad use "hurry up" techniques?** Some ads may claim that there are only limited quantities available to push you into making a quick decision.

▶ **Does the ad promise you a money-back guarantee?** You should not count on these guarantees. It is not always easy or possible to get your money back.

2 **Try to check any claims made about the product.**

▶ Before purchasing a product, read the packaging information, including the fine print. Does any of the information indicate the product is actually less effective or suitable than the claims imply?

▶ If you are unsure about the language used on the packaging, ask a healthcare professional for advice.

3 **Request more information.**

You can request more information from the product's manufacturer about any claims that seem suspicious. Or, you could visit the web site of the Federal Trade Commission to search for any customer complaints made about the particular manufacturer.

Practice the Skill

1. Analyze the ad for Acne-B-Gone.
   a. Describe the claims made by the ad.
   b. Do any of the claims make you suspicious? Why or why not?
2. Analyze three other magazine or television advertisements for personal-care products such as hairstyling products or deodorants.
   a. Evaluate whether the ads include misleading or suspicious claims.
   b. Look for one of the products in a local store. Does any of the packaging information indicate that the product is less effective than the ad implied?
3. Find an ad that makes claims about a scientific study that supports the effectiveness of the product.
   a. List some questions you would like to have answered about the study to believe its claims.
   b. How could you find this information?

Your Eyes and Ears

Objectives

▶ **Explain** how your eyes allow you to see.

▶ **Identify** two ways to keep your eyes healthy.

▶ **Explain** how your ears allow you to hear and maintain your balance.

▶ **Identify** ways to keep your ears healthy.

Vocabulary

- cornea
- pupil
- iris
- lens
- retina
- optometrist
- eardrum
- cochlea
- semicircular canals
- audiologist

Warm-Up

Dear Advice Line,

One of my friends likes to play loud music when I am at his house. Sometimes when I leave, my ears are ringing and I have trouble hearing for several hours. I've asked him to lower the music, but he just laughs at me. I don't want to stop hanging out with him. What should I do?

WRITING   Write a response to this teen to help solve the problem.

Your Eyes

Much of the information you gather about your environment reaches your brain through your eyes. Because of your eyes, you can enjoy the beauty of colorful sunsets. Your eyes warn you when a car is approaching, and help you recognize the faces of friends. **The eyes are complex organs that respond to light by sending impulses. Your brain then interprets the impulses as images.**

How Light Enters Your Eye   When rays of light strike the eye, they pass through the structures shown in Figure 11. First the light strikes the **cornea** (KAWR nee uh), the clear tissue that covers the front of the eye. The light then passes through a chamber filled with a liquid that nourishes the eye. The light then reaches the **pupil,** the opening through which light enters the eye.

The size of the pupils adjusts based on the amount of light entering the eye. In bright light, the pupil becomes smaller. In dim light, the pupil becomes larger. The **iris** is a circular structure that surrounds the pupil and regulates its size. The iris also contains pigments that give your eyes their color.

Connect to Your Life   **What color are your eyes? What part of your eyes contain this color?**

How Light Is Focused   Light that passes through the pupil strikes the lens. The **lens** is a flexible structure that focuses light. Muscles attached to the lens adjust its shape, producing an image that is in focus. The lens of your eye functions something like the lens of a camera, which focuses light on photographic film. Because of the way in which the lens of the eye bends the light rays, the image it produces is upside down and reversed.

How You See an Image   After passing through the lens, focused light rays pass through a clear, jellylike fluid. Then the light rays strike the **retina,** a layer of cells that lines the back of the eye.

The retina contains about 130 million cells called rods and cones that respond to light. Rods work best in dim light and allow you to see black, white, and shades of gray. Cones work best in bright light and allow you to see colors. One type of cone cell responds to red light, another to blue, and a third to green. This difference between rods and cones explains why you see colors best in bright light, but only gray images in dim light.

When light strikes the rods and cones, nerve impulses travel through the optic nerves to the brain. One optic nerve carries impulses from the left eye and the other from the right eye. In the cerebrum, the brain turns the flipped image right-side up. The brain also combines the information from each eye to produce a single image.

The Eye

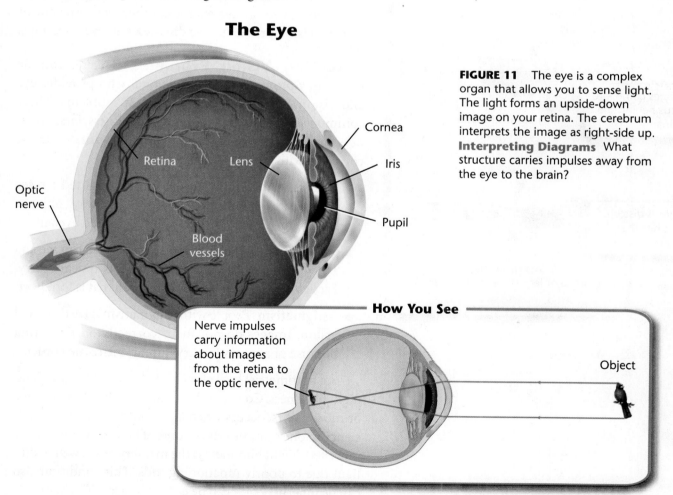

FIGURE 11   The eye is a complex organ that allows you to sense light. The light forms an upside-down image on your retina. The cerebrum interprets the image as right-side up. **Interpreting Diagrams** What structure carries impulses away from the eye to the brain?

Optic nerve

Retina   Lens

Cornea

Iris

Pupil

Blood vessels

How You See

Nerve impulses carry information about images from the retina to the optic nerve.

Object

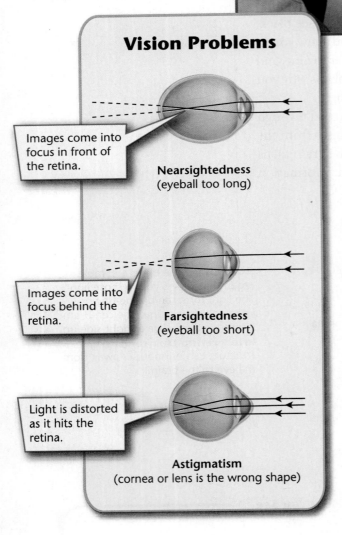

FIGURE 12 Optometrists treat nearsightedness, farsightedness, and astigmatism with different types of lenses. The lenses make light focus on the ideal portion of the retina.

Vision Problems

Images come into focus in front of the retina.

Nearsightedness
(eyeball too long)

Images come into focus behind the retina.

Farsightedness
(eyeball too short)

Light is distorted as it hits the retina.

Astigmatism
(cornea or lens is the wrong shape)

Caring for Your Eyes

There are some things you can do to help your eyes stay healthy throughout your lifetime. **It is important to protect your eyes from damage and to have regular eye exams.** To protect your eyes from damage wear protective goggles when you work with harmful substances or around machinery. Also, wear sunglasses that provide UV protection. Regular eye exams can help you prevent or identify vision problems, eye diseases, and eye infections.

Detecting Vision Problems During routine visits, an **optometrist,** a professional who provides eye and vision care, checks you for vision problems. Three common vision problems are nearsightedness, farsightedness, and astigmatism. All three problems usually can be corrected with eyeglasses or contact lenses.

▶ **Nearsightedness** People who are nearsighted can see nearby objects clearly, but not faraway objects. Nearsightedness is caused by an elongated eyeball.

▶ **Farsightedness** People who are farsighted can see faraway objects clearly, but nearby objects appear blurry. Farsightedness is caused by an eyeball that is too short.

▶ **Astigmatism** People with astigmatism have distorted vision. Images do not focus correctly on the retina because of an uneven curvature in the cornea or lens.

An optometrist may also check for colorblindness and night blindness. Colorblindness, the inability to detect one or more colors, occurs when a person is born with a deficiency in one or more sets of cones. This disorder is usually inherited. Night blindness is the inability to see well in dim light due to poorly functioning rods. This condition also can be inherited, or it can be caused by a lack of vitamin A.

Treating Eye Diseases As a person ages, the eyes become susceptible to several diseases.

▶ **Glaucoma** Age and certain diseases, such as diabetes and high blood pressure, may slow the drainage of liquid from the eye. The result is a buildup of pressure in the eye, a condition called glaucoma (glaw KOH muh). Glaucoma can damage the optic nerve and lead to sight problems. Glaucoma often develops so slowly that a person may have severe vision damage before it is detected. Regular eye exams can detect glaucoma before symptoms are noticed.

▶ **Cataracts** The clouding of the eye's lens is known as a cataract. This condition is very common among older adults. Treatment involves surgical replacement of the clouded lens with an artificial lens. Wearing sunglasses with UV-ray protection and not smoking are two behaviors that may slow or prevent the development of cataracts.

▶ **Detached Retina** Aging or an injury to the eye can cause the retina to separate from the lining of the eye. Surgery is the only effective treatment for a detached retina.

▶ **Macular Degeneration** The leading cause of eyesight problems in older adults is macular degeneration. This condition occurs when cells in the center of the retina break down. Treatment for macular degeneration is limited and often depends on the extent of the damage.

Treating Eye Infections Two common eye infections are sties and conjunctivitis. A sty is a painful swelling that occurs when an oil gland at the base of an eyelash becomes infected. Allergic reactions or infections related to colds can lead to conjunctivitis, an inflammation of the outside layer of the eye. The eye may ooze a yellowish fluid and become red and itchy. Sties and conjunctivitis can be treated with prescription medications.

Connect to Your Life Have you ever had an eye infection? How was it treated?

GO ONLINE
PearsonSuccessNet.com
For: More on eye diseases

FIGURE 13 Spending extended periods of time in front of a computer can lead to eyestrain. Although eyestrain does not cause permanent damage, it can be uncomfortable and distracting.

Eye Care Tips

▶ Blink often when using a computer.

▶ Look away from a computer or television every 30 minutes for about 10 seconds.

▶ Do not rub your eyes.

▶ If you wear contact lenses, follow your doctor's instructions.

▶ Eat foods rich in vitamin A such as carrots, red peppers, and cantaloupe.

▶ When outdoors, wear sunglasses that provide 100% UV-ray protection.

359

Your Ears

You know that your ears allow you to hear, but do you know that they also help you keep your balance? **The ears convert sounds into nerve impulses that your brain interprets. In addition, structures in the ear detect the position and movement of your head.** By sensing movement and position, your ears help you to stand upright, walk smoothly, and adjust your body's position.

The Outer Ear   Figure 14 shows the three regions of the ear—the outer ear, middle ear, and inner ear. When you look in a mirror, you can see part of the outer ear. This part, which is covered with a thin layer of skin, acts as a collecting funnel for sounds. Sounds travel to your ears as vibrations—movements in the air. In the outer ear, the vibrations are channeled into the ear canal, a narrow cavity that leads to the middle ear. At the end of the ear canal is a thin membrane called the **eardrum.** The eardrum vibrates when sound vibrations strike it.

The Middle Ear   Vibrations from the eardrum pass to the middle ear, which contains three small bones—the hammer, the anvil, and the stirrup. The vibrating eardrum causes the hammer to vibrate, which pushes against the anvil, which then moves the stirrup.

Have you ever felt your ears pop in an elevator? This happens because the air pressure in the outer ear suddenly changes. Usually the pressure in the outer ear and the middle ear is the same. The auditory tube, which connects the middle ear with the back of the throat, keeps the pressure equal so that your eardrum vibrates correctly. Most of the time the auditory tube is closed. When you cough, swallow, or yawn, however, it opens. You hear a popping sound as the air pressure in the middle ear and outer ear equalize.

FIGURE 14   Sound vibrations enter the outer ear and cause structures in the middle ear to vibrate. When the vibrations reach the inner ear, nerve impulses travel to the brain via the auditory nerve.

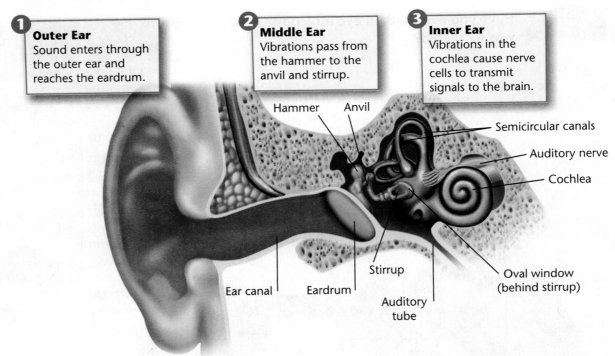

1 Outer Ear
Sound enters through the outer ear and reaches the eardrum.

2 Middle Ear
Vibrations pass from the hammer to the anvil and stirrup.

3 Inner Ear
Vibrations in the cochlea cause nerve cells to transmit signals to the brain.

Hammer   Anvil

Semicircular canals

Auditory nerve

Cochlea

Ear canal   Eardrum

Stirrup

Auditory tube

Oval window (behind stirrup)

FIGURE 15 Structures in the surfer's inner ear, together with his eyes, muscles, and brain, help him keep his balance as he rides the waves.

Waves, car trips, and rides give some people **motion sickness.** They feel ill when their **brains** receive **conflicting information** from their **ears and eyes.**

The Inner Ear   After the anvil passes vibrations to the stirrup, the stirrup pushes on the oval window. The oval window is a membrane-covered opening that separates the middle ear from the inner ear. Vibrations are passed through the oval window to a hollow, coiled tube filled with fluid called the **cochlea** (KAWK lee uh).

The cochlea is lined with cells with hairlike extensions that sense vibrations. When the cochlear fluid moves, the cells stimulate impulses in nerves. The impulses travel through the auditory nerve to the brain, where they are interpreted as sound.

The Inner Ear and Balance   Above the cochlea in your inner ear are the **semicircular canals,** structures that send information to your brain about the movements of your head. Two sacs located behind the canals capture information about your head's position. The canals and sacs are also lined with tiny cells that have hairlike extensions.

When your head moves, the fluid inside the semicircular canals and sacs causes the "hairs" to move. The movement stimulates nerve cells, which send impulses to your brain. Your brain interprets these impulses to determine the position of your body. In response, the brain sends signals to your muscles to help you keep your balance.

What part of your ear helps you to walk down a flight of stairs?

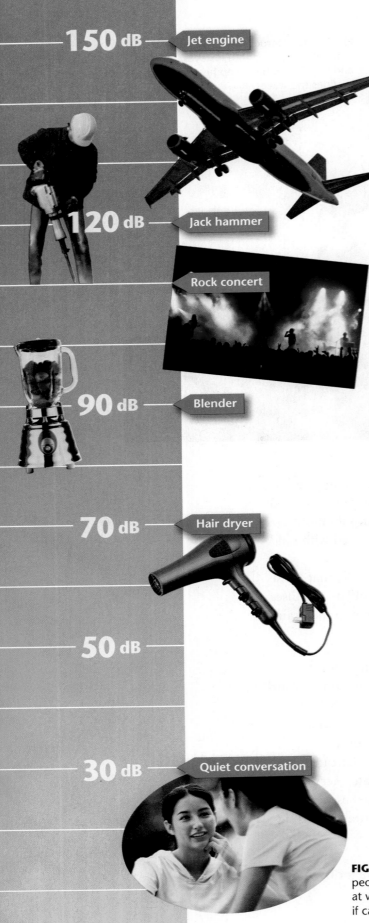

150 dB — Jet engine

120 dB — Jack hammer

Rock concert

90 dB — Blender

70 dB — Hair dryer

50 dB

30 dB — Quiet conversation

0 dB

Caring for Your Ears

Proper ear care is fairly simple. **Besides keeping your ears clean, you also need to monitor noise levels. In addition, you should see a doctor if you experience ear pain or hearing difficulties.**

Ear Care Use a wet washcloth to clean your outer ear and the front part of your ear canal. Dry your ears thoroughly after you wash them.

Never insert a cotton-tipped swab or any other object into your ear canal. The swab can damage your eardrum. Swabs may also compress the earwax. Earwax, which is secreted by glands lining your ear canal, traps dust and microorganisms. If the earwax is compressed, it will not drain normally.

Monitoring Noise Levels Partial hearing loss or deafness can result from damage to nerves or to the vibration-sensing cells in the cochlea. This type of hearing damage is generally permanent. The longer and more often a person is exposed to loud noise, the more likely it is that noticeable hearing damage will occur.

The intensity, or loudness, of sound is measured in units called decibels (DES uh bulz). Exposure to sounds above 80 decibels (dB) for several hours at a time can damage hearing. Exposure to sounds above 120 dB for even a few seconds can damage hearing. Ringing in your ears or difficulty hearing normal conversation are signs that you have exposed yourself to ear-damaging noise levels.

To avoid hearing damage, keep your television and stereo low enough that you can comfortably hear a person speaking at a normal level. When listening to music with headphones or ear buds, you should never turn the music player up to more than 60 percent of its potential volume.

 Connect to Your Life **In what ways do you try to protect your hearing?**

FIGURE 16 Many sounds that people are exposed to at home and at work can lead to hearing damage if care is not taken.

Treating Ear Infections Bacterial infections of the middle ear can sometimes result in some hearing loss—especially if the infections occur frequently and are not treated. A middle-ear infection may cause the eardrum to break, or rupture. Although the eardrum will heal, scarring will result. Scar tissue makes the eardrum less flexible and less able to transmit sound.

Middle-ear infections are especially common in young children. An infected ear usually aches, feels warm, and may feel filled with fluid. If you have an earache, see a doctor. If you are prone to ear infections or have ever had a damaged eardrum, you should wear earplugs when swimming.

Treating Hearing Problems Hearing loss, whether temporary or permanent, can be caused by factors other than loud noise or infections. Some types of hearing loss can be inherited. Diseases, high fevers, and certain medications can also cause hearing loss. A buildup of wax in the ear can cause temporary hearing loss when the wax blocks the passage of sound vibrations. A doctor can remove the wax or prescribe treatments to soften the wax.

People with hearing problems see an audiologist (aw dee AHL uh jist). **Audiologists** are professionals who are trained to evaluate hearing and treat hearing loss. In some cases, people with hearing loss use hearing aids. Most hearing aids increase the volume of sounds and transmit the sounds into the ear canal. Another treatment, called a cochlear implant, does not increase the volume of sounds. Instead, it acts as a replacement cochlea by converting sound waves to impulses that can be sent to the brain.

FIGURE 17 Cochlear implants do not restore hearing, but they do help a deaf person understand speech and other sounds going on around them.

Section 3 Review

Key Ideas and Vocabulary

1. List the structures in the eye through which light passes to allow you to see an image.

2. List two ways you can keep your eyes healthy.

3. Trace the path of sound from your outer ear until it is perceived by your brain.

4. How do the **semicircular canals** help you keep your balance?

5. List three ways you can keep your ears healthy.

Critical Thinking

6. Classifying If nearby objects seem blurry, what type of vision problem might you have? What does this indicate about the shape of your eyes?

Health and Community

Music and Hearing Loss Going to a concert with friends can be a lot of fun, but it can also put the health of your ears at risk. Research some strategies that allow you to protect your ears from loud music and still enjoy a concert. Make a pamphlet that shares these strategies with your classmates. **WRITING**

7. Predicting If a person were born with only green and blue cone cells, which color would the person have trouble seeing? How might this condition affect the person?

8. Relating Cause and Effect Why may an infection of the inner ear cause you to lose your balance?

Sleep and Feeling Fit

Objectives

▶ **Describe** why sleep is important for health.

▶ **Explain** how circadian rhythms influence the sleep patterns of teens.

Vocabulary

- insomnia
- sleep apnea
- narcolepsy
- circadian rhythm

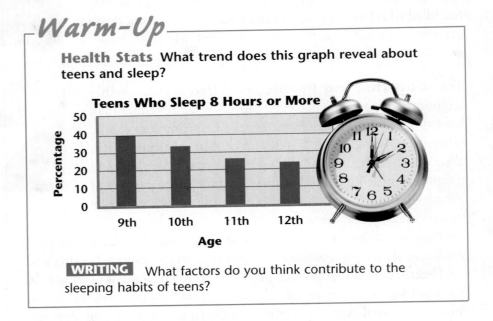

Warm-Up

Health Stats What trend does this graph reveal about teens and sleep?

Teens Who Sleep 8 Hours or More

(bar graph: Percentage vs. Age — 9th: ~42, 10th: ~35, 11th: ~28, 12th: ~26)

WRITING What factors do you think contribute to the sleeping habits of teens?

What Is Sleep?

Sleep is the deep relaxation of the body and mind during which the eyes are usually closed and there is little conscious thought or movement. During sleep, your muscles relax, your breathing and heart rate decrease, and your body temperature drops slightly. **Although some people think of sleep as wasted time, it is actually just as important to the body as air, water, and food.**

Benefits of Sleep Scientists have yet to agree on the reason why people sleep. But their research has uncovered a number of possible benefits of sleep.

▶ During sleep, your brain sorts the day's information. Learning and the storage of memories may occur.

▶ The healing of body tissues occurs during sleep. For example, the damage done to muscle tissue after a workout heals while you sleep.

▶ Adequate sleep helps the immune system to function properly.

▶ Adequate sleep may help prevent some diseases, such as diabetes.

Connect to Your Life How does your body feel after a night of too little sleep? How does your mind function?

The Sleep Cycle As you sleep, your body and brain go through periods of light and heavy sleep. Figure 18 shows the typical sleep cycle. At first, you enter nonrapid eye movement sleep (NREM). As you pass through the four stages of NREM sleep, your body gradually reaches a state of deep relaxation.

After the stages of NREM sleep, you enter rapid eye movement sleep (REM). During REM sleep, your eyes flicker rapidly behind closed eyelids, and there is a high level of brain activity. This is also the stage of sleep in which you dream. Your muscles are paralyzed during REM sleep, which prevents you from acting out your dreams.

Notice in Figure 18 that you alternate between NREM and REM sleep during the night. About 25 percent of your sleeping time is REM sleep. This percentage decreases as you age. REM sleep may be when you form long-term memories and when your brain discards unneeded information.

Sleep Disorders A number of sleep disorders can affect your health. Sleep disorders should not be ignored. If you experience symptoms of any of these disorders, you should see a doctor for treatment.

▶ **Insomnia** refers to difficulties falling asleep or staying asleep. Insomnia can be caused by stress or some physical problems.

▶ **Sleep apnea** (AP nee uh) is a disorder in which a person stops breathing for short periods during sleep and then suddenly resumes breathing. This may happen 20 to 30 times an hour without the person being aware of it. However, he or she may be extremely tired during the day.

▶ **Narcolepsy** is a disorder in which a person experiences severe sleepiness during the day, or falls asleep suddenly. The brain of someone with narcolepsy does not regulate the wake-sleep cycle normally.

GO ONLINE
PearsonSuccessNet.com
For: More on teens and sleep

FIGURE 18 During a typical eight-hour period, you cycle between NREM sleep and REM sleep several times. **Reading Graphs** How many times was this person in REM sleep? In stage 4 NREM sleep?

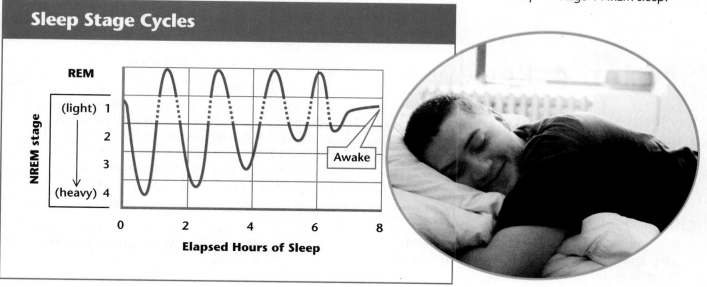

Sleep Stage Cycles

REM

NREM stage

(light) 1
2
3
(heavy) 4

Awake

0   2   4   6   8
Elapsed Hours of Sleep

FIGURE 19 Sleeping less than you should leads to several negative consequences that will impact your daily life.

Some Effects of Sleep Loss
- Depression
- Problems with focusing and paying attention
- Difficulties learning
- Increased risk of illness
- Increased risk of motor vehicle crashes

Teens and Sleep

Do you have a hard time waking up for school, but do not feel tired at night? This is a common problem for teens. The sleep cycle is under the influence of the body's **circadian rhythm** (sur KAY dee un)—the body's internal system for regulating behavior patterns during a 24-hour cycle. **Puberty affects the body's circadian rhythm. One result is that teens want to sleep later into the day and stay awake later at night than adults.**

Most teens need about nine hours of sleep each night. However, teens sleep an average of seven hours. Some of the consequences of not getting enough sleep on a regular basis are listed in Figure 19. Here are some tips to help you develop good sleep habits.

▶ Go to bed and wake up at the same times each day, even on weekends.

▶ Avoid bright lights at night. After waking, expose yourself to bright light as soon as possible.

▶ Avoid caffeine and sugary foods after noon.

▶ Exercise regularly, but not right before bedtime.

▶ Don't fall asleep with the television on.

▶ Avoid all-nighters, which disrupt your sleep patterns.

▶ If you nap, do not let your naps interfere with your regular sleep patterns.

▶ If you can't fall asleep, get up and do something relaxing until you feel tired.

Section 4 Review

Key Ideas and Vocabulary

1. List three possible health benefits of sleep.
2. Explain the symptoms of **insomnia** and **narcolepsy**.
3. Describe how the typical circadian rhythm of teens affects their sleep patterns.

Critical Thinking

4. **Relating Cause and Effect** Why do people with sleep apnea feel tired even after sleeping for eight hours or more?

Health at Home

Sleep Journal For two weeks, keep track of what time you go to bed and wake up. Also note how you feel each day, both mentally and physically. At the end of the two weeks, review your journal. In a paragraph, describe any connections you notice between your sleep pattern and your health status. **WRITING**

5. **Evaluating** List four reasons why you think teens do not get enough sleep. What can be done to address these reasons?

GO ONLINE PearsonSuccessNet.com | Audio Summary Section 14.4

Chapter 14
At a Glance

VIDEO **TEENS** Talk ◐
Taking Care of You How has watching this video changed your attitudes about personal care?

Section 1   Your Teeth and Gums

Key Ideas

▶ Healthy teeth allow you to chew your food properly and speak clearly.

▶ Healthy gums fit tightly around the neck of each tooth like a collar, holding it firmly in place.

▶ The changes that occur in the jaws throughout the growing years can lead to structural problems.

▶ A healthy diet, proper tooth care, and regular dental checkups can prevent tooth decay and gum disease.

Vocabulary
• enamel (342) • cementum (342) • dentin (342)
• pulp (342) • malocclusion (343) • orthodontist (343)
• halitosis (344) • plaque (344) • tartar (346)
• periodontal disease (346)

Section 2   Your Skin, Hair, and Nails

Key Ideas

▶ The skin protects the body from injury, infection, and water loss. It also helps to regulate body temperature and gathers outside information.

▶ Care for your skin by avoiding damage from UV-rays. Also, you should monitor your moles carefully.

▶ Hair protects the scalp from sunlight and provides insulation from the cold. Hairs in the nostrils and ears and your eyelashes keep out debris.

▶ Tough, platelike nails cover and protect the tips of your fingers and toes.

Vocabulary
• epidermis (348) • keratin (348)
• melanin (348) • dermis (348)
• pore (348) • follicle (348)
• sebaceous gland (348) • melanoma (349)
• acne (350) • dermatologist (350) • eczema (350)

Section 3   Your Eyes and Ears

Key Ideas

▶ The eyes are complex organs that respond to light by sending impulses to your brain.

▶ It is important to protect your eyes from damage and to have regular eye exams.

▶ The ear converts sounds into impulses that your brain interprets. In addition, structures in the ear detect the position and movement of your head.

▶ Keep your ears clean. You should also monitor noise levels and see a doctor if you experience ear pain or hearing difficulties.

Vocabulary
• cornea (356) • pupil (356) • iris (356)
• lens (357) • retina (357) • optometrist (358)
• eardrum (360) • cochlea (361)
• semicircular canals (361) • audiologist (363)

Section 4   Sleep and Feeling Fit

Key Ideas

▶ Although some people think of sleep as wasted time, it is actually just as important to the body as air, water, and food.

▶ Puberty affects the body's circadian rhythm. One result is that teens want to sleep later into the day and stay awake later at night than adults.

Vocabulary
• insomnia (365) • sleep apnea (365)
• narcolepsy (365) • circadian rhythm (366)

Chapter 14 Review

GO ONLINE

PearsonSuccessNet.com

For: Chapter 14 review activity

Reviewing Key Ideas

Section 1

1. What material covers the crown of a tooth?
   - **a.** dentin
   - **b.** enamel
   - **c.** pulp
   - **d.** gums

2. Which of the following is a condition in which the lower and upper teeth do not meet properly?
   - **a.** malocclusion
   - **b.** gingivitis
   - **c.** cementum
   - **d.** tooth decay

3. Explain the process by which tooth decay occurs.

4. What is an impacted wisdom tooth?

5. Why are regular visits to the dentist so important?

6. **Critical Thinking** Sometimes people lose their molars due to periodontal disease. How do you think this might affect their diet?

Section 2

7. Which of these structures are found in the dermis, but not the epidermis?
   - **a.** blood vessels
   - **b.** pores
   - **c.** living cells
   - **d.** hairs

8. How does your skin help to regulate your body temperature?

9. What characteristics of a new or changed mole might be signs of melanoma?

10. How can keeping your nails smooth and clean help you stay healthy?

11. **Critical Thinking** Soaps that dry out your skin can make acne breakouts worse. Why do you think this is true?

Section 3

12. The transparent structure that covers the front of the eye is the
    - **a.** pupil.
    - **b.** lens.
    - **c.** retina.
    - **d.** cornea.

13. How do the iris and the pupil work together to control the amount of light entering the eye?

14. What is astigmatism?

15. **Critical Thinking** What would happen if the bones of the middle ear were stuck together and could not move?

Section 4

16. Which sleep disorder involves the inability to fall asleep or stay asleep?
    - **a.** insomnia
    - **b.** narcolepsy
    - **c.** sleep apnea
    - **d.** circadian rhythm

17. What happens during NREM sleep? What happens during REM sleep?

18. What are some things you can do to help yourself get a good night's sleep?

19. **Critical Thinking** Studies have shown that night workers have a higher injury rate on the job than day workers. What do you think might account for the higher rate of injuries?

Building Health Skills

20. **Analyzing Influences** Watch an hour of children's television programs. Count the ads for sugary cereals and snacks. What techniques are used to capture the attention of children? How could these ads affect children's oral health?

21. **Communicating** Write a letter to your school newspaper offering reasons why school should start later in the day. **WRITING**

22. **Practicing Healthful Behaviors** Create a comic strip that uses humor to remind people about the importance of protecting the skin from the sun.

23. **Setting Goals** Come up with a plan for getting more sleep during the school week. Monitor your progress for one week, then make changes to your plan. Continue to monitor your sleep habits over the next few weeks.

Health and Community

Volunteering to Read Volunteer to read to people with impaired vision. You usually can find such programs at senior centers, nursing homes, or organizations for the blind. Once you have been reading for two weeks, write an editorial describing your experience. **WRITING**

Standardized Test Prep

Math Practice

The graph compares the percentage of total sleep that is spent in REM sleep in different age groups. Use the graph to answer Questions 24–26.

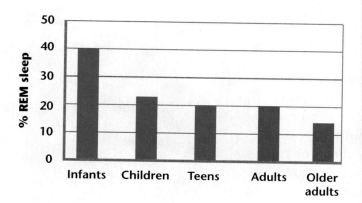

24. Which of the following statements is true according to the graph?
 A Infants spend the most time sleeping.
 B Children spend the same amount of time sleeping as adults.
 C The oldest adults spend the lowest percentage of time in REM sleep.
 D Not every age group spends time in REM sleep.

25. Which age group(s) spend 50% less time in REM sleep than infants?
 F Children
 G Children and teens
 H Teens and adults
 J Adults and older adults

26. Which title would be the best one for this graph?
 A Total REM Sleep
 B Total Percentage of Sleep
 C Total Sleep and Age
 D REM Sleep and Age

Test-Taking Tip

Get plenty of sleep the night before a test. You will be more alert and perform better if you are not tired.

Reading and Writing Practice

Read the passage. Then answer Questions 27–30.

UVA and UVB are two types of ultraviolet rays that reach Earth. Many people once thought that UVA rays caused tans, while UVB rays caused burns. Because tanning booths emit primarily UVA rays, people assumed that tanning booths were safer than sun exposure. However, recent research has shown this to be false. Although the two types of UV rays affect the skin in different ways, they both contribute to the development of skin cancer. Overexposure to either type of UV ray also damages proteins in skin, leading to signs of premature aging. In addition, the rays cause cataracts and suppress the immune system.

27. Which of the following statements is true according to this passage?
 A UVB rays are emitted from tanning beds, but not from the sun.
 B UVA rays are not dangerous to the skin, but UVB rays are.
 C Overexposure to the sun may make people look older than they actually are.
 D It is not yet known whether UVA rays contribute to the development of skin cancer.

28. In this passage, the word *premature* means
 F early.
 G abnormal.
 H excessive.
 J embarrassing.

29. What is the main idea of this passage?
 A No amount of exposure to sunlight is safe.
 B Both UVA and UVB rays have effects that are harmful to the body.
 C Scientists continue to study the effects of UV rays on the skin.
 D Overexposure to UV rays causes cataracts.

Constructed Response

30. In a paragraph, discuss the effects of UVA and UVB rays on the skin.

CAREERS

Physical Fitness

People in physical fitness careers help patients keep their bodies in top condition or rehabilitate from injuries.

Athletic Trainer

Athletic trainers work with athletes to help them prevent, treat, or recover from sports injuries. They may also provide first aid and non-emergency medical care at games and practices. Athletic trainers may work for college or professional sports teams, at sports medicine clinics, or in health clubs. For this career, you need a bachelor's degree in athletic training or a related field, and state certification. Some athletic trainers may also have a graduate degree.

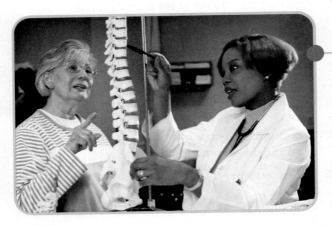

Chiropractor

Chiropractors diagnose and treat problems of the skeletal, nervous, and muscular systems. For some conditions, chiropractors might use a treatment technique called spinal manipulation. They also might recommend exercise and rest rather than medications. This career requires two to four years of premedical undergraduate study, a four-year chiropractic degree, and state licensing.

Orthodontist

Orthodontists are dentists with specialized training in treating dental and facial irregularities. They use corrective appliances such as braces, retainers, and headgear to align teeth, jaws, and lips. To become an orthodontist, a person must obtain degrees from both a dental program and an orthodontic program after college. Licenses in dentistry and orthodontics are also required.

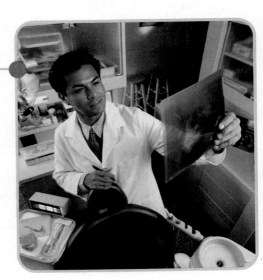

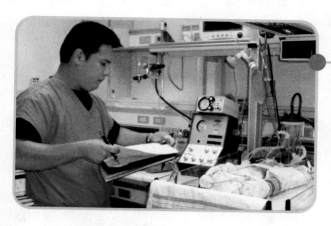

Respiratory Therapist

Respiratory therapists provide care for patients with chronic breathing problems such as asthma or emphysema. They may also treat premature infants whose lungs are not fully developed. This career requires a minimum of an associate's degree in respiratory therapy. Most states also require certification by the National Board for Respiratory Care and a state license.

Career Focus

Teodoro Tovar, Jr., Respiratory Therapist

How did you become interested in respiratory therapy?

"I became interested in respiratory therapy when my father was hospitalized after a near-fatal accident. While at his bedside, I witnessed the one-on-one care provided to him by the respiratory therapist. I was impressed by the therapist's knowledge and experience, and gained a lot of respect for the profession. After that experience I knew I wanted to become a respiratory therapist."

What does a respiratory therapist do?

"As a respiratory therapist, my job is to maintain an airway, assess oxygen needs, and give my patients ventilation assistance. I have worked with patients of all ages, but, for the past 15 years, I have specialized in neonates (premature babies)."

What challenges do the babies face?

"Because these babies have underdeveloped lungs, they can't get enough oxygen. I place them on special ventilators that breathe for them up to 400 times a minute."

What is the best part of your job?

"My favorite part is watching parents take their new baby home. The parents are so thankful, appreciative, and respectful of what respiratory therapists do. I become very close with the families. Sometimes the parents bring the baby back to the hospital just so I can see how well they are doing and how big and strong the baby has grown."

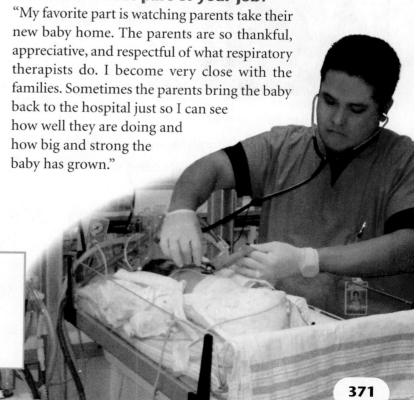

Health and Careers

Careers in Physical Fitness Research other physical fitness careers. Choose a career that interests you. Explain how keeping physically fit yourself would help you be successful at the career. **WRITING**

Alcohol

▶ **GO ONLINE** PearsonSuccessNet.com

VIDEO 15

TEENS Talk

Drinking Dangers

Preview **Activity**

What's Your Take on Drinking?

Complete this activity before you watch the video.

1. Ask five students your age to complete each sentence with the first thought that comes into mind.

   a. Alcohol is __?__ .

   b. Teens who refuse alcohol are __?__ .

   c. Teens who get drunk are __?__ .

   d. Driving after drinking alcohol is __?__ .

2. In a paragraph, describe what your survey revealed about teens' attitudes towards alcohol. **WRITING**

SOMETIMES IT TAKES A FAMILY OF FOUR TO STOP A DRUNK DRIVER. MADD

Alcohol Is a Drug

Objectives

▶ **Describe** how alcohol acts as a depressant in the body.

▶ **Identify** three major factors that influence underage drinking.

Vocabulary

• drug
• depressant
• fermentation
• zero-tolerance policy

Warm-Up

Quick Quiz See how many of these questions you can answer "yes" to.

1 Do you observe the law that prohibits people under age 21 from purchasing or possessing alcohol?

2 Do you avoid riding with drivers who have been drinking?

3 Do you say *no* to friends who pressure you to drink?

4 Do you know how to seek help for an alcohol problem?

WRITING What other things can you do to avoid the risks associated with drinking alcohol?

Facts About Alcohol

You may not think of alcohol as a drug, but it is. A **drug** is a chemical substance that is taken to cause changes in a person's body or behavior.

Alcohol Is a Depressant Alcohol acts as a powerful depressant. A **depressant** (dih PRES unt) is a drug that slows brain and body reactions. **In slowing the body's normal reactions, alcohol may cause confusion, decreased alertness, poor coordination, blurred vision, and drowsiness.**

The depressant effects of alcohol are very strong. If a person drinks large amounts of alcohol, vital functions such as heartbeat and breathing can be seriously affected. Death can result.

Alcohol Production The alcohol in beverages such as beer, wine, and liquor is produced by the process of fermentation. During **fermentation,** microorganisms called yeast feed on the sugars in foods such as malted grains, grapes, or berries. In the process, carbon dioxide and alcohol are produced.

How Much Alcohol Is in a Drink?

This 1.25-oz shot of liquor contains 40% alcohol, or 0.5 oz.

This 12-oz beer contains 4% alcohol or 0.5 oz.

This 5 oz-glass of wine contains 10% alcohol, or 0.5 oz.

To Calculate Alcohol Content
Multiply drink volume by percent alcohol.
Example: 5 oz wine × 0.10 = 0.5 oz

FIGURE 1 All of these drinks contain the same amount of alcohol—0.5 oz.
Calculating How much alcohol is in an 18-oz beer? **MATH**

Alcohol Content Not all alcoholic beverages contain the same amount of alcohol. The alcohol content of alcoholic beverages typically ranges from 4 percent to 50 percent.

Beverages with a greater percentage of alcohol, such as whiskey, gin, and rum, list their proof on the label. To calculate alcohol content from proof, divide by two. Thus 100-proof vodka is 50 percent alcohol.

Teens and Alcohol

For teens and others under the age of 21, using alcohol is illegal. In addition, many schools have adopted a **zero-tolerance policy.** Under such a policy, students face stiff consequences—including suspension—starting with the first time they are caught with alcohol or other drugs. Even so, alcohol is the most widely abused drug among high school students.

What influences teens' decisions about drinking? **The attitudes of peers, family, and the media strongly influence underage drinking.** Teens who refuse alcohol avoid the serious health and legal risks of this dangerous drug.

Influence of Peers Some teens say they drink to fit in, or just to do what their classmates seem to be doing. Teens often mistakenly believe that everyone is drinking. In fact, millions of teens never use alcohol.

Teens who choose friends who avoid alcohol will have an easier time refusing it themselves. Some teens refuse because they have a friend with an alcohol problem and don't want to turn out that way. Some teens refuse because they know a friend or family member who was killed because of drinking.

GO ONLINE
PearsonSuccessNet.com
For: More on drunk driving

Connect to Your Life How can you and your friends help each other avoid alcohol?

Media Wise

Sports and Alcohol

Think back to the last time you watched a sports event on TV. What kinds of products were advertised during the commercials? Chances are, some of the ads were for beer. Besides being aired during sports events, how do the ads try to connect sports and alcohol in people's minds?

Does the ad have a competitive or a sports-related theme?	Yes No
Does the beer have a "mascot," as many sports teams do?	Yes No
Is beer shown to improve athletic performance or increase enjoyment of sports?	Yes No
Does the ad make other connections to sports?	Yes No

A "Yes" answer to one or more questions indicates a link connecting an alcohol ad to sports.

Activity Watch two beer commercials that air during sporting events. Use the checklist above to evaluate whether the ads make a connection between sports and alcohol. Then explain how the connection to sports is misleading. **WRITING**

Influence of Family Teens report that parents and other family members are important influences on their decisions about alcohol. A majority of teens want their parents' guidance in making decisions about alcohol use. Although your parents may seem tough on you, their rules and advice can help you steer clear of alcohol and other drugs.

Influence of the Media Alcohol's wide availability makes it relatively easy to obtain. Alcohol use is also seen as generally acceptable in people who are over 21—even though it can be dangerous at any age.

Companies that sell alcohol bombard the public with advertisements for beer, wine, liquor, and other beverages. Television commercials and magazine ads often show drinkers in beautiful outdoor settings, at fun-filled parties, or enjoying sports. Although the ads never show underage drinking, the scenarios tend to appeal to teens as much as to adults.

Usually the message accompanying an alcohol ad says nothing about the product. Unlike ads for some drugs, alcohol ads are not required to list negative side effects. Instead, the ads promote a one-sided image of drinkers as athletic, healthy, and successful. The ads give the false impression that drinking will make you more popular and attractive.

Risks of Underage Drinking   Teen alcohol use can have very serious consequences. In fact, alcohol is a huge factor in injury deaths, the leading cause of death among teens. Teens who use alcohol increase their risk of the following:

▶ Being injured or killed in a motor vehicle crash

▶ Committing or being the victim of sexual assault or other violence

▶ Long-term brain damage

▶ Problems with alcohol later in life

▶ Suspension from school, sports teams, or other school activities

FIGURE 2 Each year, crashes and other injuries related to underage drinking kill about 5,000 youth in the United States.

Legal Risks   Laws prohibiting minors—people under the age of 21—from buying or possessing alcohol are enforced with heavy fines and lawful seizure of property. For example, law-enforcement officers in some states can seize a car in which a minor is in possession of alcohol. Selling alcohol to someone under the age of 21 is a criminal offense for the seller. In many states, it is against the law to serve alcohol to people under the legal drinking age, even at a private party.

People found to be driving under the influence of alcohol may have their driver's licenses taken away or face other stiff penalties. In some states, those found guilty repeatedly can be sent to prison. You will learn more about driving laws in the next section.

Section 1 Review

Key Ideas and Vocabulary

1. What is a **depressant**?

2. List at least three of the depressant effects alcohol may cause.

3. Describe how **fermentation** produces alcohol.

4. What are three major factors that influence underage drinking?

Critical Thinking

5. Making Judgments Some people argue that alcohol should not be considered a drug. After all, it is legal for adults to use alcohol. What do you think? **WRITING**

Health at School

School Policy on Alcohol Find out your school's policy on alcohol. Make a poster that informs your peers of the rules and the consequences. **WRITING**

6. Predicting What legal consequences could you face by possessing alcohol as a minor?

7. Relating Cause and Effect Students who use alcohol regularly are more likely than nondrinkers to get lower grades, drop out of school, and use other drugs. Offer some reasons why you think this is so. **WRITING**

Communicating

Developing Refusal Skills

Erica's friends are pressuring her to drink alcohol with them. Though Erica does not use drugs of any kind, she worries about what her friends will think if she refuses. Perhaps you have felt this way about saying no to your friends. Maybe you worried that if you refused, your friends would be disappointed or not want to hang out with you. You might even have decided to go along with your friends just to avoid the discomfort of saying no.

Refusing your friends is never easy. Nevertheless, being true to yourself and honest with friends are two important values. To refuse an offer convincingly, you may need to do more than say *no*. These guidelines can help you learn to say *no* in a way that tells others you mean it.

When You Refuse...

Do
- Make eye contact.
- Stand up tall.
- Use a firm voice.

Don't
- Look at the ground or glance away.
- Show that you're nervous.
- Speak softly.

1 **Give a reason for your refusal.**
When you say no, also state reasons for your refusal. Be honest—honest answers are more easily accepted by others. Some reasons might be:

"I want to keep a clear head."

"I could get suspended from the team."

"I'd rather have a soft drink."

2 **Use body language to reinforce what you say.**
Your body language can either strengthen or weaken your message.

3 **Show your concern for others.**
Express your concern for those trying to persuade you. In the case of friends who have decided to drink, you might say things like:

"I'd be really sad if anything happened to you."

"Your parents would ground you for months if they ever found out."

4 **Provide alternatives.**
Try to persuade your friends to do something safer or more comfortable. Here are some suggestions:

"I'm bored. Let's hang out at the Teen Center."

"This isn't fun. Let's go to a movie."

5 **Take a definite action.**
If your friends still try to persuade you after you have made your feelings clear, it is best not to continue repeating the point. Instead, take a definite action that removes you from the situation. This will make it clear that you cannot be persuaded to change your mind.

If All Else Fails...

Get up and leave the party.

Call other friends and do something else.

Always call for help rather than ride with someone who has been drinking.

Practice the Skill

1. Suppose that a friend asks you to sit close by during a test and share your answers.
   a. How would your friend's request make you feel? Why?
   b. If you were to refuse, what honest reason could you give? How would you express yourself?
   c. What are some possible consequences of saying no? What are some possible consequences of saying yes?

2. Think of two situations in which you said no to people who tried to convince you to do something you did not want to do.
   a. Describe each situation. List the things that allowed you to refuse in each case.
   b. In which situation was it more difficult to say no? Why?
   c. Did you use any of the steps presented in this skill when you refused? If so, describe the steps and how effective they were.

Alcohol's Effects on the Body

Objectives

▶ **Summarize** the effects of intoxication on the body systems.

▶ **List** four factors that affect blood alcohol concentration.

▶ **Identify** three ways that intoxication may lead to death.

Vocabulary

- intoxication
- blackout
- blood alcohol concentration (BAC)
- hangover
- driving while intoxicated (DWI)
- overdose
- binge drinking

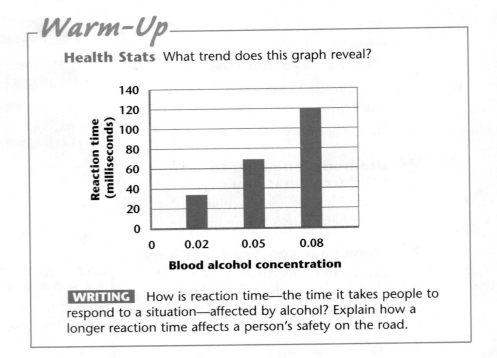

Warm-Up

Health Stats What trend does this graph reveal?

WRITING How is reaction time—the time it takes people to respond to a situation—affected by alcohol? Explain how a longer reaction time affects a person's safety on the road.

Physical and Behavioral Effects

When a person drinks alcohol, the alcohol follows the same pathway through the digestive system as food. But unlike food, alcohol does not have to be digested in the stomach before it is absorbed into the blood. Thus, alcohol gets into a person's bloodstream within minutes of being consumed. Once in the blood, alcohol circulates throughout the body, where it has widespread effects.

Effects on Body Systems When people drink alcohol faster than the body can break it down into harmless compounds they become intoxicated. **Intoxication** is the state in which a person's mental and physical abilities are impaired by alcohol or another substance. **Many negative effects on a drinker's body and behavior accompany intoxication by alcohol.** Some of these effects are shown in Figure 3.

Connect to Your Life **Think of a movie or book in which a character became intoxicated. Describe the effects.**

Effects of Intoxication

FIGURE 3 Intoxication has many effects on a drinker's body and behavior. **Predicting** Which effects would reduce a person's ability to drive safely?

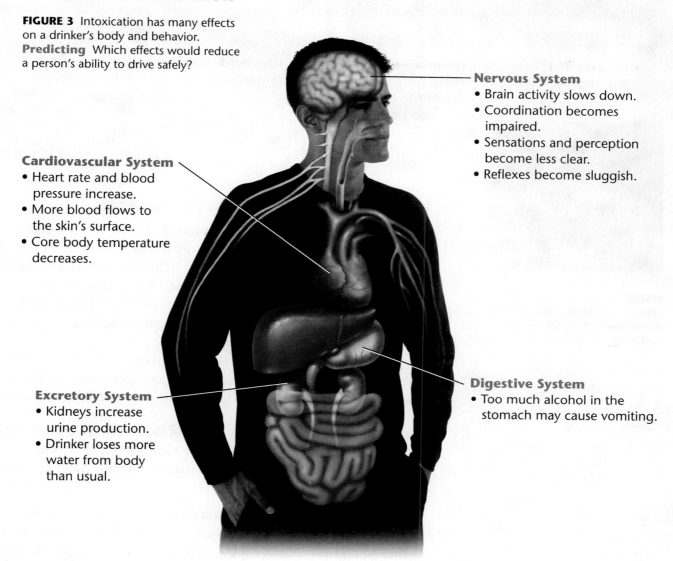

Nervous System
- Brain activity slows down.
- Coordination becomes impaired.
- Sensations and perception become less clear.
- Reflexes become sluggish.

Cardiovascular System
- Heart rate and blood pressure increase.
- More blood flows to the skin's surface.
- Core body temperature decreases.

Excretory System
- Kidneys increase urine production.
- Drinker loses more water from body than usual.

Digestive System
- Too much alcohol in the stomach may cause vomiting.

Effects on Behavior As intoxication takes effect, drinkers begin to lose judgment and self-control. At the same time, alcohol decreases drinkers' natural fears. When these two effects are combined, drinkers may behave in ways they normally would never consider. For example, a person under the influence of alcohol may express anger in violent or destructive ways. Shy people may behave in outgoing ways, and serious people may act foolishly.

A person who drinks a lot of alcohol may suffer a blackout. A **blackout** is a period of time that the drinker cannot recall. Other people may recall seeing the drinker talking, walking, and seemingly in control. The following day, however, the drinker may have no memory of some events from the day before. The drinker may harm others or be harmed during a blackout. Blackouts can happen to first-time drinkers as well as to experienced drinkers.

0.02–0.03	0.04–0.06	0.07–0.09	0.12–0.15
• Reflexes and alertness decline.	• Judgment and self-control are impaired. • Reaction time slows.	• Muscle coordination decreases.	• Vomiting usually occurs. • Emotions become exaggerated, unstable, or violent.

FIGURE 4 As blood alcohol concentration increases, physical and behavioral effects get more and more severe.

Blood Alcohol Concentration

Two people who drink the same amount of alcohol may not be equally affected. Why? The effects of alcohol depend on how much is actually circulating in a person's bloodstream. This amount is termed the **blood alcohol concentration (BAC).** BAC is the amount of alcohol in a person's blood, expressed as a percentage. For example, a BAC of 0.1 percent means that one-tenth of 1 percent of the fluid in the blood is alcohol.

The higher a person's blood alcohol concentration, the more severe the physical and behavioral effects. Blood alcohol concentration is a more reliable measure of intoxication than the number of drinks consumed.

Factors Affecting BAC A variety of factors affect a drinker's BAC. You can see the effects of some of these factors in Figure 5. **The rate of alcohol consumption, the gender and size of the drinker, and how much food is in the stomach all affect BAC.**

▶ **Rate of Consumption** A person's liver chemically breaks down, or metabolizes, alcohol at a fairly constant rate. That rate is about one half to one ounce of alcohol per hour—the approximate amount of alcohol in one can of beer, one shot of liquor, or one glass of wine. Therefore, people who have a few drinks in one hour have a higher BAC than people who drink the same amount over several hours.

▶ **Gender** At the same rate and amount of alcohol consumption, males generally will have a lower BAC than females. This is because, for males, a larger portion of the alcohol gets metabolized in the stomach before it enters the bloodstream. In addition, the liver is more efficient at metabolizing alcohol in males.

▶ **Body Size** In general, smaller people—by weight and height—feel the effects of alcohol more than larger people. They will have a higher BAC after a similar number of drinks.

▶ **Amount of Food in the Stomach** Drinking on an empty stomach increases the rate of alcohol absorption into the bloodstream. A higher BAC will result.

GO ONLINE

PearsonSuccessNet.com
For: More on blood alcohol concentration

0.20	0.30	0.40	0.50 and higher
• Confusion, dizziness, and disorientation occur. • Vision and speech are impaired. • Blackouts are typical.	• Ability to stand or walk is lost. • Loss of consciousness may occur.	• Loss of consciousness usually occurs. • Death may occur.	• Death usually occurs.

After Drinking Ends

Once a person stops drinking, BAC begins to decrease. The intoxicating effects of alcohol slowly diminish, and the person's reflexes and coordination return to normal. Many people refer to this process as "becoming sober" or "sobering up."

You may have heard that cold showers, exercise, fresh air, or coffee will help a person sober up more quickly. But this is not true. Nothing can speed the liver's ability to break down alcohol. Fresh air may keep a person awake, but it does not eliminate the intoxicating effects of alcohol.

Hangovers

Drinking heavily usually causes a person to wake up the next day with a hangover. **Hangover** is a term used to describe the after-effects of drinking too much alcohol. Symptoms of a hangover include nausea, upset stomach, headache, and a sensitivity to noise. It is not clear why some drinkers get a hangover and others do not. The only way a person can be sure to prevent one is to avoid alcohol altogether.

Connect to Your Life Your friend says he'll drive you home after he "sobers up" with a cup of coffee. What do you say?

FIGURE 5 Several factors besides number of drinks affect blood alcohol concentration. **Predicting** Predict the BAC of a 110-pound woman after she consumes three drinks in one hour.

Estimating Blood Alcohol Concentration

Number of Drinks* (per hour)	Males			Females		
	100–120 lb	120–140 lb	140–160 lb	100–120 lb	120–140 lb	140–160 lb
1	0.04	0.03	0.02	0.05	0.04	0.03
3	0.10	0.08	0.07	0.13	0.11	0.07
5	0.18	0.15	0.12	0.21	0.18	0.15
7	0.24	0.20	0.17	0.30	0.25	0.22

*One drink is 1.25 oz of 80-proof liquor, 5 oz of wine, or 12 oz of beer.

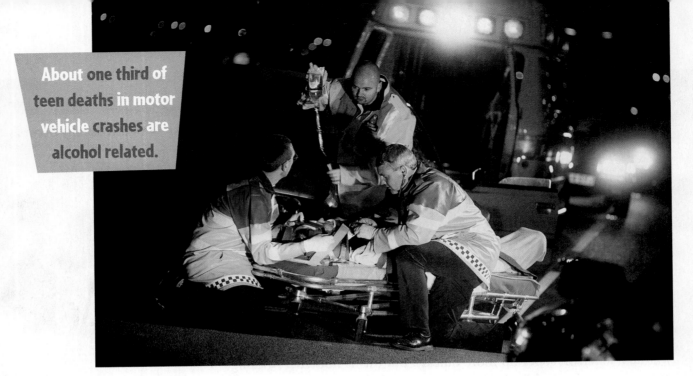

About one third of teen deaths in motor vehicle crashes are alcohol related.

FIGURE 6 Alcohol has a dramatic effect on fatality risk in motor vehicle crashes.

Life-Threatening Effects

The short-term effects of intoxication can put a drinker at serious risk. **Intoxication increases the risk of death from motor vehicle crashes, alcohol overdose, and interactions of alcohol with other drugs.**

Motor Vehicle Crashes Alcohol is involved in about 40 percent of fatal motor vehicle crashes. Driving can be impaired by any amount of drinking, even if it falls below legal limits.

Alcohol especially impairs the driving skills of underage drinkers. Because of their relative lack of driving experience, underage drivers are already more likely to crash, even without the influence of alcohol. The effects of alcohol and driving inexperience together are a particularly dangerous combination.

▶ **Driving Under the Influence** A driver over age 21 caught driving with a BAC that exceeds the legal limit of 0.08 is charged with **driving while intoxicated (DWI).** Law enforcement officers often measure BAC with a breath alcohol testing device. The device measures the alcohol level in the breath from the lungs, from which BAC is accurately estimated. Or a blood sample may be drawn and tested directly. People whose BAC is above the legal limit can have their driver's license taken away and can be prosecuted. They may have to pay stiff fines or serve jail time.

▶ **Zero Tolerance Laws** For drivers under the age 21, the law is different. The purchase and possession of alcohol by minors is already illegal. Therefore, there is no acceptable BAC for underage drivers. Laws vary a little from state to state, but in all cases, it is illegal for minors to drive after consuming any amount of alcohol. The penalties for underage drivers may be more strict than those for other drivers.

Overdose Taking an excessive amount of a drug that leads to coma or death is called an **overdose.** Alcohol overdose, also called alcohol poisoning, can cause the heart and breathing to stop. Many drinkers assume that they will pass out before drinking a fatal amount. This is not necessarily true. Alcohol continues to be absorbed into the blood for 30 to 90 minutes after a person's last drink. The drinker's BAC can increase even if the drinker becomes unconscious.

A person need not be a regular drinker or an alcoholic to die from an overdose. Even someone drinking for the first time can overdose and die from binge drinking. **Binge drinking** is the consumption of excessive amounts of alcohol at one sitting. Binge drinking is a particular problem among underage drinkers, who may consume many drinks on a bet or dare, or during a "drinking game." Binge drinking also affects teens more severely than older drinkers—teens enter comas at lower blood alcohol concentrations than adults.

Interactions With Other Drugs Sometimes, two drugs can interact to produce effects that are greater than either drug would produce by itself. Recall that alcohol is a depressant drug. When a person drinks alcohol and takes another depressant, such as sleeping pills, the combination can cause drastic changes in the body. Together, the two depressants' effects are more than doubled and can dangerously slow breathing and heart rates. In extreme cases, combining alcohol and other depressants leads to coma or death.

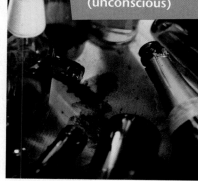

Warning Signs of Alcohol Poisoning
- Cold, clammy, pale, or bluish skin
- Slow or irregular respiration
- Vomiting while "sleeping"
- Cannot be wakened (unconscious)

FIGURE 7 If someone you know shows any of these warning signs, contact emergency medical services.

Section 2 Review

Key Ideas and Vocabulary

1. What is **intoxication?**
2. Describe the effects of intoxication on four body systems.
3. List four factors that affect blood alcohol concentration.
4. What are three ways that intoxication can lead to death?
5. For drivers over age 21, how is **driving while intoxicated (DWI)** defined?
6. What is an **overdose?** How could **binge drinking** cause an alcohol overdose?

Health and Community

BAC and Driving Laws Since state governments lowered the legal limit for adult drivers from a BAC of 0.10 to 0.08, thousands of lives have been saved. Is 0.08 low enough? Take a poll of teens and adults in your community. Summarize your findings in a letter to a local politician. **WRITING**

Critical Thinking

7. **Relating Cause and Effect** Teens who use alcohol are more likely to get into fights than those who don't. Relate this fact to the effects of intoxication on the nervous system. **WRITING**
8. **Comparing and Contrasting** How do drinking-and-driving laws differ for teens and adults?

Long-Term Risks of Alcohol

Objectives

▶ **Identify** five serious physical effects of long-term alcohol abuse.

▶ **Describe** the three stages of alcoholism.

▶ **List** in order three steps taken during recovery from alcoholism.

Vocabulary

• fetal alcohol syndrome
• cirrhosis
• alcoholism
• tolerance
• dependence
• addiction
• reverse tolerance
• detoxification
• withdrawal
• rehabilitation

Warm-Up

Myth Alcoholics sleep on park benches and wear shabby clothes.

Fact Alcoholics come from all cultures, backgrounds, and levels of education.

WRITING In what ways does the media contribute to this myth about alcoholics? How else does the media shape people's perception of alcoholics?

Damage to the Body

Adults over age 21 who use alcohol responsibly usually are not at risk of developing long-term health problems related to alcohol. But heavy drinking can cause serious damage to the body over time. **Long-term alcohol abuse may harm the brain, liver, heart, and digestive system. Furthermore, drinking any amount of alcohol during pregnancy may permanently harm the developing baby.**

Brain Damage Long-term alcohol abuse destroys nerve cells in the brain. Destroyed nerve cells usually cannot grow again. The loss of many nerve cells causes permanent changes that impair memory, the ability to concentrate, and the ability to make sound judgments. These losses interfere with normal everyday functions.

Effects on the brain can be especially damaging for underage drinkers. When teens drink, they expose the brain to alcohol during a critical time in its development. Teenage drinkers may suffer long-term learning and memory problems.

Connect to Your Life

Why are teens especially vulnerable to brain damage caused by alcohol?

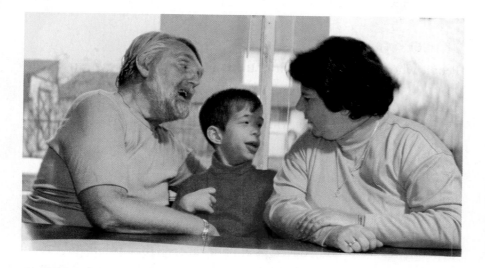

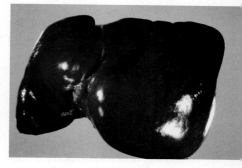

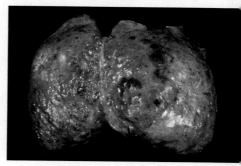

FIGURE 8 Drinking any amount of alcohol during pregnancy may cause fetal alcohol syndrome. This boy, shown with his adoptive parents, has severe symptoms.

Fetal Alcohol Syndrome   Pregnant women who drink put the health of their future children at risk. **Fetal alcohol syndrome** is a group of birth defects caused by the effects of alcohol on an unborn child.

Babies born with this syndrome may suffer from heart defects, malformed faces, delayed growth, poor motor development, and mental retardation. Some show only brain and behavioral problems, without the other physical effects.

Tragically, drinking during pregnancy is the leading preventable cause of mental retardation in the United States. Even small amounts of alcohol consumed during pregnancy can cause brain damage. Any woman who is planning to become pregnant, or who is already pregnant or breast-feeding, should not drink any alcohol.

Liver Damage   Alcohol interferes with the liver's ability to metabolize, or break down, fats. As a result of heavy drinking, the liver begins to fill with fat, which blocks the flow of blood in the liver. The fat-filled liver cells die, leaving behind useless scar tissue. This disease, called **cirrhosis** (sih ROH sis), may lead to liver failure and death.

Heavy drinkers also may suffer from alcoholic hepatitis, an inflammation of the liver caused by the toxic effects of alcohol. It too can cause the drinker to die.

▼ **Healthy liver**

▼ **Liver damaged by cirrhosis**

FIGURE 9   A healthy liver contains smooth tissue. The liver of a heavy drinker contains useless scar tissue.

Heart Disease   Excessive drinking contributes to heart disease, the leading cause of death in the United States. Over time, alcohol causes increased blood pressure and heart rate, irregular heartbeat, and a buildup of fatty deposits in the heart muscle.

Digestive Problems   Ongoing drinking also irritates the tissues that line the digestive system, causing inflammation. Repeated irritation increases the risk of

► cancers of the mouth, tongue, esophagus, and stomach.

► recurring diarrhea.

► chronic indigestion, heartburn, or ulcers.

Alcoholism

People who can no longer control their use of alcohol suffer from the disease known as **alcoholism.** Physically, an alcoholic's body requires alcohol to function. Psychologically, alcoholics consider drinking a regular, essential part of coping with daily life.

Changes to the Brain   With repeated use of alcohol, its effects in the brain become reduced—the body has developed **tolerance** to alcohol. Tolerance causes a drinker's body to need increasingly larger amounts of alcohol to achieve the original effect.

With increasing tolerance, the body will eventually develop **dependence**—the brain develops a chemical need for alcohol and cannot function normally without it. Finally, **addiction** results—the drinker no longer has control over his or her drinking. Alcohol addiction is characterized by a craving, or strong emotional need, to use alcohol.

Because alcoholics can no longer control their alcohol use, they must receive help to recover from this disease. Scientists have found that during addiction, the structure and the chemistry of the brain changes—addiction is a disease of the brain.

Who Is at Risk?   Anyone who drinks is at risk of becoming an alcoholic. However, some people seem to be at higher risk than others. For example, alcoholism is four to five times more common among the children of alcoholics than in the general population. The reason for this is likely a combination of the influence of genetics and the environment in which a person grows up.

Attitudes towards drinking and the availability of alcohol in the home play a strong role in determining whether or not a person will develop a drinking problem. Underage drinking also increases a person's risk of becoming an alcoholic.

FIGURE 10 Teenage drinking affects the brain dramatically in the short term. Shown here (in red) is brain activity in two teens asked to perform the same task.
Interpreting Photos Which brain has more activity?

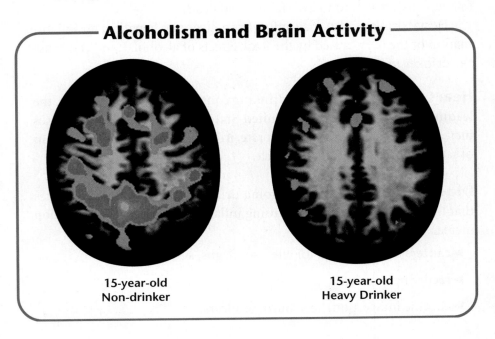

Alcoholism and Brain Activity

15-year-old
Non-drinker

15-year-old
Heavy Drinker

The Stages of Alcoholism Alcoholics progress through several stages as their dependence strengthens. **What begins as problem drinking becomes absolute dependence, and finally, late-stage alcoholism.** Each stage may last weeks, months, or years. Teenage alcoholics tend to go through the stages faster than adult alcoholics.

Stage 1: Problem Drinking Even a "social drinker"—someone who occasionally drinks small amounts with meals, at parties, or on special occasions—can become an alcoholic. If social drinkers start to use alcohol to try to relieve stress or escape from problems at home, school, or work, their drinking habit may quickly become a problem. Some warning signs of problem drinking are listed in Figure 11.

Stage 2: Absolute Dependence At this stage, the drinker becomes totally dependent on the drug. Alcohol dominates the drinker's life. He or she usually cannot stop after one drink, and feels a constant need to drink.

Some alcoholics are able to hide their problem and appear to be fine. Others show signs of excessive alcohol consumption. Signs of alcoholism may include frequent absences from work or school and strained relationships.

Stage 3: Late Stage of Alcoholism During this stage, alcoholics rapidly lose their mental, emotional, and physical health. Because their entire lives revolve around drinking, they become isolated from society. Late-stage alcoholics also experience **reverse tolerance** for alcohol, a condition in which less and less alcohol causes intoxication.

Serious health problems, including malnutrition, liver and brain damage, cancer, lung disease, and heart disease, are common among alcoholics. Without medical and psychological help, an alcoholic may die.

 How can you reduce your risk of alcoholism? Explain.

A Problem Drinker's Self-Test

	Yes	No
Do you drink to avoid facing problems or when you are angry?	☐	☐
Do you prefer to drink by yourself rather than with others?	☐	☐
Do you try to stop drinking, but fail?	☐	☐
Do you lie to others about how often or how much you drink?	☐	☐
Do you ever forget whole blocks of time when you are drinking?	☐	☐
Do you get drunk even when you do not intend to do so?	☐	☐
Are your school grades dropping because of your drinking?	☐	☐
Do you drink in the morning?	☐	☐
Do you ever get into trouble when you drink?	☐	☐
Is it important to you to show others that you can drink alcohol?	☐	☐

FIGURE 11 One or two "yes" answers to these questions may indicate a drinking problem.

FIGURE 12 Alcoholism has many negative effects on families.

Effects of Alcoholism on the Family
• Unpredictable behavior
• Embarrassment
• Violence
• Neglect
• Money problems
• Legal problems
• Divorce

Effects on Others Alcohol abuse and alcoholism affect many people other than the drinker. Consider some of the financial and emotional costs to society and individual families.

▶ In one year, alcohol-related crimes, medical expenses, lost productivity on the job, and motor vehicle crashes cost the United States over 220 billion dollars.

▶ Alcohol is involved in over 80,000 deaths per year. Most of these deaths are due to violence committed under the influence of alcohol and to motor vehicle crashes involving drunk drivers.

▶ About one in every five Americans grows up in an alcoholic family. Spouses and children of alcoholics live in homes filled with stress arising from uncertainty and embarrassment.

▶ In some cases, alcoholics verbally or physically abuse family members. Family life centers around the drinking member as the needs of other family members are ignored.

Treating Alcoholism

With appropriate treatment, the progress of alcoholism can be stopped. Alcoholics can lead productive, happy lives if they stop drinking completely. **There are three stages in an alcoholic's recovery: acknowledging the problem, detoxification, and rehabilitation.**

Acknowledging the Problem In the first step of recovery, alcoholics must acknowledge their problem and ask for help. For some alcoholics, the shock of losing a job, being arrested, or being separated from their families motivates them to enter a treatment program.

GO ONLINE
PearsonSuccessNet.com
For: More on alcoholism

Detoxification   The next step in recovery is **detoxification,** which involves removing all alcohol from a person's body. The alcoholic will suffer from **withdrawal,** a group of symptoms that occur when a dependent person stops taking a drug. Withdrawal symptoms last from three to seven days. They include shakiness, sleep problems, irritability, rapid heartbeat, and sweating. The drinker also may see, smell, or feel imaginary objects. Severe withdrawal symptoms can be extremely dangerous, requiring medical care or a hospital stay.

Rehabilitation   After detoxification, the recovering alcoholic begins **rehabilitation**—the process of learning to cope with everyday living without alcohol. During rehabilitation, alcoholics receive counseling to help them understand their disease and behavior. In some cases, the recovering alcoholic takes medications that may help prevent a return to alcohol use.

Support Groups   Community, religious, and health organizations often sponsor support groups for alcoholics. In one of the most successful groups, Alcoholics Anonymous (AA), recovering alcoholics offer encouragement and support to help other alcoholics stop drinking.

Two other groups, Al-Anon and Alateen, are designed to help friends and family members of alcoholics. Al-Anon helps adult friends and family members learn how they can help in the alcoholic's recovery process. Alateen provides help for teenagers living with alcoholics. You can find the phone numbers for local AA, Al-Anon, and Alateen groups on the Internet or in a telephone book.

FIGURE 13   Al-Anon members use understanding and education in their efforts to help alcoholics cope.

Section 3   Review

Key Ideas and Vocabulary

1. What are five long-term physical effects of alcohol abuse?

2. What is **cirrhosis?** Explain how the disease can be fatal.

3. What is **tolerance** to alcohol? How does it relate to **dependence?**

4. Describe each stage of alcoholism. What happens during absolute dependence?

5. List in order three steps alcoholics must take to recover from their alcohol dependence.

Health at School

Support for Teens   What kinds of school programs do you think would help teenagers who have drinking problems? What elements would the program need to be effective?
Prepare an oral report to present to school officials.   **WRITING**

Critical Thinking

6. Evaluating   "Alcoholism only affects the alcoholic." Do you agree or disagree with this statement? Explain your answer.

7. Comparing and Contrasting   How are the goals of Alcoholics Anonymous, Al-Anon, and Alateen similar? How are they different?

Section 4

Choosing Not to Drink

Objectives

▶ **Evaluate** how refusal skills help you stick to your decision not to drink.

▶ **Identify** two benefits of avoiding situations where alcohol is present.

Vocabulary

• refusal skills

Warm-Up

Dear Advice Line,

I was at a friend's house and we were bored. My friend got some liquor and offered me a drink. I said I couldn't because I had a game that night. The real reason is that I've decided not to drink at all. Was it wrong to give an excuse? What if she asks me again when I don't have a game?

WRITING Write a response to this teen. Offer advice on how to handle future situations.

Abstaining from Alcohol

You know that underage drinking is illegal and could risk your health and future plans. The best decision you can make is to abstain from alcohol, meaning not to drink at all. Once you turn 21, drinking will no longer be illegal, but the risks will remain. Many adults abstain from, or choose not to drink, alcohol.

At different times in your life—now or years from now—you will likely find yourself in situations where you are pressured to drink when you don't want to. How will you stick to your decision? **Sticking to your decision not to drink means being able to say no with confidence in situations where other people are drinking.**

The skills needed to say *no* are sometimes referred to as **refusal skills.** Refusal skills are especially important when others are pressuring you to do something against your will. You will feel better about yourself by sticking to your beliefs.

What to Say When Offered a Drink

"No thanks, I don't drink."

"I'm not old enough to drink."

"I want to stay in control."

FIGURE 14 There's more than one way to refuse a drink.

Prepare for Pressure   To prepare yourself for the pressure you may face, ask yourself the following questions:

▶ What are my reasons for not drinking alcohol at this time in my life?

▶ How can I come across as confident in my decision?

▶ In what situations will I most likely encounter pressure to drink?

▶ Why are my friends pressuring me to drink?

▶ Are there other friends who can help me stick to my decision?

You may want to practice saying *no* in role-playing situations with friends or classmates. That way you can develop the refusal skills you will need in actual social situations.

Stick to Your Decision   You may find that some people will not accept your decision not to drink. Many people who drink want to see others around them drink so that they can feel accepted.

Remember that you never need to apologize for not drinking. Most people will respect your decision, especially if you are clear in your response. Refer to the Building Health Skills on pages 378–379 for other tips for developing your refusal skills.

 GO ONLINE

PearsonSuccessNet.com
For: More on alcohol-free celebrations

 How would you say no to alcohol if it were offered to you?

Avoiding High-Pressure Situations

Besides using refusal skills, teens who choose not to drink also do something else that's smart: they stay away from situations where alcohol is present. **Avoiding situations in which alcohol is present will help you stay alcohol free. It will also help you avoid related risks, like being injured by someone who has been drinking.**

Alternatives to Parties   Teenagers who abstain from alcohol are likely to participate in healthy activities. Think about the kinds of activities that interest you. You may be interested in sports, hobbies, playing an instrument, helping an organization raise money, or organizing a school activity. Try taking up a new activity or spending more time with a current activity as an alternative to parties.

Refusing Rides From Drinkers   Even if you don't drink alcohol, you may have to deal with people who have had too much to drink. Remember that intoxicated people must not be allowed to drive. The driver may be a friend, a relative, or the parent of a child for whom you babysit. You should *never* get into a car with anyone who has been drinking. Don't worry about being rude—your life is more important than the driver's feelings. You should also do everything you can to prevent that person from driving.

If you find yourself dependent on a drinker for a ride home, ask someone for help. Some teens have an understanding with a parent or other adult that they can call for a ride home, no questions asked. Do not risk riding with an intoxicated driver.

A Safe Ride Home
- Find a sober driver.
- Call a parent or another adult.
- Take a taxi or bus.

FIGURE 15   Don't risk your life with a driver who has been drinking, even if they don't seem drunk.

Section 4 Review

Key Ideas and Vocabulary

1. What are **refusal skills**?
2. How can you stick to a decision not to drink?
3. What are two benefits of staying away from situations where alcohol is present?

Critical Thinking

4. **Applying Concepts** What reasons would you give for postponing drinking until you are of legal age?
5. **Evaluating** Make a list of pros and cons of going to a party where alcohol may be served. Then evaluate the list and decide what you would do.

Health at Home

Reminder Card Cut an index card to fit in your wallet. On it, list three ways that you would feel comfortable saying *no* if you were offered alcohol. Also list the names and phone numbers of three friends and family members you could contact if you needed a ride home. Carry the card with you so it's always handy.

6. **Making Judgments** The father of a child you've been baby-sitting is intoxicated when he returns. He offers you a ride back to your house. What would you do? **WRITING**

Chapter 15
At a Glance

VIDEO **TEENS** Talk ⊙
Drinking Dangers List three things that you learned from the video about refusing alcohol.

Section 1 Alcohol is a Drug

Key Ideas

▶ In slowing the body's normal reactions, alcohol may cause confusion, decreased alertness, poor coordination, blurred vision, and drowsiness.

▶ The attitudes of peers, family, and the media strongly influence underage drinking.

Vocabulary
• drug (374)
• depressant (374)
• fermentation (374)
• zero-tolerance policy (375)

Section 2 Alcohol's Effects on the Body

Key Ideas

▶ Many negative effects on a drinker's body and behavior accompany intoxication by alcohol.

▶ The rate of alcohol consumption, the gender and size of the drinker, and how much food is in the stomach all affect blood alcohol concentration.

▶ Intoxication increases the risk of death from motor vehicle crashes, alcohol overdose, and the interactions of alcohol with other drugs.

Vocabulary
• intoxication (380) • blackout (381)
• blood alcohol concentration (BAC) (382)
• hangover (383) • driving while intoxicated (DWI) (384)
• overdose (385) • binge drinking (385)

Section 3 Long-Term Risks of Alcohol

Key Ideas

▶ Long-term alcohol abuse may harm the brain, liver, heart, and digestive system. Furthermore, drinking any amount of alcohol during pregnancy may permanently harm the developing baby.

▶ As alcoholism progresses, what begins as problem drinking becomes absolute dependence, and finally, late-stage alcoholism.

▶ There are three stages in an alcoholic's recovery: acknowledging the problem, detoxification, and rehabilitation.

Vocabulary
• fetal alcohol syndrome (387) • cirrhosis (387)
• alcoholism (388) • tolerance (388)
• dependence (388) • addiction (388)
• reverse tolerance (389) • detoxification (391)
• withdrawal (391) • rehabilitation (391)

Section 4 Choosing Not to Drink

Key Ideas

▶ Sticking to your decision not to drink means being able to say no with confidence in situations where other people are drinking.

▶ Avoiding situations in which alcohol is present will help you stay alcohol free.

Vocabulary
• refusal skills (392)

Chapter 15 Review

Reviewing Key Ideas

GO ONLINE

PearsonSuccessNet.com

For: Chapter 15 review activity

Section 1

1. Alcohol is classified as a depressant drug because it
   a. slows brain and body reactions.
   b. reduces blood flow to skin.
   c. causes liver failure.
   d. increases heart rate.

2. The percentage of alcohol in 80-proof liquor is
   a. 4 percent.   b. 8 percent.
   c. 40 percent.   d. 80 percent.

3. Identify three ways that teens who drink put themselves at risks for physical harm.

4. **Critical Thinking** How do peers influence teens' decision whether to drink?

Section 2

5. Blood alcohol concentration measures
   a. the number of drinks consumed in one hour.
   b. the rate at which a person drinks alcohol.
   c. a person's risk of a car crash.
   d. the amount of alcohol in a person's blood.

6. Which organ breaks down alcohol?

7. How can alcohol's interaction with other drugs be fatal?

8. **Critical Thinking** Why is blood alcohol concentration a more reliable indicator of intoxication than number of drinks consumed?

Section 3

9. A condition in which less and less alcohol causes intoxication is called
   a. tolerance.   b. reverse tolerance.
   c. dependence.   d. problem drinking.

10. What are the physical and psychological signs of alcohol addiction?

11. What are some signs that a person may be a problem drinker?

12. During detoxification, why might an alcoholic need to be in a hospital?

13. **Critical Thinking** Doctors recommend that former alcoholics should avoid drinking even one drink. Why do you think so?

Section 4

14. The skills you need to say no to alcohol are called
    a. denial skills.   b. problem-solving skills.
    c. tolerance skills.   d. refusal skills.

15. List three reasons why teens should abstain from alcohol. Then, turn each reason into a way to say *no* to alcohol.

16. **Critical Thinking** What activities do you enjoy that take place in alcohol-free settings?

 ## Building Health Skills

17. **Making Decisions** Your 18-year-old sister has a date with her boyfriend. He is driving. When he arrives you smell alcohol on his breath. What do you do?

18. **Accessing Information** What are the laws that regulate alcohol purchases in your community? Do you think they are effective at preventing underage drinking? What more could be done? Explain. **WRITING**

19. **Advocacy** What advice would you give someone who has an alcoholic parent? Be specific.

20. **Communicating** Three members of the football team were suspended from playing for the rest of the season because they were caught drinking at a private party. Write a letter to the editor of the school newspaper giving your opinion about the situation. **WRITING**

21. **Setting Goals** Develop a list of strategies you can use to refuse alcohol. Review your list over the course of the school year. Refine your strategies as necessary to make them more effective.

Health and Community

Public Service Announcement Work with a group of your classmates. Design a public service announcement (PSA) to educate the public about the dangers of binge drinking. **WRITING**

Standardized Test Prep

Math Practice

The graph shows the effect of a driver's blood alcohol concentration on motor vehicle crashes. Use the graph to answer Questions 22–24.

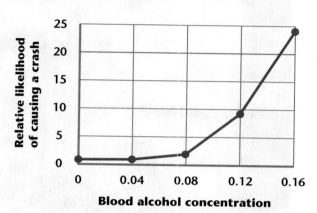

22. About how much higher is crash likelihood at a BAC of 0.08 compared with a BAC of zero?
    A About the same
    B 2 times
    C 5 times
    D 10 times

23. By about what percentage does crash risk increase between a BAC of 0.08 and a BAC of 0.1?
    F 25%
    G 50%
    H 100%
    J 400%

24. What mathematical term best describes the relationship between BAC and crash risk?
    A inverse correlation
    B exponential
    C linear
    D constant

Test-Taking Tip

Read *all* of the answers to a question before you make your choice. An answer that seems correct at first might not be the best answer when you weigh it against all the other choices.

Reading and Writing Practice

Read the poem below. Then answer Questions 25–28.

My Papa's Waltz
by Theodore Roethke

The whiskey on your breath
Could make a small boy dizzy;
But I hung on like death:
Such waltzing was not easy.

We romped until the pans
Slid from the kitchen shelf;
My mother's countenance
Could not unfrown itself.

The hand that held my wrist
Was battered on one knuckle;
At every step you missed
My right ear scraped a buckle.

You beat time on my head
With a palm caked hard by dirt,
Then waltzed me off to bed
Still clinging to your shirt.

25. From the context of the poem, what's the best definition of *countenance?*
    A a waltz step
    B anger
    C dizziness
    D facial expression

26. Which two words make a soft, or inexact, rhyme?
    F head, bed
    G wrist, missed
    H dizzy, easy
    J dirt, shirt

27. Which of the following verbs contributes most to the poem's violent feeling?
    A waltzed
    B scraped
    C romped
    D battered

Constructed Response

28. What does the poem suggest are the boy's feelings about his father's alcoholism? Explain.

Tobacco

GO ONLINE PearsonSuccessNet.com

VIDEO 16

TEENS Talk

Tackling Tobacco

Preview **Activity**

Why Do Teens Start to Smoke?

Complete this activity before you watch the video.

1. List three reasons why you think that some teens start to smoke.
2. Get together with a partner to discuss the reasons you each wrote down. Between the two of you, how many different reasons did you come up with?
3. Design a T-shirt or bumper sticker with an anti-smoking message. The message should address at least one of the reasons why you and your partner think that some teens start to smoke.

Teens and Tobacco

Objectives

▶ **Identify** three factors that influence teens' decisions about tobacco use.

▶ **Describe** the various forms of tobacco products.

Vocabulary

- nicotine
- smokeless tobacco
- chewing tobacco
- snuff

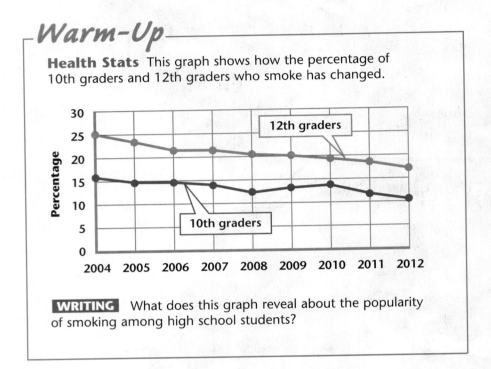

Warm-Up

Health Stats This graph shows how the percentage of 10th graders and 12th graders who smoke has changed.

WRITING What does this graph reveal about the popularity of smoking among high school students?

Why Teens Use Tobacco

When your parents were teens, they lived in a much smokier environment than you do today. Only a few decades ago, people smoked on airplanes, in movie theaters, in restaurants, and at work. Today, people know a lot more about the dangers of tobacco use. As a result, tobacco use has fallen sharply and it is not as socially acceptable as it once was.

Despite all of the health warnings, some people do start using tobacco. Few users can pinpoint the exact reason they started smoking or using smokeless tobacco. But, both users and nonusers refer to the same factors when discussing their decision. **Friends, family, and the media greatly influence whether someone starts to use tobacco.**

Influence of Friends Most people who become addicted to tobacco start using it during their teens. Friends are an important influence. Teens with friends who use tobacco are more likely to also use tobacco. They may feel pressure to be part of the group.

On the other hand, if a teen's friends do not use tobacco, it is less likely that he or she will make the decision to use it. Many teenagers credit their friends for helping them resist the temptation to use tobacco.

Influence of Family   Your parents may have first made you aware of tobacco's negative health effects. They also may have offered you advice on how to avoid tobacco use. Other family members, such as older sisters or brothers, may be positive role models for you.

Studies show that children of smokers are much more likely to smoke, even if their parents try to discourage them. Why are children of smokers more likely to smoke? These children may think of smoking as a behavior related to adulthood. They may simply assume that they will use tobacco just like their parents do.

Influence of Media   Anti-tobacco advertising in magazines, television, and other media also may have influenced your decision not to smoke. You probably have read or heard much about the dangers of tobacco through the media. Many anti-tobacco ads are designed to get the attention of teens. Anti-tobacco programs were designed to compete with the appealing ads created by tobacco companies.

The advertising of tobacco products on radio and television has been banned for over 30 years. In the 1990s, further regulations were placed on tobacco advertising. Ads placed near schools were banned. Tobacco companies were told to discontinue cartoon-like ads that appeal to children and teens. In addition, tobacco companies were required to help pay for anti-smoking education.

Despite all these regulations, tobacco companies still find ways to promote their products. They advertise on Web sites and in places where cigarettes are sold. They use direct mail. The companies also sponsor events and offer discounts to keep prices low.

 Connect to Your Life   What people or factors have influenced your decisions about tobacco use?

 GO ONLINE
PearsonSuccessNet.com
For: More on teens and tobacco

Media

FIGURE 1   Friends and family can be positive influences that steer teens away from tobacco use. However, the media, especially the movies, have long been criticized for glamorizing tobacco use.

Friends

Family

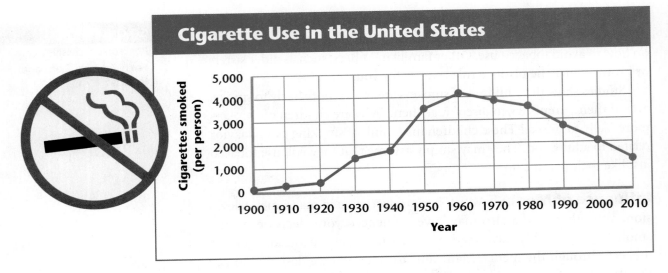

Cigarette Use in the United States

FIGURE 2 Cigarette use has fallen sharply since people have become more aware of its negative health effects. **Reading Graphs** In 1964, the Surgeon General issued the first report on the negative health effects of smoking. What effect did the report seem to have on cigarette use? Explain.

Tobacco Products

Tobacco products are made from the dried, processed leaves of tobacco plants. Tobacco plants naturally produce a chemical that acts as an insecticide to protect the plants' leaves from insects. This insecticide is **nicotine,** a very addictive chemical in tobacco products.

In its pure liquid form nicotine is extremely poisonous. In fact, each year thousands of young children are poisoned from eating cigarettes and cigars. Tobacco users are not immediately poisoned by nicotine because only a small amount enters the body at a time.

As you will learn in Sections 2 and 3, even small amounts of nicotine can have profound effects on several body systems. **Tobacco users take in nicotine whenever they use cigarettes, cigars, pipes, or smokeless tobacco products.**

Products That Are Smoked   There is a wide variety of tobacco products that are smoked. When the tobacco is processed for these products, preservatives, flavorings, and other substances may be added. Some of these substances contribute to the harmful effects of smoking.

▶ Cigarettes are the most frequently used tobacco product. Cigarettes consist of cured and shredded tobacco leaves rolled in paper.

▶ *Bidis,* which are imported from India, are cigarette-like products that consist of tobacco wrapped in a leaf and tied with string.

▶ *Kreteks,* which are imported from Indonesia, contain ground clove. The clove alters the cigarette's flavor and numbs the lungs.

▶ Cigar and pipe tobacco is less processed than cigarette tobacco. It usually contains more nicotine than cigarette tobacco.

Many people think that products such as *bidis, kreteks,* cigars, pipes, and water pipes are safe alternatives to cigarettes. This is not true. No matter how tobacco is burned, cancer-causing chemicals and other harmful substances are produced.

Smokeless Tobacco Tobacco that is chewed, placed between the lower lip and teeth, or sniffed through the nose is known as **smokeless tobacco.** As you will read in Sections 2 and 3, these products cause direct harm to the lining of the mouth, tongue, teeth, and gums. Smokeless tobacco also contains many of the same harmful chemicals found in tobacco smoke, including nicotine. In 1986, the Surgeon General concluded that smokeless tobacco is not a safe substitute for cigarettes.

▶ **Chewing tobacco,** also known as "dip" or "chew," consists of poor-quality, ground tobacco leaves mixed with flavorings, preservatives, and other chemicals. Wads of chewing tobacco are placed between the cheek and gum.

▶ **Snuff** is finely ground, powdered tobacco. It may be a dry powder, or oil may be added to make the snuff moist. Most snuff users place it in their mouths, between the lower lip and teeth. Some users sniff it through their nose.

When chewing tobacco and snuff are held in the mouth, the products cause increased saliva production. The user often spits out the excess saliva and tobacco juice. This is why smokeless tobacco is often called "spit" or "spitting tobacco."

FIGURE 3 Most smokeless tobacco products are held in the mouth. Although they do not harm the lungs like smoking does, these products pose other risks to a user's health.

Section 1 Review

Key Ideas and Vocabulary

1. Describe three factors that influence a person's decision about tobacco use.

2. What is **nicotine?**

3. List the types of tobacco products that are smoked and the smokeless tobacco products.

4. What part of the body is most affected by the use of smokeless tobacco?

Critical Thinking

5. Sequencing Consider the three factors that may influence a teen's decision about tobacco use—friends, family, and media. Which do you think has the greatest influence? Which has the least influence? Explain.

Health and Community

Smoking in Movies For many years, filmmakers have been accused of glamorizing smoking. Watch two movies in which one of the main characters smokes. In a report describe how smoking was treated in each film. Was smoking portrayed in an accurate way? Present your observations to your class. **WRITING**

6. Evaluating Which do you think have a greater influence on a teen's thoughts about smoking—tobacco ads or anti-tobacco ads?

7. Making Judgments At most schools, teens caught with alcohol face stronger punishments than teens caught with tobacco products. Do you think fewer teens would use tobacco if they faced stronger punishments?

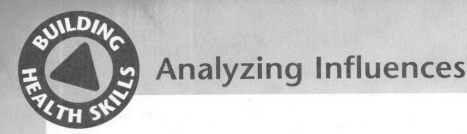

Analyzing Influences

Examining Advertising Tactics

Tobacco companies used to spend billions of dollars a year to advertise their products. Their ads appeared on television, in magazines, in newspapers, and on billboards.

Why do companies spend so much money on advertising? The ultimate goal of advertising, of course, is to increase a company's profits. To do this, advertising is used to attract new users, increase customer use of a product, or to persuade people to switch brands. On a daily basis, you are bombarded with hundreds of advertisements. Use the following guidelines to help you identify and resist the techniques that advertisers use to influence you.

① Identify the tactics being used to sell the product.

These are some common advertising techniques.

► **Humor** Funny ads may cause you to associate a product with fun or feeling good.

► **Slogans and Jingles** Catchy phrases or tunes may help you remember the product.

► **Testimonials** "Satisfied customers" may convince you that the product works.

► **Attractive Models** The use of attractive models communicates the idea that attractive or successful people use the product.

► **Positive Images** The ad may imply that you need the product to be strong, independent, and successful.

► **Bandwagon Approach** The ad makes you think that everyone uses the product. You may want to "jump on the bandwagon" too.

► **Appeal to the Senses** The use of beautiful or exciting scenery, colors, or music appeals to the senses.

► **Price Appeal** The ad may imply the product is a better bargain than other products.

② Identify the ad's target audience.

These questions can help you determine whom an ad is trying to reach.

► In what setting does the ad take place? If it is a sporting event, for example, the ad is probably targeted at sports fans.

► What are the characters in the ad doing? If they are doing the latest fad, the ad may be targeted at teens or young adults.

► Where does the ad appear? Advertisers know which television shows and magazines attract the audience they want to reach.

③ Identify the ad's message.

What exactly is the ad trying to convince you to believe?

► Write a one-sentence statement that describes what the ad wants you to believe about the product. Start your sentence as follows, "If I use this product, then . . ." For example, "If I use this product, then I will be happier and have more friends."

► Reread the statement you wrote. Do you think it could be true? Why or why not?

Practice the Skill

1. Examine the ad for a tobacco product on the previous page.
   a. Identify the tactics being used by the advertiser.
   b. Who do you think the ad is trying to reach? What is its message?

2. Search the Internet for vintage print ads for tobacco products. In this case, *vintage* means classic or old. Some Web sites have print ads grouped by decade.

3. Select and print three different cigarette ads. For each ad, describe the setting, characters, and behaviors. Decide which tactic is being used to sell the product. Then write a one-sentence statement that expresses the ad's message as you see it.

4. Work in a small group and compare ads. Identify the most common messages in cigarette ads. Are there different messages for different audiences? How have the messages changed over time?

5. Use one or more of the advertising tactics described to make an anti-tobacco poster.

Chemicals in Tobacco Products

Objectives

▶ **Explain** how nicotine affects the body.

▶ **Identify** two other dangerous substances in tobacco smoke.

▶ **Examine** why using smokeless tobacco is not a safe alternative to smoking.

Vocabulary

- stimulant
- tar
- carcinogen
- carbon monoxide

Warm-Up

Myth Low-tar and low-nicotine cigarettes are safer than regular cigarettes.

Fact Although the amount of tar and nicotine in these cigarettes may be reduced, carbon monoxide levels are not. Also, smokers tend to smoke more of these cigarettes and inhale more deeply in order to feel the same effects as they felt from regular cigarettes.

WRITING Where do you think that most teens get their information about tobacco products? How factual do you think this information is?

Nicotine and the Body

Nicotine is a type of drug called a stimulant. **Stimulants** are drugs that increase the activity of the nervous system. In smokers, nicotine enters the blood mainly through the lungs. In smokeless tobacco users, nicotine enters the blood through the lining of the mouth or nose.

Once in the blood, nicotine reaches the brain within seconds. There, it takes the place of certain neurotransmitters—chemicals that send signals between cells. By mimicking these neurotransmitters, nicotine affects breathing, movement, learning, memory, mood, and appetite.

Nicotine's Short-Term Effects   The immediate effects of nicotine on the body depend largely on how much nicotine is used and on the user's history of tobacco use. **The major short-term effects of nicotine use are increased heart rate, increased blood pressure, and changes in the brain that may lead to addiction.** Figure 4 outlines nicotine's short-term effects on several body systems.

First-time tobacco users may experience mild signs of nicotine poisoning, which include rapid pulse, clammy skin, nausea, and dizziness. However, in frequent users, nicotine stimulates the area of the brain that produces feelings of reward and pleasure. These effects last for about 30 minutes. It is these feelings that make the continued use of tobacco seem appealing.

Effects of Nicotine

FIGURE 4 Nicotine acts as a stimulant. It has many immediate effects on several body systems. **Interpreting Diagrams** How does nicotine affect the heart? How does it affect the brain?

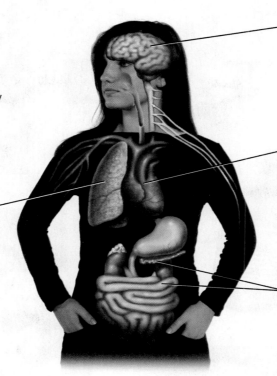

Nervous System
- Increases activity level
- Mimics neurotransmitters
- Decreases some reflex actions
- Activates the brain's "reward pathway"

Cardiovascular System
- Increases heart rate and the force of contractions
- Increases blood pressure
- Reduces blood flow to skin
- Increases risk of blood clotting

Respiratory System
- Increases mucus production
- Decreases muscle action in the lungs' airways
- Causes breathing to become more shallow

Digestive System
- Increases saliva production
- Decreases the amount of insulin released from the pancreas
- Increases bowel activity

Nicotine Addiction   People who use tobacco frequently begin to rely on it for feelings of alertness and pleasure. Ongoing use of nicotine causes the body to develop a tolerance to nicotine. With tolerance, the user needs more and more nicotine to produce the same effects on the mind and body.

As tolerance increases, nicotine addiction develops. Once people are addicted, they experience strong cravings for nicotine. They might feel irritable or anxious in places or situations in which they cannot use tobacco.

The time it takes to become addicted depends on several factors including genetics, frequency of use, and age. Studies show that teens may become addicted faster and more intensely than adults. In fact, it may take only a few cigarettes for some teens to become addicted.

Psychological Dependence   Tobacco users might also become dependent on nicotine for psychological reasons. Tobacco use may become a habit used to cope with stressful situations. Or, it may become associated with social situations, such as hanging out with friends. These psychological factors can make quitting difficult.

Nicotine Withdrawal   If a nicotine addict goes without nicotine for even a short time, he or she may experience nicotine withdrawal. Symptoms of nicotine withdrawal include headaches, irritability, difficulty sleeping, inability to concentrate, and intense nicotine cravings. Withdrawal effects may begin as soon as 30 minutes after the last dose of nicotine.

 GO ONLINE
PearsonSuccessNet.com
For: More on nicotine

Have you ever observed someone experiencing nicotine withdrawal? Describe his or her behavior.

FIGURE 5 Tobacco products contain many harmful chemicals. Some of these chemicals are a natural part of tobacco. Others are added when the tobacco is processed or form when tobacco is burned.

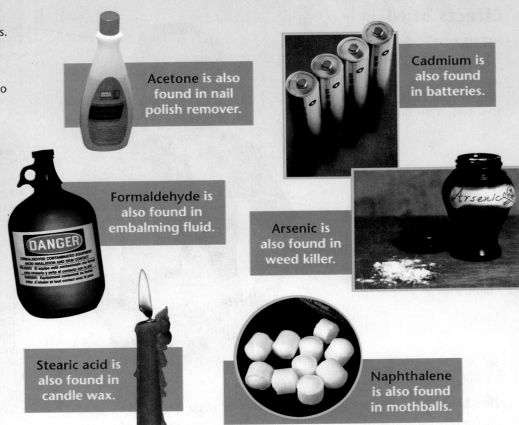

Acetone is also found in nail polish remover.

Cadmium is also found in batteries.

Formaldehyde is also found in embalming fluid.

Arsenic is also found in weed killer.

Stearic acid is also found in candle wax.

Naphthalene is also found in mothballs.

Some Chemicals in Tobacco Smoke
- Acetone
- Ammonia
- Arsenic
- Benzene
- Butane
- Cadmium
- Carbon monoxide
- Formaldehyde
- Hydrogen cyanide
- Methanol
- Naphthalene
- Nickel
- Propane
- Stearic acid
- Uranium
- Vinyl chloride

Other Dangerous Chemicals

As you can see in Figure 5, nicotine is only one of many chemicals in tobacco that can harm your body. In fact, tobacco smoke contains more than 4,000 chemicals. **In addition to nicotine, two of the most harmful substances in tobacco smoke are tar and carbon monoxide.**

Tar The dark, sticky substance that forms when tobacco burns is known as **tar.** Tar is a mixture of hundreds of chemicals. Smokers of any type of tobacco product—including cigarettes, herbal cigarettes, cigars, and pipes—expose their bodies to the short-term effects of tar.

▶ Brown stains on fingers and teeth

▶ Smelly hair and clothes

▶ Bad breath

▶ Paralysis of cilia lining the airways

▶ Increased number of respiratory infections, such as colds and the flu

▶ Impaired lung function, which leads to reduced athletic ability

In addition to these short-term effects, tar also causes long-term damage to the body. Tar contains many chemicals that are known **carcinogens** (kahr SIN uh junz), or cancer-causing agents. Tar can also damage the respiratory system to the point that it can no longer function. You will read more about the long-term effects of tar in Section 3.

Carbon Monoxide When substances—including tobacco—are burned, an odorless, poisonous gas called **carbon monoxide** is produced. Once inhaled and absorbed into the blood, carbon monoxide binds to the hemoglobin molecules in red blood cells in place of oxygen. When this happens, red blood cells cannot transport as much oxygen as the body cells need.

To make up for the shortage of oxygen, a smoker's breathing and heart rates increase. Over time, this strain can damage the cardiovascular system and other organs.

Chemicals in Smokeless Tobacco Some people think that using smokeless tobacco products is safe because no smoke is produced or inhaled. **However, smokeless tobacco contains many of the same dangerous chemicals that are in tobacco smoke.** There are no safe tobacco products.

Smokeless tobacco is at least as addictive as cigarettes. In fact, with each dose of chewing tobacco, a user absorbs about two and a half times the nicotine as a person who smokes one cigarette. A snuff user absorbs about twice the nicotine as a person who smokes one cigarette.

The life-threatening effects of smokeless tobacco use, such as cancer, will be discussed in Section 3. Smokeless tobacco also has a number of other effects that are unpleasant or may lead to health problems.

► Stained teeth

► Bad breath and drooling

► Receding gums and tooth decay

To avoid these unpleasant side effects, many smokeless tobacco users eventually turn to smoking to satisfy their nicotine craving. Then they expose their bodies to the additional hazards of tar and carbon monoxide.

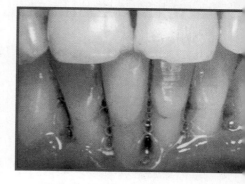

FIGURE 6 In addition to other harmful chemicals, many smokeless tobacco products contain sand and sugars. Both of these can damage the gums. Note how smokeless tobacco caused the gums to pull away from the teeth in this photo.

Section 2 Review

Key Ideas and Vocabulary

1. What type of drug is nicotine? How does nicotine affect the body?

2. What effects do tar and carbon monoxide have on the bodies of smokers?

3. What is a **carcinogen**?

4. Explain how smokeless tobacco products harm the body.

Critical Thinking

5. Applying Concepts What facts about tobacco would you use to convince a friend not to start using tobacco?

Health at Home

Life After Quitting Interview two family members, neighbors, or friends who have quit smoking. Ask them how they stopped smoking, how difficult it was, and how their lives have changed. In a paragraph, compare and contrast their experiences. **WRITING**

6. Making Judgments Do you think that drugstores, which sell medicines, should also sell tobacco products? Why or why not? **WRITING**

7. Evaluating Why do you think that tobacco users are willing to live with unpleasant side effects, such as stained teeth and bad breath?

Risks of Tobacco Use

Objectives

▶ **Describe** the long-term health risks of tobacco use.

▶ **Identify** the long-term risks of exposure to secondhand smoke.

▶ **Examine** how smoking by a pregnant woman can affect her baby.

Vocabulary

- chronic obstructive pulmonary disease (COPD)
- chronic bronchitis
- emphysema
- leukoplakia
- mainstream smoke
- sidestream smoke
- secondhand smoke

Warm-Up

Quick Quiz All of the following statements are true except for one. Which statement do you think is false?

① **In the United States, over 400,000 people die from smoking each year.**

② **Children of people who smoke have a greater risk of developing asthma.**

③ **Scientists have developed cures for chronic bronchitis and emphysema.**

④ **Smokers die about 14 years earlier than nonsmokers.**

⑤ **Smokeless tobacco increases one's risk of cardiovascular disease.**

WRITING Explain why you gave the answer that you did.

Long-Term Risks

In Section 2, you read about the immediate effects that tobacco has on a person's health. You may have noticed some of these effects, such as stained teeth and bad breath, in tobacco users you know. What you cannot notice, however, is the development of much more serious problems. **With every dose of tobacco, users increase their risk of developing respiratory diseases, cardiovascular disease, and several different forms of cancer.**

Did you know that tobacco use is the leading cause of preventable death in the United States? Cigarette smoking alone is directly responsible for the deaths of over 400,000 Americans each year. Many more people die each year from cigar, pipe, and smokeless tobacco use. More than 6 million children living today may die early because of a decision they will make during their teen years—the decision to use tobacco.

What warning label would you put on cigarette packages? Why?

FIGURE 7 Over time, smoking can affect the function of many body systems and processes. Although some of these effects may be merely unpleasant, serious damage to the respiratory system can be life threatening.

Smoking also leads to . . .
- Increased risk of stomach ulcers
- Slower healing of injuries
- Increased colds and flus
- Increased allergies and asthma
- A constant runny nose
- Frequent headaches
- Dulled sense of taste and smell
- Premature wrinkling

Respiratory Diseases

You may know smokers who suffer from a hacking cough that does not go away. "Smoker's cough" is the result of damage caused by tar. Cells that line the respiratory tract have hairlike extensions called cilia. The cilia move in a sweeping motion and push mucus and particles away from the lungs and toward the throat to be swallowed.

Tar sticks to the cilia, prevents them from moving, and damages them over time. Dust, tobacco smoke toxins, and mucus then accumulate in the airways. Coughing is the body's attempt to clear the airways.

Tobacco smoke and other accumulating toxins also irritate the lining of the bronchi. Bronchi are the tubes that carry air between the trachea and the lungs. The bronchi become inflamed, which restricts the amount of air that can enter and leave the lungs.

Chronic Obstructive Pulmonary Disease If a person continues to smoke over a long period of time, the damage that occurs to the respiratory system becomes permanent. He or she may develop chronic obstructive pulmonary disease (COPD), a disease that results in a gradual loss of lung function.

COPD develops slowly, but its effects are severe. People with COPD find it difficult to fill their lungs with air. Simple activities, such as climbing stairs, may leave them gasping for breath. Chronic bronchitis and emphysema are two types of COPD. Many people with COPD have both chronic bronchitis and emphysema.

▶ **Chronic Bronchitis** In people with chronic bronchitis, the airways are constantly inflamed. Over time, mucus-producing cells increase in size and number, producing more and more mucus. The constricted airways and overproduction of mucus make breathing difficult.

Hands-On *Activity*

Make a Model of a Smoker's Lungs

In this activity, you will construct a simple smoking machine to demonstrate how smoking affects the lungs.

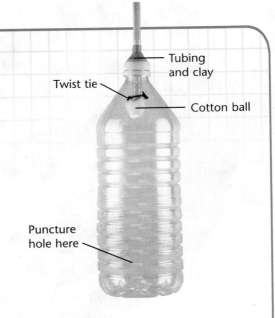

Tubing and clay

Twist tie

Cotton ball

Puncture hole here

Materials
- plastic bottle with cap • plastic tubing • clay
- cotton ball • twist tie • cigarette • safety matches

Try This

1 Your teacher will make a hole in the bottle cap about the size of the tubing. Your teacher will also poke a hole in the side of the bottle.

2 Thread the tubing into the hole in the bottle cap, and seal the edges with clay.

3 Place the cotton ball over the tubing on the underside of the cap. Use the twist tie to secure it.

4 Insert the cigarette into the other end of the tubing so that the side you light points up.

5 Screw the cap onto the bottle.

6 Squeeze the bottle to force some air out of it. Then cover the hole with your thumb.

7 Have your teacher light the cigarette. With your thumb over the hole, pump the bottle slowly and steadily. This will draw air in through the cigarette.

8 When the bottle is full of air, uncover the hole to let some air out. Cover the hole before drawing air in through the cigarette again.

9 Your teacher will extinguish the cigarette and dispose of it.

Think and Discuss

1 Describe the appearance of the cotton ball after the smoking test.

2 What does the inside of the bottle look like?

3 Use the model to describe what smoking does to a smoker's teeth, throat, and lungs.

▶ **Emphysema** Recall that your lungs contain millions of tiny alveoli, or air sacs. Normally, the alveoli expand as you breathe in oxygen and contract as you breathe out carbon dioxide. Tobacco smoke damages alveoli tissue. The damage can lead to **emphysema,** a disorder in which alveoli in the lungs can no longer function properly.

With emphysema, the alveoli lose shape and elasticity. Less oxygen can get into the alveoli and less carbon dioxide can get out. Eventually, the alveoli walls start to break down, which reduces the area in which gas exchange can occur. As a result, people with emphysema are always short of breath.

COPD Treatments Cigarette smoking is responsible for about 90 percent of all COPD deaths. Although there is no cure for COPD, quitting smoking will prevent symptoms from getting worse. Treatments focus on relieving symptoms and slowing the progress of the disease. Possible treatments include medications that open airways, breathing exercises, oxygen treatments, and in severe cases, lung transplants.

Cardiovascular Disease

Cardiovascular disease—diseases of the heart and blood vessels—kill about 138,000 smokers in the United States every year.

▶ A smoker is two to three times more likely to have a heart attack than a nonsmoker.

▶ Cigarette smoking doubles a person's chances of suffering a stroke.

▶ Smokers are 10 times more likely to develop circulation problems in blood vessels that bring blood to the stomach, kidneys, legs, and feet.

These statistics are not surprising when you consider the damage that substances in tobacco products do to the heart and blood vessels. **The combined effects of nicotine, tar, and carbon monoxide force the cardiovascular system to work harder to deliver oxygen throughout the body.** Tobacco use also raises blood pressure, which, over time, weakens blood vessels and places strain on many organs.

Studies also show that the chemicals in tobacco smoke increase blood cholesterol levels and promote atherosclerosis—the thickening and hardening of artery walls. In addition, nicotine increases the blood's tendency to clot. Clots may block blood flow through narrowed arteries, leading to a heart attack or stroke.

Connect to Your Life How do you think smoking would affect your ability to stay active as you age?

Cancer

Both tobacco smoke and smokeless tobacco contain many ingredients that are known carcinogens. **Tobacco use is a major factor in the development of lung cancer, oral cancers, and several other cancers.**

Many factors influence a tobacco user's risk of developing cancer. Some of these factors include when the person started using tobacco, how much tobacco the person has used, and how often the person is exposed to other people's smoke.

FIGURE 8 Most smokers are not fully aware of the damage occurring to their lungs until it is too late.
Comparing and Contrasting Compare the lungs of a person with emphysema and a person with lung cancer to the healthy lung.

▲ Healthy lung

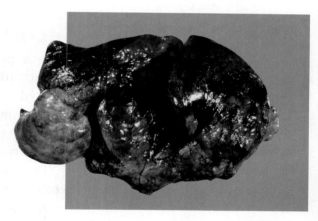
▲ Lung with emphysema

▲ Lung with cancer

Lung Cancer   Lung cancer is the leading cause of cancer death for both women and men. Scientists estimate that more than 85 percent of all deaths caused by lung cancer are related to smoking. Unfortunately, by the time most lung cancers are diagnosed successful treatment is unlikely. Only 15 percent of lung cancer patients survive for more than five years.

Oral Cancer   Smoking and smokeless tobacco are also associated with oral cancers—cancers of the mouth, tongue, and throat. About 90 percent of oral cancers occur in people who use or have used tobacco. The survival rate for oral cancer is higher than for lung cancer. However, surgery to remove the cancer may be disfiguring.

Tobacco users may develop white patches on their tongues or the lining of their mouths called **leukoplakia** (loo koh PLAY kee uh). Because the sores sometimes become cancerous, they should be monitored by a doctor.

Other Cancers   Tobacco carcinogens affect many organs in the body. As a result, tobacco users also have an increased risk of cancers of the esophagus, larynx, stomach, pancreas, kidney, bladder, and blood, among other sites.

Secondhand Smoke

When a person smokes, smoke enters the air from two sources. **Mainstream smoke** is exhaled from a smoker's lungs. Both the cigarette filter and the smoker's lungs trap a lot of substances before they can enter the air in mainstream smoke. The other source, **sidestream smoke,** is smoke that goes into the air directly from the cigarette. Sidestream smoke contains twice as much tar and nicotine as mainstream smoke.

The combination of mainstream and sidestream smoke is called **secondhand smoke,** or environmental tobacco smoke. Secondhand smoke is inhaled by everyone near the smoker.

Quit... *for them.*

Secondhand smoke kills.

Sponsored by the Somerset County Department of Health

Dangers of Secondhand Smoke Long-term exposure to secondhand smoke can cause **cardiovascular disease, many respiratory problems, and cancer.** In fact, secondhand smoke exposure increases the risk of a sudden heart attack by about 30 percent. Each year, secondhand smoke causes about 50,000 deaths from heart attacks and lung cancer.

Children are especially vulnerable to secondhand smoke. Each year, secondhand smoke contributes to between 150,000 and 300,000 respiratory infections in children younger than 18 months. Children who are exposed to secondhand smoke are more likely to develop allergies and asthma. Their asthma symptoms are more likely to be worse than those of children who are not exposed. Inhaled secondhand smoke can cause recurring, long-lasting ear infections—a leading cause of hearing loss.

Avoiding Secondhand Smoke Although secondhand smoke is still a serious problem, great progress has been made to eliminate it. Federal, state, and local laws now prohibit or restrict smoking in many public places and workplaces. As smoking becomes less socially acceptable, smoking in public will become even less common.

Breathing clean air is a serious issue for everyone. The government and several health organizations have made great strides to protect you from secondhand smoke. But it is important that you also protect yourself.

▶ Ask smokers not to smoke around you.

▶ Be firm when telling guests that they can't smoke in your home or car.

▶ Pick restaurants that do not allow smoking or at least sit in no-smoking areas.

GO ONLINE **PLANETDIARY**

PearsonSuccessNet.com
For: More on secondhand smoke

Connect to Your Life **Describe how you feel when you are exposed to secondhand smoke.**

FIGURE 9 About 22 percent of children in the United States are exposed to secondhand smoke at home on a regular basis.

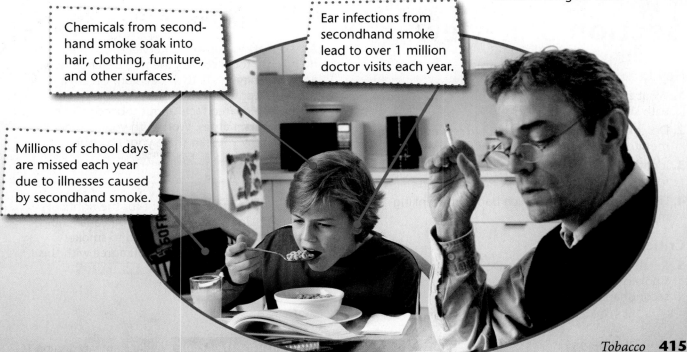

Chemicals from second-hand smoke soak into hair, clothing, furniture, and other surfaces.

Ear infections from secondhand smoke lead to over 1 million doctor visits each year.

Millions of school days are missed each year due to illnesses caused by secondhand smoke.

Tobacco Use and Pregnancy

Many of the harmful chemicals in tobacco smoke pass directly from a pregnant woman to her developing baby. **Pregnant women who smoke put their babies at risk for many health problems.** Tobacco smoke increases the baby's heart rate, reduces the baby's oxygen supply, and slows cell growth.

The babies born to mothers who smoke weigh, on average, six ounces less than the babies of nonsmokers. Low birthweight is a risk factor for many problems that could affect a baby throughout his or her entire life.

▶ Cerebral palsy

▶ Sight impairment

▶ Hearing problems

▶ Learning difficulties

Pregnant women who smoke also have higher rates of miscarriages, premature births, and stillbirths than women who do not smoke. Babies whose mothers smoked during pregnancy are also at much higher risk for sudden infant death syndrome (SIDS). SIDS is an unexplained disorder in which a seemingly healthy baby dies suddenly, usually while sleeping.

In addition, nursing mothers who smoke produce less milk than nonsmoking mothers. The nicotine in their milk can cause vomiting and diarrhea in nursing babies.

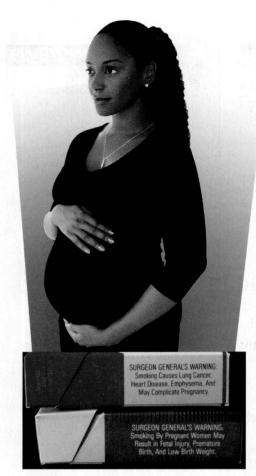

FIGURE 10 Despite warning labels, some pregnant women continue to smoke. However, the numbers are falling.

Section 3 Review

Key Ideas and Vocabulary

1. What are three long-term health risks associated with smoking?
2. Describe **leukoplakia.** Why should leukoplakia be monitored by a healthcare professional?
3. Identify three health risks associated with exposure to secondhand smoke.
4. List four problems for which babies of smoking mothers are at risk.

Critical Thinking

5. **Relating Cause and Effect** Do you think that smokers are also vulnerable to the dangers of secondhand smoke? Explain.

Health at School

Anti-Smoking Quotes Interview your peers who do not use tobacco. Ask them to describe how and why they made their decision. Create a brochure containing the most notable quotes along with related facts about tobacco. Do not use students' names. Work with your teacher to find out how you can share your brochure with younger students. **WRITING**

6. **Evaluating** People who fight for the rights of smokers claim that smoking is a personal choice and that they should be allowed to smoke anywhere they want to. Do you agree with this argument? Why or why not? **WRITING**

Saying No to Tobacco

Objectives

► **Examine** how refusal skills will help you stick with your decision not to use tobacco.

► **Describe** the benefits of quitting tobacco use.

► **Identify** the most important factor for successfully quitting tobacco.

Vocabulary

• nicotine substitute

Warm-Up

Dear Advice Line:

A bunch of my friends chew tobacco, especially when we get together to play sports. I know that it is not good for you, but I feel like a wimp when everyone else is chewing and I'm not. What if I just use chewing tobacco when we are playing?

WRITING Write a response to this teen to help with the decision he is facing.

Avoiding Tobacco Use

Your decision not to use tobacco will help you stay healthy now and reduce your risk of developing life-threatening diseases in the decades to come. As a nonuser, you are part of the growing majority of teens and adults who do not use tobacco. Your example may encourage others not to use tobacco.

At some point during your teen years, it is likely that someone will offer you a cigarette or another tobacco product. What will you do if this situation arises? **Sticking to your decision not to use tobacco involves being able to say no clearly and with confidence.**

It may be helpful to have a response prepared in advance so that you are not caught off guard. Simply stating, "I do not smoke," should be enough to end the conversation. Or, you could explain that you work hard to stay in shape and you do not want to spoil it. Fewer than one out of four teens smoke, which indicates that most teens do say no.

Do not assume that you can start using tobacco now and then quit. Studies show that people who start using tobacco in their teens have a more difficult time quitting than people who start using tobacco as adults. Refer to pages 378–379 for help in developing refusal skills.

Connect to Your Life How would you say no to a cigarette or other tobacco product offered to you?

Changes in a Smoker's Body After Quitting

First Days

After 20 minutes
- Blood pressure and heart rate return to normal
- Temperature of hands and feet increases to normal

After 8 hours
- Oxygen and carbon monoxide levels return to normal

After 24 hours
- Risk of sudden heart attack decreases

After 48 hours
- Senses of smell and taste start to improve

After 3 months
- Circulation improves; lung function improves

After 9 months
- Coughing and nasal congestion diminish
- Respiratory infections are less frequent
- Energy level increases

After 1 year
- Excess risk of heart disease is half that of a current smoker

FIGURE 11 Immediately after a person kicks the tobacco habit, the body begins to repair damage from the harmful substances to which it was exposed. Some of these repairs occur within days, while others may take decades. **Classifying** What benefits occur to the respiratory system after a smoker quits?

Benefits of Quitting

Surveys show that about nine out of ten smokers want to quit. Quitting tobacco use is not easy because it involves breaking an addiction. Nicotine may be just as addictive as some other drugs, such as cocaine and heroin. Quitting also involves breaking many habits associated with smoking. Taking time to consider the benefits of quitting, however, can make the difficult process seem even more worthwhile.

The tobacco user who quits can expect many immediate and long-term benefits. **The health benefits of quitting tobacco use begin immediately and continue throughout life. Society also benefits every time a tobacco user quits.** Figure 11 displays the changes that occur in a smoker's body after quitting.

Cardiovascular Benefits Immediately after quitting tobacco use, blood pressure lowers and heart rate returns to normal. As time passes, circulation improves and the risk of heart disease and stroke becomes similar to that of nonsmokers.

Respiratory Benefits Gradually, the cilia lining the air passages regain normal function. Breathing becomes easier as the lungs become free of tar, excess mucus, and other debris.

Psychological Benefits People who quit tobacco use usually feel increased confidence. They feel that they have regained control over their lives rather than allowing the tobacco to control them.

Benefits to Society Quitting tobacco also benefits society. Tobacco use costs society almost $200 billion per year. These expenses pay for healthcare for tobacco-related illnesses, damages and injuries from smoking-related fires, and loss of earnings from disease and early death.

After 5 years
- Stroke risk is the same as a nonsmoker
- Risk of mouth and throat cancer is half that of a current smoker

After 10 years
- Lung cancer death rate is about half the rate of a current smoker
- Life expectancy is comparable to a nonsmoker

Tips for Quitting

Breaking an addiction to tobacco is not easy, but millions of people have done it. **The most important factor in successfully quitting tobacco is a strong personal commitment.** Most people quit on their own. Others attend classes or seek other forms of professional help.

Some people who quit find that quitting abruptly, or going "cold turkey," works for them. Other people may quit by gradually reducing their use of tobacco over an extended period of time. No single method works best for everyone.

Quitting is most difficult within the first week or two after the last cigarette. By then, symptoms of nicotine withdrawal have usually subsided, but psychological symptoms may continue. There are many things you can do to help cope with withdrawal symptoms.

▶ Make a list of the reasons why you quit. Keep it handy.

▶ Throw away all tobacco products and anything that reminds you of tobacco use, such as ashtrays.

▶ Do little things to change your daily routine, such as sitting in a different seat at the kitchen table.

▶ Tell your family and friends that you have quit so that they can be there for support.

▶ Avoid being around people who use tobacco.

▶ Put aside the money you save. Reward yourself with a present.

▶ Exercise or call a friend to take your mind off smoking.

GO ONLINE
PearsonSuccessNet.com
For: More on quitting tobacco use

Connect to Your Life

What would you do to support a friend or family member who is trying to quit tobacco use?

FIGURE 12 With the help of nicotine patches or gum, tobacco users can gradually overcome their nicotine addiction.

Getting Help Many resources are available to help tobacco users quit. For those who want to quit on their own, several health organizations offer booklets and pamphlets containing tips for quitting. Contact groups such as the American Lung Association or the American Cancer Society for more information and tips on quitting tobacco use.

Those who feel that they need professional help can attend local workshops or support groups. Some programs offer counseling on the phone or online. Local hospitals and other healthcare facilities frequently offer programs for helping tobacco users quit. A healthcare professional can advise you about where to get help.

Nicotine Substitutes Some tobacco users have such a strong addiction to nicotine that quitting can be very uncomfortable and difficult. These people may benefit from nicotine substitutes. A **nicotine substitute** is a product that contains nicotine, but not the other harmful chemicals found in tobacco. By slowly cutting back on the dose of a nicotine substitute, the user can reduce withdrawal symptoms.

The two most common types of substitutes are nicotine gum and nicotine patches. Inhalers and nasal sprays are also available. People younger than 18 need a prescription for any of these products.

Nicotine substitutes are only the first step in a program to break a nicotine addiction. People who use nicotine substitutes still expose their bodies to the negative effects of nicotine. Nicotine substitutes should never be used along with tobacco products.

Section 4 Review

Key Ideas and Vocabulary

1. Describe how refusal skills can help you say no to tobacco.

2. Identify four major benefits of quitting tobacco use.

3. What is the most important factor for successfully quitting tobacco? What are two ways that a person may choose to quit?

4. What is a **nicotine substitute?** Identify two types of nicotine substitutes.

Critical Thinking

5. Evaluating Do you think government money should be spent on programs to help people quit smoking? Why or why not? **WRITING**

Health and Community

Resources for Quitting What resources are available to help people in your community quit tobacco use? Create a poster that informs people of the services that are available, their costs, and other important details. With permission, hang the poster in the school library, nurse's office, or other visible location.

6. Calculating Brent used to spend $5 a day on cigarettes. Now that he has quit smoking, about how much extra money will he have each month? Each year? **MATH**

GO ONLINE PearsonSuccessNet.com   Audio Summary Section 16.4

Chapter 16
At a Glance

VIDEO **TEENS** Talk
Tackling Tobacco What misconceptions did you have about tobacco products before watching this video?

Section 1   Teens and Tobacco

Key Ideas

▶ Friends, family, and the media greatly influence whether someone starts to use tobacco.

▶ Tobacco users take in nicotine whenever they use cigarettes, cigars, pipes, or smokeless tobacco products.

Vocabulary
- nicotine (402)
- smokeless tobacco (403)
- chewing tobacco (403)
- snuff (403)

Section 2   Chemicals in Tobacco Products

Key Ideas

▶ The major short-term effects of nicotine use are increased heart rate, increased blood pressure, and changes in the brain that may lead to addiction.

▶ In addition to nicotine, two of the most harmful substances in tobacco smoke are tar and carbon monoxide.

▶ Smokeless tobacco contains many of the same dangerous chemicals that are in tobacco smoke.

Vocabulary
- stimulant (406)
- tar (408)
- carcinogen (408)
- carbon monoxide (409)

Section 3   Risks of Tobacco Use

Key Ideas

▶ With every dose of tobacco, users increase their risk of developing respiratory diseases, cardiovascular disease, and several different forms of cancer.

▶ If a person continues to smoke over a long period of time, the damage that occurs to the respiratory system becomes permanent.

▶ The combined effects of nicotine, tar, and carbon monoxide force the cardiovascular system to work harder to deliver oxygen throughout the body.

▶ Tobacco use is a major factor in the development of lung cancer, oral cancers, and many other cancers.

▶ Long-term exposure to secondhand smoke can cause cardiovascular disease, many respiratory problems, and cancer.

▶ Pregnant women who smoke put their babies at risk for many health problems.

Vocabulary
- chronic obstructive pulmonary disease (COPD) (411)
- chronic bronchitis (411) • emphysema (412)
- leukoplakia (414) • mainstream smoke (414)
- sidestream smoke (414) • secondhand smoke (414)

Section 4   Saying No to Tobacco

Key Ideas

▶ Sticking to your decision not to use tobacco involves being able to say no clearly and with confidence.

▶ The health benefits of quitting tobacco use begin immediately and continue throughout life. Society also benefits every time a tobacco user quits.

▶ The most important factor in successfully quitting tobacco is a strong personal commitment.

Vocabulary
- nicotine substitute (420)

Chapter 16 Review

Reviewing Key Ideas

GO ONLINE

PearsonSuccessNet.com

For: Chapter 16 review activity

Section 1

1. In nature, nicotine acts as a(n)
   a. growth agent in plants.　　b. insecticide.
   c. plant pigment.　　d. nutrient.

2. Why is tobacco use less socially acceptable than it used to be?

3. How can friends be both positive and negative influences in regard to tobacco?

4. **Critical Thinking** Do you think there should be more or fewer restrictions on the advertising and sale of tobacco products? Explain.

Section 2

5. The odorless gas in tobacco smoke that binds to hemoglobin is
   a. carbon dioxide.　　b. carbon monoxide.
   c. tar.　　d. nicotine.

6. Describe how nicotine affects the brain.

7. How does the development of nicotine addiction differ in teens and adults?

8. How does tobacco smoke affect a smoker's air passages?

9. **Critical Thinking** Why do you think some people believe they can use tobacco without becoming addicted?

Section 3

10. The smoke that a smoker exhales into the air is called
    a. environmental tobacco smoke.
    b. mainstream smoke.
    c. sidestream smoke.
    d. secondhand smoke.

11. What are three types of cancer that have been linked to tobacco use?

12. Name one disorder that babies of mothers who smoked are at risk for.

13. **Critical Thinking** What do you think are the most effective ways to protect nonsmokers from the effects of secondhand smoke? Explain.

Section 4

14. Which benefit occurs first after someone quits smoking?
    a. Blood oxygen levels return to normal.
    b. Lung function improves.
    c. The risk of having a stroke returns to normal.
    d. Senses of taste and smell return to normal.

15. What would you suggest to an ex-smoker to help him or her not start smoking again?

16. Discuss the different methods a person could use to quit smoking.

17. **Critical Thinking** Some employers prefer not to hire smokers because their healthcare costs are higher. Do you think it is appropriate not to hire someone because he or she smokes? Why or why not? **WRITING**

Building Health Skills

18. **Making Decisions** Suppose that your favorite uncle has come to visit. He asks you for an ashtray. Smoking is not allowed in your home. How would you handle this situation tactfully?

19. **Advocacy** Suppose that you work for an advertising firm. The Surgeon General has hired your firm to work on a new anti-smoking campaign. Develop a 30-second public service commercial that will discourage young people from smoking. **WRITING**

20. **Setting Goals** Evaluate how smoking could affect your career goals.

Health and Community

Volunteering to End Smoking Contact a local chapter of the American Cancer Society, American Lung Association, or other similar agency. Find out about their efforts to reduce smoking in your community. Ask about volunteer opportunities for teens. Create a flyer describing the possible opportunities and share it with your health class. **WRITING**

Standardized Test Prep

Math Practice

The graph shows the number of cigarettes smoked per person from 1920 to 2000, and the number of lung cancer deaths from 1940 to 2000. Use the graph to answer Questions 21–23.

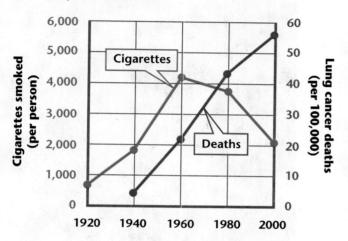

21. When did the number of cigarettes smoked per person reach its peak?
   A 1940   B 1960
   C 2000   D It has not reached its peak.

22. Why do you think that this graph does not show a significant decrease in lung cancer deaths?
   F There is no relationship between cigarette smoking and lung cancer deaths.
   G There has not been a significant decrease in cigarette smoking.
   H Lung cancer takes years to develop.
   J People survive longer with lung cancer now than in 1940.

23. What would be the best title for this graph?
   A Lung Cancer Deaths From 1920–2000
   B Causes of Lung Cancer
   C Cigarettes Smoked vs. Lung Cancer Deaths
   D The Rise and Fall of Cigarette Smoking

Reading and Writing Practice

Read the passage. Then answer Questions 24–27.

In 1998, a settlement between the states and tobacco companies prohibited the companies from directly or indirectly targeting youth in their advertising or promotions. Some people argue that the order has been violated. For example, several companies introduced fruit or candy-flavored cigarettes. Anti-smoking activists complained that these flavors clearly appeal to young people who are not used to the taste of cigarettes. The flavored cigarettes are a way to attract young people to smoking. One tobacco company has agreed to stop selling fruit or candy-flavored cigarettes.

24. In this passage, the word *settlement* means a(n)
   A establishment.
   B colony.
   C agreement.
   D punishment.

25. Why are anti-smoking activists against the production of candy-flavored cigarettes?
   F The tobacco companies did not have permission to produce candy-flavored cigarettes.
   G The tobacco companies are violating the settlement by marketing a product to youth.
   H The flavors hide the real taste of the cigarettes.
   J The flavorings may be toxic.

26. From the context of this passage, you can conclude that
   A the tobacco companies clearly violated the settlement.
   B the settlement has a lot of room for interpretation.
   C fewer young people have started smoking since the 1998 settlement.
   D candy-flavored cigarettes are more harmful than regular cigarettes.

Constructed Response
27. In a paragraph, describe the anti-smoking activists' argument. Do you agree with this argument? Why or why not?

CHAPTER 17

Preventing Drug Abuse

GO ONLINE PearsonSuccessNet.com

VIDEO 17

TEENS Talk

The Risks of Drug Abuse

Preview **Activity**

What Do Different Generations Say?

Complete this activity before you watch the video.

1. Survey ten teens in your community, asking them which three drugs they think are abused by teens the most. Then ask what they think the greatest risk of teen drug abuse is.
2. Ask the same survey questions to ten adults in your community.
3. How were the perceptions of teens and adults alike? How were they different? Summarize the results of your survey. **WRITING**

Section 1

Legal and Illegal Drugs

Objectives

▶ **Define** drug abuse and distinguish it from both appropriate use and misuse.

▶ **Describe** how psychoactive drugs affect the brain.

▶ **Summarize** the risks of drug abuse.

Vocabulary

- medicine
- over-the-counter drug
- prescription drug
- illegal drug
- drug misuse
- drug abuse
- psychoactive drug
- side effect
- drug antagonism
- drug synergism

Warm-Up

Myth Medicines from a drugstore can't harm you.

Fact Medicines can be just as dangerous as "street drugs" if they are used inappropriately.

WRITING What other myths do teens believe about drugs? Write down some statements you have heard from your peers. Which ones do you think are true? Which are false?

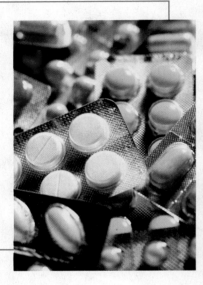

Facts About Drug Use

Drug use is part of life in the United States. Every year, doctors write countless prescriptions and consumers spend millions of dollars on non-prescription (over-the-counter) drugs. When taken as directed, prescription and nonprescription drugs treat many illnesses effectively. However, if drugs are not used as directed, serious health problems can result.

Recall from Chapter 15 that a drug is any chemical substance that is taken to cause changes in a person's body or behavior. **Medicines** are legal drugs that help the body fight injury, illness, or disease. Medicines can be classified into two groups: over-the-counter drugs and prescription drugs.

Over-the-Counter Drugs A medicine that is sold legally in pharmacies and other stores without a doctor's prescription is called an **over-the-counter drug.** Some examples are pain relievers such as aspirin, cold and cough remedies, and some sleep aids. Any over-the-counter drug can cause harm if the instructions on the label are not followed.

 Which over-the-counter drugs have you used? Did you read the labels?

Prescription Drugs A drug that can be obtained only with a written order from a doctor and can be purchased only at a pharmacy is known as a **prescription drug.** Prescription drugs require more government control than over-the-counter drugs because of their potential for harm. A doctor determines the correct amount of the medication that the individual patient needs at the time the prescription is written.

Illegal Drugs An **illegal drug** is a chemical substance that people of any age may not lawfully manufacture, possess, buy, or sell. Illegal drugs are also called street drugs.

Drug Misuse The improper use of medicines—either prescription or over-the-counter drugs—is called **drug misuse.** Examples of drug misuse include taking more than the prescribed amount of a drug, taking drugs with the wrong foods or at the wrong time of day, and not taking a drug for the correct period of time. Drug misuse is often by mistake or because of a patient's misunderstanding of a doctor's orders.

Drug Abuse When a drug is intentionally used improperly or unsafely, it is known as **drug abuse.** For example, a person is abusing prescription painkillers or over-the-counter cough medicines if he or she takes them to cause a "high," rather than to treat pain or a cough. And *any* use of illegal drugs is drug abuse. **Drug abuse occurs when people intentionally use any kind of drugs for nonmedical purposes.**

Proper Use
Using per label instructions to treat a cough

Misuse
Mistakenly taking more than is recommended to treat a cough

Abuse
Deliberately taking more than is recommended or taking for purposes other than treating a cough

FIGURE 1 Even legal drugs, such as cough syrup, can be misused or abused.

How Drugs Affect the Brain

FIGURE 2 Drug users may eventually have trouble enjoying normal activities because they have harmed the brain's ability to feel pleasure.
Interpreting Diagrams How do brain cells change after repeated drug use?

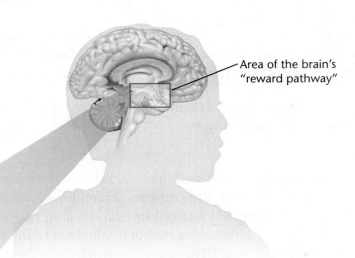
Area of the brain's "reward pathway"

1 **Under Normal Conditions**
The chemical dopamine travels between brain cells, producing pleasurable sensations.

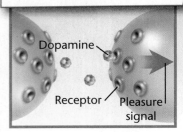
Dopamine
Receptor
Pleasure signal

2 **On Drugs**
Cells release extra dopamine, causing a stronger signal.

3 **After Repeated Drug Use**
Brain cells lose receptors for dopamine, becoming less able to process the chemical. The pleasure signal weakens.

Drug Abuse and the Brain

You have probably heard the phrase "mood-altering" used to refer to some drugs. A mood-altering drug, also called a **psychoactive drug** (sy koh AK tiv), is a chemical that affects brain activity. Most abused drugs are psychoactive. You will learn about commonly abused psychoactive drugs in Section 3.

The "Reward Pathway" Psychoactive drugs typically create a pleasurable feeling that the user wants to repeat. **Many psychoactive drugs trigger activity along a pathway of cells in the brain called the "reward pathway."**

As shown in Figure 2, brain cells along the activated reward pathway release a chemical called dopamine (DOH puh meen). Dopamine itself is not a dangerous chemical—your brain also releases it when you engage in healthy activities such as eating a delicious dessert or cuddling a puppy. In association with drug abuse, however, dopamine can have dangerous effects.

▶ The extra dopamine released during drug use can cause the user to ignore the harmful effects of the drug and want to continue using it.

▶ Flooding the reward pathway with dopamine may lead to intense cravings for the drug when it is not available.

▶ After a time, drug abuse can dull the brain's reactions to natural levels of dopamine. The user no longer feels pleasure from normal activities.

Addiction Abuse of psychoactive drugs may result in addiction. Recall from Chapter 15 that addiction is the compulsive use of a drug, despite any cost to health, family, or social standing. Addiction is a disease that changes the structure and chemistry of the brain.

Dangers of Drug Misuse and Abuse

Drugs can produce powerful changes in the body. These changes are medically useful when a person uses a drug properly. **But when drugs are misused or abused, many serious health effects can result.**

Side Effects   Whereas the immediate effect of a medicine may feel good, unpleasant side effects may follow. A **side effect** is an unwanted physical or mental effect caused by a drug. Side effects can include nausea, dizziness, and drowsiness. Because each person's body is unique, side effects of a particular drug vary from person to person. This is one reason why prescriptions should never be shared.

Medicines have been thoroughly tested to minimize side effects with appropriate use. On the other hand, drugs that are misused or abused often have side effects that can't be predicted and may be severe or even life threatening.

 Connect to Your Life   **What would you say to a friend who offers you her prescription medicine when you are sick? Why?**

Tolerance and Dependence   When a person uses a drug repeatedly, the body may develop tolerance to the drug. Recall from Chapter 15 that as tolerance grows, the user needs increasingly larger amounts of the drug to achieve the original effect. Tolerance may lead to drug dependence—the body develops a chemical need for the drug and can't function normally without it.

Withdrawal   If a person who is dependent on a psychoactive drug stops taking the drug, that person will experience withdrawal symptoms. These symptoms are the body's reaction to not having the drug. Withdrawal symptoms range from mild to life threatening, depending on the drug that was used. Withdrawal symptoms include

- ▶ Nausea or vomiting
- ▶ Headaches or dizziness
- ▶ Fever
- ▶ Digestion problems
- ▶ Paranoia or panic
- ▶ Tremors, seizures, or death

FIGURE 3 Withdrawal symptoms range from mild to severe.

FIGURE 4 It is important to read prescription and over-the-counter drug labels to avoid dangerous drug interactions.

Drug Interactions When a person takes more than one drug at a time, the drugs may interact. The result of this interaction is effects not seen when the drugs are taken alone.

▶ **Antagonism** A **drug antagonism** (an TAG uh niz um) occurs when each drug's effect is canceled out or reduced by the other. Neither drug has the predicted effect. For example, because nicotine causes blood pressure to rise, it can cancel out the beneficial effect of medications taken to lower high blood pressure.

▶ **Synergism** A **drug synergism** (SIN ur jiz um) occurs when drugs interact to produce effects greater than those that each drug would produce alone. For example, the combination of certain sleep medications with small amounts of alcohol may cause rapid loss of consciousness.

 Connect to Your Life **When taking medicines, what precautions can you follow to prevent drug interactions?**

Impurities The manufacture of illegal drugs is not regulated by law. Thus, there is no guarantee that they are pure. Many illegal drugs are contaminated with chemicals that may themselves be harmful or cause dangerous drug interactions. For example, a drug dealer may "cut," or dilute, heroin by adding cleansing powders or rat poison. Illegal drugs may also vary widely from batch to batch in the concentration of psychoactive chemicals they contain. Thus, the user can't easily predict what effect the drug will have each time.

GO ONLINE

PearsonSuccessNet.com

For: More on drug misuse and abuse

Other Health Risks There are other serious health risks associated with drug abuse.

▶ **Hepatitis and HIV** If drug users share needles to inject drugs, contaminated blood left in the needle can carry disease-causing viruses from user to user. The viruses that cause hepatitis B and C can lead to serious, sometimes fatal, liver disease. The human immunodeficiency virus (HIV) causes AIDS, a disease that has no cure.

▶ **Risks to Fetus and Newborn** Drug abuse by a pregnant woman places her baby at risk for a broad range of developmental problems. This is because the drugs cross the placenta, the membrane separating the baby's blood from the mother's blood. The baby may even be born with a drug dependency. For example, "crack babies" are born dependent on the crack cocaine their mothers took during pregnancy. Drugs can also pass through a mother's breast milk to a nursing newborn and cause harm.

Legal Risks and Other Costs

In addition to health risks, people who abuse drugs face other risks. **Drug abusers risk facing serious legal penalties, damaging their relationships with family and friends, and causing significant costs to society.**

Legal Risks Penalties for individuals who produce, possess, transport, or sell illegal drugs include long prison terms and heavy fines. Sometimes the punishment for a drug-related crime is less severe. But the person will still have a criminal record. This record makes it difficult to get a job or to be admitted into schools and the military. In addition, many drug abusers commit other crimes, such as shoplifting and robbery, to support their drug addiction. The legal penalties for these drug-related crimes include fines and imprisonment.

FIGURE 5 Arrest rates for drug violations by juveniles age 10–17 were higher in 2000 than they were in 1990.
Interpreting Graphs Calculate the percentage change in juvenile drug violations between 1990 and 2000. **MATH**

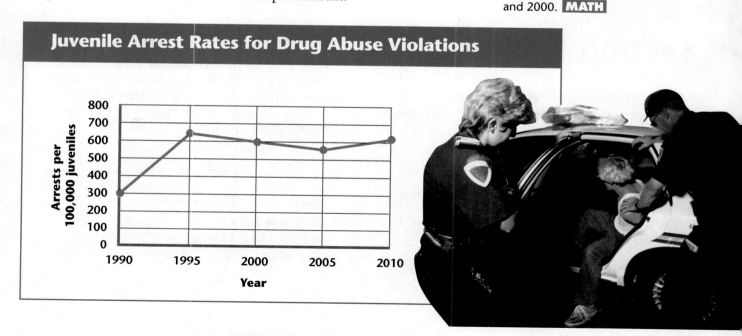

Juvenile Arrest Rates for Drug Abuse Violations

FIGURE 6 Millions of tax dollars are spent each year in an effort to prevent illegal drugs from entering the United States.

Effects on Family and Friends Relationships with family and friends often become strained as the behavior and personality of a drug abuser change. A drug abuser may have unpredictable mood swings, become violent, or withdraw from relationships and responsibilities. The interests and activities that helped bind the person with family and friends may no longer exist. Drugs can cause friends to drift away and families to break up.

Costs to Society The United States government has spent billions of dollars in efforts to stop illegal drug manufacture and sales. Significant financial resources also go toward drug abuse prevention, education, treatment, and rehabilitation programs. These programs provide hope for many drug abusers. However, the demand for such programs often exceeds available funding.

Drug abuse affects many more people than just the abusers themselves. Consider a few of the other costs of drug abuse.

▶ The cost of imprisoning thousands of people for drug-related crimes

▶ Medical costs for drug-related illnesses and injuries, including many of the nation's cases of HIV/AIDS

▶ Premature deaths from drug-related homicides and motor vehicle crashes

▶ Lost work productivity because of drug dependency

Section 1 Review

Key Ideas and Vocabulary

1. How is an **over-the-counter drug** different from a prescription drug?
2. Define drug abuse. Give an example.
3. Briefly describe how psychoactive drugs affect the brain.
4. What is a **side effect**?
5. List three health risks and two other risks that drug abusers face.

Critical Thinking

6. Comparing and Contrasting How is drug abuse different from drug misuse?

Health and Community

Drug Penalties Find out what some of the penalties are for illegal drug possession in your state. Visit the Web sites of local law enforcement agencies for information. Prepare a chart that summarizes your findings. **WRITING**

7. Relating Cause and Effect How can drug dependence affect a person's family? How can it affect a person's community?
8. Making Judgments How do you think tax dollars could best be spent to prevent teen drug abuse? **WRITING**

GO ONLINE PearsonSuccessNet.com Audio Summary Section 17.1

Technology & Health

The Brain on Drugs

Exactly how do different drugs affect the brain? A brain scanning technique called positron emission tomography (PET) can help scientists answer this question. PET scans measure the brain's ability to process brain chemicals, including dopamine and serotonin. These chemicals are critical to normal experiences of mood, emotion, and pain.

WRITING How might brain scans lead to new ways to treat drug addictions?

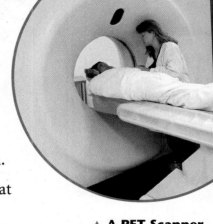

▲ A PET Scanner

The scanner produces images of the brain after specific chemicals in the brain are tagged with radioactive markers.

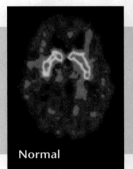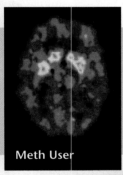

Normal | Meth User

◄ Effects of Meth

Notice the dramatic decrease in dopamine receptor activity (shown in red) compared with a normal brain. With fewer receptors to process dopamine, normal everyday feelings of pleasure are reduced.

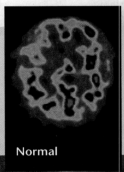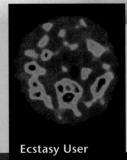

Normal | Ecstasy User

◄ Effects of Ecstasy

PET scans of an Ecstasy user show a significant decrease in the brain's ability to process serotonin. This effect makes it more difficult for the user to sleep, learn, and remember.

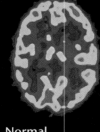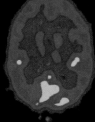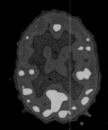

Normal | 10 Days After Quitting | 100 Days After Quitting

◄ Recovering from Cocaine Addiction

Even months after quitting cocaine, PET scans show that the brain's return to normal is very slow. Some addicts may never recover completely.

Factors Affecting Drug Abuse

Objective

▶ **Evaluate** how family, friends, and personal factors can influence an individual's decisions about drugs.

Vocabulary

• protective factor

Warm-Up

Quick Quiz See how many of these questions you can answer "yes" to.

(1) **Do you avoid situations where you think drugs might be used?**

(2) **Have you practiced refusing an offer of drugs?**

(3) **Are there adults in your life whom you trust and with whom you can talk about your problems?**

(4) **Do you manage stress in your life in healthy, constructive ways?**

WRITING Each question you answer "yes" to is a way you protect yourself from drug abuse. What other factors in your life help protect you from using drugs? Explain.

Risk Factors

Why do some people abuse drugs? Some people turn to drugs as a way of coping with life's problems and stresses. Others use drugs because their friends do. Still others use drugs because they say they like the feeling of being "high." But, no matter the reason, the risks related to drug abuse are serious.

A number of factors make it either more or less likely that a teen will abuse drugs. They include family factors, social factors, and personal factors. Often, it is a combination of factors that influences drug use.

Family Factors Consider the following situation.

Since her mom died last year, Julie's dad has withdrawn into his own world. He rarely asks Julie or her brother about their weekend plans. One night, Julie was invited to a "rave" party where everyone seemed to be using drugs. Julie figured her dad would never find out, so she joined in.

FIGURE 7 Are your friends a good influence on you?

One risk factor for teen drug abuse is poor family relationships. When family relationships are not close and supportive, teenagers may not get needed guidance. The teen may feel alienated from the family. This alienation may make teens more vulnerable to the influence of peers who abuse drugs. In addition, if family members abuse drugs, a teen is at higher risk of using drugs, too.

Social Factors Do you know someone like Mike?

Mike has smoked marijuana almost every day for two years. Some of Mike's friends were using the drug and they offered it to him. Now, whenever Mike and his friends hang out, they smoke. Mike says that he can stop using marijuana at any time, although he has yet to try.

In addition to family factors, there are a number of social factors that influence teens to use drugs.

▶ **Peer Group** Many teens, like Mike, were first introduced to drugs by friends or by peers whose acceptance they wanted. They may have initially tried drugs because they were curious or felt pressured. Some continue to abuse drugs because they want to be "part of the crowd."

▶ **Role Models** Teens may see their role models—such as favorite actors—using drugs in movie roles or in real life, without seeing the negative effects. Such "glamorization" of drugs may influence their decision to try drugs.

▶ **Competitive Pressure** For some teens, a strong desire to excel at athletics may be a risk factor for drug use. For example, some teen athletes believe the myths that painkillers will allow them to play through an injury. Others mistakenly think that steroids will allow them to bulk up safely.

In fact, athletes who use painkillers during competition are more likely to sustain serious injuries that could end their athletic careers. Steroid abuse, especially in the teen years, can lead to lifelong or life-threatening disorders.

 GO ONLINE
PearsonSuccessNet.com
For: More on signs of drug dependency

 How would you react to news that your favorite professional athlete was abusing drugs?

FIGURE 8 Drugs don't solve problems; they add problems.

"I can't concentrate in class anymore."

"What if my parents found out?"

"I need another hit!"

"What if I get suspended from the team?"

Personal Factors From time to time, all teens experience stress. But not all of them handle it like Keith.

Talia broke up with Keith after they had been going out for two years. Keith kept to himself and pretended the breakup did not bother him. Eventually, Keith began to feel depressed. He had heard that "uppers" improve mood. Soon, he was dependent on uppers and needed them just to get through the day.

There are many causes for stress in a teen's life—for example, a breakup like Keith's, an academic or social problem, or an illness or death in the family. Some teens might turn to drugs in an attempt to temporarily escape the negative feelings associated with stress. But, abusing drugs does nothing to address the underlying causes of stress. In fact, drug abuse ultimately makes life more stressful.

Another personal factor that may influence drug use is low self-esteem. When teens don't feel good about themselves, they are more likely to ignore the serious risks of drug abuse.

Protective Factors

Review the stories involving Julie, Mike, and Keith. Did their stories have to end in drug abuse? No. Even with the risk factors they faced—a distant parent, drug-abusing peers, and personal stress—their decision to use drugs was ultimately their own.

Just because risk factors exist in a teen's life does not mean the teen will abuse drugs. While most teens face at least some risk factors for drug abuse, protective factors can help them overcome those risks. A **protective factor** is a factor that reduces a person's potential for harmful behavior. **Having strong protective factors in your life will help you stay drug free.**

Family Factors Teenagers who have good relationships with their parents and other family members are better equipped to deal with life's problems and stresses. With close, supportive relationships, teens can seek guidance from parents or siblings and discuss the problems they face. Protective family factors include

- ▶ strong and positive family bonds
- ▶ parental awareness of a teen's social activities and peer group
- ▶ clear rules that are consistently enforced

Social Factors Strong social bonds and supports can cushion the negative effects of stress in your life and act as powerful buffers against drug use. Protective social factors include

- ▶ having strong bonds to school and other community institutions
- ▶ associating with peers who are drug free
- ▶ having friends who are supportive and accepting

Personal Factors Stress and negative feelings are a part of life. With guidance from adult or peer role models, teens can learn healthy techniques for managing stress. Other protective personal factors include

- ▶ a commitment to success in academics and extracurricular activities
- ▶ a personal belief that drug abuse is unacceptable

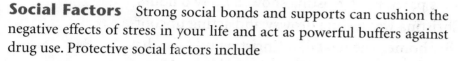

FIGURE 9 Spending quality time with family members can help protect teens from drug abuse.

Section 2 Review

Key Ideas and Vocabulary

1. What three general types of factors can either increase one's risk of drug abuse or protect against drug abuse?

2. What is a **protective factor**?

3. Why is it important to strengthen protective factors in your life?

Critical Thinking

4. Applying Concepts Explain how a teen's family life can either be a risk factor for drug abuse or a protective factor.

Health at Home

Anti-Drug Messages For one week, keep a record of all the information you receive from television, the Internet, and other media about drug use. What risk factors and protective factors do the media emphasize? Summarize your findings. **WRITING**

5. Communicating What advice would you give a friend who is abusing drugs to help him or her cope with negative feelings?

6. Evaluating Despite facing many risk factors, a person ultimately can still say "no" to drugs. Do you agree with this statement? Explain.

Intervening to Help a Friend

Jen had been concerned about her friend Christina's marijuana use for some time, but last night was the final straw. Jen and Christina were to meet at a friend's party, but Christina showed up two hours late and was "high." Christina was feeling drowsy and acting uncoordinated, so Jen drove her home. The next day, Christina told Jen that she was perfectly fine at the party and could have driven herself home. Christina also claimed that she could quit smoking marijuana at any time.

Jen wants to help Christina, but how can she when Christina is so out of touch with reality? Intervening to help a friend who abuses drugs is difficult. Here are some tips for helping a friend.

① Talk to your friend.

Talking to your friend about his or her behavior will not be easy, but it is worthwhile.

▶ **Express Your Concern** Tell your friend that you are intervening because you are worried about his or her well-being.

"I was worried something had happened to you when you showed up late."

▶ **Help Your Friend Face Facts** Share examples of your friend's destructive behavior as specific evidence of the problem. Describe behaviors accurately and simply, using dates and times when possible.

▶ **Describe Your Feelings** Tell how your friend's behavior affects you.

"When you showed up 'high,' it made me feel like you didn't care about my feelings."

▶ **Don't Criticize or Argue** Resist the temptation to be judgmental. You are objecting to the behavior, not the person. Do not get drawn into "No-I-didn't, Yes-you-did" arguments. Expect your friend to deny drug dependency or other destructive patterns of behavior. If your friend argues, say "I just want you to know how I feel," and then leave.

▶ **Offer Specific Help** Prepare a list of resources that your friend can go to for help. Include names, addresses, and phone numbers. Offer to go with your friend to the school counselor, a social service center, a member of the clergy, a health professional, or other local resource.

"Let's go talk to Mr. Ford together."

② Ask another friend to help.

The more people speaking the truth and offering support, the better. Be sure to discuss your concerns and guidelines for intervening with the second friend. Work together.

③ Follow through.

Do what you said you would do to help your friend. Be sure your friend knows that your offers of support can be counted on.

④ Seek adult or professional help.

If you think your friend is in a life-threatening or similarly serious situation, find a more experienced person to intervene directly.

⑤ Recognize your limitations.

Remember, you can only be responsible for yourself. You cannot make another person get help or change behavior. If you have followed these guidelines, then you have done all you can, and you are a good friend.

Practice the Skill

1. Review Jen's situation. Write a dialogue between Jen and Christina following the guidelines presented in Step 1. **WRITING**

2. Under what circumstances do you think Jen should consider asking for adult or professional help for Christina? Explain.

3. Prepare a list of local resources for people facing drug dependency issues. Include addresses and phone numbers, as well as a brief description of the services.

Commonly Abused Drugs

Objectives

▶ **Compare** the effects of depressants, stimulants, and hallucinogens on the body.

▶ **Describe** the effects of marijuana.

▶ **Name** three classes of drugs of increasing concern in recent years.

Vocabulary

- depressant
- barbiturates
- opiate
- heroin
- stimulant
- amphetamines
- methamphetamine
- cocaine
- hallucinogen
- marijuana
- club drugs
- inhalant

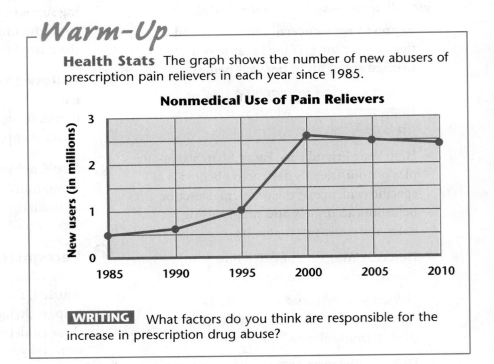

Warm-Up

Health Stats The graph shows the number of new abusers of prescription pain relievers in each year since 1985.

WRITING What factors do you think are responsible for the increase in prescription drug abuse?

Depressants

Drugs are categorized according to their actions and effects on the body. A psychoactive drug that slows brain and body reactions is called a **depressant.** Figure 10 lists some commonly abused depressants and their effects. **Depressants slow body functions by decreasing heart and breathing rates and lowering blood pressure.**

Barbiturates One class of depressants is the **barbiturates** (bahr BICH ur its)—also called sedative-hypnotics. In small doses, barbiturates are sedatives—they relax a person. In high doses, barbiturates are hypnotics—they induce sleep. Today, physicians rarely prescribe barbiturates for sleep problems because barbiturates are dangerous and they have a high potential for abuse.

A barbiturate abuser develops tolerance to the drug quickly. As tolerance increases, the abuser becomes dependent. Barbiturate abusers walk slowly, slur their speech, and react more slowly to their environment. Withdrawal from barbiturates can be fatal.

CNS Depressants   A CNS depressant is a sedative that slows the activity of the central nervous system (CNS). This class of drugs used to be called tranquilizers. CNS depressants slow nerve activity, relax muscle tension, lower alertness, and cause drowsiness. CNS depressants have generally replaced barbiturates for medical uses. Doctors may prescribe CNS depressants to treat anxiety, sleep disorders, muscle spasms, and convulsions. However, as with barbiturates, abuse of CNS depressants can cause tolerance and dependence.

Opiates   An **opiate** (OH pee it) is any drug made from psychoactive compounds contained in the seed pods of poppy plants. Some opiates can also be produced in a laboratory. In small doses, opiates act to dull the senses, relieve pain, and induce sleep. The opiates morphine and codeine, for example, are used in some prescription medications to reduce severe pain. Both morphine and codeine can produce tolerance and lead to dependence.

A growing area of concern is the use of opiate-containing painkillers or cough syrups for a "high." This kind of abuse usually involves taking a larger dose than is recommended for the intended medical purpose. Abusing opiates in this way can have dangerous or even life-threatening side effects.

Another frequently abused opiate in the United States is **heroin,** an illegal opiate made from morphine in a laboratory. Abusers of heroin appear dazed and disoriented. Heroin is also highly addictive.

 What news about painkiller abuse have you seen in the media?

▲ **Poppy seed pod**

FIGURE 10   Depressants have a number of dangerous side effects and long-term health effects when they are abused.

Depressants		
Drug	**Side Effects**	**Long-Term Effects**
Barbiturates	Poor coordination, slurred speech, decreased alertness	Sleepiness, irritability, confusion
CNS Depressants	Blurred vision, dizziness, slurred speech, drowsiness, headache, skin rash	Blood and liver disease
Opiates	Nausea, vomiting, decreased alertness, drowsiness, depressed respiration	Constipation, infections associated with injecting
Alcohol	Impaired judgment, decreased alertness, lack of coordination, memory problems, vomiting	Liver damage, brain damage, anxiety and depression, malnutrition, memory loss

Stimulants

A **stimulant** is a drug that speeds up activities of the central nervous system. **Stimulants increase heart rate, blood pressure, breathing rate, and alertness.** Physicians sometimes prescribe certain stimulants to treat sleep disorders and behavioral disorders such as attention-deficit hyperactivity disorder (ADHD). Abusers of stimulants may develop tolerance, some amount of dependence, and strong addiction. Figure 12 lists some commonly abused stimulants and their effects.

Amphetamines One group of powerful stimulants is the **amphetamines** (am FET uh meenz). Amphetamines are prescription drugs that are sometimes sold illegally as "speed" or "uppers." Amphetamine abuse produces feelings of well-being and high energy. However, the effects wear off quickly and the abuser is often left feeling depressed. The "down" often leads to taking another—and another—dose. The result may be drug dependence.

Methamphetamine A stimulant that is related to amphetamines, but is even more powerful, is **methamphetamine.** Abuse of this highly addictive drug, which is sometimes called "meth," "crank," "crystal," or "ice," is on the rise. The drug is made from relatively inexpensive over-the-counter ingredients in illegal laboratories called "meth labs."

Methamphetamine initially produces a rush, or "high." But, after the rush wears off, the user may become confused, shaky, anxious, irritable, or violent. Meth users ultimately become paranoid and psychotic due to brain damage. Meth use may also cause strokes and deadly convulsions.

▲ **Amphetamine powder**

FIGURE 11 In recent years, crimes linked to methamphetamine have soared. **Reading Graphs** By what percentage did domestic violence crimes linked to meth use increase?

Connect to Your Life

How do you think drug nicknames affect the perceptions teens have of the drugs?

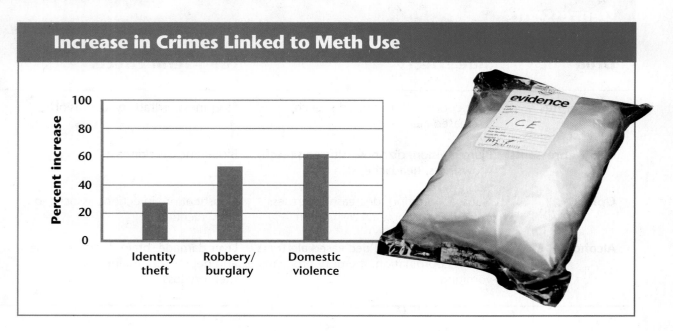

Increase in Crimes Linked to Meth Use

Stimulants		
Drug	**Side Effects**	**Long-Term Effects**
Amphetamines	Restlessness, rapid speech, blurred vision, dizziness	Hyperactivity, irritability, irregular heart rate, liver damage, paranoia
Methamphetamine	Increased respiration, elevated body temperature, convulsions, stroke	Psychotic behavior, memory loss, aggression, brain damage, heart damage, severe tooth and gum disease, stroke
Cocaine	Sleep disorders, loss of appetite, increased blood pressure and heart rate	Depression, paranoia, irritability, weight loss, irregular heartbeat, seizures, respiratory failure, cardiovascular failure, liver damage
Nicotine/ Tobacco Smoke	Nausea, loss of appetite, headache, increased blood pressure	Hacking cough, difficulty breathing, increased number of colds, heart and lung disease

Cocaine   Cocaine is a powerful but short-acting stimulant. Cocaine abusers sniff the drug into the nose, smoke it, or inject it directly into their bloodstream.

Cocaine is highly addictive. Tolerance develops rapidly, causing abusers to need larger and larger amounts. When cocaine's effects wear off, abusers often experience depression, which can be severe. An overdose of cocaine, which can be caused by even a small amount, may result in seizures, heart failure, or respiratory failure. A cocaine overdose can be fatal.

A process called "free-basing" changes cocaine into a concentrated, smokable form known as *crack*. Crack is the strongest form of cocaine. The short but powerful effects produced by crack occur within eight seconds after it is smoked.

FIGURE 12   Stimulants have a number of dangerous side effects and long-term health effects.

▲ **Crack cocaine**

Hallucinogens

A **hallucinogen** (huh LOO sih nuh jun) is a drug that distorts perception, thought, and mood. **Hallucinogens overload the brain with sensory information, causing a distorted sense of reality.** Hallucinogens are illegal and have no medical use.

Hallucinogens can produce frightening and unpredictable mood swings. Sometimes abusers cannot tell what is real. They may also experience memory loss and personality changes, be unable to perform normal activities, or lose track of time and their surroundings. Tolerance to the mind-altering effects of hallucinogens develops quickly.

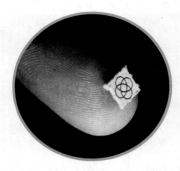

▲ LSD

▲ Psilocybin

LSD   The strongest known hallucinogen is lysergic acid diethylamide, or LSD. LSD is also called "acid." LSD's effects are unpredictable—it can either stimulate or depress the central nervous system. Abusers experience hallucinations in which they may see colorful visions and mistakenly feel they have superhuman powers. The drug may also shorten a person's attention span, causing the mind to wander.

LSD use can lead to frightening episodes known as "bad trips." Another unpredictable effect of LSD is a "flashback." A flashback is an unexpected reoccurrence of a bad trip, sometimes years after LSD was taken. Flashbacks can happen at any time without warning.

Psilocybin   Another hallucinogen is psilocybin (sil uh SY bin)—sometimes called "shrooms." Psilocybin is a chemical found in a certain type of mushroom. The mushrooms are eaten raw or mixed with food. The effects of psilocybin are much like those of LSD, but not as strong. Tolerance to psilocybin develops quickly. An added risk of this drug is that a similar-looking, but deadly, mushroom is sometimes mistaken for psilocybin.

PCP   One of the most dangerous of all drugs is PCP, short for phencyclidine. PCP was once used as an anesthetic, or painkiller, for large animals. Today, PCP, or "angel dust," is only available illegally. Abusers may smoke the white powder with tobacco or marijuana, or inject, sniff, or eat it. Because the drug eliminates the sensation of pain, abusers may unintentionally injure or even kill themselves. Some PCP abusers develop signs of schizophrenia, a mental illness. PCP's effects remain long after drug use ends, and flashbacks may occur.

FIGURE 13 The hallucinogen PCP, a white powder, is sometimes added to marijuana joints.

Marijuana

Marijuana (mar uh WAH nuh) is the leaves, stems, and flowering tops of the hemp plant *Cannabis sativa.* It is also called "pot," "dope," "weed," or "grass." Marijuana is smoked in a pipe or from a "joint" or "blunt," or mixed with food and eaten. The hemp plant is also the source of the illegal drug hashish (HASH eesh), or "hash."

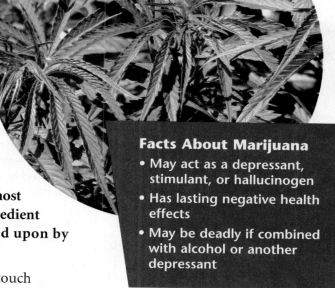

Effects of Marijuana Marijuana is one of the most frequently abused psychoactive drugs. Its main ingredient changes the way information reaches and is acted upon by the brain. Side effects of marijuana use include

▶ distorted perceptions—sights, sounds, time, and touch

▶ difficulties with thinking and problem solving

▶ loss of motor coordination

▶ increased heart rate

▶ feelings of anxiety or paranoia

Frequent use of marijuana may permanently affect the brain. Users may damage their short-term memory and lose the motivation to perform at school or work. Smoking marijuana also increases the risk of certain cancers.

Marijuana and Driving Because marijuana can act as a depressant, users often feel sleepy or drowsy. Marijuana use can also make it difficult to judge distances and react quickly to signals and sounds on the road. Driving a car is extremely dangerous when under the influence of marijuana.

A Gateway to Other Drugs You may have heard the phrase "gateway drug" used to describe marijuana. This phrase reflects the fact that marijuana use is often a gateway to using other "harder" drugs, such as cocaine. As marijuana users build up tolerance, they may seek out other drugs to experience the "high" they first got from marijuana. In addition, a marijuana user is likely to be in contact with people who use and sell other illegal drugs. Studies show that almost all young people who use other illegal drugs first used marijuana.

 How can refusing marijuana help you stay away from drugs in general?

Facts About Marijuana

- May act as a depressant, stimulant, or hallucinogen
- Has lasting negative health effects
- May be deadly if combined with alcohol or another depressant

FIGURE 14 Contrary to what some people may think, marijuana is a dangerous drug.

 GO ONLINE

PearsonSuccessNet.com

For: More on commonly abused drugs

Club Drugs

Drug	Classification	Side Effects	Other Facts
Ecstasy (MDMA) *Also called XTC, X, Adam, clarity, love drug*	Combined stimulant and hallucinogen	Increased heart rate and blood pressure, blurred vision, muscle tension, severe sweating and chills, nausea, increased body temperature that can lead to organ failure	Drugs called "Ecstasy" often contain other substances besides MDMA that make them even more dangerous.
Rohypnol *Also called roofies, rophies, forget-me pill*	CNS depressant	Decreased blood pressure, drowsiness, dizziness, confusion, memory loss	Associated with "date rapes"; a small dose can impair a user for up to 12 hours.
GHB (Gamma-hydroxybutyrate) *Also called grievous bodily harm, G, liquid ecstasy*	CNS depressant; also has anabolic (body-building) effects	Drowsiness, nausea, headache, loss of reflexes	Associated with "date rapes"; high doses may result in sleep, coma, or death.
Ketamine *Also called K, Vitamin K, cat valium*	Hallucinogen	Hallucinations, increased heart rate and blood pressure, impaired motor function, memory loss, numbness, nausea	High doses may cause delirium and fatal respiratory problems.

FIGURE 15 Some of the known effects of club drugs are listed here. **Reading Tables** Which club drugs are CNS depressants?

▲ **Ecstasy**

Club Drugs, Inhalants, and Steroids

So far, you have learned about the traditional classes of drugs that are commonly abused. **Three classes of drugs that are of growing concern in recent years are club drugs, inhalants, and anabolic steroids.** The effects of club drugs and inhalants are extremely unpredictable and dangerous. The dangers of steroid abuse are less immediate. However, abuse of steroids causes lifelong damage to the body and brain.

Club Drugs Club drugs got their name from the fact that they first gained popularity at dance clubs and raves. They are now more widely available, but their use is still often associated with the club scene. The strength and quality of club drugs are highly unpredictable—their effects are different from person to person and very dangerous. Figure 15 summarizes the dangers of four of the more common club drugs. Other drugs associated with the club scene include methamphetamine and the hallucinogens LSD and PCP.

Some people are unknowing victims of club drugs. For example, rohypnol (roh HYP nawl) can be slipped into someone's drink without his or her knowledge. While under the effects of the drug, the person may be hurt or raped and not even be able to recall the event later on.

The effects of rohypnol are most severe when it is taken with an alcoholic drink. This is because of the synergism of combining two depressant drugs. However, rohypnol can be dangerous in any drink. The best advice for avoiding club drugs is to stay away from places where these drugs are used.

Inhalants A breathable chemical vapor that produces mind-altering effects is called an **inhalant** (in HAYL unt). Some inhalants have appropriate medical uses. For example, nitrous oxide is an anesthetic used by dentists and doctors during surgery. But most inhalants are not meant for human use.

Abusing inhalants—including glue and household cleaners—may produce brief feelings of excitement or giddiness, but the feelings are far from harmless. In fact, they are a sign that the oxygen in the inhaled breath has been replaced with a chemical that has either stimulated the heart or depressed brain function. Even a single session of inhalant abuse can cause death by cardiac arrest or suffocation.

Anabolic Steroids Anabolic steroids are synthetic drugs that are similar to the hormone testosterone. Legal uses of this drug include treating growth disorders and certain types of anemia. But steroids are also abused, primarily by people who want bigger muscles.

You can review the many dangerous side effects of steroid abuse in Chapter 13. Steroid use is especially dangerous for teenagers, whose growing bodies can suffer permanent damage. Unlike other commonly abused drugs, steroids are not considered psychoactive. However, they can have serious long-term effects on a user's brain. Have you ever heard the phrase "roid rage"? Steroids can make a user's personality very aggressive. In addition, some steroid users become severely depressed.

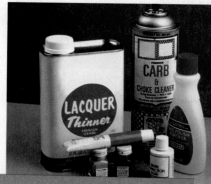

FIGURE 16 Inhalant abuse is extremely dangerous.

Some Dangers of Inhalant Abuse
- Liver and kidney damage
- Loss of bladder control
- Permanent hearing loss
- Brain cell death
- Loss of consciousness, coma, or death

Section 3 Review

Key Ideas and Vocabulary

1. Briefly describe the overall effects that depressants, stimulants, and hallucinogens have on the body.
2. What is an **opiate?** Give three examples.
3. What is **methamphetamine?** List three long-term effects of methamphetamine use.
4. How does marijuana affect the brain? List three side effects.
5. Name three classes of drugs of increasing concern today. In three sentences, summarize the dangers of each.

Health and Community

Steroid Abuse Rules Choose three different sports where steroid abuse is a problem. Find out what rules and testing procedures are applied to professional athletes in these sports. Summarize your findings in a one-page report. **WRITING**

Critical Thinking

6. **Relating Cause and Effect** Explain why prescription depressants or stimulants are dangerous when used for nonmedical purposes.
7. **Comparing and Contrasting** How is methamphetamine different from other amphetamines?

Choosing to Be Drug Free

Objectives

▶ **Identify** three treatment options for people who abuse drugs.

▶ **Name** three steps you can take to stay drug free.

Vocabulary

• therapeutic community

Warm-Up

Dear Advice Line,

My friend Greg tried methamphetamine at a party a few months ago. Soon he started doing it regularly. He gets defensive and aggressive when I ask him if he needs help. I'm scared to talk to him anymore, but I want to help.

WRITING What advice would you give Greg's friend? How can she help Greg?

Treating Drug Abuse

What can you do to help someone who is abusing drugs? Before a person can be helped, the person needs to acknowledge that he or she has a drug problem. The next step would be for the person to explore possible treatment options.

Acknowledge the Problem Before drug abusers can be helped, they need to recognize their problem. Unfortunately, this may be difficult. Many abusers deny their behavior; others deny the underlying problems that led them to drug abuse.

Figure 17 lists some of the signs of drug abuse that you may recognize in yourself or in a friend or classmate. Review the Building Health Skills on pages 438–439 for tips on how to convince a friend that he or she has a drug problem.

Connect to Your Life

What trusted adult could you turn to for advice about a friend's drug problem?

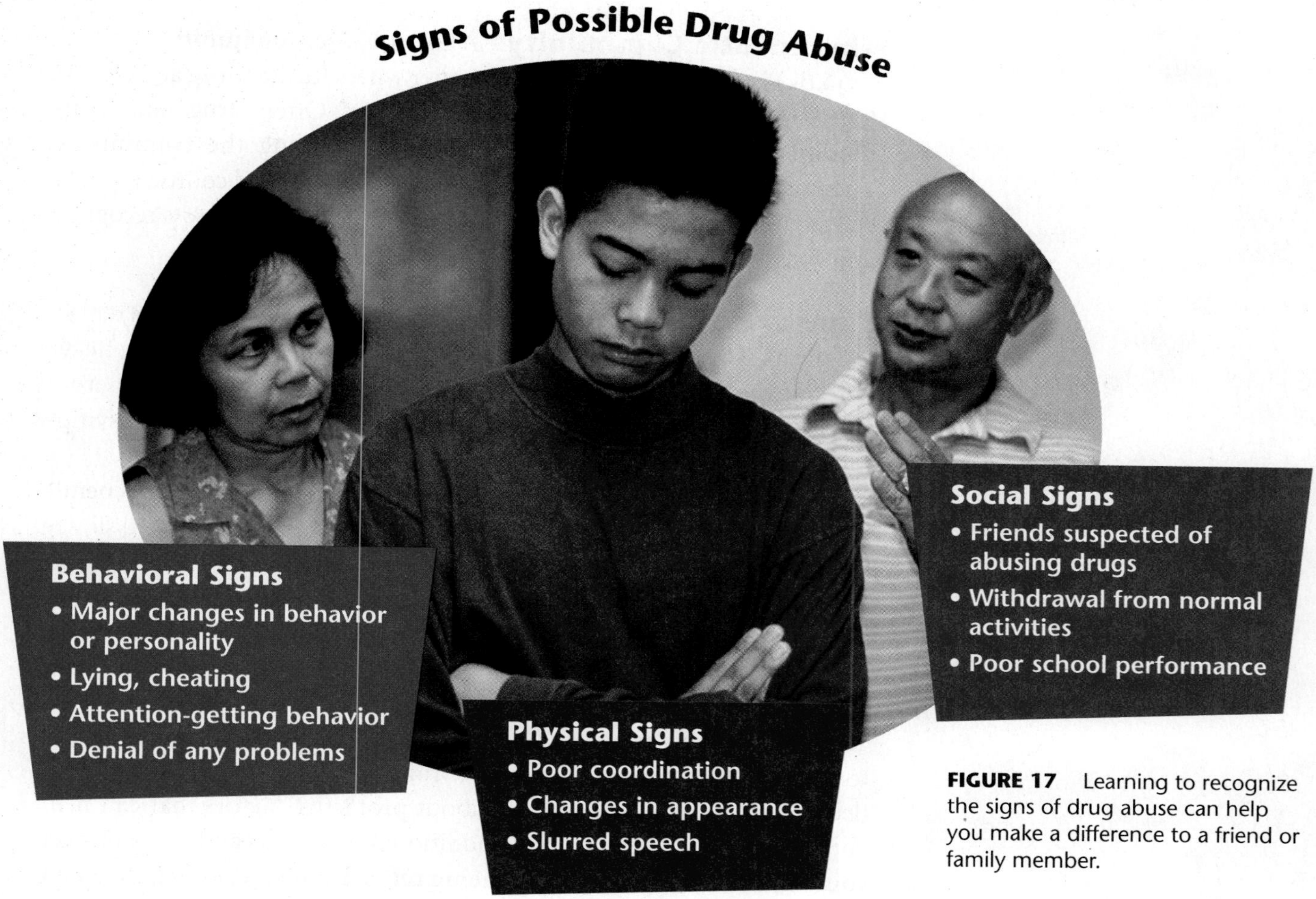

Signs of Possible Drug Abuse

Behavioral Signs
- Major changes in behavior or personality
- Lying, cheating
- Attention-getting behavior
- Denial of any problems

Physical Signs
- Poor coordination
- Changes in appearance
- Slurred speech

Social Signs
- Friends suspected of abusing drugs
- Withdrawal from normal activities
- Poor school performance

FIGURE 17 Learning to recognize the signs of drug abuse can help you make a difference to a friend or family member.

Explore Treatment Options Once drug abusers recognize their problem, several treatment options are available to them. **Treatment options for drug abusers include detoxification, therapeutic communities, and supervised medication.** Programs also exist for family members trying to understand their loved one's drug problem. Understanding the underlying cause for a loved one's drug abuse and getting involved in the person's treatment can help restore family stability.

Some drug treatment programs are available at little or no cost. Community hospitals, for example, may offer clinics or programs that provide low-cost or volunteer counseling for teenagers and adults. Local schools and governments also schedule parent meetings, peer group counseling, and drug-free programs.

Detoxification A person who enters a detoxification program undergoes gradual but complete withdrawal from the abused drug under medical supervision. Most detoxification programs are in hospitals. Doctors may reduce the drug dosage slowly to avoid painful withdrawal symptoms, or they may supervise the total withdrawal all at once. Detoxification programs include counseling to help people deal with their abuse and cope with the underlying problems.

 GO ONLINE
PearsonSuccessNet.com
For: More on treating drug abuse

Therapeutic Community A **therapeutic community** (thehr uh PYOO tik) is a residential treatment center where former drug abusers live together and learn to adjust to drug-free lives. Often, drug abusers are required to undergo detoxification before joining the community. Therapeutic communities provide both medical care and counseling. The counseling may involve behavioral therapy to help drug abusers recognize and correct negative behaviors associated with their drug use.

Supervised Medication A third treatment option involves replacing the abused drug with a drug that produces some of the same effects, without the "high." For example, the drug methadone can help heroin abusers. Small, regular doses of methadone prevent withdrawal symptoms and craving for heroin.

Because methadone and other drug replacements can cause dependency, a trained professional must carefully monitor treatment and slowly lower the dosage. Long-term methadone use causes side effects such as liver damage.

Staying Drug Free

You face decisions every day. You need to decide what to eat, what clothes to wear, and how much to exercise. You may also face decisions about drugs. In Section 2, you learned about protective factors that can help you avoid drugs. There are some additional steps you can take to protect yourself from using drugs. **Practicing refusal skills, seeking help when you need it, and getting involved in drug-free activities can help you stay away from drugs.**

FIGURE 18 Teens in many communities are taking a stand against drugs. The teens at right are part of a program in Florida called "Drug Free Youth in Town."

Hands-On *Activity*

Resisting Peer Pressure

Materials
bag of jelly beans
set of five role-playing cards per group

Try This
❶ Form a group with four other students.
❷ Your teacher will distribute a different role-playing card to each group member.
❸ Do not discuss your role with other group members.
❹ Imagine that you are at a party with friends. Spend five minutes thinking about your assigned role and how you will act during the imagined party.
❺ At your teacher's signal, begin acting out your role with the other members of your group.

Think and Discuss
❶ Explain how you felt playing your role during the imagined party.
❷ How do you think player 4 felt being pressured to eat the jelly beans?
❸ How might player 3 have felt about eventually giving in?
❹ How do you think player 1 felt about pressuring all the other players?
❺ What refusal skills will you use to resist pressure from friends to use drugs?

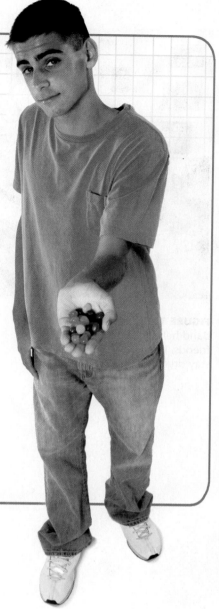

Refusing Drugs   Refusing drugs can be difficult when you are faced with pressure to take them. You can sharpen your refusal skills by reviewing the Building Health Skills in Chapter 15 on pages 378–379. To be effective, be sure to clearly state your personal reasons for not wanting to take drugs. For example, you could say, "No thanks — I want to keep a clear head," or "I don't want to become addicted," or simply, "I don't do drugs."

If the person offering you drugs continues to pressure you, take a definite action and remove yourself from the situation. Your action will make it clear that you cannot be persuaded to change your mind.

Seeking Help   If you decide that the stresses and problems in your life are too much to manage, find someone to talk to. Many people are willing to help, but you must first let them know that you need help. Parents, teachers, friends, siblings, school counselors, school nurses, and members of the clergy are usually available for guidance and support. A second option is to call a national drug-abuse hotline. Staffers can help you find support in your local community.

What are your personal reasons for refusing drugs?

FIGURE 19 Participating in a band helps these teens make friends, build self-confidence, and stay drug free.

Alternatives to Drugs Turning to drugs to try to feel good or to deal with problems is a risky choice. Imagine how you would feel if you had to tell lies, hide your physical condition, worry about police, and deal with the drug's side effects. People who become dependent on drugs spend almost all of their time either thinking about drugs, getting the money for drugs, or taking drugs. Drugs end up controlling their lives. By deciding not to use drugs, you can stay in control of your life.

There are many healthy and constructive activities that can lift your mood and help you handle the pressures in your life. In addition, you may make new friends who share your commitment to stay drug free.

▶ **Engage in physical activity.** Physical activity boosts your mood and relieves the negative effects of stress. Getting enough exercise and getting involved in sports can help you feel energetic, positive, and self-confident.

▶ **Volunteer.** Helping other people can give you a good feeling about yourself, too. Many social service agencies need volunteers. You can read to someone with a visual handicap, visit elderly people in a nursing facility, or teach a hobby or sport to young children.

▶ **Join a youth group.** Youth group leaders serve as role models and help you explore your values in a supportive environment. Youth groups often participate in community service projects. Participating in a youth group can give you a sense of belonging and a connection to others.

Section 4 Review

Key Ideas and Vocabulary

1. What are three options for drug abuse treatment?
2. Describe a **therapeutic community**. Identify two ways it helps drug abusers overcome their problems.
3. What are three steps you can take to stay away from drugs?

Critical Thinking

4. Applying Concepts What activities do you participate in that keep you away from drugs?

Health at School

Drug Prevention Speech Prepare a 5-minute speech for sixth graders about healthy alternatives to drug use. Use examples that will relate to this age group. Also pay attention to the style of speech that will most appeal to them. Practice your speech with friends and get suggestions for improvements. **WRITING**

5. Comparing and Contrasting How are detoxification and medication treatment programs similar? How are they different? **WRITING**

GO ONLINE PearsonSuccessNet.com   Audio Summary Section 17.4

Chapter 17
At a Glance

VIDEO **TEENS** Talk ⊙
The Risks of Drug Abuse What did you learn from the video about the risks of drug abuse?

Section 1   Legal and Illegal Drugs

Key Ideas

▶ Drug abuse occurs when people intentionally use any kind of drugs for nonmedical purposes.

▶ Many psychoactive drugs trigger activity along a pathway of neurons in the brain called the "reward pathway."

▶ When drugs are misused or abused, many serious health effects can result.

▶ Drug abusers risk facing serious legal penalties, damaging their relationships with family and friends, and causing significant costs to society.

Vocabulary
• medicine (426) • over-the-counter drug (426)
• prescription drug (427) • illegal drug (427)
• drug misuse (427) • drug abuse (427)
• psychoactive drug (428) • side effect (429)
• drug antagonism (430) • drug synergism (430)

Section 2   Factors Affecting Drug Abuse

Key Ideas

▶ A number of factors make it either more or less likely that a teen will abuse drugs. They include family factors, social factors, and personal factors.

▶ Having strong protective factors in your life will help you stay drug free.

Vocabulary
• protective factor (436)

Section 3   Commonly Abused Drugs

Key Ideas

▶ Depressants slow body functions by decreasing heart and breathing rates and lowering blood pressure.

▶ Stimulants increase heart rate, blood pressure, breathing rate, and alertness.

▶ Hallucinogens overload the brain with sensory information, causing a distorted sense of reality.

▶ Marijuana is one of the most frequently abused psychoactive drugs.

▶ Three classes of drugs that are of growing concern in recent years are club drugs, inhalants, and anabolic steroids.

Vocabulary
• depressant (440) • barbiturate (440) • opiate (441)
• heroin (441) • stimulant (442) • amphetamines (442)
• methamphetamine (442) • cocaine (443)
• hallucinogen (443) • marijuana (445)
• club drugs (446) • inhalant (447)

Section 4   Choosing to Be Drug Free

Key Ideas

▶ Treatment options for drug abusers include detoxification, therapeutic communities, and supervised medication.

▶ Practicing refusal skills, seeking help when you need it, and getting involved in drug-free activities can help you stay away from drugs.

Vocabulary
• therapeutic community (450)

Chapter 17 Review

GO ONLINE
PearsonSuccessNet.com
For: Chapter 17 review activity

Reviewing Key Ideas

Section 1

1. Unwanted physical and mental effects caused by a drug are called
   a. psychoactive effects.
   b. withdrawal symptoms.
   c. side effects.
   d. tolerance.

2. How does drug addiction affect the brain?

3. Contrast two kinds of drug interactions.

4. How do drugs taken by a pregnant woman reach the fetus?

5. **Critical Thinking** In what ways are drug abuse and crime linked? Give at least three examples.

Section 2

6. Something that reduces a person's potential for harmful behavior is called a
   a. risk factor.
   b. social factor.
   c. protective factor.
   d. personal belief.

7. Give three examples of social risk factors and three examples of social protective factors for drug use.

8. **Critical Thinking** Explain why you think good stress management skills are a protective factor against drug use.

Section 3

9. Drugs that slow body functions are called
   a. depressants.
   b. stimulants.
   c. hallucinogens.
   d. club drugs.

10. What is a flashback and with which category of drugs does it occur?

11. What are the immediate and long-term effects of smoking marijuana?

12. **Critical Thinking** Is a drug dangerous only if it is addictive? Explain your position. **WRITING**

Section 4

13. The objective of supervised medication in treating drug addicts is to
    a. provide a safe "high."
    b. prevent withdrawal symptoms and cravings.
    c. produce a controlled form of addiction.
    d. increase side effects.

14. Where can drug treatment programs be found for little or no cost?

15. Why does detoxification require close medical supervision?

16. List three alternative activities to doing drugs.

17. **Critical Thinking** Analyze the risks and benefits of a drug replacement such as methadone. When would the benefits outweigh the risks? **WRITING**

 ## Building Health Skills

18. **Analyzing Influences** Studies show that students who regularly abuse drugs tend to get lower grades in school and are more likely to lie or steal. Why do you think this is true?

19. **Making Decisions** If you were an editor of a teen magazine, would you print a story about a movie star who overdoses on illegal drugs? Explain your answer. **WRITING**

20. **Communicating** How might you tell a friend that you suspect he or she is abusing drugs?

21. **Setting Goals** Pick an area of your life in which you feel you could add a protective factor for drug abuse. Write a goal to work on—for example, "Always let mom know where I'm going." Monitor your progress over the course of the school year.

Health and Community

Club Drugs Warning Write a public service announcement that warns people of the dangers of Ecstasy and other club drugs. Consider the audience you want to address. Choose words and images that best reach that audience. **WRITING**

Standardized Test Prep

Math Practice

The graphs below track changes in marijuana use and perceptions of marijuana risk among tenth and twelfth graders. Use the graphs to answer Questions 22–24.

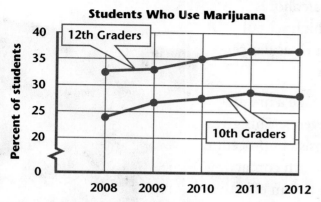

Students Who Use Marijuana

22. In what year was marijuana abuse by tenth and twelfth graders at its lowest level?
    A 2008
    B 2009
    C 2010
    D 2011

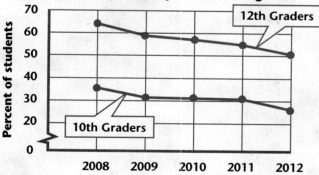

Students Who Agree Marijuana Use Is High Risk

23. In what year did most tenth and twelfth graders agree that marijuana use is high risk?
    F 2008
    G 2009
    H 2010
    J 2012

24. What phrase best summarizes the general trend shown by the graphs?
    A Marijuana abuse rises as perception of its risk falls.
    B More More tenth graders agree that marijuana use is high risk than do twelfth graders.
    C Marijuana use harmed more students in 2008 than in 2012.
    D Teaching youth the risks of marijuana use will make them want to try marijuana.

Reading and Writing Practice

Read the passage. Then answer Questions 25–27.

Many rewarding activities of everyday life, such as laughing with friends or winning a game, raise dopamine levels in the brain. Many psychoactive drugs "hijack" this natural process—the drugs synthetically boost dopamine concentration to unnaturally high levels, causing intense euphoria and the desire for more. Consequently, over time, other previously pleasurable activities like hobbies and athletics can lose their appeal. People who are addicted to drugs organize their lives around the drug use because their brains have been tricked into valuing drugs more than anything else.

25. From the context of this passage, what is the best synonym for euphoria?
    A confusion
    B aggression
    C hallucination
    D pleasure

26. According to this passage,
    F drug addiction releases a toxic chemical into the brain.
    G drugs are the only way to feel pleasure.
    H drug addicts can make a full recovery.
    J drugs interfere with a natural process in an unhealthy way.

Constructed Response

27. Addiction has been called a "disease of the brain." How does this passage support this view? Explain.

Test-Taking Tip

Plan to study for your test well ahead of time. Avoid "cramming" for a test the night before. Your brain is more likely to retain and synthesize information if you study over a longer period of time.

Focus on ISSUES

Should Students Be Tested for Alcohol Use Before School Events?

Even though underage drinking is illegal, alcohol is the most commonly abused drug among high school students. Drinking before school events, such as dances and sporting events, is a growing problem.

Some schools now require students to take a breath-alcohol test before they can enter school events. This gives school administrators an unbiased and consistent procedure for screening all students. Penalties range from contacting parents to suspension. Is a breath-alcohol test an effective way to reduce student drinking?

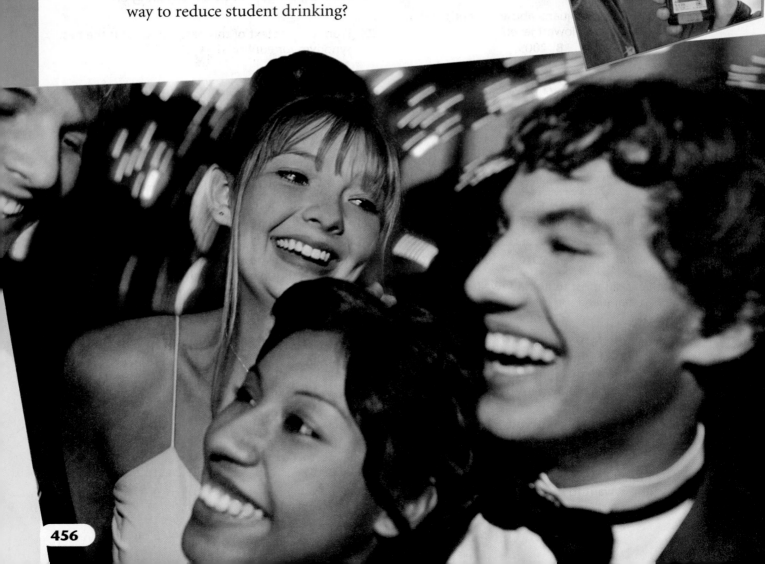

The Case for Alcohol Testing

School districts that test for alcohol use have seen significant reductions in student drinking before school events. Alcohol testing clearly reinforces the school's "zero tolerance policy" for underage drinking. Testing might not stop every student from drinking. However, a strict testing policy significantly reduces the number of injuries and behavior problems that result from drinking.

" I think it's a great idea to test everyone. Last year, I worked for months to earn enough money for the prom. That night, a few kids showed up drunk and got rowdy. It was horrible. This year, my school plans to test everyone at the entrance to the prom. Anyone testing positive will have to wait outside with a teacher for their parents to pick them up. I'm sure everyone will have a much better time this year. And I'll feel safer on the roads driving home. "

The Case Against Alcohol Testing

Alcohol testing may prevent students from drinking before school events, but it doesn't address the core problem. Schools should spend their time and money educating and counseling students about the dangers of underage drinking in general. If students know the facts, they will be able to make smarter decisions.

" Alcohol-testing policies punish all of us for the actions of a few. Just because some students may make bad decisions, it's not fair to treat all of us like criminals. Testing makes me feel that my privacy is being invaded and that school officials have no trust in us. Who will want to attend a school event knowing that you'll have to wait in a long line? Besides, testing won't stop those who want to drink from doing so. They just won't show up at school events. "

What do YOU think?

Use these steps to analyze and express your opinion about alcohol testing.

1. Analyze the Issue Carefully consider both sides of the issue. Make a table listing the pros and cons of alcohol testing at school events.

2. Consider Your Values Suppose your friend tested positive and was refused entrance to a school event. How would you feel? How would you react?

3. Take a Stand Write a paragraph expressing your opinion about alcohol testing at school events. Make sure you state your opinion clearly and offer several strong supporting reasons. **WRITING**

CHAPTER 18

Reproduction and Heredity

GO ONLINE PearsonSuccessNet.com

VIDEO 18

TEENS Talk

Hormones in the Balance

Preview **Activity**

What Are Hormones?

Complete this activity before you watch the video.

1. When you hear the word *hormone,* what things do you think about? Jot down your impressions of what hormones are and what they do.

2. Based on what you know, write a definition for *hormone.*

3. Compare your answers with a partner. Then revise your definition. **WRITING**

The Endocrine System

Objectives

▶ **Describe** the general roles of the endocrine system.

▶ **Identify** the glands of the endocrine system.

Vocabulary

• endocrine gland
• hormone
• hypothalamus
• pituitary gland
• puberty

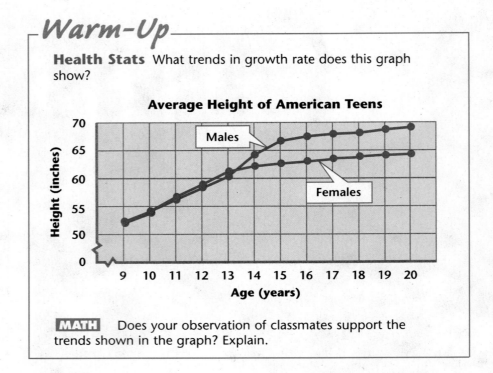

Warm-Up

Health Stats What trends in growth rate does this graph show?

Average Height of American Teens

MATH Does your observation of classmates support the trends shown in the graph? Explain.

What Is the Endocrine System?

How much have you grown in the past year? When will you reach your adult height? Your growth rate is one of the many functions controlled by your body's endocrine system. **The endocrine system regulates long-term changes in the body such as growth and development. It also controls many of your body's daily activities.** Two examples of daily activities include your body's use of energy from a meal and its response to stress.

Endocrine Glands Your endocrine system is made up of a group of organs, called endocrine glands (EN duh krin). An **endocrine gland** produces and releases chemical substances that signal changes in other parts of the body. Some of your body's glands, such as sweat glands, release their chemicals into tiny tubes called ducts. The ducts carry the chemicals to the place where they will be used. Endocrine glands, on the other hand, do not have ducts. Instead, they release substances directly into the bloodstream. The blood then carries those substances throughout the body.

Adrenaline directs your response to sudden stress or fear.

Testosterone controls beard growth in males.

Growth hormone regulates your growth to adult height.

FIGURE 1 Hormones play many roles in the body.

Hormones A chemical substance produced by an endocrine gland is known as a **hormone.** You can think of a hormone as a chemical messenger. Each hormone has a specific function and specific "targets" in the body. Once released into the bloodstream, a hormone travels to its target cells, where it turns on, turns off, speeds up, or slows down the activities of those cells. For example, targets of the hormone adrenaline include cells in your heart, muscles, and brain. Adrenaline causes a faster heartbeat, tensing of the muscles, and increased alertness—your "fight-or-flight" response.

The endocrine system is kept in balance by the coordinated action of various hormones. For example, a hormone from one gland may turn on the production of a different hormone by a second gland. In turn, the hormone from the second gland signals the first gland to stop releasing its hormone. By this system of checks and balances, the endocrine system keeps the body's activities functioning smoothly.

 Describe a time when you experienced a surge of adrenaline.

Functions of Endocrine Glands

Each of your endocrine glands plays a specific, important role in your body. **The endocrine glands include the hypothalamus, pituitary gland, thyroid gland, parathyroid glands, thymus gland, adrenal glands, pancreas, and reproductive glands.**

Hypothalamus The **hypothalamus** (hy poh THAL uh mus), an endocrine gland located in the brain, is actually part of both the nervous and the endocrine systems. For example, nerve signals from the hypothalamus control body temperature and feelings of sleep and hunger, and hormones from the hypothalamus control the body's water levels. The hypothalamus also produces a class of hormones called "releasing hormones" that signal the release of hormones from another region of the brain.

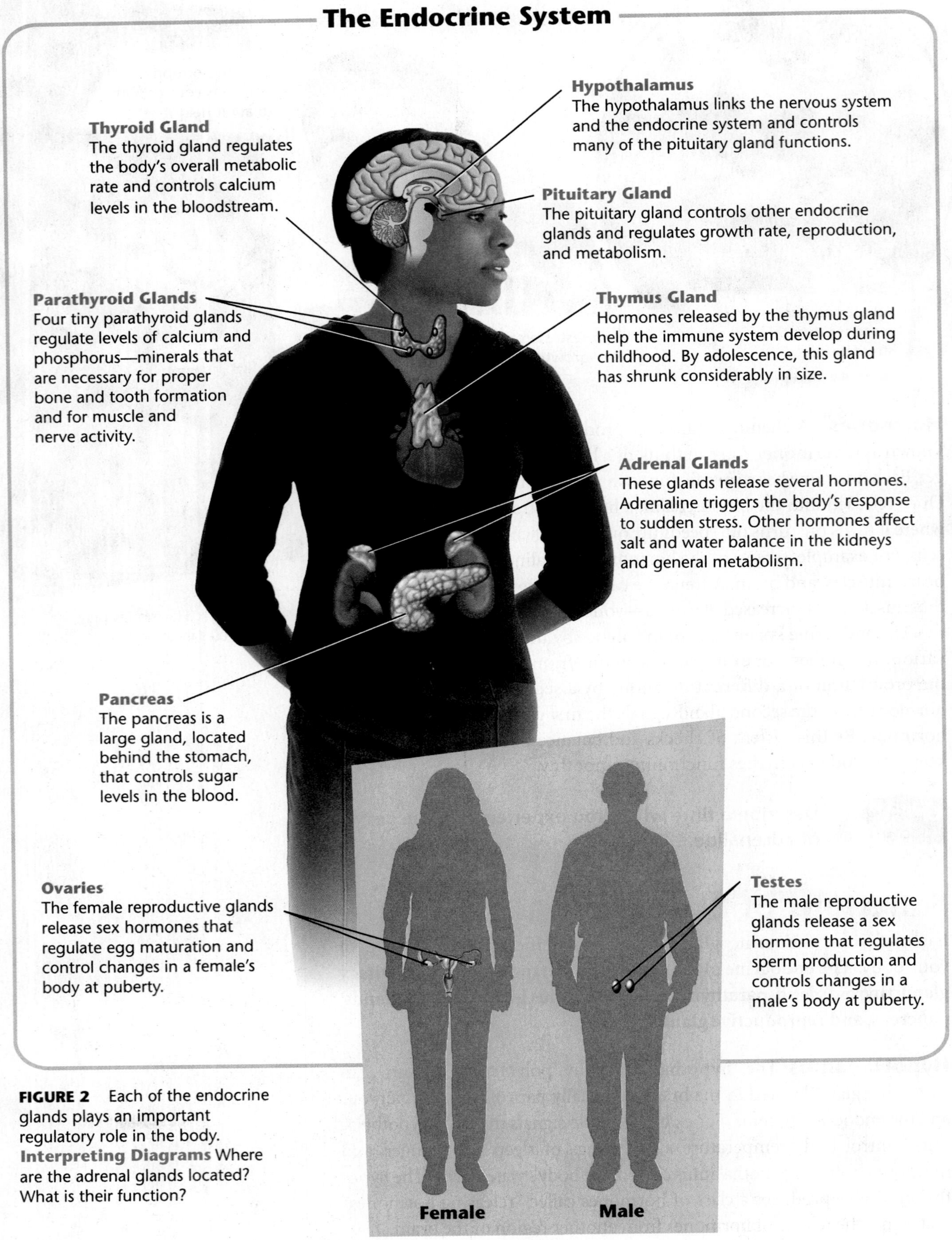

The Endocrine System

Thyroid Gland
The thyroid gland regulates the body's overall metabolic rate and controls calcium levels in the bloodstream.

Parathyroid Glands
Four tiny parathyroid glands regulate levels of calcium and phosphorus—minerals that are necessary for proper bone and tooth formation and for muscle and nerve activity.

Pancreas
The pancreas is a large gland, located behind the stomach, that controls sugar levels in the blood.

Ovaries
The female reproductive glands release sex hormones that regulate egg maturation and control changes in a female's body at puberty.

Hypothalamus
The hypothalamus links the nervous system and the endocrine system and controls many of the pituitary gland functions.

Pituitary Gland
The pituitary gland controls other endocrine glands and regulates growth rate, reproduction, and metabolism.

Thymus Gland
Hormones released by the thymus gland help the immune system develop during childhood. By adolescence, this gland has shrunk considerably in size.

Adrenal Glands
These glands release several hormones. Adrenaline triggers the body's response to sudden stress. Other hormones affect salt and water balance in the kidneys and general metabolism.

Testes
The male reproductive glands release a sex hormone that regulates sperm production and controls changes in a male's body at puberty.

Female   **Male**

FIGURE 2 Each of the endocrine glands plays an important regulatory role in the body.
Interpreting Diagrams Where are the adrenal glands located? What is their function?

Pituitary Gland "Releasing hormones" from the hypothalamus signal the release of hormones from a pea-sized endocrine gland in the brain, called the **pituitary gland** (pih TOO ih tehr ee). The pituitary controls many of your body's functions. These functions include growth, reproduction, and metabolism. Metabolism is the process by which you obtain energy from food.

Some pituitary hormones act as "on" switches for other endocrine glands. For example, one pituitary hormone signals the thyroid gland to release hormones essential for normal metabolism. Other pituitary hormones control body activities directly. For example, growth hormone released by the pituitary gland regulates growth throughout your body from infancy to adulthood.

Other Endocrine Glands Endocrine glands are found throughout the body, as shown in Figure 2. Notice the range of body functions that your endocrine system controls—from your blood sugar level over the course of a day to the long-term changes in your body that you experience as a teen.

The reproductive glands are an important part of the endocrine system. In males, the reproductive glands consist of two testes, and in females, two ovaries. The reproductive glands work at low levels in both boys and girls until about the age of ten, when puberty typically begins. **Puberty** is the period of sexual development during which a person becomes sexually mature and physically able to reproduce.

Puberty starts when the hypothalamus signals the pituitary gland to begin producing two hormones. Those hormones in turn signal the reproductive glands to produce sex hormones. Sex hormones activate several changes in your outward appearance during puberty. Sex hormones also control reproductive functions inside your body. You will learn more about the reproductive glands and their hormones in the next two sections.

GO ONLINE

PearsonSuccessNet.com
For: More on endocrine glands

Section 1 Review

Key Ideas and Vocabulary

1. What roles does the endocrine system play in the body?

2. What is a **hormone**? Explain how hormones reach the cells where they have their effect.

3. List the glands of the endocrine system.

4. What is the **hypothalamus**? How does it interact with the **pituitary gland**?

Critical Thinking

5. Relating Cause and Effect How is the onset of puberty related to the endocrine system?

Health at School

Adrenaline in Action Interview a musician or an athlete at your school about the role that adrenaline might play during a performance or game. Find out the conditions under which they have noticed this response and whether it helped their performance. Write a transcript of your interview. **WRITING**

6. Applying Concepts A driver brakes suddenly when a dog darts out in front of her car. How did the endocrine system aid her quick response?

The Male Reproductive System

Objectives

▶ **Describe** three functions of the male reproductive system.

▶ **Identify** five ways to keep the male reproductive system healthy.

Vocabulary

- sperm
- fertilization
- testes
- testosterone
- scrotum
- penis
- semen
- ejaculation
- infertility

Warm-Up

Myth Cancers of the male reproductive system only affect older men.

Fact Cancer of the testes (testicular cancer) most often occurs in teens and young men.

WRITING Why do you think that teens may have a number of misconceptions about the reproductive system?

Structure and Function

One essential function of all living things is reproduction, the process by which organisms produce offspring. In humans, the process begins with the development of reproductive cells in the bodies of males and females. In males, the reproductive cells are called **sperm. The functions of the male reproductive system are to produce sex hormones, to produce and store sperm, and to deliver sperm to the female reproductive system.** There, a sperm cell may join with an egg in a process called **fertilization.** Under the right conditions, a fertilized egg develops into a baby.

Testes Look at Figure 3 to see the organs of the male reproductive system. Locate the two oval-shaped **testes** (TES teez), the male reproductive glands. The testes (singular, *testis*) have two major functions—the production of testosterone and the production of sperm. The sex hormone **testosterone** affects the production of sperm and signals certain physical changes at puberty, such as the growth of facial hair.

The testes, also called testicles, hang outside the main body cavity, within a sac of skin called the **scrotum.** Because they are located outside the body, the temperature of the testes is a few degrees lower than the temperature inside the body. Sperm need this lower temperature to develop properly and survive.

In some males, one or both of the testes may not descend into the scrotum before birth, a condition called *undescended testis*. Sperm will not develop properly in an undescended testis because the temperature is too high. The condition is also a risk factor for testicular cancer. Surgery is usually performed before age two to correct this condition.

Penis The **penis** is the external sexual organ through which sperm leave the body. The tip of the penis is covered with loose skin, called the foreskin. In some males the foreskin is removed shortly after birth. This surgical procedure is known as circumcision. The decision to circumcise an infant is usually based on cultural or religious reasons.

Other Structures Besides the external structures of the male reproductive system, there are internal ducts and accessory glands that play an important role in storing and releasing sperm.

Sperm Production Once a male reaches puberty, millions of sperm are produced in his testes each day. Sperm production begins when the hypothalamus signals the pituitary gland to release two hormones—luteinizing hormone (LH) and follicle-stimulating hormone (FSH). LH signals the testes to begin making testosterone. Testosterone and FSH then signal the production of sperm. Sperm production continues throughout adulthood.

Why do you think some people are uncomfortable using the proper terms for reproductive structures?

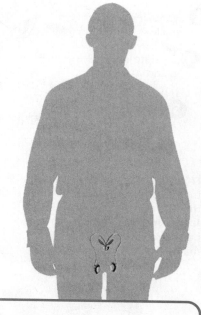

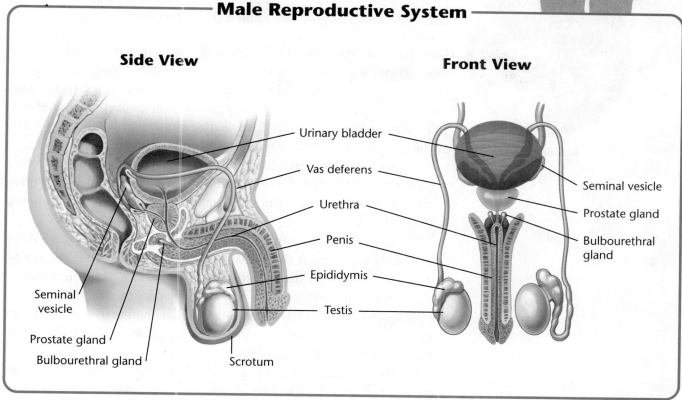

Male Reproductive System

Side View

Front View

- Urinary bladder
- Vas deferens
- Urethra
- Penis
- Epididymis
- Testis
- Seminal vesicle
- Prostate gland
- Bulbourethral gland
- Seminal vesicle
- Prostate gland
- Bulbourethral gland
- Scrotum

FIGURE 3 The male reproductive system produces, stores, and releases sperm.

The Pathway of Sperm

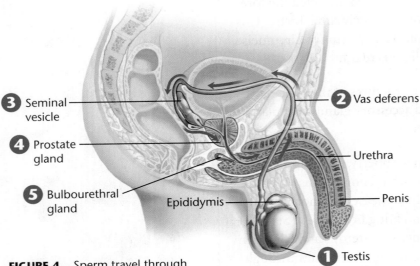

1 Sperm are produced in the **testes.** They mature and are stored in the **epididymis.**

2 Sperm travel through the **vas deferens** to the seminal vesicles.

3 **Seminal vesicles** add a fluid that provides a source of energy for the active sperm.

4 The **prostate gland** adds a fluid that protects the sperm.

5 The **bulbourethral glands** add a fluid that protects sperm from acidic conditions in the **urethra.**

3 Seminal vesicle
4 Prostate gland
5 Bulbourethral gland

2 Vas deferens
Urethra
Penis
Epididymis
1 Testis

FIGURE 4 Sperm travel through the reproductive system before they are released.
Interpreting Diagrams Where do sperm complete their maturation?

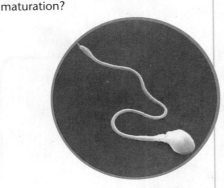

▲ **A sperm cell**

The Pathway of Sperm Look at Figure 4 to track the pathway of sperm through the male reproductive system. Note that during their passage through the male reproductive system, sperm cells mix with fluids produced by the prostate and two other glands. The mixture of sperm cells and these fluids is called **semen** (SEE mun).

Release of Sperm The ejection of semen from the penis is called **ejaculation.** Ejaculation occurs when muscles in the male reproductive system and at the base of the bladder contract, forcing semen through the urethra. The urethra—a tube that passes through the penis to the outside of the body—carries urine as well as sperm, but not at the same time. A valve within the urethra prevents the two fluids from mixing.

Several million sperm cells are released during one ejaculation. What happens to sperm that are not ejaculated? Sperm stored in the male reproductive system eventually degenerate, meaning they break down, and are disposed of.

Ejaculation can occur when the penis is in an erect state. An erection is a condition in which the penis becomes larger and stiffer as blood chambers in the penis become filled with blood. An erection does not need to result in ejaculation—in fact, most do not. Erections can be caused by different factors, including sexual excitement or tight clothing. Sometimes an erection may occur for no apparent reason at all. This is especially common during puberty.

It is also common for a teenage male to experience a nocturnal emission, or "wet dream," which is erection and ejaculation during sleep. Nocturnal emissions occur for various reasons, including sexually arousing dreams. They are a normal occurrence and may happen frequently. It is also normal not to experience nocturnal emissions.

Keeping Healthy

A number of medical conditions can affect the male reproductive system. However, teens who adopt healthy habits can reduce their risk of problems. **Caring for the male reproductive system involves cleanliness, sexual abstinence, protection from trauma, self-exams, and regular medical checkups.**

GO ONLINE

PearsonSuccessNet.com
For: More on male reproductive health

Cleanliness   Healthy habits start with cleanliness. It is important to thoroughly clean the external organs—the penis and scrotum—daily, preferably during a shower or bath. Each day, an uncircumcised male should gently pull the foreskin back to clean the head of the penis. Drying the groin area well after showering can prevent fungal infections that can cause jock itch.

Sexual Abstinence   A number of serious infections of the reproductive system and other body systems can result from sexual contact. Healthy choices regarding sexual behavior can prevent such infections. The only way to eliminate your risk of sexually transmitted infections is to abstain—or refrain from—sexual activity. In other words, practice sexual abstinence. Sexually transmitted infections will be discussed further in Chapter 22.

Protection From Trauma   Good health also requires protection and prevention. During athletic activities, males should wear a protector, also called a "cup," or supporter. Tight clothing should be avoided, since tight pants or underwear can irritate or cause pain in the groin area.

Males should also be careful when lifting heavy objects. Pressure in the abdomen during lifting can push a loop of intestine out of the area that usually contains it, causing a hernia. An inguinal (ING gwuh nul) hernia results if part of the intestine pushes into the scrotum. Surgery is almost always necessary to correct an inguinal hernia.

Self-Exams   It is important for males to monitor their own bodies for any signs of possible medical problems. Pain when urinating, unusual discharges, or sores on the genitals require a medical examination. Such conditions should not be self-treated.

Males, especially teens and young men, should also examine their testes for signs of testicular cancer. Almost a third of testicular cancer cases occur in young men in their teens and twenties. The Building Health Skills on pages 476–477 includes instructions on how to perform a self-examination. As with all cancers, treatment is most effective when the cancer is caught in its early stages.

FIGURE 5 This catcher protects himself with a helmet, face guard, body padding, and a "cup" that protects his reproductive organs from injury.

Connect to Your Life

Why is it important for males in their teens to know the symptoms of testicular cancer?

Medical Checkups Medical exams throughout life can help ensure reproductive health. The prostate gland is of particular concern after middle age. In many older men, the prostate becomes enlarged or develops cancer. An enlarged prostate does not necessarily indicate either disease or illness, but it can cause discomfort. Since the prostate gland surrounds the urethra, an enlarged prostate may make urination painful or difficult. If that happens, surgery is usually required. Furthermore, starting at age 50, men are encouraged to get screened for prostate cancer during their regular medical exams. Prostate cancer is the second most common cause of cancer death of older men.

Another condition a doctor can diagnose is **infertility** —the condition of being unable to reproduce. Infertility can affect both males and females. In males, infertility is marked by the inability to produce healthy sperm or the production of too few sperm. Three causes of infertility are exposure to certain chemicals, having mumps after puberty, and having an undescended testis. Scientists are learning more about the causes of infertility and how to prevent or treat it.

FIGURE 6 Your doctor can answer any questions you have about your reproductive health.

Section 2 Review

Key Ideas and Vocabulary

1. What are three main functions of the male reproductive system?
2. What is the name of the sac in which the **testes** are located?
3. What is **semen**, and how is it formed?
4. List five things that males should do to maintain reproductive health.
5. What are two kinds of problems with sperm that lead to **infertility** in males?

Health at Home

Reminder Card Write an e-mail to a male family member reminding him of the importance of regular medical checkups and self-exams. **WRITING**

Critical Thinking

6. **Sequencing** Arrange the following structures in the order in which sperm pass by or travel through them: epididymis; vas deferens; testes; prostate gland; seminal vesicles
7. **Applying Concepts** How could more young men be convinced to follow the recommendations for reproductive health? **WRITING**

The Female Reproductive System

Objectives
▶ **Describe** three functions of the female reproductive system.

▶ **Summarize** the stages of the menstrual cycle.

▶ **Identify** five ways to keep the female reproductive system healthy.

Vocabulary
- ova
- ovaries
- estrogen
- progesterone
- ovulation
- fallopian tubes
- uterus
- vagina
- menstrual cycle
- menopause
- Pap smear
- mammogram

Warm-Up

Dear Advice Line,
I've been going to the same male doctor since I was a little kid. My doctor is really nice, but since my body started developing, I just don't feel comfortable having my checkups with him anymore. I'd like to see a female doctor. Is it OK to feel this way? What should I do?

WRITING Do you think this girl's feelings are normal? Write back with your advice.

Structure and Function

You learned that the reproductive cells in males are called sperm. In females, they are called eggs, or **ova** (singular, *ovum*). **The functions of the female reproductive system are to produce sex hormones, to produce eggs, and to provide a nourishing environment in which a fertilized egg can develop into a baby.**

Ovaries The reproductive glands in which eggs are produced are called **ovaries.** The ovaries are located a few inches below the waist, one on each side of the body. Each ovary is about the size of an almond. The ovaries have two important functions: they produce the female sex hormones estrogen and progesterone, and they release mature egg cells. The sex hormone **estrogen** activates certain physical changes at puberty, such as breast development, and controls the maturation of eggs. **Progesterone** activates changes to a woman's reproductive system before and during pregnancy.

When a girl is born, each ovary contains hundreds of thousands of immature eggs. The eggs begin to mature, or ripen, when the girl reaches puberty. Once puberty begins, one of the ovaries releases a ripened egg about once every month in a process called **ovulation.** The tiny egg that is released is no larger than the period at the end of this sentence.

Fallopian Tubes   Look at Figure 7 to locate the two **fallopian tubes** (fuh LOH pee un)—passageways that carry eggs away from the ovaries. When the ovary releases an egg during ovulation, the fingerlike ends of the fallopian tube draw the egg into the tube. Eggs, unlike sperm, cannot swim. Tiny hairlike extensions called cilia line the fallopian tube and sweep the egg toward the uterus. If sperm are present around the egg, it may be fertilized. The fallopian tubes are where fertilization usually occurs.

Uterus   The **uterus** is a hollow, muscular, pear-shaped organ. In the uterus, a fertilized egg can develop and grow. The uterus has several layers of tissue and a rich supply of blood that protect and nourish the developing baby. The narrow base of the uterus is called the cervix. When a baby is ready to be born, the cervix expands to allow the baby to pass through.

Vagina   The **vagina,** or birth canal, is a hollow, muscular passage leading from the uterus to the outside of the body. Sperm enter a female's body through the vagina. During childbirth, the baby passes out of the mother's body through the vagina. The walls of the vagina are very elastic, which allows it to expand dramatically during childbirth.

Connect to Your Life

Where could you find reliable information about the female reproductive system?

Female Reproductive System

Front View

Side View

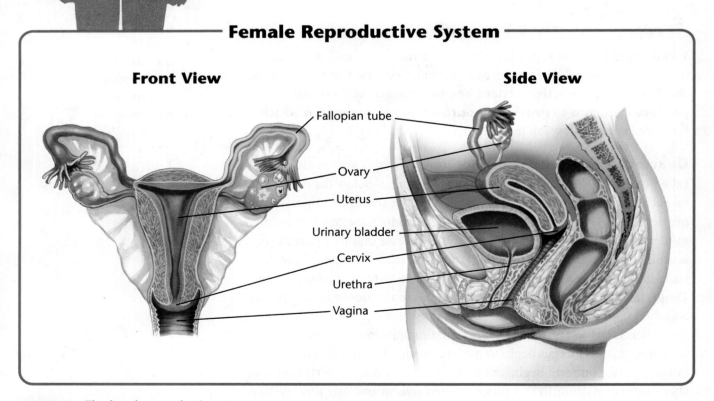

- Fallopian tube
- Ovary
- Uterus
- Urinary bladder
- Cervix
- Urethra
- Vagina

FIGURE 7   The female reproductive system produces eggs and provides a nourishing environment for a fertilized egg to develop.

Media Wise

Sexuality in Music Videos

When watching your favorite music videos, you may not think about the hidden, or not-so-hidden, meanings they contain. What messages are conveyed about sex? Consider these questions as they relate to music videos.

1. Are there suggestive close-ups on body parts? **Yes** **No**

2. Is there non-verbal flirting (such as suggestive body positions or touching)? **Yes** **No**

3. Does anyone dress suggestively or take off any clothing? **Yes** **No**

4. Does anyone use force to touch or kiss someone? **Yes** **No**

5. Is there sexual bias—a greater emphasis on women's or men's bodies? **Yes** **No**

A "Yes" answer to one or more questions may indicate a video that presents sex in an unhealthy way.

Activity Think about how music videos make you feel about your body. In general, do they represent sex in a healthy or unhealthy way? Explain. **WRITING**

The Menstrual Cycle

As you learned, males typically produce millions of sperm cells every day after reaching puberty. Females, on the other hand, usually produce only one mature egg cell each month during a process called the **menstrual cycle** (MEN stroo ul). **During the menstrual cycle, an ovary releases a mature egg. The egg travels to the uterus. If the egg is not fertilized, the uterine lining is shed and a new cycle begins.**

Factors Affecting the Menstrual Cycle   On average, a menstrual cycle lasts 28 days. However, cycles as short as 21 days or as long as 35 days can be normal for some individuals. The endocrine system controls the menstrual cycle. The hormones involved include FSH and LH, which are released by the pituitary gland, and estrogen and progesterone, which are released from the ovaries. Factors such as diet, stress, exercise, and weight gain or loss also affect the menstrual cycle. The menstrual cycle may be irregular at times, especially during puberty.

Except during pregnancy, menstrual cycles occur each month from puberty until about the age of 45 to 55. At that time of life, called **menopause,** the ovaries slow down their hormone production and no longer release mature eggs. Gradually, the menstrual cycle stops, and the woman is no longer able to become pregnant.

The Menstrual Cycle

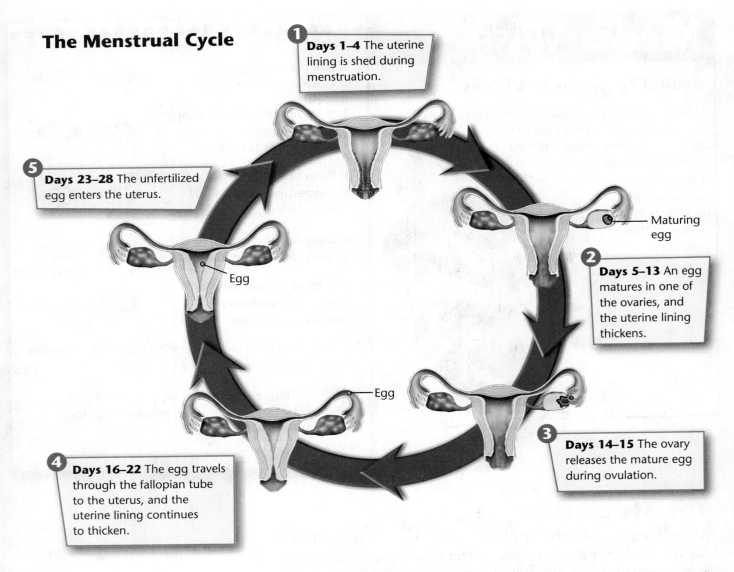

1 Days 1–4 The uterine lining is shed during menstruation.

2 Days 5–13 An egg matures in one of the ovaries, and the uterine lining thickens.

Maturing egg

3 Days 14–15 The ovary releases the mature egg during ovulation.

4 Days 16–22 The egg travels through the fallopian tube to the uterus, and the uterine lining continues to thicken.

5 Days 23–28 The unfertilized egg enters the uterus.

Egg

Egg

FIGURE 8 The thickening of the lining of the uterus, ovulation, and menstruation are key events of the menstrual cycle.
Interpreting Diagrams
Through which structure does an egg travel before reaching the uterus?

Stages of the Menstrual Cycle Follow the stages of a typical menstrual cycle in Figure 8. During the first half of the cycle, an egg matures inside one of the ovaries. Meanwhile, the lining of the uterus thickens. At about the middle of the cycle—typically on day 14—ovulation occurs. The mature egg is released by the ovary and travels into the fallopian tube. A female is most fertile, or able to become pregnant, around the time of ovulation.

It takes about seven days for the egg to travel through the fallopian tube into the uterus. During this time the uterine lining continues to thicken, and the blood supply to it increases. If the egg has not been fertilized by the time it reaches the uterus, the uterine lining breaks down.

The blood and tissue of the thickened lining pass out of the body through the vagina in a process called menstruation, or the menstrual period. As menstruation is taking place, another egg begins to mature in one of the ovaries. Thus menstruation marks the end of one cycle and the beginning of another. In general, a menstrual period lasts about 3 to 5 days. Most women wear either a sanitary pad or a tampon to absorb the menstrual flow.

Menstrual Discomfort During the menstrual period, some women may experience abdominal cramps or other discomfort. Cramps are caused by contractions of the uterus. See Figure 9 for some ways to relieve menstrual cramps. For severe cramps or for any other menstrual concerns, women should see a medical professional.

Some women experience discomfort some time before the menstrual period. This condition, known as premenstrual syndrome, or PMS, is marked by nervous tension, mood swings, headaches, bloating, and irritability. The dramatic change in hormone levels that occurs before menstruation begins may cause PMS. Some doctors recommend that PMS sufferers reduce their intake of salt, sugar, and caffeine, get regular exercise, and try other stress-reduction techniques.

Toxic Shock Syndrome A rare but serious medical condition associated with tampon use is toxic shock syndrome. This syndrome is caused by a bacterial infection. Symptoms of toxic shock syndrome include a sudden high fever, a rash, vomiting, diarrhea, and dizziness. Because toxic shock syndrome can lead to death, a woman with any of these symptoms during her period should seek medical attention immediately. To decrease the risk of toxic shock syndrome, women should use tampons with the lowest possible absorbency for their needs and change tampons often.

What misconceptions did you hold about menstruation before reading this section?

GO ONLINE
PearsonSuccessNet.com
For: More on the menstrual cycle

Menstrual cramps ? Try this ...
- Engage in moderate exercise.
- Take a warm bath.
- Apply a heating pad to the abdomen.
- Take aspirin or ibuprofen with doctor's approval.

FIGURE 9 Following these simple tips can help relieve menstrual cramps.

Reproduction and Heredity **473**

Keeping Healthy

A number of medical conditions can affect the female reproductive system. Teens who adopt healthy habits can reduce their risk of problems. **Caring for the female reproductive system involves cleanliness, sexual abstinence, prompt treatment for infections, self-exams, and regular medical checkups.**

Cleanliness   One important health habit is cleanliness, including daily washing of the external vaginal area. Cleanliness is especially important during menstruation, as is the regular changing of sanitary pads or tampons. Feminine hygiene sprays, douches, and deodorant tampons are not necessary. In fact, they may be harmful if they cover up signs of an infection or cause irritation. If washing does not get rid of normal body odors, or if any unusual discharge is noted, seek medical attention.

Sexual Abstinence   A number of serious infections can result from sexual contact. Healthy choices regarding sexual behavior can prevent such infections. The only way to eliminate your risk of sexually transmitted infections is to abstain from sexual activity.

Prompt Treatment for Infections   Some infections of the reproductive system are not related to sexual behavior. Many women experience vaginitis, a vaginal infection caused by yeast, bacteria, or other microorganisms. Symptoms include a thick discharge, odors, vaginal itching, and a burning sensation during urination. Only a doctor can diagnose the specific cause of vaginitis and provide appropriate treatment.

Self-Exams   It is important for women to monitor their own bodies for signs of possible medical problems. Symptoms of vaginitis, sores on the genitals, or any unusual pain in the abdomen require a medical exam. A woman should also consult a doctor if she notices heavier bleeding than normal during menstruation, if her periods stop completely, or if she notices bleeding at times between her regular periods.

For the early detection of breast cancer, all women, including teens, should perform a monthly breast self-examination. Instructions can be found in the Building Health Skills on pages 476–477.

FIGURE 10   Daily washing is an important part of keeping the reproductive system healthy.

Medical Checkups   A yearly checkup of the reproductive system is recommended for all females who have reached puberty. During the exam, the doctor will examine the breasts and genitals and may perform a pelvic exam and a Pap smear. In a **Pap smear,** a sample of cells is taken from the cervix and examined under a microscope. Pap smears can detect cancer of the cervix.

Starting at about age 40, women may get a **mammogram,** an X-ray of the breast that can help detect breast cancer. A woman with a family history of breast cancer or other risk factors may have her first mammogram at a younger age. A mammogram may detect cancers that are too small for a woman or her doctor to feel in a breast exam.

A doctor can also detect and treat other reproductive problems, including cancers of the ovary or uterus, and

FIGURE 11   This doctor is using a magnifying glass to more closely examine a mammogram.

▶ **Ovarian cysts** Ovarian cysts are growths on the ovary. Large ones may be painful and need to be surgically removed.

▶ **Endometriosis** This is a condition in which tissue from the lining of the uterus—the endometrium—grows outside the uterus, in the pelvic cavity. This condition can be very painful and is usually treated with hormones or surgery.

▶ **Infertility** Causes of infertility in women include blocked fallopian tubes and problems with ovulation.

Section 3   Review

Key Ideas and Vocabulary

1. What are three main functions of the female reproductive system?
2. What is **ovulation**?
3. Where are the **fallopian tubes** located? What is their function?
4. What event marks the end of one menstrual cycle and the beginning of another?
5. List five things that females should do to maintain reproductive health.

Health at School

Medication Regulations Many girls suffer from menstrual cramps, sometimes during school hours. Ask your school nurse or an administrator what the policies are for taking pain medications on school grounds to treat menstrual cramps and other common aches and pains. Write a memo detailing your findings. **WRITING**

Critical Thinking

6. **Calculating** If a woman's ovaries release one egg per month for 30 years, how many eggs in total will she have released? **MATH**
7. **Applying Concepts** How could more young women be convinced of the importance of regular breast exams? **WRITING**

Breast and Testicular Self-Exams

Breast Self-Exam

Breast cancer is one of the most common forms of cancer in women. Although it is rare in young women, breast cancer becomes more common as women age. If breast cancer is found early, the disease can be effectively treated and often cured.

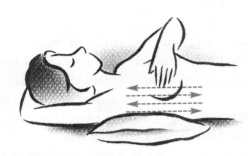

The teenage years are a good time to establish the habit of regular self-exams. The best time to do a breast self-exam is the week after a menstrual period, when the breasts are least swollen. For women who have reached menopause or have irregular periods, the exam should be done on the same day each month. If you forget a month, don't worry. Start the routine exams again once you remember.

1 Check your breasts while lying down.

- ► Lie down and place your right arm behind your head.

- ► Use the finger pads of the three middle fingers on your left hand to feel for lumps in the right breast. Use overlapping dime-sized circular motions of the finger pads.

- ► Use three different levels of pressure. Use light pressure to feel the tissue closest to the skin. Use medium pressure to feel a little deeper. Use firm pressure to feel the tissue closest to the chest and ribs.

- ► Feel the breast in an up-and-down pattern starting at an imaginary line drawn straight down your side from the underarm, and move inward until you reach the bone in the middle of your chest, your sternum (See diagram above).

- ► Check the entire breast area, moving down until you can feel only ribs and up to the neck or collar bone.

- ► Repeat the exam on your left breast, using the fingers of the right hand.

2 Look at your breasts while standing in front of the mirror.

- ► While pressing your hands down firmly on your hips, look for any change in breast shape or appearance, such as dimpling of skin, redness or swelling, or changes to the nipples.

- ► Slightly raise your right arm and feel your underarm with your lefthand fingers. Repeat on the left side.

3 Report any abnormalities to your doctor immediately.

Many lumps are cysts or harmless tumors that are not cancerous. But only a doctor can make a diagnosis.

Testicular Self-Exam

Cancer of the testes, or testicular cancer, is the most common cancer found in young men between 15 and 34 years of age. Testicular cancer can be cured if it is detected early and treated promptly. Most testicular cancers are noticed by men themselves, not by their doctors. The American Cancer Society recommends discussing with your doctor how frequently you should perform the exam. Unlike the breast self exam, it is generally not recommended as often as once a month.

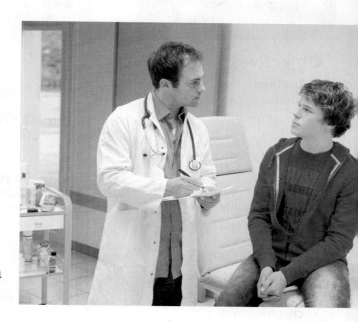

The best time to do a testicular self-exam is after a hot shower or bath, when the scrotum is relaxed and the testes can be felt more easily.

1 Examine each testis separately with both hands.

> ▶ Roll each testis between the thumbs and fingers of both hands, feeling for lumps or hard places about the size of a pea. If a lump is present, it is usually found in the front or on the sides of a testis.

> ▶ Look and feel for any hard lumps or smooth, rounded masses, or any change in the size, shape, or texture of the testes.

> ▶ Learn to recognize what the epididymis feels like so you won't confuse it with a lump. The epididymis appears as a small "bump" on the back side of the testis.

2 Report any abnormalities to your doctor immediately.

Lumps may not be cancerous, but only a doctor can make a diagnosis. Other signs of testicular cancer are enlargement of a testis, a dull aching in the genital area, or a feeling of heaviness in the scrotum. However, testicular cancer is not typically painful when it first develops.

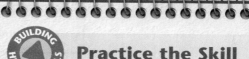

Practice the Skill

Breast Self-Exam

1. Do the breast self-exam lying down and standing in front of the mirror, and again one week after your next menstrual period (or in one month if you haven't started your menstrual periods).

2. Describe the steps of the self-exam to a female family member. Find out if you have any history of breast cancer in your family.

Testicular Self-Exam

1. After a shower or hot bath, practice the testicular self-exam.

2. Describe the steps of the self-exam to a male family member. Find out if you have any history of testicular cancer in your family.

Heredity

Objectives

▶ **Explain** how genetic information passes from one generation to the next.

▶ **Identify** the causes of genetic disorders.

▶ **Compare** the role of genes, environment, and behavior in affecting a person's risk for disease.

Vocabulary

• heredity
• chromosome
• gene
• genetic disorder

Warm-Up

Quick Quiz Take a brief self-inventory of some of your physical traits, or characteristics.

(1) **Do you have a widow's peak or a smooth hairline?**

Widow's Peak   Smooth

(2) **Do you have free or attached earlobes?**

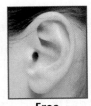 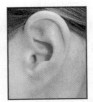

Free   Attached

WRITING A widow's peak and free earlobes are examples of dominant traits. What do you think a "dominant trait" is?

The Basic Rules of Heredity

When a baby is born, people may say, "She looks just like her father," or "He has his grandmother's ears." Think about how children resemble their parents, grandparents, and other relatives. Their eye color, the shape of their ears, their height—these traits are determined in part from the genetic information they inherit from their parents. **Heredity** is the passing on, or transmission, of biological traits from parent to child. People are similar to each of their parents in some ways but different from their parents in other ways. What determines the combination of traits that are passed on?

Chromosomes To answer these questions, you must first learn about chromosomes. **Chromosomes** (KROH muh sohmz) are tiny structures found within cells that carry information about the characteristics you will inherit. Most of the cells in your body contain 23 pairs of chromosomes— 46 chromosomes in all. However, sex cells—sperm or eggs—contain half this number, or 23 chromosomes. When a sperm and egg unite, the fertilized egg ends up with 46 chromosomes—23 from each parent.

FIGURE 12 Your looks are determined in part by the traits you inherit.

Genes Every chromosome in your body is made up of many genes. A **gene** is a section of a chromosome that determines or affects a characteristic, or trait. Like the chromosomes that contain them, genes come in pairs. Since a sex cell contains only one half of each chromosome pair, it also has only one half of each gene pair. Once a sperm fertilizes an egg, however, the fertilized egg contains two copies of the gene for each trait—one from the father and one from the mother. **Hereditary information passes from one generation to the next through genes contained on the two sets of chromosomes that a person receives from their parents.**

Dominant and Recessive Traits Suppose a father has one trait and the mother has another. Which trait will their child have? The answer depends on the makeup of the pair of genes that the child inherits.

Consider earlobe shape. Earlobes can be either free or attached. There are two forms, or versions, of the gene for earlobe shape. One form of the gene carries information for free earlobes—the dominant trait. A dominant trait is one that appears in an offspring whenever its gene is present. The other form of the gene carries information for attached earlobes—the recessive trait. A recessive trait appears in an offspring only when the dominant form of the gene is *not* present.

You need two copies of the recessive form of the gene to have attached earlobes. You need just one dominant form of the gene to have free earlobes. Receiving a dominant form of the gene from both parents will also result in free earlobes.

Note that the rules of heredity for most traits, such as height and eye color, are more complex than those for earlobe shape. This is because many different genes plus factors other than genetics affect most traits.

 Do you get dimples in your cheeks when you smile? Smile dimples are a dominant trait.

 GO ONLINE
PearsonSuccessNet.com
For: More on genetic disorders

Genetic Disorders

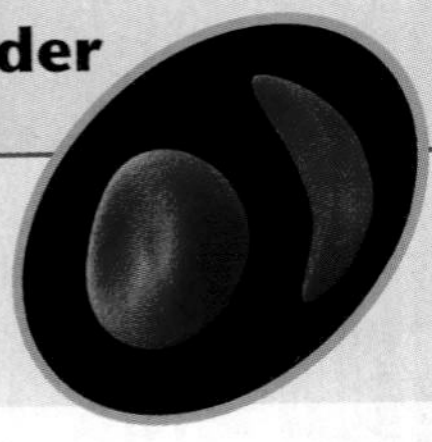

Disorder	Type of Disorder	Effect on the Body
Sickle cell disease	Recessive disorder	High number of red blood cells have an abnormal sickle shape; blood cells clump and block small blood vessels, causing severe pain and weakness
Tay-Sachs disease	Recessive disorder	Lack of important chemical in the brain results in brain damage and death in childhood
Cystic fibrosis	Recessive disorder	Mucus in lungs becomes thick and sticky, trapping bacteria that cause infections and lung damage; mucus also affects pancreas
Phenylketonuria (PKU)	Recessive disorder	Body cannot break down phenylalanine, a chemical found in food; causes brain damage if not diagnosed and treated early
Duchenne muscular dystrophy	Recessive disorder that primarily affects males	Lack of important protein needed for muscle function leads to loss of muscle control
Hemophilia	Recessive disorder that primarily affects males	Blood does not clot properly, leading to internal bleeding that can damage the joints
Huntington's disease	Dominant disorder	Cells in brain start to die in middle age; mental abilities decline and movements become uncontrollable, resulting in early death
Down syndrome	Chromosomal disorder	Mental retardation and heart defects; characteristic facial features; severity of disease ranges from mild to severe

FIGURE 13 Genetic disorders may be dominant or recessive, or caused by errors in chromosome inheritance.
Reading Tables Name two disorders that are more common in males.

Heredity and Disease

Just like earlobe shape, eye color, and other inherited traits, an abnormal condition known as a **genetic disorder** can be passed from parent to child. **Genetic disorders are caused by the inheritance of an abnormal gene or chromosome.**

Genetic Disorders Figure 13 provides information about some of the more common genetic disorders. Many genetic disorders, such as cystic fibrosis and hemophilia, are recessive traits. A child must receive two abnormal copies of the gene—one from each parent—in order for the disorder to develop. A few disorders, such as Huntington's disease, are dominant traits. Such disorders require just one abnormal copy of the gene. Other genetic disorders, such as Down syndrome, are the result of too few or too many chromosomes.

Family Medical History You have probably heard that certain diseases run in families. What does that mean? Scientists know that a person's risk for many diseases increases when close relatives have the disease. Therefore, it is important to develop a family medical history—a record of diseases and disorders that your parents, siblings, or grandparents experienced. Some diseases for which a genetic link is suspected or has been identified are breast cancer, colon cancer, high blood pressure, diabetes, and some forms of Alzheimer's disease. In addition, some genes do not typically cause disease, but they do increase a person's risk.

 Connect to Your Life What diseases run in your family? How can you decrease your risk for these diseases?

The Effect of Environment and Behavior Even if you have genes that increase your risk for certain diseases, many other factors also affect your risk. **For most diseases, your environment and your behavior affect your risk as much as or even more than your genes.** Environmental factors include such things as exposure to air pollution and certain chemicals. The typical climate where you live may be an environmental risk factor. Suppose, for example, that skin cancer runs in your family. Living in a warm, sunny climate would further increase your risk for developing the disease.

Exposure to environmental risk factors is sometimes not in your control, especially as a child. Other risk factors, however, are. Among the factors you can control are your habits or behaviors. For example, using sunscreen can reduce your risk of skin cancer. Regular physical activity can lower your risk of high blood pressure, diabetes, and breast cancer. Eating more fruits and vegetables can reduce your risk of colon cancer. Making wise choices now will greatly decrease your risk for disease later on in life.

Risk Factors You Can Control
- Unprotected or excessive exposure to the sun
- Use of tanning beds
- Sunburns

Risk Factors You Can't Control
- Fair complexion
- Multiple or abnormal moles
- Family history of skin cancer
- Climate in which you live

FIGURE 14 Using plenty of sunscreen can reduce your risk of skin cancer. **Classifying** Which risk factors for skin cancer are genetic? Environmental? Behavioral?

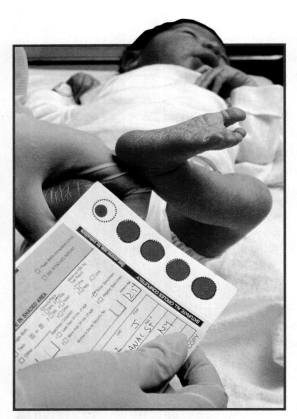

Medical Advances Today, scientists are working hard to develop new ways to identify and treat genetic disorders and diseases with a genetic link. Areas of research include genetic testing and gene therapy.

▶ **Genetic Testing** Genetic testing involves the analysis of a blood sample for the presence of abnormalities in specific genes. Genetic testing has become more common in recent years. The symptoms of some genetic disorders and most diseases don't show up early in life. By knowing someone has the defective gene as early as possible—in some cases, even before birth— doctors may be able to start therapies that can prevent or reduce future symptoms.

▶ **Gene Therapy** Scientists are currently researching a technique in which healthy copies of a gene are delivered to the cells of a person who has a defective copy of the gene. This therapy would ideally restore normal function to people with a genetic disorder. Unfortunately, gene therapy has yet to be proven as an effective treatment, but the research effort continues.

FIGURE 15 In the future, blood samples from newborns may routinely undergo genetic testing for both rare disorders and common diseases.

Section 4 Review

Key Ideas and Vocabulary

1. How is genetic information passed from one generation to the next?

2. What are **genes**? How are they related to **chromosomes**?

3. What are the causes of genetic disorders? Give two examples of genetic disorders.

4. What three factors influence your risk for disease? Which factors are under your control?

Critical Thinking

5. Predicting A man with free earlobes—who has two dominant forms of the gene—marries a woman with attached earlobes. What kind of earlobes will their children have? Explain.

Health and Community

Supporting a Cause Contact an organization that supports research for a genetic disorder. Find out how you can help support the cause. Write an e-mail to your friends telling them about the disease, its causes and treatment, and how people can help. **WRITING**

6. Making Judgments Government funding for research of some genetic disorders is very low because the disorders are so rare. Is that reasonable? Explain your position.

7. Evaluating Research shows that proper use of sunscreen can reduce the risk of skin cancer. However, nearly one third of Americans report never using sunscreen. Write a paragraph evaluating this statistic. Why might people choose not to use sunscreen despite the risk? **WRITING**

GO ONLINE PearsonSuccessNet.com Audio Summary Section 18.4

Chapter 18
At a Glance

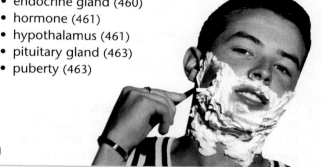

VIDEO

TEENS Talk ▶

Hormones in the Balance Give three examples of hormone disorders presented in the video.

Section 1 The Endocrine System

Key Ideas

▶ The endocrine system regulates long-term changes in the body such as growth and development. It also controls many of your body's daily activities.

▶ The endocrine glands include the hypothalamus, pituitary gland, thyroid gland, parathyroid glands, thymus gland, adrenal glands, pancreas, and reproductive glands.

Vocabulary
• endocrine gland (460)
• hormone (461)
• hypothalamus (461)
• pituitary gland (463)
• puberty (463)

Section 2 The Male Reproductive System

Key Ideas

▶ The functions of the male reproductive system are to produce sex hormones, to produce and store sperm, and to deliver sperm to the female reproductive system.

▶ Caring for the male reproductive system involves cleanliness, sexual abstinence, protection from trauma, self-exams, and regular medical checkups.

Vocabulary
• sperm (464) • fertilization (464) • testes (464)
• testosterone (464) • scrotum (464) • penis (465)
• semen (466) • ejaculation (466) • infertility (468)

Section 3 The Female Reproductive System

Key Ideas

▶ The functions of the female reproductive system are to produce sex hormones, to produce eggs, and to provide a nourishing environment in which a fertilized egg can develop into a baby.

▶ During the menstrual cycle, an ovary releases a mature egg. The egg travels to the uterus. If the egg is not fertilized, the uterine lining is shed and a new cycle begins.

▶ Caring for the female reproductive system involves cleanliness, sexual abstinence, prompt treatment for infections, self-exams, and regular medical checkups.

Vocabulary
• ova (469) • ovaries (469) • estrogen (469)
• progesterone (469) • ovulation (469)
• fallopian tubes (470) • uterus (470) • vagina (470)
• menstrual cycle (471) • menopause (471)
• Pap smear (475) • mammogram (475)

Section 4 Heredity

Key Ideas

▶ Hereditary information passes from one generation to the next through genes contained on the two sets of chromosomes that a person receives from their parents.

▶ Genetic disorders are caused by the inheritance of an abnormal gene or chromosome.

▶ For most diseases, your environment and your behavior affect your risk as much as or even more than your genes.

Vocabulary
• heredity (478) • chromosome (478) • gene (479)
• genetic disorder (480)

Chapter 18 Review

GO ONLINE
PearsonSuccessNet.com
For: Chapter 18 review activity

Reviewing Key Ideas

Section 1

1. Which of the following is *not* an endocrine gland?
   a. pituitary gland   **b.** adrenal gland
   c. prostate gland   **d.** ovary

2. Which hormone regulates the "fight-or-flight" response?

3. What are the reproductive glands called in females? In males?

4. **Critical Thinking** Steroids abused by some athletes to build muscle contain chemicals similar to sex hormones. Why do you think steroid use can have a harmful effect on the reproductive system, especially in teens?

Section 2

5. In males, straining to lift heavy objects may result in
   a. an inguinal hernia.   **b.** an enlarged prostate.
   c. testicular cancer.   **d.** infertility.

6. What are two effects of testosterone?

7. Describe the roles played by hormones during sperm production.

8. List two causes of infertility in men.

9. **Critical Thinking** If only one sperm is needed to fertilize an egg, why do you think many sperm are released during ejaculation?

Section 3

10. Which organ releases mature eggs?
    a. uterus   **b.** pituitary gland
    c. vagina   **d.** ovary

11. How long is the average menstrual cycle?
    a. 3 to 5 days   **b.** 14 days
    c. 28 days   **d.** 9 months

12. Which four hormones play a role in the menstrual cycle?

13. Which kind of cancer may be detected by a Pap smear?

14. **Critical Thinking** Your 13-year-old sister does not mentruate regularly. Should she be concerned? Explain.

Section 4

15. How many chromosomes are contained in each of your sex cells?
    a. 2   **b.** 23
    c. 46   **d.** 92

16. Which of the following is *not* a genetic disorder?
    a. sickle cell disease   **b.** breast cancer
    c. cystic fibrosis   **d.** hemophilia

17. Explain the difference between dominant and recessive traits. Give one example of each.

18. Identify two diseases that may be affected by genetics. What other factors influence the onset of these diseases?

19. **Critical Thinking** Explain how two parents without a genetic disorder could have a child that has the disorder.

Building Health Skills

20. **Accessing Information** Suppose that your younger brother is worried because he's been hearing a lot of myths about puberty from his classmates. How could you help him find accurate information?

21. **Advocacy** Suppose that a friend has confided in you that during a breast self-exam, she detected a lump. She is reluctant to see a doctor. Write an e-mail to your friend with advice. **WRITING**

22. **Setting Goals** Set a personal goal to decrease your risk of skin cancer. Describe a specific change to your behavior that will help you reach your goal. Monitor your progress over the next year.

Health and Community

Cancer Awareness Write a script for a public service announcement to raise awareness about prostate or breast cancer. Think about the age of the people you want to target with your message. Develop your message to best reach that audience. **WRITING**

Standardized Test Prep

Math Practice

The graph shows the approximate breakdown of new reproductive cancers diagnosed each year. Use the graph to answer Questions 23–25.

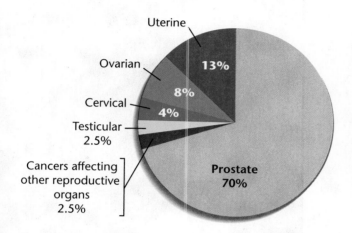

23. Which type of reproductive cancer is most common?
  A ovarian cancer
  B testicular cancer
  C prostate cancer
  D cervical cancer

24. About how much more common is ovarian cancer than cervical cancer?
  F half as common
  G equally common
  H twice as common
  J four times as common

25. What percentage of the total do prostate and testicular cancers represent?
  A 50%   B 70.25%
  C 72.5%   D 85%

Reading and Writing Practice

Read the passage. Then answer Questions 26–29.

Two hormones regulate calcium concentration in the bloodstream: calcitonin from the thyroid glands and parathyroid hormone (PTH) from the parathyroid glands. When blood calcium levels are too high, the thyroids release calcitonin. Calcitonin signals cells in the intestine to absorb less calcium from food and signals calcium deposition by bone tissue. If calcium levels drop too low, the parathyroids release PTH. PTH signals the intestine to absorb more calcium from food and signals bone cells to release some of the calcium stored in bone tissue into the bloodstream.

26. After the release of PTH,
  A blood calcium levels decrease.
  B bone tissue deposits calcium.
  C thyroid glands release calcitonin.
  D the intestine absorbs more calcium from food.

27. In this passage, the word *deposition* means
  F reduction.
  G storage.
  H destruction.
  J release.

28. What can you summarize from this passage?
  A Calcitonin and PTH have similar effects.
  B Calcium levels in the body are controlled by hormones.
  C Bones manufacture calcium.
  D Each hormone released by the body targets only one location.

Constructed Response

29. In a paragraph, explain how the body's regulation of blood calcium level is an example of "checks and balances."

CHAPTER 19

Pregnancy, Birth, and Childhood

GO ONLINE PearsonSuccessNet.com

VIDEO 19

TEENS Talk

Teen Pregnancy

Preview **Activity**

How Would Your Plans Change?

Complete this activity before you watch the video.

1. Make a list of your plans for the weekend. Make a second list of your plans for after graduation.

2. Now suppose that you were a teen parent. Describe all the ways you think your weekend plans and your long-term plans would need to change. **WRITING**

Development Before Birth

Objectives

▶ **Summarize** the events that occur during the first week after fertilization.

▶ **Describe** the structures that protect and nourish the embryo and fetus.

Vocabulary

- zygote
- embryo
- blastocyst
- implantation
- amniotic sac
- placenta
- umbilical cord
- fetus

Warm-Up

Quick Quiz Which of the following statements made by a married couple do you think are good reasons for having a baby? Choose one or more.

(1) "It's now or never. We're almost 40."

(2) "We have lots of love to give a child."

(3) "If we have one more, maybe it will be a girl."

(4) "Our marriage will improve if we have a baby."

(5) "With our new jobs, we've finally saved enough money to start a family."

WRITING In a paragraph, describe the factors that a married couple should consider before they have children.

The Beginning of the Life Cycle

Parenthood has many joys and satisfactions, but it is also stressful and involves a lot of hard work. The responsibilities of parenthood go far beyond those of most other occupations. Babies are demanding and totally helpless.

Along with the loving feelings, smiles, and cuddles, new parents face sleepless nights, worries about illness, and the loss of many freedoms they used to enjoy. Parents must also be prepared to give their child love and guidance throughout his or her life, not just as a baby.

Once a couple has decided to start a family, they may try to conceive, or get pregnant. Recall from Chapter 18 that, in a fertile woman's body, about once a month an egg enters one of the fallopian tubes and begins its journey to the uterus. During sexual intercourse, sperm from the man are deposited into the vagina. Some of these sperm swim through the uterus to the fallopian tubes. If the egg is on its way to the uterus, a sperm may fertilize it. This moment of fertilization is also called conception.

① Fertilization In Figure 1, you can track the events that occur in the first week after fertilization. Only a few hundred sperm of the hundreds of millions that enter the vagina usually make it to the egg, and only one can fertilize it. Within seconds of fertilization, the surface of the egg changes so that no more sperm can enter the egg. **In the first week after fertilization, the fertilized egg undergoes many cell divisions and travels to the uterus.**

② The Zygote The united egg and sperm is called a **zygote** (ZY goht). Within 36 hours, while the zygote is still traveling through the fallopian tube, it begins to divide.

③ Cell Division The original cell divides to make two cells. From the two-cell stage until about nine weeks after fertilization, the growing structure is called an **embryo** (EM bree oh). The two-celled embryo divides into four cells, and so on.

④ The Blastocyst About five days after fertilization, the embryo reaches the uterus, where it floats free for a few days. By this time, it is made up of about 50 to 100 cells. The structure, called a **blastocyst** (BLAS tuh sist), is no longer a solid mass of cells, but a sphere of cells surrounding a hollow center.

⑤ Implantation Once the blastocyst forms, it begins to attach itself to the wall of the uterus. The process of attachment is called **implantation.**

FIGURE 1 The fertilized egg travels to the uterus in the first week of pregnancy.
Interpreting Diagrams Through which structure does the embryo travel before reaching the uterus?

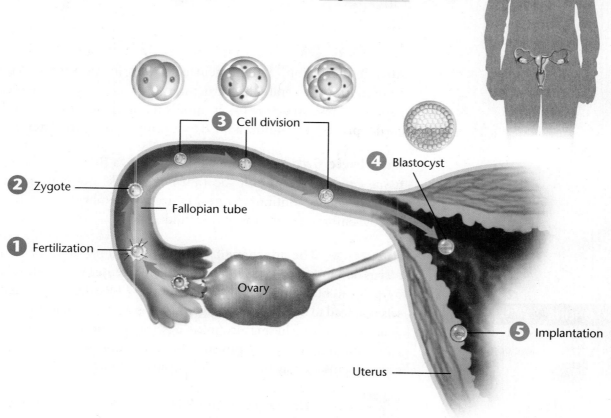

③ Cell division
④ Blastocyst
② Zygote
Fallopian tube
① Fertilization
Ovary
⑤ Implantation
Uterus

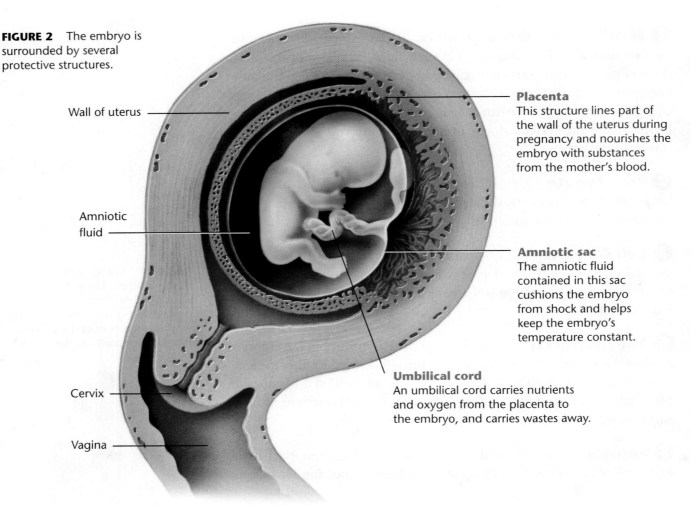

FIGURE 2 The embryo is surrounded by several protective structures.

Wall of uterus

Amniotic fluid

Cervix

Vagina

Placenta
This structure lines part of the wall of the uterus during pregnancy and nourishes the embryo with substances from the mother's blood.

Amniotic sac
The amniotic fluid contained in this sac cushions the embryo from shock and helps keep the embryo's temperature constant.

Umbilical cord
An umbilical cord carries nutrients and oxygen from the placenta to the embryo, and carries wastes away.

Development in the Uterus

After implantation, development continues in the uterus. While the embryo grows, several other structures that you can see in Figure 2 also develop. **These structures—the amniotic sac, placenta, and umbilical cord—protect and nourish the developing embryo, and later the fetus.**

Amniotic Sac Soon after implantation, a fluid-filled bag of thin tissue called the **amniotic sac** (am nee AHT ik) develops around the embryo. The sac continues to grow in size as the embryo grows. Inside the sac, the embryo floats in amniotic fluid.

Placenta The attachment holding the embryo to the wall of the uterus develops into a structure called the **placenta.** Within the placenta, oxygen and nutrients move from the mother's blood into tiny blood vessels that lead to the embryo. Dangerous substances can pass from mother to embryo, too, including alcohol, drugs, the chemicals in tobacco smoke, and some microscopic organisms that cause disease. Any of these substances can seriously harm the developing embryo.

GO ONLINE

PearsonSuccessNet.com

For: More on development before birth

Connect to Your Life

How do you think the fluid-filled sac helps protect a fetus during pregnancy?

Umbilical Cord About 25 days after fertilization, a ropelike structure called the **umbilical cord** (um BIL ih kul) develops between the embryo and the placenta. The umbilical cord is the embryo's lifeline. Blood vessels in the umbilical cord carry nutrients and oxygen from the placenta to the embryo and wastes from the embryo to the placenta.

The Growing Embryo During the first two months of development, the major body systems and organs start to form in the embryo. For example, a beating heart, major blood vessels, kidneys, and endocrine glands develop. By the end of eight weeks, the embryo is about an inch long and has recognizable external features such as eyes, ears, arms, and legs. The head is large in proportion to the body—it makes up nearly 50 percent of the length of the embryo.

The Fetus From the third month until birth, the developing human is called a **fetus.** During the third to sixth month, the fetus begins to move and kick, a sign that its skeleton and muscles are developing. As its nervous system matures, the sense organs begin to function. The fetus becomes sensitive to light and sound and alternates periods of activity with periods of sleep.

From the seventh to the ninth month, the fetus continues to grow and develop. The size of the body increases so that it is more in proportion to the size of the head, and body fat accumulates. The eyelids open and close. By the end of the ninth month, the fetus is ready to be born.

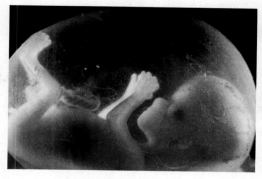

▲ **Fetus at 3 months**

▼ **Fetus at 8 months**

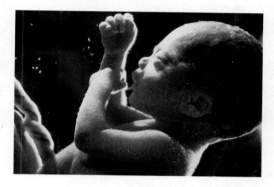

FIGURE 3 Between the third and eighth month of development, the facial features and limbs of a fetus change dramatically.

Section 1 Review

Key Ideas and Vocabulary

1. What happens during the first week of human development?
2. What happens during **implantation**?
3. What three structures protect and nourish the embryo, and later the fetus?
4. What is the **placenta**? What is its function?
5. How does a **fetus** change between the third and sixth months of pregnancy?

Critical Thinking

6. Calculating Suppose that only 200 sperm out of the original 400 million sperm deposited in the vagina survive the journey to the egg. What percentage is this? **MATH**

Health and Community

Support for New Parents Many communities offer free support groups for new parents. At the support group, parents can share the joys and frustrations of caring for their newborn. They may also learn new skills, such as how to bathe, diaper, and give first aid to their baby. Find out what services your community offers and make a pamphlet for new parents. **WRITING**

7. Relating Cause and Effect Why is it an unhealthy decision for a pregnant woman to drink alcohol?
8. Sequencing List in order the following steps of development: eyelids open and close, legs kick, embryo is about an inch long, amniotic sac develops.

A Healthy Pregnancy

Objectives

▶ **Identify** four behaviors that are essential for a healthy pregnancy.

▶ **Explain** the importance of prenatal care throughout pregnancy.

Vocabulary

- prenatal care
- obstetrician
- trimester
- ultrasound
- chorionic villus sampling
- amniocentesis
- ectopic pregnancy
- miscarriage
- preeclampsia
- gestational diabetes

Warm-Up

Myth A pregnant woman doesn't need to visit the doctor until she begins to show, or look pregnant.

Fact Regular doctor visits from the beginning of pregnancy until the birth are recommended to ensure health.

WRITING List some other do's and don'ts for pregnant women. Review and update your list when you complete this section.

Doctor's Appt. 10:00 AM

Staying Healthy During Pregnancy

Amanda starts her day with a bowl of oatmeal. Later, she and her husband go out for a brisk walk. At night, she skips a party where people will be smoking.

Amanda and her husband are thinking about having a baby. Even before she becomes pregnant, Amanda started taking extra care to have a healthy pregnancy. **Getting proper nutrition and exercise and avoiding drugs and environmental hazards are especially important both before and throughout pregnancy.**

Proper Nutrition "Now you're eating for two," people sometimes say to pregnant women. This is because a pregnant woman needs to eat more calories to support the growth of her own body and the developing embryo or fetus. During pregnancy, a woman needs to consume about 300 more calories than usual. The best way to obtain these extra calories is to eat a well-balanced diet rich in the key nutrients listed in Figure 4.

One vitamin that is especially important during pregnancy is folic acid, or folate. Folic acid is essential for proper development of an embryo's neural tube, which later develops into the spinal cord and brain. The neural tube forms early in an embryo's development, often before a woman knows she is pregnant. Therefore, a woman should not wait until she knows she is pregnant to get enough folic acid. Doctors recommend that all women of childbearing age consume at least 0.4 mg (400 micrograms) of folic acid every day.

Exercise Regular physical activity is also important for a healthy pregnancy. A fit woman will better meet the extra energy demands of carrying the fetus. She also reduces her risk for diabetes and other health problems during pregnancy. A woman should get her doctor's approval for her exercise program. Some forms of exercise should be avoided—for example, horseback riding, where there is a high risk of falling.

Avoiding Alcohol and Other Drugs As soon as she plans to become pregnant, a woman should abstain from all alcohol, tobacco, and any other drugs not prescribed or approved by her doctor. These substances, even in small amounts, can harm or kill the developing baby, decrease the newborn's chance to live, or cause lifelong problems. For example, women who drink alcohol during pregnancy risk having a baby with fetal alcohol syndrome. As you read in Chapter 15, symptoms of fetal alcohol syndrome may include mental retardation, minor to severe heart defects, and delayed growth.

Some drugs that are typically safe outside of pregnancy can cause harm to a fetus. A pregnant woman should talk to her doctor before using any prescription drugs or over-the-counter drugs, such as pain medications; creams and lotions; and vitamins. Likewise, a woman should get her doctor's approval before using herbal teas or herbal supplements.

 Connect to Your Life Which recommendations for pregnant women are also good everyday advice for yourself?

FIGURE 4 Proper nutrition contributes to the healthy development of a baby.
Reading Tables Name three nutrients that play a role in the development of the nervous system.

Important Nutrients During Pregnancy

Nutrient	Needed For
Folic acid	Formation of neural tube; brain and spinal cord development
Protein	Muscle formation and growth
Calcium	Bone and tooth formation; nerve and muscle development
Iron	Oxygen delivery by blood cells
Vitamin A	Cell and bone growth; eye development
Vitamin B complex	Nervous system development

Avoiding Environmental Hazards Some common substances found in the environment, including many chemicals and disease-causing organisms, can seriously harm a fetus. Pregnant women should take care to avoid exposure to these substances.

▶ **X-rays** The radiation from X-rays can harm a developing embryo or fetus. This is why doctors and dentists ask women if they could possibly be pregnant before taking an X-ray.

▶ **Lead** The main source of exposure to lead is from lead-based paint present in older homes. If a pregnant woman lives in a home built before 1978, she should contact her state health department for information on getting her home tested for lead.

▶ **Mercury** Most exposure to this dangerous metal comes from eating contaminated fish. Pregnant women should eat commercially caught fish only once a week, and should not eat swordfish or shark.

▶ **Cat litter** Cat feces can contain a parasite that is especially dangerous to a developing fetus. Pregnant women should avoid contacting soiled cat litter or garden soil.

Prenatal Care

Besides taking care of herself at home, a woman also needs to plan for **prenatal care,** or medical care during her pregnancy. Her doctor visits should be under the supervision of an **obstetrician,** a doctor specialized in pregnancy and childbirth. **The chances of having a healthy baby greatly increase if the mother visits her doctor or clinic for regular checkups throughout pregnancy.**

The Three Trimesters A pregnancy is divided into three periods of time—**trimesters**—each of which is approximately three months long. Figure 5 lists things the parents-to-be can expect at routine visits.

FIGURE 5 A doctor monitors the health of the mother-to-be and her fetus during regular prenatal visits.

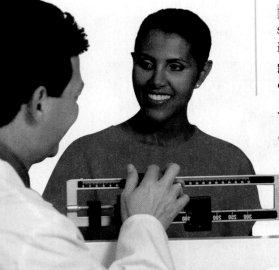

First Trimester
- Record medical history and weight
- Note conditions that could affect the pregnancy
- Prescribe prenatal vitamins as needed

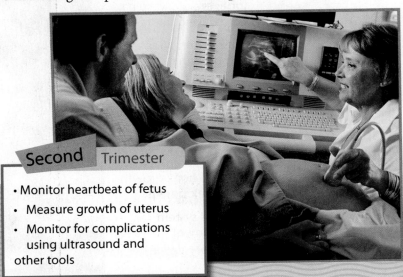

Second Trimester
- Monitor heartbeat of fetus
- Measure growth of uterus
- Monitor for complications using ultrasound and other tools

Monitoring Tools Prenatal care gives a pregnant woman access to the latest medical tests and technologies.

▶ **Ultrasound** Did you know that your first pictures may have been taken months before you were born? High-frequency sound waves, or **ultrasound,** are used in most pregnancies to create an image of the developing fetus. Ultrasound may be used at any point during pregnancy, although it is typically used in the sixteenth to twentieth week. Using ultrasound, a doctor can tell the age of the fetus, whether it is a boy or girl, and if the heart, muscles, and bones are developing normally. Ultrasound may also detect the presence of more than one fetus or confirm the position of the fetus in the uterus.

▶ **Chorionic Villus Sampling** Around the eighth week of pregnancy, some women will undergo a test called **chorionic villus sampling,** or CVS. To perform the test, the doctor removes and tests a small piece of the developing placenta. CVS can detect inherited disorders in the embryo such as hemophilia or extra chromosomes. The test is only done when risk factors are present, such as a family history of genetic disorders or when the mother is over the age of 35. An older mother has an increased risk of having a baby with Down syndrome or other chromosomal abnormalities.

▶ **Amniocentesis** Another test that may be done around the fourteenth to sixteenth week of pregnancy is **amniocentesis** (am nee oh sen TEE sis). The procedure involves inserting a needle into the woman's abdomen and uterus to remove a small amount of amniotic fluid surrounding the fetus. The doctor then tests fetal cells naturally found in this fluid for abnormalities. Like CVS, amniocentesis is only performed when the fetus is at higher risk for a genetic disorder. CVS and amniocentesis are not routine tests because they slightly increase the risk of miscarriage, or death of the fetus.

Connect to Your Life

Have you ever seen an ultrasound picture of a fetus? What features could you recognize?

Third Trimester
- Check position and size of fetus
- Check for warning signs of premature, or early, birth
- Continue to monitor for complications
- Discuss birth process

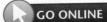
GO ONLINE
PearsonSuccessNet.com
For: More on pregnancy care

Complications Problems can occur at any time during pregnancy. For some of these complications, timely treatment can reduce negative consequences or even save the life of the woman or fetus.

▶ **Ectopic pregnancy** In the very rare case of an **ectopic pregnancy,** the blastocyst implants in the fallopian tube or elsewhere in the abdomen, instead of in the uterus. It cannot develop normally and may put the mother's life at risk. Surgery is necessary to remove the embryo and repair the damaged fallopian tube.

▶ **Miscarriage** The death of an embryo or fetus in the first 20 weeks of pregnancy is called a **miscarriage.** Almost all miscarriages take place during the first trimester. They can occur before or after a woman knows she is pregnant. At least 15 percent of recognized pregnancies end in miscarriages. Miscarriage is usually caused by a serious genetic defect, but it is sometimes due to illness or a drug the mother has taken. In other cases, there is no apparent reason for a miscarriage.

▶ **Preeclampsia** **Preeclampsia** (pree ih KLAMP see uh), which is also called toxemia, is characterized by high blood pressure, swelling of the wrists and ankles, and high levels of protein in the urine. Its onset is usually in the second or third trimester. Preeclampsia prevents the fetus from getting enough oxygen. This serious condition is treated with bed rest or medication.

▶ **Gestational Diabetes** Diabetes that develops in pregnant women is called **gestational diabetes** and is marked by high blood sugar levels. It usually develops later in pregnancy. If untreated, excess blood sugar can pass through the placenta to the fetus. The fetus may grow too large, which increases the risk of a difficult birth. The birth may also occur early, resulting in breathing problems for the newborn.

Section 2 Review

Key Ideas and Vocabulary

1. List four healthy habits that a pregnant woman should adopt before and during pregnancy.
2. Why is prenatal care so important throughout pregnancy?
3. About how long is each **trimester** of a pregnancy?
4. What is **chorionic villus sampling**? Under what conditions is it sometimes recommended?
5. Describe three symptoms of **preeclampsia**. How is it treated?

Health at Home

Ultrasound Pictures Ask your mother or other relative with children if she saved any ultrasound pictures from her pregnancy. Ask permission to see the pictures. Ask about her emotions during the ultrasound—were she and the father scared, happy, excited? Write a paragraph about the pictures and the parents' experience. **WRITING**

Critical Thinking

6. **Evaluating** From the following list, which food choice is generally recommended for pregnant women: swordfish, spinach, wine, herbal tea?
7. **Comparing and Contrasting** How are chorionic villus sampling and amniocentesis alike? How are they different?

Technology & Health

Surgery Before Birth

What can be done if prenatal tests reveal a life-threatening condition in a fetus? In some cases, doctors can perform prenatal surgery—that is, surgery before birth. Prenatal surgery has been performed successfully on fetuses with heart conditions and neural tube defects. It has also been used to correct unbalanced blood flow between identical twins.

WRITING Any surgery has risks. What questions must parents consider with a doctor as they weigh the risks of prenatal surgery?

❶ Diagnosis

Doctors can diagnose an unbalanced blood flow between identical twins using tests that produce images of the fetuses. The imaging would show that a shared blood vessel between the fetuses is depleting blood from one twin—the donor. The other twin—the recipient—is getting too much blood. Without intervention, both twins would likely die.

❷ Surgery

The doctor makes a small incision in the mother's abdomen and uterus. Using a tiny instrument called an endoscope, the doctor locates the shared blood vessel and closes it off. Now each twin will have a separate blood supply.

❸ A Successful Outcome

The surgery is successful. Here, the twins are 5 months old.

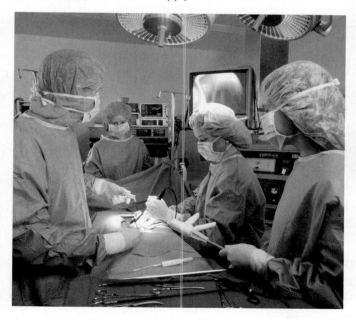

Childbirth

Objectives

▶ **Identify** the three stages of the birth process.

▶ **Describe** four complicating factors that may arise at birth.

Vocabulary

- certified nurse-midwife
- labor
- postpartum period
- stillbirth
- cesarean section
- premature birth
- low birthweight
- multiple birth

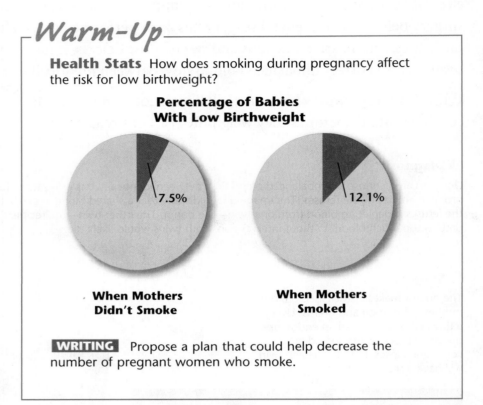

Warm-Up

Health Stats How does smoking during pregnancy affect the risk for low birthweight?

Percentage of Babies With Low Birthweight

7.5%

12.1%

When Mothers Didn't Smoke

When Mothers Smoked

WRITING Propose a plan that could help decrease the number of pregnant women who smoke.

The Birth Process

As the baby's due date approaches, the mother and father prepare. Most couples choose to have their baby in a hospital, where obstetricians, specially trained nurses, and medical equipment are available should something go wrong. If the pregnancy has gone well and the mother is in good health, a couple may choose to have the baby at home or at a home-like setting with the help of a certified nurse-midwife. A **certified nurse-midwife** is a nurse who is trained to deliver babies.

Near the end of the ninth month of pregnancy, the head of the fetus moves lower in the uterus. The birth process begins when the muscular walls of the uterus begin a series of contractions that will push the fetus out of the mother. **Birth takes place in three stages—labor, delivery of the baby, and delivery of the afterbirth.** Refer to Figure 6 to see what happens during each stage.

Connect to Your Life What mix of emotions might expectant parents feel during the birth process?

FIGURE 6 The three stages of birth include labor, delivery of the baby, and delivery of the afterbirth.

❶ Labor The work performed by the mother's body to push the fetus out is called **labor.** Labor for a first child may last from about 2 to 24 hours or longer. During this stage, strong contractions of the muscles of the uterus cause the cervix to increase in width, or dilate.

Each contraction typically lasts from 30 to 90 seconds. At first, the contractions may be minutes apart, but by the end of labor, they are usually only a few seconds apart. Near the end of this first stage, the amniotic sac breaks, and the cervix becomes softer and wide enough for the fetus to pass through.

❷ Delivery of Baby Stage two involves the actual birth, or delivery, of the baby. This stage can take from half an hour to more than two hours. Contractions of the uterus continue, and the baby is pushed out, usually head first, through the cervix and vagina.

Once the baby is out, the doctor clamps and cuts the umbilical cord. There are no nerve endings in the cord, so this does not hurt the baby or the mother. The baby's nose and mouth are suctioned to remove mucus and make breathing easier. Eye drops are put in the baby's eyes to prevent infection, and an injection of vitamin K is given to prevent excessive bleeding from the cut umbilical cord. The doctor may also prick the baby's heel for a blood sample, which will be tested for abnormal protein levels. Abnormal test results may indicate a genetic disorder.

❸ Delivery of Afterbirth Even though the baby is born, the birth process is not complete. The third stage involves contractions of the uterus that push out the placenta, also called the afterbirth. This stage typically takes about 15 to 30 minutes.

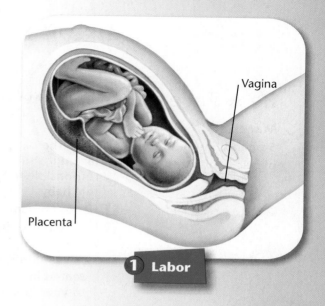

❶ Labor

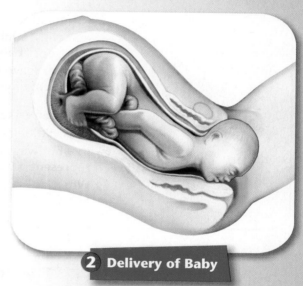

❷ Delivery of Baby

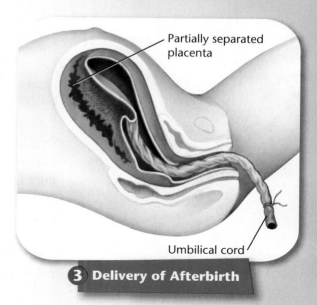

❸ Delivery of Afterbirth

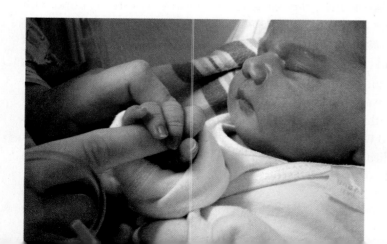

Hands-On *Activity*

Be a Parent for a Day

Materials
5-pound bag of flour
plastic bag with tie

Try This

❶ Place the bag of flour inside the plastic bag and fasten it shut. For the next 24 hours, you will be responsible for your bag of flour as if it were a real baby.

❷ Choose a name for your "baby."

❸ Follow these rules for taking care of your "baby."

- Every 5 hours, including night, feed your "baby" for 20 minutes. During this time, you must remain seated in one place and devote your full attention to your "baby."

- Every 3 hours during the time that you are awake, allow 5 minutes for changing your "baby's" diaper.

- Spend 15 minutes in the evening talking or reading to your "baby."

- Never leave your "baby" alone. If necessary, arrange for someone to babysit.

Think and Discuss

❶ How did being a parent of a bag of flour affect your lifestyle?

❷ In what ways is a bag of flour an appropriate object to use to represent a baby?

❸ When do you think is the best time for a person to become a parent? Explain.

The Postpartum Period   After the birth, a period of adjustment for the parents and their newborn begins. During the first six weeks, called the **postpartum period,** many changes take place. Immediately after the birth, the newborn's lungs begin to function for the first time. The circulatory system and heart undergo changes that send more blood to the lungs, where the baby now gets oxygen from the air. The nervous system reacts to new sensations: light, air against the skin, a parent's touch, hunger, and pain. While its organs adjust to life outside the uterus, the newborn is learning to get what it needs by forming a strong bond with its mother and father.

For the mother, changing hormone levels signal the breasts to produce milk and cause the uterus to gradually shrink back to its normal size. Hormonal changes and fatigue may cause the mother to feel overwhelmed, or even very sad, during the postpartum period. Usually, these "baby blues" pass within a few days. If, however, the sadness lasts longer or causes the mother to withdraw from the baby and other people, she should seek prompt medical attention. She may need to be treated for a serious condition called postpartum depression.

Complications at Birth

Although the birth process usually proceeds smoothly, problems can sometimes occur. **Some complications result in a surgical delivery or premature birth. Low birthweight and the birth of more than one baby also may cause complications.** In addition, very rarely, a pregnancy may end with a stillbirth. A **stillbirth** occurs when a fetus dies and is expelled from the body after the twentieth week of pregnancy.

Surgical Delivery Sometimes delivery through the cervix and vagina is not possible because of the position of the fetus in the uterus or the narrowness of the mother's hips. Other times, illness or other conditions may make labor and vaginal delivery dangerous for the mother or the fetus.

In these circumstances, the obstetrician will perform a cesarean section. A **cesarean section** (suh ZEHR ee un) is a surgical method of birth. The operation takes about one hour to complete, and the mother may be awake or asleep during the procedure. First the doctor makes an incision in the lower abdomen into the uterus. Then he or she removes the baby and placenta. About 30 percent of all babies born in the United States are delivered by cesarean section.

Premature Birth Sometimes a baby is born before it has developed fully. Delivery of a live baby before the 37th week of pregnancy is called **premature birth.** The earlier the birth, the more problems the baby tends to have. The lungs of a premature baby are usually not fully developed, and in some cases, the baby cannot breathe by itself. The baby may also have additional problems if other organs aren't fully developed. A premature baby may receive care in an incubator, a chamber designed to protect the baby until it has developed more.

What misconceptions about premature babies did you hold before reading this section?

GO ONLINE

PearsonSuccessNet.com
For: More on the birth process

FIGURE 7 A premature baby may need extended hospital care until it becomes more fully developed.

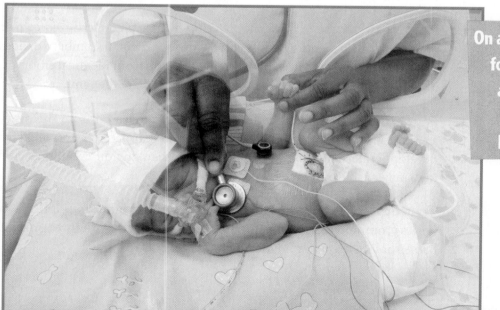

On average, hospital costs for premature babies are 14 times as high as costs for healthy newborns.

FIGURE 8 Risk factors for having a baby with low birthweight include smoking or dieting during pregnancy and teenage pregnancy.

Babies born to teen mothers are at increased risk for low birthweight.

Low Birthweight   A newborn that weighs less than 5.5 pounds at birth is considered to have **low birthweight.** Some low-birthweight babies are also premature. Others are full-term, but they just didn't grow enough before birth.

Premature and low-birthweight babies face an increased risk of health problems as newborns, chronic lifelong health problems, and even death. Not all cases are preventable. However, the number of premature and low-birthweight babies could dramatically decrease if more women adopted healthy habits during pregnancy. For example, a woman reduces her risk of having a baby with low birthweight by about 40 percent by not smoking during pregnancy.

Multiple Births

The delivery of more than one baby—for example, twins, triplets, or quadruplets—is called a **multiple birth.** These births carry greater risk to the mother and babies, and are closely monitored by doctors. Delivery by cesarean section is more likely for a multiple birth than for a single birth.

What causes more than one fetus to develop? Figure 9 shows how the two types of twins develop.

Identical Twins   Twins that develop from a single fertilized egg, or zygote, are called identical twins. Early in development, the embryo divides into two identical embryos. Because they develop from identical embryos, identical twins have the same inherited traits and are the same sex.

Fraternal Twins   Sometimes two eggs are released from the ovary and are fertilized by two sperm. When this happens, fraternal twins develop. Fraternal twins are no more alike than any other siblings, and they may or may not be the same sex.

Triplets or More   Triplets, quadruplets, and other multiple births are less common than twins. But the number of births with three or more babies has increased dramatically in the last 30 years.

Identical Twins

A sperm fertilizes a single egg.

Early in development, the embryo splits and forms two identical embryos.

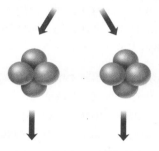

Identical twins result.

Fraternal Twins

Two different sperm fertilize two eggs.

Each of the fertilized eggs develops into an embryo.

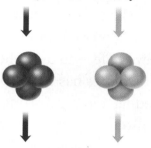

Fraternal twins result.

FIGURE 9 Identical twins inherit identical traits, whereas fraternal twins do not. **Applying Concepts** Why can fraternal twins be different sexes while identical twins cannot?

Section 3 Review

Key Ideas and Vocabulary

1. What are the three stages of birth?
2. Describe what happens during **labor**.
3. What is the **postpartum period**? List two changes that happen in the newborn and two changes that happen in the mother during this period.
4. What are four complicating factors that may arise at birth?
5. What is a **cesarean section**? Give two reasons why a cesarean section may be performed.

Health at School

Twins Interview Interview twins you know at your school or in your community. Ask them how they think being twins affects their relationship as siblings. Write a transcript of your interview. **WRITING**

Critical Thinking

6. **Relating Cause and Effect** Describe two risk factors for low birthweight.
7. **Comparing and Contrasting** How do fraternal twins differ from identical twins?

BUILDING HEALTH SKILLS

Coping With Change

Dolores and Miguel brought their first baby home from the hospital last week. They had been planning for the birth of their first child for months, but now they are feeling overwhelmed.

Dolores has been up every night, feeding and comforting the baby. Miguel is also feeling stress because of all his new responsibilities. How can they cope with all these changes in their lives?

The period between the old and new ways of life, called the transition time, can be difficult. The following guidelines can help you deal with transition times in your life, no matter what type of change you are facing.

1 Accept change as normal.
Change is a natural part of life. Some changes are a result of your decisions, and others are beyond your control. In either case, the transition is often stressful.

2 Expect mixed feelings.
Because some fear and loss accompany even the most desirable new experience, change usually brings mixed feelings—both positive and negative.

When you are faced with a significant change, make a chart listing the advantages and disadvantages the change will bring into your life. This "change chart" can help you understand your mixed feelings.

3 Understand your resistance.
Moving on to "unexplored territory" is stressful, and resistance is common. There are a couple things you can do to reduce your resistance to change.

▶ Review your "change chart" to identify those disadvantages that are the immediate, or short-term, stresses associated with the change. Cross those out. They will disappear as soon as you integrate the new situation into your life.

▶ Now circle the disadvantages over which you have no control. Remind yourself that you often must "let go" of things you cannot control.

Change Chart

Change: Moving to a new school

Advantages
- Academics are better
- School is safer
- Can make new friends
- Walking distance to home
- Soccer team

Disadvantages
- Won't see old friends every day
- Won't know anyone
- Can't find my way to class
- Have to memorize new schedule
- Lunch costs more

4 Build an inside support system.

► Use lessons from the past to help you get through the current situation. Think about how you coped with past changes. How can you build on your past successes and apply them to your current situation?

► Focus on the positive aspects of the change you are now facing. Jot down the most important benefits of the change and add a reassuring message, such as "I can handle . . . and feel good!" Place your list where you will see it often.

5 Build an outside support system.

► Enlist the support of friends and family members who were helpful to you in the past. Let them know you would appreciate their support again.

► Seek new sources of support. You may want to join organized groups that are working on similar issues.

6 Start with small steps.

Even a small step can make you feel confident that you can handle the change in your life.

► Decide on a goal and put it in words, such as "to feel more a part of my new school."

► Take a small, positive step toward that goal, such as attending a meeting of one after-school club.

7 Work through setbacks.

It is not unusual to feel scared, even as you are making progress. Your natural tendency may be to go back to what was safe and comfortable. Instead, remind yourself of your successes and the steps you have already taken toward your goal. Tell yourself that you can do it . . . and you can!

Practice the Skill

1. Think back to a major change you faced in the recent past. List the positive and negative reactions you felt about the change. Did you use any of the strategies above in coping with the change? Explain.

2. Think about a change you are currently facing or are about to face.
   a. Make a "change chart" that lists the advantages and disadvantages of the change.
   b. Cross out the short-term disadvantages that will go away after a short time. Circle those disadvantages that are out of your control so you can "let them go."
   c. List the people that you could ask to be your outside support system.
   d. Decide on a first small step toward making the change a part of your life. Explain your choice.

Childhood

Objectives

▶ **Describe** the changes that children undergo during early childhood.

▶ **Identify** key areas of development that occur during middle and late childhood.

Vocabulary

• pre-adolescence

Warm-Up

Dear Advice Line,

I babysit a 2-year-old. She can't do things by herself like pour milk into her cup or put on her pajamas, but she gets mad at me when I try to help and insists on doing it herself. What should I do?

WRITING Explain what factors might be contributing to this two-year-old's behavior. What advice can you give the babysitter?

Early Childhood

Do you have younger siblings or cousins? Do you babysit for young children? If so, you have probably noticed that they do not behave or think the way that older children or adults do. Babies and young children are not miniature adults. Their bodies and brains are still growing and developing rapidly. **From birth to age six, children change from helpless babies into confident individuals who can do many things for themselves.**

Birth to Eighteen Months Have you ever seen or held a newborn baby? A newborn is born with some physical skills. It can nurse, cry, and direct its gaze right at you. However, it will not learn to smile until it is about one month old. At birth, many of the baby's organs and systems are not yet fully developed. A newborn's bones are still soft and flexible.

FIGURE 10 Children change dramatically during childhood.

Birth to 18 Months
• Cries for help
• Learns to sit, crawl, stand, and walk

By the time a baby is 3 or 4 months old, the brain, nerves, and muscles are ready for more coordinated movement. The baby recognizes its parents and siblings, cries to get what it needs, and responds to attention with smiles. By 18 months of age, the baby has probably learned to sit, crawl, stand, and walk. He or she now has some "baby" teeth and can chew solid food.

GO ONLINE

PearsonSuccessNet.com
For: More on growth and development

Eighteen Months to Three Years
Most children learn to talk sometime between 18 months and 3 years of age. This is also the age when children lose their babylike appearances—baby fat is lost and the arms and legs get longer. Appetite decreases as growth slows down. Physical coordination improves.

During this time, most children gain abilities to do things for themselves. They may show off around family and friends but be shy around strangers. When they are with others their age, toddlers tend to play alongside, but not with, each other. They are not ready to share or to play together because they are busy learning to do things for themselves. With encouragement from parents and caregivers, the child's confidence grows.

Three to Six Years
Between the ages of 3 and 6, most children lose all traces of babyhood. They become more independent and active. Muscles grow, energy is high, and the curious child is "into everything." Communication skills advance rapidly. Most 4-year-olds talk in sentences.

During this stage, children learn to play together and to make friends. They begin school and learn how to behave in a group. They also start to develop a sense of right and wrong.

Connect to Your Life **Think back to when you were in first grade. How did you look and act?**

18 Months to Three Years
- Plays alongside others
- Learns many words

Three to Six Years
- Plays with others
- Has lots of energy

Six to Twelve Years
- Becomes less self-centered
- Has many interests and hobbies

Middle and Late Childhood

Think about some of the things you did between the ages of 6 and 12. Maybe you learned to play a sport, developed a hobby, or made a best friend. **Physical growth, mastering new skills, and making friends are key areas of development during middle and late childhood.** Middle childhood is defined as the period between age 6 and 8, and late childhood as ages 9 through 12. Late childhood is also called **pre-adolescence** or the "tween" years. It is the stage of development before adolescence.

FIGURE 11 Having a best friend is important during pre-adolescence.

Physical Growth   Many changes occur during middle and late childhood. For example, at around age 6 or 7, a child's facial structure changes with the appearance of permanent teeth. Muscles and bones continue to grow, and coordination develops further. As children enter pre-adolescence, their bones begin to grow faster, mostly in the legs. Their appetite also increases.

Mental Development   Mental development continues during these years, as children learn higher-level thinking skills. Children will feel pride in accomplishing tasks and attempting new challenges. Praise from teachers and parents helps increase their self-confidence.

During middle and late childhood, the self-centeredness of early childhood lessens, and children continue to learn values, such as honesty and fairness. They may start taking on responsibilities at home, such as chores, during this stage.

Importance of Friends   When did the approval of friends and the need to fit in with a social group become very important to you? Often, this occurs at about age 10. These feelings help children learn to work well in group situations. Having a best friend also becomes important in pre-adolescence and will remain so into the teen years.

Section 4 Review

Key Ideas and Vocabulary

1. In a sentence, describe a typical newborn. Then describe a typical 18-month-old, a 3-year-old, and a 6-year-old.

2. List three key areas of development that occur during middle and late childhood.

3. What is **pre-adolescence**? At about what ages does it begin and end?

Health and Community

Babysitter's Guide Choose one age range of children described in this section. Create a brochure that contains information and tips for babysitters of children in that age range. Be sure to include suggestions for keeping the children both entertained and safe from injury. **WRITING**

Critical Thinking

4. **Comparing and Contrasting** In what ways are you similar to how you were at age 10? In what ways are you different?

GO ONLINE PearsonSuccessNet.com   Audio Summary Section 19.4

Chapter 19
At a Glance

VIDEO **TEENS** Talk 🔘
Teen Pregnancy Describe how pregnancy affected the long-term plans of the teens in the video.

Section 1   Development Before Birth

Key Ideas

▶ In the first week after fertilization, the fertilized egg undergoes many cell divisions and travels to the uterus.

▶ The amniotic sac, placenta, and umbilical cord protect and nourish the developing embryo and later the fetus.

Vocabulary
- zygote (489)
- embryo (489)
- blastocyst (489)
- implantation (489)
- amniotic sac (490)
- placenta (490)
- umbilical cord (491)
- fetus (491)

Section 2   A Healthy Pregnancy

Key Ideas

▶ Getting proper nutrition and exercise and avoiding drugs and environmental hazards are especially important both before and throughout pregnancy.

▶ The chances of having a healthy baby greatly increase if the mother visits her doctor or clinic for regular checkups throughout pregnancy.

Vocabulary
- prenatal care (494)
- obstetrician (494)
- trimester (494)
- ultrasound (495)
- chorionic villus sampling (495)
- amniocentesis (495)
- ectopic pregnancy (496)
- miscarriage (496)
- preeclampsia (496)
- gestational diabetes (496)

Section 3   Childbirth

Key Ideas

▶ Birth takes place in three stages—labor, delivery of the baby, and delivery of the afterbirth.

▶ Some complications at birth result in a surgical delivery or premature birth. Low birthweight and the birth of more than one baby also may cause complications.

Vocabulary
- certified nurse-midwife (498)
- labor (499)
- postpartum period (500)
- stillbirth (501)
- cesarean section (501)
- premature birth (501)
- low birthweight (502)
- multiple birth (502)

Section 4   Childhood

Key Ideas

▶ From birth to age six, children change from helpless babies into confident individuals who can do many things for themselves.

▶ Physical growth, mastering new skills, and making friends are key areas of development during middle and late childhood.

Vocabulary
- pre-adolescence (508)

Chapter 19 Review

GO ONLINE

PearsonSuccessNet.com

For: Chapter 19 review activity

Reviewing Key Ideas

Section 1

1. During implantation
   a. the egg is fertilized.
   b. the blastocyst travels to the uterus.
   c. the blastocyst attaches to the wall of the uterus.
   d. the embryo grows to about an inch in length.

2. Describe how a fetus obtains nutrients and gets rid of wastes.

3. What changes occur in a fetus between the 7th and 9th month of development?

4. **Critical Thinking** Why do you think many expectant parents keep pregnancy a secret until after the first trimester?

Section 2

5. Which nutrient is critical for proper neural tube development?
   a. iron   b. folic acid
   c. sodium   d. vitamin A

6. List four environmental hazards of particular concern to pregnant women.

7. During which trimester of a pregnancy should a woman start prenatal care?

8. **Critical Thinking** Besides prenatal care, how can expectant parents prepare for the experience of birth?

Section 3

9. All of the following happen during a typical labor *except*
   a. the uterus contracts.
   b. the cervix dilates.
   c. the amniotic sac breaks.
   d. the umbilical cord breaks.

10. What are some warning signs of postpartum depression?

11. **Critical Thinking** Newborns who form a close, loving bond with their parents grow faster and are healthier than newborns who do not form this bond. Why do you think this is so?

Section 4

12. During what stage does a child typically begin to get his or her permanent teeth?
   a. newborn
   b. early childhood
   c. middle childhood
   d. late childhood

13. Between which ages do children typically learn to dress themselves?

14. **Critical Thinking** Explain why parents of 2-year-olds must "keep an eye on them" all the time.

Building Health Skills

15. **Advocacy** How could you help an older cousin stop smoking before she decides to have a baby?

16. **Accessing Information** How would someone go about choosing an obstetrician or certified nurse-midwife? What resources could they use?

17. **Making Decisions** A 26-year-old pregnant woman with no genetic disorders in her family says she wants an amniocentesis done so that she "gets all that medical science has to offer." Do you agree with her reasoning? Explain. **WRITING**

18. **Setting Goals** Identify one habit you could change that would help you be a better parent in your 20s or 30s. It may seem a long way off, but changing habits is easiest when you are young. Write down the habit you would like to change, and monitor your progress over the school year.

Health and Community

Folic Acid Awareness Many health organizations recommend that all women increase their folic acid consumption, starting in their teen years. Create a public service announcement to deliver this important message to teenaged girls. In it, describe the importance of folic acid and offer tips for adding more of it to one's diet. **WRITING**

Standardized Test Prep

Math Practice

The graphs below display data on multiple births in the U.S. between 1980 and 2010. The first graph shows births of triplets or more. The second graph shows births of twins. Use the graphs to answer Questions 19–21.

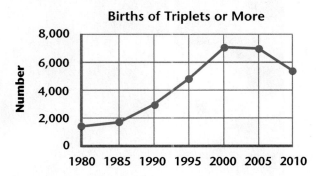

Births of Triplets or More

19. About how many more births of triplets or more were there in 2000 compared with 1980?
    A 4,000   B 2,000
    C 5,500   D 7,000

20. Which of the following best describes the change in the number of births of triplets or more between 1980 and 2005?
    F They increased slightly.
    G They increased by 50 percent.
    H They doubled.
    J They nearly quadrupled.

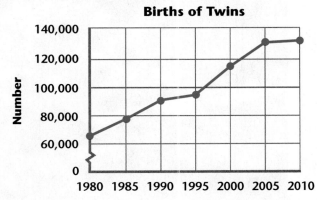

Births of Twins

21. Approximately how much greater was the number of twin births compared with births of triplets or more in the year 2005?
    A 2 times   B 4 times
    C 8 times   D 18 times

Reading and Writing Practice

Read the passage. Then answer Questions 22–25.

In the United States, more than 20 percent of women smoke. More than half of these women smoke while they are pregnant. This is a major public health problem because, not only can smoking harm a woman's health, but smoking during pregnancy can lead to pregnancy complications and serious health problems in newborns. The statistics are compelling. If all pregnant women in the United States stopped smoking, there would be an estimated 11 percent reduction in stillbirths and a 5 percent reduction in deaths of newborns.

22. In this passage, the word *compelling* means
    A interesting.   B doubtful.
    C convincing.   D reliable.

23. According to the passage, which of these statements is true?
    F There is no correlation between smoking and newborn deaths.
    G More than 20 percent of women smoke during pregnancy.
    H If more women chose not to smoke during pregnancy, more newborns would survive.
    J Smoking during pregnancy does not affect the number of stillbirths.

24. What word best describes the tone of this passage?
    A poetic   B angry
    C sarcastic   D persuasive

Constructed Response

25. Write a sentence summarizing the viewpoint of the author of this reading passage. Then, in a paragraph, explain how the author uses statistics to defend this viewpoint.

Test-Taking Tip

Skip difficult questions. You can return to them later. Don't get stuck on them and waste time.

CHAPTER 20

Adolescence and Adulthood

GO ONLINE PearsonSuccessNet.com

VIDEO 20

TEENS Talk

Pictures of "Perfection"

Preview **Activity**

What's Important to You?

Complete this activity before you watch the video.

1. Rank the following qualities by how important you think they are to *your* overall attractiveness (with 1 being most important).

_____ body shape
_____ facial features
_____ mature appearance
_____ personality
_____ intelligence

2. Now rank the list by how important you think each quality is to *other* people's attractiveness. How do your two rankings differ?

3. Now reflect. Do you think that your rankings for yourself and others are as they *should* be? Explain. **WRITING**

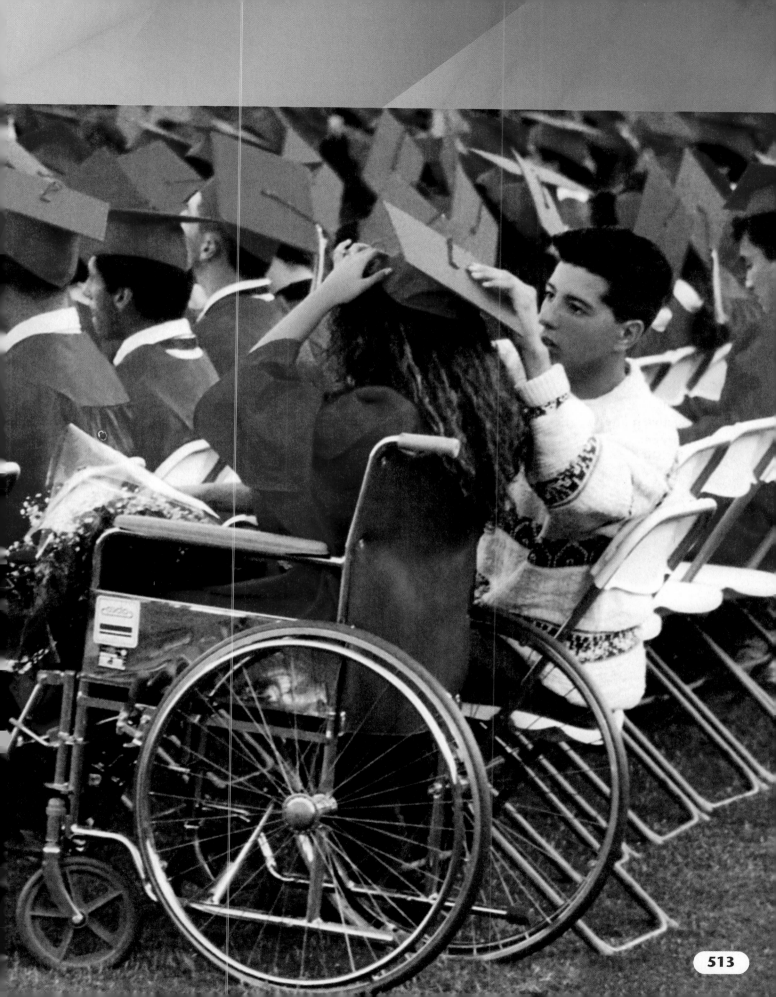

Adolescence: A Time of Change

Objectives

▶ **List** three main categories of physical changes that occur during adolescence.

▶ **Describe** three mental changes that adolescents experience.

▶ **Summarize** the emotional changes of adolescence.

Vocabulary

- adolescence
- reproductive maturity
- secondary sex characteristics

Warm-Up

Dear Advice Line,

I'm very self-conscious because I look more grown up than all of my friends. I'm tired of people staring at me and making comments about my body. What can I do?

WRITING What advice and reassurances would you offer this teen?

Changes in Your Body

If you were to compare a recent photograph of yourself to one taken three years ago, you would notice many changes. From about the ages of 12 to 19, you gradually change from a child into an adult. This period of gradual change is called **adolescence.** During adolescence, a person undergoes many physical, mental, and emotional changes.

As photographs reveal, adolescence is a period of rapid physical growth. However, photos show only some of the physical changes taking place. Important physical changes are also occurring inside the body during this time. **During adolescence, the reproductive system matures, adult features appear, and height and muscle mass increase.**

Reproductive System Puberty usually begins before you reach adolescence and ends during mid-adolescence. As you learned from Chapter 18, puberty is the period of sexual development when a person becomes sexually mature and able to reproduce. You may have heard the term *puberty* used in many different ways. Some people use the term to refer to all of the changes of adolescence. However, the term refers specifically to the changes that happen to your reproductive system.

Also recall from Chapter 18 that sex hormones control the changes that occur during puberty. At some point between the ages of 9 and 16, the pituitary gland in the brain signals a girl's ovaries or a boy's testes to begin producing sex hormones. The ovaries produce estrogen and progesterone while the testes produce testosterone.

The release of sex hormones causes girls to begin to ovulate and menstruate, and boys to begin to produce sperm. Ovulation in girls and sperm production in boys signal **reproductive maturity,** or the ability to produce children. Early in puberty, the body does not produce sex hormones consistently. In girls, this affects the regularity of the menstrual cycle. Many girls begin to ovulate before their menstrual cycles become regular. In fact, in some girls, menstrual cycles do not become regular for many years. As the glands mature, hormone production becomes more regular.

Appearance The sex hormones also cause the development of **secondary sex characteristics,** which are physical changes that develop during puberty, but are not directly involved in reproduction. Secondary sex characteristics are listed in Figure 1.

The physical changes at puberty can be overwhelming at times. Some adolescents have difficulty adjusting to their changing body shape, or may be embarrassed or confused about the sexual changes occurring to their bodies. Having someone to talk to, especially a trusted adult, can help adolescents understand and accept their feelings.

FIGURE 1 At puberty, sex hormones cause the development of secondary sex characteristics.

Connect to Your Life Whom can you talk to when you feel concerned about the changes in your body?

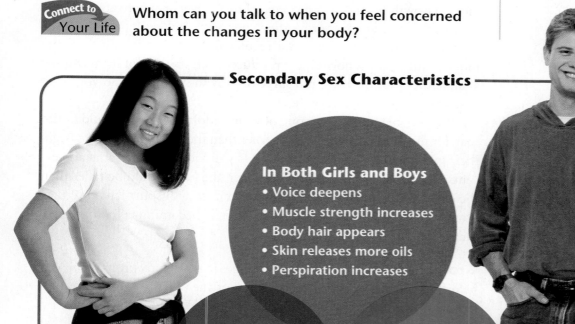

Secondary Sex Characteristics

In Both Girls and Boys
- Voice deepens
- Muscle strength increases
- Body hair appears
- Skin releases more oils
- Perspiration increases

In Girls Only
- Breasts develop
- Hips widen
- Body fat increases

In Boys Only
- Shoulders broaden
- Hair appears on face and chest

FIGURE 2 Girls typically begin their growth spurt earlier than boys, but don't grow as much overall.

8th Grade Dance

Senior Prom

Height and Muscle Mass Around the same time that puberty starts, the pituitary gland also increases its production of growth hormone. Growth hormone is a chemical messenger that activates growth. First your hands and feet grow, then your arms and legs.

Growth does not occur in a regular fashion, but in spurts. Some months little growth hormone is produced, and you do not seem to grow at all. Other months there is a surge of growth hormone, and you seem to jump shoe sizes in a very short time.

If you were to look at a group of young adolescents, you would notice that, for the most part, the girls are taller than the boys. Girls tend to begin their growth spurt earlier than boys. If you looked at the same adolescents at the end of high school, however, the boys would be taller than the girls, for the most part. Boys start their growth spurt later, but they grow for a longer period of time—eventually becoming taller than girls, on average.

Growing Pains Adjusting to changes in your body proportions can be difficult at times. Rapid lengthening of the bones in your arms and legs can cause aches and cramps. It can also make you feel awkward. You may feel as if you are tripping over your own feet, or you may find that you are no longer comfortable in your favorite chair.

If you challenge your growing body with a variety of physical activities, you will adjust more rapidly to your new size and shape. Physical activity will also help to develop your muscles and your coordination. As unlikely as it may seem, your feelings of discomfort and awkwardness will soon disappear.

Energy Demands You may also notice another effect that growth has on your body—it makes you hungry. Your family may remark that your stomach seems to be a "bottomless pit." This is normal during adolescence because you need extra energy to fuel your growing body. It is important, however, to eat nutritious meals and snacks to supply your body with the nutrients it needs. You should not gain excessive weight.

Early Bloomers and Late Bloomers If you are like most adolescents, you have probably compared your own physical development to that of your peers. Some of your classmates may already look like adults, while others may be just starting to show signs of puberty. You can see in Figure 4 that the age range for the "normal" onset of puberty is wide. Some people start puberty before middle school, some start puberty toward the end of high school, and others start somewhere in between.

Adolescents who develop at an early age, before most other adolescents, are sometimes called early bloomers. Those who develop at a late age, after most other adolescents, are called late bloomers. Although they may not think so, most early bloomers and late bloomers are developing at a normal rate.

What accounts for the wide range of ages at which puberty and the growth spurt begin? The ages at which people mature sexually and grow to their adult height are determined in large part by heredity. You are probably maturing at about the same age and speed as your parents did. Another factor that influences your unique timetable of development is your overall state of health.

FIGURE 3 It's normal to feel an increase in your appetite during adolescence—your body needs extra fuel for growth.

Connect to
Your Life

Do you consider yourself an early bloomer, late bloomer, or somewhere in between? Why?

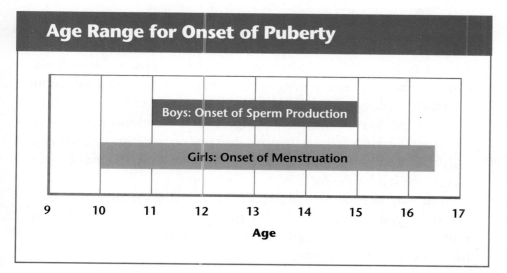

Age Range for Onset of Puberty

Boys: Onset of Sperm Production

Girls: Onset of Menstruation

| 9 | 10 | 11 | 12 | 13 | 14 | 15 | 16 | 17 |

Age

FIGURE 4 There is no "typical" age at which puberty begins. This timeline shows that the age range for onset of puberty is wide. **Calculating** What is the range in years between the earliest and latest onset of menstruation in girls? **MATH**

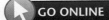

GO ONLINE

PearsonSuccessNet.com

For: More on adolescence

Mental Changes

Hormones control most of the outward physical changes of adolescence. But changes in the way you think and feel have more to do with changes occurring in your brain. In your first few years of life, millions of brain cells and the pathways connecting them formed. Then, when you were between 10 and 13 years old, a second dramatic wave of growth and development took place. In fact, your brain grew a bit too much! During the rest of your adolescence, your brain will be "pruned back." Only the brain cells and connections that you use will survive and flourish.

Scientists are discovering how changes in the brain affect teenage development. Figure 5 shows four regions of the brain in which significant changes occur. **Mental changes during adolescence include improved abstract thinking, reasoning skills, and impulse control.**

Abstract Thinking   When you were a child, your thoughts and feelings were tied directly to your physical experiences at each moment. For example, you thought about hunger only when your stomach was empty. Now, however, it is easier for you to think abstractly—to consider ideas that are not concrete or visible. For example, you can now think about the problem of chronic hunger in communities around the world. Your growing ability to think abstractly is partly due to the dramatic growth in your brain's frontal cortex, shown in Figure 5.

 How have you used abstract thinking skills today at school? Explain.

Reasoning Skills   During adolescence, changes to your brain also help to expand your reasoning abilities—including the way you solve problems and make decisions. You are becoming increasingly able to see more than one side of a question and to think through the pros and cons of decisions you face. As you gain experience making wise choices in simple everyday dilemmas, you find it easier to make wise choices when more difficult situations arise.

Impulse Control   Some teenagers find that their impulses, or tendencies to act rapidly based on emotional reactions, are sometimes clouding their decision-making abilities. Maybe a friend dares them to do something dangerous, and before they consider the consequences, they go ahead and do it. As described in Figure 5, the emotional region of an adolescent's brain is more active than the same region in an adult's brain. Scientists hypothesize that greater activity in the amygdala may be one reason why it is harder for teens to ignore impulses.

You may not like the consequences of acting on your impulses. Removing yourself from an intense situation and taking some time to think things through can help you stay in control. As you mature, your impulse control will improve.

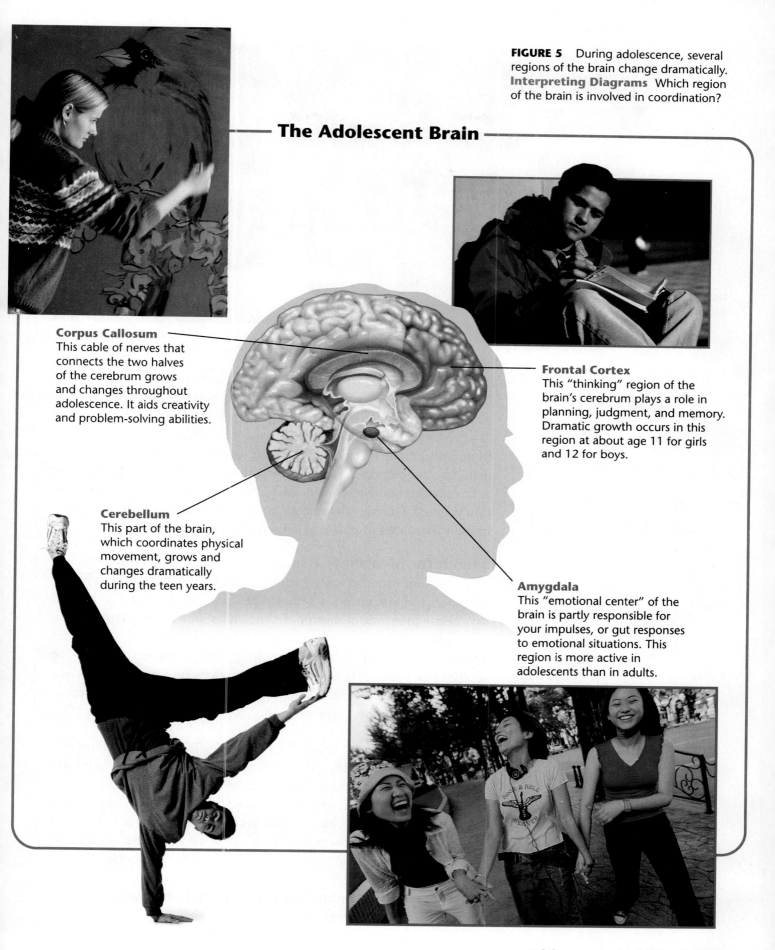

The Adolescent Brain

Corpus Callosum
This cable of nerves that connects the two halves of the cerebrum grows and changes throughout adolescence. It aids creativity and problem-solving abilities.

Frontal Cortex
This "thinking" region of the brain's cerebrum plays a role in planning, judgment, and memory. Dramatic growth occurs in this region at about age 11 for girls and 12 for boys.

Cerebellum
This part of the brain, which coordinates physical movement, grows and changes dramatically during the teen years.

Amygdala
This "emotional center" of the brain is partly responsible for your impulses, or gut responses to emotional situations. This region is more active in adolescents than in adults.

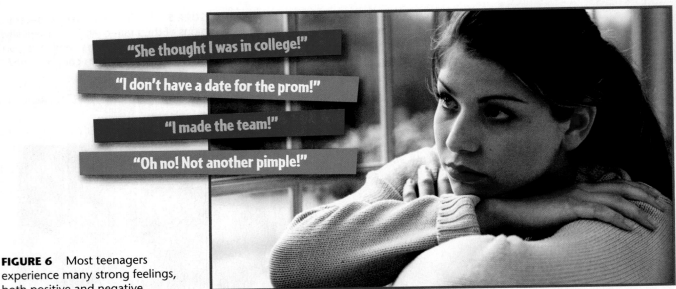

"She thought I was in college!"

"I don't have a date for the prom!"

"I made the team!"

"Oh no! Not another pimple!"

FIGURE 6 Most teenagers experience many strong feelings, both positive and negative.

Emotional Changes

During adolescence, you may feel like you are on an emotional roller coaster—very happy one moment, and miserable the next. You are not alone in having these strong feelings—all teens experience them.

For many teens, adolescence is a time for questioning. You may begin to question many things that you have simply accepted until now. You may start to question the actions and values of people around you, such as friends and family members. Most important, you may start to question yourself. **During adolescence, individuals start to define meaning in their lives, a set of personal values, and a sense of self.**

Search for Meaning   During adolescence, it is not unusual to suddenly question whether your friends are really true friends and whether happiness and love are possible to attain. These questions signal that you have begun to search for meaning in life. This search is important because you are beginning to choose a way of life that is right for you. Some teens find answers to these questions by talking with parents or other trusted adults. Others explore these questions through their own experiences. For example, some teens volunteer in hospitals or food pantries. Such experiences often help them figure out what is important to them.

Search for Values   Have you started to question the opinions and beliefs of others, especially those of your parents? This process helps you discover your values—those beliefs that are important to you. Although you may disagree with your parents at times, they can offer you guidance and serve as role models. Parents, teachers, and other adults can help you clarify your values. For the most part, many of the values that adolescents eventually come to accept are similar to those of their parents.

Connect to Your Life

What important values do you share with your parents?

Search for Self Some of the most difficult questions that adolescents ask concern themselves and their place in the world. These questions are signs of a search for who you are— your identity. This search for identity may take many forms. You might discuss the question of identity with others, or you might compare yourself to people you admire. Exploring your racial and ethnic traditions can be an important part of your search for identity. You may experiment with new hairstyles, different clothing, and even new behaviors.

As you explore ways to express your identity, think about the long-term social consequences of your actions. Some changes are difficult to reverse. What will the person in Figure 7 think about her tattoo when she is 50?

If you are like many adolescents, your self-esteem may not be as high today as it was a few years ago. Right now your feelings about yourself are strongly influenced by the opinions of others, particularly your peers. You may worry whether your peers approve of your clothing, your looks, your personality, and your interests. It is normal to have these worries. In time, these feelings will lessen.

It is not always easy to keep a clear and consistent picture of yourself, or to feel positive about who you are. Try writing about your accomplishments and talents in a journal. When the question "Who am I?" comes up, you can find some good answers in your journal.

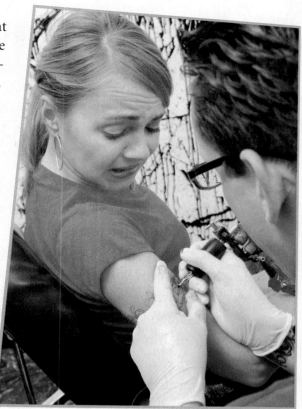

FIGURE 7 Sometimes people use a tattoo to express their identity.
Evaluating Could having a tattoo affect a person's ability to get a job?

Section 1 Review

Key Ideas and Vocabulary

1. What are three categories of physical changes that occur during adolescence?
2. What is **reproductive maturity**? How is it related to puberty?
3. What are **secondary sex characteristics**? List two for males and two for females.
4. Describe three mental changes that occur during adolescence.
5. How do teens develop emotionally during adolescence? Give three examples of questions teens may ask themselves.

Health at Home

Advertising Appeal Choose two magazine or television advertisements that target adolescents. Make a list of the products being advertised and answer these questions for each: How does the ad take advantage of a teen's search for self? Do the ad's images promote a particular identity? Is the identity related to the product or not? Explain your answers. **WRITING**

Critical Thinking

6. **Making Judgments** In your opinion, is it more difficult to be an early bloomer or a late bloomer? Explain.
7. **Predicting** How have your values changed since you were young? How do you think your values might change as you get older? Explain. **WRITING**

Setting a Goal

Now that Diego is a senior in high school, everyone is asking him about his goals. When his uncle tells him to consider "where he'll be in ten years," his father complains that Diego doesn't know where he'll be next week.

Diego knows he should start looking ahead, but how far ahead? He's always said he wants to be an architect, but he's never done anything about it. His attention and energies seem to skip from one thing to another. The following guidelines could help Diego focus his energies on achievable goals. You can use them, too, to help set your own realistic and reachable goals.

1 Know yourself.
Before deciding on specific goals, jot down what you know about yourself. What are your long-term interests? What activities do you enjoy? What are your abilities? What are the most important things in your life? Goals that correspond to your interests and values will be more desirable. Goals tied to your abilities will be easier to reach.

2 Make goals clear, specific, and positive.
A clear, specific, positive goal accurately describes what you want to be doing when you achieve it. An example of a well-written goal is: "I want to get all Bs this term." This is clearer and more specific than "I want to do better in school." It allows you to measure your success by counting the number of Bs you receive. In contrast, you cannot measure "doing better."

Getting all Bs is also more positive than "I don't want any Fs this term." Making progress toward a positive goal will give you a sense of pride and inspire you to keep going.

③ Include deadlines.

Set a reasonable time limit for your goals. Deadlines make goals more specific, add a sense of urgency, and provide a good way to measure success. If you cannot meet the deadline, you may need to consider a more realistic time limit. For example, if you were able to raise four out of five grades to Bs this term, this would be good progress, not failure. The goal of earning all Bs can be rescheduled for next term.

④ Break long-term goals into small steps.

Long-term goals, such as running a marathon, should be broken into smaller, more manageable, measurable steps. Future marathoners begin their training with short distances. Only when they have built the speed and endurance necessary for long distances do they go on to run the full marathon course.

⑤ Keep written goals visible.

Write your goals down. Then tape them to your closet door, mirror, notebook, or other place you look at frequently. This repeated reinforcement of a goal will keep you focused on achieving it.

> Review class notes every day.
>
> Ask teacher for extra help.
>
> Study in library before track practice.

⑥ Evaluate your progress.

At times, stop and ask yourself if you are making progress toward your goal. If so, good. If not, how can you get on track?

Practice the Skill

1. Review Diego's situation. How could Diego use the steps given here to help set some long-term and short-term goals? How could he use a career goal to focus his energies during his senior year?

2. Evaluate each of the goals below. Is each one as clear, specific, and positive as it could be? Revise each goal to increase its chances of being met. Break up the goal into smaller steps if necessary. Also include realistic deadlines.
   a. I don't want to gain any more weight.
   b. I want to be a professional tennis player.
   c. I want to stop fighting with my parents so much.
   d. I want to eat better.
   e. I want to be happy.

3. Think about a time when you set a goal and tried to reach it. Did you use any of the steps described here? Explain. Did you reach your goal? Why or why not?

4. Get to know yourself better by listing your interests, abilities, and values. Keeping that list in mind, write three clear, specific, positive goals you want to achieve by
   a. the end of the school year.
   b. the end of high school.
   c. the end of ten years.

   Then break each goal down into manageable steps, or short-term goals, that will allow you to measure your progress toward the overall goal.

5. Review the list of your interests from question 4. Using the guidelines described here, set a goal with a realistic deadline of two weeks or less. After two weeks, evaluate your success. How did the guidelines help make your goal achievable?

Adolescence and Responsibility

Objective
▶ **Identify** the responsibilities that adolescents have to themselves and others.

Vocabulary
• autonomy

Warm-Up

Quick Quiz See how many of these questions you can answer "yes" to.

1. Do you do what is best for you even if friends urge you to do otherwise?

2. Are your decisions consistent with your values?

3. Do you think about how your behavior impacts others?

4. Do you accept responsibility for your actions?

WRITING In a paragraph, describe some steps teens can take to be able to answer "yes" to all the questions.

Responsibilities to Yourself

With adolescence comes increased privileges. You are treated more like an adult, and you make decisions that direct your life. However, the flip side of privilege is responsibility. You are expected to behave consistently and to assume responsibility for yourself and others. Often the move to this new status is not a smooth one. You may be anxious for the privileges but not so anxious for the responsibilities. Some days you may want to make all your own decisions. Other days you may wish you could hide your head under your pillow and let someone else take charge. **Your pathway to adulthood will be marked by a growing responsibility for your own decisions and actions.**

Making Everyday Decisions During adolescence you become responsible for taking care of yourself. Adults may still remind you, but ultimately, it's up to you to eat nutritious meals, exercise, and visit the dentist. You are responsible for other decisions, too, such as what to wear. If you pay for some or all of your clothes and other personal items, you also become responsible for managing a budget.

Resisting Negative Influences While following the clothing styles of your peers may be harmless, following all of their behaviors may have more serious consequences. Many decisions you will face can affect your health and safety, including decisions about smoking, drinking, drugs, and sexual activity. Parents and other adults may make rules for you early in your teens. Eventually, however, you make these decisions on your own and take responsibility for the results.

Thinking About Your Future Adolescence is also a time to begin looking toward the future. During these years, you make many decisions that can affect your future career opportunities. You now know that you have to plan and work for what you want—these things do not just happen on their own. There is plenty of time to figure out what you want to do, or to change your mind. However, making responsible decisions now can help keep your options open.

 What are you doing now to take responsibility for your future?

Responsibilities to Others

Your responsibilities to your family, friends, and community increase greatly during adolescence. At the same time that you are gaining more independence, others may be relying more on you for help.

Your Role in the Family How does your status as an adolescent affect your relationships with your family? In many families, the family unit and family rules are valued more highly than a teenager's **autonomy,** or independence. This may lead to friction between generations. Parents may expect their teens to stick to the older ways. At the same time, teens may be pulled in other directions by their peers.

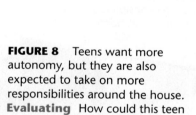
GO ONLINE
PearsonSuccessNet.com
For: More on responsibility

FIGURE 8 Teens want more autonomy, but they are also expected to take on more responsibilities around the house. **Evaluating** How could this teen and his dad work out a solution to their conflict?

Responsibility to Family Despite images in the media that show teenagers as angry, rude, and rebellious, most teenagers are happy, healthy people who value their families. Research shows that most families are able to work out the conflicts that normally arise as teenagers strive for more autonomy.

Working out these conflicts involves some give and take on the part of both parents and teens. It helps to show respect for the feelings, tastes, and values of family members on minor issues, such as clothing styles. This sets the stage for increased independence on bigger issues, such as borrowing the family car.

With increased independence at home comes increased responsibilities. What are your responsibilities to your family?

▶ **Helping Out** You may now be responsible for more of the physical work needed to maintain your household. You may need to learn new skills, such as house painting, grocery shopping, or laundering. You may be responsible for taking care of a younger brother or sister after school. Perhaps you are contributing to the family finances with money you bring home from an after-school job.

▶ **Giving Back** You are responsible for becoming more of a "giver" in your family relationships. You are now mature enough to offer understanding and support to other family members. You can participate more fully in the emotional life of your family. For example, if your sister is studying for a test, you can offer encouraging words and help her study.

▶ **Playing by the Rules** Another responsibility is to follow your family guidelines about clothing, curfews, and other activities. This does not mean that your parents make all of the rules all of the time. You can help your parents establish guidelines that are right for you.

FIGURE 9 Helping out more around the house and looking after a younger sibling are just two of the new responsibilities you may encounter at home.

Hands-On *Activity*

Living on a Budget

Materials

employment ad section of newspaper
apartment ad section of newspaper
sample utility bills
supermarket circulars

Try This

❶ Look through the employment ads and find a job for which you think you are qualified. Calculate an average monthly salary. Subtract 30 percent for taxes and other deductions—this amount is your spendable monthly income.

❷ Use the apartment ads to find out how much it costs to rent a one-bedroom apartment.

❸ Use sample utility bills to estimate the monthly costs of electricity, gas, heat, and telephone.

❹ Use supermarket circulars to estimate your total food costs for a month.

❺ Estimate how much it costs to operate a car for a week, and multiply by four. Include gas, insurance, and repairs. Alternatively, calculate the cost of public transportation.

❻ Estimate how often you like to go out for entertainment, such as movies and restaurants, and how much these would cost for a month.

❼ Calculate how much you spend on clothing during a month.

Think and Discuss

❶ Total the monthly amounts in items 2 through 7. Is it more or less than your monthly spendable income?

❷ If your expenses are more than your income, what could you do to either increase your monthly income or to decrease your monthly expenses?

❸ What did you learn by doing this activity?

Responsibility to Friends   During adolescence, you may realize that your friends are more than just people with whom to have fun. Friends are people who really listen when you talk and who support you when you have a problem. You have similar responsibilities toward them. You should be willing to take time away from your activities to help out a friend, to be a good listener, and to offer comfort and encouragement when needed.

You may also witness some friends engaging in destructive or dangerous behaviors. When you have a concern about a friend's health, safety, or well-being, you have a responsibility to try to help. Peer pressure—in spite of the way the term is often used—can be a positive force. You can use peer pressure to influence your friends in positive directions and to provide a network of support in times of stress or crisis.

When did you last help out a friend? What did you do?

FIGURE 10 During adolescence, you take on more responsibility to your community.

Responsibility to Community As you continue through your teen years, you will begin to see yourself as an important part of your larger community. You may also recognize that your actions directly affect community life. For example, you probably appreciate clean streets and parks, and you like knowing that cars will stop at red lights when you are crossing the street. Now you are mature enough to see that these benefits depend on you and people like you.

Littering, vandalism, or reckless driving endanger the quality of life in a community. Some of these irresponsible behaviors are also dangerous, and many of them are against the law. During your teen years, you become responsible for knowing the laws of your community and for obeying them. You are expected to think about the effect that your actions will have, not only on yourself and your friends but on the community as a whole. Acting responsibly is a way of showing your new maturity.

You may even want to go further in helping to improve your community. Participating in cleanup or fund-raising activities or giving aid directly to less fortunate community members can be satisfying. During adolescence, many teens become more interested in public issues, and they find that their actions can have a noticeable positive effect on their community.

Section 2 Review

Key Ideas and Vocabulary

1. What responsibilities do adolescents have to themselves?

2. What is **autonomy**? How might it lead to conflicts with family members during adolescence?

3. List one example each of increasing responsibilities that teens may have to their family, their friends, and their community.

Critical Thinking

4. **Relating Cause and Effect** A teen who often breaks her parents' rules may feel she has less autonomy than her friends who follow family rules. Explain why this might be the case. **WRITING**

Health at School

School Responsibility Identify a problem at your school—for example, littering or tardiness—that could be solved by an increase in responsibility by the student body. What strategies would you propose to increase the student body's sense of responsibility for the problem? Write a one-page action plan. **WRITING**

---

5. **Evaluating** A teen decides not to use his cell phone while driving. To whom is he being responsible? Explain.

6. **Applying Concepts** Describe one way you "give back" to your community. How has this experience affected you? **WRITING**

🔊 **GO ONLINE** PearsonSuccessNet.com | Audio Summary Section 20.2

Adulthood and Marriage

Objectives

▶ **Summarize** the changes that people undergo during adulthood.

▶ **List** three keys to a successful marriage.

▶ **Analyze** how decisions made in youth can affect the aging process.

Vocabulary

• physical maturity
• emotional maturity
• dementia
• Alzheimer's disease

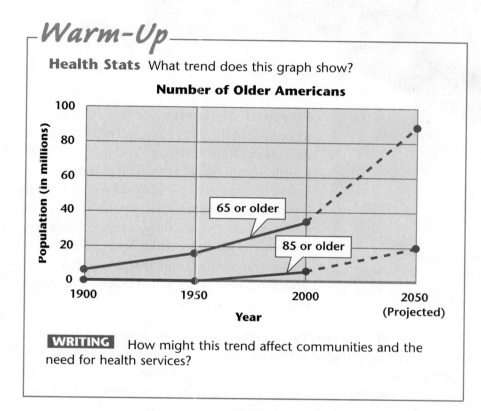

Warm-Up

Health Stats What trend does this graph show?

Number of Older Americans

(graph: Population (in millions) vs Year, showing "65 or older" and "85 or older" lines from 1900 to 2050 (Projected))

WRITING How might this trend affect communities and the need for health services?

Young Adulthood

At what point do you become an adult? On a certain birthday? When you are financially independent? When you marry? When you have physically matured? From a legal standpoint, Americans are considered to be adults at the age of 18 for some activities and at the age of 21 for others. From a physical and emotional standpoint, however, it is difficult to say when adulthood begins.

During the next few years, you will begin the transition from adolescence to adulthood. **You will change physically and emotionally during the transition from adolescence into young adulthood. In fact, changes continue throughout your life as an adult.**

Connect to Your Life At what age do you think adulthood begins? Explain your answer.

To Stay at Your Physical Peak
- Maintain a healthy diet.
- Avoid tobacco and other drugs.
- Exercise regularly.
- Get adequate rest.
- Have regular medical and dental checkups.

FIGURE 11 It's not all downhill after reaching your physical peak. You can adopt the habits listed above to keep your physical strengths for many years.

Physical Maturity   If you look up the term *adult* in the dictionary, you might find this definition: "fully developed and mature." Most people reach **physical maturity,** the state of being full-grown in the physical sense, by their late teens or early twenties. By this time, all of your body systems are fully developed, and you are as tall as you will ever be. Your physical abilities—your strength and speed, as well as your breathing and heart efficiencies—will reach their peak during young adulthood.

Emotional Maturity   Unlike physical maturity, adults reach **emotional maturity,** or full development in the emotional sense, over their lifetime. There are three major factors that contribute to emotional maturity—developing close relationships with others, giving back to society, and learning to accept yourself for who you are.

In young adulthood, an important emotional milestone is the establishment of close relationships with individuals outside your family. As an adult, you are more likely to form long-lasting friendships than you are forming now as an adolescent. Why? You will have a better sense of who you are, and be better able to choose friends with interests and values similar to your own. Having a clear idea of who you are and trusting others will also give you the foundation for emotional intimacy. Emotional intimacy is the openness, sharing, affection, and trust that can develop in a close relationship.

Your Career   One major concern of young adults is finding a career in which they feel productive and satisfied. During adolescence, you need to think, plan, and prepare for your life's work. During young adulthood, you make decisions and take action towards your career goals. You need to know what skills, education, and training are necessary to achieve your goal. You also should consider the income you will need to earn to be self-supporting. If you get married and have children, you will have to juggle your work responsibilities with the needs of your family.

Marriage

More than 70 percent of all Americans marry at some time during their lives. Therefore, it is likely that you will marry someday. If you do choose to marry, it will probably be one of the most important decisions you will make. It will affect you, your spouse, your family, your friends, and future generations.

Why People Marry People marry for a variety of reasons. Some people marry because they desire another person's love and companionship. Others marry for financial, social, or cultural reasons. Some couples marry in order to start a family of their own.

You need to know yourself fairly well before you select a marriage partner. You need to know what your goals are and how you are going to achieve them. You need to know what is important to you. When it comes time to marry, people usually select marriage partners who have similar interests, values, level of education, and social background to themselves. People who are quite different from each other can also have successful marriages, but they may have to work harder to overcome their differences.

Successful Marriages You probably feel, as most people do, that successful marriages are based on love. But what is love? Often young people mistake sexual attraction or short-lived crushes for love. Real love is part of a long-lasting relationship in which people really know, like, and accept each other as they are. People who are truly in love appreciate the things they like about each other and accept the things they dislike. When you love someone, his or her well-being becomes as important to you as your own.

Although love is a basic element in a successful marriage, it is not the only one. **Love, compatibility, and commitment are key factors in a successful marriage.** Compatibility is the ability to live together in harmony. Couples who share many qualities tend to be more compatible. Commitment is the strong determination by the couple to make their marriage a fulfilling lifelong relationship, despite the challenges. Other important factors to consider when thinking about marriage are listed in Figure 12.

Connect to Your Life

What do you think is most important in a successful marriage?

What Qualities Make a Marriage Successful?
- Love
- Friendship
- Commitment
- Compatibility
- Communication
- Mutual respect
- Physical attraction
- Ability to compromise

FIGURE 12 There are many elements of a successful marriage besides love.

FIGURE 13 Many married couples share responsibilities both inside and outside the home.

Stresses in Marriage Throughout marriage, a couple must be willing to make adjustments to meet each other's needs. The changes in attitudes and expectations that these adjustments require can produce stress.

One difficult adjustment in marriage can be determining the responsibilities that each spouse will have. Some couples decide early in their marriage how each person will contribute financially and who will do certain household tasks. Who will do the cooking? Who will pay the bills?

By compromising and accepting tasks that fit their abilities and schedules, a couple usually can develop a comfortable give-and-take relationship. When changes occur, such as the birth of a child or a new job, the couple may need to redefine their responsibilities.

Marriages can become strained when unexpected problems arise. One spouse may lose his or her job. A spouse or child may become seriously ill. There may be an unplanned pregnancy. Effective communication can be an important tool in helping a couple get through a crisis. Sometimes a couple may need to seek help from community agencies that provide financial or counseling services. Turning to family or friends for emotional support is another way to get through hard times.

Parenthood For some people, young adulthood is not only a time for marriage but also a time to become parents. The relationship between parent and child is critical to the child's healthy development. As you read in Chapter 19, parents need to be able to commit a lifetime of love, guidance, and attention to their children.

At least one part of making the decision to become parents is purely practical. A couple should review their budget to find out whether or not they can afford to provide food, clothing, and medical care for a child. They need to discuss who will care for the child if both spouses continue to work. They need to find out if their employers grant maternity or paternity leave, so that at least one of them can stay home with the baby for a few months and still return to the same job. They may also need to investigate the costs and availability of child care.

Teens and Marriage When teens marry, they often face additional challenges compared with those who marry later. Adjusting to a new relationship, earning a living, and completing an education can feel overwhelming. Many married teens drop out of school. Without a high-school diploma, it can be difficult to find a good job. Even if both teens work, they may have difficulty earning enough money for rent and food. The couple may end up living with parents or other relatives. Such an arrangement can limit a couple's opportunities to get to know each other, to make decisions, and to develop as a couple.

Teens who marry may experience changes in their friendships. Friends who are not married often do not have the same interests and goals as a married couple, especially if the couple has a baby. A married couple may be concerned about stretching a small income. Single friends may be more concerned about school or dating.

It is difficult to know when you are 17 or 18 just how you will feel when you are 25 or 30. People change a great deal during their teens and early twenties. For this reason, many teenagers choose to wait before making a long-term commitment. They want to find out more about themselves, to meet people, and to have other experiences.

In spite of all the obstacles, some teenage marriages are successful. The couple must be willing to put in the effort needed to make their marriage work. They need to learn to communicate, to compromise, and to develop the qualities that are important for a fulfilling relationship.

Connect to Your Life

What would you say to a friend who is thinking about getting married?

FIGURE 14 Divorce rates are higher for couples who marry in their teens.
Reading Graphs What percentage of teens who marry under age 18 will divorce in the first five years of marriage?

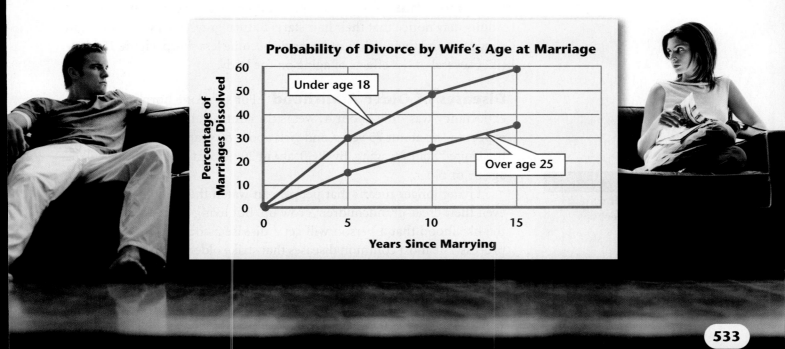

Probability of Divorce by Wife's Age at Marriage

Percentage of Marriages Dissolved

Under age 18

Over age 25

Years Since Marrying

FIGURE 15 Aging affects many of the body systems. Exercising in water can help maintain joint flexibility.

Healthy Aging

After about the age of 30, adults begin to experience changes associated with the aging process. Aging is a normal biological process that you cannot avoid. However, there are many things you can do over your lifetime to slow the effects of aging. **People tend to reduce or delay the physical signs of aging when they establish healthy behaviors during their youth.**

 What hobbies will you engage in to stay active as you age?

Physical Changes What physical changes occur as people age? Adults may notice that their hair starts to turn gray, facial wrinkles begin to appear, and their vision and hearing become less sharp. Figure 15 identifies several of the effects of aging on the body.

Diseases of Older Adulthood For someone born in 1900, life expectancy was only about 47 years. In contrast, boys born today can expect to live about 75 years, and girls about 80 years. The population of the United States is aging. By 2030, about 20 percent of Americans will be age 65 or older.

Living longer means that people can watch their grandchildren, or even their great-grandchildren, grow up. But living longer also increases the likelihood that a person will get a disease associated with the aging process. The most common diseases that strike older adults include heart disease, cancer, and lung disease. Other common diseases of older adulthood are listed on the next page.

GO ONLINE
PearsonSuccessNet.com
For: More on perceptions of aging

▶ **Arthritis** This disease attacks the body's joints. It can make simple tasks, such as holding a pencil or climbing stairs, very painful. Arthritis can be managed with pain medication and physical activities that are gentle on the joints, such as exercising in water.

▶ **Osteoporosis** The bones of older people tend to break easily and heal slowly. This is due to osteoporosis, a condition caused by a loss of bone calcium. Medications can help slow calcium loss. In addition, railings installed along stairs and in bathtubs can help prevent falls that could fracture bones.

▶ **Parkinson's disease** This disease of the nervous and muscular systems causes the muscles to become stiff. A person experiences shaky movements and progressive loss of muscle function. Medications can slow the progression of this disease.

▶ **Dementia** Approximately 14 percent of adults over 70 and 37 percent of adults over 90 suffer from **dementia** (dih MEN shuh). This disorder is characterized by loss of mental abilities, abnormal behaviors, and personality changes. Dementia has several causes, some of which can be treated.

▶ **Alzheimer's disease** About two thirds of people with dementia have **Alzheimer's disease** (AHLTS hy murz). This disease causes brain cells to die, resulting in the gradual loss of mental and physical function. There is no cure, but some medications may slow the progression of the disease.

Emotional and Social Changes Maintaining emotional and social health during adulthood is also important for healthy aging. For many people, adulthood is a time of contribution to their family and community. For example, adults in midlife may help take care of their grandchildren or their aging parents, or may serve as volunteers in their community. They must find a healthy balance between meeting their own needs and helping others.

You may have heard the phrase "midlife crisis" used to describe the emotions that some adults experience. Many adults do undergo a period of self-evaluation—comparing the dreams they had in young adulthood with their actual accomplishments. But despite the phrase, this period of self-evaluation does not usually have a bad outcome. A midlife crisis can lead to positive change—a different career, a return to school, or travel.

Older adults may begin to reflect on their lives. Accepting the good and the bad in their past without regrets helps them enjoy the time they have left. Older adults can best maintain their emotional health if they continue to stay psychologically connected to others. It also helps if they stay committed to something that gives meaning to their lives, such as family, friends, religion, or community activities.

FIGURE 16 Many adults in middle adulthood enjoy spending time with their grandchildren.

Section 3 Review

Key Ideas and Vocabulary

1. How do people continue to change in adulthood?

2. Define **physical maturity**. When is it reached?

3. What are three keys to a successful marriage?

4. How do healthy behaviors during youth affect aging?

5. What is **dementia**? How is it similar to **Alzheimer's disease**?

Critical Thinking

6. Applying Concepts How can you help your grandparents or other older adults stay connected to others?

Health and Community

Reaching Across Generations Write a proposal to the officials in your city or town for a project in which young people can work side by side with senior citizens. Focus on something that will beautify or in some other way improve the quality of life in your town. **WRITING**

7. Predicting Two 17-year-olds marry in their senior year of high school and start living in their own apartment. How could the marriage affect their academic goals?

8. Evaluating How might a midlife crisis contribute to an adult's emotional maturity?

Death and Dying

Objectives

▶ **List** the five stages of dying that some people experience.

▶ **Summarize** healthy strategies for coping with a dying loved one and coping after a death.

Vocabulary

• hospice
• terminal illness

Warm-Up

Myth When visiting a dying person, you should never talk about the person's condition or about death.

Fact Many dying people want to talk about what is happening to them, but you should let them raise the subject.

WRITING Is this myth common around the world? Write about your knowledge of different cultural attitudes towards death.

Dying With Dignity

Death is part of the normal cycle that all living things go through. No amount of fame, money, or love prevents death. As strange as it sounds, dying is a part of living. Still, it is never easy to face death, whether one's own or that of a loved one. However, understanding the process and learning some strategies for coping can help.

End of Life Care The process of dying has changed in the last few decades. In the past, most people died in their homes, surrounded by family and friends. The medical advances that have lengthened the average life span have also given doctors the ability to prolong the life of a dying person. Today, a person is more likely to die in a nursing home or hospital than at home.

Some people who are dying choose to be cared for in a **hospice** (HAHS pis). A hospice is a facility or program that provides physical, emotional, and spiritual care for dying people and support for their families. Some hospice programs have their own facilities where dying patients can be given round-the-clock care by hospice workers. Other hospice workers visit the dying person at home or in the hospital. Hospice workers help patients and their families to accept death and to enjoy whatever time is left. To make hospice affordable, most of the workers, except for medical personnel, are trained volunteers.

Stages of Dying

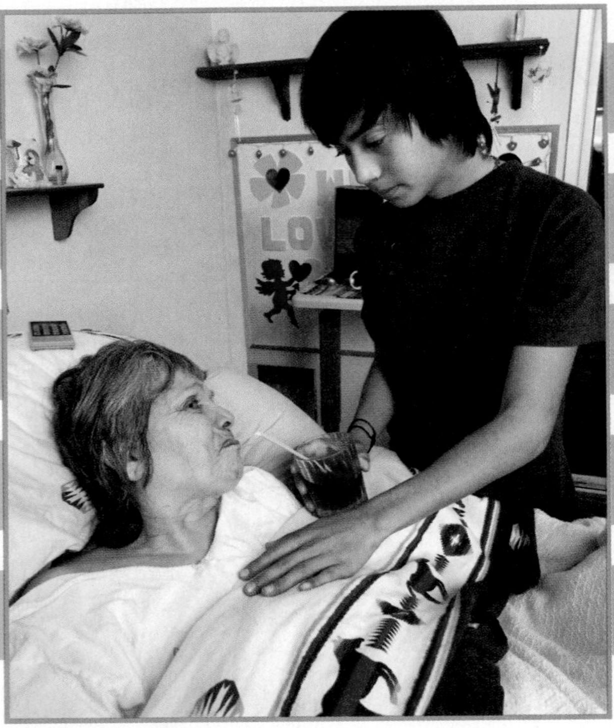

Stage	Patient		Family Member
1 Denial	"No, it's not my time to die."		"The doctor can't be right."
2 Anger	"It's not fair!"		"Why not somebody else?"
3 Bargaining	"If I stop smoking, I'll get better."		"I'd do anything to keep her here."
4 Depression	"It hurts so much. What's the use?"		"I can't stand to lose her."
5 Acceptance	"I've said my good-byes. I'm at peace."		"Soon she won't be in pain anymore."

FIGURE 17 The dying person and their loved ones may go through similar stages of emotion as death draws near.

Stages of Dying   When you think about death and grief, you may first think about the feelings of family and friends left behind when a loved one dies. But people who know they are dying also experience grief.

Consider the case of a person who has been diagnosed with a terminal illness. A **terminal illness** is an illness for which there is no chance of recovery. When the American psychiatrist Elisabeth Kübler-Ross studied the reactions of terminally ill people and their families, she discovered that they typically go through five emotional stages. **The five stages of dying are denial, anger, bargaining, depression, and acceptance.** These stages may be experienced by both the dying person and their loved ones, as shown in Figure 17.

It is important to note that not everyone reacts in the same way. The way people deal with an approaching death depends on their expectations, their emotional strengths, and the reactions of loved ones. Some people do not experience all five stages, and others may experience them in a different order.

Coping Skills

Suppose your grandparent, parent, or friend is dying. Like most people, you may find it very uncomfortable to deal with death and dying. Some people try to cover up their grief by false cheer—they pretend that everything is fine and that they are happy. Others may refuse to talk about their grief. Some keep away from the dying person. These are generally not healthy strategies. What should you do if a person close to you is dying?

 GO ONLINE

PearsonSuccessNet.com
For: More on the grieving process

Emotional Support Staying silent or absent doesn't help either the dying person or your grieving process. **Staying actively involved in a dying loved one's life will help both you and the dying person cope.**

► Visit the person as often as you can. Make dying a time for loving and sharing, not loneliness and despair.

► Listen to what the dying person has to say. Let the dying person direct the conversation. Let him or her talk about the past. Others may want to talk about what is happening to them.

► Try not to be shy about discussing death. If death frightens you, think of the dying person as someone who is about to set out on a long journey. Try to share your feelings of loss before a loved one goes.

► Talk about your plans and hopes. Even though the person will not be there to share the future with you, it will cheer the person to think about things other than the present.

Grieving After Death Dealing with your grief after a loved one dies is not easy. It may be even more difficult if the death is sudden—for example, if a loved one dies in a car crash. **After the death of a loved one, it is important not to deny your feelings. However, don't become so overwhelmed with emotion that you forget to take care of yourself.**

► Try to talk about your loss. Discuss your feelings with family and friends or write them in a journal. Talk about how you miss the person. Think of how you would like to remember the person.

► Continue your usual routine as much as possible. This will help you focus your mind on something other than the death. It will also help get you out of the house and interacting with other people.

► Allow yourself some time to grieve. However, if your feelings of grief do not lessen or pass after a time, seek the help of a parent, counselor, or other trusted adult.

FIGURE 18 Different families and cultures honor the memories of dead loved ones in different ways.

▼ **Jewish funeral**

Honoring Chinese ancestors ▶

▼ **Jazz funeral procession**

FIGURE 19 Supporting your friends through their grief shows that you care about them.

Helping Others Through Their Grief How can you support your friends when they have lost a loved one?

▶ **Be a good listener.** Your grieving friend may want to sort through some emotions by talking to you.

▶ **Write a sympathy note.** Remember that your friend will be feeling his or her loss in a unique and personal way. Don't say things like "I know how you must feel," or "You'll get over it soon." Instead, say "I'm thinking of you," or "I'm here if you want to talk."

▶ **Help with everyday errands.** Offer to bring homework assignments home for your friend, bring the family a meal, or run other errands.

▶ **If necessary, help your friend get counseling.** If your friend doesn't seem to be making any progress after time, ask a trusted adult to help you get your friend in touch with a grief counselor.

Section 4 Review

Key Ideas and Vocabulary

1. What is **hospice**? What are the benefits of a hospice program?

2. What is a **terminal illness**?

3. Describe the five stages of dying as defined by Elisabeth Kübler-Ross.

4. What is one healthy strategy for coping with a dying loved one? What is one strategy for grieving after a death?

Health at Home

Note of Sympathy Suppose a close friend's grandparent has died. Write an imaginary letter to your friend, expressing your sympathy and offering your help. **WRITING**

Critical Thinking

5. **Classifying** Into which stages of dying would you classify the following reactions:

   a. "It must be a mistake. I don't really have cancer."

   b. "I just don't care about anything anymore."

6. **Applying Concepts** Suppose your neighbors experience a death in the family. How could you offer support?

GO ONLINE PearsonSuccessNet.com   Audio Summary Section 20.4

Chapter 20
At a Glance

VIDEO **TEENS** Talk
Pictures of "Perfection" How did the video change your perception of models? Of yourself?

Section 1   Adolescence: A Time of Change

Key Ideas

▶ During adolescence, the reproductive system matures, adult features appear, and height and muscle mass increase.

▶ Mental changes during adolescence include improved abstract thinking, reasoning skills, and impulse control.

▶ During adolescence, individuals start to define meaning in their lives, a set of personal values, and a sense of self.

Vocabulary
- adolescence (514) • reproductive maturity (515)
- secondary sex characteristics (515)

Section 2   Adolescence and Responsibility

Key Ideas

▶ Your pathway to adulthood will be marked by a growing responsibility for your own decisions and actions.

▶ Your responsibilities to your family, friends, and community increase greatly during adolescence.

Vocabulary
- autonomy (525)

Section 3   Adulthood and Marriage

Key Ideas

▶ You will change physically and emotionally during adulthood.

▶ Love, compatibility, and commitment are key factors in a successful marriage.

▶ People tend to reduce or delay the physical signs of aging when they establish healthy behaviors during their youth.

Vocabulary
- physical maturity (530)
- emotional maturity (530)
- dementia (535)
- Alzheimer's disease (535)

Section 4   Death and Dying

Key Ideas

▶ The five stages of dying are denial, anger, bargaining, depression, and acceptance.

▶ Staying actively involved in a dying loved one's life will help both you and the dying person cope.

▶ After the death of a loved one, it is important not to deny your feelings. However, don't become so overwhelmed with emotion that you forget to take care of yourself.

Vocabulary
- hospice (537) • terminal illness (538)

Chapter 20 Review

Reviewing Key Ideas

GO ONLINE
PearsonSuccessNet.com
For: Chapter 20 review activity

Section 1

1. Secondary sex characteristics
   a. occur in girls, but not boys.
   b. are associated with puberty.
   c. are directly involved in reproduction.
   d. cause a growth spurt.

2. One mental characteristic that develops over the course of adolescence is
   a. a reduction in memory.
   b. decision-making based on immediate physical experiences.
   c. improved reasoning skills.
   d. stronger impulses.

3. Contrast height trends in girls versus boys at the start of adolescence.

4. **Critical Thinking** You are the parent of a teenager who "tries on" an identity you dislike. How could you show disapproval without destroying your child's self-confidence?

Section 2

5. Autonomy is
   a. independence.   b. a value or belief.
   c. emotional maturity.   d. a curfew.

6. List three ways teens show responsibility to their families.

7. **Critical Thinking** How could a teen use peer pressure to help be responsible to his friends? Give a specific example.

Section 3

8. When you are full-grown in the emotional sense, you will reach
   a. emotional intimacy.   b. your physical peak.
   c. emotional maturity.   d. a midlife crisis.

9. Explain the importance of commitment to a successful marriage.

10. Describe two big challenges most married teenagers face.

11. **Critical Thinking** Compare and contrast physical and emotional maturity. When in life are they reached? Explain. **WRITING**

Section 4

12. According to Elisabeth Kübler-Ross, the final stage of dying is
    a. acceptance.   b. denial.
    c. bargaining.   d. depression.

13. Describe four ways you can give emotional support to a dying loved one.

14. Name three healthy ways to cope with grief after a death.

15. **Critical Thinking** Why do you think some people are more afraid of the process of dying than of dying itself?

Building Health Skills

16. **Communicating** Your 14-year-old friend is worried because he is shorter than other guys and still looks the same as he did in seventh grade. Write him with your advice. **WRITING**

17. **Making Decisions** You really want to play on the softball team, but you worry that your grades will suffer if you do. How would you decide what to do?

18. **Advocacy** Since her mother died, your friend has dropped out of all social activities and barely talks to anyone. It's been a month now and you are very concerned. What could you do to help your friend?

19. **Setting Goals** What daily habits could you adopt to reduce the aging of your bones and skin? Explain the specific steps you will take. Monitor your progress over the school year.

Health and Community

An Interview With Adults Interview three adults—a young adult, a middle-aged adult, and an older adult. Ask them what advice they would offer to teenagers who are trying to set goals for the future. Compare the responses of the people you interviewed. What did you learn about planning for the future? **WRITING**

Standardized Test Prep

Math Practice

The graph shows the average age at which people in the United States first marry. Use the graph to answer Questions 20–22.

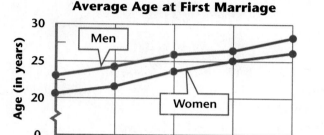

Average Age at First Marriage

20. For men, by about how much did the average age at marriage increase from 1970 to 1990?
    A 0.5 year
    B 3 years
    C 5 years
    D 6 years

21. About how much younger were women than men at first marriage in 2000?
    F 1 year   G 3 years
    H 4 years   J 6 years

22. What trend does the graph show?
    A Men marry at a younger age than women.
    B People were more likely to get married in 1970 than today.
    C Age at first marriage has risen steadily since 1970.
    D Age at first marriage rose until 1990, then declined.

Test-Taking Tip

On test day, remember your supplies. You will likely need several sharpened #2 pencils with good erasers. If you are allowed other supplies, such as a calculator, bring those as well.

Reading and Writing Practice

Read the passage. Then answer Questions 23–26.

Grief takes a toll on the body as well as the mind. Physical symptoms of grief include sagging energy levels, loss of appetite, and too much or too little sleep. Disrupted sleep patterns make the immune system less effective, sometimes leading to illness. In fact, individuals experience more sick days and hospital admissions in the year following their loss than do non-grieving individuals.

Pre-existing stress and depression are significant contributors to disrupted sleep after bereavement. On the other hand, people who have worked out effective coping strategies, have good social support networks, and maintain a healthy sleep profile are the most physiologically resilient.

23. From the context of this passage, the best definition for the word *bereavement* is
    A depression brought on by grief.
    B a coping strategy.
    C the death of a loved one.
    D lack of sleep.

24. What does the author suggest is the link between depression and physical illness in grieving people?
    F It disrupts sleep patterns.
    G It increases resiliency.
    H It reduces appetite.
    J It is a bad coping strategy.

25. According to this passage, who is most resilient after experiencing a loss?
    A Those who spend time alone
    B Those who maintain a healthy sleep profile
    C Those who take time off from work
    D Those who go to the hospital

Constructed Response

26. In a paragraph, summarize the main point of this passage in your own words.

CAREERS

Human Development

Careers in human development focus on the needs of people at all life stages—from babies to adults to people facing terminal illnesses.

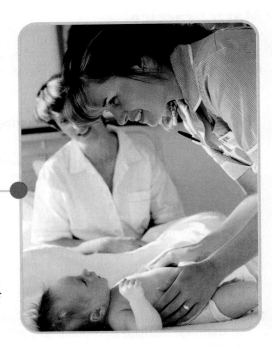

Certified Nurse-Midwife

Certified nurse-midwives care for women during pregnancy, supervise labor, and perform deliveries. They also teach new mothers about breastfeeding, nutrition, and child care. This career requires a bachelor's degree as a registered nurse, a minimum of one year of training in midwifery, and certification by the American College of Nurse Midwives.

Guidance Counselor

Guidance counselors help students with behavioral, social, and personal problems. They also advocate for at-risk students and for those with special needs. Guidance counselors in high schools assist students with college planning and job-search skills. A career as a guidance counselor usually requires a master's degree in school counseling as well as state certification.

Ultrasound Technician

Ultrasound technicians operate machines that use high frequency sound waves—ultrasound—to create images of internal parts of the body. The images help doctors diagnose diseases in various organs, including the heart and brain. Ultrasound is also used during pregnancy to determine the size and health of the fetus. To pursue this career, an associate's degree in ultrasound technology is typically required.

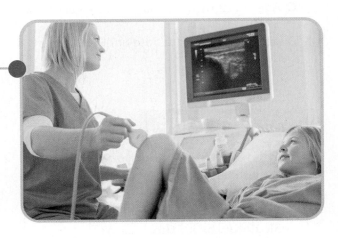

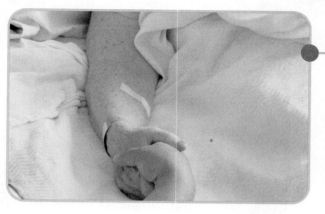

Hospice Caregiver

Hospice caregivers care for terminally ill patients. Their primary concern is to ensure that the patient is as pain-free as possible. Hospice caregivers also provide psychological and social support to help make the patient's final days comfortable. A career as a hospice caregiver requires a bachelor's degree in nursing or social work.

Career Focus

John Williams, Hospice Caregiver

What is the most important part of your job?

"People at the end of life, for the most part, know how they want their final days to play out. We help them by honoring their wishes. Most people want to be at home with their families when they die—most of our patients do just that."

How do you help your patients deal with their physical and emotional pain?

"Physical and emotional pain are often tied together. Managing pain with the most beneficial medication is only part of the picture. Actively listening to the patient and their loved ones is as important. Sometimes listening to what people are saying 'between the lines' and validating their fears and concerns can bring a large measure of relief."

Are the patients' families involved with their care?

"Family members are really on the 'front line' of care. We do a lot of teaching with family members, such as how to care for a bed-bound patient, how to follow a medication schedule, and anything else that can make the home environment more comfortable for their loved one. Ongoing teaching empowers family members and helps make the process of seeing their loved one approaching death less frightening."

Health and Careers

Careers in Human Development Research other careers in human development. Think about what stage of life and what skills you would like to focus on if you pursued a career in this field. Which career would best fit your preferences? Explain your choice. **WRITING**

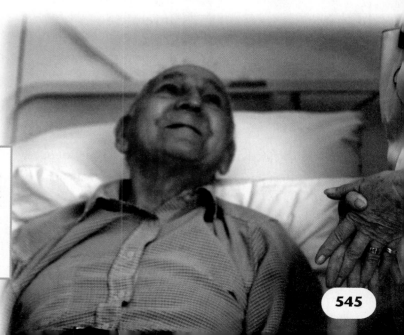

545

Infectious Diseases

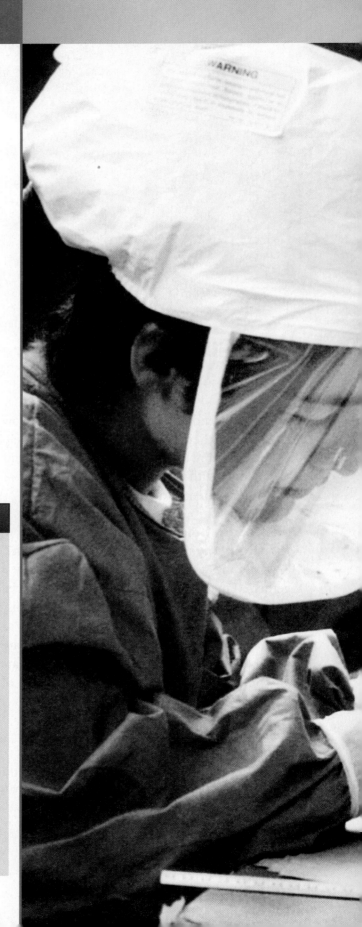

GO ONLINE PearsonSuccessNet.com

VIDEO 21

TEENS Talk

Protection From Infection

Preview **Activity**

What Behaviors Put You at Risk for Infectious Diseases?

Complete this activity before you watch the video.

1. With a partner, prepare a list of five behaviors that might put you at risk for an infectious disease.

2. On your own, rank the five behaviors from most risky to least risky.

3. Get together with your partner and compare your rankings. Discuss why you ranked the behaviors as you did.

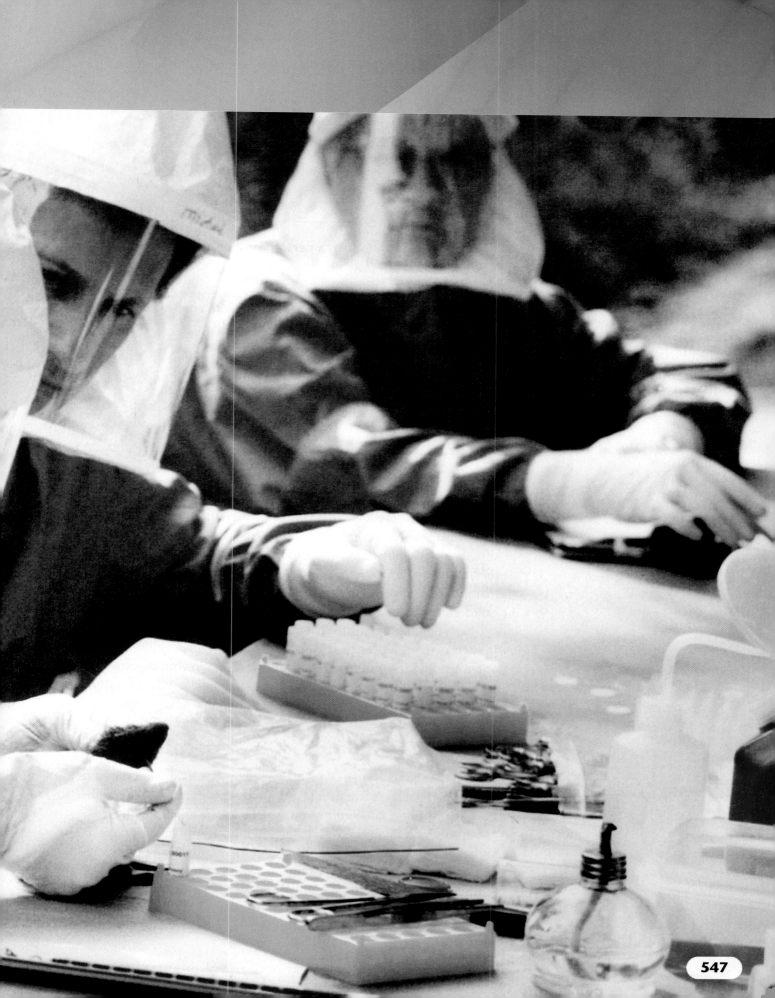

Understanding Infectious Diseases

Objectives

▶ **Identify** the causes of infectious diseases.

▶ **Describe** four ways in which infectious diseases are spread.

Vocabulary

- infectious disease
- microorganism
- pathogen
- bacteria
- toxin
- virus
- fungi
- protozoan

Warm-Up

Myth There isn't much a person can do to avoid spreading or catching a cold or the flu.

Fact About 80% of infectious diseases are spread by hand contact. Washing your hands with soap and water is a simple and effective way to prevent the spread of colds and the flu.

WRITING Do you think most teens wash their hands as much as they should? What do you think are some ways to encourage more frequent hand washing?

Causes of Infectious Diseases

For as long as there have been humans, there have been infectious diseases. Also known as communicable diseases, **infectious diseases** (in FEK shus) are caused by organisms or viruses that enter and multiply within the human body. Most disease-causing organisms and viruses are so small that they can be seen only through a microscope. Organisms this small are called **microorganisms** (my kroh AWR guh niz ums).

Not all microorganisms that enter and live in your body cause disease. In fact, many are present in your body all the time. Billions of microorganisms live in your mouth, on your skin, and in your digestive tract.

Microorganisms and viruses that cause disease are called **pathogens** (PATH uh junz). Pathogens do not belong in your body. **Pathogens can cause an infectious disease when they enter your body and multiply.** There are many kinds of pathogens. Some examples are shown in Figure 1.

Bacteria **Bacteria** (bak TEER ee uh) are simple, single-celled microorganisms. Bacteria live in air, soil, food, and in and on the bodies of plants and animals, including you. Most bacteria are not pathogens.

Some bacteria injure cells by giving off poisons called **toxins** (TAHK sinz). Certain bacteria that grow on food, for example, give off toxins that can cause food poisoning. A type of bacteria found in soil produces a toxin that causes tetanus (TET n us). These bacteria can also grow inside deep wounds. In the body, tetanus toxin damages the nervous system, causing uncontrollable muscle contractions, paralysis, and even death.

Viruses The smallest pathogens are **viruses.** They are about 100 times smaller than most bacteria. Unlike most bacteria, a virus can multiply only after entering a living cell. The virus then takes over the cell's reproductive mechanisms, resulting in cell damage or death.

Some viruses, such as those that cause the common cold, invade the cells of the respiratory tract. Other viruses invade other regions of the body. The virus that causes chickenpox, for example, invades skin cells.

Fungi Organisms such as yeasts, molds, and mushrooms are known as **fungi** (FUN jy). Fungi grow best in warm, dark, moist areas. Two examples of disease caused by fungi are athlete's foot and ringworm, a skin infection that forms a reddish circle on the skin.

Protozoans Single-celled organisms that are much larger and more complex than bacteria are known as **protozoans** (proh tuh ZOH unz). Protozoans have the ability to move through fluids in search of food. Malaria, a disease that is common in tropical areas, is caused by a protozoan that infects red blood cells, causing weakness and nausea. Amebic dysentery is caused by a different protozoan. Dysentery is characterized by stomach pain and diarrhea.

Other Pathogens Some infectious diseases are caused by animals such as mites, lice, and certain worms. For example, the trichina worm can live in the muscle tissue of some animals, such as pigs. If the meat of an infected animal is not thoroughly cooked, a person who eats the meat can become infected.

What types of pathogens do you think you commonly encounter?

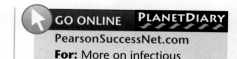
GO ONLINE PLANETDIARY
PearsonSuccessNet.com
For: More on infectious diseases

FIGURE 1 Different types of pathogens cause different infectious diseases. **Classifying** What type of pathogen causes tuberculosis? Polio?

Infectious Diseases by Type of Pathogen

Bacteria	Viruses	Fungi	Protozoans
strep throat, Lyme disease, anthrax, tuberculosis, cholera, diphtheria, pertussis, tetanus, typhoid fever, staph infection, **food poisoning** ▼	common cold, hepatitis, chickenpox, measles, mononucleosis, mumps, polio, rabies, rubella, West Nile virus, **influenza** ▼	athlete's foot, **ringworm** ▼	malaria, amebic dysentery, **African sleeping sickness** ▼

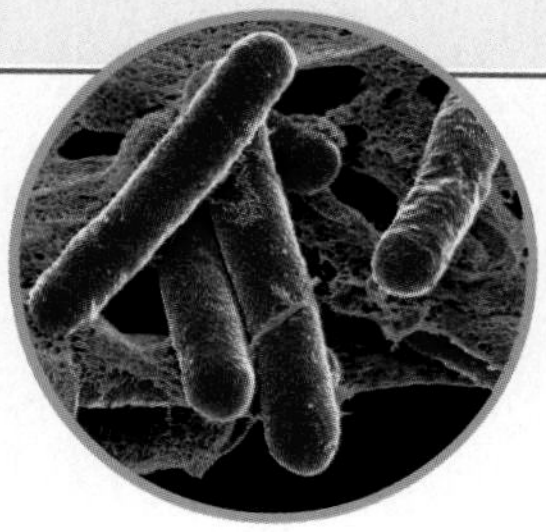

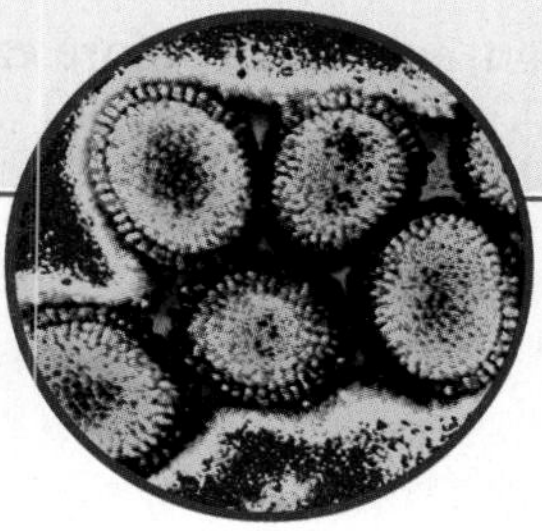

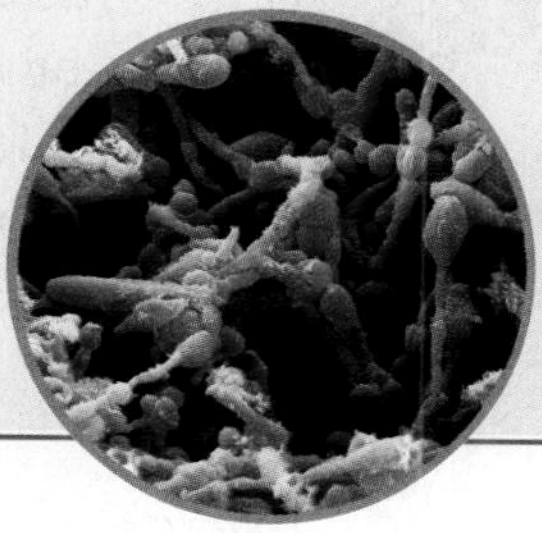

How Pathogens Are Spread

How does a person come in contact with pathogens? **Pathogens can spread through contact with an infected person; an infected animal; contaminated objects; or contaminated food, soil, or water.** The pathogens can then enter the body through breaks in the skin or through the moist linings of the eyes, ears, nose, mouth, or other openings.

Infected People Many infectious diseases are spread through some form of contact with a person who has the disease. The contact may be direct physical contact, such as shaking hands or kissing. If you kiss someone with a cold sore, for example, the cold sore viruses could enter your body. Sexually transmitted infections are transmitted through direct physical contact.

Infectious diseases can also spread through indirect contact. For example, if an infected person coughs or sneezes, you can inhale the pathogens in tiny droplets of moisture in the air. Influenza, measles, mumps, and chickenpox can spread by droplet inhalation. Contact with an infected person's blood, such as when needles are shared to inject illegal drugs, is another form of indirect contact that can spread disease.

Infected Animals Some infectious diseases are transmitted to humans through the bites of animals. For example, rabies, a deadly disease of the nervous system, can be transmitted by bites from infected dogs, bats, or raccoons. People contract malaria through mosquito bites. Lyme disease and Rocky Mountain spotted fever are spread through tick bites.

Contaminated Objects Some pathogens can survive for a period of time outside a person's body. These pathogens can be spread from person to person on objects such as doorknobs, eating utensils, towels, and needles used for body piercings and tattoos. If you drink from a cup used by an infected person, you can become infected as well. If you touch a desktop or money that has been sneezed or coughed on, or contaminated in some other way, you can become infected when you touch your eyes, your mouth, or your food. This is why it is always a good idea to wash your hands often, especially before eating.

Infected Person
Pathogens can be spread when you shake hands with someone.

Infected Animal
A raccoon can transmit pathogens when it bites you.

Contaminated Object
You can pick up pathogens from an object that an infected person has touched, coughed on, or sneezed on.

FIGURE 2 Infectious diseases can be spread in several different ways.

Contaminated Food, Soil, or Water   Some pathogens are naturally present in food and soil. One common type of food poisoning is caused by *Salmonella* bacteria, which can live in poultry and eggs. Another type of food poisoning is caused by *E. coli* bacteria, which can live in beef. It is important to cook foods thoroughly to kill these bacteria. It is also important to refrigerate food promptly to prevent the growth of harmful bacteria.

Other bacteria can live in foods that have been improperly canned. These bacteria cause botulism (BAHCH uh liz im), a very serious and often deadly type of food poisoning. The bacteria that cause tetanus are naturally present in soil. These bacteria can enter your body through cuts on your skin.

Sometimes, water and food become contaminated with pathogens from infected people. Drinking water contaminated by sewage is a common source of disease in many areas of the world. Cholera, for example, is a bacterial disease of the digestive system that causes severe diarrhea. Cholera outbreaks can occur after floods and earthquakes, when water and sanitation systems are disrupted.

Contaminated Food
Some foods have bacteria that can make you sick if the food isn't cooked or stored properly.

Connect to Your Life   List some things you can do to avoid contact with pathogens.

Section 1 Review

Key Ideas and Vocabulary

1. What is a **pathogen**? Name four types of pathogens.

2. How do pathogens cause infectious diseases?

3. What is a **virus**? How are viruses different from bacteria?

4. What are four ways that infectious diseases can spread?

Critical Thinking

5. Applying Concepts   If you were traveling to a country where mosquito-borne diseases were common, how would you protect yourself from getting infected?

Health at Home

Food Safety   Evaluate the way your family handles food at home. Do you wash fruits and vegetables thoroughly before eating or cooking them? Do you cook meats thoroughly? Do you promptly clean countertops and wash your hands after handling raw meat? Create a checklist to hang in your kitchen to remind yourself of practices that prevent the spread of infectious diseases. **WRITING**

6. Relating Cause and Effect   Why do you think that communities boil their drinking water after a water line break?

Defenses Against Disease

Objectives

▶ **Identify** the body's physical and chemical defenses against infectious disease.

▶ **Describe** the inflammatory response.

▶ **Summarize** how the immune system works.

▶ **Compare** passive and active immunity.

Vocabulary

- mucous membrane
- inflammation
- phagocyte
- immune system
- lymphocyte
- immunity
- T cell
- B cell
- antibody
- lymphatic system
- immunization
- vaccine

Warm-Up

Quick Quiz Complete each of these statements with *always, sometimes,* or *never.*

1 I __?__ wash my hands before meals.

2 When preparing fruits and vegetables, I __?__ wash them thoroughly.

3 I am __?__ careful to use only my own eating utensils, drinking cups, towels, toothbrush, and grooming items.

4 I __?__ cover my mouth when I cough or sneeze.

5 If I spend time in wooded areas, I __?__ wear insect repellent.

WRITING For each of your responses, explain how your behavior could affect your chances of getting or spreading an infectious disease.

Physical and Chemical Defenses

If pathogens are everywhere, why aren't you sick all the time? When you do get sick, what keeps the pathogens from multiplying until they take over your body? The answer to these questions is that your body has a number of defenses against infection. **Your body's first line of defense against infectious disease includes both physical and chemical defenses that prevent pathogens from entering your body.** Figure 3 shows the body's first line of defense.

Skin Your skin serves as both a physical and a chemical barrier against pathogens. The surface cells are hard and have no gaps between them. Sweat acts as a chemical barrier because it contains acids that kill many bacteria. Finally, old skin cells are shed constantly, and the pathogens on these cells are shed, too. In fact, microorganisms usually cannot get through your skin unless you have a cut, scrape, burn, or other injury.

 Connect to Your Life **Have you ever had a cut in your skin that became infected? Why did that happen?**

Mucous Membranes   The openings into your body, such as your mouth, eyes, and nose, are covered by protective linings called **mucous membranes** (MYOO kus). Mucous membranes secrete a liquid called mucus. The mucus traps many pathogens and washes them away. Mucus also contains chemicals that attack pathogens.

Cilia   Some of your body's mucous membranes are lined with tiny hair-like structures called cilia (SIL ee uh). Your air passages, for example, are lined with cilia. Together, cilia and mucus help trap and remove pathogens. When you inhale, dust and pathogens get trapped in the mucus of your air passages. The cilia beat rhythmically, moving the mucus up your windpipe toward your mouth and nose. When you cough, sneeze, or blow your nose, the pathogens are removed along with the mucus.

Saliva and Tears   Your saliva and tears can trap pathogens and wash them away. Like mucus, saliva and tears also contain chemicals that attack pathogens.

Digestive System   Chemicals in your digestive system, including acids in your stomach, kill many pathogens. In addition, the normal motions of the digestive system not only move food through your system but also move pathogens out. Finally, bacteria that normally live in your digestive system produce substances that can harm or kill invading bacteria.

FIGURE 3 Your body's physical and chemical defenses prevent many pathogens from entering your body and causing disease.

Your Body's Physical and Chemical Defenses

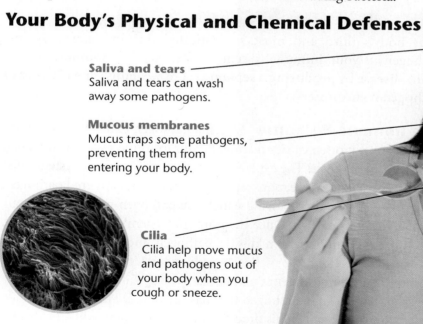

Saliva and tears
Saliva and tears can wash away some pathogens.

Mucous membranes
Mucus traps some pathogens, preventing them from entering your body.

Cilia
Cilia help move mucus and pathogens out of your body when you cough or sneeze.

Skin
Your skin is an effective barrier against many pathogens.

Stomach acid
When you swallow certain pathogens with food, water, or mucus, acids in your stomach can kill those pathogens.

Inflammation

If pathogens are able to get past the physical and chemical defenses and begin to injure cells, your body is ready with its second line of defense—**inflammation** (in fluh MAY shun). **Inflammation is your body's general response to all kinds of injury, from cuts and scrapes to internal damage.** Inflammation fights infection and promotes the healing process.

Phagocytes   Within seconds after your body is injured, the damaged cells release chemicals that cause blood vessels in the injured area to enlarge. Blood, other fluids, and white blood cells called **phagocytes** (FAG uh syts) leak out of the enlarged vessels. The phagocytes engulf and destroy pathogens. Meanwhile, the infected area becomes red, swollen, and sore—in other words, inflamed.

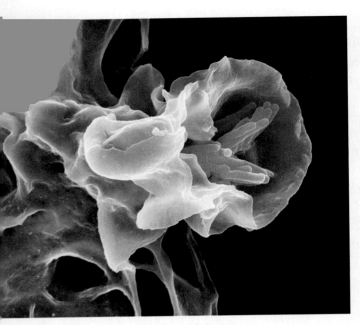

FIGURE 4   This micrograph shows a phagocyte (blue) attacking bacteria (pink). Phagocytes kill pathogens by engulfing and then digesting them.

Healing   Phagocytes also give off substances that cause healing to begin. The fluids, phagocytes, and dead cells that accumulate at the injury site often result in the formation of a thick, white liquid called pus. Eventually, the inflammation process heals the damage, and the inflammation subsides.

The Immune System

Your body's third and most sophisticated line of defense against pathogens is your **immune system** (ih MYOON). **The immune system fights disease by producing a separate set of weapons for each kind of pathogen it encounters.**

The Immune Response   When a pathogen enters your body for the first time, it often causes disease. If your immune system is working, why does this happen? The explanation is that your immune system must build up its arsenal of weapons against the newly encountered pathogen. This process takes time, during which the pathogen multiplies in your body and causes disease. Once the immune system's arsenal is built up, however, the immune system kills the pathogen, and your body gradually recovers. White blood cells called **lymphocytes** (LIM fuh syts) carry out most of the immune system's functions.

What happens if a pathogen that has previously attacked your body enters your body again? This time, your immune system will quickly recognize the pathogen and launch an immediate attack. When this happens, you are said to be immune to the disease. **Immunity** (ih MYOON ih tee) is your body's ability to destroy pathogens that it has previously encountered before the pathogens are able to cause disease.

Connect to Your Life   **When you experience inflammation, what blood cells are fighting the pathogens in your body?**

T Cells There are two types of lymphocytes—T lymphocytes, or T cells, and B lymphocytes, or B cells. **T cells** perform several functions.

▶ **Killer T cells** destroy any body cell that has been infected by a pathogen.

▶ **Helper T cells** produce chemicals that stimulate other T cells and B cells to fight off infection.

▶ **Suppressor T cells** produce chemicals that "turn off" other immune system cells when an infection has been brought under control.

T cells also help your immune system "remember" pathogens. This memory capacity, along with the memory capacity of B cells, is what causes you to develop immunity to a previously encountered pathogen.

B Cells The B lymphocytes, or **B cells,** produce antibodies. **Antibodies** (AN tih bahd eez) are proteins that attach to the surface of pathogens or to the toxins produced by pathogens. This binding action keeps the pathogen or toxin from harming the body. Each type of B cell produces antibodies that attack a specific pathogen or toxin. Figure 5 shows how T cells and B cells work together in destroying a pathogen.

Once an infection is overcome, your B cells stop producing antibodies, but they do not "forget" how to produce them. Those B cells continue to circulate in your body for years. They are ready to produce antibodies quickly if the same pathogen reenters your body. This memory capacity of B cells explains why you develop immunity to some diseases you've already had.

GO ONLINE

PearsonSuccessNet.com
For: More on the immune response

FIGURE 5 T cells and B cells work together when fighting pathogens, such as viruses.
Interpreting Diagrams Which type of lymphocyte destroys infected body cells?

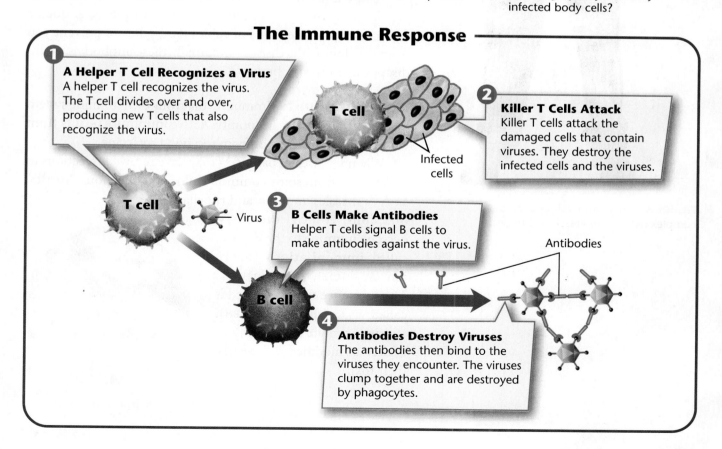

The Immune Response

1 A Helper T Cell Recognizes a Virus
A helper T cell recognizes the virus. The T cell divides over and over, producing new T cells that also recognize the virus.

T cell

2 Killer T Cells Attack
Killer T cells attack the damaged cells that contain viruses. They destroy the infected cells and the viruses.

Infected cells

T cell

Virus

3 B Cells Make Antibodies
Helper T cells signal B cells to make antibodies against the virus.

Antibodies

B cell

4 Antibodies Destroy Viruses
The antibodies then bind to the viruses they encounter. The viruses clump together and are destroyed by phagocytes.

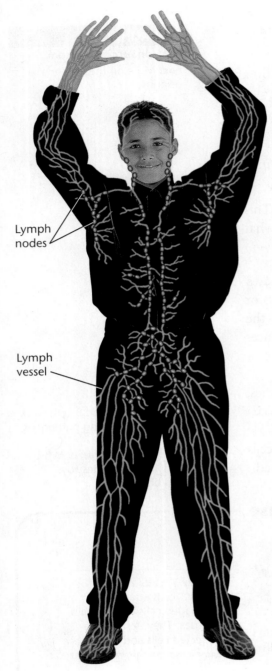

Lymph nodes

Lymph vessel

FIGURE 6 Your lymphatic system is a complex network of vessels and nodes.

The Lymphatic System Much of your immune system is contained within your lymphatic system. The **lymphatic system** (lim FAT ik) is a network of vessels that collects fluid from your tissues and returns it to the bloodstream. The fluid flowing through the lymphatic system is called lymph (limf).

As shown in Figure 6, the lymphatic vessels have hundreds of small stations, called lymph nodes. Each lymph node acts as a sort of filter. Phagocytes and lymphocytes are present in the lymph nodes and attack pathogens as they pass through.

Passive and Active Immunity

There are two types of immunity—passive and active. Both types are important in protecting your body against infections.

Passive Immunity People can develop immunity if they are given antibodies against a pathogen. **Immunity acquired by receiving antibodies from a source other than one's own immune system is called passive immunity.** This type of immunity is temporary, not lifelong. It occurs naturally in babies, who receive antibodies from their mothers before birth. After birth, antibodies also pass to an infant in the mother's breast milk. These antibodies protect newborns before their own immune systems have fully developed.

Passive immunity also can be artificially acquired. For example, suppose you were bitten by a dog with rabies. A doctor would give you injections of rabies antibodies to prevent you from developing the disease. Eventually these antibodies would disappear from your body.

Active Immunity Immunity that your own immune system creates is called active immunity. **Active immunity results from either having a disease or from receiving a vaccine.**

When you were a baby, you may have received injections to protect you from some common childhood infectious diseases, such as measles, mumps, and rubella. These injections, which caused you to become immune to the disease, are called **immunizations** (im yuh nih ZAY shunz), or vaccinations. The substance that is injected is called a **vaccine** (vak SEEN). Vaccines contain small amounts of dead or modified pathogens or their toxins.

▲ **Immunization**

Recommended Immunizations

Birth–4 months	6 months–18 months	4 years–12 years
• Diphtheria, Tetanus, Pertussis	• Diphtheria, Tetanus, Pertussis	• Diphtheria, Tetanus, Pertussis
• *Haemophilus influenzae* type b	• *Haemophilus influenzae* type b	• Polio
• Pneumococcal conjugate	• Pneumococcal conjugate	• Measles, Mumps, Rubella
• Hepatitis B	• Hepatitis A and B	• Meningococcal
• Polio	• Polio	• HPV
	• Varicella	
	• Influenza	
	• Measles, Mumps, Rubella	

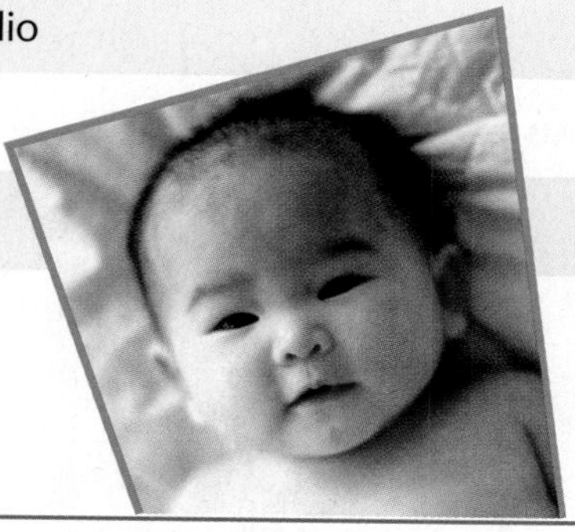

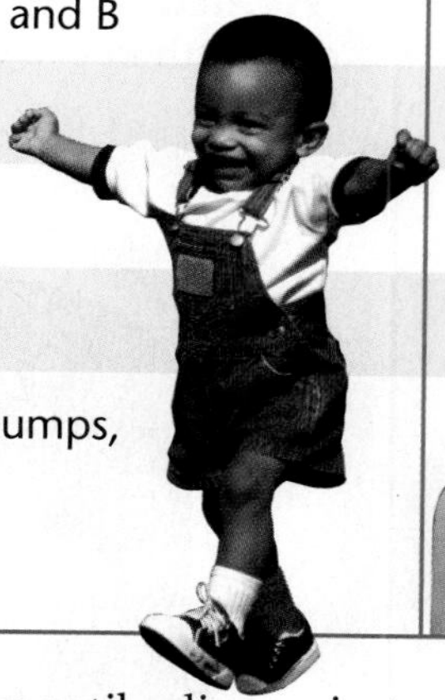

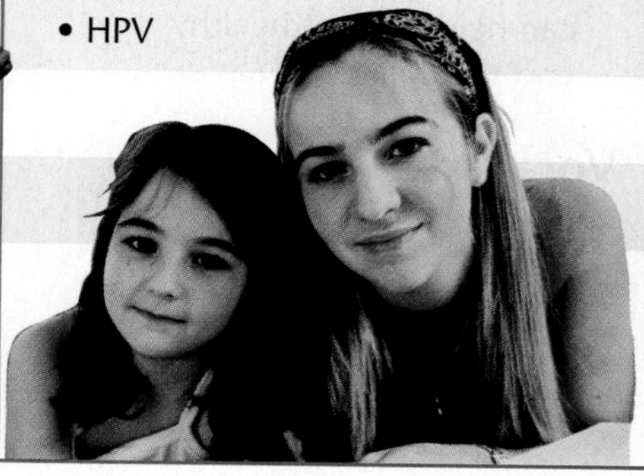

A vaccine causes your immune system to produce antibodies against the pathogen, as if you had actually been infected. You develop immunity without having to experience the disease. After a few years, you may receive a booster dose of some vaccines to "remind" your immune system to maintain your immunity.

Many people need additional immunizations because of the work they do, the places to which they travel, or their exposure to an unusual pathogen. Other people may need to be immunized because of risk factors such as age or poor health. Influenza vaccines, for example, are given to elderly people to protect them from the flu.

FIGURE 7 Different immunizations are given at different ages. If you missed any of the recommended immunizations, talk to your doctor about catch-up vaccines.

Section 2 Review

Key Ideas and Vocabulary

1. Name five physical and chemical defenses that prevent pathogens from entering your body.

2. How does the inflammation process fight an infection in the body?

3. What is a **lymphocyte**?

4. How do the T cells and B cells of your immune system respond to pathogens?

5. How are passive immunity and active immunity similar? How are they different?

Health at School

Immunizations Find out which immunizations are required in order for students to be allowed to attend your school. Your school nurse should have this information. Write a paragraph summarizing your findings. Why do you think these immunizations are required? **WRITING**

Critical Thinking

6. Applying Concepts Name two physical defenses that would protect your body against pathogens that might be found in a swimming pool.

7. Classifying What type of immunity—passive or active—does a polio vaccine trigger? Explain.

Common Infectious Diseases

Objectives

▶ **Identify** some diseases caused by bacteria and by viruses.

▶ **Describe** behaviors that can help you get healthy and stay healthy.

Vocabulary

• antibiotic

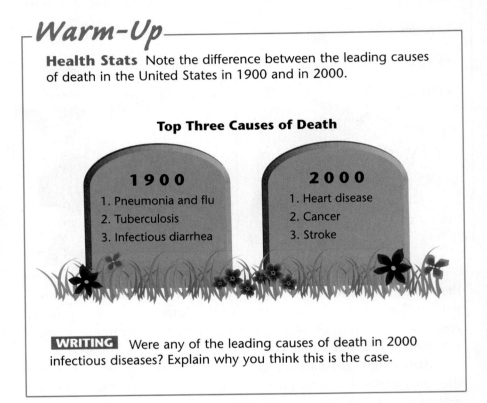

Warm-Up

Health Stats Note the difference between the leading causes of death in the United States in 1900 and in 2000.

Top Three Causes of Death

1900
1. Pneumonia and flu
2. Tuberculosis
3. Infectious diarrhea

2000
1. Heart disease
2. Cancer
3. Stroke

WRITING Were any of the leading causes of death in 2000 infectious diseases? Explain why you think this is the case.

Bacterial Diseases

Despite all your body's defenses, occasionally pathogens are able to enter your body and cause disease. In most cases, your immune system fights the infection and you gradually recover. There are thousands of infectious diseases, and over 40 kinds commonly occur in the United States. **Four infectious diseases caused by bacteria are strep throat, Lyme disease, meningitis, and tuberculosis.**

Strep Throat A bacterial disease that is common among teens is strep throat. "Strep" is short for *Streptococcus,* the bacterium that causes the disease. Strep bacteria, which are usually found in the nose and throat, can be spread by contact with mucus from an infected person. Symptoms include sore throat, swollen lymph nodes on the sides of the neck, headache, and fever. A fever is a body temperature above 98.6°F and usually indicates that your body is fighting an infection. A doctor can diagnose strep throat by swabbing the back of your throat and identifying the bacteria in the sample.

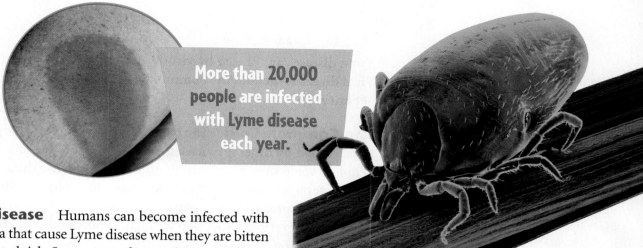

More than 20,000 people are infected with Lyme disease each year.

FIGURE 8 The deer tick can carry the bacteria that cause Lyme disease. One of the symptoms of Lyme disease is a bull's eye-shaped rash that forms at the site of the bite.

Lyme Disease Humans can become infected with the bacteria that cause Lyme disease when they are bitten by an infected tick. Symptoms of Lyme disease include a red rash at the site of the tick bite, fever, chills, and body aches. The best way to protect yourself from Lyme disease is by avoiding tick bites. In wooded areas, wear long-sleeved shirts and long pants, and tuck your pants into your socks.

Bacterial Meningitis An infection of the fluid in the spinal cord and the fluid that surrounds the brain is called meningitis. Symptoms of meningitis include high fever, headache, vomiting, and a stiff neck. Anyone who experiences these symptoms should seek medical attention immediately. There are two types of meningitis—one is caused by bacteria, the other by a virus. Bacterial meningitis tends to be more serious than the viral kind. Early treatment of bacterial meningitis is critical to prevent serious illness and death.

Tuberculosis A highly contagious bacterial infection of the lungs is tuberculosis (too bur kyuh LOH sis), or TB. It is transmitted when droplets from an infected person's cough or sneeze are inhaled. Symptoms, which include fatigue, weight loss, a mild fever, and a constant cough, may not show up for many years after the initial infection. One-third of the world's population is infected with TB, and nearly two million people die of TB each year.

Treating Bacterial Diseases If your doctor determines that you have a bacterial disease, he or she may treat your infection with an **antibiotic** (an tih by AHT ik), a drug that inhibits or kills bacteria. An antibiotic is a prescription medicine—a medicine that is available only with a written order from a qualified healthcare professional.

Using antibiotics exactly as they are prescribed is very important to prevent bacteria from developing resistance to the medicine. Antibiotic resistance can result if you don't finish your prescription and some of the bacterial pathogens in your body survive. For instance, some TB bacteria have developed antibiotic resistance, making them very difficult to treat.

Connect to Your Life When was the last time you took an antibiotic? What was it for?

Viral Diseases

Some diseases are caused by viruses that enter the body and multiply. **Viral diseases include the common cold, influenza, pneumonia, and hepatitis.**

The Common Cold   The common cold is really a group of symptoms caused by different viruses. Soon after exposure to a cold virus, people develop sneezing, sore throats, runny noses, coughing, chest congestion, fever, headaches, and muscle aches. Most colds last three to seven days. Colds spread when a person touches a contaminated object or inhales droplets from a sneeze or a cough. Unfortunately, there is no cure for the common cold.

Influenza   The flu, or influenza, is a common viral infection of the upper respiratory system. Like the common cold, influenza is spread by airborne droplets and contact with contaminated objects. Typical symptoms are high fever, sore throat, headache, and a cough. When you have the flu, you will most likely go through the stages shown in Figure 9.

Influenza viruses can cause more serious illness than cold viruses, especially in infants, the elderly, and people with heart and lung diseases. During an average year in the United States, between 3,000 and 49,000 people die of the flu. Some types of influenza can be prevented by an immunization, commonly called a "flu shot." An annual flu shot is especially important for children aged 6 months to 4 years and adults aged 50 and over. Sometimes, antiviral medications can help reduce the severity of the illness for those already infected. Currently, such medications are given only to groups of people at high risk for complications from influenza.

Pneumonia   In people who are elderly, or who have heart disease or breathing problems, flu may develop into pneumonia (noo MOHN yuh), a serious infection of the lungs. Many people die each year from pneumonia, which can be caused by viruses, bacteria, or even fungi.

FIGURE 9   The flu usually passes through five stages.
Predicting If you went to school during the fourth or fifth day of your illness, would you be likely to infect others? Explain.

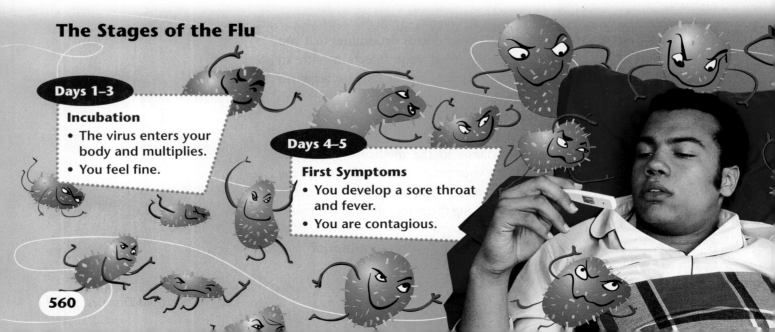

The Stages of the Flu

Days 1–3

Incubation
- The virus enters your body and multiplies.
- You feel fine.

Days 4–5

First Symptoms
- You develop a sore throat and fever.
- You are contagious.

Hepatitis A group of viruses that infect the liver can cause hepatitis (hep uh TY tis), or inflammation of the liver. Because the liver is important to so many bodily functions, hepatitis is a serious disease. Symptoms of hepatitis include fever, nausea, pain in the abdomen, and jaundice (JAWN dis), or yellowing of the skin. People with hepatitis need medical care. The most common types of hepatitis are identified as A, B, or C.

▶ **Hepatitis A** is transmitted in human wastes and in contaminated water and food. Illness begins about four weeks after exposure, and recovery takes several weeks. A vaccine for hepatitis A can effectively prevent the disease.

▶ **Hepatitis B** is more severe than type A. The virus can be transmitted in blood or during sexual contact. It can also be transmitted during tattooing or body piercing if tools are not properly sterilized. Over a million Americans carry hepatitis B, for which there is a vaccine.

▶ **Hepatitis C** is also more severe than type A. Like hepatitis B, it can be transmitted in blood, during sexual contact, or during tattooing or body piercing. Hepatitis C is the number one reason for liver transplants in the United States. Approximately three million Americans carry hepatitis C.

Treating Viral Diseases In most cases, there is no particular medicine that can cure a viral infection. Antibiotics, for instance, are only effective against bacteria—not viruses. Although antiviral medications may shorten the length of infection in some cases, the best treatments for viral infections are rest, a well-balanced diet, and plenty of fluids. In addition, many over-the-counter medicines—those available without a prescription—can treat the symptoms of viral infections. They may make you feel better, but they do not cure the infection.

Connect to Your Life When you have a cold, how do you treat your illness?

GO ONLINE

PearsonSuccessNet.com
For: More on infectious diseases

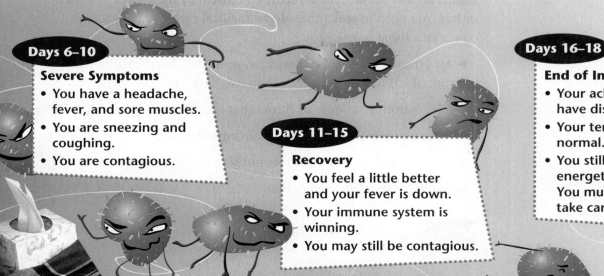

Days 6–10

Severe Symptoms
- You have a headache, fever, and sore muscles.
- You are sneezing and coughing.
- You are contagious.

Days 11–15

Recovery
- You feel a little better and your fever is down.
- Your immune system is winning.
- You may still be contagious.

Days 16–18

End of Infection
- Your aches and pains have disappeared.
- Your temperature is normal.
- You still do not feel as energetic as usual. You must continue to take care of yourself.

Media Wise

Evaluating Antibacterial Products

Products claiming to rid your home of pathogens seem to be everywhere. Do you think these products stand up to their claims? Evaluate products claiming to have antibacterial action using this questionnaire.

Does the product claim to inhibit or destroy all pathogens?	Yes No
Does the product seem to be using scare tactics to get you to buy it?	Yes No
Does the product use non-scientific words, such as "germs" or "bugs"?	Yes No
Do the benefits sound too good to be true?	Yes No
Are the ingredients identical to those in non-antibacterial products?	Yes No

A "Yes" answer to one or more questions indicates that the product may not live up to its claims.

Activity Choose a product from a local store that claims to be antibacterial. Devise an experiment to test the effectiveness of the product.
WRITING

Getting Healthy, Staying Healthy

Infectious diseases are unpleasant at best, but they are part of life. When you do get sick, you can help your body recover by going to bed and resting. This treatment and well-balanced meals are all that you need to recover from most mild infections. However, what if you have a more serious infection? Do you know when to see a doctor?

When to Seek Medical Care If you are worried about your health for any reason, see a doctor and discuss your concerns with him or her. You need to seek professional medical care if you have any of the conditions listed below:

► An extremely sore throat, earache, vomiting, diarrhea, or a temperature of 101°F that lasts more than two days

► Mucus from your nose or throat that is thick and yellowish green

► Difficulty breathing, or severe pain anywhere

► A cut, scrape, or sore that does not seem to be healing as it should

► An illness that lasts longer than usual

Connect to Your Life When was the last time you had to see a doctor because you weren't feeling well?

Preventing Infectious Diseases You can protect yourself from infectious diseases in three ways: avoiding contact with pathogens, making sure that your immunizations are current, and choosing healthful behaviors. But as you know, it is impossible to avoid all pathogens, and immunizations are not available for all infectious diseases. However, choosing healthful behaviors—the best long-term strategy for preventing disease—is something you can always do.

Here are some healthful behaviors you should practice to help you avoid disease.

▶ Wash your hands several times a day, especially before eating and after using the bathroom (or use hand sanitizer if running water is not available).

▶ Do not share items that can transfer pathogens, such as towels, eating utensils, cups, or hairbrushes.

▶ Cook and store foods properly. Meats should be cooked thoroughly. Keep hot foods hot, and cold foods cold.

▶ Avoid close contact with people who are ill. Stay home when you are not feeling well.

▶ Sneeze into your sleeve or elbow to prevent spraying germs onto others.

▶ Learn to manage stress in healthful ways, and get at least eight hours of sleep each night.

▶ Eat well-balanced meals, and do not skip meals. Exercise regularly, at least three or more times a week.

▶ Avoid unhealthful substances, such as tobacco, alcohol, and illegal drugs.

FIGURE 10 Never share your toothbrush with a friend.

Section 3 Review

Key Ideas and Vocabulary

1. List four bacterial diseases.

2. What is an **antibiotic**? What type of pathogen does it work against?

3. List four viral diseases. Describe how a mild viral infection might be treated.

4. Describe five symptoms that should prompt you to seek medical care.

5. Identify three healthful behaviors that can help you avoid infectious diseases.

Health at School

Good Hygiene Count the number of times you wash your hands at school in one day. Do you wash your hands before eating lunch? Where are sinks with soap and paper towels located? Create a poster to remind students of the importance of hand washing. **WRITING**

Critical Thinking

6. Evaluating If you had the flu, how would you try to reduce the chances of spreading it to other members of your family?

7. Relating Cause and Effect Children usually have more infectious diseases per year than adults. Why do you think this is so?

BUILDING HEALTH SKILLS

Practicing Healthful Behaviors

Using Medicines Correctly

Felicia got home from her after-school job, ate dinner, and sat down to study. All of a sudden, she realized she had forgotten to take an antibiotic tablet earlier that day. Her doctor had prescribed the antibiotic for her strep throat. Should Felicia take two tablets now to make up for the one she missed? Or should she take just one tablet now?

To be safe and effective, medicines must be used according to their directions. When should you use a medicine, and how can you make sure that you use it correctly? These guidelines will help you decide.

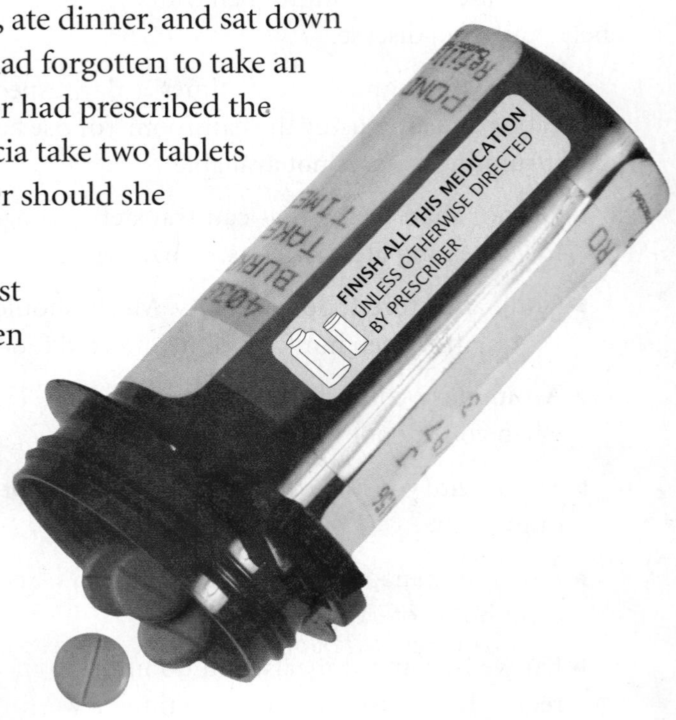
FINISH ALL THIS MEDICATION
UNLESS OTHERWISE DIRECTED
BY PRESCRIBER

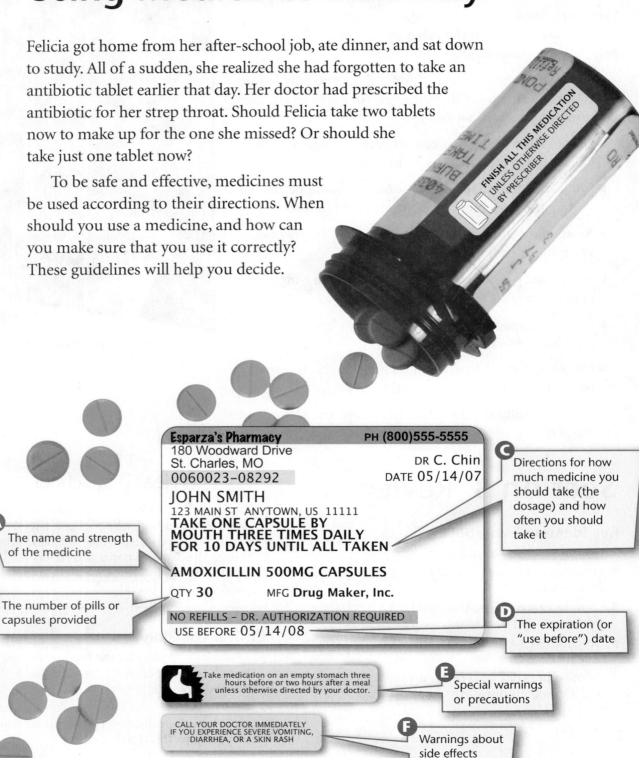

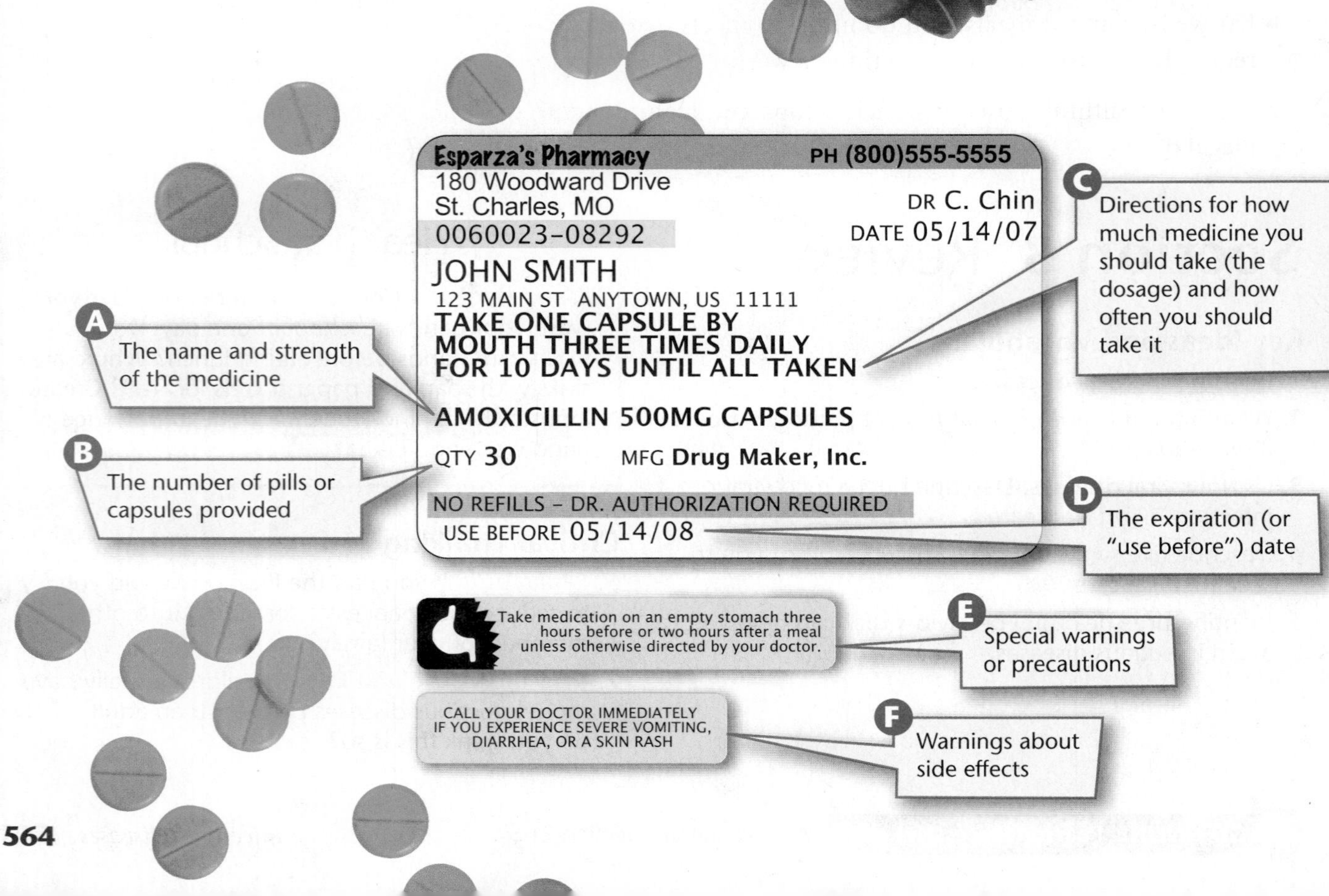
Esparza's Pharmacy
PH (800)555-5555
180 Woodward Drive
St. Charles, MO
DR C. Chin
0060023-08292
DATE 05/14/07
JOHN SMITH
123 MAIN ST ANYTOWN, US 11111
TAKE ONE CAPSULE BY MOUTH THREE TIMES DAILY FOR 10 DAYS UNTIL ALL TAKEN
AMOXICILLIN 500MG CAPSULES
QTY 30
MFG Drug Maker, Inc.
NO REFILLS – DR. AUTHORIZATION REQUIRED
USE BEFORE 05/14/08
Take medication on an empty stomach three hours before or two hours after a meal unless otherwise directed by your doctor.
CALL YOUR DOCTOR IMMEDIATELY IF YOU EXPERIENCE SEVERE VOMITING, DIARRHEA, OR A SKIN RASH
A The name and strength of the medicine
B The number of pills or capsules provided
C Directions for how much medicine you should take (the dosage) and how often you should take it
D The expiration (or "use before") date
E Special warnings or precautions
F Warnings about side effects

① Read all the information on the label and follow the directions.

▶ Be sure to take your medicine as prescribed. Keep a record of the times when you take your medicine.

▶ If you forget to take your medicine at a scheduled time, do not take a double dose to try to make up for it. Take a single dose and get back on the original schedule. If you miss more than one dose, consult with your doctor or pharmacist.

▶ With an antibiotic, continue taking it until you have used all of it. If you do not finish the entire prescription, your infection may return.

② Only take medicines prescribed for you.

Medicines are prescribed according to factors that are specific to each person, such as age, weight, health conditions, and other medicines being taken. It is dangerous to use medicines prescribed for another person.

③ Call your doctor if a medicine causes serious side effects.

All medicines have side effects, some more serious than others. Side effects might include headache, dizziness, drowsiness, and nausea. Common allergic reactions to medicines include a skin rash, runny nose, breathing difficulties, and rapid heartbeat. If you develop serious side effects, contact your doctor or a hospital emergency room immediately.

④ Never combine medicines without checking with your doctor.

Sometimes it is necessary to use different medicines at the same time to treat a single problem or to treat several problems. Not all medicines, however, can be used in combination with each other. Before you start using more than one medicine at a time, check with your doctor or pharmacist.

⑤ Never drink alcohol while taking medicines.

Alcohol and medicines can be a dangerous, or even deadly, combination. Anyone taking medicines should avoid alcohol.

⑥ Store medicines according to the label's instructions.

▶ Keep medicines in their original containers so that their directions for use, precautions, and expiration dates are always known. Keep medicines out of the reach of children.

▶ Many medicines lose their effectiveness over time and should not be used after their expiration date. Dispose of medicines properly so they are kept away from children and animals.

Practice the Skill

1. Study the prescription medicine label on the facing page and answer these questions.
   - What medicine has been prescribed?
   - What is the dosage?
   - How often should the person take the medicine?
   - Should this medicine be taken with meals?
   - Are there specific foods or fluids that should not be taken with this medicine?
   - Should the person stop taking the medicine as soon as symptoms of the illness disappear?

2. At your local drugstore, read the label of an over-the-counter medicine, such as aspirin or a cold-relief medicine. What is the medicine used for? What warnings or cautions are on the label? What is the recommended dosage? Under what conditions should you consult a doctor?

Emerging Infectious Diseases

Objectives
▶ **Define** the term *emerging disease.*
▶ **Identify** five reasons why diseases emerge.

Vocabulary
• epidemic
• emerging disease

Warm-Up

Health Stats The map shows how dengue fever, a viral disease carried by mosquitoes, has spread since 1960.

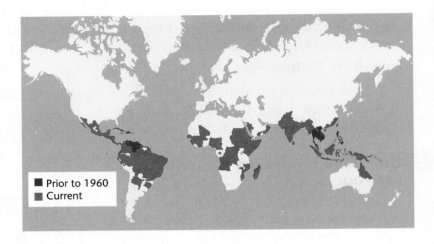

■ Prior to 1960
■ Current

WRITING Should the United States be concerned about dengue fever? Explain.

What Is an Emerging Disease?

In the winter of 1918, just as World War I was coming to an end, an influenza virus spread around the globe. Unlike previous flu viruses, this one was especially deadly. More than 20 million people died from the flu between 1918 and 1919, including almost 700,000 Americans.

The deadly flu outbreak of 1918 is an example of an epidemic. An **epidemic** (ep uh DEM ik) is an unusually high occurrence of a disease in a certain place during a certain time period. When an epidemic affects many areas of the world, as the 1918 flu outbreak did, it is sometimes called a *pandemic.*

You have probably heard news reports about epidemics of various diseases occurring today. Some of the diseases are known as **emerging diseases.** **An emerging disease is an infectious disease that has become increasingly common in humans within the last 20 years or threatens to become more common in the near future.** Figure 11 describes some emerging diseases that scientists are currently monitoring around the world.

Why Do Diseases Emerge?

Emerging diseases are a reminder that the human immune system is in a never-ending battle with pathogens. No matter how many medicines or vaccines are developed, certain pathogens will cause disease anyway.

A number of different factors are responsible for emerging diseases around the world. **Diseases can emerge when humans come into contact with infected animals; pathogens become resistant to existing drugs; or people lack appropriate immunizations. In addition, the increased frequency of international travel and a global food supply can enable emerging diseases to spread very quickly.**

Contact With Infected Animals Some diseases that are common in animals can spread to humans. For example, avian flu is caused by a virus that infects certain birds. There have been recent cases in Asia in which people have become sick after being exposed to infected birds. Even more worrisome is that a high percentage of those who got sick died. Some scientists fear that another deadly flu epidemic could result if the virus takes on a form that can spread easily between people.

GO ONLINE

PearsonSuccessNet.com
For: More on modern epidemics

FIGURE 11 Several viral diseases threaten to become more common. There are no specific treatments for these diseases.

Viral Diseases to Watch

Disease	How Spread	Where	Symptoms	Prevention
Avian flu	Close contact with an infected bird; person-to-person transmission may become possible	Asia	Severe, flu-like symptoms	Vaccines in development; avoiding close contact with birds and poultry farms
SARS (Severe Acute Respiratory Syndrome)	Droplet inhalation from an infected person's cough or sneeze	Currently contained in Asia	High fever, headache, body aches, dry cough, pneumonia	Frequent hand washing
Yellow fever	Bite from an infected mosquito	Africa, South America, Caribbean islands	Fever, muscle pain, headache, nausea, jaundice	Vaccine; avoiding mosquito bites; mosquito control
Dengue fever	Bite from an infected mosquito	Widespread throughout many tropical and sub-tropical regions (see map on facing page)	High fever, severe headache, joint and muscle pain, vomiting	Vaccines in development; avoiding mosquito bites; mosquito control
West Nile virus	Bite from an infected mosquito	United States, Africa, Australia, Europe, the Middle East, and West Asia	Fever, headache, body aches, nausea, vomiting, muscle weakness, vision loss	Avoiding mosquito bites; mosquito control

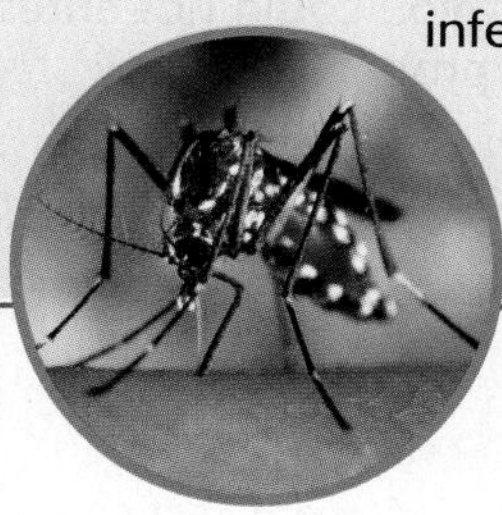

◀ **West Nile mosquito**

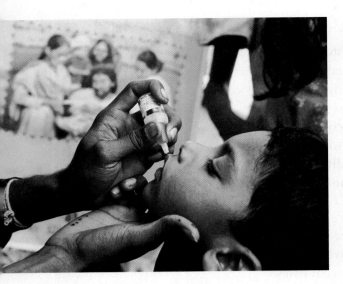

Drug Resistance Some diseases are caused by pathogens that can mutate, or change, over time. Sometimes these mutations result in a strain, or type, of pathogen that no longer responds to medicine. As mentioned earlier, some strains of tuberculosis are antibiotic resistant. Thus, people who become infected with a resistant strain cannot be treated with existing antibiotics and can spread the disease to others.

Lack of Immunization Diseases that were common many years ago can pose a threat again if people don't get the proper immunizations. For example, polio was nearly eliminated 50 years ago by an effective vaccine. But the polio virus remains a threat in several Asian and African countries because many people in those countries have not received the vaccine.

FIGURE 12 Health officials in India hope to eradicate polio by giving an oral vaccine to all children under age five.

International Travel You may have heard the term *globalization*. That term refers to the fact that people around the world are no longer geographically isolated from each other. In a 12-hour plane ride, you could be on the other side of the world. Not only can people travel much more easily, but so can any pathogens that live in their bodies. This is one reason that globalization is a concern when disease outbreaks occur. World travelers could spread the pathogen around the world in a short amount of time.

Global Food Supply Food also travels all over the world. For example, you may have eaten an apple from China or a mango from Mexico. If a pathogen is present in a food product, it can spread quickly.

An infectious disease known as mad cow disease caused a global food scare when contaminated beef was distributed to several countries. A number of people who ate the beef became very sick. Cattle and meat are closely monitored to make sure that mad cow disease does not enter the global food supply again.

Section 4 Review

Key Ideas and Vocabulary

1. What is an **epidemic**?
2. Explain what is meant by the term *emerging disease*. Give an example of an emerging disease.
3. List five factors that contribute to the development of emerging diseases.

Critical Thinking

4. **Relating Cause and Effect** Federal agencies closely monitor meats and produce that are brought into the United States from other countries. Why is this important?

Health and Community

Flu Season Find out where in your community flu shots are offered. For what groups of people are the flu shots recommended? Create an announcement for your local newspaper detailing the information about flu shots for people in your community. **WRITING**

5. **Predicting** If you were traveling from a country with high rates of yellow fever, you could not enter some other countries without proof of a yellow fever vaccination. Predict what might happen if vaccinations were not required.

Chapter 21
At a Glance

VIDEO

TEENS Talk 🔘

Protection From Infection According to the video, what are three ways to protect yourself from infectious diseases?

Section 1   Understanding Infectious Diseases

Key Ideas

▶ Pathogens can cause an infectious disease when they enter your body and multiply.

▶ Pathogens can spread through contact with an infected person; an infected animal; contaminated objects; or contaminated food, soil, or water.

Vocabulary
- infectious disease (548)
- microorganism (548)
- pathogen (548)
- bacteria (548) • toxin (548)
- virus (549) • fungi (549)
- protozoan (549)

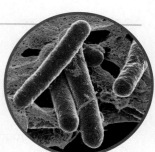

Section 2   Defenses Against Disease

Key Ideas

▶ Your body's first line of defense against infectious disease includes both physical and chemical defenses that prevent pathogens from entering your body.

▶ Inflammation is your body's general response to all kinds of injury.

▶ The immune system fights disease by producing a separate set of weapons for each kind of pathogen it encounters.

▶ Passive immunity is acquired by receiving antibodies from oustide your own immune system. Active immunity results from having a disease or from receiving a vaccine.

Vocabulary
- mucous membrane (553) • inflammation (554)
- phagocyte (554) • immune system (554)
- lymphocyte (554) • immunity (554) • T cell (555)
- B cell (555) • antibody (555) • lymphatic system (556)
- immunization (556) • vaccine (556)

Section 3   Common Infectious Diseases

Key Ideas

▶ Bacterial diseases include strep throat, Lyme disease, meningitis, and tuberculosis.

▶ Viral diseases include the common cold, influenza, pneumonia, and hepatitis.

▶ You can protect yourself from infectious diseases in three ways: avoiding contact with pathogens, making sure that your immunizations are current, and choosing healthful behaviors.

Vocabulary
- antibiotic (559)

Section 4   Emerging Infectious Diseases

Key Ideas

▶ An emerging disease is an infectious disease that has recently become more common or could become more common in the near future.

▶ Diseases can emerge when humans come into contact with infected animals; pathogens become drug-resistant; or people lack immunizations.

▶ International travel and a global food supply also can enable emerging diseases to spread.

Vocabulary
- epidemic (566) • emerging disease (566)

Chapter 21 Review

GO ONLINE

PearsonSuccessNet.com

For: Chapter 21 review activity

Reviewing Key Ideas

Section 1

1. Infectious diseases are caused by
   a. phagocytes. b. cilia.
   c. pathogens. d. vaccines.

2. Give an example of a disease caused by a protozoan.

3. Why is it not a good idea to share a drinking glass with someone?

4. **Critical Thinking** Do you think that all microorganisms are pathogens? Explain your answer.

Section 2

5. White blood cells that carry out most of the immune system's functions are called
   a. antibodies. b. lymphocytes.
   c. vaccines. d. antibiotics.

6. What role do phagocytes play in inflammation?

7. What types of cells produce antibodies?

8. Explain how a vaccine can make you immune to a particular infectious disease.

9. **Critical Thinking** How does your immune system "remember" a particular pathogen?

10. **Critical Thinking** Multiple sclerosis is a disease in which T cells attack parts of the central nervous system. How are these T cells acting differently from normal T cells?

Section 3

11. Antibiotics are usually prescribed for diseases caused by
    a. viruses. b. protozoans.
    c. fungi. d. bacteria.

12. What part of the body does hepatitis affect? What type of pathogen causes hepatitis?

13. Why is it important to make sure that your immunizations are current?

14. **Critical Thinking** More people get the flu during the winter months than at any other time of year. Why do you think this is true?

Section 4

15. An epidemic refers to a disease that
    a. affects very   b. affects many people
       few people.   in one area.
    c. is caused by   d. doesn't spread.
       bacteria.

16. Explain how antibiotic resistance could lead to a bacterial disease epidemic.

17. **Critical Thinking** During the SARS outbreak of 2003, the World Health Organization issued a warning against traveling to countries where SARS was present. Explain why this warning was issued.

Building Health Skills

18. **Practicing Healthful Behaviors** Sometimes, over-the-counter medicines that you might take for a cold or the flu can make you feel well enough to go about your usual routine even though your body is still fighting the infection. Why might this be a problem?

19. **Analyzing Risks and Benefits** Matt's doctor prescribed an antibiotic for his skin infection. One of his friends has a similar looking sore on his arm. Should Matt share his medicine with his friend? Why or why not?

20. **Accessing Information** A friend is going to the pharmacy to pick up a prescription medicine. Write down a list of questions that she should ask the pharmacist about the medicine. **WRITING**

21. **Setting Goals** Make a list of things you do that put you at risk for infectious diseases. Choose two items from your list and set goals for lessening your risk. Monitor your behavior over the next week to see how you did.

Health and Community

Prevention Poster Evaluate the risk of getting Lyme disease or West Nile virus in your community. Prepare a poster that warns people about the risk and offers tips about how to avoid getting bitten by ticks or mosquitoes. **WRITING**

Standardized Test Prep

Math Practice

The graph below compares the amount of time it takes the immune system to produce antibodies upon first exposure to a pathogen and upon second exposure to the same pathogen. Use the graph to answer Questions 22–25.

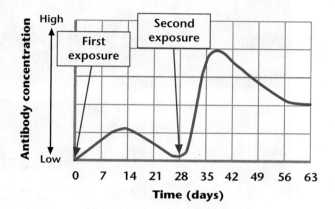

22. The first exposure to the pathogen generated
   - **A** more antibodies than the second exposure.
   - **B** fewer antibodies than the second exposure.
   - **C** the same number of antibodies as the second exposure.
   - **D** no antibodies.

23. The second exposure occurred how many days after the first?
   - **F** 14 days
   - **G** 21 days
   - **H** 28 days
   - **J** 30 days

24. The amount of time for the antibody concentration to reach its peak after the first exposure was
   - **A** 4 days.
   - **B** 6 days.
   - **C** 8 days.
   - **D** 12 days.

25. The amount of time for the antibody concentration to reach its peak after the second exposure was
   - **F** 4 days.
   - **G** 8 days.
   - **H** 12 days.
   - **J** 14 days.

Reading and Writing Practice

Read the passage. Then answer Questions 26–29.

The social, economic, and human toll exacted by malaria globally is widespread and profound. Each year, acute malaria occurs in more than 300 million people and results in more than one million deaths worldwide. Malaria is caused by one of four species of *Plasmodium*, a single-cell parasite transmitted by mosquitoes. Drug-resistant *Plasmodium* strains are widespread, as are insecticide-resistant strains of the mosquitoes that carry the parasites.

26. *Plasmodium* is
   - **A** a type of mosquito.
   - **B** a type of insecticide.
   - **C** a parasite.
   - **D** a malaria drug.

27. In this passage, the word *exacted* means
   - **F** decreased.
   - **G** preserved.
   - **H** survived.
   - **J** harmed.

28. According to the passage, which of these statements is true?
   - **A** Malaria is decreasing worldwide.
   - **B** About 0.33% of those who get malaria die from the disease.
   - **C** Insecticide-resistant mosquitoes don't carry the *Plasmodium* parasite.
   - **D** All types of malaria can be treated with drugs.

Constructed Response
29. In a paragraph, explain how drug resistance relates to the spread of malaria.

Test-Taking Tip

In the days leading up to a test, stay healthy by getting plenty of rest and eating balanced meals.

CHAPTER 22

Sexually Transmitted Infections and AIDS

GO ONLINE PearsonSuccessNet.com

TEENS Talk

Risks and STIs

VIDEO 22

Preview **Activity**

How Risky Is Sexual Activity?

Complete this activity before you watch the video.

1. Complete each of the following statements by filling in the blank.
  a. Being sexually active as a teen is ___?___.
  b. There are ___?___ risks that come with sexual activity.
  c. A person should not be sexually active until ___?___.
2. Look over your responses. In a paragraph, summarize what you learned about your self by completing the statements. **WRITING**

The Risks of Sexual Activity

Objectives

▶ **Identify** risky behaviors associated with the current epidemic of sexually transmitted infections.

▶ **Describe** behaviors that can help prevent the spread of sexually transmitted infections.

Vocabulary

• sexually transmitted infection (STI)

Warm-Up

Quick Quiz Which of these statements do you think are true? Which are false?

1 **It can take only one sexual contact with an infected person to get a sexually transmitted infection.**

2 **Even if you've been infected with a sexually transmitted infection before, you can get that same infection again.**

3 **You can have more than one sexually transmitted infection at a time.**

4 **You can get a sexually transmitted infection from sharing needles.**

WRITING For each of your responses, explain why you gave the answer you did. Review your answers after reading this section.

The Silent Epidemic

Any pathogen that spreads from one person to another during sexual contact is called a **sexually transmitted infection,** or **STI.** (Such infections are sometimes called sexually transmitted diseases, or STDs.) There are approximately 20 million new cases of STIs in the United States each year. Of those cases, about half occur in people between the ages of 15 and 24.

Harmful Effects of STIs The STI epidemic is a serious concern for several reasons. STIs are harmful in terms of physical and emotional suffering. And yearly healthcare expenses related to STIs in the United States amount to well over $10 billion.

In the short term, STIs may cause pain, discomfort, and embarrassment. The long-term consequences of STIs may include an increased risk of certain cancers and an increased risk of infertility in both men and women. Infertility is the condition of being unable to have children.

Many STIs can be treated with medicines, but some are incurable. If left untreated, some STIs are fatal. Unlike many other infectious diseases, people do not develop immunity to STIs after being infected. A person can be cured and then reinfected with the same STI again.

Risky Behaviors and the STI Epidemic There are several risky behaviors that account for the current STI epidemic, including ignoring the risks of sexual activity, having sexual contact with multiple partners, and not getting proper treatment when necessary.

GO ONLINE
PearsonSuccessNet.com
For: More on sexually transmitted infections

▶ **Ignoring Risks** Being sexually active puts a person at risk for STIs. Many people who are sexually active do not take precautions against infection. They often do not realize the risks of contracting STIs, or they choose to ignore the risks. Adolescents in particular tend to ignore the risks, thinking "It can't happen to me." But the reality is that it can, and it does happen to many teens.

▶ **Multiple Partners** Many people begin to engage in sexual activity at a young age, and some may have multiple sexual partners during their lifetimes. The more sexual partners a person has, the greater the chance of getting an STI.

▶ **Not Seeking Treatment** Some people who become infected do not seek immediate medical treatment. Sometimes people are too embarrassed to seek treatment. Others don't know that they have an STI because they do not recognize the symptoms. In some cases, STIs have no symptoms and can only be detected by laboratory tests. Sometimes the symptoms go away temporarily, leading the person to think the infection has been cured. In all of these situations, the infection may go untreated, increasing the chances that the person will spread it to others.

Connect to Your Life What advice would you give a friend who seems to be ignoring the risks of sexual activity?

FIGURE 1 This graph shows data for one STI, chlamydia, that is common among young people. **Evaluating** Why do you think young people are especially at risk for STIs?

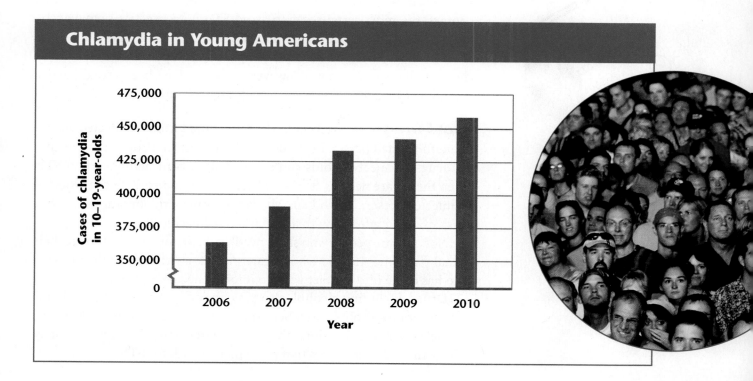
Chlamydia in Young Americans

Graph: Cases of chlamydia in 10–19-year-olds vs. Year

Year	Cases
2006	~363,000
2007	~390,000
2008	~432,000
2009	~440,000
2010	~457,000

FIGURE 2 Educating yourself about STIs can help you make healthy decisions.

Avoiding STIs

STIs are transmitted mainly through sexual contact, but a few are also transmitted through contact with the blood of an infected person. The good news about STIs is that they are preventable. **Healthy behaviors such as practicing abstinence, avoiding drugs, and choosing responsible friends are ways to avoid STIs.**

Practice Abstinence   Because STIs are spread mainly by sexual contact, the most certain way to avoid STIs is to practice sexual abstinence. Sexual abstinence means not having sexual intercourse, oral sex, or anal sex. Even teens who have not been abstinent up to this point can still choose to be abstinent now. However, teens who have been sexually active should be tested for STIs.

Avoid Drugs   Some STIs can be transmitted from an infected person to an uninfected person by blood-to-blood contact. People who use illegal drugs or inject steroids run a high risk of contracting certain STIs when they share needles that have been contaminated with the blood of an infected person. Individuals who get body piercings or tattoos also run a risk of being infected with a contaminated needle.

Not only are people who share needles at risk for STIs, but so are their sexual partners. Anyone who engages in sexual activity with someone who has come into contact with an infected needle is at risk.

Drugs, including alcohol, also play an indirect role in the STI epidemic. Because alcohol and other drugs impair the ability to think clearly, people may make decisions they later regret. For example, they may engage in sexual behaviors that place them at risk for STIs.

Choose Responsible Friends It might sound obvious, but the best way to ensure that you practice abstinence and avoid drugs is to choose friends who have also chosen those behaviors. Friends who support your healthy decisions can make it easier to resist the pressure to use drugs or engage in sexual behavior. Furthermore, going out in groups, rather than as couples, can make it easier to choose abstinence.

Parents, teachers, and other adults can also provide support for healthy behavior choices. It may feel uncomfortable at first to talk to a parent or other adult about the pressures to engage in sexual activity. But most adults can offer helpful advice about choosing abstinence as the responsible and healthy choice.

FIGURE 3 Choosing friends and activities that encourage abstinence can greatly reduce your risk of becoming infected with an STI.

Section 1 Review

Key Ideas and Vocabulary

1. What is a **sexually transmitted infection**?

2. What are three risky behaviors that contribute to the current STI epidemic?

3. Explain how practicing abstinence, avoiding drugs, and your choices of friends can help you avoid STIs.

Critical Thinking

4. Relating Cause and Effect How is the fact that some STIs have few or no symptoms related to the STI epidemic?

Health and Community

STI Education Create a poster or a web page to educate teens about the risks of sexual activity and STIs. Include statistics about the incidence of STIs in teens. Include other facts that you think teens should be aware of. **WRITING**

5. Evaluating Explain how refusal skills and effective communication are important skills that teens can use to avoid STIs.

Kinds of STIs

Objectives

▶ **Identify** three of the most common STIs, including their symptoms and treatments.

▶ **List** four other STIs and describe their symptoms.

▶ **Know** when a person should seek treatment for an STI.

Vocabulary

- trichomoniasis
- urethritis
- vaginitis
- human papilloma virus
- chlamydia
- pelvic inflammatory disease
- gonorrhea
- genital herpes
- syphilis
- chancre

Warm-Up

Myth All STIs can be treated with antibiotics.

Fact STIs caused by viruses cannot be treated with antibiotics. Antibiotics are only used to treat STIs caused by bacteria. Several STIs caused by viruses cannot be cured and can cause lifelong health problems.

WRITING Do you think most teens are aware that some STIs are not easily treated? And that some may persist for years? Explain your answer.

The Most Common STIs

Like other infectious diseases you have learned about, STIs are caused by pathogens, including bacteria, viruses, and protozoans. The pathogens that cause STIs live in the reproductive organs of males and females. Some also live in the blood. STIs can be spread from person to person through blood and body fluids such as semen, vaginal secretions, and breast milk.

Early diagnosis and treatment of STIs is essential in preventing long-term health problems. Although some STIs do not have obvious symptoms, many do have distinct symptoms. Anyone experiencing symptoms of an STI should see a doctor immediately.

Three of the most common STIs in the United States are trichomoniasis, human papilloma virus, and chlamydia. It is important to be able to recognize the symptoms of these infections.

Trichomoniasis The STI known as **trichomoniasis** (trik uh moh NY uh sis) is caused by a protozoan that infects the urinary tract or vagina. In males, symptoms include painful urination, a clear discharge from the penis, and some itching. Most males experience no symptoms at all. Symptoms in females include itching and burning in the vagina, an unpleasant-smelling, yellowish discharge, and pain when urinating.

A doctor can prescribe medicine to cure a trichomoniasis infection. In males, if trichomoniasis is not treated, it can lead to inflammation of the lining of the urethra, called **urethritis** (yoor uh THRY tis). In females, untreated trichomoniasis can lead to **vaginitis** (vaj uh NY tis), which is a vaginal infection or irritation.

Human Papilloma Virus   The most common viral STI in the U.S. is caused by a group of viruses called **human papilloma virus** (pap uh LOH muh), or HPV. Often, HPV causes no symptoms. So people may not know that they are infected. The body's immune system may destroy the virus. But in some people, HPV remains in the body for life.

Some forms of HPV cause genital warts, which may itch or burn. A doctor can remove the warts, but they may reappear. A more serious condition associated with HPV is cervical cancer in women. Regular pap tests help detect cervical cancer before it becomes life-threatening.

The FDA has licensed a vaccine for use in girls and young women ages 9 to 26. The vaccine protects against the four types of HPV virus that cause 70 percent of cervical cancers and 90 percent of genital warts. Research is ongoing to see if the HPV vaccine has benefits for males.

Chlamydia   The most common STI caused by bacteria in the U.S. is **chlamydia** (kluh MID ee uh). People who are sexually active should be checked regularly for chlamydia, which can be cured with antibiotics.

Infected males often experience painful, frequent urination and discharge from the penis. If untreated, chlamydia may lead to urethritis.

In females, often the only symptom is a yellowish vaginal discharge. If untreated, chlamydia can cause a serious infection of the reproductive organs called **pelvic inflammatory disease,** or PID. PID can lead to infertility or an ectopic pregnancy, a potentially fatal condition where a fertilized egg implants somewhere other than in the uterus. Also, a pregnant woman can transmit chlamydia to her baby during birth. If an infected infant survives, it may suffer damage to the lungs or eyes.

GO ONLINE

PearsonSuccessNet.com
For: More on sexually transmitted infections

FIGURE 4   The micrographs show the pathogens that cause trichomoniasis, HPV, and chlamydia. These STIs affect millions of Americans every year.

Connect to Your Life   For each STI, list the symptoms that a person needs to watch for.

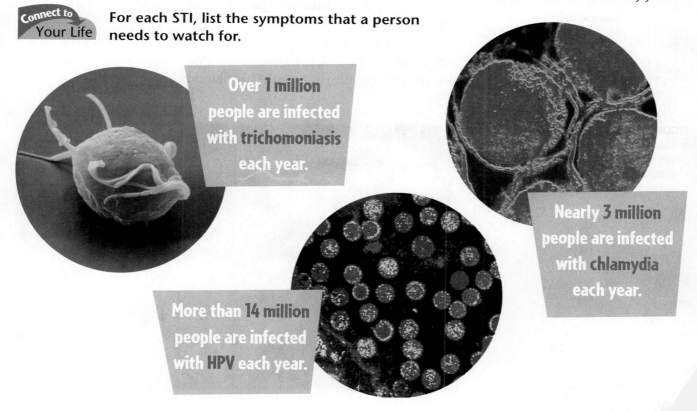

Over 1 million people are infected with **trichomoniasis** each year.

More than 14 million people are infected with **HPV** each year.

Nearly 3 million people are infected with **chlamydia** each year.

Other STIs

Other STIs can also cause health problems and require medical treatment. Information about some of these STIs is summarized in Figure 6. **Other STIs include hepatitis, gonorrhea, genital herpes, and syphilis.**

Hepatitis   Hepatitis B and C, also called HBV and HCV, are sexually transmitted infections that attack the liver. They are also spread by blood-to-blood contact, such as when people share needles.

Individuals with HBV or HCV are often unaware of their infection. The most common symptoms are fatigue, abdominal pain, nausea, and jaundice. Both infections may lead to liver cancer or cirrhosis (sih ROH sis), a condition in which normal liver tissue is replaced by scar tissue.

Hepatitis B and C can be diagnosed by a blood test. Medications may relieve symptoms, but there is no cure for HBV or HCV. Children are now routinely vaccinated against HBV. Currently, there is no vaccine for HCV.

Gonorrhea   A bacterial STI that infects the urinary tract of males and females and the reproductive organs of females is **gonorrhea** (gahn uh REE uh). Researchers estimate that about 820,000 Americans are infected with gonorrhea each year. Males usually have a thick, puslike discharge from the penis and painful urination. Females sometimes experience painful urination and a puslike discharge from the vagina or urinary tract. More often, however, symptoms in a woman are very mild and may not be noticed. If left untreated, gonorrhea can lead to urethritis and infertility in males. In females it may lead to PID and infertility.

An infected woman can transmit gonorrhea to her baby during birth. In the United States, babies are given medicated eyedrops at birth to prevent infection of the eyes.

Because gonorrhea often has no noticeable symptoms, people participating in high-risk behaviors should get regular medical checkups. Treatment for gonorrhea requires antibiotics.

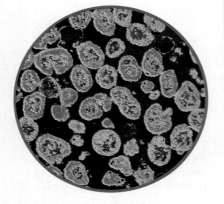

▲ **Gonorrhea**

FIGURE 5   Newborn babies are routinely given medicated eyedrops to prevent gonorrhea infection. The micrograph above shows the bacteria that cause gonorrhea.

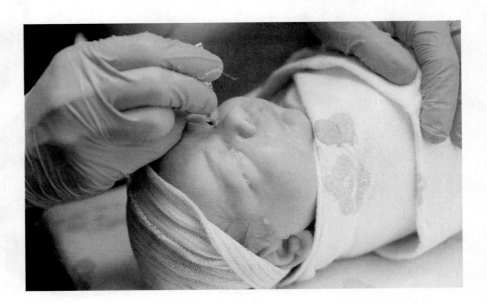

FIGURE 6 Chancroid, bacterial vaginosis, pubic lice, and scabies are all treatable STIs. **Classifying** Which of these STIs can affect both males and females?

◀ Chancroid

Other STIs

Infection	Pathogen	Symptoms	How Spread	Treatment
Chancroid	Bacteria	Painful sores around the genitals	Contact with sores	Antibiotics
Bacterial vaginosis	Bacteria	In women, discharge, pain, itching, or burning in or around the vagina	Role of sexual activity in the spread of bacterial vaginosis is unclear	Antibiotics
Pubic lice and Scabies	Insects and mites that infest the hair around the genitals	Itching around the genitals; a rash	Direct physical contact with an infested person or with infested clothing or bedding	Medicated shampoo; washing infested clothing or bedding in very hot water

▲ Pubic louse

Genital Herpes Another STI caused by a virus is **genital herpes** (HUR peez). The virus that causes genital herpes is a herpes simplex virus. Researchers estimate that one out of six people aged 14 to 49 has had a genital herpes infection.

In some people, the symptoms may be hardly noticeable, and they may not realize they are infected. In other people, symptoms may be more severe, including painful blisters that appear on or around the genitals. A doctor can prescribe medicine to relieve the discomfort and dry up the blisters, but there is no cure for genital herpes. Infected people can experience periodic outbreaks of blisters throughout their lives.

An infected individual can pass the herpes simplex virus to a sexual partner whether blisters are present or not. A woman with genital herpes can infect her infant during childbirth, causing blindness and possibly death. A doctor may recommend that an infected woman have a cesarean section to prevent the baby from being infected.

Connect to Your Life
If a friend were considering a body piercing, what would you say about the risk of hepatitis?

Syphilis Although far less common than it used to be, thousands of people in the United States become infected with syphilis each year. **Syphilis** (SIF uh lis) is a serious bacterial STI that progresses through three distinct stages.

► In the first stage, a painless sore called a **chancre** (SHANG kur) appears at the site of exposure. The bacteria may spread from the sore to different parts of the body.

► In the second stage, sores appear in the mouth and flulike symptoms develop. A nonitchy skin rash often appears on the hands and feet.

► In the third stage, symptoms may disappear for years. During this time, however, the bacteria attack internal parts of the body, such as the brain and heart. Eventually, untreated syphilis can cause brain damage, paralysis, and heart disease. This damage can lead to death.

In its early stages, syphilis can be treated and cured with antibiotics. Once it progresses beyond the second stage, the bacteria can be killed, but any damage that has already occurred is permanent.

A pregnant woman with syphilis will pass the disease to her developing baby. If the mother does not receive treatment during pregnancy, syphilis can damage the baby's skin, bones, eyes, teeth, and liver. A baby born with syphilis is said to have congenital syphilis.

FIGURE 7 An itchless rash on the hands is one of the symptoms of syphilis. The bacteria that cause syphilis are spiral-shaped, as you can see in the micrograph. The poster shown here was part of a public health program in the 1940s.

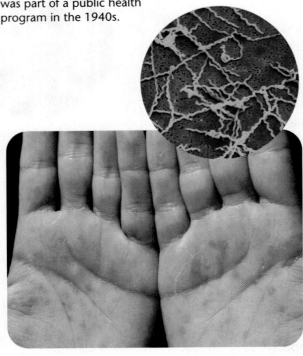

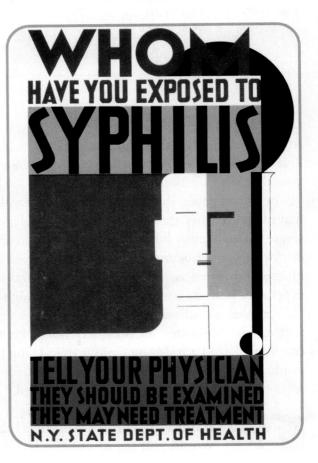

WHOM HAVE YOU EXPOSED TO SYPHILIS

TELL YOUR PHYSICIAN
THEY SHOULD BE EXAMINED
THEY MAY NEED TREATMENT
N.Y. STATE DEPT. OF HEALTH

Seeking Treatment

Being tested for STIs may be uncomfortable and embarrassing, but it is crucial for long-term health. **People who participate in high-risk behaviors should get medical checkups every six months. Individuals who suspect they may be infected should seek prompt medical attention.**

A person who suspects an STI infection should refrain from sexual activity and see a doctor. Depending on the symptoms, the doctor may need to do a physical exam or a blood test. If an infection is present and treatable, the person should start treatment immediately. It is important to finish all of the prescribed medicine, even if symptoms disappear.

If a person finds out that he or she has an STI, it is also important to notify any sexual partners, so they can seek treatment as well. If the STI is not curable, the doctor can offer advice about how to live with the disease and how to prevent passing it on to others.

Many states have clinics that test for STIs. The results of these tests are confidential. Information about clinics that test for STIs is available from state or local public health departments or from the Centers for Disease Control and Prevention.

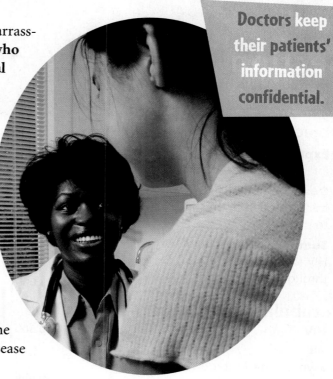

Doctors keep their patients' information confidential.

FIGURE 8 It is very important for long-term health to see a doctor if you think you might have an STI.

Section 2 Review

Key Ideas and Vocabulary

1. What are three of the most common STIs in the United States? What type of pathogen causes each STI?
2. Why is **pelvic inflammatory disease** a serious problem in women?
3. List the symptoms of hepatitis, gonorrhea, genital herpes, and syphilis.
4. Which stage of syphilis is characterized by the appearance of a **chancre**?
5. When should a person seek treatment for STIs?

Health at Home

Accessing STI Information Write down a list of questions that you have about STIs. Set up a time with a parent or other trusted adult to discuss your questions. If the person doesn't know the answers, ask for his or her help in finding the answers. **WRITING**

Critical Thinking

6. **Classifying** Which of the STIs that you learned about in this section can be treated but not cured? Which can be cured if treated early?
7. **Applying Concepts** Suppose a friend is worried about a possible STI. Write an e-mail to your friend, offering your advice about what to do. **WRITING**

HIV and AIDS

Objectives

▶ **Explain** how HIV infection leads to AIDS.

▶ **Describe** how HIV is transmitted from person to person.

▶ **Summarize** the state of HIV infection and AIDS throughout the world.

Vocabulary

• HIV
• AIDS
• asymptomatic stage
• opportunistic infection

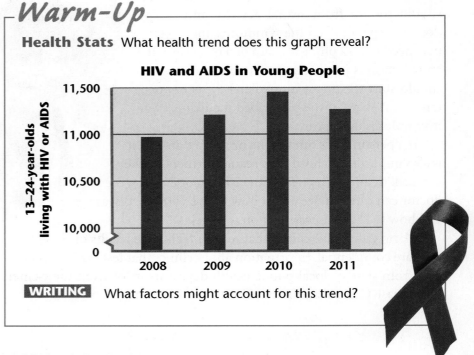

Warm-Up

Health Stats What health trend does this graph reveal?

HIV and AIDS in Young People

WRITING What factors might account for this trend?

HIV Infection

The most serious incurable STI is caused by the human immunodeficiency virus, commonly called **HIV.** As of 2011, about 1.4 million people in North America were living with HIV. In the United States, 13- to 24-year-olds account for about 13 percent of HIV cases.

HIV infection can lead to **AIDS,** or acquired immunodeficiency syndrome, which is an often fatal disease of the immune system. **HIV attacks specific cells of the immune system, disabling the body's defenses against other pathogens. When the immune system becomes severely disabled, the infected person has AIDS.**

How HIV Attacks the Immune System Inside the body, HIV infects helper T cells, which stimulate other cells of the immune system to produce antibodies against invading pathogens. Inside a helper T cell, HIV reproduces, killing the cell in the process. The new viruses are released from the cell and move on to destroy other helper T cells.

Doctors can use the number of helper T cells that remain active in the body to monitor the progression of HIV infection. The fewer helper T cells, the more advanced the disease. Figure 9 shows how helper T cell counts can be used to monitor the progression of the disease.

Stages of HIV Infection

HIV slowly destroys the immune system. Doctors describe HIV infection as progressing through three stages.

▶ **Asymptomatic Stage** Soon after exposure to HIV, an infected person may experience flulike symptoms, which usually go away after a few weeks. Many months or years may follow during which the person shows no outward signs of disease. Because of the lack of symptoms, this period is called the **asymptomatic stage.** During this stage, the virus destroys helper T cells. People in the asymptomatic stage can infect others even though they feel fine.

▶ **Symptomatic Stage** When an HIV-infected person starts to experience symptoms, he or she has entered the symptomatic stage of infection. Symptoms may include weight loss, a persistent fever, diarrhea, or fungal infections. Such symptoms may not appear until 7 to 10 years after infection with HIV.

▶ **AIDS** The onset of AIDS is usually marked by a very low number of helper T cells in the blood, as shown in Figure 9. At this stage, HIV-infected people are usually experiencing even more severe symptoms than in the symptomatic stage. Because the body's ability to fight disease has been weakened by HIV, they are susceptible to infections that a healthy person's immune system could easily fight off.

▲ **HIV viruses (red) emerging from a human helper T cell**

Connect to Your Life

Can you assume that someone who looks healthy is not infected with HIV? Explain.

FIGURE 9 The number of helper T cells in the blood decreases as HIV infects and destroys more cells. **Reading Graphs** Describe how T cell counts change over time in a person infected with HIV.

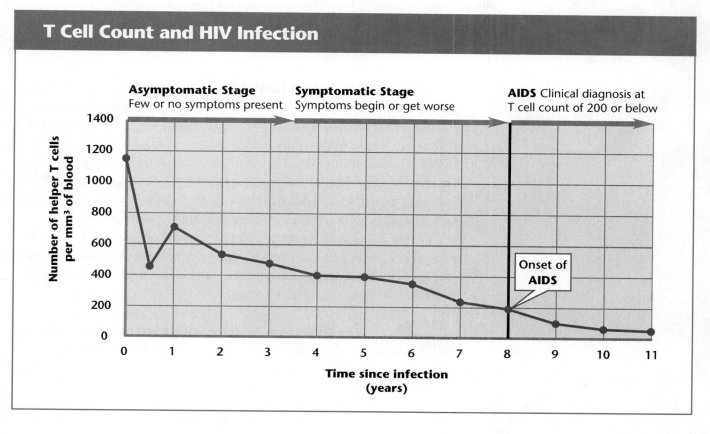

T Cell Count and HIV Infection

Asymptomatic Stage Few or no symptoms present
Symptomatic Stage Symptoms begin or get worse
AIDS Clinical diagnosis at T cell count of 200 or below

Onset of AIDS

Number of helper T cells per mm³ of blood (y-axis: 0, 200, 400, 600, 800, 1000, 1200, 1400)

Time since infection (years) (x-axis: 0, 1, 2, 3, 4, 5, 6, 7, 8, 9, 10, 11)

Hands-On *Activity*

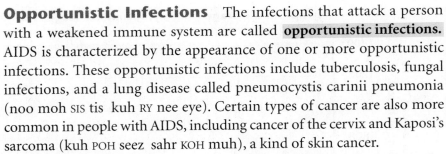

How Quickly Can HIV Spread?

Materials

cups
chocolate candies
cinnamon candies

Try This

❶ Your teacher will give you a cup filled with small candies. Do not look inside the cup.

❷ Walk around the room until your teacher tells you to stop. At that point, pair up with the student closest to you.

❸ Pour a few of the candies from your cup into your partner's cup. Your partner should also pour some candies into your cup.

❹ Repeat steps 2 and 3 two more times.

❺ Look at the candies in your cup. If you have a cinnamon candy, you have been "infected" with HIV.

Think and Discuss

❶ How many people in your class ended up with a cinnamon candy (HIV) in their cup? Would it surprise you to learn that only one person was infected to begin with?

❷ Suppose that each person you exchanged candies with represents a sexual partner. How many people other than you did each of your partners exchange candies with? What does this suggest about having multiple sexual partners and the chances of getting infected with HIV or another STI?

Opportunistic Infections The infections that attack a person with a weakened immune system are called **opportunistic infections.** AIDS is characterized by the appearance of one or more opportunistic infections. These opportunistic infections include tuberculosis, fungal infections, and a lung disease called pneumocystis carinii pneumonia (noo moh SIS tis kuh RY nee eye). Certain types of cancer are also more common in people with AIDS, including cancer of the cervix and Kaposi's sarcoma (kuh POH seez sahr KOH muh), a kind of skin cancer.

People living with AIDS often experience severe weight loss. As the disease progresses, the virus may attack the brain and nervous system, causing blindness, depression, and mental deterioration. Death is usually caused by an opportunistic infection.

Connect to Your Life

Would you spend time with a friend who is HIV-positive if you were sick with the flu? Explain.

Transmission of HIV

People with HIV are infectious whether or not they have any symptoms of disease. **Individuals infected with HIV can pass the virus on to someone else through the exchange of blood, semen, vaginal secretions, or breast milk.**

Risky Behaviors   There are four main ways that HIV spreads from person to person.

▶ **Sexual Contact** HIV can be transmitted through any form of sexual contact that involves contact with an infected person's body fluids, including vaginal, oral, and anal sex. Infected fluids can enter a person's bloodstream through sores or tiny cuts in the lining of the mouth, vagina, rectum, or opening of the penis.

▶ **Shared Needles** HIV can be transmitted through shared needles or syringes that are contaminated with the blood of an infected person. Therefore, sharing needles for tattoos or body piercings and injecting illegal drugs put you at risk for HIV infection.

▶ **Contact With Blood** HIV can be transmitted if a person has an open cut or sore that comes into contact with the blood or blood parts of an infected person. Avoid all contact with others' blood.

▶ **Mother to Baby** HIV can pass from an infected mother to her child, either during pregnancy, birth, or breast-feeding. Certain drugs can decrease the chances of transmission during pregnancy, and the doctor might deliver the baby by cesarean section to reduce the risk of transmission during birth. In addition, mothers infected with HIV should not breast-feed their babies.

GO ONLINE

PearsonSuccessNet.com
For: More on AIDS

FIGURE 10   It is safer for an HIV-positive mother to bottle-feed, rather than breast-feed, her baby.

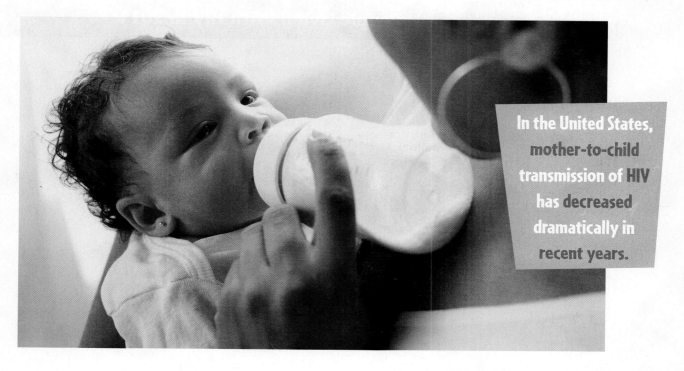

In the United States, mother-to-child transmission of **HIV** has decreased dramatically in recent years.

FIGURE 11 Playing contact sports such as rugby does not put you at risk for HIV infection.

FIGURE 12 The global distribution of HIV infections is uneven. **Sequencing** List the areas of the world from greatest number of infected people to smallest number of infected people. What position does North America have on the list?

Safe Behaviors HIV is not transmitted by casual contact. You cannot get HIV by going to classes or eating lunch with an infected person. You cannot get HIV by holding hands or hugging an infected person. Families who live with an infected person are not at risk of contracting HIV unless they engage in high-risk behaviors. Small amounts of HIV occur in saliva, tears, and perspiration. However, the amounts are so small that infection from contact with these fluids is unlikely.

The Safety of Donated Blood The risk of getting HIV from blood transfusions is extremely small. Since 1985, all of the blood collected in the United States has been tested for the presence of HIV. Blood that tests positive for HIV antibodies is discarded. Potential donors are interviewed and are not allowed to give blood if they have engaged in behaviors that place them at risk for HIV infection.

A Global Problem

Figure 12 shows the global distribution of HIV infections. **With approximately 34 million people infected around the world, HIV and AIDS represent a global health problem.**

▶ **Africa** Sub-Saharan Africa accounts for 69% of all global infections. Some estimates indicate that, if infections continue to rise at the current rate, 80 million Africans may die from AIDS by 2025.

▶ **Asia** HIV infections are also increasing in certain parts of Asia. For example, researchers estimate that about 2.5 million people are living with HIV and AIDS in India.

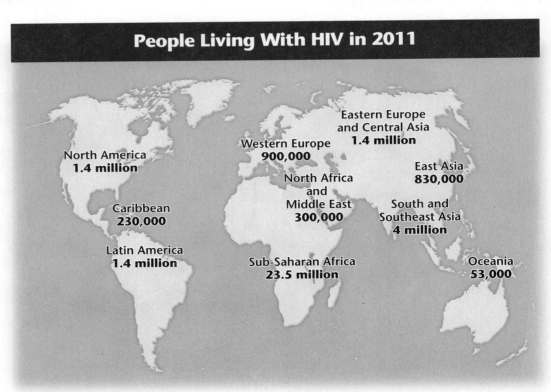

People Living With HIV in 2011

North America
1.4 million

Caribbean
230,000

Latin America
1.4 million

Western Europe
900,000

Eastern Europe
and Central Asia
1.4 million

North Africa
and
Middle East
300,000

Sub-Saharan Africa
23.5 million

East Asia
830,000

South and
Southeast Asia
4 million

Oceania
53,000

High-Risk Groups In all areas of the world, HIV is spreading among people who share needles to inject drugs and people who engage in high-risk sexual behaviors. In many countries, young women represent the majority of new HIV infections. In sub-Saharan Africa, for example, 75% of young people infected with HIV are female. The higher infection rates in women are often due to a lack of information about how to protect themselves or, in some cases, a lack of power to protect themselves.

Education and Prevention Several international organizations are working to lessen the toll that HIV and AIDS are taking on populations all over the world. The World Health Organization and the Joint United Nations Programme on HIV/AIDS monitor the situation and recommend steps for stemming the epidemic in different countries.

The main goal of international organizations is HIV education. Making people in high-risk countries aware of how to protect themselves from HIV infection is a huge step toward prevention. Because treatment can be very expensive and inaccessible for the people at highest risk, much effort is put toward preventing HIV infection in the first place.

In addition to prevention education, international organizations coordinate treatment efforts for people already living with HIV and AIDS. Efforts are being made to provide medicine to millions of infected people in countries most affected by HIV and AIDS.

FIGURE 13 A girl from Zambia, a country in Africa, holds a sign she made for World AIDS Day.

Section 3 Review

Key Ideas and Vocabulary

1. Explain how HIV affects the immune system and how it eventually leads to AIDS.

2. What is meant by an **opportunistic infection**? Give an example.

3. What are four ways that HIV can be transmitted from an infected person to an uninfected person? List three ways HIV is *not* transmitted.

4. Which region of the world accounts for the majority of HIV infections?

Critical Thinking

5. Making Judgments Should teens in the United States be concerned about the global AIDS problem? Why or why not?

Health at School

AIDS Awareness Plan an AIDS Awareness Day at your school. Divide your class into groups to make posters about different aspects of HIV and AIDS. For example, one poster could focus on how HIV is transmitted. Another poster could focus on the status of the AIDS epidemic. Display your posters at school to help educate other students. **WRITING**

6. Evaluating HIV is more common in poorer countries than in wealthier countries. Why do you think this might be the case?

Evaluating Internet Sources

The amount of health information available on the Internet can be overwhelming. For example, suppose you wanted to learn more about one of the sexually transmitted infections discussed in this chapter. If you typed the name of the STI into a search engine, you would likely come up with thousands of hits. You can't possibly visit every site, so how do you decide which sites have accurate information? The following guidelines will help you evaluate the reliability of Internet sources. These guidelines apply to Internet sources on all kinds of topics, not just health topics.

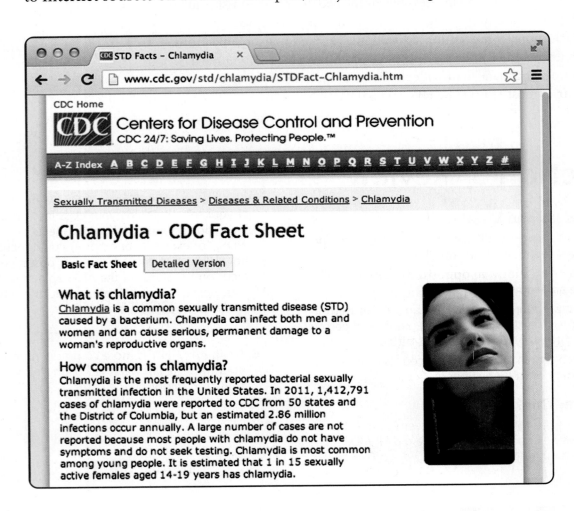

STD Facts – Chlamydia

www.cdc.gov/std/chlamydia/STDFact–Chlamydia.htm

CDC Home

CDC Centers for Disease Control and Prevention
CDC 24/7: Saving Lives. Protecting People.™

A-Z Index A B C D E F G H I J K L M N O P Q R S T U V W X Y Z #

Sexually Transmitted Diseases > Diseases & Related Conditions > Chlamydia

Chlamydia - CDC Fact Sheet

Basic Fact Sheet | Detailed Version

What is chlamydia?
Chlamydia is a common sexually transmitted disease (STD) caused by a bacterium. Chlamydia can infect both men and women and can cause serious, permanent damage to a woman's reproductive organs.

How common is chlamydia?
Chlamydia is the most frequently reported bacterial sexually transmitted infection in the United States. In 2011, 1,412,791 cases of chlamydia were reported to CDC from 50 states and the District of Columbia, but an estimated 2.86 million infections occur annually. A large number of cases are not reported because most people with chlamydia do not have symptoms and do not seek testing. Chlamydia is most common among young people. It is estimated that 1 in 15 sexually active females aged 14-19 years has chlamydia.

① Determine the type of Web site you are looking at and its purpose.

The Web address tells you what type of company or organization operates the site.

▶ A **.gov** in the address indicates that the site is run by a government organization. This type of site will usually provide reliable information. It may also represent the current administration's point of view.

▶ A **.com** or a **.net** indicates that it is a commercial site. A commercial site may provide information about products that are for sale. If the site is sponsored by the business that would profit from sales of those products, you probably will not find any negative information about the products on that site.

▶ A **.edu** indicates that an educational institution runs the site. Professors and students often post their own research on such sites.

▶ A **.org** indicates that a non-profit organization runs the site. Be aware of the organization's agenda as you consider its content.

② Identify the author(s) of the site.

The author(s) should be indicated clearly at the top or bottom of the page, or on a page that is linked to the page you are looking at. What are the author's credentials? Is there contact information for the author? If it is not clear who takes responsibility for the content, it may not be reliable.

③ Determine if the information is current.

Many Web sites indicate when their content was last updated. Information on some topics may become out of date quickly. For example, if you are looking for the number of people who have been diagnosed with AIDS this year, you should look for a site that has been updated recently.

④ Determine the quality of the site.

Does the site look organized and professional, or does it look like it was put together haphazardly? Is the information presented in a straightforward way, or does it ramble?

⑤ Verify the information on the site with information from another source.

Does the site provide sources for the information it provides? If not, look elsewhere for information.

Practice the Skill

1. Go online and use a search engine to find a Web site on sexually transmitted infections and AIDS. See if you can answer the following questions based on the page you find:
   a. Who is the author of the site?
   b. What bias might the author have regarding the topic?
   c. When was the site last updated?
   d. What sources did the author use?

2. Based on your answers to the questions above, evaluate the reliability of the information on that Web site. Would you trust the information provided there? How would you verify that information?

Section 4

Protecting Yourself From HIV and AIDS

Objectives

▶ **Identify** three behaviors that can prevent the spread of HIV.

▶ **Describe** how a person gets tested for HIV.

▶ **Describe** the goal of HIV treatment.

Vocabulary

• universal precautions
• HIV-positive
• viral load

Warm-Up

Dear Advice Line,

Lately my boyfriend has been asking me to have sex. I really like him, but I'm not ready for that. Plus I'm not sure he's telling me everything about his past. What should I do?

WRITING Write a response to this teen, encouraging her to choose abstinence. What would you tell her about the risk of becoming infected with HIV and other STIs?

Preventing HIV Infection

At present there is no cure for HIV or AIDS. But, the good news is that you can choose behaviors that will help you avoid this very serious disease. **You can protect yourself from HIV by practicing abstinence, avoiding drugs, and avoiding contact with others' blood and body fluids.**

Practice Abstinence Choosing sexual abstinence is the best way to avoid HIV and AIDS. Even if you have been sexually active, you can choose abstinence. It is much easier to be abstinent if you have friends who are also abstinent. Spending time with responsible friends can reduce the pressure you may feel to engage in sexual behavior.

Avoid Drugs Avoiding drug use is also extremely important for reducing the risk of HIV infection. People who share contaminated needles to inject themselves with drugs are at a high risk for contracting HIV. People who have sex with drug abusers are also at high risk. Do not inject illegal drugs, and avoid sexual contact with anyone who uses illegal drugs.

Using alcohol or other drugs can impair a person's judgment. People with impaired judgment are more likely to engage in behaviors that place them at risk. To guard against infection, you need to be able to think clearly so you can make healthy decisions.

Connect to Your Life **How can your choice of friends help you avoid risky behaviors?**

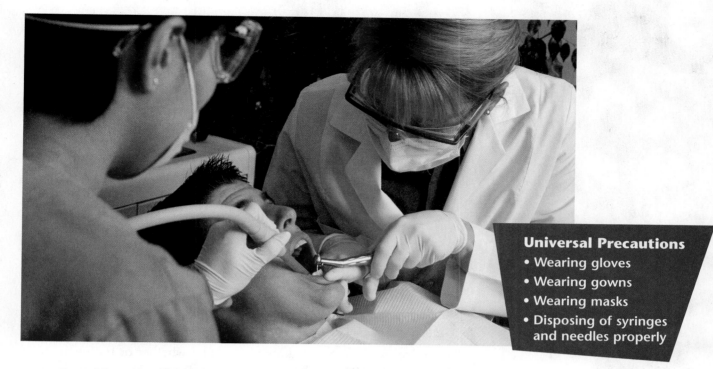

Universal Precautions
- Wearing gloves
- Wearing gowns
- Wearing masks
- Disposing of syringes and needles properly

FIGURE 14 Healthcare providers protect themselves and their patients by following universal precautions.

Avoid Contact With Blood or Body Fluids Never share any personal items that may have blood or other body fluids on them. For example, razors, syringes, and piercing or tattoo needles should never be shared. In addition, mothers who are infected with HIV should not breast-feed their babies because the virus can be transmitted through breast milk.

Healthcare providers often come into contact with the blood and body fluids of patients. To reduce the risk of HIV transmission, doctors, nurses, dentists, dental hygienists, and other healthcare providers practice **universal precautions,** as listed in Figure 14.

Sexual Fidelity For people in a sexual relationship it is important to practice sexual fidelity. Sexual fidelity is practiced when both partners agree to have sexual contact only with one another—to be monogamous. If both partners are uninfected, sexual fidelity eliminates the risk of getting HIV or another STI. If either partner has practiced risky behaviors in the past, he or she should be tested for HIV and other STIs.

Barrier Protection People in relationships may not be sure that their partners are faithful and uninfected. They can reduce the risk of HIV infection by using a condom during every sexual encounter. The condom must be made of latex or polyurethane, be free of tears, and be used in accordance with the directions on the package. Condoms serve as a physical barrier against HIV and some other pathogens that cause STIs. It is important to know that condoms are not 100 percent effective in preventing the transmission of HIV. Abstinence is the best way to protect yourself from HIV and other STIs.

FIGURE 15 A blood test can reveal if a person is infected with HIV. Getting an HIV-positive result can be frightening and depressing. Therefore, it is important that HIV-positive individuals receive counseling to help them deal with the emotional impacts of their infection.

Testing for HIV

The only way a person can know for certain whether or not he or she is infected with HIV is to have a blood test. People who engage in risky behaviors should have their blood tested at a clinic or by a private physician. The names of clinics that provide confidential HIV testing are available from each state's department of public health or from the Centers for Disease Control and Prevention. People who think they may have been exposed to HIV should practice abstinence to avoid spreading the virus.

In an HIV test, a person's blood is tested for antibodies to HIV. If antibodies are detected, a second test is done to verify the result. A person who is diagnosed as being infected with HIV is said to be **HIV-positive.**

An HIV-Positive Diagnosis If a person is diagnosed as HIV-positive, he or she needs to notify all previous sexual partners so that they can also be tested. Early diagnosis is important to prevent the spread of the disease and to start treatment as soon as possible.

It is difficult to cope with an HIV-positive diagnosis. For this reason, it is recommended that individuals receive counseling from a healthcare professional before being tested. People who learn they are HIV-positive should receive additional counseling.

Reasons for Follow-Up Testing If an HIV infection is recent, a blood test may not be accurate. This is because there is a lapse between the time of infection and the time when antibodies show up in a person's blood. Antibodies usually show up within three months after infection. So even if no antibodies are detected in the person's first blood test, he or she should avoid all high-risk behaviors and be tested again in three months.

Connect to Your Life **How could you convince someone of the importance of follow-up testing?**

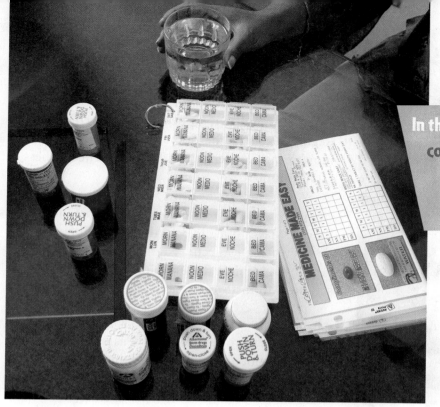

In the United States, medical costs for a person living with HIV are about $25,000 a year.

FIGURE 16 A common treatment regimen requires an HIV-positive person to take many pills each day. If the person misses too many doses, the virus may develop resistance to the medication.

Treatment for HIV and AIDS

Although there is no cure for HIV infection and AIDS, some treatments can add many years to a patient's life. The sooner a person begins treatment, the more effective it can be in slowing the progress of the disease.

The Goal of Treatment **The main goal of HIV treatment is to keep the person's immune system functioning as close to normal as possible.** To achieve this goal, the treatment must

▶ keep the person's **viral load**—the number of virus particles circulating in the body—as low as possible, and

▶ keep the person's T cell count as high as possible.

If both of these goals are achieved, the patient's immune system is more capable of fighting off opportunistic infections. Remember that current treatments do not rid the body of HIV. They try to stop HIV from destroying the immune system.

Combination Drug Therapy The most common treatment for HIV infection today is known as Highly Active AntiRetroviral Therapy, or HAART. HAART uses a combination of drugs to reduce the viral load in the blood. Multiple drugs are necessary to prevent the virus from reproducing inside helper T cells. A doctor prescribes a combination of drugs that is right for each individual patient.

Some drawbacks to HAART are its complicated dosage schedules, its cost, and its side effects, which can include liver and kidney damage. Furthermore, if a person is not consistent about taking the drugs exactly as prescribed, drug resistance can develop quickly.

 GO ONLINE
PearsonSuccessNet.com
For: More on HIV/AIDS prevention

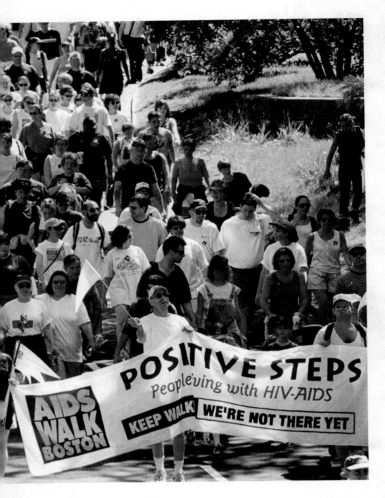

Living With HIV People who are HIV-positive must take extra care to practice healthful behaviors. Eating right, exercising, and getting plenty of sleep are especially important for people who are HIV-positive. Regular visits to the doctor are also important for monitoring a patient's health and the effectiveness of HIV treatment.

When they are healthy, HIV-positive people can carry on with their careers and other activities. But they do have to avoid high-risk behaviors that put them at risk for infecting someone else. And because HIV compromises the immune system, they should stay away from anyone who has an infectious disease.

The Need for Support As with any serious disease, people who are HIV-positive as well as their loved ones need a lot of support to help them deal with their distress and anxiety. Support may include counseling, healthcare services, and financial assistance.

HIV-positive individuals should be treated with compassion. They also should be allowed to live their lives with dignity. Because HIV cannot be transmitted by casual contact, such as hugging or shaking hands, no one needs to be fearful of working or going to school with someone who is HIV-positive.

FIGURE 17 Every year, thousands of people participate in walks to help raise money for AIDS research and education.

Section 4 Review

Key Ideas and Vocabulary

1. What are three behaviors that can help you avoid HIV infection?

2. What does an HIV test involve?

3. What does **HIV-positive** mean?

4. What is the main goal of HIV treatment? How is that goal achieved?

Critical Thinking

5. **Evaluating** Depression can be a serious problem in people who are HIV-positive. What do you think are some ways to help people deal with the mental and emotional effects of this disease?

Health at School

HIV Prevention Some schools introduce HIV prevention education in grades six to eight. Find out if you or a group of classmates could prepare a program to help educate these younger students about protecting themselves from HIV infection. Then, develop an outline for your program. **WRITING**

---

6. **Relating Cause and Effect** Doctors recommend that people who are HIV-positive should stay as healthy as possible, eating well, getting enough sleep, and avoiding exposure to anyone with an infectious disease. Why do doctors recommend this?

GO ONLINE PearsonSuccessNet.com Audio Summary Section 22.4

Chapter 22
At a Glance

VIDEO **TEENS** Talk
Risks and STIs List three things you learned from the video about the importance of sexual abstinence.

Section 1   The Risks of Sexual Activity

Key Ideas

▶ Risky behaviors that account for the current STI epidemic include ignoring the risks of sexual activity, having sexual contact with multiple partners, and not getting proper treatment.

▶ Practicing abstinence, avoiding drugs, and choosing responsible friends are ways to avoid STIs.

Vocabulary
• sexually transmitted infection (STI) (574)

Section 2   Kinds of STIs

Key Ideas

▶ Trichomoniasis, human papilloma virus, and chlamydia are common STIs in the United States.

▶ Other STIs include hepatitis, gonorrhea, genital herpes, and syphilis.

▶ People who participate in high-risk behaviors should get medical checkups every six months. Individuals who suspect they may be infected should seek prompt medical attention.

Vocabulary
• trichomoniasis (578) • urethritis (578)
• vaginitis (578) • human papilloma virus (579)
• chlamydia (579) • pelvic inflammatory disease (579)
• gonorrhea (580) • genital herpes (581)
• syphilis (582) • chancre (582)

Section 3   HIV and AIDS

Key Ideas

▶ HIV attacks the immune system, disabling the body's defenses. When the immune system becomes severely disabled, the infected person has AIDS.

▶ Individuals infected with HIV can pass the virus on to someone else through the exchange of blood, semen, vaginal secretions, or breast milk.

▶ With 40 million people infected around the world, HIV and AIDS represent a global health problem.

Vocabulary
• HIV (584) • AIDS (584)
• asymptomatic stage (585)
• opportunistic infection (586)

Section 4   Protecting Yourself From HIV and AIDS

Key Ideas

▶ You can protect yourself from HIV by practicing abstinence, avoiding drugs, and avoiding contact with others' blood and body fluids.

▶ In an HIV test, a person's blood is tested for antibodies to HIV. If antibodies are detected, a second test is done to verify the result.

▶ The main goal of HIV treatment is to keep the person's immune system functioning as close to normal as possible.

Vocabulary
• universal precautions (593) • HIV-positive (594)
• viral load (595)

Chapter 22 Review

GO ONLINE
PearsonSuccessNet.com
For: Chapter 22 review activity

Reviewing Key Ideas

Section 1

1. A reduced ability to have children is
   a. STI.　　　　　　**b.** epidemic.
   c. infertility.　　　**d.** abstinence.

2. Describe two ways to avoid getting an STI.

3. **Critical Thinking** If you found out that the person you were dating had injected illegal drugs in the past, how would that affect your relationship?

Section 2

4. A serious infection of the female reproductive organs that can be caused by chlamydia is
   a. pelvic inflammatory disease.
   b. genital warts.
   c. syphilis.
   d. trichomoniasis.

5. An STI that cannot be treated with antibiotics is
   a. gonorrhea.　　　　**b.** chlamydia.
   c. human papilloma virus.　**d.** syphilis.

6. How can genital herpes affect a newborn baby?

7. What steps should be taken by a person who suspects that he or she is infected with an STI?

8. **Critical Thinking** Why should someone who is diagnosed with an STI notify all of his or her sexual partners?

Section 3

9. The virus that causes AIDS is
   a. herpes.　　　**b.** HPV.
   c. PID.　　　　　**d.** HIV.

10. HIV destroys
    a. neurons.　　**b.** antibodies.
    c. B cells.　　　**d.** T cells.

11. Why do people with AIDS fall victim to opportunistic infections?

12. Describe four ways that HIV is spread.

13. **Critical Thinking** Jason has engaged in high-risk sexual behavior, but he feels fine. He sees no reason to get tested for HIV or any other STI. What would you tell Jason about the importance of getting tested?

Section 4

14. Which of these behaviors is *not* a way to protect yourself from HIV?
    a. avoiding contact with blood
    b. practicing abstinence
    c. sharing needles
    d. avoiding alcohol

15. HIV-positive people receive treatments to keep
    a. their viral load as high as possible.
    b. their viral load as low as possible.
    c. their viral load equal to their T cell count.
    d. their T cell count as low as possible.

16. In what ways can HIV treatment be difficult?

17. **Critical Thinking** Alyssa has engaged in high-risk sexual behavior in the past three months. She had an HIV test a month ago that came back negative. Should she be tested again? Explain.

18. **Critical Thinking** Experts consider education critical in preventing HIV infection. Do you agree? Explain your answer.

Building Health Skills

19. **Analyzing Influences** Do the media do a good job in educating people about HIV and other STIs? Give examples to support your answer.

20. **Advocacy** What could teens do to make abstinence an easier choice for their peers?

21. **Setting Goals** List some goals you have for the next ten years. How could practicing abstinence help you achieve those goals? **WRITING**

Health and Community

Public Service Announcement Some people behave in sexually risky ways. And in many cases, they don't get tested regularly for HIV or other STIs. Create a public service announcement that emphasizes the risks of certain behaviors and the importance of getting tested. Indicate where people in your community can go to get tested for HIV and other STIs. **WRITING**

Standardized Test Prep

Math Practice

The graph shows the helper T cell counts recorded for a person who is HIV-positive. Use the graph to answer Questions 22–24.

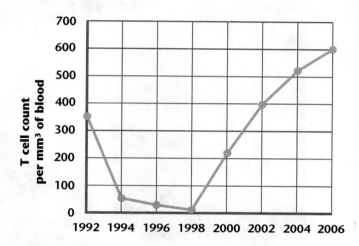

22. What is the lowest helper T cell count recorded for this patient?
    A 300 T cells per mm^3 of blood
    B 100 T cells per mm^3 of blood
    C 50 T cells per mm^3 of blood
    D 10 T cells per mm^3 of blood

23. During which year do you think this patient started treatment for HIV?
    F 1996   G 1998
    H 2000   J 2002

24. Between 2002 and 2006, the patient's T cell count
    A increased steadily.
    B decreased steadily.
    C fluctuated.
    D remained the same.

Test-Taking Tip

Underline important words and phrases as you read. Then when answering questions, you can access the important content quickly.

Reading and Writing Practice

Read the passage. Then answer Questions 25–28.

Researchers are working to develop preventive HIV vaccines to protect people who are HIV-negative and control the spread of HIV. Multiple HIV vaccines may be necessary to prevent infection in the same way that multiple drugs are needed to treat people who are already infected. Researchers are also evaluating therapeutic HIV vaccines to treat people who are HIV-positive. A therapeutic vaccine could theoretically be given during early infection to delay the need for antiretroviral therapy and reduce the risk of transmission.

25. A therapeutic vaccine would
    A prevent HIV infection.
    B treat people who are HIV-positive.
    C be given prior to HIV infection.
    D increase the need for antiretroviral therapy.

26. In this passage, the word *antiretroviral* refers to
    F drugs that treat HIV infection.
    G an HIV vaccine.
    H T cell count.
    J viral load.

27. According to the passage, which of these statements is true?
    A Only one vaccine will be needed to prevent HIV infection.
    B If a vaccine works to prevent HIV infection, it will also be able to treat someone who is HIV-positive.
    C Preventive vaccines will not control the spread of HIV.
    D A therapeutic vaccine should delay the need for antiretroviral therapy.

Constructed Response
28. In a paragraph, compare the two different types of HIV vaccines being developed.

CHAPTER 23

Chronic Diseases and Disabilities

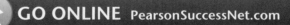

GO ONLINE PearsonSuccessNet.com

TEENS Talk

VIDEO 23

Living With Disabilities

Preview **Activity**

What Does a Disability Mean to You?

Complete this activity before you watch the video.

1. Write down your own definition of the word *disability*.
2. Form a group with two of your classmates. Share and discuss the definitions you wrote.
3. As a group, write a new definition of *disability* that you all can agree on. **WRITING**

Cardiovascular Diseases

Objectives

▶ **List** six types of cardiovascular disease.

▶ **Describe** the ways in which cardiovascular disease is detected and treated.

▶ **Identify** risk factors for cardiovascular disease and ways to lower your risk.

Vocabulary

- chronic disease
- cardiovascular disease
- angina pectoris
- heart attack
- fibrillation
- stroke
- cerebral hemorrhage
- aneurysm

Warm-Up

Quick Quiz Complete each of these statements with *always, sometimes,* or *never.*

1. I __?__ eat foods rich in vitamins, minerals, and fiber, and I __?__ avoid foods high in saturated fats and salt.

2. I __?__ exercise on a regular basis.

3. I __?__ avoid tobacco products and alcohol.

4. I __?__ include relaxation time in my schedule.

WRITING Predict how your behavior may affect your chances of developing cardiovascular disease.

Types of Cardiovascular Disease

In the United States today, the leading causes of death are not infectious diseases. Instead they are **chronic diseases,** diseases that persist for a long period or recur throughout life. Chronic diseases are usually caused by risk factors that are behavioral, environmental, or hereditary—not by pathogens. The most common chronic diseases are **cardiovascular diseases** (KAHR dee oh VAS kyuh lur), which are diseases of the heart (cardio) and blood vessels (vascular). **Cardiovascular diseases include hypertension, atherosclerosis, heart attack, arrhythmia, congestive heart failure, and stroke.**

Hypertension A person whose blood pressure consistently measures 140/90 or higher has hypertension, or high blood pressure. Since many people experience no obvious symptoms, hypertension frequently goes undetected and is known as the "silent killer." The only way to know if you have hypertension is to have your blood pressure measured.

Over time, hypertension can lead to heart disease. This is because the increased blood pressure puts a strain on the heart and blood vessels. Hypertension can be controlled with behavior changes and medications.

Nearly one out of three American adults has hypertension, and the number of teens with hypertension is on the rise. You can reduce your risk of developing hypertension by exercising regularly, maintaining a healthy weight, reducing stress, and eating foods that are low in sodium.

Atherosclerosis Atherosclerosis (ath uh roh skluh ROH sis) is a disease in which fatty substances, including cholesterol (kuh LES tur awl), build up inside artery walls. These deposits, called plaque (plak), cause the artery walls to thicken and narrow, as shown in Figure 1. As it becomes more difficult for blood to flow in the narrowed vessels, blood pressure rises.

A diet high in saturated fats can increase your risk of developing atherosclerosis. This is because saturated fats tend to increase levels of cholesterol in the blood. Other major risk factors include a family history of heart disease, smoking, diabetes, obesity, and lack of exercise.

Atherosclerosis can also increase your risk of developing other cardiovascular conditions.

▶ **Arteriosclerosis** People who suffer from atherosclerosis often have arteriosclerosis (ahr teer ee oh skluh ROH sis) as well. Arteriosclerosis, or hardening of the arteries, develops when arteries lose their elasticity and become stiff.

▶ **Coronary Heart Disease** When atherosclerosis starts to develop in the arteries that supply blood to the heart, it can lead to coronary heart disease. As the coronary arteries narrow, blood flow to the heart decreases. **Angina pectoris** (an JY nuh PEK tur is) is the chest pain that occurs when an area of the heart does not get enough oxygen-rich blood. Coronary heart disease can lead to a heart attack.

How do your exercise habits affect your chances of developing atherosclerosis?

FIGURE 1 An artery with atherosclerosis offers more resistance to blood flow than a healthy artery. This increases blood pressure and causes the heart to work harder.
Relating Cause and Effect What kind of eating habits could lead to atherosclerosis?

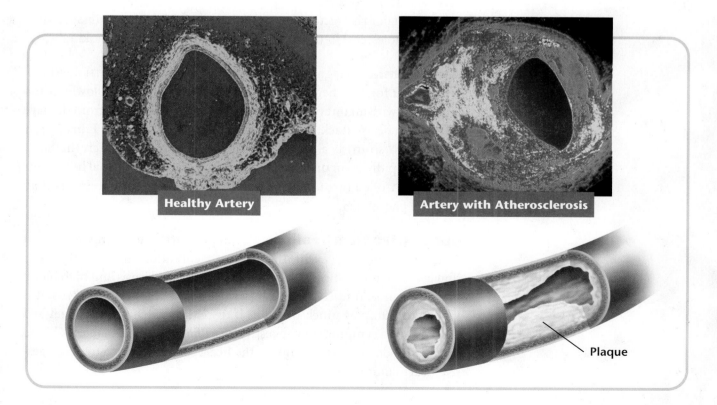

Healthy Artery

Artery with Atherosclerosis

Plaque

▶ Uncomfortable pressure or pain in the center of the chest lasting for two minutes or longer

▶ Pain spreading to the shoulder, neck, or arms

▶ Severe pain, dizziness, fainting, sweating, extreme anxiety, nausea, or shortness of breath

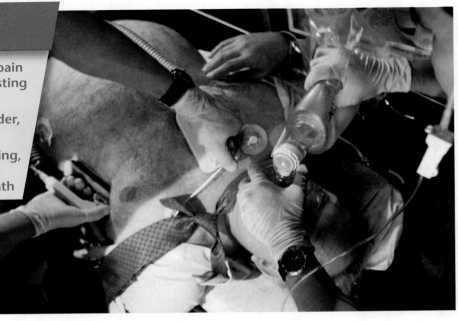

FIGURE 2 Learn to recognize the warning signs of a heart attack. Automated external defibrillators, located in public places such as malls and airports, can help save a heart attack victim's life.

Heart Attack   A **heart attack** occurs when some of the tissue in the heart doesn't receive its normal blood supply and dies. The cause is usually a blood clot that forms in a coronary artery that has been narrowed by atherosclerosis. The clot blocks blood flow to the heart. The more heart tissue that dies due to lack of oxygen, the more severe the heart attack.

Each year, over a million people in the United States suffer a heart attack. Of those people, about 500,000 die. Figure 2 lists the warning signs of a heart attack. Immediate medical attention can mean the difference between life and death.

Four major risk factors for heart attacks are high blood pressure, high levels of cholesterol in the blood, physical inactivity, and smoking.

Arrhythmia   Irregular heartbeats, or arrhythmias (uh RITH mee uhs), are another form of heart disease. The heart may beat too slowly or too quickly, or with an uneven rhythm. Arrhythmias may result from damage caused by a heart attack, or they may develop spontaneously. **Fibrillation** (fib ruh LAY shun) is a life-threatening arrhythmia in which the heart twitches rapidly in an uncoordinated fashion. Some abnormal heartbeats can be controlled by medications. Others require surgery to implant an artificial pacemaker.

Congestive Heart Failure   Unlike a heart attack, congestive heart failure is not a single event. Instead it is a condition in which the heart slowly weakens over time. Usually, years of atherosclerosis and high blood pressure can lead to congestive heart failure. As the heart weakens, it is unable to pump as much blood as it once did. Swelling of the feet and lower legs is a symptom of congestive heart failure. Drugs that relax blood vessels and decrease the strain on the heart may be used to treat congestive heart failure.

Stroke   A **stroke** is a sudden disruption of blood flow to part of the brain. Strokes can occur when an artery that supplies blood to an area of the brain is blocked. The blockage may be caused by atherosclerosis or by a blood clot.

Strokes also can occur when a weakened artery in the brain bursts, flooding the area with blood. If the burst artery is located in the cerebrum, the main portion of the brain, the stroke is called a **cerebral hemorrhage** (suh REE brul HEM ur ij). Cerebral hemorrhage may also be caused by a head injury or by an aneurysm that bursts. An **aneurysm** (AN yuh riz um) is a blood-filled weak spot that balloons out from the artery wall.

Without a supply of blood, brain cells soon die from lack of oxygen. The effects of a stroke depend on its location and severity.

► Brain damage from a stroke can affect the senses, speech, comprehension, behavior, thought patterns, and memory.

► Paralysis on one side of the body is common. Many people who survive a stroke become severely disabled. Sometimes normal function can be regained with therapy.

► Over one third of stroke cases result in death.

Each year in the United States, more than 750,000 people experience a stroke. Risk factors for stroke include high blood pressure, high blood cholesterol, smoking, excessive use of alcohol, physical inactivity, and obesity. Figure 3 lists some of the warning signs of a stroke.

Connect to Your Life   **List some ways you can lower your risk for a stroke.**

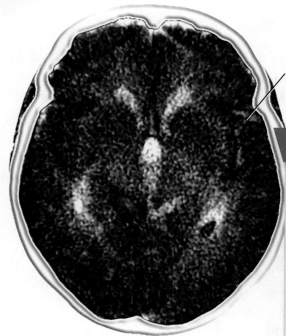

Top View of Brain

Cerebral hemorrhage

FIGURE 3   A blockage or break in an artery in the brain can cause a stroke. A person who experiences any of the warning signs of a stroke should seek prompt medical attention.

Warning Signs of a Stroke

► Sudden, severe headache with no apparent cause

► Sudden weakness or numbness of the face, arm, or leg on one side of the body

► Loss of speech, trouble talking, or trouble understanding speech

► Sudden dimness or loss of vision, particularly in one eye

► Unexplained dizziness, nausea, unsteadiness, or sudden falls

Treating Cardiovascular Disease

Cardiovascular diseases cannot be cured, but they often can be controlled or prevented from getting worse. **There are many medical technologies and surgical methods available for detecting and treating cardiovascular diseases.** Some of these are described in Figure 4. In addition, medicines are often used to control cardiovascular diseases. Certain drugs may lower blood pressure, lower cholesterol levels in the blood, or lessen the chance of blood clots forming.

FIGURE 4 There are many testing and treatment options for patients with cardiovascular disease. New technologies are being developed that may replace these methods in the future.

Testing and Treatment for Cardiovascular Disease

Testing Tools

Magnetic Resonance Imaging (MRI)
Magnetic energy is used to produce a clear image of the heart. Doctors can analyze the image for heart damage.

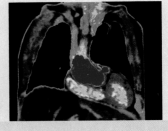

Electrocardiogram (ECG)
Electrodes attached to the skin detect the heart's electrical activity. Abnormalities in heart rhythm or other heart problems are revealed in the recorded pattern.

Echocardiogram
A device that generates sound waves is placed against the chest. The sound waves create a moving picture of the heart. A doctor can evaluate the heart's valves and chambers from the picture.

Arteriography
A flexible tube is threaded through an artery in an arm or leg until it reaches the heart. A dye is then released into the coronary arteries, and X-rays are taken. The X-rays can reveal blockages.

Treatment Methods

Balloon Angioplasty
A thin tube with an expandable tip is guided into a coronary artery. As the tip is inflated, it flattens fatty deposits in the artery wall, improving blood flow. Metal structures called stents are sometimes inserted to keep the artery open.

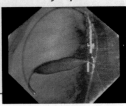

Coronary Bypass Surgery
Surgeons use a vein from the patient's leg or an artificial blood vessel to construct a detour around a blocked coronary artery. This procedure creates an alternate route for blood flow.

Artificial Pacemaker
An artificial pacemaker is a small, battery-operated device that is surgically implanted in the chest. It produces electrical impulses that regulate the heartbeat.

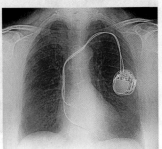

Heart Transplant
When a person's heart cannot function adequately, it may be replaced with a heart from an organ donor. This surgical procedure carries some risk because the immune system may reject the new heart. To lower rejection rates, doctors use drugs to suppress the immune system.

FIGURE 5 Some people inherit a tendency to develop cardiovascular disease. Healthy behaviors are even more important for people with risk factors that they cannot control.

Preventing Cardiovascular Disease

Some risk factors for cardiovascular disease are out of your control. Others are within your control. **Choosing behaviors that lower your risk for cardiovascular disease is important for your health, both now and throughout your life.**

Risks You Cannot Control   Certain risk factors for cardiovascular disease are not within your control. If you have any of these risk factors, it is even more important that you practice healthy behaviors to combat cardiovascular disease.

▶ **Heredity** Having a family history of certain cardiovascular diseases, such as hypertension, may increase your risk of developing those diseases. It is important to be aware of your family's health history so that you can practice behaviors that may reduce your risk.

▶ **Ethnicity** Some diseases strike people of certain ethnicities disproportionately. For example, African Americans and Latinos tend to have higher rates of coronary heart disease.

▶ **Gender** Some cardiovascular diseases strike men and women at different rates. For example, men are more likely to suffer heart attacks than women. On the other hand, women are more likely to suffer strokes than men.

▶ **Age** As people age, their risk of cardiovascular disease increases. However, more young people today are being diagnosed with cardiovascular disease than ever before.

Connect to Your Life

Which of these factors increase your risk of cardiovascular disease?

GO ONLINE
PearsonSuccessNet.com
For: More on cardiovascular disease

FIGURE 6 Healthy behavior patterns in your teen years can give you a head start in preventing cardiovascular disease.

Risks You Can Control   There are many things you can do to avoid cardiovascular disease. Because the damage to your body can begin when you are young, it is important to develop healthy habits now.

▶ **Maintain a Healthy Weight** If you are overweight, your heart has to work harder than it should. Being overweight also raises blood pressure and blood cholesterol levels. Obese adults are more likely to develop diabetes, which is a major risk factor for cardiovascular disease.

▶ **Eat a Healthy Diet** Choose a diet that is high in plant products and low in saturated fat and cholesterol. Limit your intake of red meat, high-sodium snacks, and sugary foods, such as soda and candy.

▶ **Be Physically Active** Regular exercise strengthens your cardiovascular system and can lower blood pressure.

▶ **Manage Stress** Take time to relax each day. Feelings of stress and anxiety can raise blood pressure and contribute to cardiovascular disease.

▶ **Monitor Your Blood Pressure** Have your blood pressure checked regularly by a doctor or nurse. If your blood pressure is high, discuss ways to lower it.

▶ **Avoid Smoking and Drinking** Do not start smoking. And if you smoke, quit. Smokers have a higher risk of heart attack and stroke than nonsmokers. Excessive alcohol intake can also damage the heart.

Section 1 Review

Key Ideas and Vocabulary

1. Name six types of cardiovascular disease.
2. What is **fibrillation**?
3. What is an **aneurysm** and how can it lead to a stroke?
4. What medical test might be used to detect an arrhythmia? How might an arrhythmia be treated?
5. List four things you can do to lower your risk for cardiovascular disease.

Critical Thinking

6. **Comparing and Contrasting** Distinguish between a heart attack and a stroke.

Health at School

Heart Health Write an advertisement, song, or skit that informs teens about ways to prevent cardiovascular disease. Think about how you can motivate other students to practice healthy behaviors. Present your advertisement, song, or skit to the class. **WRITING**

7. **Applying Concepts** Suppose you have a friend who has a family history of cardiovascular disease. If you noticed your friend eating meals high in saturated fat and salt, what would you say?

Cancer

Objectives

▶ **Describe** how cancer affects the body.

▶ **Identify** the tests and treatments for cancer.

▶ **List** seven ways you can prevent cancer.

Vocabulary

• cancer
• tumor
• malignant
• metastasis
• oncogene
• carcinogen
• biopsy

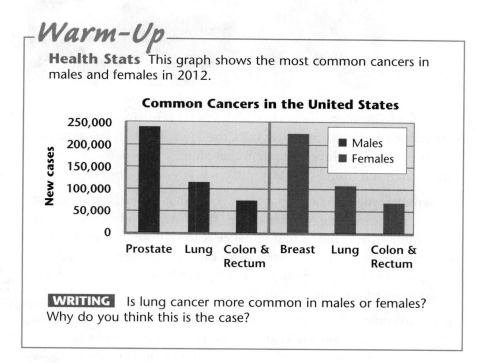

Warm-Up

Health Stats This graph shows the most common cancers in males and females in 2012.

Common Cancers in the United States

New cases (y-axis): 0, 50,000, 100,000, 150,000, 200,000, 250,000

Categories: Prostate, Lung, Colon & Rectum, Breast, Lung, Colon & Rectum

Legend: ■ Males ■ Females

WRITING Is lung cancer more common in males or females? Why do you think this is the case?

How Cancer Affects the Body

In the United States, cancer is the second leading cause of death in adults, just behind cardiovascular disease. **Cancer** is a group of diseases that involves the rapid, uncontrolled growth and spread of abnormal cells. **Cancer harms the body by destroying healthy body tissues.**

Cancer cells typically form a mass of tissue called a **tumor.** The word **malignant** (muh LIG nunt) is used to describe a cancerous tumor. A tumor that is not cancerous is called a benign tumor.

The cells of a malignant tumor grow into surrounding tissues and destroy them. In addition, some cancer cells may break away from the original tumor. The cells travel through blood vessels or lymph vessels to other parts of the body. There the cancer cells may start new tumors. The spread of cancer from where it first develops to other parts of the body is called **metastasis** (muh TAS tuh sis).

Many cancers can be cured if they are detected early and treated promptly. Because cancer cells eventually replace normal cells, death may result if the cancer is not treated.

Connect to Your Life How much do you know about cancer? What questions do you have?

FIGURE 7 This man is wearing a respiratory mask to protect himself from carcinogens such as asbestos.

Causes of Cancer In normal body cells, a control system keeps cell reproduction in check. In cancer cells, the control system has gone haywire, and cells reproduce more than they should. This damaged control system can result from hereditary and environmental factors.

▶ **Heredity** All human cells contain genes that control cell reproduction. But some people inherit genes that have a tendency to change, or mutate, into forms that allow cells to reproduce too rapidly. A normal gene that has changed into a cancer-causing gene is called an **oncogene** (AHN kuh jeen). People whose cells contain oncogenes may develop certain forms of cancer.

▶ **Environment** The environment contains cancer-causing agents known as **carcinogens** (kahr SIN uh junz). Carcinogens can cause mutations in genes that control cell reproduction. The range of possible carcinogens is broad. Ultraviolet light and X-rays can cause mutations. So can tobacco products, asbestos, arsenic, and some pesticides. Some types of viruses are also carcinogens.

Types of Cancer Cancer can occur in almost any part of the body. A cancer is named according to the part of the body where it first develops. Figure 8 surveys some different types of cancer.

Some cancers are rare. Others are more common. For example, one form of skin cancer—basal cell carcinoma—is the most common cancer that occurs in the United States. Fortunately, this common form of skin cancer is rarely life-threatening, especially if it is detected early. Another form of skin cancer, called melanoma (mel uh NOH muh), is less common but can be much more serious.

Many cancers are curable if they are caught early, including testicular cancer and breast cancer. Other cancers are hard to detect early in their development and pose a bigger challenge for treatment. Symptoms of lung cancer, for example, usually do not appear until the disease has spread.

Connect to Your Life What carcinogens are you exposed to? How can you protect yourself from them?

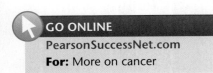

GO ONLINE

PearsonSuccessNet.com
For: More on cancer

FIGURE 8 Symptoms, screening methods, and prevention strategies vary for each type of cancer. **Classifying** Which cancers affect both males and females?

Types of Cancers

Cancer	Symptoms	Screening	Prevention
Skin	A mole that changes size, shape, or color; tenderness, itching, or pain around a mole	• Check skin regularly for moles	• Avoid extended time in the sun • Wear sunblock • Do not use tanning salons
Prostate	If advanced, painful or burning urination, blood in the urine, or pain in the lower back or pelvis	• Regular checkups for men • Rectal examination • PSA (prostate-specific antigen) blood test	
Breast	Unusual lump in the breast	• Perform monthly breast self-exams • Mammogram	
Lung	Persistent cough; chest pain; recurrent pneumonia or bronchitis	• Chest X-ray	• Do not smoke
Colorectal	Bleeding from the rectum; blood in the feces; changes in bowel habits	• Colonoscopy	• Eat a diet low in saturated fat and high in fiber
Cervical	Abnormal vaginal bleeding	• Have regular Pap tests	• Avoid HPV infection by practicing abstinence
Oral	Lumps in the mouth; a sore in the mouth that bleeds easily; a red or white patch in the mouth	• Have regular dental checkups	• Do not smoke and do not use smokeless tobacco products • Do not drink alcohol
Non-Hodgkin's Lymphoma	Swollen lymph nodes	• X-ray • CT scan	
Ovarian	Usually no early symptoms	• Regular and thorough pelvic exams for women	
Leukemia	Weight loss; recurrent infections; fatigue; swollen lymph nodes	• Blood test	

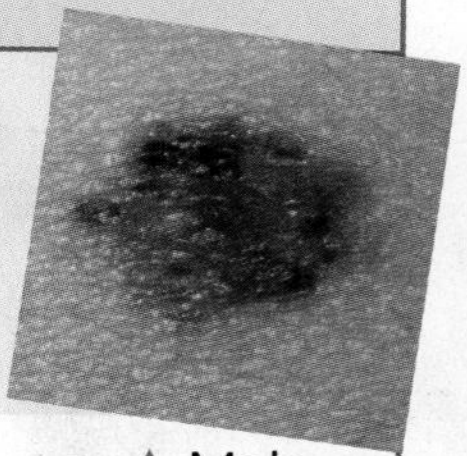
▲ Mole

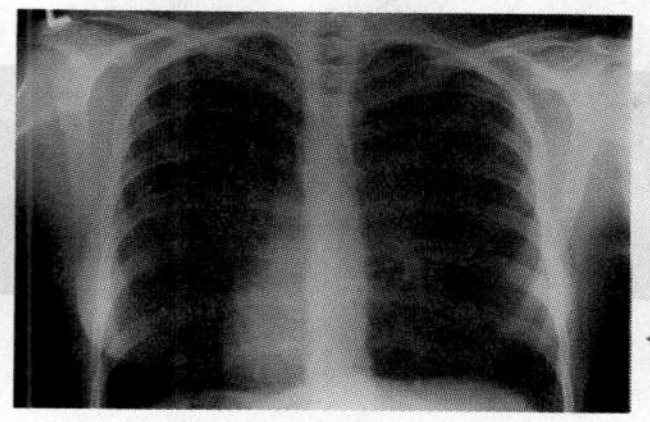
◀ Chest X-ray

Dental checkup ▼
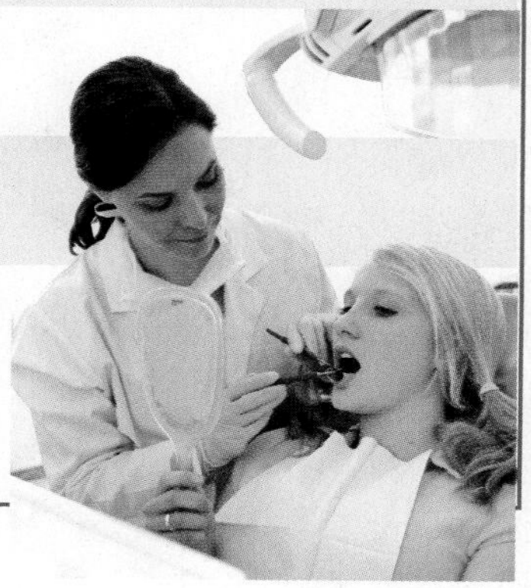

Media Wise

Evaluating Tanning Products

There is a lot of information available about the dangers of too much sun exposure. But, many young people still tan. Evaluate products that claim to give you a "healthy tan" using this questionnaire.

Does the product's labeling caution about the dangers of ultraviolet (UV) radiation?	Yes	No
Does the product provide SPF (sun protection factor) information?	Yes	No
Does the product encourage you to minimize your exposure to the sun or other UV radiation?	Yes	No
Does the product recommend other precautions—such as wearing sunglasses or a hat?	Yes	No

A "No" answer to one or more questions indicates that using the product may endanger your skin.

Activity Use the checklist to evaluate a tanning product. Then write a paragraph explaining why the tanning product you chose may or may not be healthy for your skin. **WRITING**

Detecting and Treating Cancer

Seven common warning signs of cancer are listed in Figure 9. If you experience any of these warning signs, you should seek medical attention. **The key to curing cancer is early detection and treatment.**

Tests Screening tests, such as mammograms, chest X-rays, and endoscopies, can detect cancers before any symptoms appear. If cancer is suspected from screening test results, surgeons may remove a small piece of the tissue in question to examine it for signs of cancer. This procedure is called a **biopsy** (BY ahp see).

Treatments Cancer treatments depend on the type of cancer, its location, and its stage of development.

► Surgery can remove part or all of a malignant tumor.

► Radiation therapy can kill cancer cells and slow tumor growth.

► Chemotherapy (kee moh THEHR uh pee) uses drugs to slow the reproduction of cancer cells. Immunotherapy (im yuh noh THEHR uh pee) uses drugs to stimulate the body's immune system to attack cancer cells.

When the signs or symptoms of cancer disappear, the cancer is said to be in remission. Most cancers that stay in remission for five years are considered cured. Sometimes, however, the cancer returns after five years. A second occurrence of the same cancer is usually more difficult to treat.

Preventing Cancer

Early detection of cancer cannot prevent the disease, but it may prevent the cancer from killing you. Regularly examining your skin and breasts or testicles for abnormal lumps or growth is a good habit to start. Self-exams and seeing your doctor regularly can help you prevent the further development of a cancer—if one is present in your body—by catching it early.

Detecting cancer early is very important, but avoiding cancer altogether is ideal. **Although the specific cause of most cancers is unknown, certain behaviors have been shown to decrease the risk of cancer.**

▶ Do not use any form of tobacco. Tobacco and tobacco smoke contain carcinogens. Smokeless tobacco, or snuff, can cause oral cancer.

▶ Avoid alcohol. Drinking, especially along with smoking, greatly increases the risks of oral cancer and liver cancer.

▶ Avoid the sun's ultraviolet rays. Wear protective clothing and use sunscreen. Do not use tanning beds.

▶ Choose a diet low in saturated fat and cholesterol. Instead, eat plenty of vegetables, fruits, and whole grains. Such a diet is rich in vitamins and fiber, which may reduce the risks of some cancers.

▶ Exercise regularly and maintain a healthy weight.

▶ Avoid unnecessary X-rays, especially during pregnancy.

▶ Avoid known carcinogens. If you cannot avoid them, wear protective clothing or equipment.

Seven Warning Signs of Cancer

- **C**hange in bowel or bladder habits, such as constipation, diarrhea, or incomplete emptying of the bowel
- **A** sore throat that does not heal
- **U**nusual bleeding or discharge, particularly from the rectum or vagina
- **T**hickening or lump in the breast or elsewhere
- **I**ndigestion or difficulty in swallowing
- **O**bvious change in a wart or mole, such as growth, discharge, or unusual appearance
- **N**agging cough or hoarseness

FIGURE 9 If you experience any of these warning signs, see your doctor. Notice that the first letters of the warning signs spell "caution."

Section 2 Review

Key Ideas and Vocabulary

1. How does cancer harm the body? What changes in cells allow cancer to develop?
2. What is a **tumor?** When is a tumor considered **malignant?**
3. What is a **carcinogen?**
4. How does a doctor determine if a person has cancer? If cancer is present, what types of treatment might the patient receive?
5. Name four ways you can reduce your risk of developing cancer.

Health at Home

Cancer Prevention Many types of cancer can be prevented by practicing healthy behaviors. Discuss some cancer prevention tips with your family. Together, list some changes family members can make in their current behaviors. Post the list on your refrigerator or in another visible location. **WRITING**

Critical Thinking

6. **Comparing and Contrasting** Distinguish between a normal gene and an oncogene.
7. **Applying Concepts** Some cancer cells live much longer than noncancerous cells. How might this play a role in the development of a tumor?

Other Chronic Diseases

Objectives

▶ **Distinguish** between the two types of diabetes.

▶ **Describe** how allergies and asthma affect the body.

▶ **Identify** the symptoms of arthritis.

Vocabulary

- diabetes
- insulin
- allergy
- allergen
- histamine
- arthritis
- osteoarthritis
- rheumatoid arthritis

Warm-Up

Dear Advice Line,

My older brother was just diagnosed with diabetes. Is he going to be okay? Should I be worried about getting diabetes, too? What can I do to avoid it?

WRITING Write a draft of a response to this question. Revise your answer after reading this section.

Diabetes

About 26 million Americans are affected by diabetes. But some do not know that they have it. **Diabetes** (dy uh BEE teez) is a disease in which the body's ability to use glucose (blood sugar) is impaired. Diabetes involves **insulin** (IN suh lin), a hormone produced by the pancreas. Insulin stimulates body cells to take up and use blood sugar.

If not controlled, diabetes can be life-threatening. People with diabetes are also at risk for heart disease, stroke, kidney disease, blindness, infections requiring amputation, and complications during pregnancy. There are two common types of diabetes, type 1 and type 2.

Type 1 Diabetes About 5 to 10 percent of diabetics have insulin-dependent diabetes, or type 1 diabetes. **A person with type 1 diabetes produces little or no insulin. Without insulin, glucose levels in the blood remain high.** Symptoms include thirst, frequent urination, nausea, hunger, fatigue, and weight loss.

Although it can strike at any age, type 1 diabetes usually first appears in childhood. Type 1 diabetics must monitor their blood glucose levels and give themselves doses of insulin on a strict schedule. In addition, they need to eat the proper amounts of carbohydrates and other nutrients on a regular schedule.

Taking too much insulin, missing a meal, or exercising too much can result in low blood sugar levels. The opposite condition—high blood sugar—occurs when too little insulin is taken or too much food is eaten. If not treated promptly, both of these conditions can be life-threatening.

Type 2 Diabetes Also known as noninsulin-dependent diabetes, type 2 diabetes occurs mostly in people over the age of 30. However, it can strike children and teens, especially if they are overweight and do not get enough exercise. **People with type 2 diabetes produce sufficient insulin, but their body cells do not respond normally to insulin. As with type 1 diabetes, the result is a high level of glucose in the blood.**

Type 2 diabetes usually develops slowly and often goes undetected until symptoms become severe. Symptoms are the same as for type 1 diabetes, but also include drowsiness, itching, blurred vision, numbness in the hands or feet, and frequent, hard-to-heal infections. Risk factors for type 2 diabetes include a family history of diabetes, being overweight, and a lack of physical activity.

Fortunately, many people can prevent type 2 diabetes by maintaining a desirable body weight and by exercising regularly. Some people who develop the disease can control it if they follow a weight-loss and exercise program. In other cases, medications may be used. Excessive sugar consumption is not thought to be a direct cause of type 2 diabetes. However, a high-sugar diet can lead to obesity, which can increase the risk of developing type 2 diabetes.

 What can you do to lower your risk for type 2 diabetes?

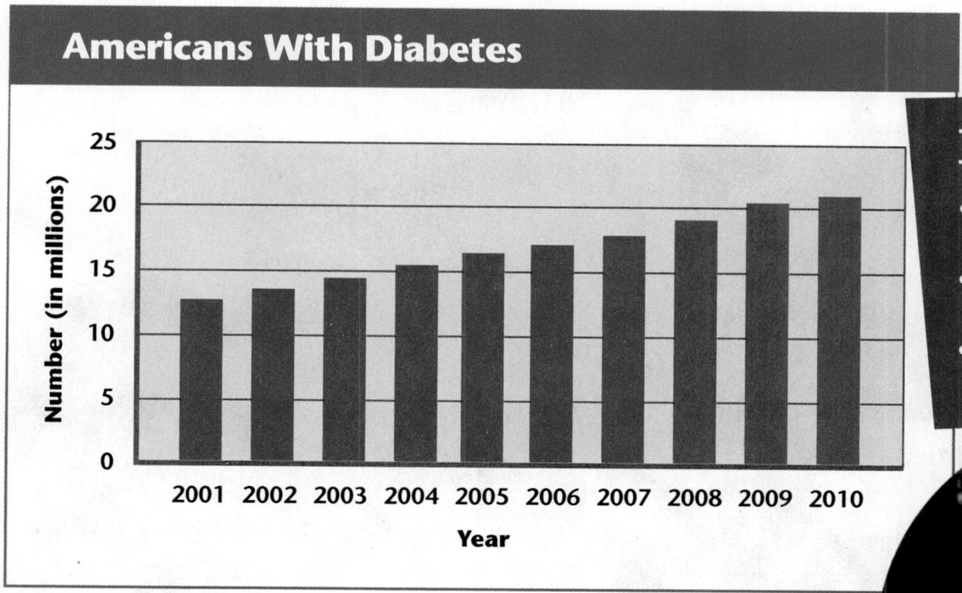

Americans With Diabetes

Number (in millions) vs Year (2001–2010), values rising from about 12.5 in 2001 to about 20.5 in 2010.

Tips for Preventing Type 2 Diabetes
- Maintain a healthy body weight.
- Eat nutritious meals low in sugar and saturated fats.
- Exercise for at least 30 minutes every day.

FIGURE 10 Diabetes is a major risk factor for cardiovascular disease. If you follow the guidelines for preventing type 2 diabetes, you can also reduce your risk of cardiovascular disease. **Predicting** How do you think the trend in diabetes will affect trends in other chronic diseases?

Allergies and Asthma

Some people's bodies overreact to harmless substances, and as a result, they may feel sick. An **allergy** is a disorder in which the immune system is overly sensitive to a particular substance not normally found in the body. One type of allergic reaction can lead to a condition called asthma, which you learned about in Chapter 12.

Causes of Allergies   **Allergies develop when foreign substances enter the body and set off a series of reactions.** Any substance that causes an allergy is called an **allergen.** Common allergens include plant pollen, dust, molds, some foods, and even some medicines. Allergens may get into your body when you inhale them, eat them in food, or touch them with your skin.

The immune system's overly sensitive response to an allergen causes large quantities of a chemical called **histamine** (HIS tuh meen) to be released. Histamine is responsible for the symptoms of an allergy, such as sneezing and watery eyes. Antihistamines—medicines that interfere with the action of histamine—may relieve symptoms. However, the best strategy is to try to avoid any substance to which you are allergic.

Some allergic reactions can be very serious and require immediate medical attention. For example, people who are severely allergic to bee stings must carry medicine with them in case they get stung.

FIGURE 11 Some people have allergic reactions to plant pollen, dust mites, or cats.

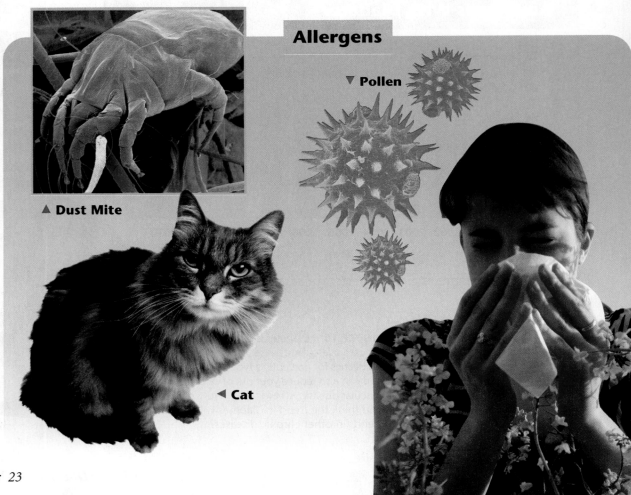

Allergens

▼ **Pollen**

▲ **Dust Mite**

◄ **Cat**

An Asthma Attack

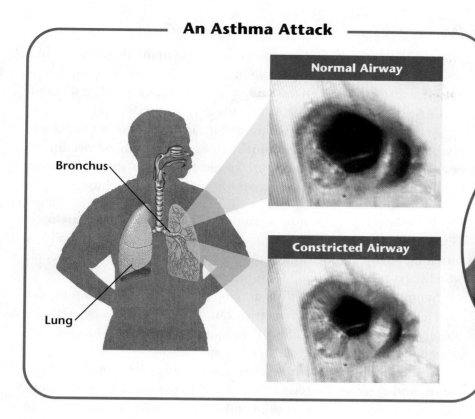

Normal Airway

Constricted Airway

Bronchus

Lung

About 60% of children have missed school because of asthma.

FIGURE 12 During an asthma attack, the respiratory passages in the lungs become narrower and secrete extra mucus. Both responses make breathing difficult. Using an inhaler with medicine can stop an asthma attack.

Asthma Asthma is a disorder in which a person's respiratory passages become inflamed and narrow significantly in reaction to certain "triggers." Figure 12 shows a narrowed airway of a person having an asthma attack.

Asthma attacks can be triggered by many things, including certain allergens, stress, cold weather, tobacco smoke, or exercise. During an attack, a person may wheeze, cough, or become short of breath. Some people describe an asthma attack as trying to breathe through a straw.

Managing Asthma About 40 million people in the United States have asthma. Of these, about 10 million are children. Asthma can be serious, but it can be managed so that asthma sufferers can lead normal, active lives.

Managing asthma involves avoiding the triggers that bring on asthma attacks. It may also involve the use of medicines. Asthma medicines are either "controllers" or "rescue drugs." A person with asthma can use a controller each day to prevent asthma attacks from occurring. When the person has an attack, he or she uses a rescue drug to relieve the symptoms. Rescue drugs relax the muscles in the airways, making it easier to breathe.

Do you know someone who has asthma? What does he or she do to manage it?

 GO ONLINE
PearsonSuccessNet.com
For: More on allergies

Arthritis

Inflammation or irritation of a joint is known as **arthritis** (ahr THRY tis). Arthritis is one of the most common chronic diseases, affecting nearly one in every three adults in the United States. In fact, arthritis is the leading cause of disability among Americans over age 15.

Arthritis is not life-threatening, but it can be extremely painful and disabling. **Arthritis results in joint stiffness, joint pain, or swelling in one or more joints.** There is no cure for most types of arthritis. However, treatments and exercise can reduce the severity of the symptoms.

Osteoarthritis   The most common type of arthritis is **osteoarthritis** (ahs tee oh ahr THRY tis). This form of arthritis is caused by wear and tear on a joint after years of use or by repeated injuries to a joint. Most people who live past 60 will develop some form of osteoarthritis.

Symptoms of osteoarthritis develop slowly, usually beginning as a mild ache or soreness. Osteoarthritis can occur in almost any joint, but most commonly occurs in hips, knees, spine, and fingers. When it occurs at the finger joints, bony growths often appear.

Treatment for osteoarthritis may involve drugs, heat and cold treatments, and exercise. Exercise is important to maintain joint flexibility. Sometimes, weight loss is recommended to ease stress on the joints. In severe cases of osteoarthritis, surgery may be required to repair or replace affected joints.

FIGURE 13   Regular stretching and exercise can help prevent osteoarthritis. The inset shows an X-ray of a knee with osteoarthritis. Much of the cartilage between the two bones has been worn away.

Rheumatoid Arthritis In **rheumatoid arthritis** (ROO muh toyd), the membrane surrounding a joint becomes inflamed. The inflammation then spreads to other areas of the joint. An affected joint becomes hot, red, and swollen. Areas of the body other than joints may also become inflamed.

Rheumatoid arthritis affects both the young and the old. Over two million Americans suffer from rheumatoid arthritis. The exact cause of rheumatoid arthritis is still unclear. Much evidence suggests that the immune system malfunctions and attacks some of the body's own tissues. This "self-attack" leads to the inflammation that is characteristic of rheumatoid arthritis.

Any joint in the body may be affected by rheumatoid arthritis, although joints in the wrist and knuckles are most commonly affected. If not treated, rheumatoid arthritis can cause joints to stiffen in deformed positions. The damage can be so severe that it changes the shape of the joint, as you can see in Figure 14.

Treatment includes aspirin or other anti-inflammatory drugs, exercise, and rest. Early diagnosis and treatment by a doctor are the best ways to reduce the severity of the disease.

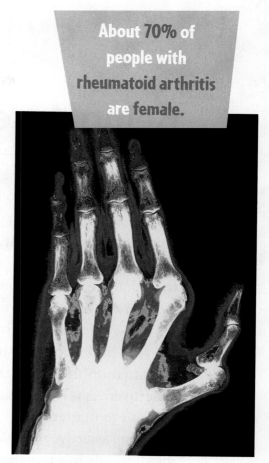

About 70% of people with rheumatoid arthritis are female.

FIGURE 14 In rheumatoid arthritis, joints become inflamed. Over time, the joints may become deformed, as shown in this X-ray.

Section 3 Review

Key Ideas and Vocabulary

1. Distinguish between type 1 and type 2 diabetes. How are their effects on the body similar?
2. Where is **insulin** produced, and what does it do?
3. How do allergies and asthma affect the body?
4. What is **histamine**?
5. What are the symptoms of arthritis?

Critical Thinking

6. **Comparing and Contrasting** How are osteoarthritis and rheumatoid arthritis similar? How do they differ?

Health at School

Reducing Asthma Triggers Asthma is one of the most common chronic diseases that occur in childhood. An important aspect of managing asthma is to reduce asthma triggers in the environment. Evaluate your school environment for asthma triggers. Write a paragraph summarizing your findings. **WRITING**

7. **Relating Cause and Effect** Why do you think that people with diabetes often feel tired?

Being Assertive

While walking to his car at the mall, Mark noticed a person parking in a spot reserved for people with disabilities. At first, Mark was going to ignore the situation. But he knew it wasn't right for someone who is not disabled to park there. So Mark politely informed the woman that she needed to move her car.

Mark behaved assertively in this situation. Do you think you could be assertive in a similar situation? If not, you are not alone. Assertiveness is a skill that many people find difficult to master.

Being assertive means expressing your feelings honestly in a way that respects your rights and the rights of others. Acting assertively can help you feel more self-confident and more in control of factors that affect your life. This step-by-step process can help you master the skill of assertiveness. The process is especially helpful in situations where you would like to act assertively but find it difficult to do so.

1 Evaluate your current behavior.
To understand why you didn't act assertively in a situation, ask yourself these questions:

▶ What outcome did I desire?

▶ What outcome did I get?

▶ What negative thoughts kept me from acting assertively in this situation?

▶ What was I afraid might have happened if I had acted assertively?

2 Observe a role model in action.
Identify a person who acts assertively in difficult situations. Observe the person as he or she handles a situation in an assertive manner. Pay attention to the words, tone of voice, and body language the person uses.

3 **Conduct a mental rehearsal.**

Imagine yourself being assertive in a situation you expect to be involved in. Mental rehearsal helps you think about how you will look, act, and feel in the actual situation.

4 **Use assertive verbal behavior.**

When the situation you have rehearsed presents itself, put your plan into action.

▶ Ask for what you want by using "I" messages. Begin statements with "I feel" or "I want." Do not try to blame or demand things by saying "You should …" or "You did…."

▶ Be specific about what you want to say. Do not speak in terms that are too general.

▶ Be direct and unapologetic. For example, say "I believe I was ahead of you." Do not assume that the other person did something on purpose.

▶ Speak calmly and clearly. Take time to think things through. When listening, pay full attention to the other person.

5 **Use assertive nonverbal behavior.**

▶ Pay attention to your body language. Be sure to use gestures and facial expressions that match what you are saying.

▶ Look directly at the other person when speaking. Make direct eye contact.

▶ Stand a comfortable distance from the person to whom you are speaking. Standing too close may seem uncomfortable or threatening to some people.

6 **Evaluate yourself.**

After the encounter, ask yourself these questions:

▶ Did I say what I intended to say?

▶ Was I direct and unapologetic, yet still considerate?

▶ Did I stand up for myself without becoming defensive and without infringing on the other person's rights?

▶ Was my body language assertive?

▶ Did I feel good about myself after the encounter?

▶ Do I think the other person felt comfortable with my interaction?

Questions to which you answered *no* indicate areas you should work to improve for future encounters.

Practice the Skill

1. What would you have done in Mark's position? Would you have approached the person who parked illegally? Why or why not?

2. List some situations in which you need to be assertive. Some examples are saying *no* to a friend who asks for a favor, or returning a defective product to a store.

3. Mentally rehearse how you would act assertively in those situations. Write out what you would do and say. What verbal and nonverbal behavior would you use? Then, when the situations arise, use your assertiveness skills to take action.

Technology & Health

Vital Signs on the Go

Suppose you could go about your normal activities while your doctor gathers data about your asthma or other health condition. That's the idea behind "wearable monitoring technology." These vests and shirts can record your every breath, as well as your heart rate, body temperature, oxygen levels, coughing, and even your posture. The data can then be downloaded and sent to your doctor over the Internet. With this new technology, your doctor can monitor your health without disrupting your life.

WRITING In a paragraph, give three reasons why wearable technology is a good alternative to monitoring patients in a hospital or doctor's office.

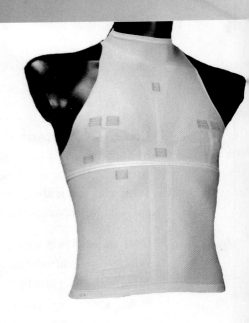

Monitoring Vest ▲

Leads from sensors woven into the fabric of this vest attach to the patient's body and record vital signs.

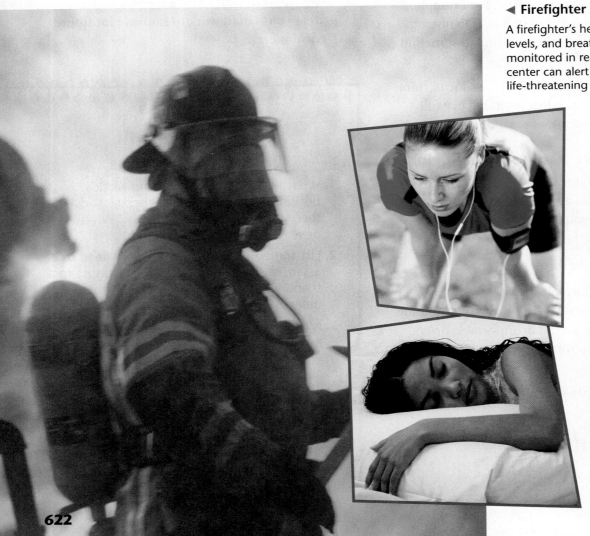

◀ Firefighter Safety

A firefighter's heart rate, oxygen levels, and breathing can be monitored in real time. A command center can alert the firefighter to any life-threatening conditions.

◀ Asthma

Doctors can monitor how things like activity level, temperature, stress, and medications affect asthma or other respiratory conditions.

◀ Sleep Apnea

Instead of going to a hospital sleep lab, patients can be monitored in their own beds for sleep apnea, a condition in which breathing stops for short periods of time during sleep.

Disabilities

Objectives

▶ **Identify** the three most common physical disabilities.

▶ **Explain** how the rights of people with disabilities are protected.

Vocabulary

• disability
• macular degeneration
• tinnitus
• Americans with Disabilities Act

Warm-Up

Myth People with physical disabilities always need someone's help.

Fact Most people with physical disabilities can function independently. Allow a person with a physical disability to take the lead when performing a particular task. Wait for the person to perform the task independently or to ask you for help.

WRITING What other misconceptions do you think people hold about disabilities?

Types of Disabilities

A **disability** is any physical or mental impairment that limits or reduces normal activities, such as attending school or caring for oneself. **The three most common physical disabilities are impaired vision, impaired hearing, and impaired mobility.** The severity of a disability can vary, but in many cases, there are devices or ways to modify the physical environment to reduce a person's limitations.

Impaired Vision Nearly 4 million Americans over age 40 are visually impaired, and a million of them are blind. Young people may also be visually impaired, often due to birth defects or eye injuries. The leading causes of vision impairment in the United States are diabetes, cataracts (cloudiness in the lens), glaucoma (pressure buildup in the eyeball), and macular degeneration. **Macular degeneration** is a condition affecting the retina and is the leading cause of vision loss in older Americans.

Technologies enable some people with vision impairment to see more clearly. For example, cornea transplants can restore vision in some people. Unfortunately, not every type of vision impairment can be treated at this time. In such cases, people usually depend on sound as a primary means of gathering information. Material written in Braille, a system that uses characters made up of raised dots, is also available. Canes may be used to detect obstacles, such as curbs, and trained guide dogs allow mobility for many vision-impaired people. Figure 15 on the next page lists some guidelines for interacting with someone who is visually impaired.

Interacting With a...

Vision-Impaired Person

► Speak right away so that the person knows you are there.

► If the person asks to be guided, extend your arm and place the person's hand on it. Do not grab the person by the arm.

► Ask for permission before touching or talking to a guide dog.

► Describe where things are and who is present.

Hearing-Impaired Person

► Touch the person gently to gain attention.

► Have the person look directly at you. Do not shout.

► Find out if the person hears better on one side and position yourself on the "good" side.

► Speak slowly and clearly and be sure your mouth is visible to the person.

► Use sign language if both of you know it.

FIGURE 15 Many people with physical disabilities can navigate their environment and communicate effectively.
Evaluating By following these guidelines, how are you showing respect for a disabled person's independence?

Impaired Hearing Hearing loss is more common in older people than in younger people. In fact, about 1 in 3 Americans over the age of 60 has some degree of hearing impairment. Nevertheless, some young people, including infants, may also experience hearing impairment and deafness. Some causes of hearing impairment include birth defects, genetic disorders, exposure to excessive noise, and ear infections.

Tinnitus is a condition in which ringing is heard in the ears, even when there is no external sound. Tinnitus can be so severe that it impairs a person's hearing. A major cause of tinnitus is prolonged exposure to loud sounds. You can protect your hearing by limiting your exposure to loud sounds, such as those at music concerts, car races, or sports events.

A variety of devices and techniques can help people with hearing impairments.

► Hearing aids increase the volume of sounds for people who are not completely deaf.

► Devices called cochlear implants can be surgically implanted to help people who are completely deaf to sense sounds.

► Sign language and lip reading enable people with severe hearing impairment to communicate. Signing is a language consisting of hand positions and movements.

► Special telephones and doorbells amplify sound or use lights.

► The Internet and e-mail allow people who are hearing impaired to gather information and communicate.

Impaired Mobility   The body's ability to move depends on the nervous, muscular, and skeletal systems functioning together in a coordinated fashion. Disease in, or injury to, any of these body systems may result in impaired mobility.

▶ **Diseases** In children, impaired mobility can be caused by diseases such as cerebral palsy and muscular dystrophy. Multiple sclerosis can develop in young people and may result in impaired mobility. In the elderly, arthritis, Alzheimer's disease, Parkinson's disease, and heart disease are common causes of impaired mobility.

▶ **Injuries** Paralysis of the arms or legs due to injuries to the brain or spinal cord is a major cause of impaired mobility. These kinds of injuries are frequently the result of unnecessary risk-taking, substance abuse, or violence. Nearly 80% of spinal cord injury victims are young males.

The loss of arms or legs due to injury is another cause of impaired mobility. Diseases such as diabetes and cancer can also require the surgical removal of a limb to save the person's life.

Individuals with impaired mobility can use canes, walkers, wheelchairs, crutches, braces, or artificial limbs to be mobile. Elevators, curb cuts, and ramps at building entrances allow people in wheelchairs access to places and services. For people who are paralyzed, research on nerve cell function holds some promise.

Connect to Your Life   In what ways is your school accessible to people with impaired mobility?

GO ONLINE

PearsonSuccessNet.com

For: More on disabilities

Living With Disabilities

People adapt to physical disabilities in different ways, depending on the extent of the disability, their feelings about it, and the support they receive. Many organizations help people adapt to disabilities by providing equipment, education, and emotional support.

People with disabilities have the same life goals as people who do not have disabilities. And these goals require that they be integrated into school, the workplace, and the community. People with disabilities are capable of great things and should not be underestimated.

An important move toward integrating people with disabilities into the workplace and community came in 1990 when the Americans with Disabilities Act was signed into law. The Americans with Disabilities Act (ADA) guarantees the civil rights of Americans who have physical or mental disabilities. This includes people who are physically impaired or mentally retarded, as well as those who have cancer, epilepsy, and HIV or AIDS. It also protects people who are undergoing or have completed rehabilitation for alcoholism or drug abuse. The law guarantees that people with disabilities have access to the same employment opportunities, public services, public transportation, public accommodations, and communications capabilities as everyone else.

In addition, the Individuals with Disabilities Education Act (IDEA) of 1997 helps ensure that children with disabilities receive quality education alongside other students.

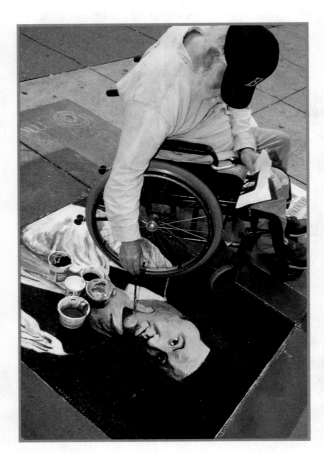

FIGURE 16 People with disabilities contribute in all areas of society.

Section 4 Review

Key Ideas and Vocabulary

1. What is a **disability**?
2. What are the three most common physical disabilities?
3. What is **tinnitus** and how can it be prevented?
4. How are the rights of Americans with disabilities protected?

Critical Thinking

5. **Evaluating** If one of your friends were making fun of a person with a disability, how would you react?

Health and Community

Protecting Your Hearing Create a public service announcement informing people in your community about the dangers of prolonged exposure to loud noises. Include information about different types of noises and how they can affect your hearing. Describe ways you can protect your hearing at work and at play. **WRITING**

6. **Relating Cause and Effect** Some disabilities can be prevented. Choose a disability you read about in this section that is preventable. What behaviors could you practice now to avoid that disability?

Chapter 23
At a Glance

VIDEO **TEENS** Talk ○

Living With Disabilities Did the video change your view of disabilities? In what way?

Section 1 Cardiovascular Diseases

Key Ideas

▶ Cardiovascular diseases include hypertension, atherosclerosis, heart attack, arrhythmia, congestive heart failure, and stroke.

▶ There are many medical technologies and surgical methods available for detecting and treating cardiovascular diseases.

▶ Choosing behaviors that lower your risk for cardiovascular disease is important for your health, both now and throughout your life.

Vocabulary
- chronic disease (602) • cardiovascular disease (602)
- angina pectoris (603) • heart attack (604)
- fibrillation (604) • stroke (605)
- cerebral hemorrhage (605) • aneurysm (605)

Section 2 Cancer

Key Ideas

▶ Cancer harms the body by destroying healthy body tissues. The key to curing cancer is early detection and treatment.

▶ Although the specific cause of most cancers is unknown, certain behaviors have been shown to decrease the risk of cancer.

Vocabulary
- cancer (609)
- tumor (609)
- malignant (609)
- metastasis (609)
- oncogene (610)
- carcinogen (610)
- biopsy (612)

Section 3 Other Chronic Diseases

Key Ideas

▶ People with type 1 diabetes produce little or no insulin, and blood glucose levels remain high.

▶ People with type 2 diabetes produce sufficient insulin, but their cells do not respond. Blood glucose levels remain high.

▶ Allergies develop when foreign substances enter the body and set off a series of reactions.

▶ With asthma, the respiratory passages become inflamed in reaction to certain "triggers."

▶ Arthritis results in joint stiffness, pain, or swelling.

Vocabulary
- diabetes (614) • insulin (614) • allergy (616)
- allergen (616) • histamine (616) • arthritis (618)
- osteoarthritis (618) • rheumatoid arthritis (619)

Section 4 Disabilties

Key Ideas

▶ The three most common physical disabilities are impaired vision, impaired hearing, and impaired mobility.

▶ An important move toward integrating people with disabilities into the workplace and community came in 1990 when the Americans with Disabilities Act was signed into law.

Vocabulary
- disability (623)
- macular degeneration (623)
- tinnitus (624)
- Americans with Disabilities Act (626)

Chapter 23 Review

Reviewing Key Ideas

GO ONLINE
PearsonSuccessNet.com
For: Chapter 23 review activity

Section 1

1. Hardening of the arteries is known as
   a. atherosclerosis.
   b. congestive heart failure.
   c. arteriosclerosis.
   d. angina pectoris.

2. An artificial pacemaker can help control
   a. arrhythmia.
   b. heart attack.
   c. cerebral hemorrhage.
   d. hypertension.

3. How is hypertension related to other forms of cardiovascular disease?

4. **Critical Thinking** How could a drug that lowers cholesterol levels in the blood affect the development of atherosclerosis?

Section 2

5. A mass of cancerous cells is called a(n)
   a. malignant tumor.   b. benign tumor.
   c. oncogene.   d. carcinogen.

6. A cancer-causing substance in the environment is
   a. a melanoma.   b. a carcinogen.
   c. a tumor.   d. an oncogene.

7. What role does a biopsy play in detecting cancer?

8. **Critical Thinking** Smoking is now banned in many public places. Do you think the health benefits to society justify this restriction? Explain.

Section 3

9. Which hormone regulates blood sugar levels?
   a. diabetes   b. histamine
   c. insulin   d. allergen

10. Name three risk factors for type 2 diabetes.

11. What is the most common form of arthritis? What is its cause?

12. **Critical Thinking** Whenever Julie visits her grandmother's house, she sneezes and sometimes has trouble breathing. How could Julie determine if she has an allergy to something there?

Section 4

13. A common cause of vision impairment in older people is
    a. eye injury.   b. spinal cord injury.
    c. tinnitus.   d. macular degeneration.

14. Describe three devices that may help people who are hearing impaired communicate effectively.

15. What devices are available to help mobility-impaired people be more mobile?

16. What needs are addressed by the Americans with Disabilities Act?

17. **Critical Thinking** What recommendations would you make to provide more job and other opportunities for disabled people in your community?

Building Health Skills

18. **Advocacy** What kinds of health programs would you want the government to support to help reduce type 2 diabetes in the United States? Would such programs save money? Explain.

19. **Making Decisions** After shoveling snow from his driveway, your elderly neighbor sits down suddenly, clutching his chest. What should you do?

20. **Setting Goals** Choose a disease from this chapter that you might be at risk for. List some behavior changes you can make to lower your risk. Monitor your behavior for a few weeks and evaluate your progress in a short report. **WRITING**

Health and Community

Disability Assistance Many communities have services that assist people with both physical and mental disabilities. Find out what services are available in your community for helping people with disabilities. You may look in the telephone directory, on the Internet, or on posting boards around your community. Share your findings with your class. **WRITING**

Standardized Test Prep

Math Practice

The graph shows the occurrence of cardiovascular diseases in men and women of different ages. Use the graph to answer Questions 21–23.

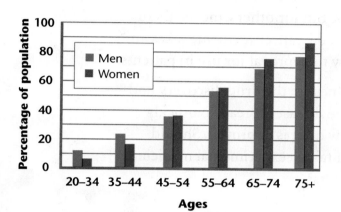

21. At what ages are more men than women affected by cardiovascular diseases?
    A 20–44
    B 35–44
    C 45–54
    D 65–75

22. What happens to the percentage of women with cardiovascular diseases between age 40 and age 60?
    F It stays the same.
    G It increases slightly.
    H It doubles.
    J It more than triples.

23. According to the graph, which of the following statements is true?
    A Men over 55 don't need to worry about cardiovascular disease.
    B Men are more at risk for cardiovascular disease than women.
    C As people age, the risk of cardiovascular disease decreases.
    D As people age, the risk of cardiovascular disease increases.

Reading and Writing Practice

Read the passage. Then answer Questions 24–27.

Scientists have been studying the link between the hormone leptin and breast cancer. Leptin helps regulate energy balance and weight. Leptin can increase the amount of estrogen in the breast tissue of obese women. Perhaps blocking leptin's activity could be a novel approach for treating some breast cancers. To test this idea, scientists designed non-toxic inhibitors of leptin, which they tested in mice. The inhibitors reduced both the number and size of mammary tumors in the mice. The incidence of metastasis to the liver was also reduced.

24. Leptin inhibitors may
    A increase the size of mammary tumors.
    B increase the number of mammary tumors.
    C decrease the number and size of mammary tumors.
    D increase estrogen in breast tissue.

25. In this passage, the word *novel* means
    F book-like.   G new.
    H beneficial.   J ill-timed.

26. According to the passage, which of these statements is true?
    A Leptin may contribute to tumor growth.
    B Leptin hasn't been linked to breast cancer.
    C Leptin inhibitors have been used for years to treat breast cancer.
    D Leptin inhibitors only work if they are toxic.

Constructed Response
27. In a paragraph, summarize the leptin inhibitor experiment and the results.

Test-Taking Tip

When taking a test, be sure to read the directions first. Then start answering the questions.

Focus on **ISSUES**

Should Experimental Medicines Be Available to the Terminally Ill?

Over half a million Americans die every year from cancer. Some forms of cancer can be treated with medicines. But for other cancers, there are currently no effective treatments. A new cancer medicine takes an average of 12 years to go from discovery to approval for use in patients.

For patients with life-threatening illnesses, the drug discovery and approval process can feel too slow. Some diseases spread so quickly that a patient will likely die before a new drug is approved. Should terminally ill patients have the option of taking experimental medicines that show promise for treating their illness?

The Case for Experimental Medicines

Medicines should be made available to seriously ill patients as soon as the medicines show signs of promise and some degree of safety. It is not ethical to withhold these medicines from patients with very little time and hope left. If patients understand the risks of taking an experimental medicine, they should be allowed to make their own decision in consultation with their doctor.

❝ **I lost a cousin last year to leukemia. While she was sick, we found out that there was a new medicine being tested. She was told that there was no way to get the new drug. I felt angry, like they were not giving her a chance to be cured. People should have the right to try anything that might slow or cure their disease.** ❞

The Case Against Experimental Medicines

Using a medicine that is not yet approved may expose patients to serious side effects that might be worse than their disease. Approximately 1,000 possible cancer medicines, for example, are studied in the laboratory before one emerges as a candidate for testing in humans. The odds are too great that an experimental medicine might pose serious health risks to the patient.

❝ **If I were terminally ill, I would only want treatments that have been proven to work and be safe. I wouldn't want to have false hope in a medicine that might even make me sicker. The testing process is in place to protect patients from harm. As slow as the process is, people need to let drug companies and the government thoroughly test new medicines.** ❞

What do **YOU** think?

Use these steps to analyze and express your opinion about whether experimental medicines should be available to the terminally ill.

1. Analyze the Issue Carefully consider both sides of the issue. Make a table listing the pros and cons of making experimental medicines available to the terminally ill.

2. Consider Your Values Look at the different pros and cons you listed. Which of them are most important to you? Which are less important? Explain.

3. Take a Stand In a paragraph, express your opinion on whether experimental medicines should be available to the terminally ill. State your opinion clearly, and give several reasons that support your view. **WRITING**

631

CHAPTER 24

Safeguarding the Public

GO ONLINE PearsonSuccessNet.com

VIDEO 24

TEENS Talk

Taking Charge of Your Health

Preview **Activity**

Where Do You Get Your Health Information?

Complete this activity before you watch the video.

1. Choose a health topic you would like to know more about.
2. Write down a list of different sources that could provide you with more information on that topic. **WRITING**
3. Rank the sources you listed from most reliable to least reliable.
4. When you have looked for health information in the past, did you go to the most reliable source? Why or why not?

The Healthcare System

Objectives

▶ **Identify** the healthcare providers who work together to care for patients.

▶ **Describe** different types of healthcare facilities.

▶ **Analyze** how technology has affected healthcare.

Vocabulary

- healthcare system
- primary care physician
- diagnosis
- medical specialist
- primary healthcare
- outpatient
- secondary healthcare
- inpatient
- tertiary healthcare

Warm-Up

Quick Quiz Only one of the following statements is true. Which statement do you think it is?

(1) You only need to see a doctor when you are sick.

(2) A doctor will keep your personal information confidential.

(3) Health insurance covers 100% of your medical expenses.

(4) Doctors know what's best for you, and you shouldn't question their opinions.

WRITING Explain why you gave the answer you did.

Healthcare Providers

When you go to a doctor for regular checkups and immunizations, you participate in the healthcare system. The **healthcare system** includes all available medical services, the ways in which individuals pay for medical care, and programs aimed at preventing disease and disability. **Within the healthcare system, doctors work with nurses and other healthcare providers to care for patients.**

Doctors **Primary care physicians** take care of most people's routine medical needs. Most primary care physicians are medical doctors who have specialized in one of three areas of medicine—family practice; internal medicine; or pediatrics, children's medical care.

After medical school and further training, a doctor must pass the medical licensing test of the state in which he or she intends to practice. Once licensed, a doctor can diagnose medical conditions, provide treatment, and write prescriptions for medication. A **diagnosis** (dy ug NOH sis) is a doctor's opinion of the nature or cause of a medical condition. A prescription is a written order to a pharmacist authorizing that a patient be given a particular medicine.

Medical Specialists If you have a condition that requires specialized treatment, a primary care physician will refer you to a medical specialist. A **medical specialist** is a doctor who has received additional training in a particular branch of medicine. Figure 1 describes some medical specialists.

FIGURE 1 If a doctor is not planning to become a primary care physician, he or she usually specializes in one area of medicine.

Neurologists treat nervous system disorders.

Dermatologists treat skin disorders.

Oncologists treat cancers.

Allergists treat allergies and other immune disorders.

Pediatricians provide primary care for children.

Orthopedic surgeons treat bone and joint disorders.

Ophthalmologists treat eye diseases.

Nurse ▶

FIGURE 2 A variety of providers care for patients' different needs. **Applying Concepts** What other types of healthcare providers have you heard of? What do they do?

◀ Registered dietitian

Nurses Nurses are licensed healthcare providers who work in collaboration with doctors to care for patients. There are several types of nurses that differ in their levels of training. Registered nurses (RNs) observe and assess patient symptoms, plan the best approach to promoting recovery, and evaluate progress. They also counsel patients of all ages about ways to stay healthy and prevent injury.

Registered nurses who have received additional training may become registered nurse practitioners. Nurse practitioners are trained to do many tasks that only doctors used to perform. For example, they may take medical histories, perform physical exams, order tests, treat routine medical problems, and prescribe medications. When nurse practitioners see patients for routine medical needs, they may be referred to as *primary care providers*. A nurse practitioner usually works with a doctor.

Other Providers A variety of healthcare professionals provide services that complement the work of doctors and nurses.

▶ **Physician assistants** Physician assistants perform many tasks previously done by doctors. These tasks may include taking medical histories, performing physical exams, and prescribing medications. Physician assistants work under the supervision of a doctor.

▶ **Physical therapists** Physical therapists help patients with arthritis, muscle pain, fractures, burns, strokes, or sports injuries. Physical therapists supervise exercise programs and may use heat and massage to relieve pain and improve strength and mobility.

▶ **Registered dietitians** Registered dietitians, sometimes called nutritionists, may set up and supervise food services for institutions such as hospitals. They may also provide nutritional counseling to patients in a healthcare facility or in private practice.

Connect to Your Life When was the last time you visited a healthcare provider?

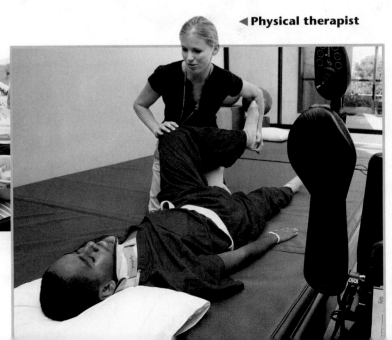

◀ Physical therapist

Media Wise

Evaluating TV Doctors

Many television shows are set in hospitals. How do different shows portray healthcare providers? What effect might these shows have on viewers' attitudes toward doctors? Evaluate a TV doctor using this questionnaire.

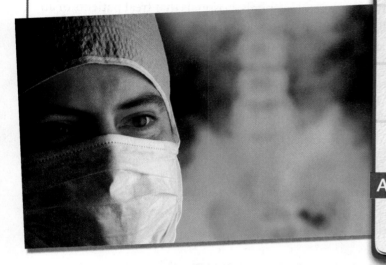

Does the doctor give each patient the time and attention he or she needs? **Yes No**

Does the doctor make patients feel comfortable discussing personal information? **Yes No**

Does the doctor explain each patient's condition in terms that are easy to understand? **Yes No**

Is the doctor knowledgeable about patients' conditions and medical options? **Yes No**

Does the doctor readily admit when he or she has made a mistake? **Yes No**

"Yes" answers indicate positive qualities that patients should look for in a doctor.

Activity Use the checklist to evaluate a doctor from a television show. Then write a paragraph explaining whether you would be comfortable being treated by that doctor. Why or why not? **WRITING**

Healthcare Facilities

Healthcare facilities include doctors' offices, clinics, hospitals, and long-term care centers. These facilities offer different levels of care.

Doctors' Offices   Perhaps the most frequently used healthcare facility is the doctor's private office, which may be in a hospital or in a private building. Here doctors, nurse practitioners, or physician assistants do routine examinations and tests to diagnose and treat minor illnesses and injuries. Minor surgery, such as removing a wart, may also be done in a doctor's office. Routine healthcare provided in a doctor's office is called **primary healthcare.**

Clinics   When a medical test or procedure cannot be performed in a doctor's office, a person may go to an outpatient clinic. A clinic is a facility in which primary healthcare is provided by one or more doctors and other healthcare providers. An **outpatient** is a person admitted to a clinic for tests or treatments that do not require an overnight stay.

A variety of tests and surgical procedures can be performed at clinics. For example, cataract surgery, which involves removing a cloudy lens from an eye, can be performed at an outpatient clinic. Outpatient care is less costly than a hospital stay.

GO ONLINE

PearsonSuccessNet.com
For: More on healthcare professionals

Hospitals Diagnosis and treatment of serious disorders require the services of a hospital. Hospitals are equipped to provide healthcare services requiring complicated procedures. Most hospitals also have emergency departments to treat sudden conditions or injuries.

Healthcare that is given to a patient in a hospital is known as **secondary healthcare.** Hospitals provide overnight accommodations for patients who need it. A patient who is required to stay in a hospital overnight or longer is called an **inpatient.** The patient's primary care physician and specialists, such as surgeons, visit the patient every day to note progress and adjust the patient's care.

Some hospitals are general hospitals, hospitals that treat patients of all ages and with all kinds of illnesses. Specialty hospitals, such as children's hospitals, specialize in treating one age group or one type of disorder. Hospitals located near medical schools may be "teaching hospitals." Doctors train medical students and other healthcare providers at these hospitals. Because many doctors at teaching hospitals carry out medical research, these hospitals often offer advanced and experimental medical care. Care provided in specialty hospitals and teaching hospitals is called **tertiary healthcare.**

Long-Term Care Long-term care facilities provide services for patients with a variety of medical needs. Figure 4 describes some long-term care facilities.

Connect to Your Life Have you ever stayed overnight in a hospital? If so, describe your experience.

FIGURE 3 Hospital emergency rooms provide care for people who are injured or who are suffering from a sudden onset of serious illness.

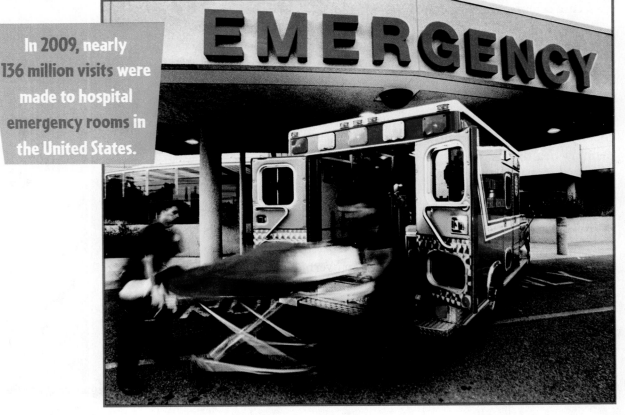

In 2009, nearly 136 million visits were made to hospital emergency rooms in the United States.

Long-Term Care Facilities

Skilled Nursing Facilities	Patients recovering from surgery, illness, or injury may require basic nursing care for an extended time before returning to their homes. A skilled nursing facility provides care for people in these situations.
Assisted Living Facilities	People who can no longer live by themselves, but do not require constant nursing care, may live in assisted living facilities. These facilities provide help with preparing meals, housekeeping, and taking medications.
Nursing Homes	Nursing homes provide long-term care for elderly or chronically ill people who cannot care for themselves.
Home-Health Care	Some patients who need long-term care are cared for in their own homes. The medical care is provided by nurses who visit the person's home.
Hospice	A special kind of nursing care is available for patients who are terminally ill. This care, called hospice, is usually given in the home. Hospice care focuses on helping a dying patient live as comfortably as possible.

FIGURE 4 Long-term care facilites offer a variety of services depending on the level of care needed. **Classifying** Which type of facility provides nursing care for those recovering from surgery? For those who are chronically ill?

Technology and Healthcare

If you've been to a doctor's office or hospital lately, then you know that computers and other technology play a huge role in healthcare today. **The Internet, e-mail, and other technologies can make healthcare more efficient, and can make patients feel more involved in their care.**

The Internet and E-mail Many people today gather health information on the Internet. Some doctors appreciate that their patients are better informed. Others, however, worry that patients can get incorrect or biased information. Doctors often spend time with patients correcting misconceptions that stem from information the patients found on the Internet. This is why you should never rely on information you find on the Internet without first discussing it with your doctor.

Some doctors now use e-mail to communicate with their patients about non-emergency health issues. One benefit is that patients and doctors no longer need to be free at the same time to discuss things, as was the case with the telephone. There is also a written record of the communication, unlike with telephone calls. However, not everyone is comfortable communicating private health information via e-mail.

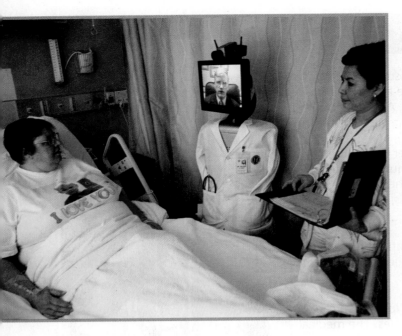

FIGURE 5 Telemedicine allows doctors to communicate with each other and receive training over long distances. It also allows doctors to monitor the condition of patients in different locations. The device shown here is equipped with a camera and microphone.

Computerized Imaging Many imaging techniques, including MRIs, CT scans, and X-rays, are performed with computerized equipment. Digital images allow doctors to share a patient's results more easily with other specialists. This can allow for quicker or more accurate diagnoses.

Telemedicine In a growing number of settings, healthcare providers may make "virtual visits" to their patients. Providers use two-way video, electronic monitoring, smart phones, and other electronic forms of communication to follow patients closely from distant locations. Telemedicine is useful for hospitals in which medical specialists are not always on site, in rural settings, or when one doctor rotates around to several hospitals in one region.

Electronic Health Records Patients benefit when their body scans, test results, or medical records can be shared efficiently between providers. For example, in an emergency situation, a doctor being able to access the patient's records quickly could save the patient's life. This type of file sharing, however, is not available everywhere. The Affordable Care Act requires providers and hospitals to completely convert from paper to electronic health records. Electronic health records cut down on medical mistakes that are sometimes made when a provider does not have access to a patient's medical history.

Section 1 Review

Key Ideas and Vocabulary

1. Describe the roles that three types of healthcare providers play in the healthcare system.

2. What is a **primary care physician?** What kind of care does a primary care physician provide?

3. What is a **diagnosis?**

4. Compare and contrast these healthcare facilities—doctors' offices, clinics, and hospitals.

5. How does an **inpatient** differ from an **outpatient?**

6. How has technology such as the Internet and e-mail affected the relationship between patients and doctors?

Health at School

Provider Brochure Find out what healthcare providers and services are available in your school district. Create a brochure for students that provides information about the different types of healthcare providers and services that are available to them. **WRITING**

Critical Thinking

7. **Comparing and Contrasting** Distinguish between an assisted living facility and a nursing home.

8. **Evaluating** Would you feel comfortable if a doctor handled some of your healthcare using telemedicine? What advantages and disadvantages might there be with that technology?

GO ONLINE PearsonSuccessNet.com Audio Summary Section 24.1

Participating in Your Healthcare

Objectives
- ▶ **Describe** how to choose and participate fully in your healthcare.
- ▶ **Compare** different options for paying for healthcare.

Vocabulary
- medical history
- physical examination
- premium
- copayment
- deductible

Warm-Up

Dear Advice Line,

I just moved with my family to a new city, and I don't have a doctor here yet. How can I make sure that the doctor we choose is the right one for me?

WRITING Write a draft of a response to this question. Revise your answer after reading this section.

Your Healthcare

Up to now, adults have probably made most of the decisions about your healthcare. As you grow older, however, you will take on these responsibilities for yourself. Knowing some basics about your healthcare choices can help you choose what is best for you.

Choosing Healthcare Choosing your doctor is one healthcare responsibility that will eventually be yours. **Deciding what doctor to see for routine healthcare deserves careful consideration. After all, you want your healthcare delivered by qualified people with whom you feel comfortable.**

Some people prefer to see a doctor in a clinic. At some clinics you can arrange to see the doctor of your choice. At others, you may see the first available doctor. Some clinics also give you the option of seeing a nurse practitioner as your primary care provider.

Rather than seeing a doctor at a clinic, some people prefer to see a doctor who is in private practice. Often several doctors in private practice have their offices together in the same building and work together in a group practice.

Finding a Doctor Here are some tips for finding a doctor who is suited to your needs.

▶ **Ask for recommendations.** The best way to begin your search for a doctor is to ask for recommendations from family members and friends. Also, you can ask the opinion of other healthcare providers you know, such as your school nurse.

▶ **Do your research.** When you have the names of some recommended doctors, you might go to your local library and check the *American Medical Directory*. This directory lists the names of doctors, the year they received their medical degrees, their areas of specialization, and whether or not they are board-certified. A board-certified physician has completed three or more years of additional training in a medical specialty and has passed a certification exam.

▶ **Identify your preferences.** Once you have the basic information, begin to think about your own preferences. Do you want a young doctor, or would you prefer an older one? Would you be more comfortable with a male or a female doctor? Do you want a doctor with an outgoing personality, or one who is more reserved?

The best time to make your first visit to a doctor is while you are well. Figure 6 lists some questions you might ask yourself about the doctor after your initial visit. These questions can help you decide if that doctor is right for you.

What qualities do you look for in a doctor? Why are these qualities important to you?

FIGURE 6 It is very important that you feel comfortable with your doctor. **Evaluating** Use this checklist to evaluate your current doctor.

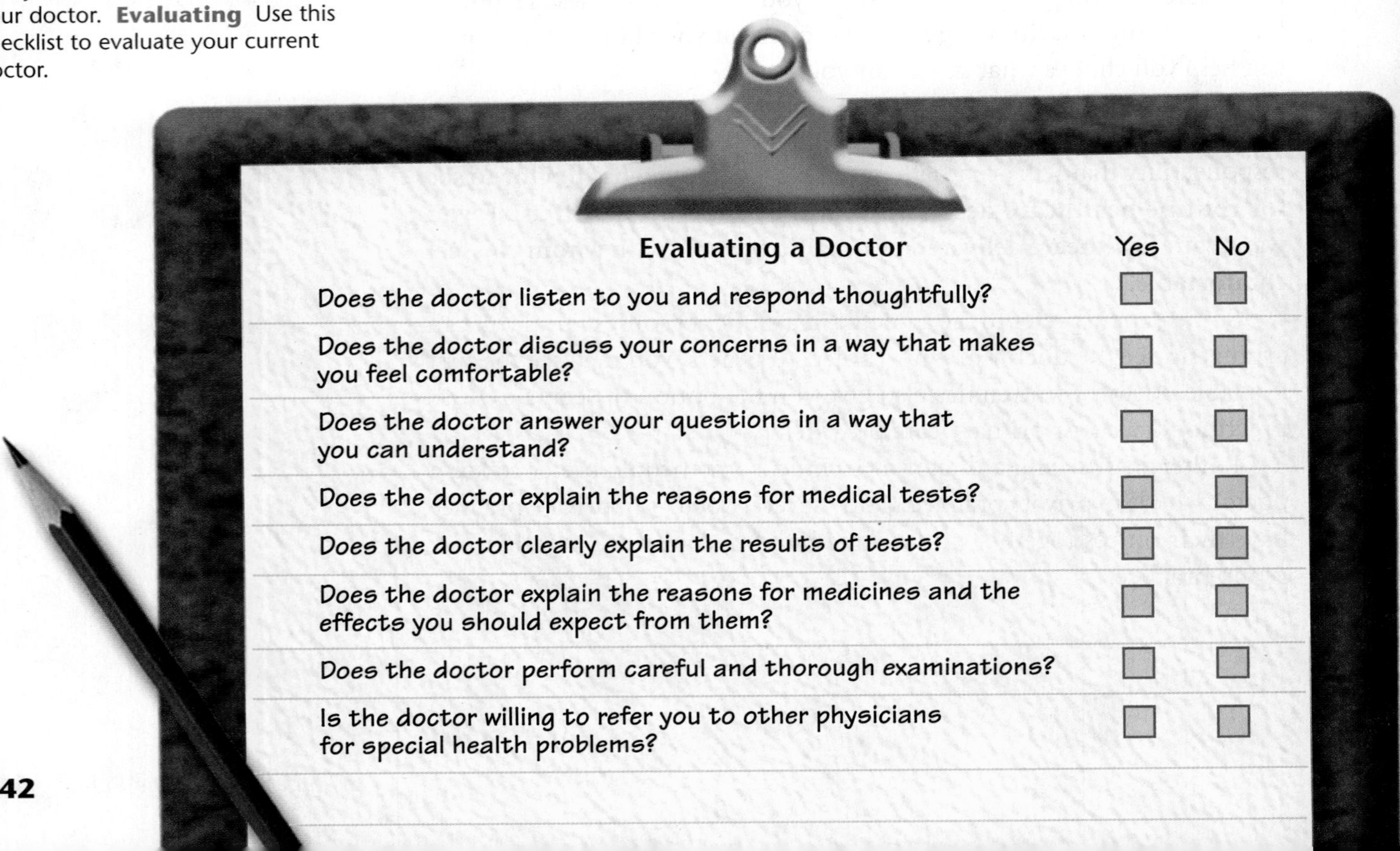

Evaluating a Doctor	Yes	No
Does the doctor listen to you and respond thoughtfully?	☐	☐
Does the doctor discuss your concerns in a way that makes you feel comfortable?	☐	☐
Does the doctor answer your questions in a way that you can understand?	☐	☐
Does the doctor explain the reasons for medical tests?	☐	☐
Does the doctor clearly explain the results of tests?	☐	☐
Does the doctor explain the reasons for medicines and the effects you should expect from them?	☐	☐
Does the doctor perform careful and thorough examinations?	☐	☐
Is the doctor willing to refer you to other physicians for special health problems?	☐	☐

FIGURE 7 It is normal to feel anxious about going to the doctor. The list of tips shown here can help you reduce your anxiety.

The Doctor Appointment Have you ever put off seeing your doctor because you were afraid of getting a shot or dreaded getting undressed in the examining room? If so, you are like many other people. Instead, try thinking of a doctor's appointment as an opportunity. A visit to your doctor allows you to find out more about your body and prevent future health problems.

A doctor will usually first take your **medical history,** a record of your present and past health as well as the health of members of your family. You may have to fill out a medical history form, which the doctor will review with you.

Next, you will have a **physical examination,** a head-to-toe check of your body to identify any medical problems you may have. During the physical exam, the doctor may do some or all of the following:

► measure your height, weight, blood pressure, and body temperature

► check your skin, eyes, ears, nose, and throat

► listen to your lungs and heart

► check your muscles and bones, including your arms, legs, hands, and feet for signs of joint swelling or bone problems

► check your nervous system

► check your spine for abnormal curvature

► test your reflexes, balance, and coordination

If the doctor finds a medical condition requiring attention, he or she will discuss it with you. The doctor should explain what the condition means in terms of treatment, testing, and short-term and long-term effects.

Your medical examination should also include time for you to ask questions. Regardless of how foolish you think your questions are, keep asking them. Getting answers to questions about your body will help you participate more fully in your own healthcare.

FIGURE 8 You and your doctor must work together as a team. If you feel that you and your doctor are not a good match, you have the right to choose another provider.

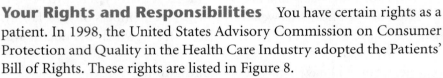

The Patients' Bill of Rights

▶ **Information** You have the right to accurate and easily understood information about your healthcare. If you speak another language, have a physical or mental disability, or just don't understand something, you will be provided with assistance.

▶ **Choice** You have the right to a choice of healthcare providers and to high-quality healthcare.

▶ **Access** If you have severe pain, an injury, or a sudden illness that may put your health in serious danger, you have the right to emergency care whenever and wherever needed, without prior authorization or financial penalty.

▶ **Participation** You have the right to know your treatment options and to participate in decisions about your care.

▶ **Respect** You have the right to considerate, respectful, and nondiscriminatory care from your healthcare providers.

▶ **Confidentiality** You have the right to talk in confidence with healthcare providers and to have your healthcare information protected. You also have the right to review and copy your own medical record.

▶ **Complaints** You have the right to a fair, fast, and objective review of any complaint you have against your healthcare providers or facilities.

Your Rights and Responsibilities You have certain rights as a patient. In 1998, the United States Advisory Commission on Consumer Protection and Quality in the Health Care Industry adopted the Patients' Bill of Rights. These rights are listed in Figure 8.

As a patient you also have certain responsibilities. You must fulfill these responsibilities in order to receive the best healthcare possible.

▶ Ask your doctor about anything that concerns your health. Most doctors expect questions. If a doctor seems annoyed by your questions, it would be wise to look for another doctor.

▶ Answer your doctor's questions honestly. Information about symptoms, medications you are taking, and any activities or behaviors that may affect your health or treatment are important for your doctor to know. The more information you can provide, the more likely your doctor can provide an accurate diagnosis.

Doctors and other healthcare providers vary in their attitudes, professional styles, and how they relate to people. If you are not satisfied with the services provided by a doctor or clinic, you do not have to continue there. Receiving good healthcare means being satisfied with the medical as well as the personal treatment you receive.

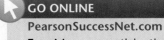

GO ONLINE

PearsonSuccessNet.com

For: More on participating in your healthcare

Connect to Your Life

How did you fulfill your patient responsibilities the last time you saw your doctor?

Paying for Healthcare

One way to pay for healthcare is to pay for all of your own medical expenses out-of-pocket, which can be very expensive. Another way is through health insurance. **Health insurance pays for a major part of an individual's medical expenses.** Some companies offer health insurance options to their employees and their families. Individuals can also purchase their own health insurance.

Health Insurance Currently, the most commonly held health insurance plans in the United States are managed care insurance plans. Plan members pay a monthly or yearly fee called a **premium.** Whenever they visit the doctor, they may also be required to pay a small fee called a **copayment.** Managed care plans characteristically have a network of doctors who agree to provide healthcare at lower costs. Members are encouraged to see only doctors within the plan's network.

▶ **Health Maintenance Organizations** The most common managed care plans are health maintenance organizations, or HMOs. Members of an HMO choose a primary care physician who provides routine care and makes referrals to specialists within the network when necessary. HMOs usually only cover the costs of health services provided within the network.

▶ **Point of Service Plans** Like HMOs, point of service (POS) plans require you to choose a primary care physician. The difference is that your primary care physician may refer you to specialists outside the network. However, to see a doctor outside the network, you will have to pay a higher copayment.

▶ **Preferred Provider Organizations** A preferred provider organization (PPO) also has a network of doctors—the preferred providers—who charge reduced fees to plan members. Unlike HMOs and POS plans, however, you can see a specialist without a referral. In addition, a PPO covers services by out-of-network doctors, but at a higher cost to the patient. In general, PPOs are more expensive than HMOs and POS plans, but they allow members more flexibility.

FIGURE 9 Average healthcare spending for an American family of four totals $19,000 per year. If the family has PPO insurance coverage through an employer, they pay about $3,280 every year out-of-pocket. The rest is covered by the employer and insurance.
Reading Graphs What percentage of the total healthcare spending is for medications?

Yearly Healthcare Spending (Total: $19,000)

Inpatient care 31%

Physician visits 33%

Other 4%

Outpatient care 17%

Medications 15%

Traditional Insurance   Historically, health insurance in the United States has been made available through an employer. Traditional health insurance plans offer more flexibility than managed healthcare plans by permitting you to use any doctor or facility you choose. In most cases, out-of-pocket expenses with these plans are more costly than those of managed care plans. Children up to 18 years of age and unemployed spouses are insured through a family plan purchased by an employed parent. Employers pay monthly premiums to a private insurance company. This premium or some part of it is usually deducted from the employee's salary. Individuals without a job or who work for an employer who does not offer health insurance may purchase insurance directly from an insurance company at a higher rate.

Not all adults are employed. Some people work in settings where health insurance is not offered, and others may have elected not to purchase insurance. For these reasons, the United States struggles with caring for its uninsured citizens. Many states have created models for covering the costs of care for uninsured adults and their children.

Because of the high cost of healthcare and health insurance, there have been many efforts to reduce premium costs. Employers may limit the number of options from which employees can choose. Employees may have to use only certain healthcare providers. Employees may be required to pay a co-payment or a deductible. A **deductible** is a fixed amount of money that employees must pay for medical expenses each year before the insurance company begins paying for procedures. Other methods to reduce premium costs include excluding some services from coverage and not covering care for pre-existing conditions.

Government-Sponsored Insurance   Some people in the United States who cannot afford private health insurance are eligible for government health insurance programs. Medicare is the federally financed insurance program for people over age 65 and for younger people who are disabled or who have chronic kidney disease. Medicaid is a state program funded by both the state and federal governments. Medicaid pays for the healthcare of people whose incomes are below a certain level.

FIGURE 10 The Affordable Care Act puts in place comprehensive health insurance reforms outlined here.

The Affordable Care Act

- Creates a Health Insurance Marketplace that allows individuals and small businesses to buy affordable, qualified health benefit plans

- Creates a new type of non-profit health insurer called a Consumer Operated and Oriented Plan (CO-OP)

- Prohibits health insurers from charging more for, or denying coverage to, people with a pre-existing condition

- Allows children to stay on their parents' insurance plans until age 26

Rising Healthcare Costs There are many factors that contribute to the rising costs of healthcare in the United States.

▶ **An Aging Population** The growing population of elderly Americans is a major force in driving up costs. People live longer on average than they used to. The result is a growing number of people who are likely to need extensive medical services. Taxpayers of all ages contribute to federal programs such as Medicare that provide healthcare support for older Americans.

▶ **Chronic Diseases** The increasing incidence of chronic diseases such as cardiovascular disease and diabetes affects all Americans. When individuals require more and more medical care, health insurance companies must raise everybody's premiums to offset the extra costs.

▶ **Prescription Drug Costs** The research and development of prescription drugs is very expensive, and this cost is usually passed on to consumers. One way to relieve some of the burden is to use generic drugs. Generic drugs have the same active ingredients as brand-name drugs, but they usually cost significantly less. Unfortunately, there is not a generic version of every brand-name drug.

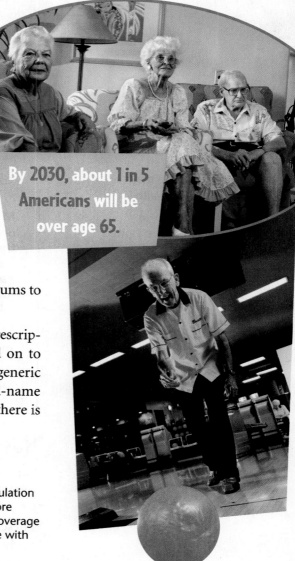

By 2030, about 1 in 5 Americans will be over age 65.

FIGURE 11 As the elderly population grows, Medicare will require more funding to keep up. Medicare coverage for older Americans may change with future legislation.

Section 2 Review

Key Ideas and Vocabulary

1. Why is it important to choose your doctor carefully? What are your responsibilities as a patient?
2. What is included in a **medical history**?
3. Briefly describe the three types of health insurance.
4. What is the difference between a **premium** and a **deductible**?

Critical Thinking

5. Evaluating Which of the patients' rights listed in Figure 8 is most important to you? Explain.

Health at Home

Family Health Talk to members of your family about your medical history. Is there a disease that is common in your family? Make a list of the information that is important to share with your doctor. **WRITING**

6. Making Judgments What, if anything, do you think should be done to help Americans deal with rising healthcare costs? Explain.

7. Calculating Suppose your family spends a total of $2,000 for healthcare in one year. If 40% of your healthcare spending is for visits to the doctor, what amount does your family spend on doctor visits in one year? **MATH**

Public Health

Objectives

▶ **Summarize** the main goal of public health programs today.

▶ **Describe** how the United States' public health system is organized.

Vocabulary

- public health
- quarantine
- epidemiology
- health code
- vital statistics

Warm-Up

Myth Public health officials only deal with natural disasters and infectious disease outbreaks that threaten large populations.

Fact Many public health efforts focus on preventing disease and injury in daily life, not just when catastrophes strike.

WRITING Why do you think prevention is a major focus in the field of public health?

What Is Public Health?

Suppose that you could find no clean drinking water. What if restaurants were not required to be clean and pest-free? What if children could attend school without being immunized against serious infectious diseases? These are all matters that would affect public health. **Public health** is the study and practice of protecting and improving the health of people in a group or community.

Fortunately, health-threatening conditions like those mentioned above rarely exist in the United States. That is because a public health system is in place to prevent them. The public health system includes all the government and private organizations that work with the public to prevent disease and promote positive health behaviors.

The History of Public Health Throughout history, people associated disease with unclean or unsanitary conditions and took measures to promote cleanliness. The ancient Hebrews, for example, established rules for the sanitary preparation of foods. The ancient Romans built efficient systems to supply people with clean water and to remove wastes.

In Europe during the Middle Ages, however, cities became crowded with people and animals, and their wastes. Epidemics swept across Africa, Asia and Europe. One of the only ways people knew to combat these disease outbreaks was through quarantine. **Quarantine** (KWAWR un teen) is a period of isolation imposed on people who may have been exposed to an infectious disease. Quarantine prevents people who may be infected from spreading the disease.

New Understandings

During the latter half of the 1800s, scientists began to understand that microorganisms cause many diseases. In 1850, London physician John Snow studied an outbreak of cholera (KAHL ur uh), an infectious disease that causes severe diarrhea and vomiting. Dr. Snow learned that all of the outbreak victims had drunk water from the same well. He was able to show that this well was contaminated with cholera-causing bacteria.

Starting in the early 1900s, vaccines against a variety of serious diseases became available. The United States government launched nationwide programs to immunize the public. As a result, the incidence of many infectious diseases, such as measles, was greatly reduced.

The field of epidemiology has also contributed to new understandings in the field of public health. **Epidemiology** (ep ih dee mee AHL uh jee) is the study of disease among populations. Epidemiologists look for patterns in the occurrence of infectious and chronic diseases. Their findings are used to develop policies and programs for disease control and prevention.

Public Health Goals Today

The public health system continues to combat infectious diseases but also seeks to prevent a broad range of other health problems. **Public health programs today emphasize the need for prevention in order to avoid disease and other health problems.** Many public health problems today relate to people's behaviors. For example, drug and alcohol abuse, teenage pregnancy, obesity, violence, and child abuse are major public health problems related to people's behaviors.

The Department of Health and Human Services, or HHS, is the major public health agency in the United States. HHS developed an important public health document, *Healthy People 2020,* that identifies prevention as the key to improving the health of all Americans. Chapter 1 discusses the goals of *Healthy People 2020.*

FIGURE 12 In the 1950s, immunizing people against polio was a top public health priority. The photo above shows a drive-through polio vaccination clinic.

▲ **A Tennessee girl in quarantine for scarlet fever, 1949**

When did you last take part in a public health program, such as getting immunized?

Public Health in the United States

GO ONLINE

PearsonSuccessNet.com

For: More on public health

As the United States has grown and changed, so have its public health needs. The public health system today addresses many more problems than ever before. Most programs, however, fall into one of three main categories.

▶ **Fighting Chronic Diseases** As in most countries with high standards of living, deaths from chronic diseases exceed those from infectious diseases in the United States. Today, many public health programs emphasize the importance of behaviors such as regular exercise and proper nutrition to reduce people's risks of many chronic diseases.

▶ **Helping Populations at Risk** One of the greatest challenges in public health is to provide services to high-risk populations. High-risk populations are groups of people who, because of age, economic conditions, or some other factor, are more likely to contract a particular disease or disorder than the general population.

▶ **Safety and Environmental Health** Many public health regulations focus on safety issues in all areas of society. Safety standards, for example, must be met in the workplace, in the design and construction of buildings, in the transportation industry, and in many household and medical products. The public health system also addresses environmental concerns. For example, there are laws that limit pollution levels from industries and motor vehicles.

In the United States, public health is primarily a governmental responsibility that is managed at the federal, state, and local levels. A variety of private organizations also contribute significantly to the advancement of public health.

FIGURE 13 Workers from the federal Environmental Protection Agency monitor the environment for substances that could endanger public health.

The Federal Government As mentioned earlier, the federal agency with the widest range of responsibilities for public health is the Department of Health and Human Services (HHS). HHS provides many services, including:

▶ sponsoring health research and education

▶ compiling and analyzing health information

▶ setting health and safety standards

▶ supporting state and local health departments

▶ funding programs for people in need of public health services

Figure 14 summarizes the services provided by different federal agencies. The Centers for Disease Control and Prevention (CDC) and the National Institutes of Health (NIH) are particularly important research agencies that are reliable sources of health information.

Federal Public Health Agencies

Department of Health and Human Services

Administration for Children and Families	Administers programs that improve the lives of children from low-income families and people with disabilities
Administration on Aging	Provides services to older persons and their caregivers
Agency for Healthcare Research and Quality	Promotes improvements in the practice of medicine, the organization and financing of healthcare, and access to quality care
Agency for Toxic Substances and Disease Registry	Investigates and assesses risks to human health from hazardous materials
Centers for Disease Control and Prevention (CDC)	Collects data and conducts research on nearly all types of diseases, disorders, and disabilities
Centers for Medicare and Medicaid Services	Supervises Medicare and Medicaid
Food and Drug Administration (FDA)	Inspects, tests, and assesses the safety of food, drugs, and a variety of consumer goods
Health Resources and Services Administration	Funds health services and resources for underserved populations such as migrant workers, people with AIDS, and homeless people
Indian Health Service	Provides comprehensive healthcare for Native Americans
National Institutes of Health (NIH)	Serves as the primary biomedical research facility of the federal government; provides grants to support medical research at institutions throughout the country
Substance Abuse and Mental Health Services Administration	Supports programs that prevent and treat substance abuse and mental illness. It assists states, communities, and healthcare facilities in substance-abuse and mental-health services

Other Federal Agencies

Occupational Safety and Health Administration (OSHA)	In the Department of Labor, identifies occupational hazards and enforces laws requiring minimum safety standards in the workplace
Department of Agriculture (USDA)	Is responsible for inspecting and grading meat, poultry, and other agricultural products; manages nutrition programs such as school-lunch programs and food stamps
Environmental Protection Agency (EPA)	Protects the public from environmental hazards; enforces laws that regulate pollution and sets standards for safe levels of exposure to toxic substances and radiation

State Government The federal government depends on the states to carry out programs to meet its public health objectives. States distribute federal funds to their local health departments or to private health-service providers. These agencies then carry out specific health programs, such as drug rehabilitation and prenatal care.

Most states have several departments or agencies involved in public health. State departments of public health, mental health, rehabilitation, environmental health, and social services are some common examples.

State health departments are also responsible for other services needed to maintain public health within the state. For example, they inspect healthcare and food-handling facilities; test water, food, and medical samples; compile health statistics; and monitor pollution levels.

Local Government In most states, public health services are provided directly by local health departments. Their services are usually free or have a fee based on a person's income. Figure 15 lists some of the services provided by local health departments.

Local health departments are also responsible for enforcing state health codes. **Health codes** are standards established by the state for certain factors that affect health, such as water quality, sanitation in restaurants, and sewage treatment facilities. Local health departments also collect **vital statistics**—the numbers of births and deaths and the numbers and kinds of diseases that occur within a population.

Connect to Your Life

How do the services provided by your local health department protect your health?

FIGURE 15 Local health departments provide many health services directly to members of the community.

Local Health Department Services

- ▶ Insect control for prevention of mosquito-borne diseases
- ▶ Counseling for people with drug or alcohol problems
- ▶ Testing for and treatment of sexually transmitted infections
- ▶ Health education
- ▶ Prenatal care
- ▶ Immunizations
- ▶ Screening for tuberculosis, high blood pressure, cholesterol, and diabetes
- ▶ Home health services for people confined to their homes

FIGURE 16 Volunteering at a soup kitchen is one way to help deliver public health services in your community.

Private Organizations   Many private organizations play important roles in providing public health services. Some of these are national organizations. Others exist only at the local level, in the communities they serve.

A number of national organizations raise funds to support specific health causes. You may be familiar with organizations such as the American Heart Association, American Cancer Society, and March of Dimes. Funds raised by these and other organizations pay for medical research, health services, and educational programs.

In most communities, churches and other community-based organizations offer public health services. These organizations may run programs such as food banks, counseling services, training programs, soup kitchens, and homeless shelters.

Section 3 Review

Key Ideas and Vocabulary

1. What is **epidemiology**?

2. What is the main goal of public health programs today? Why is this goal important?

3. Briefly describe how the public health system in the United States is organized.

4. What are **health codes**? What level of government is responsible for enforcing health codes?

Critical Thinking

5. Evaluating Which of the three major categories of public health challenges in the United States today do you feel should be given highest priority? Explain your answer.

Health and Community

Locating Community Resources Suppose that a family in your community was homeless and you wanted to help. Find out what services are available in your community to help homeless families. Summarize your findings in the form of a letter to your local newspaper. **WRITING**

6. Applying Concepts Many of today's public health problems result from people's behaviors. For example, obesity is a growing public health problem that results mainly from poor eating habits and lack of exercise. What public health approach would be most effective for combating obesity? Explain.

Working in Groups

Sumiko sat listening as the other student council members argued about how they should raise money for the March of Dimes.

"We should have a walk-a-thon," said Sam.

"No, that's a bad idea," said Sylvia. "Let's have a…"

"I say we have a car wash," Tom interrupted.

Finally, Sumiko stood up and pointed out that no one was listening to anyone else's ideas. "If we're going to get anything accomplished," said Sumiko, "we have to start working together."

Have you ever wondered why some groups get a lot done and others do not? Group success often depends on group dynamics, how members work together. Since you participate in many groups— your family, friends, a sports team, this class—learning about group dynamics can be helpful. The following guidelines will help you work successfully in groups.

❶ Set goals and priorities.

As a group, set clear and realistic goals. If there are several goals, decide which ones are most important. All members should be involved in prioritizing the group's goals. Post your goals and priorities as a way to keep group members focused. Refer to them if you think the group is getting sidetracked.

❷ Choose a leader.

Groups work best when members select a leader who is respected by the group. A good leader has the time, interest, and patience to see that things run smoothly.

❸ Delegate tasks and make a schedule.

As a group, decide what steps are necessary to reach your goals. Which members have special skills or resources for these tasks? Divide activities so that everyone is involved. Finally, work together to come up with a realistic schedule for all tasks. Put the schedule in writing and distribute it to all group members.

❹ Monitor group dynamics.

People play different roles in groups. Use the examples below to help you identify the roles that people are playing in your group. To improve group dynamics, urge everyone to adopt a positive role.

▶ **Starter:** Often begins discussions. Introduces new ideas.

▶ **Clarifier:** Requests additional information. Restates points so they are clear to all.

▶ **Peacemaker:** Suggests common ground and compromise when people disagree.

▶ **Supporter:** Is friendly and responsive to others and to their ideas.

▶ **Clown:** Uses jokes to attract attention. Disrupts group.

▶ **Blocker:** Always disagrees with others' ideas or focuses on trivial issues.

▶ **Dominator:** Tries to control group. Bullies other group members.

❺ Evaluate group progress.

At different points, stop and consider the following questions.

▶ Are group members working together productively?

▶ Are tasks being completed on time? If not, the group should discuss why. Maybe the goals or schedule were unrealistic, or only a few people were doing all the work.

▶ Are there conflicts, and are they being handled well?

▶ Are there any communication problems within the group?

Remember that a group functions best when all members share in the process of helping the group meet its goals.

Practice the Skill

1. Choose a group that you belong to. Use the following questions to analyze how well the group works together.
   a. What are the goals of the group? How are the group's priorities decided?
   b. Who is the group leader? How was that person selected? Does the leader guide the group well? Explain.
   c. Does the group have a schedule for accomplishing its goals? Is the schedule realistic? Do all members have tasks that are suited to their own strengths?
   d. Identify the roles members play in the group. Who plays positive roles? Negative roles? What roles do you play?
   e. Is your group accomplishing its goals? Do members communicate well and meet deadlines?
   f. Is working with your group enjoyable? Why or why not?

2. Look over your answers to the questions above. For each, give your group an overall grade. Where does it do best? Worst?

3. List some suggestions for improving the dynamics and productivity of your group.

Global Public Health

Objectives

▶ **Explain** the importance of global public health efforts.

▶ **Describe** the types of public health problems that international health organizations work to overcome.

Vocabulary

- developing nation
- World Health Organization (WHO)
- United Nations Children's Fund (UNICEF)

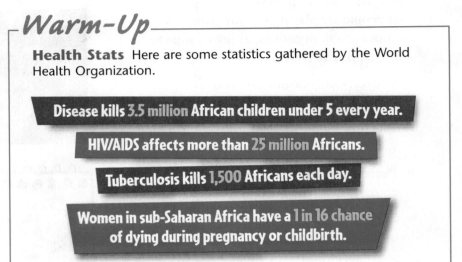

Warm-Up

Health Stats Here are some statistics gathered by the World Health Organization.

> Disease kills **3.5 million** African children under **5** every year.

> HIV/AIDS affects more than **25 million** Africans.

> Tuberculosis kills **1,500** Africans each day.

> Women in sub-Saharan Africa have a **1 in 16** chance of dying during pregnancy or childbirth.

WRITING How do you think the United States and other countries can help improve the lives of people in Africa?

Why Are Global Efforts Important?

In December 2004, a powerful tsunami struck South Asia. Because there was no warning of the tsunami, people did not know to evacuate coastal areas. As a result, hundreds of thousands of people in Indonesia, Thailand, India, and Sri Lanka died.

Threats of disease and a lack of clean drinking water were immediate concerns after the tsunami. Within days, governments and organizations from all over the world sent help in the form of money, supplies, and medical personnel.

In times of crisis, people around the world work together to combat public health problems in developing nations. **Developing nations** are countries with weak economies and low standards of living. Roughly 75 percent of the world's people live in developing nations. Many suffer from serious health problems. **Global efforts provide services and funding to developing nations that might not otherwise have the resources to make their public health programs succeed.**

Connect to Your Life **What global public health efforts have you heard about recently?**

International Health Organizations

In the aftermath of the tsunami, many international health organizations arrived on the scene to help. These organizations do work all over the world, in countries that have been devastated by natural disasters, wars, disease, or famine. Famine is a widespread lack of food. **International health organizations work in developing nations to overcome public health problems such as malnutrition, lack of basic medical care, poor sanitation, and lack of clean water.**

The United Nations   A number of United Nations agencies are directly involved in improving the living conditions of people in developing countries.

▶ The **World Health Organization (WHO)** sends people trained in medicine, agriculture, water quality, engineering, and other health-related skills to countries in need. WHO workers seek to boost food production and prevent diseases through education and immunization programs. WHO also collects worldwide health statistics to evaluate and predict future health threats.

▶ The **United Nations Children's Fund (UNICEF)** focuses on programs that aid children, such as immunization programs, day-care and health centers, and school food programs. UNICEF also runs training programs for nurses and teachers.

International Committee of the Red Cross

The world's largest private international public health organization is the International Committee of the Red Cross, known in Muslim countries as the Red Crescent. This privately funded organization began in 1859 to aid victims on the battlefield. Today, its services have greatly expanded. The Red Cross organizes assistance anywhere in the world for victims of disasters. The organization provides medical care, food, water, clothing, and temporary shelter.

GO ONLINE

PearsonSuccessNet.com
For: More on global public health

FIGURE 17   The 2004 tsunami killed nearly 300,000 people and prompted millions of dollars of donations from countries around the world.

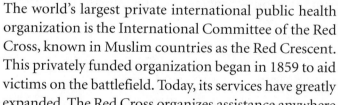

International organizations coordinated relief efforts for victims of the 2004 tsunami.

The Agency for International Development The United States Agency for International Development (USAID) was established to provide support for developing nations. A major focus of this support is the distribution of food to countries stricken by famine. USAID also funds programs for immunizations, medicines, sanitation, healthcare training, and treatment for dehydration. Dehydration occurs when the body suffers severe water loss. Dehydration resulting from diarrhea is the major cause of death among young children in developing nations.

The Peace Corps The Peace Corps is a United States government organization that trains volunteers for public health work in developing nations. The work that volunteers do depends both on their background and training and on the needs of the countries that invite them. Volunteers may help improve agricultural techniques, provide healthcare, construct shelters, or improve sanitation and water supply systems. In addition to health programs, some Peace Corps volunteers serve as advisors in the areas of education, technology, business, and industry.

Other Agencies The governments of many countries sponsor agencies that provide international public health assistance. Also, a number of privately supported organizations provide health services worldwide. For example, Oxfam International is known for its work in providing clean water and sanitation services in disaster areas. The Cooperative for Assistance and Relief Everywhere (CARE) provides healthcare, food, water, and emergency assistance to refugees and disaster victims. Many churches and missionary groups provide hospital, disease-prevention, and relief services.

FIGURE 18 Peace Corps volunteers work with people in developing nations to improve all aspects of public health.

Section 4 Review

Key Ideas and Vocabulary

1. What is a **developing nation**?
2. Explain why global public health efforts are important for helping developing nations.
3. What problems do international health organizations try to solve?
4. Describe the services provided by the **World Health Organization**.

Critical Thinking

5. **Evaluating** Sometimes, celebrities appeal to governments for aid on behalf of developing nations. Do you think this is an effective strategy? Why or why not?

Health and Community

International Aid Choose an international public health problem you are interested in, such as HIV/AIDS, childhood diseases, or famine. Create a 30-second public service advertisement for an organization that addresses the problem you chose. How will you command the attention of your audience? What kind of help will you ask for? **WRITING**

6. **Making Judgments** Many public health experts say that vaccinations were the greatest public health achievement of the 20th century. What do you think would be the greatest public health achievement so far this century? Explain your response.

Chapter 24
At a Glance

VIDEO **TEENS** Talk ⊙
Taking Charge of Your Health In what ways did the video motivate you to take charge of your health?

Section 1   The Healthcare System

Key Ideas

▶ Within the healthcare system, doctors work with nurses and other healthcare providers to care for patients.

▶ Healthcare facilities include doctors' offices, clinics, hospitals, and long-term care centers.

▶ The Internet, e-mail, and other technologies can make healthcare more efficient, and can make patients feel more involved in their care.

Vocabulary
- healthcare system (634)
- primary care physician (634)
- diagnosis (634)
- medical specialist (635)
- primary healthcare (637)
- outpatient (637)
- secondary healthcare (638)
- inpatient (638)
- tertiary healthcare (638)

Section 2   Participating in Your Healthcare

Key Ideas

▶ Deciding what doctor to see for routine healthcare deserves careful consideration.

▶ As a patient you also have certain responsibilities. You must fulfill these responsibilities in order to receive the best healthcare possible.

▶ Health insurance pays for a major part of medical expenses.

Vocabulary
- medical history (643)
- physical examination (643)
- premium (645) • copayment (645)
- deductible (646)

Section 3   Public Health

Key Ideas

▶ Public health programs today emphasize the need for prevention.

▶ In the United States, public health is primarily a governmental responsibility that is managed at the federal, state, and local levels.

Vocabulary
- public health (648)
- quarantine (648)
- epidemiology (649)
- health code (652)
- vital statistics (652)

Section 4   Global Public Health

Key Ideas

▶ Global efforts provide services and funding to developing nations that might not otherwise have the resources to make their public health programs succeed.

▶ International health organizations work in developing nations to overcome public health problems, such as malnutrition.

Vocabulary
- developing nation (656)
- World Health Organization (WHO) (657)
- United Nations Children's Fund (UNICEF) (657)

Chapter 24 Review

GO ONLINE
PearsonSuccessNet.com
For: Chapter 24 review activity

Reviewing Key Ideas

Section 1

1. A doctor who has received additional training in a particular branch of medicine is called a
   a. physician assistant. b. nurse practitioner.
   c. medical specialist. d. physical therapist.

2. A person who receives treatment but does not stay overnight in a hospital is called a(n)
   a. inpatient. b. outpatient.
   c. nurse. d. primary care physician.

3. What three things is a doctor licensed to perform?

4. **Critical Thinking** Explain why a patient might receive more advanced care at a teaching hospital than at another type of hospital.

Section 2

5. A record of your health and of your family's health is called a
   a. premium. b. deductible.
   c. physical examination. d. medical history.

6. The amount of money that a patient pays monthly for health insurance coverage is the
   a. premium. b. deductible.
   c. copayment. d. HMO.

7. What are some things to consider when choosing a doctor?

8. **Critical Thinking** Suppose you have a traditional health insurance plan that pays for 80% of your medical bills. How much would your out-of-pocket costs be for a $200 bill? **MATH**

Section 3

9. The numbers of births, deaths, and diseases in a population are called
   a. quarantines. b. health codes.
   c. vital statistics. d. deductibles.

10. What federal government agency has the major responsibility for public health?

11. **Critical Thinking** An epidemiologist studying diabetes finds that the disease is more common in people of a certain ethnicity than in the general population. How could this knowledge be used to help develop a public health policy for diabetes?

Section 4

12. A developing nation generally has
    a. a high standard of living.
    b. a strong public health system.
    c. excellent sanitation systems.
    d. a weak economy.

13. Describe two agencies of the United Nations that help people in developing nations.

14. Give an example of a public health crisis that required a global public health effort. What services did international groups provide?

15. **Critical Thinking** If you had the opportunity to join the Peace Corps, in what part of the world would you want to serve? Why?

Building Health Skills

16. **Advocacy** Michelle has an unusual rash on her leg, but she hasn't seen a doctor because her family doesn't have health insurance. What advice would you give Michelle?

17. **Making Decisions** You notice the water in your school's water fountains has an unpleasant smell and taste. You are concerned about the possible cause. What would you do?

18. **Setting Goals** Identify one career in healthcare that you might be interested in pursuing. Write down specific steps you can take to learn more about that career and to determine if it is a good match for you. **WRITING**

Health and Community

Legislation Investigation Work with other students in your class to research the Health Insurance Portability and Accountability Act (HIPAA). What patient rights are granted by this law? How does this law protect patients' privacy? Present your findings to your class. **WRITING**

Standardized Test Prep

Math Practice

The graph shows the number of people in the United States without any form of health insurance. Use the graph to answer Questions 19–21.

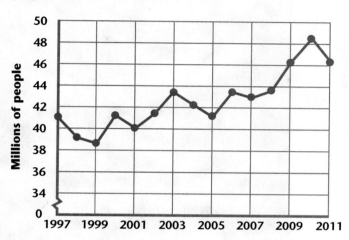

19. Approximately how many Americans were without health insurance in 1997?

 A 38 million   **B** 39 million

 C 40 million   **D** 41 million

20. By what percentage did the number of uninsured Americans increase from 2001 to 2011?

 F 8 percent   **G** 10 percent

 H 15 percent   **J** 18 percent

21. Which statement best describes the trend shown in this graph?

 A The number of Americans without health insurance has decreased since 1997.

 B The number of Americans without health insurance has increased steadily since 1997.

 C The number of Americans without health insurance has remained the same since 1997.

 D Overall, the number of Americans without health insurance increased between 1997 and 2011.

Test-Taking Tip

When taking a test, narrow down the possible answers by crossing out choices you know are wrong.

Reading and Writing Practice

Read the passage. Then answer Questions 22–25.

Prescription drug advertising and over-the-counter (OTC) drug advertisements that appear on television are among the most common forms of health communication reaching the U.S. public. The arrival of direct-to-consumer advertising has sparked both praise and criticism. Prescription drug advertising is regulated by the Food and Drug Administration, but questions remain regarding the most effective format for communicating benefit and risk information to consumers. Some health advocates fear that consumers are not well enough informed about the risks associated with certain drugs.

22. Prescription drug advertising directed at consumers is called

 A OTC advertising.

 B direct-to-consumer advertising.

 C FDA regulation.

 D risk and benefit analysis.

23. The Food and Drug Administration

 F regulates prescription drug advertising.

 G does not regulate prescription drug advertising.

 H has nothing to do with advertising.

 J is a television network.

24. According to the passage, which of these statements is true?

 A Direct-to-consumer advertising of drugs is problem-free.

 B Direct-to-consumer advertising of drugs is bad for the public.

 C Direct-to-consumer advertising of drugs has drawn both praise and criticism.

 D Drug advertisements on television do not reach many Americans.

Constructed Response

25. In a paragraph, summarize the main question that remains about direct-to-consumer drug advertising. Explain *your* opinion regarding direct-to-consumer drug advertising.

CHAPTER 25

A Healthy Community and Environment

GO ONLINE PearsonSuccessNet.com

VIDEO 25

TEENS Talk

Making a Difference

Preview **Activity**

How Can You Make a Difference?

Complete this activity before you watch the video.

1. Think about this quote.

   You must be the change you wish to see in the world.

   Mahatma Gandhi

2. Explain what you think this quote means.
3. What changes would you like to see in your neighborhood, school, or larger community?
4. How could you help put these changes into effect? **WRITING**

Section 1

Your Community, Your Health

Objectives

▶ **Identify** the different kinds of communities to which you belong.

▶ **Describe** how communities affect personal health.

Vocabulary

- social network
- community service organization
- mixed-use development
- urban sprawl

Warm-Up

Quick Quiz How connected are you to your community? See if you can answer "yes" to any of the following questions.

1. Do at least five adults in your neighborhood know you by name?

2. Can you name at least three of your community's leaders (e.g., the mayor, police chief, and the superintendent of schools)?

3. Can you describe what each of the community leaders do that influences health?

WRITING How is being connected to your community important to your overall health and well-being?

What Is Community?

If someone were to ask you, "To what community do you belong?," what would you answer? You might answer by giving the name of the city or town in which you live. However, the complete answer is more complex.

There are, in fact, many different kinds of communities to which you belong. **Besides being a resident of your city or town and your neighborhood, you are a member of a particular school, a cultural community, and probably one or more clubs or organizations.** Being a member of each of these communities is important to your sense of identity.

The people with whom you interact and look to for friendship, information, and social support in all of these different communities make up your **social network.** The extent and quality of your social network can play a major role in helping to keep you healthy.

Your City or Town   The place where you live, whether it is a big city, small town, or rural village, has a number of specific features that shape your sense of community. Physical features include the weather and the natural environment. Social characteristics include the people who live there, the kinds of work these people do, and the local government.

Your Neighborhood   Your neighborhood includes the people in the immediate vicinity of your home. The people in your neighborhood may know you and your family members by name. They are probably comfortable enough to ask you for a favor from time to time.

Your School Community   Schools are not only responsible for your education, but they are also important communities in which you form friendships and develop leadership skills. At school, you are likely to belong to particular groups, such as clubs or teams in which you and others share the same interests.

Your Cultural Community   Your cultural background is another factor that contributes to your sense of community. It determines what holidays you celebrate, what traditions you follow, and what kinds of foods you typically eat. What cultural traditions do you celebrate? How many people who share your cultural background live nearby? Answers to these kinds of questions help to define who you are and give you a sense of pride and belonging.

Other Communities   In addition to the communities described so far, your involvement in clubs or other organizations may also be important in your life. **Community service organizations** are official groups whose members act or unite for a common purpose. For example, Boys and Girls Clubs of America and 4-H clubs provide teens with a supportive environment for recreation, learning, and service.

Who are two or three adults in your community you could ask for help if you needed it?

FIGURE 1   You are a member of several communities.

Your Neighborhood

Your School

Your City or Town

Your Culture

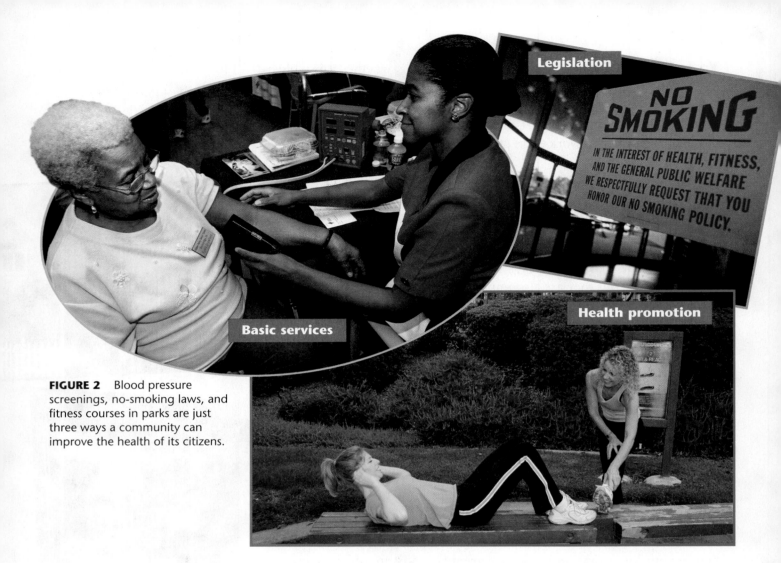

FIGURE 2 Blood pressure screenings, no-smoking laws, and fitness courses in parks are just three ways a community can improve the health of its citizens.

Image labels: Legislation; Basic services; Health promotion

NO SMOKING
IN THE INTEREST OF HEALTH, FITNESS, AND THE GENERAL PUBLIC WELFARE WE RESPECTFULLY REQUEST THAT YOU HONOR OUR NO SMOKING POLICY.

How Communities Affect Health

Your health and quality of life are affected by the communities in which you live. **Community factors contribute significantly to the physical and social health of community members.**

Your City or Town Here are some of the ways that your city or town affects your health.

▶ **Basic health services** Your local government is responsible for providing water sewage treatment, clean drinking water, emergency medical services, road and highway maintenance, and other services that protect health. Restaurant inspections, infectious disease control, immunizations, and blood pressure screenings are other basic health services that your city or town may deliver.

▶ **Health legislation** Local governments also often approve and enforce regulations to protect the health of their citizens. For example, laws that limit noise levels or that ban cigarette smoking in restaurants and public buildings protect citizens from harm.

Community Design and Physical Activity

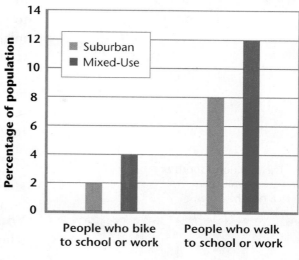

Community design

FIGURE 3 More people walk and bike in mixed-use communities.
Reading Graphs Compare the percent of people who walk to school or work in each type of community. How much greater is the percent in a mixed-used community? **MATH**

▶ **Promotion of healthy and active lifestyles** Your town or city may have recreational facilities and parks that encourage physical activity. Your community may also run blood drives, food pantries, nutritious school lunch programs, and weight-management groups.

▶ **Community design** Some communities plan new developments or redesign existing neighborhoods to promote walking, biking, and the use of public transportation. One way this is done is through **mixed-use development,** which means building homes closer to businesses and schools. In mixed-use neighborhoods, people can get to work or school and run errands easier by foot or by bike than by car.

Mixed-use development is a healthier alternative to the building of homes in suburbs away from business districts. This type of spread-out development is called **urban sprawl.** People who live in mixed-use neighborhoods rely less on cars and are more active. So they tend to suffer from fewer chronic health problems, including high blood pressure, obesity, and arthritis.

 GO ONLINE
PearsonSuccessNet.com
For: More on community actions

 Connect to Your Life How does your community's design promote health? What improvements could you suggest?

Your Neighborhood In addition to what your town or city does, your neighborhood may also organize efforts to protect the health of its members. A neighborhood might organize safety patrols, sponsor a softball game, or clean up a local park.

Many neighborhood activities also promote social health. Block parties, carpools, and group gardening projects are some ways that neighbors build social relationships.

 What could you do to improve the health of your neighborhood?

Your School Community Aside from your home, school is probably where you spend most of your time. It is not surprising, then, that your school's physical and social environment can significantly affect your health. For example, some older schools have problems with mold or crumbling ceilings and walls that expose toxic building materials. Such conditions can aggravate asthma and other respiratory conditions.

Many other factors at school can affect your health. These factors include

▶ Availability of nutritious foods for lunch and snacks

▶ Safe routes to school, including buses that are safe

▶ Policies that protect students from bullying and other types of violence

▶ Opportunities for physical activity for all students

▶ Access to school nurses and counselors

Your Cultural Community The cultural community in which you and your family live also influences your health. For example, a tightly-knit cultural community can serve as a "safety net" to support members who are in trouble or in need.

Family gatherings at which cultural traditions are celebrated also strengthen social health. In addition, foods that are important to your cultural group may enhance your health. For example, the soy proteins in tofu and other traditional Asian foods have been shown to help prevent certain cancers. The use of olive oil in Greek and Italian cooking may help prevent heart disease.

FIGURE 4 The traditional foods of your cultural community can contribute to a healthful diet.

Other Communities Community service organizations and other volunteer groups do many things to improve the health of community members. For example, Students Against Destructive Decisions (SADD) has helped to reduce the number of fatalities due to driving under the influence of alcohol in many communities through advocacy and education. Boy Scouts and Girl Scouts may organize food drives or maintain hiking trails. Other community groups may sponsor bicycle races or walk-a-thons to raise money for cancer research or other causes.

Religious organizations also have increasingly become involved in efforts to improve the health of their communities. For example, many churches, synagogues, and mosques now sponsor

▶ Programs that promote healthful eating

▶ Low-cost screenings for high blood pressure or cancer

▶ Youth groups that participate in community service projects to help people in need

FIGURE 5 This teen is a member of her local 4-H club, where she practices leadership and other life skills.

Section 1 Review

Key Ideas and Vocabulary

1. Identify five different types of communities to which people belong.

2. What is a **social network?** What people are most important to you in your social network?

3. What is a **community service organization?** Give an example.

4. Describe three ways that communities can affect a person's physical health and social health.

5. How is **mixed-use development** different from **urban sprawl?**

Critical Thinking

6. Evaluating Why do you think some communities are better at promoting health than others?

> ## Health at School
>
> **Measuring School Health** Make a list of things about your school that make it a healthy place to be. Then make a list of things about your school that need improvement. Write a letter to your school principal or school board detailing your findings. In your letter, emphasize the most important items that should be addressed to improve student health. **WRITING**

7. Predicting Many schools now restrict school buses from idling—leaving their engines running—outside of school buildings. In what ways do you think this change will improve student health?

8. Applying Concepts How do you think your cultural community improves your family's health?

Accessing Information

Locating Community Resources

Dierdra has been feeling depressed since her parents told her they were getting a divorce. She hasn't been able to concentrate in school or fall asleep at night. Dierdra doesn't want to discuss her concerns with her parents because they both seem so upset already. But she doesn't know who else in her community to turn to for help.

Where do you think Dierdra could go for help with her problems? Below are some steps that Dierdra or you could take to help find resources that are available in your community.

1 Talk to a trusted adult.
When you have a problem or feel depressed, you may find it helpful to talk to an adult you know and trust. The person might be a parent, relative, friend of the family, trusted teacher, coach, school counselor, family doctor, or a religious leader.

2 Search the Internet.
Using search engines to search the Internet can identify countless sites for health-related information and services. Keep in mind, though, that not all sources of information are equally reliable.

Try to identify and read the advice of established organizations. Many county health departments have a listing on their Web sites of community-based health services and agencies. You may also want to check the Web sites of larger voluntary health organizations to see if they have a chapter in your area.

③ Find local contact information.

Use the Internet or a telephone directory to find phone numbers for local resources. Include your location for Internet searches. Search for these terms online or in the phone book:

► "Self-Help" or "Health" (may be found at the front of white or yellow pages)

► "Community Health Services," "Human Health Services," or "Mental Health Services"

► "Government Services"

If you still can't find help, try calling people who are likely to keep "help" numbers handy. These include dialing 411 for directory assistance, your local library, or the police and fire departments. If you are in an emergency situation, dial 911.

④ Call to find out what services are provided.

After identifying what you believe to be an appropriate resource or service, call the service and briefly discuss your problem to find out whether the service can meet your needs. Be sure to ask about the location, the hours, and if there is a fee.

If the services do not meet your needs or are too costly, ask the person to whom you are speaking to suggest other places that you can call.

⑤ Select one resource and make an appointment to visit.

You may wish to ask a trusted person to accompany you to your first visit. You may want to have the person wait outside so you can talk privately with the counselor or other professional with whom you are meeting.

If you are not satisfied with the service you have selected, there may be other options. Discuss any concerns with the counselor or try a different service or organization.

Practice the Skill

1. Make a list of some common problems that young people face today. Think about issues related to families, peers, academics, drugs, finances, illness, and others to include in your list.

2. Make a class directory of resources for each problem. List each organization's name, Web site, address, phone number, hours, fees, and services.

3. With permission, distribute the directory to people in your school community.

Air Quality and Health

Objectives

▶ **Summarize** the potential health effects of air pollution.

▶ **Evaluate** factors that affect indoor air pollution.

▶ **Analyze** how government and personal actions can help improve air quality.

Vocabulary

- pollution
- fossil fuels
- smog
- ozone layer
- asbestos
- radon

Warm-Up

Dear Advice Line,

My allergies always seem to be worse when I am indoors rather than outdoors. I thought flowers and other things found outdoors caused allergies. Is something wrong with me?

WRITING Make a list of indoor conditions that might affect indoor air quality. Then, write back with your answer and advice.

Air Pollution

One factor that is central to the health of communities is the quality of the air people breathe. As you read this sentence, you are breathing in air from your surroundings. Air is a mixture of gases and small particles. The one gas you need—oxygen—makes up about 20 percent of the air you breathe. The remaining 80 percent of the air consists mainly of nitrogen plus small amounts of other naturally occurring gases.

In addition to the natural gases a breath of air contains, harmful gases and particles that have been released into the air may also be present. **Pollution** is the presence or release of substances—called pollutants—into the environment in quantities that are harmful to living organisms. **Air pollutants can damage the respiratory system, enter the bloodstream and harm other parts of the body, and reduce your protection from the sun's radiation.**

How does air get polluted? Whenever substances such as wood and other fuels are burned, particles and harmful waste gases are produced. One of the biggest sources of air pollution is the burning of **fossil fuels,** energy-rich substances mined from deep in the earth. Fossil fuels include coal, oil, and natural gas.

Harmful gases also are released into the air when liquids such as gasoline or paint thinner evaporate, or when gases are released from natural sources such as volcanoes. Figure 6 lists five major air pollutants that affect health directly.

What Is Smog?   If you live in or near a major city, you're familiar with smog. **Smog** is a brown haze that forms when air pollutants react in the presence of sunlight. It forms when there is little or no wind and a layer of air is trapped next to the ground. Without air circulation, pollutants can build up and become visible as smog. Local smog alerts warn people—especially those with respiratory conditions like asthma—to limit outdoor activity and physical exertion on days when smog levels are hazardous.

Air Pollutants and the Ozone Layer   The gas ozone is a pollutant when it is near to the ground. But naturally occurring ozone located high up in earth's atmosphere—in the **ozone layer**—plays a protective role. The ozone layer absorbs most of the harmful ultraviolet light radiated by the sun, thus preventing it from reaching Earth's surface. Ultraviolet light is harmful to all living things. In people, it may cause skin cancer or cataracts, which is a cloudiness of the eye's lens. Ultraviolet light may also damage the immune system.

Some air pollutants destroy the ozone layer. Chemicals called CFCs, short for chlorofluorocarbons (klawr oh floor oh KAHR bunz) are especially damaging. CFCs have been widely used as cooling fluids in air conditioners and refrigeration units, as propellants in aerosol spray cans, and in foam insulating materials. CFCs are now banned in new products.

Connect to Your Life   **What physical activities do you enjoy outdoors that would be affected by a smog alert?**

FIGURE 6   Air pollutants have a number of negative effects on health. **Predicting** If emissions of nitrogen oxides decrease, how are ozone levels likely to be affected?

Major Air Pollutants

Pollutant	Source	Health Effects
Carbon monoxide (CO)	Combustion of automobile engines; agricultural burning; tobacco smoke	Reduces ability of circulatory system to transport oxygen; causes headache, fatigue, nausea; reduces endurance
Sulfur dioxide (SO_2)	Combustion of fossil fuels; petroleum refining; smelting	Increases risk of chronic respiratory disease; causes shortness of breath; worsens narrowing of airways for people with asthma
Nitrogen oxides	Combustion of fossil fuels; fertilizers	May aggravate respiratory infections and symptoms; may increase risk of chest colds, bronchitis, and pneumonia in children
Ozone (O_3)	Reactions of nitrogen oxides with oxygen in presence of sunlight	Irritates upper respiratory tract and aggravates respiratory conditions such as asthma, bronchitis, and emphysema
Particulate matter	Forest fires; fuel combustion; incineration	Increases chronic and acute respiratory diseases; may irritate tissue of throat, nose, lungs, and eyes

Indoor Air Pollution

Many people think that air pollution occurs only outdoors. In fact, the levels of some air pollutants can be higher indoors than outdoors. Some common sources of indoor air pollutants are listed in Figure 7.

Indoor air pollution is most severe in homes and other buildings that have been sealed against air leaks. A building with few air leaks uses less energy for heating and cooling. Unfortunately, inside such energy-efficient buildings, pollutants can build up to high levels if the air is not conditioned properly. To reduce pollutant levels, some houses and offices are now being designed to allow for adequate ventilation year-round.

Asbestos Many older buildings contain a dangerous indoor pollutant called asbestos. **Asbestos** (as BES tus) is a fibrous mineral that was used in fireproofing and other building materials. Unfortunately, bits of asbestos flake off easily. When asbestos fibers are inhaled into the lungs, they damage the cells of the lungs and can cause lung cancer. Today, the use of asbestos is banned entirely in construction. Asbestos removal programs for schools and other buildings have helped reduce exposure to this pollutant.

Radon A naturally occurring radioactive gas called **radon** is also a serious indoor air pollutant. Radon leaks from rocks in the ground through the foundations of buildings. In some buildings, radon can rise to dangerous levels. Radon is responsible for thousands of lung cancer deaths each year. Many experts recommend that people test their homes for radon. If a radon problem exists, people should improve ventilation and seal cracks in foundation walls and floors.

GO ONLINE

PearsonSuccessNet.com

For: More on air pollution

FIGURE 7 There are many sources of indoor air pollution.

Sources of Indoor Air Pollution

- ▶ Fumes from carpets and paint
- ▶ Pesticides
- ▶ Plywood glues
- ▶ Foam insulation
- ▶ Gas stoves
- ▶ Fuel-burning indoor heaters
- ▶ Air fresheners
- ▶ Mold
- ▶ Dust mites
- ▶ Asbestos
- ▶ Radon
- ▶ Tobacco smoke

FIGURE 8 Electric buses help reduce air pollution.

Protecting Air Quality

Much progress has been made towards reducing air pollution. Decades ago, governments recognized that air pollutants harm people's health. They passed regulations to reduce emissions of harmful gases from motor vehicles and industries. **In addition to government regulations, personal actions, such as your day-to-day decisions about energy use, directly affect air quality.**

Government Regulations The Clean Air Act of 1970 identified major air pollutants and set standards for air quality. Since 1970, Congress has made changes and additions to the Clean Air Act every few years. To comply with federal laws, some factories and power plants installed scrubbers, or filters, on smokestacks to remove some of the most toxic pollutants.

Some other federal and local government measures that help reduce air pollution include

▶ Funding for developing more efficient ways to use traditional fossil fuels or alternatives to these fuels, such as wind power and solar power

▶ Laws requiring vehicles to pass annual inspections of exhaust pollutants

▶ Tax breaks for drivers who purchase hybrid automobiles that save gasoline by running partly on electric power

Air Quality Ratings Weather reports for cities and other areas with air pollution problems often include air quality ratings. The ratings, which are based on air quality standards set by the government, range from "good" to "unhealthy" to "very hazardous." In this way, communities can monitor their progress toward achieving cleaner, healthier air.

Connect to Your Life **What measures taken by your community do you think are aimed at improving air quality? Explain.**

FIGURE 9 Using public transportation is one way you can help improve air quality.

What You Can Do Reducing air pollution depends on your actions as well as those of governments and industries. Here are some steps you and your family can take to help reduce air pollution.

▶ Walk, ride a bicycle, or use public transportation instead of an automobile.

▶ When driving, avoid unnecessary trips. For example, combine errands in one trip.

▶ Make sure your vehicle is well-maintained so it produces the least pollution.

▶ Turn off lights and appliances that are not being used. Saving energy saves fuel, which reduces air pollution.

▶ Clean the cooling fans or coils on refrigerators and air conditioners so they will work efficiently.

▶ In winter, set the thermostat lower and wear extra clothes to keep warm indoors.

▶ In the summer, if you have an air conditioner, set it at the highest comfortable temperature.

▶ Make sure that any fuel-burning appliances are vented and working properly.

Section 2 Review

Key Ideas and Vocabulary

1. What is **pollution?** Give examples of three sources of air pollution.

2. What health problems are caused by air pollution?

3. In what kind of building is indoor air pollution worst?

4. What is **asbestos?** How is it dangerous to health?

5. Give examples of one government action and one personal action that improve air quality.

Critical Thinking

6. **Predicting** On a cloudy, windy day, is a smog alert likely? Explain.

Health and Community

Local Air Pollution Find out how many days your community or the nearest large city reported "unhealthy" or worse air quality ratings. What efforts is your community making to reduce this number or keep it at zero? Write a report explaining your findings and describing what residents and industries can do to help reduce air pollution. **WRITING**

7. **Evaluating** What factors in a building's design and construction materials can affect indoor air pollution?

GO ONLINE PearsonSuccessNet.com   Audio Summary Section 25.2

Protecting Land and Water

Objectives

▶ **Summarize** the threats that hazardous wastes pose to human health.
▶ **Identify** three sources of water pollution.
▶ **Describe** three solutions for protecting land and water.

Vocabulary
• biodegradable waste
• hazardous waste
• landfill
• recycling
• sewage
• runoff
• conservation

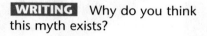

Myth It is healthier to drink bottled water than tap water.

Fact Local health departments closely monitor the quality of tap water. Bottled water is less closely regulated. By drinking tap water, you also save money and reduce plastic waste.

WRITING Why do you think this myth exists?

Waste Disposal

As part of the normal processes of life, all organisms produce wastes. These wastes usually do not cause pollution because they are broken down by microorganisms and reused by other living things. Waste that can be broken down by microorganisms is called **biodegradable waste.**

In addition to biodegradable wastes, humans create wastes that are not, or are only partially, biodegradable. Some non-biodegradable wastes are not dangerous, but they do remain in the environment for a long time instead of being broken down into useful raw materials. Other non-biodegradable wastes, however, are hazardous.

Hazardous Wastes A **hazardous waste** is any waste that is either flammable, explosive, corrosive, or toxic to humans or other living things. Each year, millions of tons of hazardous wastes are produced in the United States alone. They include motor oil, pesticides, solvents, mercury, lead, and radioactive materials. **Hazardous wastes build up in the environment and threaten the health of plants and animals, including humans.** Some hazardous wastes are carcinogens, meaning they cause cancer. Others may cause birth defects, developmental problems, or diseases.

Where Household Trash Goes

1960

Incinerated
30.6%

Landfilled
63%

Recycled
6.4%

2010

Landfilled
54.2%

Incinerated
11.7%

Recycled
34.1%

FIGURE 10 The percentage of household trash that ends up in landfills has decreased in the last few decades.
Reading Graphs How much more trash was recycled in 2010 compared with 1960? MATH

Landfills A landfill is a permanent storage area where garbage and other wastes are deposited and covered with soil. Landfills are widely used for disposal of solid and liquid wastes. One problem with landfills is that many of them are at or near full capacity. Also, suitable space to build new landfills is running out.

Another more serious problem is that some landfills contain illegally dumped hazardous wastes that may leak into water supplies. However, many federal regulations are in place to prevent this from happening. These regulations include locating landfills away from wetlands, lining landfills to prevent seepage of chemicals, and monitoring water quality near landfills.

Another piece of good news is shown in Figure 10. Compared with the past, a greater percentage of household trash today is being recycled. A smaller percentage is being landfilled or incinerated, meaning burned. Recycling is the process of reclaiming raw materials from discarded products and using them to create new products. Many states and communities now require residents to recycle materials such as newspapers, metals, plastics, and glass.

Sources of Water Pollution

Bodies of water such as lakes, rivers, and oceans have always been used to dispose of wastes. If the wastes are biodegradable and the amount is small, microorganisms can break them down. However, when both the amount and types of wastes increase, water pollution becomes more and more of a problem. **Wastes from household, industrial, and agricultural sources can cause pollution of water resources.**

Household Sewage The waste material carried from toilets and drains is referred to as **sewage.** If released into the environment too rapidly, sewage can make water foul-smelling and deadly to fish and other organisms. Sewage also contains bacteria and viruses that can cause disease. For example, in coastal areas, clams, oysters, and other shellfish exposed to sewage may become contaminated with the hepatitis A virus. People who eat raw shellfish may develop hepatitis A, a liver disease caused by this virus.

Up until the 1970s, many communities in the United States discharged raw, or untreated, sewage directly into lakes, rivers, or oceans. In 1972, the Clean Water Act required communities to treat their raw sewage before releasing it into the environment. Sewage treatment makes use of microorganisms to break down the wastes in the water. Treatment can occur in septic tanks, cesspools, or sewage treatment plants. Each provides conditions that allow microorganisms to break down wastes before they are released into the environment.

Have pollutants ever caused a pool or beach in your community to close? Explain the circumstances.

FIGURE 11 If this beach had a sign like the one shown above, these men would not be able to harvest shellfish.

GO ONLINE PLANETDIARY

PearsonSuccessNet.com
For: More on health effects
of mercury

Household Cleaners Household cleaners can be a source of pollution if they contain phosphates, which can harm water plants and animals, or harsh chemicals such as chlorine. Chlorine in high concentrations is toxic to all forms of life. Chlorine also can react with certain substances that are dissolved in water, forming carcinogens.

Industrial Wastes Waste products from industrial operations, such as mining and manufacturing, are some of the most dangerous types of water pollutants. Many industrial wastes are extremely hazardous or non-biodegradable, or both. Industrial wastes include such things as dyes, acids, solvents, and heavy metals such as mercury, lead, and cadmium.

In the past, it was common for industrial wastes to be discharged into ground and surface waters, contaminating organisms that lived in or drank the water. Today, although there is much greater regulation to prevent such contamination, some of these pollutants are still a problem. The Environmental Protection Agency (EPA) estimates that one in six American women of childbearing age has a blood mercury level that would be considered dangerous to a developing fetus.

Agricultural Runoff The water that drains from land into streams is called **runoff**. Runoff can carry with it many kinds of substances that pollute water supplies. Runoff from agricultural land, for example, often contains chemicals applied to crops to control weeds and insect pests. Many of these chemicals are toxic if ingested in large enough quantities.

Even if polluted water is not used by humans directly, game animals may pass the contamination on to people who eat them. Most states now issue advisories to help protect people from consuming such pollutants. The advisory includes a list of recommendations to limit or avoid eating certain types of fish and other game animals.

FIGURE 12 Pesticides are sometimes sprayed onto crops from an airplane. Unfortunately, runoff from fields may contaminate local water supplies.

Hands-On *Activity*

Nontoxic Housecleaning

Materials
bucket
hot water
baking soda
soap flakes
cornstarch
white vinegar
stirrer
sponge
rags or paper towels

Try This

❶ In a bucket, make a nontoxic, all-purpose cleaner by adding 1/2 tablespoon of baking soda and 1/8 cup of soap flakes to 1/2 gallon of hot water. Stir until all ingredients are completely dissolved.

❷ Moisten a sponge with the cleaning solution and clean your desktop or another surface that your teacher selects. Note how easily and effectively the cleaner works.

❸ Make a nontoxic glass cleaner by adding 1 tablespoon of cornstarch and 1/4 cup of white vinegar to 1/2 gallon of warm water. Stir well.

❹ Moisten a rag or paper towel with the glass cleaner. According to your teacher's instructions, try cleaning a window or mirror.

Think and Discuss

❶ How well did the cleaners work? How do they compare with commercially prepared products you have used?

❷ How do you think most people dispose of cleaning products? What effect do you think disposing of cleaning products has on the environment?

❸ What are the benefits and drawbacks of making your own nontoxic cleaners? **WRITING**

Maintaining Environmental Health

The environmental damage to land and water—and in turn, the damage to human health—is a serious problem, but there are solutions. **Cleaning up waste sites, improving waste management, and conserving natural resources are three solutions for protecting land and water.**

Cleaning Up Waste Sites The EPA has placed over 1,000 of the most dangerous hazardous waste sites on a national priority list for cleanup. These so-called "Superfund" sites are found in every state. Thousands of other hazardous waste sites are being cleaned up by state governments or by private companies.

Some dump sites are identified only after citizens notify authorities. If you suspect hazardous chemicals have been dumped at a site, notify your local health department or state agency for environmental protection.

Connect to Your Life Do you know if there are any Superfund sites in your community? How could you find out?

Proper Disposal of Wastes Laws now make it difficult for industries and individuals to dump wastes illegally. Today, legal dump sites for hazardous chemicals are designed to prevent the escape of wastes into the surrounding environment.

Many communities have collection centers where residents can turn in hazardous wastes, such as motor oil, pesticides, and car batteries, for proper disposal. Many companies have also developed ways to reduce the amount of wastes they generate in the first place or to recycle their wastes. Using new technologies, such as high-temperature incineration, has also helped eliminate large amounts of hazardous wastes.

Conservation Humans have been altering the land for thousands of years—for farming, settlement, and harvesting resources such as lumber. In most instances, the environment has been able to recover. In modern times, however, the demand for land development and the use of other natural resources has risen dramatically as the human population has grown rapidly.

Losing natural land areas can make pollution worse. For example, pavement cannot absorb rainwater. Therefore, paving an area may increase runoff of pollutants into streams and lakes.

Conservation is one key to slowing down the rate at which natural areas are lost. **Conservation** is the protection and preservation of the natural environment by managing natural resources wisely and developing land for new construction responsibly.

What conservation organizations are active in your community?

FIGURE 13 This community group has launched an effort to keep a local beach clean.

What You Can Do You can help reduce the problems associated with land and water pollution by following the "three Rs"—reduce, reuse, and recycle.

▶ **Reduce** by creating less waste in the first place. For example, avoid using disposable, non-biodegradable products such as plastic cups. Purchase products that have a minimum of packaging, or that are packaged in recycled or recyclable materials. Finally, buy only as much of a product or material as you need.

▶ **Reuse** by finding other uses for objects or by donating them rather than discarding them. For example, reuse cardboard boxes and empty jars for storage. Pass magazines or catalogs on to friends after you are through with them. You might also donate old clothes, furniture, and sports equipment rather than throwing them out.

▶ **Recycle** by keeping separate from the trash any materials that can be reprocessed into new products. Glass, metal, most plastics, and many types of paper can be recycled. Check with your city or town for the recycling guidelines specific to your community.

FIGURE 14 To help remind others not to pollute, this teen is stenciling a warning message next to a storm drain.

Section 3 Review

Key Ideas and Vocabulary

1. What is a **hazardous waste?** Give three examples.
2. How do hazardous wastes affect human health?
3. What is a **landfill?** What serious problem do some landfills pose to the environment?
4. What are three sources of water pollution?
5. Identify three solutions that can help protect land and water resources.

Critical Thinking

6. **Applying Concepts** What are you doing to reduce the amount of waste you contribute to landfills? What else could you do?

Health at Home

Reducing Waste Make an inventory of products you buy that come with packaging. Put each package into one of three categories: "Reuse" means you will use it again; "Recycle" means you will recycle it; "Trash" means you can't recycle or reuse it. For each product in your "Trash" category, describe how you could "Reduce" instead by either going without the product or buying a less wasteful alternative. **WRITING**

7. **Relating Cause and Effect** What health concerns in your community have been caused by land or water pollution? Explain.

Working for Community Health

Objectives

▶ **Examine** two keys to building a sense of community.

▶ **Identify** three steps to getting more involved in your community.

Vocabulary

• civic engagement
• consensus-building

Warm-Up

Health Stats What impact do teen volunteers make?

> **55% of teens do volunteer work.**

> Teens spend **1.3 billion hours volunteering each year.**

> **The typical teen volunteer contributes 29 hours per year.**

WRITING Why do you think so many teens volunteer? What benefits do the volunteers get from doing so?

A Sense of Community

Building healthy communities requires that people work together. To do this, people need to have a sense of community. When people believe that they are part of a community, they have a stake in making their community function as well as it can. **Two keys to building a sense of community are civic engagement and a shared vision of the future.**

Civic Engagement   How involved are people in your community? The level of involvement that average citizens have in the planning and decision-making that affects their community is called **civic engagement.** Some examples of civic engagement include

▶ Participating in community government

▶ Registering to vote when you turn 18

▶ Volunteering during a political campaign

▶ Attending public hearings or school board meetings

A Shared Vision   For communities to make progress and bring about positive changes, members need to share common goals. How can citizens with very different views come to a consensus on important issues? **Consensus-building** is the process by which a community arrives at an agreed-upon vision for the future. Consensus-building requires strong leadership and give-and-take among citizens.

Achieving goals for the future often means that a community has to make sacrifices in the short term. For example, suppose that a city decides to expand its subway system. The project would be paid for by tax dollars today although its benefits will not be realized until several years later. In other words, one generation pays for a benefit that the next generation will receive.

If it were not for a shared vision, many communities might not make investments in their school systems, transportation systems, or public health programs.

Your Life   **What sacrifices do you make in order to see a future benefit?**

FIGURE 15   At a public hearing, people have the opportunity to express their opinions to the decision makers in their community.

GO ONLINE

PearsonSuccessNet.com

For: More on getting involved

Getting Involved in Your Community

How can you get more involved in your commuity? **There are three steps to getting involved: become informed, volunteer your time, and be an advocate.** By following these steps, you can help bring about changes to improve the quality of life, or even save lives, in your community.

Become Informed What are some of the key health-related issues facing your community? What are people most concerned about? And what are the strengths and weaknesses of the community to address those issues? The first step in getting involved in your community is to become informed about questions like these.

By asking such questions, you can gain insight into what people are thinking about. Which concerns affect health? Maybe it's a dangerous traffic intersection, the quality of school lunches, or disease-carrying mosquitoes in the summer months. You can learn about the scope of a problem, how people view the problem, and any possible solutions that have been proposed. Several ways you can become informed are listed in Figure 16.

Connect to Your Life What community health concerns have your parents, friends, or neighbors expressed?

FIGURE 16 There are many ways to gather information about the concerns of your local community. **Applying Concepts** What sources do you rely on for information about your community?

How to Become Informed

- Read the local newspaper.
- Tune into the local radio or television stations.
- Attend a meeting of your town council, board of health, or school board.
- Interview community leaders.
- Survey your peers or other groups affected by your issue.

Volunteer Your Time Once you've become informed, the next step is to reach out, plan a strategy, and get more involved. Maybe your school has a stake in the issue and needs someone to serve as a student representative at key meetings. Or maybe you can volunteer with a community organization that has expressed concern about the issue.

Did you know that more than half of America's teenagers, ages 12 to 17, do some kind of volunteer community service work? On average, teenage volunteers devote almost four hours each week working with religious organizations, community service organizations, school groups, and other groups.

There are lots of ways that volunteering improves community health. Food drives and programs like "Meals on Wheels" help disadvantaged members of the community get food they might otherwise go without. School recycling programs can help improve your community's environment. And volunteering to coach disabled students can help improve the physical and mental health of the people you coach. It can also make you feel good about yourself simply because you've helped another person.

Volunteering helps the community at large, but it also helps the volunteers themselves. Figure 17 lists some of the many benefits of volunteering that teens report.

FIGURE 17 Volunteering benefits the community-at-large and also rewards the volunteer.

Benefits to Teen Volunteers
- Gain new perspective on community problems.
- Discover positive role models.
- Develop career goals and obtain job skills.
- Improve grades in school.
- Meet new people with shared values.

FIGURE 18 These teens have organized a campaign for more resources for tobacco prevention in their school.

Be an Advocate Remember from Chapter 1 that advocacy means speaking or writing in support of a person or issue. There are several ways you can be an advocate and take a stand on issues in your community. All of these actions require good communication skills.

▶ Speak out about an issue at public meetings.

▶ Write a letter to the editor of your local or school newspaper.

▶ Recruit your peers to meet with a government official or other decision makers.

▶ Organize a "Teen Summit" to empower others to become advocates.

▶ Establish an electronic listserv, Web blog, or Web site where you can keep other concerned teens updated on developments.

▶ Work with some friends to provide information about an important health topic, such as organ donation, at a community event.

Whatever you do, by taking a stand as an advocate, you become an agent for change. But keep in mind, it takes courage to voice your opinion, especially when people may be reluctant to change. Enlist the support of peers, teachers, and other adults who support your ideas and can help you move your ideas forward.

Section 4 Review

Key Ideas and Vocabulary

1. What are two keys to building a sense of community?

2. What is **civic engagement?** How does it apply to you?

3. Describe three steps you can take to get more involved in your community.

Critical Thinking

4. Evaluating What do you think are three health challenges facing the community in which you live? Explain.

Health and Community

Cell Phone Disposal Plan Disposing of cell phones—which often contain hazardous-materials—in an environmentally and socially responsible manner is a growing health concern. Write a plan for organizing a phone recycling program for your community. You may want to first research organizations that accept old cell phones. Describe in your plan both the benefits and challenges of such a program. **WRITING**

5. Applying Concepts What more could be done to address the challenges you cited in Question 4? What role could you play as an advocate?

Chapter 25
At a Glance

VIDEO

TEENS Talk ⊙

Making a Difference How could you volunteer more in your community?

Section 1   Your Community, Your Health

Key Ideas

▶ Besides being a resident of your city or town and neighborhood, you are a member of a particular school, a cultural community, and probably one or more clubs or organizations.

▶ Community factors contribute significantly to the physical and social health of community members.

Vocabulary
- social network (664)
- community service organization (665)
- mixed-use development (667)
- urban sprawl (667)

Section 2   Air Quality and Health

Key Ideas

▶ Air pollutants can damage the respiratory system, enter the bloodstream and harm other parts of the body, and reduce your protection from the sun's radiation.

▶ Indoor air pollution is most severe in homes and other buildings that have been sealed against air leaks.

▶ In addition to government regulations, personal actions, such as your day-to-day decisions about energy use, directly affect air quality.

Vocabulary
- pollution (672) • fossil fuels (672) • smog (673)
- ozone layer (673) • asbestos (674) • radon (674)

Section 3   Protecting Land and Water

Key Ideas

▶ Hazardous wastes accumulate in the environment and threaten the health of plants and animals, including humans.

▶ Wastes from household, industrial, and agricultural sources can cause pollution of water resources.

▶ Cleaning up waste sites, improving waste management, and conserving natural resources are three solutions for protecting land and water.

Vocabulary
- biodegradable waste (677) • hazardous waste (677)
- landfill (678) • recycling (678) • sewage (679)
- runoff (680) • conservation (682)

Section 4   Working for Community Health

Key Ideas

▶ Two keys to building a sense of community are civic engagement and a shared vision of the future.

▶ There are three steps to getting involved: become informed, volunteer your time, and be an advocate.

Vocabulary
- civic engagement (684)
- consensus-building (685)

A Healthy Community and Environment   **689**

Chapter 25 Review

Reviewing Key Ideas

GO ONLINE
PearsonSuccessNet.com
For: Chapter 25 review activity

Section 1

1. How is a social network important to health?
   a. It provides information
   b. It provides friendships
   c. It provides social support
   d. All of the above

2. What benefits do community service organizations provide for teens?

3. How can mixed-use developments improve the health of people living in a city?

4. **Critical Thinking** Describe how one condition of the town or city in which you live affects your health. **WRITING**

Section 2

5. Each of the following is an air pollutant *except*
   a. sulfur dioxide.
   b. nitrogen.
   c. carbon monoxide.
   d. particulate matter.

6. What health conditions are made worse by smog?

7. What is one health risk of excessive radon exposure?

8. **Critical Thinking** How do you think technology has helped to make people more aware of air pollution?

Section 3

9. A site where wastes are covered with soil is called a
   a. sewer.
   b. runoff.
   c. landfill.
   d. hazardous waste site.

10. What happens to most natural wastes in the environment?

11. **Critical Thinking** How could toxic substances dumped into oceans affect human health? Explain.

12. **Critical Thinking** What do you think are some of the advantages and disadvantages of burning trash?

Section 4

13. The process by which a community arrives at an agreed-upon vision for the future is called
    a. volunteerism   b. civic engagement
    c. advocacy   d. consensus-building

14. Give three examples of civic engagement.

15. Identify three ways that volunteering in their community benefits teen volunteers.

16. **Critical Thinking** Give three examples of community health programs that would require a short-term sacrifice for a long-term benefit. **WRITING**

Building Health Skills

17. **Advocacy** You recently learned that a neighbor has been changing her car's oil and dumping the used engine oil into the town sewer system. What would you do to try to discourage her from this behavior?

18. **Communicating** A friend of yours suggests that the actions of one person have little effect on the environment. What arguments could you use that might change his or her view? **WRITING**

19. **Setting Goals** Set a goal to become more active in your community on any issue by the end of the school year. Write out a stepwise plan that will help you achieve this goal. Monitor your progress along the way. **WRITING**

Health and Community

Community Cleanup Organize a community volunteer cleanup project. Select a lake, stream, road, park, or other area in your community to clean up. Submit your plan, including a list of necessary materials and safety precautions, to your teacher before beginning the project. After obtaining permission and carrying out your project, prepare a presentation about the experience. **WRITING**

Standardized Test Prep

Math Practice

The graph shows the distribution of causes for which teens volunteer. Use the graph to answer Questions 20–22.

Where Teens Volunteer

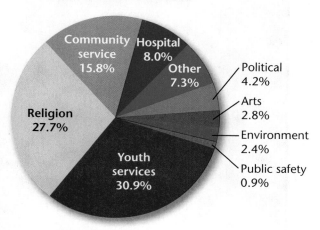

20. What percentage of teens volunteer for environmental causes?
    A 0.9%
    B 2.4%
    C 4.2%
    D 15.8%

21. In which two areas do teens volunteer the most?
    F hospital and religion
    G arts and environment
    H religion and youth services
    J political and community service

22. In a group of 1,000 teen volunteers, about how many would volunteer in youth services?
    A 16
    B 31
    C 158
    D 309

Test-Taking Tip

Take care to record your answers properly. For example, make sure you fill in the answer bubbles completely and don't make stray marks on the answer sheet.

Reading and Writing Practice

Read the passage describing a technology that is used to clean up the hazardous waste uranium. Then answer Questions 23–26.

One new development in cleaning up hazardous wastes is called bioremediation. Bioremediation uses microorganisms to convert wastes into substances that are either less toxic or easier to clean up. For uranium, the process involves pumping uranium-contaminated water into a reaction tank that contains a unique type of bacteria. These bacteria are able to convert uranium from a water-soluble form to a water-insoluble form. The water-insoluble uranium settles to the bottom of the tank. It is still radioactive, but because it is insoluble, it is much easier to separate and remove.

23. From the context of the passage, the best definition of *water-insoluble* is
    A not able to dissolve in water.
    B hazardous when in water.
    C hazardous when in air.
    D radioactive.

24. What role do bacteria play in the bioremediation of uranium?
    F They convert hazardous wastes into harmless substances.
    G They eat the uranium.
    H They convert the uranium to a form that is easier to clean up.
    J The bacteria die and sink to the bottom of the tank.

25. What is the best title for the passage?
    A Radioactive Waste
    B Insoluble Bioremediation
    C Uranium Bioremediation
    D Uranium and Bacteria

Constructed Response

26. What do you suppose the potential benefits of bioremediation are? On the other hand, what might be some of the disadvantages?

Preventing Injuries

GO ONLINE PearsonSuccessNet.com

VIDEO 26

TEENS Talk

Playing It Safe

Preview **Activity**

Which Activities Are Most Dangerous?

Complete this activity before you watch the video.

1. Pair up with another student. Together, list ten activities that teens do that you think carry a risk of injury.
2. On your own, rank the items in your list from most dangerous (1) to least dangerous (10).
3. Get together with your partner and compare your rankings.
4. Do you perceive the danger of certain activities differently from your partner? If so, why do you think that is the case? **WRITING**

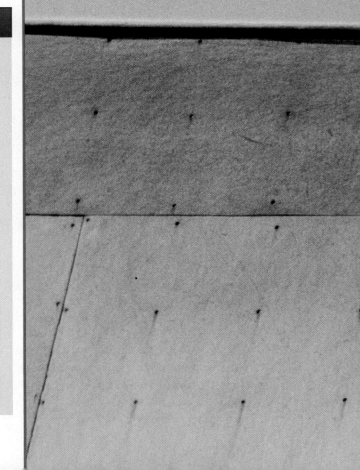

Safety at Home and in Your Community

Objectives

▶ **Describe** five factors that can help you prevent unintentional injuries.

▶ **Identify** unintentional injuries that commonly occur in the home.

▶ **Summarize** ways to stay safe in natural disasters.

▶ **Explain** how to protect yourself from crime.

Vocabulary

• unintentional injury
• flammable material
• electrocution
• assault
• rape
• stalker

Warm-Up

Myth Accidents just happen. There's nothing you can do to prevent them.

Fact Most "accidents" result from risky behaviors. They do not just happen. Many can be prevented by practicing safe behaviors or by removing hazards from the environment.

WRITING Do you think most people behave in ways to prevent injuries? Why or why not?

What Are Unintentional Injuries?

You are probably more familiar with the term *accident* than *unintentional injury*. To many people, the word *accident* refers to an event that cannot be predicted or prevented. In fact, most events that are considered accidents can be prevented.

This chapter uses the term *unintentional injury* instead of *accident* to make you aware that it is often possible to prevent injuries. An **unintentional injury** is an unplanned injury. **Five factors that can help prevent unintentional injuries or lessen their damage are awareness, knowledge, ability, state of mind, and environmental conditions.**

▶ **Awareness and Knowledge** Recognizing risks to your safety and knowing what actions to take can reduce the risk of unintentional injury.

▶ **Ability** Be realistic when you judge your abilities and those of others.

▶ **State of Mind** Be aware of your own condition and that of others. A person who is tired, rushed, distressed, or under the influence of drugs or alcohol is more likely to be injured or to cause injury to others.

▶ **Environmental Conditions** Consider the hazards in your environment that might cause an injury. For example, if the floor has just been mopped, do not run across it when the telephone rings.

Connect to Your Life

Describe a situation in which you prevented an unintentional injury.

Injuries in the Home

One third of all unintentional injuries occur in the home. **Some common causes of unintentional injuries in the home are due to falls, poisoning, suffocation, fires, electric shock, and firearms.** Unfortunately, many of these injuries happen to young children. Figure 1 lists some guidelines for preventing injuries when you are caring for young children.

Falls Hazards in the home can cause anyone to fall. The main factor in avoiding falls is to consider environmental conditions.

► Make sure stairways have nonslip treads and strong railings. Keep stairs and walkways uncluttered and well lit.

► Make sure floors are not slippery, clear them of small objects, and anchor all carpets and rugs firmly.

► Equip bathtubs and showers with grab bars and nonskid rubber mats.

► Keep outdoor steps and sidewalks in good repair and free of ice, leaves, toys, and other obstacles.

Poisoning Most poisoning incidents involve children under the age of five. A local poison control center can tell you what household substances are poisonous and what to do in the event of a poisoning.

Another form of poisoning is carbon monoxide poisoning. Carbon monoxide is a colorless, odorless gas that is produced by vehicles and fuel-burning appliances. If garages or appliances are not vented or functioning properly, carbon monoxide can build up and cause severe illness or even death. It is recommended that people install carbon monoxide detectors near furnaces and in every sleeping area of a home.

FIGURE 1 When caring for a young child, it is important to take many precautions.

Caring for Young Children

Preventing Falls	Preventing Poisoning	Preventing Suffocation
► Never leave a baby alone on a table or other raised surface.	► Keep medications, household cleaners, cosmetics, and alcohol out of reach.	► Do not let children put small toys or other objects in their mouths.
► Use safety gates at the bottom and top of stairs.	► Keep hazardous substances in a locked cabinet.	► Cut food into small pieces.
► Do not allow children to sit on windowsills or lean against screens.	► Do not let children chew or swallow leaves from houseplants.	► Keep plastic bags, cords, and scarves away from children.
► Keep children away from decks or porches without railings.	► Carefully follow the directions for giving a child medication.	► Make sure bedding and clothing do not interfere with a child's breathing.
	► If you suspect a poisoning, call a poison control center immediately.	

Suffocation   When a person's supply of air is cut off, the result is suffocation. Suffocation can be caused by choking when an object gets caught in the breathing passages, by smothering, or by being trapped in an enclosed space. Suffocation can result in death.

Fires and Burns   The seven most common causes of household fires are careless cooking, smoking, faulty or overloaded electrical wiring, unsafe heating units, improperly used fireplaces, children playing with matches, and improper storage of flammable materials. **Flammable materials** catch fire easily and burn quickly. Figure 2 lists some ways of reducing the risks of fire in your home. Most areas have 911 emergency calling, which you should use in case of a fire.

▶ If a small fire starts on the stove, put it out with a fire extinguisher.

▶ Never use water on a grease fire. Water causes the fire to spread.

▶ If a small fire begins to get out of control, leave immediately and alert other residents to the danger.

▶ If your home is on fire, leave immediately. If there is a lot of smoke, crawl along the floor to the nearest exit. Do not pause to collect any belongings. Your life is more important.

▶ Once you are outside, do not go back in. Go to a neighbor's house or to the nearest fire-alarm box and alert the fire department.

▶ If a person catches fire, roll the person on the ground, in a rug, or in a heavy coat to cut off the air the fire needs.

FIGURE 2 Fires can be prevented if you take the time to reduce the risks in your home.

Reducing Fire Risks

▶ Install smoke detectors on each floor of your home.

▶ Practice a fire escape plan.

▶ Keep fire extinguishers in the kitchen and garage.

▶ Make sure electrical outlets are not overloaded.

▶ Replace frayed or cracked appliance cords.

▶ Discourage smokers from smoking in bed.

▶ Keep matches and lighters out of reach of small children.

▶ Store flammable materials in fireproof containers.

Electric Shock Electricity and faulty or misused equipment pose other risks. Make sure that your home is properly wired. Keep all home appliances in good repair, and know how to use them safely. Never try to repair an electric appliance when it is plugged in.

Death from direct contact with electricity is called **electrocution** (ih lek truh KYOO shun). To prevent electrocution, keep young children away from electrical outlets. Place safety covers over unused electrical outlets. Never use appliances when you are wet or near water.

Firearms Each year about 600 people are unintentionally killed in the home by firearms. Many of the deaths occur among young people between the ages of 10 and 19. To prevent unintentional injuries and deaths, firearms should be kept unloaded and locked in a place where children cannot reach them. Ammunition should be locked in a separate place. Do not handle firearms if you have not been trained in their use.

Natural Disasters

Disasters are sudden, catastrophic events that affect many people. Disasters may result from human error or from a natural event. Oil spills and train derailments are examples of disasters caused by humans. **Earthquakes, tornadoes, hurricanes, floods, blizzards, and many forest fires are examples of natural disasters.**

How can you prepare for disasters or lessen their effects on you and your family? Figure 3 lists some questions that can help you evaluate how prepared your family is for a disaster. If a disaster occurs in your area, follow the instructions given over the Emergency Alert System (EAS) on your radio or television.

What can your family do to be better prepared for a disaster?

FIGURE 3 Being prepared for a disaster requires you to collect certain supplies. **Evaluating** What other supplies might be important to have in case of a natural disaster?

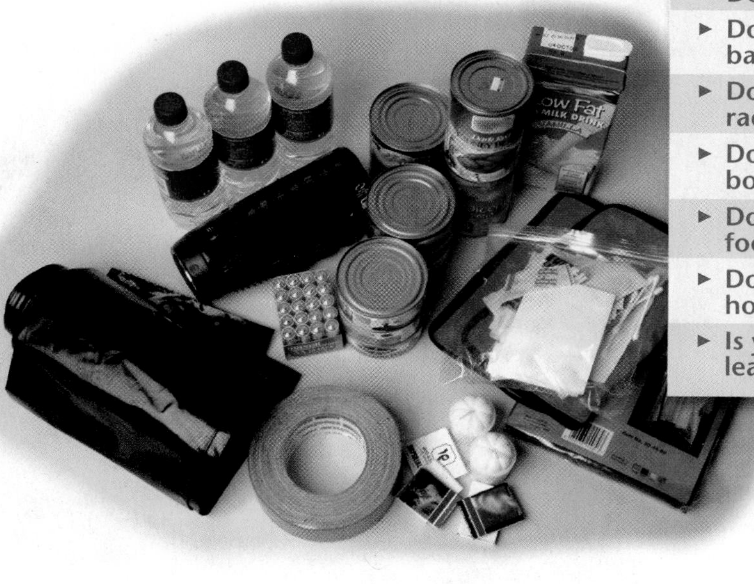

Are You Prepared for a Disaster?

- ▸ Does your family have a first-aid kit?
- ▸ Do you have flashlights and fresh batteries?
- ▸ Do you have a battery-powered radio?
- ▸ Do you have a two-week supply of bottled water?
- ▸ Do you have a supply of canned foods?
- ▸ Do you know how to turn off your home's gas, electricity, and water?
- ▸ Is your vehicle's gas tank always at least half full?

Earthquakes   An earthquake is a sudden shaking of the ground caused by the movement of rock beneath Earth's surface. If you are indoors during an earthquake, stand under the frame of an interior door or crawl under a table or desk. Stay away from windows, glass doors, heavy hanging objects, or furniture that might tip over. If you are outside, stay in the open, away from buildings, walls, and electrical wires. If you are driving, pull over and stop. After a major earthquake, turn off the gas and electricity in your home to prevent a gas leak or fire.

Tornadoes   A tornado is a rapidly rotating column of air whirling at speeds of up to 500 miles per hour. Tornadoes are fairly common in the central and southern United States. If you are caught outdoors during a tornado, move away from the tornado at right angles to its path. If the tornado is too close for you to escape, find shelter or lie flat in a low place in the ground. If you are at home, go to the lowest floor of your home. Keep some windows open to equalize pressure, but stay away from them. If you live in a mobile home, go to a tornado shelter.

Hurricanes   A hurricane is a powerful storm characterized by heavy rains and winds over 74 miles per hour. If you hear that a hurricane is coming, place tape across windows and board them up. Anchor or bring inside any furniture or other items outside your home. Hurricane-force winds can knock down power lines. Avoid contact with downed power lines. If local authorities tell you to evacuate, seek shelter elsewhere.

One of the most serious hurricanes to hit the United States in recent years was hurricane Katrina. Katrina struck the United States Gulf Coast in the summer of 2005. Figure 4 shows some of the devastation that Katrina caused, including severe flooding in New Orleans, Louisiana.

Hurricane Facts

► Hurricanes are rated on a scale of 1 (least severe) to 5 (most severe).

► Hurricanes develop from tropical storms over the ocean.

► A hurricane is named according to the tropical storm from which it developed. Tropical storms are named in alphabetical order and alternate between male and female names.

► In the Atlantic Ocean, hurricane season lasts from June 1 through November 30.

FIGURE 4 In 2005, hurricane Katrina caused damage in states along the Gulf Coast.

Satellite Image of Katrina

Fort Lauderdale, Florida

Floods In 2005, New Orleans, Louisiana, experienced some of the worst flooding ever to occur in the United States. The flooding resulted from levees that broke after hurricane Katrina struck the Gulf Coast. The city had to be evacuated because lack of food and clean water and contaminated floodwaters posed serious health threats to residents.

In the event of any flood, you should turn off your home's water, gas, and electricity and move your belongings to the highest floor before leaving home. When you are able to return home, discard any liquids or foods touched by floodwaters. Drink bottled water until local authorities tell you that the tap water is safe.

Most floods can be predicted, but a flash flood can occur suddenly, without warning, after a heavy rainfall or snowmelt. Check the history of your area to find out if there is a risk of flash flooding. If your area is at risk, find out where you should go if an evacuation is ordered.

Blizzards A blizzard is defined as a heavy snowstorm, with winds of at least 35 miles per hour, that lasts for three hours or more. These conditions usually result in very low visibility. Generally, the safest place to be during a blizzard is inside your home or other warm shelter. If you have a problem requiring special treatment, alert local authorities so that you can be evacuated safely from your home. Do not try to go out on your own.

Forest Fires Some forest fires are caused by humans, but others are the result of natural occurrences, such as lightning. Fire often serves an important "clean up" role in forests. But when fires spread near human communities, they can be very dangerous. It is important to pay attention to local authorities when they tell you to evacuate an area at risk for fire.

Connect to Your Life **Do you live in an area at high risk for certain natural disasters? Which ones?**

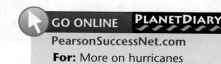
GO ONLINE **PLANETDIARY**
PearsonSuccessNet.com
For: More on hurricanes

Long Beach, Mississippi

New Orleans, Louisiana

Media Wise

Internet Safety

The Internet can be a valuable resource for all kinds of information. Unfortunately, it can sometimes prove to be a dangerous place. Use this questionnaire to determine if you protect yourself adequately on the Internet.

Do you refuse to give out personal information, such as your address, phone number, or photos, on the Internet?   **Yes**   **No**

Do you refuse to meet face-to-face with anyone you have met on the Internet?   **Yes**   **No**

Do you send messages only to people you already know?   **Yes**   **No**

Do you stay away from sites that try to convince you to join or give money to questionable organizations?   **Yes**   **No**

Do you sign off if you feel uncomfortable in a chat room?   **Yes**   **No**

"Yes" answers indicate wise practices for protecting yourself on the Internet.

Activity   Create a 30-second public service announcement about Internet safety for teens. Use a slogan or music to get your message across.   **WRITING**

Protecting Yourself From Crime

Unfortunately, some injuries are intentional. Some, for example, are the result of crime. An **assault** is an unlawful attempt or threat to harm someone. An assault can lead to intentional injuries or death.

Rape and Stalking   One type of assault that is both physically and psychologically painful is rape. **Rape** means that one person forces another to have sexual relations. Most rapes are acquaintance rapes—rapes carried out by someone the victim knows.

It is hard to tell if a person might be a potential rapist, but it is important to trust your judgment. If you feel that you might be in danger, you probably are. However, feeling "safe" with someone does not mean that you are safe. Always let a family member or friend know where you are going and when you will return home. If someone tries to rape you, do whatever you need to do to protect your life.

All rape victims should seek medical treatment immediately. Reporting a rape is not easy. Most police departments, however, have police officers who specialize in helping rape victims.

A **stalker** is someone who makes repeated, unwanted contact with a person and may threaten to kill or injure the person. If you are stalked, notify the police. Laws can help protect you from a stalker.

Avoiding Risky Situations   You can prevent assault or reduce the likelihood of injury by following certain safety guidelines. The most basic guideline is to avoid risky situations.

► Lock all doors and windows when you are home alone. Never allow a stranger inside. Never let a caller know you are alone.

► Do not keep keys in an obvious place, such as under a doormat.

► Avoid deserted places, such as dark streets, parks, and garages. If you cannot avoid them, make sure you walk with a friend.

► Stay away from dark doorways and hedges where an attacker could hide. If someone follows you, step into the nearest business.

► When driving, keep the car doors locked. Always be sure to park in a well-lit place. Before getting back into your car, always check to make sure no one is hiding in the back seat or on the floor.

► Do not hitchhike or pick up hitchhikers.

► If your car breaks down, pull over, raise your hood, and turn on your emergency flashers. If a stranger stops to help, do not unlock your car door. Just ask the person to call the police.

► If someone tries to rob you, give up your possessions. They are not as important as your life.

► If you see a crime in progress, call the police immediately. Do not try to intervene, especially if weapons could be involved.

Protecting Yourself From Rape

Stay away from people who

• act strangely and make you uncomfortable.
• pay no attention to you when you say *no* or *stop.*
• try to touch you when you do not want to be touched.
• push you to do things you do not want to do.

FIGURE 5 Both males and females of all ages are potential victims of rape. Rapists look for people who appear vulnerable.

Section 1 Review

Key Ideas and Vocabulary

1. What is an **unintentional injury**?

2. Name five factors that can help you prevent unintentional injuries. Why is each factor important?

3. List six types of unintentional injuries that occur in the home.

4. What is **electrocution**?

5. How can you be prepared for earthquakes? For tornadoes?

6. What is the single best way to protect yourself from crime? Explain.

Critical Thinking

7. Applying Concepts What changes would you make in your home to ensure a one-year-old's safety during a visit?

Health and Community

Crime Prevention Programs Find out what kinds of crime prevention organizations are at work in your community. For example, some communities form Neighborhood Crime Watch groups that report suspicious activities to the police. Create a poster encouraging community members to get involved in one of the organizations you learned about. **WRITING**

8. Making Judgments Suppose you have a weekend job at a restaurant about three miles from your house. You need to drive home alone at night. What precautions should you take?

<table>
<tr><td>

Section 2

</td><td>

Safety at Work and Play

</td></tr>
</table>

Objectives

▶ **Describe** how occupational injuries and illnesses can be prevented.

▶ **Summarize** the four basic guidelines for recreational safety.

Vocabulary

- occupational injury
- occupational illness
- survival floating
- active supervision
- capsizing

Warm-Up

Quick Quiz Complete each of these statements with *always*, *sometimes*, or *never*.

① I __?__ bring plenty of drinking water when I go hiking or camping.

② I __?__ wear a personal flotation device when participating in water sports.

③ I __?__ wear appropriate protective gear when playing sports.

④ I __?__ wear a helmet when skateboarding or riding a bicycle.

WRITING For each of your responses, predict how your behavior may affect your risk of injury.

Occupational Safety

Many unintentional injuries occur at work. Although you are not working full time yet, you probably will be some day. You may already be working at an after-school job. You should know about the possible hazards of the workplace and what you can do to protect yourself.

The Occupational Safety and Health Administration (OSHA) is the federal agency that identifies workplace hazards and sets standards for safety. Both employers and workers are responsible for following OSHA regulations.

OSHA defines an **occupational injury** as any wound or damage to the body that results from an event in the work environment. OSHA defines an **occupational illness** as any abnormal condition or disorder caused by exposure to the work environment. **Many occupational injuries and illnesses can either be prevented or made less serious by removing potential hazards from the workplace.** Figure 6 gives information about some occupations that are especially hazardous.

 Do you have an after-school job? What kinds of hazards are present in your work environment?

Teen Workers   Many teens in the United States work after school and during the summer. Unfortunately, over 80 teens die each year from occupational injuries. These injuries often result from motor vehicle crashes, electrocution, or falls on the job. In a recent year over 146,000 teens reported occupational injuries. It is the responsibility of your employer to keep your workplace as safe as possible and to inform you of any on-the-job hazards. It is your responsibility to be well rested and alert, to be sober, and to follow all safety procedures.

Farm Safety   Over a million teens in the United States work on farms. Farm jobs have the highest rate of injuries and deaths of all types of teen employment. When working on a farm, it is important to be properly trained on equipment and to use common sense.

▶ If you have to drive a truck or tractor, be sure that someone teaches you how it works and how to stop it and turn it off.

▶ Never drive a vehicle or operate a piece of machinery if you are not comfortable doing so.

▶ Never operate equipment under the influence of alcohol or other drugs.

▶ If you work around animals, approach them so that they can see you. A startled animal can be dangerous and may kick or charge.

▶ Avoid direct contact with pesticides and other chemicals. If you come into contact with a chemical, call a poison control center.

▶ Dress appropriately for farm work. Wear sturdy shoes, and avoid baggy clothing that could get caught in machinery. Tie back long hair.

▶ Wear goggles and earplugs to protect your eyes and ears. Wear sunscreen to protect your skin.

▲ **A teen working on a farm**

FIGURE 6 Some jobs carry a greater risk of fatal injury than others. **Reading Graphs** Which job shown here has the highest death rate? The lowest death rate?

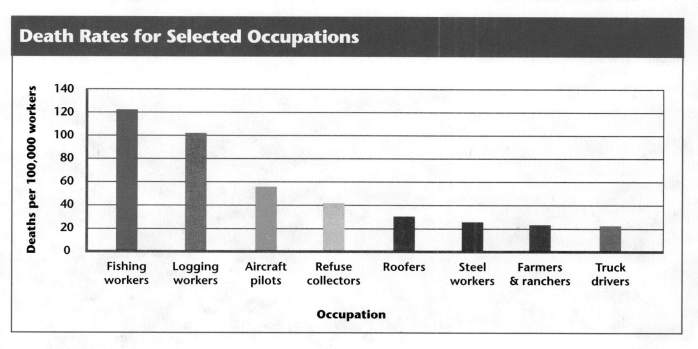

Death Rates for Selected Occupations

Deaths per 100,000 workers vs. *Occupation*

Occupation	Deaths per 100,000 workers
Fishing workers	~122
Logging workers	~101
Aircraft pilots	~55
Refuse collectors	~40
Roofers	~29
Steel workers	~24
Farmers & ranchers	~22
Truck drivers	~21

Recreational Safety

Almost everyone enjoys some kind of recreational activity. And most recreational activities involve some degree of risk. **Whatever recreational activities you enjoy, you should follow four basic safety guidelines.**

► Learn and apply the proper skills.

► Have appropriate, well-maintained equipment.

► Know the safety rules specific to the activity.

► Prepare adequately for the activity.

Safety When Hiking and Camping   Hiking and camping are great forms of exercise, but these activities also present safety risks.

► Always let someone know where you are going and when you expect to return home. Never hike or camp alone.

► Find out about any potential dangers, such as bears, ticks, or poisonous snakes and plants.

► Take along a first-aid kit. Figure 7 lists some supplies that should be included in a first-aid kit. Know how to respond to hazardous situations, such as snakebites or skin infections.

► Check the weather forecast, and dress appropriately. Layers are best when days are warm and nights are cool. Wear proper footwear.

► Wear sunscreen and a hat. Bring insect repellent if necessary.

► Be sure to take plenty of food and water. In your camp area, stow food and garbage in your car or up in a tree so as not to attract animals.

► Hike and camp only in approved areas. Follow campsite rules.

► Cook in a protected area so that sparks will not start a fire. Put a campfire out completely with water or dirt.

FIGURE 7 It is important to be prepared for outdoor conditions when hiking or camping.

First-Aid Supplies for Camping

- First-aid manual
- Sterile gloves
- Sterile bandages and gauze
- Antiseptic wipes and antibiotic ointment
- Burn ointment
- Calamine lotion
- Moleskin for blisters
- Pain reliever
- Anti-diarrhea medicine
- Scissors and tweezers
- Thermometer
- Instant cold pack
- Blanket

Survival Floating

1. Inhale and Rest
- Take a breath and hold it.
- Put your face in the water.
- Let your arms and legs dangle.
- Rest.

2. Exhale
- Tilt your head back so your mouth clears the water.
- Press your arms and legs down to help raise your head out of the water.
- Exhale.
- Repeat step 1.

Water Safety Over 3,000 unintentional drownings occur ever year in the United States. Drownings can occur in bathtubs, hot tubs, swimming pools, lakes, rivers, and oceans. Most drownings are preventable if you follow certain precautions.

▶ Take swimming lessons. Even if you never learn how to swim, however, you should know how to protect yourself from drowning. Figure 8 shows **survival floating,** a lifesaving technique that allows you to float and breathe without using much energy.

▶ Never drink alcohol or use other drugs when you're going to be swimming.

▶ Never swim alone or in unsupervised areas.

▶ Never dive into water of unknown depth. Doing so could result in serious injuries, including spinal cord injuries.

▶ Pay attention to beach warning flags. If you are caught in a rip current, a current that pulls you away from shore, swim parallel to the shore.

▶ Use only battery-powered radios around a pool or hot tub to prevent electrocution. Never go in the water during a thunderstorm.

▶ If you are on an ice-covered body of water and the ice starts to crack, immediately lie down and crawl to shore.

Drowning is the second-leading cause of injury-related deaths among children ages 1 to 14. Pools should have fences around them with self-latching gates to keep children from getting in unsupervised. If you are watching children around water, you must actively supervise them. **Active supervision** means that you keep children in your view at all times when they are in or near the water. Do not engage in other distracting behaviors, and stay close to the water in case you are needed.

Connect to Your Life

What would you tell someone who has never had swimming lessons?

FIGURE 9 Common causes of death in boating incidents are drowning, trauma, burns, and electrocution. Follow these safety tips to prevent injuries and death.

Boating Safety Millions of Americans enjoy boats and personal watercraft. Unfortunately, nearly 4,000 people each year are injured in boating incidents, and about 700 people die. Follow these safety guidelines when boating and operating personal watercraft.

► Take a boating safety class. Local Coast Guard branches, community boating facilities, the American Red Cross, and the United States Power Squadrons offer these classes.

► Make sure that your boat or watercraft is in good repair.

► Check the weather before you go out on the water. Never go out during a thunderstorm.

► Always wear a United States Coast Guard-approved personal flotation device (PFD), such as a life jacket, regardless of your swimming ability. Never allow a child to wear an air-filled swimming aid, such as "water wings," instead of a PFD.

► Never drink alcohol or use other drugs.

► If someone falls overboard, immediately toss a PFD and a towline to the person. Shut off the motor, and help the person into the boat.

► The overturning of a boat is called **capsizing.** If you are in a boat when it capsizes, grab your PFD and stay with the boat until help arrives and you are rescued.

► Keep the boat's signal lights on between dusk and dawn, and use a whistle or horn to signal when visibility is poor.

 GO ONLINE

PearsonSuccessNet.com

For: More on recreational safety

Sports Safety Sports injuries may occur when you do not warm up properly before exercising or cool down properly afterward. Remember to stretch before and after exercise.

As you learned in Chapter 11, overuse injuries can result from playing one sport year-round or from doing the same movement over and over. The best way to prevent overuse injuries is to play several different sports, instead of specializing in just one. That way, the muscle groups you use in one sport have a chance to recover while you play another sport. However, you know your body best. If you feel pain, it is your responsibility to tell your coach and your parents, and to take a break.

Injuries can also occur if you use faulty or inappropriate equipment. Always wear protective gear when playing a contact sport. A forceful collision with an object or another person can cause a concussion, an injury that occurs when the brain hits the skull.

If you hunt, wear a bright-colored vest or hat so that you will not be mistaken for prey by another hunter. Hunt only in approved areas. Keep the safety on your gun until you are ready to shoot, and keep your trigger finger outside the trigger guard. Unload your gun as soon as you are done.

Here are some other tips you should follow when participating in any sport, including hunting.

▶ Drink lots of water to stay hydrated, even in cold weather.

▶ Do not participate in a sport if you are ill.

▶ Do not participate in a sport if you have been drinking or using drugs.

What sports do you participate in? How do you protect yourself from injuries?

FIGURE 10 Always wear appropriate safety gear when playing contact sports, such as hockey.
Interpreting Photos What safety gear are these hockey players wearing? How does the gear protect the players?

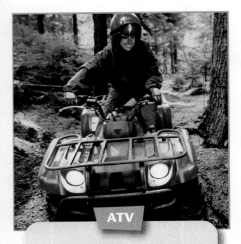

Safety Guidelines

FIGURE 11 To prevent injuries, be sure to ride bicycles, skateboards, motorcycles, and recreational vehicles responsibly.

Snowmobile

- Wear a helmet, warm clothing, boots, and goggles.
- Only ride on designated trails.
- Go slowly over rough terrain.
- Never travel alone.
- Never venture out onto an ice-covered body of water.
- Always carry drinking water, a first-aid kit, and signal flares.

ATV

- Wear a helmet, sturdy pants, boots, and gloves.
- Only ride in daylight.
- Do not ride on paved roads.
- Do not speed.
- Carry drinking water and a first-aid kit.

Skateboard

- Wear a helmet, wrist guards, elbow pads, and knee pads.
- Stay away from roads with heavy traffic.
- Skateboard in designated skate parks or only where skateboarding is permitted.

Motorcycle

- Take a motorcycle safety training course.
- Wear a helmet and sturdy clothing, including pants, boots, and gloves.
- Follow the traffic rules that apply to larger vehicles.
- Make sure you have a working headlight, taillight, and brake light.
- Signal stops, turns, or changes in direction.
- Do not speed.

Bicycle

- Wear a helmet.
- Ride single file on the right, with the flow of traffic.
- Signal your intentions with hand signals before turning or stopping.
- If you have to pull over, get your bike well off the road.
- Wear reflective clothing.
- Be alert for oil spills, gravel, potholes, opening car doors, and other hazards.

Bicycle and Recreational Vehicle Safety Many young people are killed or injured each year in incidents involving bicycles, motorcycles, all-terrain vehicles (ATVs), and snowmobiles. These incidents usually result from mechanical problems, poor judgment, or ignoring basic safety rules. Figure 11 lists some safety guidelines you should follow for bicycles, skateboards, motorcycles, snowmobiles, and ATVs. Motorcycle safety rules also apply to mopeds. These rules apply to all recreational vehicles.

▶ Never ride under the influence of alcohol or other drugs.

▶ Always wear appropriate clothing, a helmet, and other protective gear. Do not wear baggy clothing that could get caught in moving parts.

▶ Never allow someone else to ride with you unless the vehicle is intended for two people.

▶ Never ride while listening to headphones.

▶ Keep constant watch for possible hazards in your path. For some vehicles, you may need a rearview mirror.

▶ Never grab onto another moving vehicle.

▶ Make sure the vehicle is in good repair and can be seen easily by other riders. You will need reflectors or a headlight and a taillight.

Riding a motorcycle on a highway can present different challenges than riding on an ATV. On the motorcycle, you are sharing the highway with much larger vehicles. On the ATV, your trip must be limited by the hours of daylight. With both vehicles, you need to watch your speed.

Section 2 Review

Key Ideas and Vocabulary

1. What is an **occupational injury?**
2. How can many occupational injuries and illnesses be prevented?
3. List the four basic safety guidelines for recreational activities.
4. Briefly describe the steps of **survival floating.**
5. What does **active supervision** mean? How would you actively supervise a child in a pool?

Critical Thinking

6. **Predicting** If you worked on a farm that required you to operate a tractor, what kind of training would you expect to get? If you didn't receive training, what risks would you be taking?

Health at School

School Safety Survey teachers, coaches, and other school personnel to find out what kind of safety training they have had. Should further training be required? Write a letter to your principal summarizing your findings. **WRITING**

7. **Making Judgments** Suppose a friend tries to persuade you to go diving with him in a water-filled quarry at night. How would you talk your friend into doing something less hazardous?

8. **Applying Concepts** Suppose you and a group of friends wanted to go sledding after a heavy snow storm. What kinds of safety precautions would you take? Make a list of what you would wear and what you would bring. **WRITING**

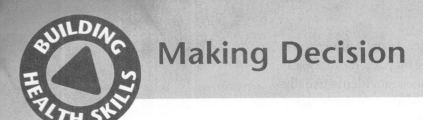
Analyzing Risks and Benefits

LaToya's friends invited her to go inline skating with them in the city park. She had never done it before, but everyone said it was fun and that she would catch on quickly. LaToya wanted to go, but she worried about getting hurt just before basketball season started. Should she take the risk?

The risk may be worth taking if LaToya decides that the benefits are greater than the possible harm. For example, skiing is another activity that involves some risk of injury. Many people decide that skiing is worth the risk, however, because it is good exercise and fun. They also realize that there are ways they can reduce the risks involved.

Making responsible decisions is a sign of maturity. It shows that you are beginning to take control of your own well-being. How can you analyze the risks and benefits of an action you might take? The guidelines that follow will help you.

① Identify the possible risks involved in taking this action.

A risk is a possible harmful outcome or consequence of taking a certain action. These negative consequences may be physical, emotional, legal, or social.

► Identify all the possible negative consequences of taking this action. Write them down.

► Determine if any of the negative consequences are likely to cause a serious injury.

► Rate the likelihood of each negative consequence actually happening, from 1 for highly likely to 5 for very unlikely.

② Identify the possible benefits of taking this action.

► Identify all the possible positive consequences of taking this action. Write them down.

► Rate the importance of these benefits to you, from 1 for very important to 5 for not very important.

③ Determine what you could do to reduce the risk of injury.

Design a strategy to reduce the degree of risk involved and maximize the benefits. For example:

► **Knowledge and awareness:** LaToya could find out if she can rent or borrow protective equipment such as wrist, elbow, and knee guards. She could also find out what skating route has the fewest hills or pedestrians.

► **Ability:** LaToya could take a lesson in in-line skating before she goes with her friends.

► **State of mind:** LaToya could make sure she is well rested and not under the influence of alcohol or other drugs when she tries skating.

► **Environmental conditions:** LaToya could agree to go only if it had not been raining, so the paths wouldn't be slippery, or if her friends would stop skating before it got dark.

④ Determine if the benefits outweigh the risks.

► Analyze the risks and benefits you wrote down, including your ratings of the likelihood of negative consequences and the importance of the benefits to you. Also review your strategies for reducing the risk of injury.

► Ask yourself if the benefits outweigh the risks for you.

► Decide whether or not to take the action.

Practice the Skill

1. Review LaToya's situation.
   a. What are all the possible risks involved in going inline skating?
   b. What are the possible benefits?
   c. What are some other ways she could reduce the risks and increase the benefits of doing this activity?
   d. What decision would you make after weighing the risks and benefits in this situation?

2. Consider a recent action you have taken or are considering taking. Analyze the action for risks and benefits following the steps described here. What strategies could minimize the possible risks and increase the benefits? Do the benefits outweigh the risks? Why or why not?

Motor Vehicle Safety

Objectives

▶ **Identify** the skills you need to be a safe driver.

▶ **List** safety rules you should follow when riding in a school bus.

Vocabulary

• defensive driving
• road rage

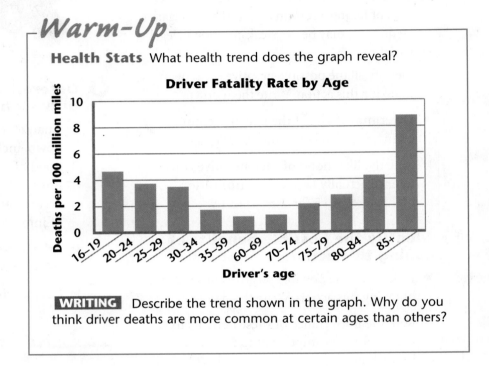

Warm-Up

Health Stats What health trend does the graph reveal?

Driver Fatality Rate by Age

(y-axis: Deaths per 100 million miles; x-axis: Driver's age — 16–19, 20–24, 25–29, 30–34, 35–59, 60–69, 70–74, 75–79, 80–84, 85+)

WRITING Describe the trend shown in the graph. Why do you think driver deaths are more common at certain ages than others?

Automobile Safety

Consider these statistics.

▶ Motor vehicle crashes are the number one cause of death for people aged 3 through 33.

▶ Each year, more than 40,000 deaths and millions of injuries occur as a result of motor vehicle crashes.

▶ On average, half of all Americans will be involved in a motor vehicle crash during their lifetimes.

Drivers between the ages of 15 and 24 are involved in more crashes than any other age group. This is due to several factors, including a lack of driving experience and a tendency to take more risks.

The use of alcohol and drugs is another major factor involved in many motor vehicle crashes. Alcohol affects a person's self-control and judgment, slows reaction time, blurs vision, and reduces coordination.

You can be a safe driver, regardless of your age. To be a safe driver, you need to practice good driving skills and know how to respond to risky situations.

Factors You Can Control Whether you are driving or riding as a passenger, certain risk factors are within your control. It is your responsibility to minimize these risks and reduce your chances of being involved in or injured in a motor vehicle crash.

► Take a course in driver education, either at your school or with a paid instructor.

► Never drive if you have been drinking alcohol or using drugs. Never get into a car with someone who has been drinking or using drugs.

► Always wear your seatbelt. When you are driving, insist that your passengers also buckle up, even those in the backseat.

► Minimize your distractions. Stay off your cell phone, do not text, keep your music down, and do not drive with too many passengers.

► Follow the speed limit. Excessive speed is a factor in many crashes.

► Follow the rules of the road.

► Allow enough distance between you and the car in front of you so that you can stop suddenly without hitting it.

► Avoid driving when you are tired, angry, or feeling stressed.

► Always tell a family member or friend where you are going and when you plan to return home.

► Never carry a flammable substance, such as extra gasoline, in the trunk of your car.

Keeping Your Vehicle Safe The condition of your vehicle can affect your chances of getting into a crash. Take your car in for regular tune-ups and make sure that it is in good repair.

► Make sure that your brakes are working properly.

► Make sure that all of your lights are working, including the brake lights.

► Make sure that your tires are in good shape and appropriate for the climate you live in.

► Make sure that your windshield wipers work properly.

How do you minimize your risk when driving or riding in a car?

Supplies to Keep in Your Vehicle
- Jumper cables
- Flashlight
- First-aid kit
- Extra windshield washer fluid
- Extra motor oil
- Blanket

FIGURE 12 Good preparation is key to being safe on the road.

FIGURE 13 Knowing how to drive in bad weather conditions can lower your risk of getting into a motor vehicle crash.
Evaluating What additional safety precautions would you take when driving near large trucks?

In bad weather, it is important that your tires and windshield wipers be in good shape.

Factors Outside Your Control Some risk factors that come with driving are outside of your control, such as road construction and bad weather. However, you are in control of how you react to such risks. The following guidelines can help you avoid a motor vehicle crash when driving under less-than-ideal conditions.

▶ Slow down. If you are driving through a construction zone, obey the lower posted speed limit.

▶ If visibility is low due to rain, fog, or snow, slow down. Follow the lines painted on the road to make sure you stay in your lane.

▶ Keep a greater distance between you and the car in front of you. It is unpredictable when you may have to stop, so give yourself more room, especially in slippery conditions.

You also have no control over the other drivers on the road. This is why it is important to practice defensive driving. **Defensive driving** means that you constantly monitor other drivers around you, and do not assume that they will do what you think they should do. Defensive driving enables you to actively avoid hazardous situations.

Road Rage You should also be a considerate driver. Allow others to merge, and do not tailgate. Being inconsiderate to other drivers can spark road rage. **Road rage** is dangerous or violent behavior by a person who becomes angry or frustrated while driving. Stay away from drivers you suspect might have road rage. If you have a problem with road rage, seek help.

 GO ONLINE

PearsonSuccessNet.com
For: More on motor vehicle safety

School Bus Safety

You may have spent a lot of time on a school bus during your younger school years. And even though you may not ride the bus regularly anymore, you still might do so occasionally for sports and other activities. **When riding in a school bus, there are rules you should follow to ensure everybody's safety.**

▶ Stay seated at all times.

▶ Do not hang any part of your body out of the windows.

▶ Avoid fighting and arguing. Do not throw things. These behaviors distract the bus driver.

▶ If someone is bullying you, tell the driver.

▶ Know where emergency exits are located.

▶ Watch for cars when getting off the bus and crossing the street.

When you start driving, be sure to look out for school buses. Do not follow a school bus too closely because it makes frequent stops. Always stop when a school bus's stop sign swings out and its red lights are flashing. You must stop whether you are behind the bus or driving in the opposite direction. The stop sign is intended to keep students safe when crossing the street.

FIGURE 14 It is important to follow bus safety rules, whether you ride the bus or not.

Section 3 Review

Key Ideas and Vocabulary

1. List five pieces of safety advice you would give to a new driver.

2. What is **defensive driving?** Why should you practice defensive driving?

3. What is **road rage?** How can you help prevent road rage?

4. List three safety rules you should follow when riding in a school bus. What rules should you observe when driving on the same street as a bus?

Critical Thinking

5. **Evaluating** Some states have a graduated licensing system, which increases young drivers' privileges over time as they gain more experience. Do you think graduated licenses are a good idea? Why or why not? **WRITING**

Health at Home

Good Driving Habits Evaluate your driving habits and the habits of others in your family. Gather a list of good driving habits that you and your family should keep up, and a list of habits you need to improve. Set goals for improving these unsafe behaviors, and reward yourselves when you meet your goals. **WRITING**

6. **Applying Concepts** Suppose you have a friend who you think is an unsafe driver. He drives at high speeds, disobeys traffic rules, and frequently takes his eyes off the road. What would you say to your friend to encourage him to drive more safely? **WRITING**

Technology & Health

A Shocking Tool to the Rescue

Sudden cardiac arrest is a condition in which the heart beats so erratically that it can no longer pump blood effectively. If a regular rhythm is not restored quickly, the person will die. Over 300,000 people do die from sudden cardiac arrest each year in the United States. A device called an automated external defibrillator, or AED, can save some of those lives. An AED delivers a shock to help restore the heart rhythm. The AED uses visual clues and voice commands that tell even untrained users exactly what to do.

WRITING Write a letter to your school board requesting that they buy an AED for your school. Explain why AEDs are important and why teens should be trained to use them.

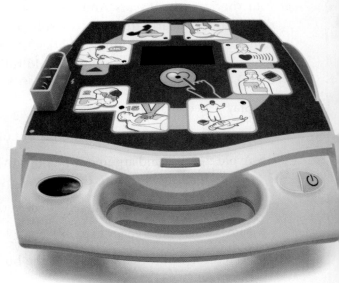

▲ **AED device**

This is one model of AED. It includes shock pads that attach to the victim's chest. Voice prompts tell rescuers what to do.

1

- Call for medical assistance.
- Press pads firmly to patient's bare skin.

2
- Do not touch the patient.
- Analyzing heart rhythm.
- Shock advised.

3

- Stand clear of patient.
- Press the shock button now.

4
- Shock delivered.
- Assessing heart rhythm.
- Do not touch the patient.

5

- It is safe to touch the patient.
- Check airway. Check breathing. Check circulation.
- If needed, begin CPR.

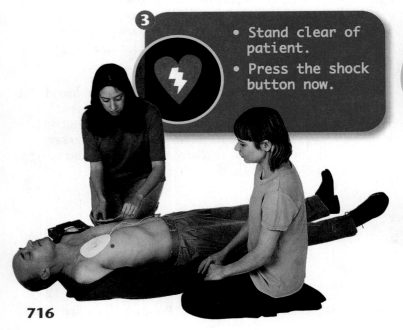

Chapter 26
At a Glance

TEENS Talk 🔿
Playing It Safe In what ways did the video influence you to practice safe behaviors in your daily life?

Section 1 Safety at Home and in Your Community

Key Ideas

▶ Five factors that can help prevent unintentional injuries or lessen their damage are awareness, knowledge, ability, state of mind, and environmental conditions.

▶ Common unintentional injuries that occur in the home are due to falls, poisoning, suffocation, fires, electric shock, and firearms.

▶ Earthquakes, tornadoes, hurricanes, floods, blizzards, and many forest fires are examples of natural disasters.

▶ You can prevent assault or reduce the likelihood of injury by following certain safety guidelines. The most basic guideline is to avoid risky situations.

Vocabulary
- unintentional injury (694)
- flammable material (696)
- electrocution (697)
- assault (700)
- rape (700)
- stalker (700)

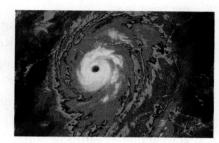

Section 2 Safety at Work and Play

Key Ideas

▶ Many occupational injuries and illnesses can be prevented or made less serious by removing potential hazards from the workplace.

▶ Whatever recreational activities you enjoy, you should follow four basic safety guidelines.

Vocabulary
- occupational injury (702)
- occupational illness (702)
- survival floating (705)
- active supervision (705)
- capsizing (706)

Section 3 Motor Vehicle Safety

Key Ideas

▶ You can be a safe driver, regardless of your age. To be a safe driver, you need to practice good driving skills and know how to respond to risky situations.

▶ When riding in a school bus, there are rules you should follow to ensure everybody's safety.

Vocabulary
- defensive driving (714)
- road rage (714)

Chapter 26 Review

GO ONLINE
PearsonSuccessNet.com
For: Chapter 26 review activity

Reviewing Key Ideas

Section 1

1. An example of an unintentional injury is
   a. electric shock. b. assault.
   c. rape. d. stalking.

2. A storm with heavy rains and winds over 74 miles per hour is a
   a. tornado. b. blizzard.
   c. forest fire. d. hurricane.

3. Why is the term *unintentional injury* usually more appropriate than the term *accident*?

4. List three ways to reduce the risk of injuries from falls in your home.

5. How should firearms be stored?

6. **Critical Thinking** Suppose you have been using electric saws for years. You have just bought a new electric saw. Should you read the instruction manual before you use it? Why or why not?

7. **Critical Thinking** How can you prevent an assault when you are at home? When you are away from home?

Section 2

8. An abnormal condition or disorder caused by exposure to the work environment is called an
   a. occupational injury. b. occupational illness.
   c. unintentional injury. d. assault.

9. The overturning of a boat is called
   a. drowning. b. survival floating.
   c. capsizing. d. PFD.

10. What federal agency provides information about workplace safety?

11. Explain why it is important for teens to think about their risk of occupational injuries.

12. Why is it important for everyone, even good swimmers, to know the technique of survival floating?

13. How can you prevent overuse injuries?

14. **Critical Thinking** Choose one recreational activity that you enjoy. Describe what you already do to prevent injuries while participating in that activity. In what ways can you better protect yourself from injuries in the future?

Section 3

15. A technique that enables you to actively avoid hazardous situations on the road is
    a. road rage. b. speeding.
    c. defensive driving. d. survival floating.

16. List three parts of your car you should have checked regularly.

17. Summarize the actions you should take when driving through a construction zone.

18. **Critical Thinking** It is a bad idea to drive when you are tired, angry, or feeling stressed. Why?

19. **Critical Thinking** There has been much debate about requiring seat belts on school buses. Do you think the extra safety that seat belts might provide justifies the cost of installing them in all school buses? Explain your answer. **WRITING**

Building Health Skills

20. **Accessing Information** Find out what laws and regulations have been established to protect people from stalking. Prepare a written report of your findings. **WRITING**

21. **Making Decisions** Lisa noticed a fire hazard at her after-school job. She reported it to her manager, but he hasn't done anything about it in over a week. What would you do if you were Lisa?

22. **Setting Goals** List three areas of vehicle safety in which your safety skills could be improved, as a driver or as a passenger. Set goals for improving your safety skills. Break your goals down into manageable sub-goals and set deadlines for yourself. **WRITING**

Health and Community

Public Safety Campaign Create a public service poster about one of the safety issues you learned about in this chapter. Think about who your target audience should be. What would be the most effective way to reach that audience? **WRITING**

Standardized Test Prep

Math Practice

The graph shows the percentage of drivers who were speeding when they were involved in a fatal vehicle crash. Use the graph to answer Questions 23–25.

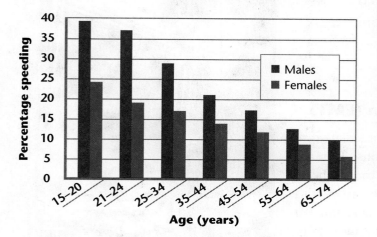

23. What age group has the highest percentage of speeding drivers involved in fatal crashes?
A Ages 15–20
B Ages 21–24
C Ages 25–34
D Ages 35–44

24. How does speeding compare between males ages 15–20 and females ages 21–24?
F The males were speeding about 50% less frequently than the females.
G The males were speeding about 50% more frequently than the females.
H The males were speeding about 100% more frequently than the females.
J There was no difference in speeding between the males and the females.

25. Which statement best describes the trend shown in this graph?
A Speed plays a greater role in fatal crashes involving female drivers than male drivers.
B Speed plays a greater role in fatal crashes involving male drivers than female drivers.
C As drivers age, speed plays a greater role in fatal crashes.
D Speed only plays a role in fatal crashes involving young drivers.

Reading and Writing Practice

Read the passage. Then answer Questions 26–29.

Most young people find paid employment, either during the summer or year-round, before graduating from high school. Young workers ages 14–24 are at risk of workplace injury because of their inexperience at work and their physical, cognitive, and emotional developmental characteristics. They often hesitate to ask questions and may fail to recognize workplace dangers. OSHA's Young Worker Initiative addresses this group's safety and health through an outreach program.

26. Young people
A always recognize workplace dangers.
B are at risk for workplace injury.
C do not usually work until after high school.
D are fully developed emotionally.

27. In this passage, the word *cognitive* means
F physical.
G emotional.
H mental.
J muscular.

28. According to the passage, which of these statements is true?
A Few young people work during the summer.
B Young people are at no greater risk for workplace injuries than older workers.
C OSHA does not address the risks that face young workers.
D Many young workers do not ask questions if they don't understand something.

Constructed Response
29. In a paragraph, summarize the reasons why young workers are at risk for workplace injury.

> ### Test-Taking Tip
> **Allow yourself plenty of time to get to the test site. You will be more relaxed if you arrive early.**

CAREERS

Community Health and Safety

Keeping people in the community healthy and safe is the goal of many health careers. Some workers treat immediate problems, while others deal with long-term health threats.

Emergency Medical Technician (EMT)

Emergency medical technicians provide immediate care to ill or injured people in emergency situations. They are trained to evaluate a patient's condition and care for heart and respiratory emergencies. They may even assist with childbirth. A career as an emergency medical technician requires a high school diploma, plus several months of training and certification by the state.

Epidemiologist

Epidemiologists investigate the medical and social aspects of diseases. For example, they may study an outbreak of meningitis to determine why a certain population got the disease. They may also recommend steps for preventing further outbreaks. A career as an epidemiologist usually requires a bachelor's degree in science or health as well as a master's or doctoral degree.

Pharmacy Technician

Pharmacy technicians assist pharmacists by entering prescription orders and patient information into a computer system. They also select and count medicines, keep track of inventory, and order drugs and other supplies. In addition to a high school diploma, pharmacy technicians usually complete a pharmacy technician program at a community college or earn state certification.

Environmental Engineer

Environmental engineers study environmental problems in order to identify solutions. They may work to improve air quality, protect water supplies, or design safe landfills. To pursue a career in environmental engineering, you must have at least a bachelor's degree in engineering.

Career Focus

Erika Bolden, Environmental Engineer for the EPA

How did you become interested in environmental engineering?

"During college, I interned at an electric power company. The region had poor air quality, due in part to emissions from a coal-fired power plant. From that experience, I became interested in air quality issues in my area."

What do you do?

"I inspect facilities such as chemical plants, automobile dealerships, and steel mills to make sure that they are not releasing too much of any air pollutant into the atmosphere. Federal law sets the limits on pollutant emissions. The air pollutants of most concern to EPA include carbon monoxide, nitrogen oxides, sulfur oxides, lead, and ozone. Any substance can be toxic if a person or the environment is exposed to too much of it."

How does your job affect people's health?

"EPA's job is to protect human health and the environment. My job specifically is to ensure that companies follow the law to minimize pollutant levels in the air. With improved air quality comes lower rates of asthma and cancer. It feels really good to know that people are breathing easier as a result of our efforts."

Health and Careers

Careers in Public Safety Research other careers that help make people's lives healthier and safer. Choose one career and write a paragraph on how you could directly affect your community by pursuing that profession. **WRITING**

First-Aid Appendix

Responding to an Emergency

In the movies, when disaster is about to strike, the music becomes louder and more dramatic. In real life, however, no such warnings alert you to emergency situations. If an emergency occurred, would you be prepared to respond?

Emergency Action Plan

If an emergency occurs, have a clear plan of action to protect yourself and to assist others by providing first aid. First aid is the immediate care given to a victim before professional medical help arrives.

The American Red Cross and the American Heart Association recommend these actions when you encounter an emergency.

1 CHECK Make sure the scene is safe for you, the victim(s), and any bystanders. Check the victim(s) for these life-threatening conditions:

- **Severe Bleeding** Signs of severe bleeding include blood pouring from an open wound, blood in vomit, pain or swelling in the abdomen, and weakness or confusion.

- **Unconsciousness** Gently tap the victim on the shoulder and ask, "Are you OK?" or say, "Open your eyes." If there is no response, the victim is probably unconscious.

- **Breathing Difficulties** Look to see if the person's chest is rising and falling. Listen for normal breathing or feel for escaping air against your cheek. The absence of these signs may indicate that the victim is not breathing normally. Gasping for breath is another sign of breathing difficulties.

2 CALL Call 911 immediately if a victim shows any life-threatening conditions. (If there is another person with you, have that person call 911 while you stay with the victim.) Be prepared to answer the 911 operator's questions and follow directions calmly and completely. If you are unsure about whether to call 911, the safest thing to do is to make the call.

3 CARE Be prepared to act quickly to provide first aid. Always care for victims with life-threatening conditions first. If you suspect a neck or spine injury, do not move the victim unless it is absolutely necessary.

Automated External Defibrillators

One important life-saving tool that you should always check for is an automated external defibrillator (AED). AEDs are found in many public places, including airports, stadiums, health clubs, and malls. By quickly locating, retrieving, and using an AED, you can make the difference between life and death.

An AED uses verbal commands and visual cues to direct even untrained users in exactly what to do. Here's how it works.

- Attach the shock pads to the victim's chest.
- The AED analyzes the person's heart rhythm.
- If an abnormal rhythm is detected, the AED automatically delivers a shock to help restore a normal rhythm.
- The AED then instructs you about what to do next.

Universal Safety Precautions

As a provider of first aid, you have a responsibility to yourself and to your victim to guard against the transmission of infectious diseases. When giving first aid, always follow these universal safety precautions.

▶ Wear disposable gloves whenever there is any chance that you will come into contact with body fluids.

▶ Use a plastic face shield or mask with a one-way valve when you perform rescue breathing.

▶ Wash your hands with soap and warm water after providing first aid.

Good Samaritan Laws

Even when first aid is applied correctly, there are times when complications can occur. Most states have a Good Samaritan Law for people who administer first aid to victims. These laws prevent the rescuer from being sued if complications arise. Rescuers should use common sense and follow these guidelines.

▶ Call 911.

▶ If someone's life is in danger and you know the correct first aid procedures, you should administer first aid.

▶ If the victim is conscious, you should ask the person's permission first to administer first aid.

▶ Be sure that your help will not further harm the victim.

Shock

With any serious injury, you need to monitor the victim closely for signs of shock. Shock is a condition in which the heart fails to circulate blood adequately to the vital organs. The more severe the injury, the more likely that shock will develop. Even if the injury or illness itself is *not* immediately life threatening, shock can lead to death.

Signs of shock include

▶ restlessness or irritability

▶ confusion or disorientation

▶ skin that is pale, ashen, bluish, cool, or moist

▶ rapid breathing

▶ rapid, weak pulse

▶ excessive thirst

▶ nausea or vomiting

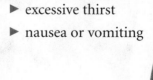

First Aid for Shock

1 Call 911 immediately if you suspect that someone is in shock.

2 Lay the victim on the floor or ground. If possible, place a blanket or jacket beneath the victim to provide insulation.

3 Raise and support the victim's legs if there is no leg or hip injury. This will improve blood flow to the vital organs.

4 Control any bleeding by applying direct pressure to the wound using a sterile gauze pad or a clean, absorbent cloth.

5 Cover the victim with a blanket or coat to keep him or her warm.

6 Monitor the victim's breathing and pulse. Be prepared to begin rescue breathing (page 725) or CPR (pages 726–727), if needed.

Choking and Rescue Breathing

You're at a restaurant when suddenly a person at a nearby table starts gasping for air. What would you do?

Choking

When food or any other object becomes lodged in a person's airway, the person may choke. Choking, also called obstructed airway, is a life-threatening emergency. Unless the object is dislodged within minutes, the person can die because the brain is deprived of oxygen.

A person who is choking may bring one or both hands to the throat, which is the universal sign for choking. The person may also gasp for air or turn blue. A choking person will not be able to speak.

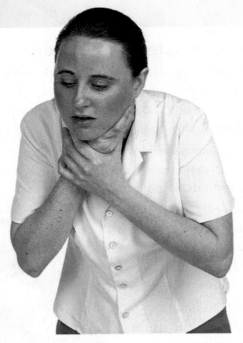

▲ **Universal sign for choking**

First Aid for Choking in an Adult or Child

The first aid procedure for choking, sometimes called the Heimlich maneuver, involves delivering abdominal thrusts. Abdominal thrusts push air from the lungs up and out of the victim's airway with enough force to expel the object.

1 Ask the victim, "Are you choking?" If the victim is able to speak or cough, there is no need to deliver first aid. If the victim cannot speak or cough, prepare to perform abdominal thrusts.

2 Stand behind the victim. Wrap both of your arms around the upper part of the victim's abdomen, just below the rib cage. Make a fist with one hand and place it, thumb inward, on the victim's abdomen between the navel and breastbone. Grasp your fist with your other hand and pull sharply inward and upward.

3 Continue delivering abdominal thrusts until either
- ► the object becomes dislodged
- ► the victim begins to cough or breathe
- ► the victim becomes unconscious

4 If the victim becomes unconscious, call 911. Then begin CPR (pages 726–727).

If You Are Alone and You Are Choking

Position your hands on your abdomen (as described in Step 2) and perform abdominal thrusts on yourself. If this is not successful, position yourself over the back of a chair or against another firm object. Push into the chair or object so the force pushes upward and inward against your abdomen.

Rescue Breathing

If a person stops breathing, the body's cells quickly run out of oxygen and begin to die. This is especially true of brain cells. If brain cells are deprived of oxygen for more than five or six minutes, some cells will begin to die. This can result in permanent brain damage or death. Rescue breathing is the first aid procedure for someone who stops breathing.

You can recognize that someone has stopped breathing normally by the absence of breathing movements, such as the chest rising and falling, or by a bluish color to the lips, tongue, and fingernails. You can also place your cheek next to the victim's mouth and nose and feel for breath on your skin.

How to Perform Rescue Breathing on an Adult or Child

1 Call 911. Then lay the victim on a firm, flat surface.

2 Place one hand on the victim's forehead. Gently tilt the victim's head back. As you do this, the mouth may fall open.

3 Wearing disposable gloves, use your fingers to pick out obvious obstructions from the victim's mouth.

4 Keep one hand on the victim's forehead to maintain the head tilt. Place the fingertips of your other hand under the victim's chin and lift the chin up. Do not press on the soft tissues of the neck.

5 Keep the head tilted back and chin lifted up so the airway remains open. Look, listen, and feel for normal breathing.

7 Place a face shield or mask over the victim's mouth. Take a normal breath, then place your lips on the shield or mask.

8 Blow into the victim's mouth for one second. Then take your mouth off the shield and look to see if the victim's chest moves. If the chest rises, this is a sign that you have given an effective breath.

9 If the victim's chest rises after the first breath, maintain the head tilt and chin lift. Then give a second breath. If the victim is still unresponsive after two breaths, begin CPR (pages 726-727).

10 If the victim's chest does not rise after the first breath, perform the head tilt and chin lift again. Then give a second breath. Whether or not the victim's chest rises, begin CPR.

6 If the victim is not breathing normally, pinch the victim's nose closed using your finger and thumb. With your other hand, continue lifting the chin.

Cardiopulmonary Resuscitation (CPR)

If an unconscious victim is not breathing normally, the person might be suffering serious heart complications. Every second is critical for the victim's survival.

Cardiac Arrest

People who suffer heart attacks, severe injuries, drug overdoses, near drownings, or breathing problems may go into cardiac arrest. In cardiac arrest, the heart stops pumping blood throughout the body. When blood does not circulate, the brain and other vital organs do not receive oxygen. Without oxygen, the victim will lose consciousness and die within minutes.

Cardiopulmonary resuscitation (CPR) is the first aid procedure for unconscious victims. If CPR is started immediately after a victim collapses, it can greatly increase the person's chances for survival.

Even if you are not trained in CPR, you can help. If you see an adult collapse from cardiac arrest, call 911. Then do chest compressions, or hands-only CPR, until help arrives.

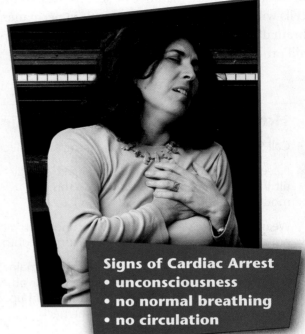

Signs of Cardiac Arrest
- **unconsciousness**
- **no normal breathing**
- **no circulation**

How to Perform Cardiovascular Resuscitation (CPR)

CPR combines rescue breathing (to force oxygen into the lungs) with chest compressions (to pump blood throughout the body). If you have confirmed that the victim is unresponsive and you have been trained in CPR, follow these steps.

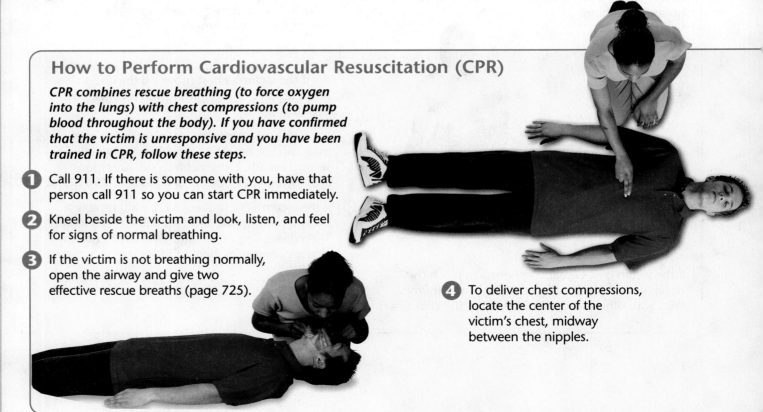

1. Call 911. If there is someone with you, have that person call 911 so you can start CPR immediately.

2. Kneel beside the victim and look, listen, and feel for signs of normal breathing.

3. If the victim is not breathing normally, open the airway and give two effective rescue breaths (page 725).

4. To deliver chest compressions, locate the center of the victim's chest, midway between the nipples.

5 Place the heel of one hand in the center of the victim's chest. Your fingers should be extended and pointing away from you.

6 Place the heel of your second hand on top of the first so that your hands are overlapped and parallel. Interlock your fingers and keep your fingers raised off the victim's chest, as shown in the photo below.

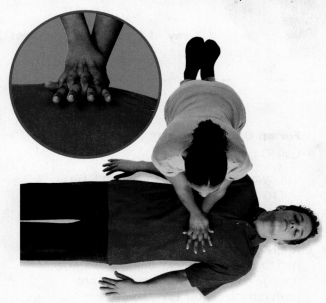

7 Lean over the victim so your shoulders are above your hands, and straighten your arms. Press down on the breastbone to compress the chest by 1.5 to 2 inches. Then release the pressure without removing your hands from the victim's chest.

8 Compress the victim's chest 30 times at the rate of 100 compressions per minute. Each compression and release should take about the same time.

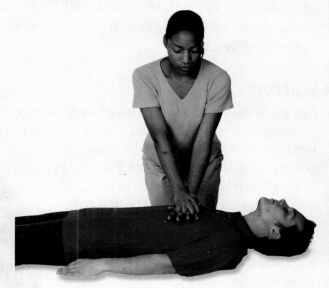

9 Establish a cycle of 2 rescue breaths and 30 chest compressions. Five cycles of breaths and compressions should take about two minutes.

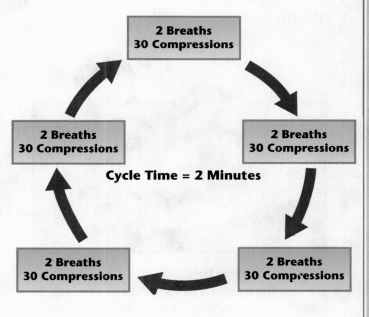

2 Breaths
30 Compressions

2 Breaths
30 Compressions

Cycle Time = 2 Minutes

2 Breaths
30 Compressions

2 Breaths
30 Compressions

2 Breaths
30 Compressions

10 Continue CPR until either medical help arrives and takes over, an AED can be located and used, or the victim starts moving on his or her own.

Bone, Joint, and Muscle Injuries

Suppose that a friend tripped and fell and his wrist began to swell. Would you know what to do? By providing proper first aid, you can reduce your friend's pain and speed up the healing process.

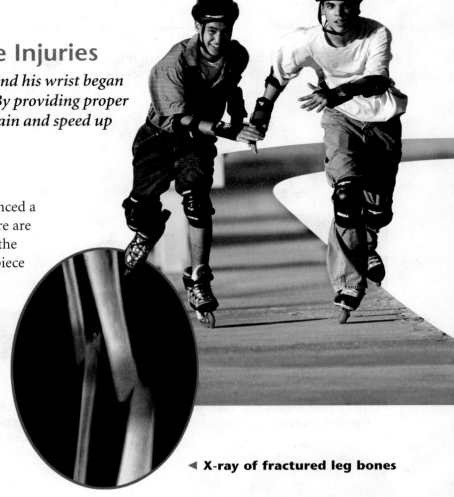

Fractures

You might know someone who has experienced a fracture—a crack or a break in a bone. There are two types of fractures. In a closed fracture, the skin remains intact. In an open fracture, a piece of the broken bone sticks out through the skin. An open fracture may bleed heavily.

The only sure way to identify a fracture is with an X-ray. However, it is important to recognize the signs of a possible fracture. These include

▶ swelling and bruising at the injured area

▶ pain in the injured area

▶ deformity of the injured area, such as a shortened, bent, or twisted limb

▶ difficulty moving the injured area

◀ **X-ray of fractured leg bones**

First Aid for Fractures

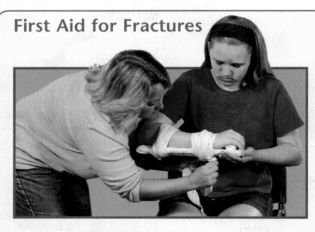

For a Closed Fracture

1 Stabilize the injured area with a sling or a splint. A splint is any material that prevents the injured part from moving. Do not try to straighten a bent bone or limb.

2 Keep the victim still and comfortable. Seek medical attention.

For an Open Fracture

1 Call 911 immediately.

2 Cut away clothing from the wound. Do not try to push the bone back through the skin. Do not try to straighten a bent bone or limb.

3 Apply gentle pressure with a large sterile pad to control bleeding. If you don't have a sterile pad, use a clean cloth. Do not push directly on the exposed bone.

4 Cover the entire wound with a sterile bandage or clean cloth.

5 If the victim needs to be moved before help arrives, first apply a splint to stabilize the injured area.

Strains and Sprains

A muscle strain can result from overexerting or pulling a muscle, such as a back muscle.

Symptoms of a muscle strain include

▶ dull pain that worsens with movement of the injured area

▶ swelling around the injured area

A sprain is an injury to a ligament—the strong, flexible bands of tissue that hold bones together at a joint.

Symptoms of a sprain include

▶ a popping sound or tearing sensation at the time of injury

▶ pain in the injured joint, especially when moving it

▶ swelling of the joint

▶ tenderness when the injured area is touched

▶ discoloration (black and blue) around the injured area

Dislocations

If a joint is twisted or overstressed, one or more of the bones that normally meet at that joint may become displaced, or dislocated.

Symptoms of a dislocation include

▶ swelling and deformity around the injured area

▶ inability to move the joint, or pain when moving the joint

▶ discoloration, tenderness, or numbness

Muscle Cramps

A muscle cramp is the sudden, painful contraction of one or more muscles.

Symptoms of a muscle cramp include

▶ severe pain in the cramping muscle

▶ inability to use the cramping muscle

First Aid for Strains and Sprains

The first aid procedure for strains and sprains can be remembered by the initials R.I.C.E.

R **Rest** the injured area and avoid using it.

I **Ice** the area during the first 24 hours to reduce swelling. After that, periodically apply moist heat to the area.

C **Compress** the area with an elastic wrap.

E **Elevate** the injured area to prevent or limit swelling.

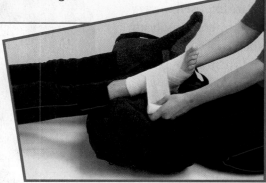

First Aid for Dislocations

The first aid procedure for a dislocated joint is similar to the procedure for a fracture.

1 Do not move the injured limb or try to put a dislocated bone back into its place.

2 Place the victim in a comfortable position.

3 Stabilize the injured body part with a sling or a splint.

4 Seek medical attention promptly.

First Aid for Muscle Cramps

1 Stretch out the cramping muscle to counteract the cramp.

2 Massage the muscle firmly, but gently.

3 Have the victim drink plenty of fluids.

4 Seek medical help if the cramps persist.

Outdoor Emergencies

Many teens enjoy outdoor activities. But those activities can expose you to extremes in temperatures and other potential dangers that may require first aid.

Frostbite

When extremities, such as hands, feet, arms, and legs, are exposed to very cold temperatures, body tissue can freeze. This is called frostbite. Frostbite is a serious condition that can result in the loss of the affected area.

Signs of frostbite include

▶ lack of feeling in the affected area

▶ skin that appears waxy or discolored and is cold to the touch

First Aid for Frostbite

1. Call 911. Then help move the victim out of the cold.

2. Remove any jewelry and wet or restrictive clothing, if possible.

3. Handle the affected area gently. Avoid rubbing the area, because rubbing could cause further injury.

4. If there is no chance that the affected area will freeze again, begin to rewarm it slowly. Gently soak the area in warm water at 100–105°F. Keep soaking until the area turns red and feels warm.

5. Wrap the affected area with dry blankets or towels.

6. If fingers or toes are frostbitten, place clean cloth between them to keep them separated.

7. Avoid breaking any blisters that may have formed.

Hypothermia

Hypothermia is the overall cooling of the entire body to a body temperature below 95°F. A person suffering from hypothermia may develop an abnormal heart rhythm, and the heart may eventually stop beating. Hypothermia can occur even when the temperature is above freezing, especially in a cold, damp, rainy environment.

Signs of hypothermia include

▶ shivering

▶ numbness or weakness

▶ glassy stare

▶ confusion or impaired consciousness

First Aid for Hypothermia

1. Call 911 immediately. Then help move the victim out of the cold.

2. Carefully remove any wet clothing and dry the victim.

3. Warm the body gradually by wrapping the victim in blankets or dry clothing.

4. Apply hot water bottles or other heat sources, wrapped in a towel, to the victim's body, if available. Do not warm the victim too quickly because this could result in dangerous heart rhythms.

5. If the victim is conscious and alert, give warm liquids, such as warm water or decaffeinated tea or coffee.

6. Monitor breathing and consciousness until medical help arrives. Be prepared to perform rescue breathing or CPR, if necessary.

Heat Exhaustion

Working outdoors in the heat or long periods of strenuous exercise can lead to heat exhaustion. With heat exhaustion, a person's body temperature can rise to dangerous levels.

Signs of heat exhaustion include

► skin that is cool, moist, pale, ashen, or flushed

► headache, nausea, or dizziness

► weakness or exhaustion

► heavy sweating

► muscle cramps

Heat Stroke

If heat exhaustion is not treated and the victim continues to overheat, heat stroke can develop. In heat stroke, body systems become so overheated that they stop functioning. As body fluids become depleted, the person stops sweating and the body can no longer cool itself. Vital organs, such as the brain, heart, and kidneys, can cease to function and death can result.

Signs of heat stroke include

► confusion or strange behavior

► red, hot, dry skin

► inability to drink or vomiting

► shallow breathing, seizures, or unconsciousness

Rescuing a Drowning Victim

If someone in the water seems to be having trouble, it is important to assess the situation quickly. Call 911 or send someone for help. Determine how to rescue the person quickly without putting yourself at risk. As soon as the victim is out of the water, perform rescue breathing or CPR, if necessary.

First Aid for Heat Exhaustion

1. Help move the victim to a cool or shady location.

2. Loosen or remove any tight clothing.

3. If the victim is conscious and alert, give fluids to replace fluids lost in sweat.

4. Cool the victim's body by wrapping it in water-soaked towels or by sponging or spraying cool water onto the victim.

5. Monitor the victim for signs of heat stroke or shock. Be prepared to call 911, if necessary.

First Aid for Heat Stroke

1. Call 911 immediately. Then help move the victim to a cool or shady location.

2. Loosen or remove any tight clothing.

3. Cool the victim quickly using whatever means are available. You can soak towels or sheets in cold water and apply them to the victim's body. You can use a hose to spray water on the victim, or wrap cold packs in a cloth and apply them to the victim.

4. Carefully monitor the victim. Be prepared to perform rescue breathing or CPR, if necessary.

Water Rescue Techniques

Bites and Stings

Poisonous Snakebites

Although about 8,000 people are bitten by poisonous snakes in the United States each year, fewer than five people die. Nevertheless, poisonous snakebites can be dangerous. Medical care needs to be administered quickly.

Signs of a poisonous snakebite include

▶ one or two distinct puncture wounds

▶ severe pain, redness, and swelling at the bite

▶ nausea and vomiting

▶ blurred vision

▶ increased salivation and sweating

▶ labored breathing

First Aid for Poisonous Snakebites

1. Call 911.

2. Gently wash the wound with clean running water.

3. Immobilize the affected area.

4. Minimize the victim's movements.

5. Make sure the victim receives medical assistance within 30 minutes of being bitten.

Insect Stings

For most people, insect stings can be painful but not life threatening. However, some people are highly allergic to substances in the venom of some insects.

Signs of an insect sting vary with each insect, but generally include

▶ pain

▶ swelling at the site of the sting

▶ hives or a rash

▶ nausea and vomiting

▶ breathing difficulties

▶ swelling of the tongue or face

First Aid for Insect Stings

1. Remove the stinger if it is visible by scraping it off with your fingernail or a credit card. Do not remove the stinger with tweezers.

2. Wash and then cover the wound.

3. Apply a cold pack wrapped in a cloth to the site of the sting.

4. Watch for signs of a severe allergic reaction (blotchy skin, swelling of the tongue or throat, puffiness around the eyes, breathing difficulties, or signs of shock).

5. At the first sign of a severe allergic reaction, call 911 immediately.

6. Monitor the victim's airway and breathing.

Animal Bites

Animal bites carry the risk of infection, including the potentially fatal disease rabies. Anyone bitten by a person or by a wild or domestic animal should seek medical help as soon as possible.

First Aid for Animal Bites

1. Wearing disposable gloves, wash the wound thoroughly with clean running water.

2. Control any bleeding with pressure.

3. Apply a clean, dry dressing.

4. Seek medical care.

Poisonings

Swallowed Poisons

A poison is any substance that can cause injury or death when it gets inside the body. Poisons that can be swallowed include cleaning products, pesticides, certain plants, paint thinner, and certain medications.

Signs that a person has swallowed a poisonous substance include

- vomiting, sometimes including blood
- confusion or impaired consciousness
- pain or a burning sensation
- empty containers in the vicinity of the victim

Inhaled Poisons

There are many harmful fumes that can poison the body if inhaled. One of the most common is carbon monoxide, a colorless, odorless gas. Carbon monoxide is a component of automobile exhaust, but can also be released by certain fires, defective furnaces or cooking equipment, and kerosene heaters.

Signs of carbon monoxide poisoning include

- skin that is pale or bluish in color
- headache
- noisy, distressed breathing
- confusion
- loss of consciousness

First Aid for Swallowed Poisons

1. Call 911. (The 911 operator may connect you to a poison control center, where medical professionals will provide specific instructions.)

2. If the victim is conscious, ask what was swallowed so you can relay that information to the medical professionals.

3. Monitor the victim's airway and breathing. Be prepared to perform rescue breathing or CPR, if necessary.

4. Do not induce vomiting. Do not give the victim anything to eat or drink unless the emergency operator tells you to do so.

First Aid for Inhaled Poisons

1. Call 911 and report your observations.

2. Carefully survey the scene to be sure that the poisonous fumes are no longer present and that it is safe for you to approach the victim.

3. If the victim is conscious and it is safe for you to do so, help the victim move into fresh air. Monitor the victim until help arrives. Be prepared to perform rescue breathing or CPR, if needed.

4. If the victim is unconscious, begin CPR immediately.

Bleeding

Severe Bleeding

Bleeding occurs when a blood vessel ruptures. The severity of the bleeding depends on the type of vessel that ruptures. For minor bleeding, applying constant pressure at the site of the wound can usually control the bleeding.

More severe bleeding may occur if an artery ruptures. Blood that is bright red in color may spurt from the wound. If the bleeding is not controlled quickly, the victim can die within a few minutes.

First Aid for Severe Bleeding

1. Call 911.

2. Wearing disposable gloves, apply direct pressure to the wound using a sterile gauze pad or a clean absorbent cloth. If disposable gloves are not available, have the victim apply pressure on the wound.

3. While continuing to apply pressure, elevate the injured area above the level of the heart, unless you suspect a fracture. In that case, follow the guidelines for providing first aid for fractures (page 728).

4. Make a "pressure bandage" by snuggly wrapping an elastic bandage (or another cloth) over the sterile gauze pad. The pressure bandage will apply continuous direct pressure to the wound.

5. If bleeding continues, apply additional bandages on top of the existing ones.

6. Monitor the victim's breathing and consciousness and watch for signs of shock. Be prepared to perform rescue breathing or CPR, if necessary.

Nosebleeds

Nosebleeds can result from a blow to the nose or from a less obvious situation. Nosebleeds seldom require medical attention. However, if a nosebleed continues for more than a few minutes and results in the loss of a lot of blood, it can become a serious emergency.

First Aid for Nosebleeds

1. Have the victim sit down and lean forward to clear the blood from the nostrils.

2. Tell the victim to breathe through the mouth and to apply pressure by pinching the nostrils closed for 10 minutes.

3. Caution the victim not to cough, spit, or sniff because this could disturb the blood clots that are forming in the nose.

4. After 10 minutes, have the victim release the pressure. If the bleeding has not stopped, have the victim reapply pressure for another 10 minutes.

5. Once the bleeding has stopped, have the victim rest quietly for a few hours. Caution the victim to avoid blowing his or her nose as this could cause the bleeding to start again.

6. If the bleeding will not stop or if the victim is having trouble breathing, call 911.

Burns

Severe Burns

Burn injuries are categorized by the depth of the burned tissue. First-degree burns affect only the epidermis, the outer layer of skin. Second-degree burns affect the dermis, the layer of skin below the surface. And third-degree burns affect all the layers of skin and possibly the tissue beneath the skin.

Large or deep burns can be life threatening and require immediate medical attention. Burns that require emergency care include

▶ burns that cover a large surface area of the body or more than one body part

▶ suspected burns to the airway

▶ burns to the head, neck, hands, feet, or genitals

▶ burns to victims under the age of 5 or over 60

▶ burns that result from chemicals, explosions, or electricity

First Aid for Severe Burns

1. Call 911.

2. Remove the victim from the source of the burn if you can do so without causing injury to yourself.

3. Check the victim's breathing and consciousness. Be prepared to perform rescue breathing and CPR, if necessary.

4. Pour cold water over the burn to cool it down and to reduce the pain.

5. Continue cooling the burn until help arrives.

6. If possible, cover the burn with a clean cloth to minimize infection. Do not apply any ointments.

Sunburns

One common first-degree burn is caused by the sun. A sunburn is actually a radiation burn because it is caused by ultraviolet radiation from the sun. The risk of sunburn can be reduced by using sunscreen with an SPF of 15 or more.

Signs of sunburn include

▶ reddened skin

▶ pain in the area of the burn

▶ blisters in the burned area

First Aid for Sunburns

1. Cover the victim's skin with light clothing or a towel.

2. Help the victim move indoors or into the shade.

3. Pour cold water on the cloth covering the burned area to cool the skin and relieve the pain.

4. Encourage the person to take frequent sips of cold water.

5. For a severe sunburn, seek medical help.

Organ Donation Appendix

An organ may become so damaged that it can no longer perform its functions in the body. Sometimes the damaged organ is replaced with an organ that is working. This procedure is called an organ transplant.

As doctors have more success transplanting organs, the list of people waiting for a transplant grows. About 4,000 new patients are added to the waiting list each month. But the number of available organs has not kept pace with the need. So some people die while waiting for "the gift of life."

The Benefits of Organ Donation

More people might become donors if they realized that one donor can save or improve the lives of many people. Organs, such as hearts and lungs, are not the only parts of the body that can be transplanted. Skin grafts can help burn victims heal. Corneas can restore a person's sight. Blood vessels are used in bypass surgeries.

Organ donation can also help a donor's family. As the family grieves the death of a loved one, they can think about all the people who are being helped.

Becoming a Possible Organ Donor

There are no limits on who can donate organs. If you are not yet 18, however, you need the consent of a parent or guardian. People can use one or more of the options listed below to register as a possible organ donor.

▶ Most states have an organ and tissue donor registry. People can often sign up online.

▶ People can download a donor card to carry in their wallets. The card must be signed by the donor and two witnesses.

▶ In many states, people can sign up when they apply for or renew a driver's license. The state will place a symbol on the license. In North Carolina, for example, the symbol is a heart.

People who want to be donors have one more important task. Families are often consulted before organs are accepted for donation. So possible donors need to tell their families about their plan. That way, family members are able to act as advocates for donation.

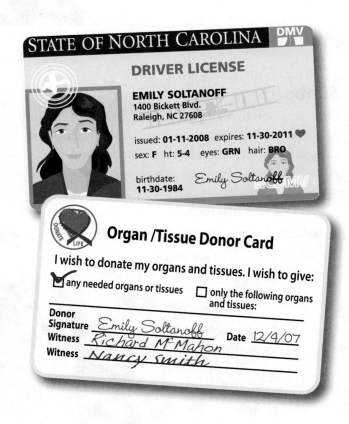

STATE OF NORTH CAROLINA
DMV
DRIVER LICENSE
EMILY SOLTANOFF
1400 Bickett Blvd.
Raleigh, NC 27608
issued: 01-11-2008 expires: 11-30-2011
sex: F ht: 5-4 eyes: GRN hair: BRO
birthdate: 11-30-1984
Emily Soltanoff

Organ /Tissue Donor Card
I wish to donate my organs and tissues. I wish to give:
☑ any needed organs or tissues ☐ only the following organs and tissues:
Donor Signature Emily Soltanoff
Witness Richard McMahon Date 12/4/07
Witness Nancy Smith

Becoming a Possible Organ Recipient

A doctor may think that a patient could benefit from a transplant. If so, the doctor will refer the patient to one of about 250 transplant centers in the United States. Each transplant center is qualified to do one or more types of transplants.

The transplant team will decide whether a patient is a good candidate for a transplant. Once patients receive approval, their names are added to a national waiting list. The list is maintained by the United Network for Organ Sharing (UNOS).

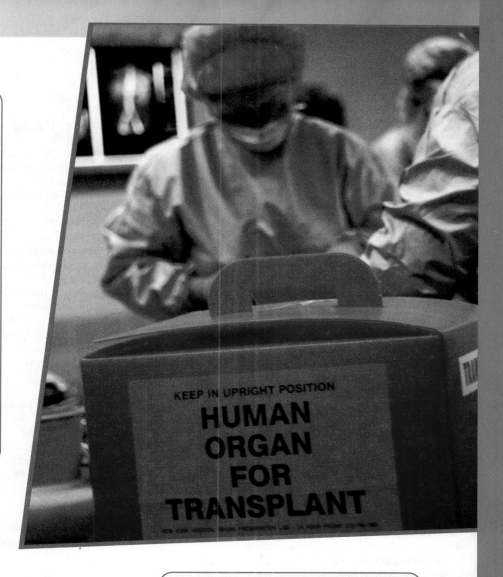

KEEP IN UPRIGHT POSITION
HUMAN ORGAN FOR TRANSPLANT

Matching Recipients and Donors

When organs become available, a match must be made between patients on the waiting list and the donor. Blood type, tissue type, and organ size are factors. So is a patient's medical condition. Where a patient lives is also a factor. A person who lives nearby is preferred. If no local match is found, an organ is offered within a region, and then nationally.

Recall that the human immune system will attack foreign antigens. This type of attack can cause a donated organ to be so damaged that it can no longer function. This outcome is called rejection. Doctors can reduce the risk of rejection. They use drugs that suppress the immune system. They also try to match donors with recipients who have many of the same antigens. Such matches are most likely between people with similar genetic profiles. So it is important for the donor pool to include people from different ethnic groups.

Organ Procurement

UNOS links transplant centers with organ procurement organizations (OPOs). An OPO is a nonprofit agency. People who work for an OPO do the following tasks.

▶ They talk with families about organ donation after a person dies.

▶ They coordinate the recovery of organs.

▶ They make sure that organs are preserved until the organs are transplanted.

▶ They arrange to transport organs to transplant centers.

▶ They educate the public about the need for organ donation.

Glossary

A

absorption The process by which nutrients pass through the lining of the digestive system. (p. 242)
absorción Proceso mediante el cual los nutrientes pasan a través de las paredes del sistema digestivo.

abstinence The act of refraining from, or not having, sex. (p. 154)
abstinencia Acción de privarse de tener relaciones sexuales.

acne A lesion that forms when excess oil and dead cells plug a hair follicle. (p. 350)
acné Lesión que se produce cuando el exceso de grasa y de células muertas obstruyen un folículo piloso.

action plan A series of specific steps you can take to achieve a goal. (p. 15)
plan de acción Serie de pasos determinados que se toman para alcanzar una meta.

active listening Focusing your full attention on what another person is saying and letting that person know you understand and care. (p. 137)
atención activa Concentrar completamente la atención en lo que otra persona dice, haciéndole saber así que se comprende y se siente interés por lo que está diciendo.

active supervision Keeping children in your view at all times when they are in or near the water. (p. 705)
supervisión activa Observar a los niños constantemente cuando están en el agua o cerca de ella.

addiction The state of losing control over the use of a drug; it is accompanied by a strong craving for the drug. (p. 388)
adicción Pérdida del control a causa del uso de una droga; viene acompañada de un intenso deseo de consumir dicha droga.

adolescence The period from about age 12 to 19 during which a child gradually changes into an adult. (p. 514)
adolescencia Período entre los 12 y los 19 años aproximadamente, durante el cual un(a) niño(a) se convierte gradualmente en adulto.

adoption The legal process by which parents take another person's child into their family to be raised as their own. (p. 114)
adopción Procedimiento legal a través del cual los padres reciben en su familia al hijo de otra persona para criarlo como suyo.

advertising The public promotion of a product or service. (p. 21)
publicidad Promoción pública de un producto o servicio.

advocacy The use of communication to influence and support others in making positive health decisions. (p. 15)
propugnación Uso de la comunicación para influir o apoyar a otros para que tomen decisiones positivas relacionadas con la salud.

aerobic exercise An ongoing physical activity that raises your breathing and heart rates. (p. 320)
ejercicio aeróbico Toda actividad física continua que aumenta los ritmos cardíaco y respiratorio.

aggressive A term that describes people who express opinions and feelings in a way that may seem threatening or disrespectful to other people. (p. 138)
agresivo(a) Término que describe a una persona que expresa opiniones y sentimientos de una manera que puede parecer irrespetuosa o amenazante para otras personas.

AIDS Acquired immunodeficiency syndrome, an often fatal disease of the immune system caused by HIV infection. (p. 584)
SIDA Sigla del síndrome de inmunodeficiencia adquirida, una enfermedad del sistema inmunológico, por lo general fatal, causada por el virus de inmunodeficiencia humana (VIH).

alcoholism A disease marked by a person being unable to control their use of alcohol. (p. 388)
alcoholismo Enfermedad que se caracteriza por la incapacidad de una persona para controlar la ingestión de bebidas alcohólicas.

allergen Any substance that causes an allergy. (p. 616)
alergeno Cualquier sustancia que provoca una alergia.

allergy A disorder in which the immune system is overly sensitive to a particular substance not normally found in the body. (p. 616)
alergia Trastorno caracterizado por una reacción excesivamente sensible del sistema inmunológico ante una sustancia particular que no se encuentra normalmente en el cuerpo.

alveoli The sacs in the lungs where gases are exchanged between the air and the blood. (p. 308)
alvéolos Pequeñas bolsas que se hallan en los pulmones, en las cuales ocurre el intercambio de gases entre el aire y la sangre.

Alzheimer's disease A disease that causes brain cells to die, resulting in the gradual loss of mental and physical function. (p. 535)
enfermedad de Alzheimer Enfermedad que causa la muerte de células cerebrales y la pérdida gradual de la facultad mental y la capacidad física.

Americans with Disabilities Act A federal law that guarantees the civil rights of Americans who have physical or mental disabilities. (p. 626)
Ley de los estadounidenses con discapacidades Ley federal que garantiza los derechos civiles de los ciudadanos estadounidenses que sufren discapacidades físicas o mentales.

amino acids Small units that are bound together chemically to form proteins. (p. 198)
aminoácidos Pequeñas unidades que, al formar enlaces químicos entre sí, forman proteínas.

amniocentesis A prenatal test in which a small amount of amniotic fluid is removed and tested for abnormalities. (p. 495)
amniocentesis Examen prenatal que consiste en extraer una pequeña cantidad de líquido amniótico y someterlo a pruebas para detectar anormalidades.

amniotic sac A fluid-filled bag of thin tissue that develops around the embryo. (p. 490)
saco amniótico Bolsa de tejido fino, llena de líquido, que se forma alrededor del feto.

amphetamines Prescription drugs that are sometimes sold illegally as "speed" or "uppers." (p. 442)
anfetaminas Fármaco de prescripción que a veces se vende ilegalmente bajo el nombre de "estimulante".

anabolic steroid An artificial form of the male hormone testosterone that is used to increase muscle size and strength. (p. 274)
esteroide anabólico Presentación artificial de la hormona masculina testosterona que se usa para aumentar el volumen y la fuerza de los músculos.

anaerobic exercise Intense physical activity that lasts for a few seconds to a few minutes. (p. 320)
ejercicio anaeróbico Toda actividad física intensa que dura desde unos segundos hasta unos minutos.

anemia A condition in which the red blood cells do not contain enough hemoglobin. (p. 206)
anemia Trastorno que se presenta cuando los glóbulos rojos no tienen suficiente hemoglobina.

aneurysm A blood-filled weak spot that balloons out from the artery wall. (p. 605)
aneurisma Punto débil en la pared de una arteria, que se llena de sangre y se distiende.

angina pectoris The chest pain that occurs when an area of the heart does not get enough oxygen-rich blood. (p. 603)
angina de pecho Dolor del pecho que se produce cuando el corazón no recibe suficiente sangre rica en oxígeno.

anorexia nervosa An eating disorder in which a person doesn't eat enough food to maintain a healthy body weight. (p. 90)
anorexia nerviosa Trastorno grave de la alimentación en el que el individuo se niega a comer los alimentos necesarios para mantener un peso corporal saludable.

antibiotic A drug that inhibits or kills bacteria. (p. 559)
antibiótico Droga que inhibe el desarrollo de las bacterias o las mata.

antibody A protein that attaches to the surface of pathogens or to the toxins produced by pathogens, keeping the pathogen or toxin from harming the body. (p. 555)
anticuerpo Proteína que se adhiere a la superficie de los patógenos o a las toxinas producidas por éstos, impidiendo que el patógeno o la toxina le haga daño al cuerpo.

antioxidant A vitamin that helps protect healthy cells from the damage caused by the normal aging process as well as from certain types of cancer. (p. 205)
antioxidante Vitamina que ayuda a proteger a las células saludables de los daños causados por el proceso normal de envejecimiento y por ciertos tipos de cáncer.

anxiety Fear caused by a source you cannot identify or a source that doesn't pose as much threat as you think. (p. 84)
ansiedad Miedo que carece de causas identificables o es producido por un peligro mínimo o inexistente.

anxiety disorder A disorder characterized by anxiety that persists for a long time and interferes with daily living. (p. 84)
trastorno de ansiedad Trastorno que se caracteriza por una ansiedad constante que interfiere en las actividades de la vida diaria.

appetite A desire for food based more on emotions and other factors rather than on nutritional need. (p. 220)
apetito Deseo de ingerir alimento cuyo origen se debe más a factores emocionales o de otro tipo que a la necesidad nutricional.

arrhythmia An irregular heartbeat. (p. 301)
arritmia Irregularidad en los latidos del corazón.

artery A thick-walled blood vessel that carries blood away from the heart. (p. 295)
arteria Vaso de paredes gruesas que transporta la sangre desde el corazón.

arthritis Inflammation or irritation of a joint. (p. 618)
artritis Inflamación o irritación de una articulación.

asbestos A fibrous mineral that was once used in fireproofing and other building materials; asbestos fibers can cause lung disease. (p. 674)
asbesto Mineral fibroso que anteriormente era usado en la fabricación de aislantes y otros materiales de construcción; las fibras de asbestos pueden causar cáncer de pulmón.

assailant A person who attacks another person. (p. 163)
agresor Persona que ataca a otro individuo.

assault An unlawful attempt or threat to harm someone. (p. 700)
asalto Ataque o amenaza ilegal contra otra persona.

assertive A term that describes people who are able to stand up for themselves while expressing their feelings in a way that does not threaten other people. (p. 138)
asertivo Término que describe a una persona que es capaz de resolver sus problemas y expresar sus sentimientos de una manera que no resulte amenazante para otras personas.

asthma A disorder in which respiratory passageways become inflamed and narrow during attacks, leading to difficulty breathing. (p. 309)
asma Trastorno en el que las vías respiratorias se inflaman y se estrechan durante los ataques, dificultando la respiración.

asymptomatic stage The stage of HIV infection in which the infected person shows no symptoms. (p. 585)
etapa asintomática Etapa de la infección del VIH durante la cual la persona infectada no muestra síntomas.

atherosclerosis A condition in which an artery wall hardens and thickens due to plaque buildup. (p. 300)
ateroesclerosis Trastorno caracterizado por el endurecimiento y engrosamiento de las paredes de una arteria debido a la acumulación de placas.

atrium An upper chamber of the heart that receives blood from the rest of the body. (p. 293)
aurícula Cada una de las dos cámaras superiores del corazón que reciben la sangre proveniente del resto del cuerpo.

atrophy A condition in which muscles that cannot contract or are not used often weaken and shrink. (p. 273)
atrofia Condición en la cual se debilitan y se encogen aquellos músculos que no se usan o que han perdido su capacidad de contracción.

audiologist A professional who evaluates hearing and treats hearing loss. (p. 363)
audiólogo Profesional que evalúa la audición y trata la pérdida de la misma.

autonomy An individual's independence from parents and family that strengthens during adolescence. (p. 525)
autonomía Independencia de un individuo respecto a sus padres y familiares, que se acrecienta durante la adolescencia.

bacteria Simple, single-celled microorganisms. (p. 548)
bacterias Microorganismos unicelulares simples.

barbiturates A class of depressant drugs; also called sedative-hypnotics. (p. 440)
barbitúrico Tipo de droga depresora; también llamada sedativo o hipnótico.

basal metabolic rate (BMR) The rate at which a person uses energy when the body is at rest. (p. 220)
tasa de metabolismo basal Tasa a la que una persona consume energía en estado de reposo.

B cell A lymphocyte that produces antibodies. (p. 555)
célula B Tipo de linfocito que produce anticuerpos.

bile A substance produced by the liver that aids in digestion by breaking up large fat droplets. (p. 245)
bilis Sustancia producida por el hígado que descompone la grasa, facilitando así la digestión.

binge drinking The consumption of excessive amounts of alcohol at one sitting. (p. 385)
ingestión excesiva de alcohol Consumir cantidades excesivas de alcohol de una vez.

binge eating disorder An eating disorder in which a person regularly has an uncontrollable urge to eat large amounts of food, but without purging. (p. 93)
ingestión excesiva de alimentos Trastorno de la alimentación en el que un individuo siente necesidad de consumir grandes cantidades de alimentos, sin purgarse luego.

biodegradable waste Waste that can be broken down by microorganisms. (p. 677)
desecho biodegradable Desecho que puede ser descompuesto por microorganismos.

biopsy The removal of a small piece of tissue to examine it for signs of cancer. (p. 612)
biopsia Extracción de una pequeña muestra de tejido para examinarla con el fin de determinar la presencia de cáncer.

blackout A period of time that an intoxicated person cannot recall. (p. 381)
pérdida del conocimiento Período que una persona intoxicada no puede recordar.

blastocyst A hollow, spherical structure made up of about 50–100 cells, formed when an embryo divides and grows. (p. 489)
blastocisto Estructura hueca de forma esférica, con aproximadamente 50–100 células, que se forma al crecer y dividirse el embrión.

blended family Consists of a biological parent, a step-parent, and the children of one or both parents. (p. 115)
familia mixta Unidad familiar que consiste en uno de los padres biológicos, un padrastro o una madrastra y el (los) hijo(s) de uno o ambos padres.

blood alcohol concentration (BAC) The amount of alcohol in a person's blood, expressed as a percentage. (p. 382)
concentración de alcohol en la sangre (CAS) Cantidad de alcohol en la sangre de una persona, expresada como porcentaje.

blood pressure The force with which blood pushes against the walls of blood vessels. (p. 296)
presión sanguínea Fuerza ejercida por la sangre contra las paredes de las venas y arterias.

body composition A measure of how much body fat a person has, as compared to muscle and bone. (pp. 227, 318)
composición corporal Proporción de tejido graso en el cuerpo con respecto al tejido muscular y a los huesos.

body language The silent messages people communicate through posture, gestures, facial expressions, and body movements. (p. 139)
lenguaje corporal Forma de comunicación no verbal que las personas realizan a través de las posturas, los gestos, las expresiones faciales y los movimientos del cuerpo.

body mass index (BMI) A ratio of a person's weight to height. BMI = [Weight (in pounds)/Height (in inches)^2] $\times$ 703. (p. 227)
índice de masa corporal (IMC) Relación entre el peso y la altura de una persona. IMC = [Peso (en libras)/Altura (en pulgadas)^2] $\times$ 703.

brain stem The area of the brain between the cerebellum and the spinal cord; it controls automatic functions such as heartbeat and blood pressure. (p. 281)
tallo cerebral Área del cerebro que se encuentra entre el cerebelo y la médula espinal; controla las funciones autónomas, como los latidos del corazón y la presión sanguínea.

bronchitis An infection that causes the mucous membranes lining the bronchi to become inflamed. (p. 310)
bronquitis Infección que causa la inflamación de las membranas mucosas de los bronquios.

bulimia An eating disorder in which a person has uncontrolled eating binges followed by purging. (p. 92)
bulimia Trastorno de la alimentación en el cual una persona ingiere comida en exceso y luego se purga.

bullying The use of threats or physical force to intimidate and control another person. (p. 169)
intimidación Uso de amenazas o de la fuerza física para amedrentar o controlar a otra persona.

calorie Unit for the amount of energy released when nutrients are broken down. (p. 193)
caloría Unidad que expresa la cantidad de energía liberada cuando el cuerpo descompone los nutrientes.

cancer A group of diseases involving the uncontrolled growth and spread of abnormal cells. (p. 609)
cáncer Grupo de enfermedades caracterizadas por el crecimiento y la diseminación rápida y descontrolada de células anormales.

capillary The smallest type of blood vessel in the body. (p. 295)
capilar Vaso sanguíneo más pequeño del cuerpo.

capsizing The overturning of a boat. (p. 706)
zozobra Voltearse o irse a pique una embarcación.

carbohydrate A nutrient made of carbon, hydrogen, and oxygen and that supplies energy. (p. 194)
carbohidrato Nutriente compuesto por carbón, hidrógeno y oxígeno, y que suministra energía.

carbohydrate loading The practice of greatly increasing carbohydrate intake and decreasing exercise on the days immediately before a competition. (p. 236)
carga de carbohidratos Práctica que consiste en ingerir grandes cantidades de carbohidratos y disminuir la cantidad de ejercicio durante los días previos a una competencia atlética.

carbon monoxide A poisonous, colorless, odorless gas produced when substances are burned. (p. 409)
monóxido de carbono Gas venenoso, incoloro e inodoro, que se produce durante la combustión.

carcinogen A substance that is known to cause cancer. (pp. 408, 610)
carcinógeno Sustancia que causa cáncer.

cardiac muscle Involuntary muscle that is found only in the heart. (p. 272)
músculo cardiaco Músculo involuntario que sólo se halla en el corazón.

cardiovascular disease A disease of the heart and blood vessels. (p. 602)
enfermedad cardiovascular Enfermedad del corazón y los vasos sanguíneos.

cartilage A tough, supportive tissue that is softer and more flexible than bone. (p. 268)
cartílago Resistente tejido que sirve de sostén y que es más blando y flexible que el hueso.

catastrophe An unexpected event that threatens lives and may destroy property. (p. 58)
catástrofe Suceso inesperado que pone en peligro o produce pérdidas de vidas y propiedades.

cementum The hard material that covers a tooth's root. (p. 342)
cemento Material duro que cubre la raíz de los dientes.

cerebellum A part of the brain that coordinates movements and balance. (p. 281)
cerebelo Parte del cerebro que coordina los movimientos y el equilibrio.

cerebral hemorrhage A type of stroke that occurs when an artery located in the cerebrum, the main part of the brain, bursts. (p. 605)
hemorragia cerebral Tipo de apoplejía que ocurre por la rotura de una arteria en el cerebro.

cerebrum A part of the brain that contains several specialized regions that receive messages from sense organs, and control movement, memory, communication, and reasoning. (p. 281)
cerebro Parte superior del encéfalo que contiene varias regiones especializadas que reciben mensajes de los órganos sensoriales; además, controla el movimiento, la memoria, la comunicación y el razonamiento.

certified nurse-midwife A nurse who is trained to deliver babies. (p. 498)
enfermera-comadrona certificada Enfermera entrenada para atender partos.

cesarean section A surgical method of birth. (p. 501)
cesárea Parto realizado a través de una intervención quirúrgica.

chancre A painless sore that appears during the first stage of syphilis infection. (p. 582)
chancro Llaga indolora que aparece en la primera etapa de la sífilis.

chewing tobacco A smokeless tobacco product that consists of poor-quality, ground tobacco leaves and is placed between the gum and the cheek. (p. 403)
tabaco de mascar Producto derivado del tabaco, hecho a partir de hojas de tabaco de baja calidad; se coloca entre la encía y la mejilla.

chlamydia A very common sexually transmitted infection caused by bacteria. (p. 579)
linfogranuloma venéreo Infección de transmisión sexual muy común, causada por una bacteria.

cholesterol A waxy, fatlike substance that is found only in animal products. (p. 197)
colesterol Sustancia grasosa y cerosa que se halla sólo en los productos de origen animal.

chorionic villus sampling A prenatal test in which a piece of the developing placenta is removed and tested for inherited disorders. (p. 495)
muestra de vellosidad coriónica Prueba prenatal que consiste en sacar un fragmento de la placenta y examinarlo para detectar trastornos hereditarios.

chromosomes The tiny structures found within cells that carry information about inherited characteristics. (p. 478)
cromosomas Estructuras diminutas que se encuentran en las células y que contienen información sobre las características hereditarias.

chronic bronchitis A condition in which the bronchi in the lungs are constantly swollen and clogged with mucus. (p. 411)
bronquitis crónica Trastorno en el que los bronquios se inflaman y se obstruyen constantemente por mucosidad.

chronic disease A disease that persists for a long period or recurs throughout life; usually caused by behavioral, environmental, or hereditary factors. (p. 602)
enfermedad crónica Enfermedad que persiste por un largo período o que aparece repetidas veces durante la vida; generalmente es causada por factores ambientales, hereditarios o de conducta.

chronic obstructive pulmonary disease (COPD) A disease that results in a gradual loss of lung function. (p. 411)
enfermedad pulmonar obstructiva crónica (EPOC) Enfermedad que causa que los pulmones pierdan gradualmente la capacidad de realizar sus funciones.

chyme A thick mixture of food and gastric juices formed in the stomach. (p. 244)
quimo Mezcla líquida espesa de alimentos y jugo gástrico que se forma en el estómago.

circadian rhythm The body's internal system that regulates behavior patterns during a 24-hour cycle. (p. 366)
ritmo circadiano Sistema interno del cuerpo que regula los patrones de conducta durante un ciclo de 24 horas.

cirrhosis A disease of the liver in which it becomes filled with useless scar tissue; cirrhosis may lead to liver failure. (p. 387)
cirrosis Enfermedad del hígado en la cual éste se llena de tejido cicatrizal; la cirrosis puede conllevar a que el hígado deje de funcionar.

civic engagement The level of involvement that average citizens have in the planning and decision-making that affects their community. (p. 684)
participación cívica Nivel de participación que los ciudadanos comunes tienen en la planificación y la toma de decisiones que afectan a su comunidad.

clinical depression The symptoms of this disorder are feeling sad and hopeless for months, being unable to enjoy activities that were once a source of pleasure, and sometimes being unable to accomplish daily tasks. (p. 94)
depresión clínica Trastorno en el cual una persona experimenta durante meses sentimientos de tristeza y desesperación, que le impiden disfrutar actividades que antes le causaban placer, y que incluso pueden impedirle realizar sus actividades cotidianas.

clinical psychologist A mental health professional who is trained to recognize and treat behavior that is not normal. (p. 103)
psicólogo(a) clínico(a) Profesional en el campo de la salud mental, especializado en identificar y tratar conductas que no son normales.

clique A narrow, exclusive group of people with similar backgrounds or interests. (p. 145)
corrillo Grupo pequeño y exclusivo de personas, con orígenes o intereses similares.

club drugs Drugs that first gained popularity at dance clubs and raves. (p. 446)
drogas de clubes Drogas que inicialmente se vuelven populares en clubes y fiestas.

cluster suicides A series of suicides that occur within a short period of time in the same peer group or community. (p. 97)
suicidio colectivo Serie de suicidios que ocurren en un breve período de tiempo dentro de un mismo grupo de iguales o una misma comunidad.

cocaine A drug that is a powerful but short-acting stimulant. (p. 443)
cocaína Droga que tiene un poderoso, pero breve efecto estimulante.

cochlea A coiled, fluid-filled tube in the inner ear that contains cells that sense sound vibrations. (p. 361)
cóclea Tubo en forma de espiral, lleno de líquido, que se encuentra en el oído interno y que contiene células sensibles a las vibraciones sonoras.

coma A prolonged period of deep unconsciousness. (p. 284)
coma Período prolongado de profunda inconsciencia.

communication The process of sharing information, thoughts, or feelings. (p. 136)
comunicación Proceso mediante el cual se transmite información, ideas o sentimientos.

community service organization An official community group whose members act or unite for a common purpose. (p. 665)
organización de servicio comunitario Grupo comunitario oficial cuyos miembros se unen o trabajan para alcanzar un objetivo común.

compromise The willingness of each person to give up something in order to reach agreement. (p. 140)
concesión Sacrificio que hacen una o varias personas para llegar a un acuerdo.

compulsion An unreasonable need to behave in a certain way to prevent a feared outcome. (p. 85)
compulsión Necesidad irracional de comportarse de determinada manera para evitar que suceda algo que se teme vaya a ocurrir.

concussion A bruiselike injury to the brain caused by brain tissue hitting the skull during a collision. (p. 284)
conmoción cerebral Lesión que sufre el cerebro cuando choca contra el cráneo durante una colisión.

consensus-building The process by which a community arrives at an agreed-upon vision for the future. (p. 685)
búsqueda de consenso Proceso mediante el cual una comunidad se pone de acuerdo sobre una visión en relación con el futuro de la misma.

conservation The protection and preservation of the natural environment by managing natural resources wisely and developing land for new construction responsibly. (p. 682)
conservación Protección y preservación de la naturaleza mediante el uso prudente de los recursos y el desarrollo responsable de nuevas áreas urbanas.

consumer Someone who buys products or services for personal use. (p. 18)
consumidor Persona que compra productos o servicios para su uso personal.

continuum A gradual progression through many stages between one extreme and another. (p. 4)
contínuum Progresión gradual, a través de muchas etapas, de un extremo a otro.

cooperation Working together toward a common goal. (p. 139)
cooperación Acción de trabajar unidos con un objetivo común.

copayment A small fee that a patient with managed care health insurance may have to pay when visiting a doctor. (p. 645)
pago parcial Pequeña suma que en ciertos casos debe pagar el paciente que tiene seguro médico cuando consulta un médico.

coping strategy A way of dealing with an uncomfortable or unbearable feeling or situation. (p. 48)
estrategia de manejo de una situación conflictiva Forma de hacer frente a las situaciones o sentimientos incómodos o insoportables.

cornea Clear tissue that covers the front of the eye. (p. 356)
córnea Tejido transparente que cubre la parte delantera del ojo.

cross-contamination The spread of microorganisms from one food to another food. (p. 251)
contaminación cruzada Propagación de microorganismos de un alimento a otro.

cross-training Participating in a wide variety of activities. (p. 326)
entrenamiento mixto Participación en una gran variedad de actividades.

culture Beliefs and patterns of behavior that are shared by a group of people and passed from generation to generation. (p. 7)
cultura Creencias y patrones de conducta comunes a un grupo de personas, que se transmiten de generación en generación.

cutting The use of a sharp object to intentionally cut or scratch one's body deep enough to bleed. (p. 96)
cortarse/automutilación Usar un objeto afilado para producir intencionalmente una herida sangrante en el cuerpo de uno mismo.

cyber bullying Bullying that takes place by e-mail, instant messaging, text messaging, or at Web sites. (p. 169)
intimidación cibernética Intimidación que se realiza a través del correo electrónico, de los mensajes instantáneos, de los mensajes de texto o en sitios de Internet.

Daily Values Recommendations that specify the amounts of certain nutrients that the average person should obtain each day. (p. 223)
Valores diarios de nutrición Conjunto de recomendaciones que indican la cantidad de ciertos nutrientes que una persona típica necesita consumir a diario.

date rape A rape that occurs during a date. (p. 151)
violación en una cita Violación que ocurre en el transcurso de una cita.

dating violence A pattern of emotional, physical, or sexual abuse that occurs in a dating relationship. (p. 150)
violencia en el noviazgo Patrón de maltrato emocional, físico o sexual que se presenta entre dos personas que son novios.

deductible A fixed amount that must be paid by the patient before traditional health insurance begins paying for covered procedures. (p. 646)
deducible Cantidad fija que debe pagar el paciente para que los seguros médicos tradicionales comiencen a cubrir el costo de algún procedimiento médico.

defense mechanism A coping strategy that helps protect a person from difficult feelings. (p. 48)
mecanismo de defensa Estrategia de manejo de una situación conflictiva con la que una persona se protege de las emociones negativas.

defensive driving A driving technique in which you constantly monitor other drivers around you. (p. 714)
conducir a la defensiva Técnica de manejo que consiste en observar atentamente lo que hacen los conductores de los autos que están alrededor del que uno conduce.

dehydration A serious reduction in the body's water content. (pp. 209, 333)
deshidratación Disminución pronunciada del contenido de agua del cuerpo.

dementia A disorder characterized by loss of mental abilities, abnormal behaviors, and personality changes. (p. 535)
demencia Trastorno caracterizado por comportamientos anormales, cambios en la personalidad y la pérdida de facultades mentales.

dentin The living material beneath enamel and cementum that makes up most of a tooth. (p. 342)
dentina Tejido sensible que se halla debajo del esmalte y el cemento, y que forma la mayor parte del diente.

dependence The condition that results when the brain develops a chemical need for a drug and cannot function normally without it. (p. 388)
dependencia Estado al que llega una persona cuando su cerebro desarrolla la necesidad química por una sustancia sin la cual ya no puede funcionar normalmente.

depressant A drug that slows brain and body reactions. (pp. 374, 440)
sedativo Droga que desacelera las funciones del cerebro y las reacciones corporales.

depression An emotional state in which a person feels extremely sad and hopeless. (p. 86)
depresión Estado emocional en el que una persona siente tristeza intensa y desesperación.

dermatologist A doctor who treats skin problems. (p. 350)
dermatólogo(a) Médico que trata las enfermedades de la piel.

dermis A tough, elastic layer of skin that lies below the epidermis. (p. 348)
dermis Capa de la piel, resistente y elástica, que se halla debajo de la epidermis.

detoxification The process of removing all alcohol or other drugs from a person's body. (p. 391)
desintoxicación Procedimiento para eliminar todo el alcohol u otras drogas del cuerpo de una persona.

developing nation A country with a weak economy and a low standard of living. (p. 656)
país en vías de desarrollo Cualquier país con una economía débil y un bajo nivel de vida.

diabetes A disease in which the body's ability to use glucose (blood sugar) is impaired. (p. 614)
diabetes Enfermedad caracterizada por la disminución de la capacidad del cuerpo para aprovechar la glucosa (azúcar de la sangre).

diagnosis A doctor's opinion of the nature or cause of a medical condition. (p. 634)
diagnóstico Opinión de un médico sobre la naturaleza o causa de un problema de salud.

dialysis A treatment for kidney failure in which a machine is used to filter wastes from blood. (p. 258)
diálisis Tratamiento que se utiliza cuando los riñones dejan de funcionar y en el cual se usa una máquina para filtrar las sustancias nocivas de la sangre.

diaphragm A dome-shaped muscle below the lungs that is involved in the breathing process. (p. 308)
diafragma Músculo en forma de cúpula, ubicado debajo de los pulmones, que interviene en la respiración.

Dietary Guidelines for Americans A document developed by nutrition experts to promote health and to help people reduce their risk for heart disease, cancer, and diabetes through diet and physical activity. (p. 210)
Normas dietéticas para los estadounidenses Documento elaborado por expertos en nutrición para promover la buena salud y ayudar a las personas a reducir el riesgo de sufrir enfermedades del corazón, cáncer y diabetes a través de la dieta y la actividad física.

dietary supplement Any product that contains one or more vitamins, minerals, herbs, or other dietary substances lacking in the diet. (p. 334)
suplemento dietético Cualquier producto que contenga una o más vitaminas, minerales, hierbas u otras sustancias que no se obtienen a través de la dieta.

digestion The process by which the digestive system breaks down food into molecules that the body can use. (p. 242)
digestión Proceso mediante el cual el sistema digestivo descompone los alimentos en moléculas que el cuerpo puede utilizar.

disability Any physical or mental impairment that limits or reduces normal activities. (p. 623)
discapacidad Impedimento físico o mental que limita o reduce la capacidad para realizar actividades normales.

discrimination The unfair treatment of a person or group based on prejudice. (p. 172)
discriminación Trato injusto hacia una persona o un grupo de personas debido a prejuicios que se tienen contra las mismas.

dislocation An injury that occurs when the ends of the bones in a joint are forced out of their normal positions. (p. 271)
dislocación Lesión que sucede cuando los extremos de los huesos dentro de una articulación son desencajados de su posición normal.

distress Stress that produces negative effects. (p. 56)
estrés negativo Estrés que produce efectos dañinos.

divorce A legal agreement to end a marriage. (p. 113)
divorcio Acuerdo legal para poner fin a un matrimonio.

domestic abuse The abuse of one spouse by the other. (p. 121)
violencia doméstica Abuso de uno de los cónyuges por parte del otro.

driving while intoxicated (DWI) The charge given to a driver over age 21 caught driving with a BAC that exceeds 0.08 percent, or to a driver under the age of 21 with any detectable BAC. (p. 384)
manejar en estado de intoxicación Delito del que se acusa a un conductor de un vehículo mayor de 21 años si es sorprendido conduciendo con una CAS superior al 0.08 por ciento, o a un conductor menor de 21 años con cualquier nivel detectable de alcohol en la sangre.

drug A chemical substance that is taken to cause changes in a person's body or behavior. (p. 374)
droga Sustancia química que se toma para alterar el funcionamiento del cuerpo o el comportamiento de una persona.

drug abuse The intentional improper or unsafe use of a drug. (p. 427)
abuso de drogas Uso intencionalmente inapropiado o peligroso de una droga.

drug antagonism A condition that occurs when one drug's effect is canceled out or reduced by another. (p. 430)
antagonismo entre drogas Condición que ocurre cuando el efecto de una droga es cancelado o reducido por el efecto de otra.

drug misuse The improper use of medicines—either prescription or over-the-counter drugs. (p. 427)
abuso de medicamentos Uso inapropiado de medicamentos, ya sean éstos de venta por prescripción o sin ella.

drug synergism A condition that occurs when drugs interact to produce effects greater than those that each drug would produce alone. (p. 430)
sinergismo entre drogas Condición que se presenta cuando distintas drogas interactúan para producir efectos superiores a los que produciría cualquiera de ellas por separado.

E

eardrum The membrane at the end of the ear canal that passes vibrations to the middle ear. (p. 360)
tímpano Membrana delgada, ubicada al final del canal auricular, que transmite las vibraciones sonoras hasta el oído medio.

eating disorder A mental disorder that reveals itself through abnormal behaviors related to food. (p. 90)
trastorno de la alimentación Trastorno mental que se manifiesta a través de conductas anormales en relación a la comida.

ectopic pregnancy A condition resulting from the implantation of the blastocyst in a location in the abdomen other than the uterus. (p. 496)
embarazo ectópico Condición causada por la implantación del blastocisto en una zona del abdomen que no sea el útero.

eczema A condition in which an area of irritated skin becomes red, swollen, hot, and itchy. (p. 350)
eczema Afección caracterizada por el enrojecimiento, la inflamación, el calentamiento y el escozor de un área de la piel irritada.

ejaculation The ejection of semen from the penis. (p. 466)
eyaculación Eyección del semen por el pene.

electrocution Death from direct contact with electricity. (p. 697)
electrocución Muerte causada por el contacto directo con la corriente eléctrica.

electrolyte A dissolved substance that regulates many processes in cells. (p. 208)
electrolito Sustancia disuelta que regula muchos procesos en las células.

embryo The stage of human development from the two-cell stage until about nine weeks after fertilization. (p. 489)
embrión Etapa del desarrollo humano que tiene lugar a partir de la división del cigoto en dos células hasta aproximadamente la novena semana después de la fecundación.

emerging disease An infectious disease that has become more common within the last 20 years or threatens to become more common in the near future. (p. 566)
enfermedad emergente Enfermedad infecciosa que se ha hecho más común en los últimos 20 años o que amenaza con volverse más común en el futuro inmediato.

emotion A reaction to a situation that involves the mind, body, and behavior. (p. 44)
emoción Reacción ante una situación, en la que intervienen la mente, el cuerpo y la conducta.

emotional abuse The nonphysical mistreatment of a person. (p. 122)
maltrato emocional Todo maltrato que no sea de índole físico.

emotional health The aspect of health that refers to how you react to events in your life. You are emotionally healthy when the feelings you experience are appropriate responses to events. (p. 3)
  salud emocional Aspecto de la salud que se refiere a cómo una persona reacciona a los sucesos que ocurren en su vida. Una persona goza de buena salud emocional si los sentimientos que experimenta son respuestas apropiadas a dichos sucesos.

emotional intimacy The openness, sharing, affection, and trust that can develop in a close relationship. (p. 154)
  intimidad emocional Franqueza, comunicación intensa, afecto y confianza que se desarrollan en una relación íntima.

emotional maturity The state of being fully developed in the emotional sense. (p. 530)
  madurez emocional Estado de desarrollo emocional completo.

empathy The ability to understand another person's thoughts or feelings. (p. 126)
  empatía Habilidad para comprender los sentimientos o ideas de otra persona.

emphysema A disorder in which damaged alveoli in the lungs can no longer take in adequate oxygen and eliminate carbon dioxide. (p. 412)
  enfisema Trastorno respiratorio en el que los alvéolos del pulmón se dañan y no son capaces de absorber suficiente cantidad de oxígeno ni de expeler suficiente cantidad de dióxido de carbono.

enamel The material, which is harder than bone, that covers a tooth's crown. (p. 342)
  esmalte Material más duro que el hueso, que cubre la corona de los dientes.

endocrine gland A gland that produces and releases chemical substances that signal changes in other parts of the body. (p. 460)
  glándula endocrina Glándula que produce y segrega sustancias químicas que regulan cambios en otras partes del cuerpo.

endorphins Chemicals that block pain messages from reaching brain cells and produce feelings of pleasure. (p. 317)
  endorfinas Sustancias químicas que impiden la llegada de sensaciones de dolor a las células del cerebro y que producen una sensación de placer.

environment All of the physical and social conditions that surround a person and can influence that person's health. (p. 7)
  ambiente Conjunto de condiciones físicas y sociales que rodean a una persona y que pueden afectar su salud.

enzyme A chemical that speeds up reactions in the body. (p. 242)
  enzima Sustancia química que acelera las reacciones del cuerpo.

epidemic An unusually high occurrence of a disease in a certain place during a certain time period. (p. 566)
  epidemia Enfermedad de la que se presenta un número inusualmente alto de casos en determinado lugar durante determinado período.

epidemiology The study of disease among populations. (p. 649)
  epidemiología El estudio de las enfermedades en las poblaciones.

epidermis The outermost layer of skin. (p. 348)
  epidermis Capa más externa de la piel.

epiglottis A flap of tissue that seals off the trachea when food or liquid is swallowed. (p. 243)
  epiglotis Lámina de tejido que ocluye la tráquea cuando se tragan alimentos sólidos o líquidos.

epilepsy A condition in which a person is prone to seizures. (p. 286)
  epilepsia Trastorno que causa que la persona sufra convulsiones.

escalate To grow more intense. (p. 175)
  intensificar Volverse algo más vigoroso.

estrogen The female sex hormone that signals certain physical changes at puberty and controls the maturation of eggs. (p. 469)
  estrógeno Hormona sexual femenina que regula ciertos cambios físicos durante la pubertad, así como la maduración de los óvulos.

eustress Stress that produces positive effects. (p. 56)
  estrés positivo Estrés que produce efectos beneficiosos.

excretion The process by which the body collects and removes wastes. (p. 254)
  excreción Proceso mediante el cual el cuerpo recoge y elimina desechos.

extended family A group of close relatives living together or near each other. (p. 114)
  familia extensa Grupo de parientes cercanos que viven juntos o cerca unos de otros.

eye contact Looking directly into another person's eyes; meeting another person's gaze. (p. 139)
  contacto visual Acto de mirar a otra persona directamente a los ojos o de mantener la mirada de otra persona.

F

fad diet A popular diet that may help a person lose or gain weight but without proper regard for nutrition and other health issues. (p. 230)
dieta de moda Régimen alimentario popular que puede ayudar a una persona a perder o ganar peso, pero que no respeta los conceptos de nutrición y otros aspectos relativos a la salud.

fallopian tubes The passageways that carry eggs away from the ovaries. (p. 470)
trompas de Falopio Tubos que conducen los óvulos fuera de los ovarios.

fat A nutrient made of carbon, hydrogen, and oxygen; supplies energy, forms cells, maintains body temperature, and protects nerves. (p. 196)
grasa Nutriente compuesto de carbono, hidrógeno y oxígeno; suminista energía, ayuda a formar las células y mantener la temperatura corporal, y protege los nervios.

fermentation The process that creates alcohol, in which microorganisms called yeast feed on sugars. (p. 374)
fermentación Proceso que produce alcohol, en el cual unos microorganismos llamados levadura se alimentan de azúcares.

fertilization The process of a sperm cell joining with an egg. (p. 464)
fecundación Proceso mediante el cual un espermatozoide se une con un óvulo.

fetal alcohol syndrome A group of birth defects caused by the effects of alcohol on an unborn child.
síndrome alcohólico fetal Conjunto de defectos congénitos causados por los efectos del alcohol sobre el feto. (p. 387)

fetus The stage of human development from the third month after fertilization until birth. (p. 491)
feto Etapa del desarrollo humano que tiene lugar a partir del tercer mes después de la fecundación hasta el nacimiento.

fiber A type of complex carbohydrate that is found in plants and is necessary for the proper functioning of the digestive system. (p. 195)
fibra Tipo de carbohidrato complejo que se halla en las plantas y que es necesario para el buen funcionamiento del sistema digestivo.

fibrillation A life-threatening arrhythmia in which the heart twitches rapidly in an uncoordinated fashion. (p. 604)
fibrilación Tipo de arritmia del corazón que pone en peligro la vida, en la que el corazón se contrae rápida y descoordinadamente.

fight-or-flight response The initial reaction of the body to stress during the alarm stage. (p. 60)
respuesta de lucha o escape Respuesta inicial del cuerpo al estrés durante la reacción de alarma.

FITT formula A fitness plan that depends on four factors of exercise: frequency, intensity, time, and type.
fórmula FIDT Plan de aptitud física que se basa en cuatro factores del régimen de ejercicio: frecuencia, intensidad, duración y tipo. (p. 326)

flammable material Any material that catches fire easily and burns quickly. (p. 696)
material inflamable Cualquier material capaz de incendiarse con facilidad y quemarse rápidamente.

follicle A skin structure in which a strand of hair grows and oil is secreted. (p. 348)
folículo Estructura de la piel en la cual crece un pelo y se segrega grasa.

food allergy The immune system's response to the proteins in certain foods. (p. 235)
alergia alimentaria Respuesta del sistema inmune a las proteínas de ciertos alimentos.

foodborne illness An illness that results from consuming a food or drink that contains either a poison or a disease-causing microorganism. (p. 250)
intoxicación alimentaria Enfermedad causada por el consumo de comidas o bebidas que contienen sustancias dañinas o microorganismos causantes de enfermedades.

food intolerance The inability to digest a particular food or food additive. (p. 235)
intolerancia alimentaria Incapacidad para digerir determinados alimentos o aditivos alimentarios.

fossil fuels Energy-rich substances mined from deep in the earth, including coal, oil, and natural gas. (p. 672)
combustibles fósiles Sustancias ricas en energía, como el carbón, el petróleo y el gas natural, que se extraen del interior de la tierra.

foster family A family in which an adult or a couple cares for children whose biological parents are unable to care for them. (p. 115)
familia adoptiva Familia en la que un adulto o una pareja se encarga de niños cuyos padres biológicos no pueden cuidarlos.

fracture A break in a bone. (p. 270)
fractura Rotura de un hueso.

fraud An illegal act that involves telling lies to obtain money or property. (p. 22)
fraude Acción ilegal en la que se miente para obtener dinero o propiedades.

friendship A relationship based on mutual trust, acceptance, and common interests or values. (p. 141)
amistad Relación basada en la confianza y la aceptación mutua entre personas que comparten intereses o valores semejantes.

fungi Organisms such as yeasts, molds, and mushrooms that grow best in warm, dark, moist areas. (p. 549)
hongos Organismos que incluyen las levaduras, los mohos y los champiñones, que crecen mejor en áreas cálidas, húmedas y con sombra.

gallbladder The organ that stores bile and releases it into the small intestine. (p. 245)
vesícula biliar Órgano que almacena la bilis y la segrega al intestino delgado.

gender A term that refers to whether you are male or female. Gender is part of heredity. (p. 6)
sexo Condición que distingue a las personas como masculinas o femeninas. El sexo es parte de la herencia.

gender roles The behaviors and attitudes that are socially acceptable as either masculine or feminine. (p. 143)
papeles sexuales Conductas y actitudes que son socialmente aceptables como masculinas o femeninas.

gene A section of a chromosome that determines or affects a characteristic, or trait. (p. 479)
gen Sección del cromosoma que determina alguna característica o rasgo.

genetic disorder A disorder caused by the inheritance of an abnormal gene or chromosome. (p. 480)
trastorno genético Trastorno hereditario causado por un gen o cromosoma anormal.

genital herpes A sexually transmitted infection caused by the herpes simplex virus. (p. 581)
herpes genital Infección de transmisión sexual causada por el virus del herpes simple.

gestational diabetes Diabetes that develops during pregnancy. (p. 496)
diabetes gestacional Diabetes que se desarrolla durante el embarazo.

glomerulus A cluster of tiny blood vessels in a nephron. (p. 256)
glomérulo Grupo de pequeños vasos sanguíneos que se encuentra en un nefrón.

goal A result that a person aims for and works hard to reach. (p. 2)
meta Resultado que una persona desea alcanzar y por el cual trabaja con dedicación.

gonorrhea A bacterial sexually transmitted infection that infects the urinary tract of males and females and the reproductive organs of females. (p. 580)
gonorrea Infección bacterial de transmisión sexual que infecta las vías urinarias del hombre y los órganos reproductores de la mujer.

grief A period of deep sorrow. (p. 44)
pesar Período de tristeza profunda.

habit A behavior that is repeated so often that it becomes almost automatic. (p. 9)
hábito Conducta que se repite tan frecuentemente que se vuelve casi automática.

halitosis Bad breath. (p. 344)
halitosis Mal aliento.

hallucinogen A drug that distorts perception, thought, and mood. (p. 443)
alucinógeno Droga que distorsiona la percepción, el pensamiento o el estado de ánimo.

hangover A term used to describe the aftereffects of drinking too much alcohol. (p. 383)
resaca Término usado para describir los efectos posteriores al consumo excesivo de alcohol.

harassment Unwanted remarks or actions that cause a person emotional or physical harm. (p. 168)
acoso Comentarios o acciones indeseables que causan daño emocional o físico a una persona.

hate violence Speech or behavior that is aimed at a person or group based on personal characteristics. (p. 172)
violencia debida al odio Pronunciamientos o conductas contra una persona o un grupo basados en las características personales de esa persona o ese grupo.

hazardous waste Waste that is either flammable, explosive, corrosive, or toxic to humans or other living things. (p. 677)
desecho peligroso Desecho que es inflamable, explosivo, corrosivo o tóxico para los seres humanos u otros seres vivos.

hazing Requiring a person to do degrading, risky, or illegal acts in order to join a group. (p. 170)
novatada El acto de exigirle a una persona que realice actos degradantes, peligrosos o ilegales como condición para formar parte de un grupo.

health The overall well-being of your body, mind, and your relationships with other people. (p. 2)
salud Bienestar general del cuerpo, de la mente y de la relación con otras personas.

healthcare system All available medical services, the ways in which people pay for medical care, and programs aimed at preventing disease and disability. (p. 634)
sistema de salud Conjunto de todos los servicios médicos, métodos de pago por la atención médica y programas dirigidos a prevenir enfermedades y discapacidades.

health code A state standard for factors that affect public health. (p. 652)
código de salud Norma fijada por el estado para regular los factores que afectan la salud.

health literacy The ability to gather, understand, and use health information to improve one's health. (p. 15)
educación sobre la salud Capacidad que tiene una persona de reunir, entender y usar información sobre la salud para mejorar su propia salud.

heart attack The condition that occurs when some of the tissue in the heart doesn't receive its normal blood supply and dies. (p. 604)
ataque de corazón Afección que ocurre cuando parte de los tejidos del corazón no reciben el suministro normal de sangre y mueren.

heredity All the traits that are passed from parent to child; the biological process of passing on, or transmitting, those traits. (pp. 6, 478)
herencia Todas aquellas características transmitidas de padres a hijos; proceso biológico de pasar, o transmitir, esas características.

heroin An illegal opiate made from morphine in a laboratory. (p. 441)
heroína Opiáceo ilegal que se produce a partir de la morfina en un laboratorio.

hierarchy of needs An arrangement of human needs in a pyramid with physical needs at the base and self-actualization at the top. (p. 40)
jerarquía de necesidades Organización de las necesidades humanas en forma de una pirámide, donde las necesidades físicas se encuentran en la base y la autorrealización se encuentra en la cima.

high-density lipoprotein A substance that picks up excess cholesterol from body tissues and artery walls and carries it to the liver. (p. 300)
lipoproteína de alta densidad Sustancia que recoge el exceso de colesterol de los tejidos del cuerpo y las paredes arteriales y lo transporta al hígado.

histamine The chemical responsible for the symptoms of an allergy. (p. 616)
histamina Sustancia química responsable de los síntomas de la alergia.

HIV The human immunodeficiency virus, an incurable sexually transmitted infection that can lead to AIDS. (p. 584)
VIH Virus de inmunodeficiencia humana, una infección de transmisión sexual incurable que puede producir el SIDA.

HIV-positive A person who is diagnosed as being infected with HIV. (p. 594)
VIH-positivo Persona que se diagnostica como infectada con el VIH.

homeostasis The process of maintaining a steady state inside the body. (p. 208)
homeóstasis Proceso que permite mantener la estabilidad en el interior del cuerpo.

homicide The intentional killing of one person by another. (p. 162)
homicidio Acción de matar intencionalmente a otra persona.

hormone A chemical substance produced by an endocrine gland. (p. 461)
hormona Sustancia química producida por una glándula endocrina.

hospice A facility or program that provides physical, emotional, and spiritual care for dying people and support for their families. (p. 537)
hospicio para moribundos Programa o instituto que ofrece cuidados físicos, emocionales y espirituales a las personas moribundas y a sus familiares.

human papilloma virus A very common viral sexually transmitted infection. (p. 579)
virus del papiloma humano Infección viral de transmisión sexual muy común.

hunger A feeling of discomfort caused by the body's need for nutrients. (p. 220)
hambre Sensación de molestia causada por la necesidad del cuerpo de obtener nutrientes.

hypertension Blood pressure that is consistently 140/90 or greater. (p. 296)
hipertensión Presión arterial que se mantiene habitualmente por encima de 140/90.

hypothalamus An endocrine gland in the brain that is part of both the nervous and endocrine systems. (p. 461)
hipotálamo Glándula endocrina, ubicada en el cerebro, que forma parte de los sistemas nervioso y endocrino.

I

identity A sense of self. (p. 35)
identidad Sentido de individualidad de una persona.

illegal drug A chemical substance that people of any age may not lawfully manufacture, possess, buy, or sell. (p. 427)
droga ilegal Sustancia química cuya manufactura, posesión, compra o venta es ilegal para toda persona, sin importar su edad.

"I" message A statement that expresses your feelings, but does not blame or judge the other person. (p. 136)
mensaje "yo" Afirmación que expresa los sentimientos de una persona, sin culpar ni juzgar a la otra persona.

immune system The body's most sophisticated defense against pathogens. (p. 554)
sistema inmunológico La defensa más sofisticada que tiene el cuerpo contra los patógenos.

immunity The body's ability to destroy a pathogen that it has previously encountered before the pathogen is able to cause disease. (p. 554)
inmunidad Capacidad del cuerpo para destruir patógenos a los que ha sido expuesto previamente, antes de que éstos puedan causar enfermedades.

immunization An injection that causes the body to become immune to an infectious disease; also called a vaccination. (p. 556)
inmunización Inyección que fomenta que el cuerpo de una persona se vuelva inmune a una enfermedad infecciosa; también se la llama vacunación.

implantation The process in which the blastocyst attaches itself to the wall of the uterus. (p. 489)
implantación Proceso mediante el cual el blastocisto se adhiere a la pared del útero.

infatuation Feelings of intense attraction to another person. (p. 148)
enamoramiento Sentimiento de atracción intensa hacia otra persona.

infectious disease A disease caused by an organism or virus that enters and multiplies within the body.
enfermedad infecciosa Enfermedad causada por organismos o virus que entran y se multiplican en el cuerpo humano. (p. 548)

infertility The condition of being unable to reproduce.
infertilidad Incapacidad para reproducirse. (p. 468)

inflammation The body's general response to all kinds of injury. (p. 554)
inflamación Respuesta generalizada del cuerpo ante cualquier lesión.

inhalant A breathable chemical vapor that produces mind-altering effects. (p. 447)
inhalante Vapor químico que se puede aspirar por la nariz y que produce alteraciones psicotrópicas.

inpatient A patient who is required to stay in a hospital overnight or longer. (p. 638)
paciente internado Paciente que debe pasar una o más noches dentro de un hospital.

insomnia A disorder in which a person has trouble falling asleep or staying asleep. (p. 365)
insomnio Trastorno en el cual existe dificultad para conciliar el sueño o para permanecer dormido.

instigator A person who encourages fighting between others while staying out of the fight himself or herself. (p. 176)
instigador Persona que fomenta disputas entre otros sin involucrarse personalmente en las mismas.

insulin A hormone produced by the pancreas that stimulates body cells to take up and use blood sugar. (p. 614)
insulina Hormona producida por el páncreas que estimula las células del cuerpo a utilizar el azúcar en la sangre.

intolerance A lack of acceptance of another person's opinions, beliefs, or actions. (p. 172)
intolerancia Incapacidad para aceptar las opiniones, creencias o acciones de otra persona.

intoxication The state in which a person's mental and physical abilities are impaired by alcohol or another substance. (p. 380)
intoxicación Estado en el cual las habilidades mentales y físicas de una persona se ven afectadas por el alcohol u otra sustancia.

iris The structure that surrounds the pupil and regulates the amount of light that enters the eye. (p. 356)
iris Estructura que rodea la pupila y que regula la cantidad de luz que entra al ojo.

isokinetic exercise Exercise performed with machines that ensure muscles contract at a constant rate. (p. 321)
ejercicio isocinético Ejercicio realizado con la ayuda de máquinas que hacen que los músculos se contraigan a un ritmo constante.

isometric exercise Exercise in which muscles contract but very little body movement occurs. (p. 320)
ejercicio isométrico Ejercicio en el cual los músculos se contraen con muy poco movimiento del cuerpo.

isotonic exercise Exercise that involves contracting and relaxing muscles through the full range of their joint's motion. (p. 321)
ejercicio isotónico Ejercicio en el que se produce la contracción y relajación de los músculos al realizar el movimiento completo de la articulación.

joint A place in the body where two or more bones meet. (p. 268)
articulación Lugar del cuerpo en el que convergen dos o más huesos.

keratin A protein in dead skin cells of the epidermis that makes skin tough and waterproof. (p. 348)
queratina Proteína que se halla en las células muertas de la epidermis y que otorga a la piel resistencia e impermeabilidad.

kidney A major organ of excretion that filters wastes from the blood and produces urine. (p. 255)
riñón Importante órgano de excreción que filtra las sustancias tóxicas de la sangre y produce orina.

labor The work performed by the mother's body to push the fetus out at the end of pregnancy. (p. 499)
trabajo de parto Función realizada por el cuerpo de la madre al final del embrazo para expulsar el feto.

landfill A permanent storage area where garbage and other wastes are deposited and covered with soil. (p. 678)
relleno sanitario Área en la que se depositan basura u otros desechos de manera permanente para después cubrirlos con tierra.

learned emotion An emotion whose expression depends on the social environment in which a person grows up. (p. 46)
emoción adquirida Emoción cuya expresión depende del ambiente social en el que crece una persona.

lens A flexible structure in the eye that focuses light on the retina. (p. 357)
cristalino Estructura flexible del ojo que enfoca la luz sobre la retina.

leukoplakia White patches on the tongue or lining of the mouth that may become cancerous. (p. 414)
leucoplasia Placas blancas que se forman en la lengua o en el interior de la boca y que pueden llegar a ser cancerosas.

life expectancy The number of years a person can expect to live. (p. 2)
esperanza de vida Cantidad de años que una persona puede esperar vivir.

lifelong fitness The ability to stay healthy and fit as you age. (p. 324)
aptitud física vitalicia Capacidad para mantenerse saludable y tener buenas condiciones físicas a medida que se envejece.

ligament A strong, fibrous band that holds bones together at a joint. (p. 269)
ligamento Tejido duro y fibroso, en forma de banda, que mantiene unidos los huesos en las articulaciones.

low birthweight A newborn weight of less than 5.5 pounds. (p. 502)
bajo peso al nacer En el recién nacido, peso inferior a las 5.5 libras.

low-density lipoprotein A substance that carries cholesterol to body tissues for storage; "bad" cholesterol. (p. 300)
lipoproteína de baja densidad Sustancia que transporta colesterol a los tejidos del cuerpo para almacenarlo; también llamada colesterol "malo".

lymphatic system A network of vessels that collects fluid from body tissues and returns it to the bloodstream; contains much of the immune system. (p. 556)
sistema linfático Red de vasos que recoge fluido de los tejidos del cuerpo y lo devuelve al torrente sanguíneo; contiene la mayoría de los componentes del sistema inmunológico.

lymphocyte A type of white blood cell that carries out functions of the immune system. (p. 554)
linfocito Tipo de glóbulo blanco que realiza diversas funciones en el sistema inmunológico.

M

macular degeneration A condition affecting the retina of the eye; the leading cause of vision loss in older Americans. (p. 623)
degeneración macular Afección de la retina del ojo; es la primera causa de pérdida de la visión entre los estadounidenses de la tercera edad.

mainstream smoke Smoke that is exhaled from a smoker's lungs. (p. 414)
humo directo Humo de tabaco que el fumador espira de sus pulmones.

malignant The term used to describe a cancerous tumor. (p. 609)
　maligno Término usado para describir los tumores cancerosos.

malocclusion A condition in which the upper and lower teeth do not meet properly. (p. 343)
　maloclusión Condición en la que los dientes superiores e inferiores no hacen contacto de forma adecuada.

mammogram An X-ray of the breast that may detect breast cancer. (p. 475)
　mamografía Radiografía de la mama que permite detectar el cáncer de mama.

marijuana A drug made from the leaves, stems, and flowering tops of the hemp plant. (p. 445)
　marihuana Droga producida a partir de las hojas, los tallos y las ramas del cáñamo.

marrow The soft tissue that fills spaces inside bones. (p. 268)
　médula ósea Tejido blando que se encuentra en el interior de los huesos.

media Forms of communication that provide news and entertainment. (p. 8)
　medios de comunicación Formas de comunicación que ofrecen noticias y entretenimiento.

mediation A process for resolving conflicts that involves a neutral third party. (p. 183)
　mediación Proceso mediante el cual se resuelven conflictos con la ayuda de una tercera persona neutral.

medical history A record of your present and past health as well as the health of members of your family. (p. 643)
　historial clínico Archivo de datos sobre el estado de salud actual y pasado de una persona, así como de los miembros de su familia.

medical specialist A doctor who has received additional training in a particular branch of medicine. (p. 635)
　médico especialista Médico con entrenamiento adicional en una rama específica de la medicina.

medicine A legal drug that helps the body fight injury, illness, or disease. (p. 426)
　medicamento Droga legal que ayuda al cuerpo a combatir lesiones, enfermedades u otros trastornos físicos.

melanin A pigment released in the epidermis that gives skin color and causes skin to tan. (p. 348)
　melanina Pigmento liberado en la epidermis, responsable del color de la piel y su capacidad para broncearse.

melanoma A serious form of skin cancer. (p. 349)
　melanoma Tipo grave de cáncer de piel.

meningitis An infection that causes inflammation of the membranes surrounding the brain and spinal cord. (p. 285)
　meningitis Infección que causa la inflamación de las membranas que rodean el cerebro y la médula espinal.

menopause The time of life during which the ovaries slow down their hormone production and no longer release mature eggs. (p. 471)
　menopausia Período de la vida en el que los ovarios disminuyen su producción de hormonas y dejan de liberar óvulos maduros.

menstrual cycle The process during which an ovary releases a mature egg that travels to the uterus; if the egg is not fertilized, the uterine lining is shed and a new cycle begins. (p. 471)
　ciclo menstrual Proceso mediante el cual el ovario libera un óvulo maduro que se dirige hacia el útero; si el óvulo no es fecundado, la capa uterina interna es expulsada y comienza un nuevo ciclo.

mental disorder An illness that affects the mind and reduces a person's ability to function, to adjust to change, or to get along with others. (p. 82)
　trastorno mental Enfermedad que afecta la mente y limita la capacidad de una persona para desempeñarse, adaptarse a los cambios o relacionarse con los demás.

mental health The state of being comfortable with yourself, with others, and with your surroundings. (p. 3)
　salud mental Estado en el cual la persona se siente bien consigo misma, con los demás y con el ambiente que la rodea.

mental rehearsal A technique used to practice an event without actually doing the event. (p. 71)
　práctica mental Técnica usada para prepararse para una actividad sin tener que realizarla.

metabolism The chemical process by which the body breaks down food to release energy. (p. 193)
　metabolismo Proceso químico mediante el cual el cuerpo descompone los alimentos para liberar energía.

metastasis The spread of cancer from where it first develops to other parts of the body. (p. 609)
　metástasis Propagación del cáncer desde el área donde se desarrolló originalmente a otras partes del cuerpo.

methamphetamine A stimulant that is related to amphetamines, but is even more powerful. (p. 442)
　metanfetamina Estimulante parecido a la anfetamina, pero de mayor potencia.

microorganism An organism that is so small it can only be seen through a microscope. (p. 548)
microorganismo Organismo de tamaño tan pequeño que sólo puede verse a través de un microscopio.

mineral A nutrient that occurs naturally in rocks or soil; needed by the body in small amounts. (p. 205)
mineral Nutriente que se halla naturalmente en las rocas o el suelo y que el cuerpo necesita sólo en pequeñas cantidades.

miscarriage The death of an embryo or fetus in the first 20 weeks of pregnancy. (p. 496)
aborto espontáneo Muerte de un embrión o feto en las primeras 20 semanas del embarazo.

mixed-use development City or town development in which homes are built close to businesses and schools. (p. 667)
urbanización mixta Desarrollo de pueblos o ciudades en los que las viviendas se construyen cerca de los negocios y las escuelas.

modeling Learning how to behave by copying the behavior of others. (p. 33)
modelar el comportamiento Aprender cierta conducta imitando el comportamiento de otros.

mood disorder A disorder characterized by extreme emotions. (p. 86)
trastorno del estado de ánimo Trastorno en el cual la persona experimenta emociones extremas.

mucous membrane The protective lining that covers any opening into the body. (p. 553)
membrana mucosa Revestimiento protector que cubre el interior de las aberturas del cuerpo.

multiple birth The delivery of more than one baby—for example, twins or triplets. (p. 502)
parto múltiple Parto de más de un bebé; por ejemplo, gemelos o trillizos.

muscle tone Contractions of limited muscle fibers that keep a muscle tense, but do not produce movement. (p. 273)
tono muscular Contracción parcial de las fibras musculares, que mantiene el músculo tenso, pero no produce movimiento.

MyPlate plan A plan that groups foods according to types and indicates how much of each type should be eaten daily for a healthy diet. (p. 213)
plan "Mi plato" Plan en el que se agrupan los alimentos de acuerdo a su tipo y que nos indica qué cantidad de cada grupo alimentario debemos comer diariamente para mantener una dieta saludable.

narcolepsy A disorder in which a person experiences severe sleepiness during the day, or falls asleep suddenly. (p. 365)
narcolepsia Trastorno en el cual una persona siente mucho sueño durante el día o se queda dormida de repente.

neglect The failure to provide for the basic needs of children. (p. 122)
abandono Falta del sustento que satisfaga las necesidades básicas de los niños.

nephron A tiny filtering unit in the kidney that removes wastes and produces urine. (p. 256)
nefrón Pequeña unidad de filtración en el riñón que elimina las sustancias tóxicas y produce orina.

neurologist A physician who treats physical disorders of the nervous system. (p. 103)
neurólogo(a) Médico especializado en la identificación y el tratamiento de los trastornos orgánicos del sistema nervioso.

neuron The basic unit of the nervous system that carries nerve impulses. (p. 278)
neurona Unidad básica del sistema nervioso, que transmite los impulsos nerviosos.

nicotine An extremely addictive chemical in tobacco products. (p. 402)
nicotina Sustancia química extremadamente adictiva que se encuentra en los productos derivados del tabaco.

nicotine substitute A product such as a gum, patch, spray, or inhaler, that contains nicotine and is designed to help a person quit tobacco use. (p. 420)
reemplazos de nicotina Productos tales como gomas de mascar, parches, aerosoles o inhaladores, que contienen nicotina y que se producen para ayudar a las personas a dejar de consumir tabaco.

nuclear family A couple and their child or children living together in one household. (p. 114)
familia nuclear Pareja y su(s) hijo(s) que viven juntos en el mismo hogar.

nutrient A substance in foods that the body needs to regulate bodily functions, promote growth, repair body tissues, and obtain energy. (p. 192)
nutriente Sustancia que se halla en los alimentos y que el cuerpo necesita para regular sus funciones, promover el crecimiento, reparar los tejidos y obtener energía.

nutrient-dense food A food that contains lots of vitamins and minerals relative to the number of calories, but is low in saturated fat, trans fat, added sugar, and salt. (p. 211)
alimento rico en nutrientes Alimento que contiene una cantidad de vitaminas y minerales muy elevada en relación con sus calorías, pero que contiene pocas grasas saturadas, grasas trans, azúcares añadidos y sal.

O

obesity Condition in adults who have a body mass index (BMI) of 30 or higher. (p. 228)
obesidad Trastorno que se presenta cuando un adulto tiene un índice de masa corporal (IMC) igual o mayor que 30.

obsession An unwanted thought or image that takes control of the mind. (p. 85)
obsesión Idea o pensamiento no deseado que ocupa la mente y no puede olvidarse.

obstetrician A doctor who specializes in pregnancy and childbirth. (p. 494)
obstetra Médico que se especializa en el embarazo y el parto.

occupational illness Any abnormal condition or disorder caused by exposure to the work environment. (p. 702)
enfermedad laboral Cualquier condición anormal o desorden causado por exposición al lugar de trabajo.

occupational injury Any wound or damage to the body that results from an event in the work environment. (p. 702)
lesión laboral Cualquier lesión o daño físico que resulta de un accidente en el lugar de trabajo.

oncogene A normal gene that has changed into a cancer-causing gene. (p. 610)
oncogen Gen normal que se ha transformado en un gen causante de cáncer.

opiate Any drug made from psychoactive compounds contained in the seed pods of poppy plants. (p. 441)
opiáceo Toda droga psicoactiva hecha a partir de ciertos compuestos de las cápsulas de amapola.

opportunistic infection An infection that attacks a person with a weakened immune system. (p. 586)
infección oportunista Infección que ataca a una persona que tiene debilitado el sistema inmunológico.

optimism A tendency to focus on the positive aspects of a situation. (p. 66)
optimismo Tendencia a concentrase en los aspectos positivos de una situación.

optometrist A professional trained to provide eye and vision care. (p. 358)
optometrista Profesional capacitado para proporcionar cuidados a los ojos y la visión.

orthodontist A specialist who corrects the position of jaws and teeth. (p. 343)
ortodoncista Dentista especializado en corregir la posición de las mandíbulas y los dientes.

ossification The process during infancy and childhood in which cartilage is replaced by bone. (p. 268)
osificación Proceso que tiene lugar durante la infancia y la niñez, mediante el cual el cartílago se convierte en hueso.

osteoarthritis A common form of arthritis that is caused by wear and tear on a joint or by repeated injuries to a joint. (p. 618)
osteoartritis Forma común de la artritis que es causada por el desgaste progresivo de una articulación o por lesiones frecuentes de la misma.

osteoporosis A condition in which a significant loss of bone mass causes bones to become weak and break easily. (p. 270)
osteoporosis Trastorno caracterizado por una pérdida significativa de masa ósea que hace que los huesos se debiliten y se fracturen fácilmente.

outpatient A person admitted to a clinic for tests or treatments that do not require an overnight stay. (p. 637)
paciente ambulatorio Persona ingresada a una clínica o a un hospital para ser sometida a exámenes o tratamientos que no requieren su permanencia nocturna en la instalación.

ova The reproductive cells in females. (p. 469)
óvulos Células reproductoras femeninas.

ovaries The female reproductive glands. (p. 469)
ovarios Glándulas reproductoras femeninas.

overdose The consequence of taking an excessive amount of a drug that leads to coma or death. (p. 385)
sobredosis Consecuencia de ingerir una cantidad excesiva de una droga que conduce al estado de coma o a la muerte.

over-the-counter drug A medicine that is sold legally in pharmacies and other stores without a doctor's prescription. (p. 426)
fármaco sin receta Medicamento que se vende legalmente en las farmacias u otras tiendas sin prescripción de un médico.

overtraining Exercising too intensely or for too long without allowing enough time for rest. (p. 335)
entrenamiento excesivo La realización de ejercicios demasiado intensos o durante demasiado tiempo sin descansar lo suficiente.

overweight Term used to describe a person who is heavier than the standard for the person's height. (p. 228)
sobrepeso Término que se usa para describir a una persona que tiene un peso superior al adecuado para su estatura.

ovulation The process during which one of the ovaries releases a ripened egg. (p. 469)
ovulación Proceso durante el cual un ovario libera un óvulo maduro.

ozone layer A section of the atmosphere that contains naturally occurring ozone; absorbs ultraviolet light from the sun. (p. 673)
capa de ozono Parte de la atmósfera que contiene ozono natural; esta capa absorbe los rayos ultravioleta del sol.

pacemaker A small group of cells in the wall of the right atrium that controls the rate at which the heart muscles contract. (p. 294)
marcapaso Pequeño grupo de células de la pared de la aurícula derecha, que regula el ritmo de las contracciones de los músculos del corazón.

Pap smear A medical procedure in which a sample of cells is taken from the cervix and examined under a microscope. (p. 475)
Prueba de Papanicolaou Procedimiento médico en que se toma una muestra de células del cuello uterino y se examinan bajo microscopio.

paralysis The loss of the ability to move and feel some part of the body. (p. 284)
parálisis Pérdida de la capacidad de movimiento y sensación en alguna parte del cuerpo.

passive A term that describes people who hold back their true feelings and go along with the other person. (p. 138)
pasivo(a) Término que describe a una persona que reprime los sentimientos propios y cede ante los demás.

pathogen A microorganism or virus that causes disease. (p. 548)
patógeno Microorganismo o virus que causa enfermedades.

peer group A group of people who are about the same age and share similar interests. (p. 33)
grupo de iguales Grupo de personas con edades e intereses semejantes.

peer pressure The need to conform to the expectations of friends. (p. 145)
presión de grupo Necesidad de adaptarse a las expectativas de los amigos.

pelvic inflammatory disease A serious infection of the female reproductive organs that can lead to infertility or an ectopic pregnancy. (p. 579)
enfermedad inflamatoria pélvica Infección grave de los órganos reproductores femeninos, que puede conducir a la infertilidad o al embarazo ectópico.

penis The external male sexual organ through which sperm leave the body. (p. 465)
pene Órgano sexual externo masculino a través del cual el cuerpo libera semen.

perfectionist A person who accepts nothing less than excellence. (p. 66)
perfeccionista Persona que no acepta más que la excelencia en todo.

periodontal disease Gum disease that can lead to tooth loss. (p. 346)
enfermedad periodontal Enfermedad de las encías que puede causar la caída de los dientes.

peristalsis Waves of muscle contractions that push food through the digestive system. (p. 243)
peristaltismo Conjunto de movimientos parecidos a una ola, producidos por las contracciones musculares del sistema digestivo para transportar los alimentos a lo largo del mismo.

personality A set of behaviors, attitudes, feelings, and ways of thinking that are unique to an individual. (p. 30)
personalidad Conjunto de conductas, actitudes, sentimientos y maneras de pensar que caracterizan a un individuo.

personality disorder A mental disorder characterized by rigid patterns of behavior, which make it difficult for a person to get along with others. (p. 88)
trastorno de personalidad Trastorno mental caracterizado por patrones de conducta inflexibles que limitan la capacidad de una persona para relacionarse con los demás.

pessimism A tendency to focus on the negative aspects of a situation and to expect the worst. (p. 66)
pesimismo Tendencia a concentrarse en los aspectos negativos de una situación y esperar que suceda lo peor.

phagocyte A type of white blood cell that engulfs and destroys pathogens. (p. 554)
fagocito Tipo de glóbulo blanco que rodea y destruye a los patógenos.

pharynx The upper portion of the throat; the junction between the digestive and respiratory systems. (p. 243)
faringe Sección superior de la garganta; es el punto de encuentro entre los sistemas digestivo y respiratorio.

phobia Anxiety that is related to a specific situation or object. (p. 84)
fobia Ansiedad relacionada con una situación o un objeto específico.

physical abuse Intentionally causing physical harm to another person. (p. 121)
maltrato físico Daño físico que se causa a otra persona de manera intencional.

physical activity Any movement that requires large muscle groups to work. (p. 316)
actividad física Cualquier movimiento que requiere el uso de un grupo importante de músculos.

physical examination A head-to-toe check of your body to identify any medical problems. (p. 643)
examen físico Revisión de pies a cabeza que se realiza para detectar problemas médicos.

physical fitness Having the energy and strength to participate in a variety of activities. (p. 318)
aptitud física Tener la energía y la fuerza para participar en una amplia variedad de actividades.

physical health The aspect of health that refers to how well your body functions. When you are physically healthy, you have enough energy to carry out everyday tasks. (p. 3)
salud física Capacidad del cuerpo para realizar bien sus funciones. Cuando una persona es físicamente saludable, tiene la energía suficiente para realizar las actividades diarias.

physical maturity The state of being full-grown in the physical sense. (p. 530)
madurez física Estado de desarrollo físico completo.

pituitary gland An endocrine gland in the brain that controls many of the body's functions, including growth, reproduction, and metabolism. (p. 463)
glándula pituitaria Glándula endocrina ubicada en el cerebro, que regula muchas de las funciones del cuerpo, como el crecimiento, la reproducción y el metabolismo.

placenta The structure that holds the embryo to the wall of the uterus. (p. 490)
placenta Estructura que mantiene al embrión unido a la pared del útero.

plaque A substance that builds up in artery walls and contributes to the development of atherosclerosis; a sticky film containing bacteria that adheres to teeth. (pp. 300, 344)
placa Sustancia que se acumula en las paredes de las arterias y que contribuye al desarrollo de la ateroesclerosis; capa pegajosa que contiene bacterias y se adhiere a los dientes.

plasma A liquid that makes up about 55 percent of the blood. (p. 297)
plasma Líquido que forma alrededor del 55 por ciento de la sangre.

platelet A cell fragment that plays an important role in the blood clotting process. (p. 297)
plaqueta Fragmento de célula que juega un importante papel en el proceso de la coagulación de la sangre.

pollution The presence or release of substances into the environment in quantities that are harmful to living organisms. (p. 672)
contaminación Presencia o liberación de sustancias al medio ambiente en cantidades que resultan dañinas para los seres vivos.

pore A tiny opening in the skin through which sweat is secreted. (p. 348)
poro Pequeña abertura de la piel a través de la cual se expulsa el sudor.

postpartum period A period of adjustment for parents and their newborn during the six weeks after birth. (p. 500)
período postparto Período de adaptación para los padres y el recién nacido durante las primeras seis semanas después del nacimiento.

pre-adolescence The stage of development before adolescence. (p. 508)
preadolescencia Etapa de desarrollo que precede a la adolescencia.

preeclampsia A serious condition during pregnancy characterized by high blood pressure, swelling of the wrists and ankles, and high levels of protein in the urine. (p. 496)
preclampsia Trastorno serio del embarazo que se caracteriza por hipertensión arterial, inflamación de las muñecas y los tobillos, y la presencia de niveles elevados de proteína en la orina.

prejudice Negative feelings about a group based on stereotypes. (p. 172)
prejuicio Sentimiento negativo hacia un grupo de personas, basado en estereotipos.

premature birth The delivery of a live baby before the 37th week of pregnancy. (p. 501)
parto prematuro Nacimiento de un bebé vivo antes de la semana 37 del embarazo.

premium A monthly or yearly fee paid for health insurance coverage. (p. 645)
prima Suma mensual o anual que una persona debe pagar por su seguro de salud.

prenatal care Medical care received during pregnancy. (p. 494)
cuidados prenatales Atención médica recibida durante el embarazo.

prescription drug A drug that can be obtained only with a written order from a doctor and can be purchased only at a pharmacy. (p. 427)
fármaco de prescripción Medicamento que se puede obtener únicamente en una farmacia, a partir de una prescripción escrita por un médico.

prevention Taking action to avoid disease, injury, and other negative health outcomes. (p. 12)
prevención Práctica que consiste en tomar medidas para evitar enfermedades, lesiones y otras consecuencias negativas para la salud.

primary care physician A doctor who takes care of people's routine medical needs. (p. 634)
médico de cabecera Médico que atiende las necesidades médicas más básicas o comunes.

primary emotion An emotion that is expressed by people in all cultures. (p. 44)
emoción primaria Emoción que expresan todas las personas, sin importar su origen cultural.

primary healthcare Routine healthcare provided in a doctor's office. (p. 637)
atención médica primaria Atención médica básica que se recibe en el consultorio médico.

progesterone A hormone that signals changes to a woman's reproductive system during the menstrual cycle and pregnancy. (p. 469)
progesterona Hormona que regula los cambios del sistema reproductor de la mujer durante el ciclo menstrual y el embarazo.

protective factor A factor that reduces a person's potential for harmful behavior. (p. 436)
factor protector Factor que reduce la posibilidad de que una persona adopte conductas perjudiciales.

protein A nutrient that contains nitrogen as well as carbon, hydrogen, and oxygen; needed for the growth and repair of body tissues. (p. 198)
proteína Nutriente que contiene nitrógeno así como carbono, hidrógeno y oxígeno; es necesaria para el crecimiento y la reparación de tejidos.

protozoan A large and complex single-celled organism. (p. 549)
protozoo Organismo unicelular grande y complejo.

psychiatric social worker A mental health professional who helps people with mental disorders and their families to accept and adjust to an illness. (p. 103)
trabajador(a) social de psiquiatría Profesional de la salud mental que ayuda a las personas con trastornos mentales y a sus familiares a aceptar una enfermedad y adaptarse a ella.

psychiatrist A physician who can diagnose and treat mental disorders. (p. 103)
psiquiatra Médico especializado en el diagnóstico y tratamiento de los trastornos mentales.

psychoactive drug A chemical that affects brain activity; also known as a "mood-altering" drug. (p. 428)
droga psicoactiva Sustancia química que afecta la actividad del cerebro; también llamada "droga que altera el estado de ánimo".

psychologist A person who studies how people think, feel, and behave. (p. 30)
psicólogo(a) Persona que estudia la manera en que las personas piensan, sienten y se comportan.

puberty The period of sexual development during which a person becomes sexually mature and physically able to reproduce. (p. 463)
pubertad Período de desarrollo sexual durante el cual la persona madura sexualmente y es capaz de reproducirse.

public health The study and practice of protecting and improving the health of people in a group or community. (p. 648)
salud pública El estudio y la aplicación de medidas para proteger y mejorar la salud de las personas de un grupo o una comunidad.

pulp The soft tissue that fills the center of each tooth. (p. 342)
pulpa dentaria Tejido blando que se encuentra en el interior de cada diente.

pupil The opening through which light enters the eye. (p. 356)
pupila Abertura a través de la cual entra la luz al ojo.

Q

quackery The selling of useless medical treatments or products. (p. 22)
charlatanería Venta de productos o tratamientos médicos que carecen de valor o utilidad.

quality of life The degree of total satisfaction that a person gets from life. (p. 2)
calidad de vida Grado de satisfacción total que una persona tiene en su vida.

quarantine A period of isolation imposed on people who may have been exposed to an infectious disease. (p. 648)
cuarentena Período de aislamiento impuesto a aquellas personas que se cree han estado expuestas a una enfermedad infecciosa.

R

radon A naturally occurring radioactive gas that is a serious indoor air pollutant. (p. 674)
radón Gas natural radioactivo que es uno de los principales contaminantes del aire en el interior de casas y edificios.

rape A type of assault in which one person forces another to have sexual relations. (p. 700)
violación Tipo de asalto en el cual una persona fuerza a otra a tener relaciones sexuales.

recycling The process of reclaiming raw materials from discarded products and using them to create new products. (p. 678)
reciclaje Proceso mediante el cual se recuperan materias primas de los productos de desecho y se vuelven a usar para fabricar nuevos productos.

red blood cell A hemoglobin-containing cell that carries oxygen from the lungs to other parts of the body. (p. 297)
glóbulo rojo Célula que contiene hemoglobina y que lleva oxígeno de los pulmones hacia las otras partes del cuerpo.

reflex An automatic response of the nervous system to the environment. (p. 282)
reflejo Respuesta automática del sistema nervioso al ambiente.

refusal skills The skills needed to say *no* when under pressure. (p. 392)
destrezas de negación Destrezas que necesita una persona para negarse a hacer algo cuando es presionada a hacerlo.

rehabilitation The process of learning to cope with everyday living without drugs. (p. 391)
rehabilitación Proceso mediante el cual se aprende a lidiar con las presiones de la vida cotidiana sin consumir drogas.

reproductive maturity The ability to produce children, signaled by the onset of ovulation in girls, and of sperm production in boys. (p. 515)
madurez reproductiva Capacidad de procrear, indicada por el comienzo de la ovulación en las niñas y la producción de espermatozoides en los niños.

resilience The ability to recover from extreme or prolonged stress. (p. 67)
capacidad de recuperación Capacidad para reponerse del estrés extremo o prolongado.

retina A layer of light-sensing cells that lines the back of the eye. (p. 357)
retina Capa de células sensibles a la luz que recubre la parte posterior del ojo.

reverse tolerance A condition in which less and less alcohol causes intoxication. (p. 389)
tolerancia inversa Condición en la cual la intoxicación es causada cada vez por una menor cantidad de alcohol.

rheumatoid arthritis A form of arthritis in which the membrane surrounding a joint becomes inflamed; the inflammation then spreads to other areas of the joint. (p. 619)
artritis reumatoide Variedad de la artritis caracterizada por la inflamación de la membrana que rodea una articulación; la inflamación se extiende después a otras áreas de la articulación.

risk factor Any action or condition that increases the likelihood of injury, disease, or other negative outcome. (p. 10)
factor de riesgo Cualquier acción o condición que aumenta la posibilidad de sufrir una lesión, contraer una enfermedad o de que se produzcan otras consecuencias negativas para la salud.

road rage Dangerous or violent behavior by a person who becomes angry or frustrated while driving. (p. 714)
violencia vehicular Comportamiento peligroso o violento de una persona que se siente enojada o frustrada mientras conduce.

runaway A child who leaves home without permission and stays away for at least one night, or two nights for teens 15 or older. (p. 123)
niño fugitivo Niño que se va de la casa sin permiso y no regresa por al menos una noche o, en el caso de los mayores de 15 años, por dos noches como mínimo.

runoff Water that drains from land into streams and other water bodies. (p. 680)
escorrentía Agua que fluye sobre la superficie de la tierra hacia los arroyos y otras masas de agua.

S

saturated fat A fat that has all the hydrogen the carbon atoms can hold. (p. 196)
grasa saturada Grasa que tiene el máximo de hidrógeno que los átomos de carbono pueden contener.

schizophrenia A disorder characterized by severe disturbances in thinking, mood, awareness, and behavior. (p. 86)
esquizofrenia Trastorno mental caracterizado por severas alteraciones del pensamiento, el estado de ánimo, la conciencia y la conducta.

scoliosis An abnormal curvature of the spine. (p. 271)
escoliosis Curvatura anormal de la columna vertebral.

scrotum A sac of skin that contains the testes. (p. 464)
escroto Bolsa de piel que contiene los testículos.

sebaceous gland A gland that secretes oil into a hair follicle in the skin; the oil softens and moistens hair and skin. (p. 348)
glándula sebácea Glándula que secreta grasa en el interior de un folículo piloso; la grasa suaviza y humecta el pelo y la piel.

secondary healthcare Healthcare given to a patient in a hospital. (p. 638)
atención médica secundaria Atención médica dada a un paciente en un hospital.

secondary sex characteristics Physical changes during puberty that are not directly involved in reproduction. (p. 515)
caracteres sexuales secundarios Cambios físicos que ocurren durante la pubertad y que no están directamente relacionados con la reproducción.

secondhand smoke A combination of mainstream smoke and sidestream smoke; also known as environmental tobacco smoke. (p. 414)
humo de segunda mano Combinación de humo directo e indirecto; también conocido como humo de tabaco ambiental.

seizure An episode of erratic nerve impulses in the brain that may lead to loss of consciousness, muscle spasms, and other uncontrollable symptoms. (p. 286)
convulsión Serie de impulsos nerviosos irregulares dentro del cerebro que causan pérdida de la consciencia, espasmos musculares y otros síntomas incontrolables.

self-actualization The process by which people achieve their full potential. (p. 40)
autorrealización Proceso mediante el cual una persona alcanza su pleno potencial como individuo.

self-esteem Your opinion of yourself; how much you respect and like yourself. (p. 36)
autoestima Opinión que tiene una persona de sí misma; la medida en que una persona se respeta y se aprecia a sí misma.

semen The mixture of sperm and fluids produced by the glands of the male reproductive system. (p. 466)
semen Mezcla de espermatozoides y fluidos producidos por las glándulas del sistema reproductor masculino.

semicircular canals Structures in the inner ear that help control balance. (p. 361)
conductos semicirculares Estructuras del oído interno que ayudan a controlar el equilibrio.

separation An arrangement in which spouses live apart and try to work out their problems. (p. 120)
separación Arreglo en el que los cónyuges viven aparte mientras tratan de solucionar sus problemas maritales.

sewage Waste material carried from toilets and drains. (p. 679)
aguas negras Desechos que se transportan desde los servicios sanitarios y los desagües.

sexual abuse A criminal offense in which an adult uses a child or adolescent for sexual purposes.
abuso sexual Acto criminal por parte de un adulto que utiliza a un(a) niño(a) o a un(a) adolescente para actividades sexuales. (p. 122)

sexual harassment Any uninvited and unwelcome sexual remark or sexual advance. (p. 171)
acoso sexual Todo comentario o acción de carácter sexual que es mal recibido por una persona.

sexually transmitted infection (STI) An infection caused by any pathogen that spreads from one person to another during sexual contact. (p. 574)
infección de transmisión sexual (ITS) Infección causada por cualquier patógeno que se transmite de una persona a otra por contacto sexual.

sibling A brother or sister. (p. 127)
hermano / hermana Personas que tienen los mismos progenitores.

side effect An unwanted physical or mental effect caused by a drug. (p. 429)
efecto secundario Efecto físico o mental indeseado, causado por drogas o medicamentos.

sidestream smoke Smoke that goes directly into the air from a burning tobacco product. (p. 414)
humo indirecto Humo que se libera directamente al aire por la combustión de productos derivados del tabaco.

single-parent family A family in which only one parent lives with the child or children. (p. 114)
familia monoparental Familia en la que sólo uno de los padres vive con uno o varios hijos.

skeletal muscle Voluntary muscle that is attached to and moves your bones. (p. 272)
músculo esquelético Músculo voluntario que conecta los huesos y los mueve.

sleep apnea A disorder in which a person stops breathing for short periods during sleep. (p. 365)
apnea del sueño Trastorno a causa del cual la persona afectada deja de respirar por breves períodos mientras duerme.

smog A brown haze that forms when air pollutants react in the presence of sunlight. (p. 673)
smog Neblina de color café que se forma cuando los contaminantes del aire reaccionan en presencia de la luz solar.

smokeless tobacco Tobacco products that are chewed, placed between the lower lip and teeth, or sniffed. (p. 403)
tabaco sin humo Cualquier producto derivado del tabaco que es masticado, aspirado por la nariz o colocado entre el labio inferior y los dientes.

smooth muscle Involuntary muscle that causes movements inside your body, such as those involved in breathing and digestion. (p. 272)
músculo liso Músculo involuntario que controla los movimientos internos del cuerpo, como los de la respiración y la digestión.

snuff A smokeless tobacco product that consists of dry or moist powder. It may be placed between the lower lip and teeth or sniffed. (p. 403)
rapé Polvo seco o húmedo, derivado del tabaco, que se consume colocándolo entre el labio inferior y los dientes o aspirándolo por la nariz.

social health The aspect of health that refers to how well you get along with others. (p. 3)
salud social Aspecto de la salud que se refiere a la habilidad de llevarse bien con los demás.

socialization The process by which children are taught to behave in a way that is acceptable to family and society. (p. 116)
socialización Proceso mediante el cual los niños aprenden a comportarse de forma aceptable dentro de su familia y su sociedad.

social network The people with whom you interact and look to for friendship, information, and social support. (p. 664)
red social Conjunto de personas con las que un individuo interactúa y entre las que busca amigos, información y apoyo social.

sperm The reproductive cells in males. (p. 464)
espermatozoides Células reproductoras masculinas.

spinal cord A thick column of nerve tissue in the central nervous system that links the brain to most of the nerves in the peripheral nervous system. (p. 282)
médula espinal Columna gruesa de tejido nervioso, que pertenece al sistema nervioso central y que conecta el cerebro con la mayoría de los nervios del sistema nervioso periférico.

sprain An overstretched or torn ligament. (p. 271)
esguince Lesión producida cuando un ligamento es estirado excesivamente o se desgarra.

stalker Someone who repeatedly makes unwanted contact with a person and may threaten to kill or injure the person. (p. 700)
acosador Persona que constantemente se pone en contacto con otra, sin que ésta lo desee, y que puede llegar a amenazarla con atacarla o matarla.

stereotype An exaggerated belief or overgeneralization about an entire group of people. (p. 172)
estereotipo Creencia excesivamente simplificada o generalizada sobre un grupo de personas.

stillbirth The expulsion of a fetus that has died after the twentieth week of pregnancy. (p. 501)
parto de un mortinato Expulsión de un feto muerto después de la vigésima semana del embarazo.

stimulant A type of drug that increases the activity of the nervous system. (pp. 406, 442)
estimulante Toda droga que acelera la actividad del sistema nervioso.

strain A pulled muscle. (p. 275)
distensión Lesión causada cuando se estira demasiado un músculo.

stress The response of your body and mind to being challenged or threatened. (p. 56)
estrés Respuesta del cuerpo y de la mente al enfrentarse a un desafío o una amenaza.

stressor An event of situation that causes stress. (p. 57)
evento estresante Suceso o situación que causa estrés.

stroke A sudden disruption of blood flow to part of the brain. (p. 605)
apoplejía Interrupción repentina del flujo de sangre a una parte del cerebro.

suicide The intentional killing of oneself. (p. 96)
suicidio Acción que realiza un individuo intencionalmente para matarse a sí mismo.

support group A network of people who help each other cope with a particular problem. (p. 130)
grupo de apoyo Red de personas que se ayudan entre sí para enfrentar un problema específico.

survival floating A technique that allows a person to float in the water and breathe without using much energy. (p. 705)
supervivencia por flotación Técnica que permite a una persona flotar en el agua y respirar sin usar mucha energía.

syphilis A serious bacterial sexually transmitted infection that progresses through three distinct stages. (p. 582)
sífilis Enfermedad bacterial grave de transmisión sexual que se desarrolla en tres etapas distintas.

T

tar A dark, sticky substance that forms when tobacco burns. (p. 408)
alquitrán Sustancia oscura y pegajosa que se forma al quemarse el tabaco.

target heart rate The heart rate at which your cardiovascular system receives the most benefits from exercise without working too hard. (p. 326)
frecuencia cardíaca ideal Frecuencia a la cual el sistema cardiovascular obtiene la mayor cantidad de beneficios del ejercicio sin tener que realizar un esfuerzo excesivo.

tartar A hardened form of plaque that irritates the gums. (p. 346)
sarro Tipo de placa dental muy dura que irrita las encías.

T cell A type of lymphocyte that helps the immune system destroy pathogens. (p. 555)
célula T Tipo de linfocito que ayuda al sistema inmunológico a destruir a los patógenos.

tendon A think strand of tissue that attaches a muscle to a bone. (p. 272)
tendón Tejido grueso y fibroso que une músculos y huesos.

tendonitis Painful swelling and irritation of a tendon, often caused by overuse. (p. 275)
tendinitis Inflamación e irritación dolorosa de un tendón, habitualmente causada por su uso excesivo.

terminal illness An illness for which there is no chance of recovery. (p. 538)
enfermedad terminal Enfermedad en la cual no hay posibilidad de recuperación.

territorial gang A group that is organized to control a specific neighborhood or "turf." (p. 167)
pandilla territorial Grupo organizado de personas que ejerce control sobre un vecindario o "territorio".

tertiary healthcare Healthcare provided in specialty hospitals and teaching hospitals. (p. 638)
atención médica especializada Atención médica dada a un paciente en un hospital docente o especializado.

testes The male reproductive glands. (p. 464)
testículos Glándulas reproductoras masculinas.

testosterone The sex hormone that affects the production of sperm and signals certain physical changes at puberty. (p. 464)
testosterona Hormona sexual que determina la producción de espermatozoides y regula ciertos cambios físicos durante la pubertad.

therapeutic community A residential treatment center where former drug abusers live together and learn to adjust to drug-free lives. (p. 450)
comunidad terapéutica Centro de tratamiento residencial donde las personas que abusaban de las drogas viven juntas y aprenden a adaptarse a una vida libre de drogas.

therapy A treatment method. (p. 104)
terapia Método de tratamiento.

tinnitus A condition in which ringing is heard in the ears, even when there is no external sound. (p. 624)
tinnitus Trastorno que hace que la persona escuche un zumbido en los oídos, aun cuando no se produce ningún sonido externo.

tolerance The condition that results when repeated use of a drug causes it to have less of an effect on the brain. (p. 388)
tolerancia Condición en la que el uso repetido de una droga hace que ésta tenga cada vez menos efecto sobre el cerebro.

toxin A poison given off by some bacteria that can injure cells. (p. 548)
toxina Sustancia venenosa, producida por algunas bacterias, que puede dañar las células.

trans fat The type of fat produced when manufacturers add hydrogen to the fat molecules in vegetable oils. (p. 197)
grasa trans Tipo de grasa producida por los fabricantes al añadir hidrógeno a las moléculas de grasa de los aceites vegetales.

trichomoniasis A sexually transmitted infection caused by a protozoan that infects the urinary tract or vagina. (p. 578)
tricomoniasis Infección de transmisión sexual causada por un protozoo que infecta las vías urinarias o la vagina.

trimester One of three periods of time that divide a pregnancy. Each trimester is approximately three months long. (p. 494)
trimestre Cada uno de los tres períodos en el que se divide el embarazo. Cada trimestre dura aproximadamente tres meses.

tumor An abnormal mass of tissue. (p. 609)
tumor Masa anormal de tejido.

ultrasound High-frequency sound waves used to create an image of a developing fetus. (p. 495)
ultrasonido Ondas sonoras de alta frecuencia utilizadas para crear una imagen del feto en desarrollo.

umbilical cord The cordlike structure that connects the embryo and the placenta. (p. 491)
cordón umbilical Estructura en forma de cuerda que conecta al embrión con la placenta.

underweight Term used to describe a person who is lighter than the standard for the person's height. (p. 229)
de bajo peso Término que se usa para describir a una persona que tiene un peso inferior al adecuado para su estatura.

unintentional injury An unplanned injury. (p. 694)
lesión accidental Lesión que se produce sin que se planifique o desee.

United Nations Children's Fund (UNICEF) A United Nations agency that aids children in developing nations. (p. 657)
Fondo de las Naciones Unidas para la Infancia (UNICEF) Agencia de las Naciones Unidas dedicada a brindar ayuda a los niños de los países en vías de desarrollo.

universal precautions Actions taken by healthcare providers that reduce their risk of coming into contact with blood and body fluids. (p. 593)
precauciones universales Medidas que toman los profesionales de la salud para reducir el riesgo de entrar en contacto con la sangre y otros fluidos corporales.

unsaturated fat A fat with at least one unsaturated bond in a place where hydrogen can be added to the molecule. (p. 196)
grasa no saturada Grasa que tiene al menos un enlace no saturado en un lugar donde se podría añadir hidrógeno a la molécula.

urban sprawl City or town development in which homes are built in spread-out suburbs that are not near business districts. (p. 667)
expansión urbana Desarrollo urbano de una ciudad o pueblo en el que las viviendas se construyen en suburbios lejanos a las zonas comerciales.

urea A substance formed in the liver from a waste product of protein breakdown. (p. 254)
urea Sustancia de desecho que se forma en el hígado al ser descompuestas las proteínas.

urethritis Inflammation of the lining of the urethra. (p. 578)
uretritis Inflamación del revestimiento interno de la uretra.

urine A watery fluid containing urea and wastes that is excreted from the body. (p. 255)
orina Líquido que contiene urea y otros desechos y que se excreta del cuerpo.

uterus The hollow, muscular, pear-shaped organ in which a fertilized egg develops and grows. (p. 470)
útero Órgano muscular hueco, en forma de pera, en el cual se desarrolla y crece el óvulo fecundado.

vaccine A substance containing small amounts of dead or modified pathogens or their toxins that is injected during an immunization. (p. 556)
vacuna Sustancia que contiene pequeñas cantidades de patógenos muertos o modificados, o sus toxinas, y que se inyecta durante la inmunización.

vagina The hollow, muscular passage leading from the uterus to the outside of the female body. (p. 470)
vagina Canal muscular que comunica el útero con el exterior del cuerpo femenino.

vaginitis A vaginal infection or irritation. (p. 578)
vaginitis Infección o irritación de la vagina.

values The standards and beliefs that are most important to you. (p. 14)
valores Normas y creencias que son muy importantes para una persona.

vandalism Intentionally damaging or destroying another person's property. (p. 173)
vandalismo Daño o destrucción intencional de la(s) propiedad(es) de otra persona.

vegan A person who does not eat food from any animal source. (p. 234)
vegetariano(a) estricto(a) Persona que no come alimentos de procedencia animal.

vegetarian A person who does not eat meat. (p. 234)
vegetariano(a) Persona que no come carne.

vein A large, thin-walled blood vessel that carries blood to the heart. (p. 295)
vena Vaso sanguíneo grande, de paredes delgadas, que lleva la sangre hacia el corazón.

ventricle A lower chamber of the heart that pumps blood out of the heart. (p. 293)
ventrículo Cada una de las dos cámaras inferiores del corazón que bombea sangre desde el corazón al resto del cuerpo.

victim The person who is attacked during a violent act. (p. 163)
víctima Toda persona que es atacada en un acto violento.

villi Tiny fingerlike projections lining the small intestine, through which nutrients are absorbed into the blood. (p. 245)
vellosidades Pequeñas formaciones con aspecto de dedo que cubren la pared interna del intestino delgado; los nutrientes son absorbidos y pasan a la sangre a través de ellas.

violence The threat of or actual use of physical force against oneself or another person. (p. 162)
violencia La amenaza de usar o el uso de la fuerza física contra uno mismo o contra otra persona.

viral load The number of virus particles circulating in the body. (p. 595)
carga viral Cantidad de partículas de un virus que circulan en el cuerpo.

virus The smallest type of pathogen. (p. 549)
virus El tipo más pequeño de patógeno.

vital statistics The numbers of births and deaths and the numbers and kinds of diseases that occur within a population. (p. 652)
estadísticas vitales Número de nacimientos, muertes, y cantidades y tipos de enfermedades que ocurren en determinada población.

vitamin A nutrient that is made by living things, is required in small amounts, and assists in chemical reactions in the body. (p. 203)
vitamina Nutriente producido por los seres vivos, es necesario en pequeñas cantidades, e interviene en las reacciones químicas del cuerpo.

warranty An offer to repair or replace a product if there is a problem with the product. (p. 19)
garantía Acción de asegurar la reparación o el reemplazo de un producto si éste tuviese algún problema.

wellness A state of high-level health. (p. 4)
bienestar Estado en el que se goza de excelente salud.

white blood cell A cell that helps protect the body from diseases and foreign substances. (p. 297)
glóbulo blanco Célula que ayuda a proteger al cuerpo de las enfermedades y los cuerpos ajenos.

withdrawal A group of symptoms that occur when a dependent person stops taking a drug. (p. 391)
síndrome de abstinencia Conjunto de síntomas que se manifiestan cuando una persona adicta a una droga deja de consumirla.

World Health Organization (WHO) A United Nations health organization that provides aid to developing nations and collects worldwide health statistics. (p. 657)
Organización Mundial de la Salud (OMS) Agencia de las Naciones Unidas que brinda ayuda a los países en vías de desarrollo y recopila datos estadísticos sobre la salud a nivel mundial.

zero-tolerance policy A policy that enforces strict consequences for underage drinking. (p. 375)
política de intolerancia total Norma que consiste en imponer castigos estrictos al consumo de alcohol por parte de menores de edad.

zygote The united egg and sperm. (p. 489)
cigoto Óvulo y espermatozoide ya unidos.

Index

Page numbers for key terms are printed in **boldface** type.
Page numbers for illustrations, maps, and charts are printed in *italics*.

A

ABCD rule *349*
abdominal thrusts *724*
absorption **242**
abstinence 152–153, **154**, 155–156
  from alcohol 392–394
  from drugs 450–452
  from sex 152–156, 467, 474, 576,
    577, 592, 593
acceptance 35, *538*
accessing information **14**
  on community resources 670–671
  on food labels *224–225*
  Internet sources 590–591
  on sexually transmitted infections
    583
accidents 694
acid, stomach 63, 244, *553*
acne *350*
acquaintance rape 151, 700
acquired immunodeficiency
  syndrome. *See* AIDS
action plan **15**, 201
active immunity **556**–557
active listening **137**, 147
active supervision 705
activity level, weight and 227, 316
addiction **388**, 407, 428
ADHD 82, *83*, 88, 442
adolescence **514**–528
  body changes in 514–517
  emotional changes in 520–521
  mental changes in 518–*519*
  nutrition in 517
  reproductive system in 514–515
  responsibility and 524–528
  self-esteem in 38
  setting goals in 522–523
adoption 114
adrenal glands *462*
adrenaline 60, *461*, *462*
adulthood **529**–536
  family responsibilities of 116
  healthy aging 534–536
  marriage in 531–533
  self-esteem in 38
  stages of *35*
advertising *21*, 404–405, 521. *See also*
  media
advocacy *15*
  for community 688
  intervening to help a friend
    438–439
  mediating conflicts 178–179
  supporting friends 146–147
AED *716*, 722
aerobic exercise *320*
Affordable Care Act 640, *646*
afterbirth, delivery of *499*
aggressive communication *138*

aging **534**–536
  eye diseases and 359
  healthcare costs and 647
agoraphobia *84*
agreeableness 31
AIDS 431, **584**
  cancer and 586
  education about and prevention of
    589
  global distribution of *588*
  onset of 585
  opportunistic infections and **586**
  preventing 592–593
  treatment for 595–596
  in young people *584*
air pollution 309, 672–674, 676
air quality ratings 675
Al-Anon 120, 391
alarm stage 60, *61*, 64
Alateen 391
alcohol 374–394, *441*
  abstaining from 392–394
  addiction **388**
  behavioral effects of 381
  blood alcohol concentration (BAC)
    380, **382**, *383*, 384, 385
  body systems and 380–*381*
  brain damage from 386
  cancer and 613
  death related to *377*, *384*, 385, 390
  dependence on **388**
  as depressant 374, 385
  digestive problems caused by 387
  fetal alcohol syndrome *387*, 493
  hangovers **383**
  heart disease from 387, 608
  interactions with other drugs 385
  life-threatening effects of 384–385
  liver damage from *387*
  long-term risks of 386–391
  motor vehicle crashes related to
    384, 712
  overdose of *385*
  pregnancy and 386, 387, 493
  sexual activities and 156
  sports and 376
  STI transmission and 576, 592
  testing students for 456–457
  tolerance to **388**
  underage drinking 375, 376, 377,
    384, 385, 386, 388, 456–457
  violence and 166
Alcoholics Anonymous (AA) 130, 391
alcoholism **388**–391
  brain activity and *388*
  effects on others *390*
  risk of 388
  stages of 389
  treatment of 390–391
allergen *616*
allergies 235, **616**

allergists *635*
all-terrain vehicles *708*
alveoli (air sacs) *307*, **308**, 412
Alzheimer's disease **535**
amebic dysentery 549
Americans with Disabilities Act
  (ADA) **626**
amino acids **198**
amniocentesis 495
amniotic fluid *490*
amniotic sac *490*
amphetamines *442*, *443*
amygdala *519*
anabolic steroids **274**, *334*, 435, 446,
  447
anaerobic exercise *320*
analyzing influences **14**. *See also*
  media
  of advertising 404–405
  of health news 252–253
  of misleading claims 354–355
  of violence in video games 165
anemia 206
aneurysm **605**
anger 42–43, 45, 174, 181, *538*
angina pectoris **603**
angioplasty, balloon *606*
animal bites, first aid for 732
animals, infected *550*, 567
anorexia nervosa **90**–91
antibacterial products 562
antibiotic **559**, 561, 580
antibiotic resistance **559**
antibodies *555*
antioxidants **205**
antisocial personality disorder 88
anxiety 84, *643*
anxiety disorder **84**–85
aorta 295
apnea, sleep **365**, *622*
appendicitis *249*
appetite **220**
appreciation, in healthy families 126
arguments 174–175
arrhythmia **301**, 604
arteries *294*, **295**
arteriography *606*
arteriosclerosis 603
arthritis 535, **618**–619
arthroscopic surgery *271*
asbestos 674
ascorbic acid *204*
assailant 163
assault **700**, 701
assertive communication *138*
assertiveness 138, 156, **620**–621
assisted living facilities *639*
asthma 63, *309*, 415, 616, *617*, *622*
  medicine for 617
  triggers 309
astigmatism *358*

Page numbers for key terms are printed in **boldface** type.
Page numbers for illustrations, maps, and charts are printed in *italics*.

Page numbers for key terms are printed in **boldface** type.
Page numbers for illustrations, maps, and charts are printed in *italics*.

Page numbers for key terms are printed in **boldface** type.
Page numbers for illustrations, maps, and charts are printed in *italics.*

Page numbers for key terms are printed in **boldface** type.
Page numbers for illustrations, maps, and charts are printed in *italics*.

travel, emerging diseases and 568
triceps *273*
triceps stretch 277
trichina worm 549
trichomoniasis **578**, *579*
trimesters *494–495*
trust, development of *34*
tsunami, Asian 656, *657*
tuberculosis 559
tumor **609**. *See also* **cancer**
twins 32, 502, *503*
type 1 diabetes 614
type 2 diabetes 228, 233, 234, *615*

ulcers 63, *249*
ultrasound **495**
ultrasound technician 544
ultraviolet (UV) radiation *349*, 613, 673
umbilical cord *490*, **491**
unconsciousness 722
underage drinking 375, 376, 377, 384, 385, 386, 388, 456–457
underbite 343
underweight 229
undescended testis 464
unintentional injuries 694
United Nations Children's Fund (UNICEF) **657**
United Nations Programme on HIV/AIDS 589
United States Agency for International Development (USAID) 658
United States Department of Agriculture (USDA) 210, 213, *651*
U.S. Department of Health and Human Services 12, 210, 649, 650
universal precautions *593*, 723
unsaturated fats *196*
urban planning *667*
urban sprawl **667**
urea 254, 255
ureter *255*
urethra *255*, *465*, *466*, *470*
urethritis **578**
urinary tract infections 257
urine **255**, 256
uterus *470*, *489*, 490–491

vaccine 556–557, *649*
vagina *470*, *490*
vaginitis 474, **578**
vaginosis, bacterial *581*
values 14, 17, 39
  adolescent search for 520
  sexual intimacy and 152
  about violence 164
valve, cardiac 293

vandalism 173
varicella (chickenpox) *557*
vas deferens *465*, *466*
vegans **234**
vegetarian diets 199, 234
vegetarians 234
veins 294, **295**
ventricle **293**
vertebrae 266, *282*
vertebral column (backbone) 266, *267*
victim **163**, *177*
video games, violence in 165
videos, music 471
villi *245*
violence 162–184. *See also* **fighting**
  bullying **169**
  costs of 162–163
  cycle of *150*
  in dating 150–151, 177
  domestic 177
  drug and alcohol abuse and 166
  in families 121–122, 123, 164
  gang membership and *167*
  hate violence **172–173**
  hazing **170**
  in media 165
  poverty and *164*
  race and 164
  risk factors for 164–167
  in schools 168–173
  sexual harassment **171**
  weapons availability and 166, 168
viral diseases 560–561, *567*
viral load **595**
virtual reality, phobias and 89
viruses 250, **549**. *See also* **HIV**
vision impairment 623–624
vital statistics **652**
vitamin poisoning 208
vitamins 192, 202–**203**, *204*–205, 208, 246
  antioxidants **205**
  fat-soluble *203*, 208
  insufficiency 234
  during pregnancy 492, *493*
  production in large intestine 246
  supplements 208
  water-soluble *204*, 208
volunteering 75, 452, *653*, 684, *687*

Wain, Louis *86*
warming up 276, *328*
warranty 19
warts 351, 579
waste(s)
  biodegradable **677**
  cellular 256, 292, 295, 297
  disposal of 677–678, 682
  hazardous **677**
  industrial 680

waste sites, cleaning up 681
water 192, 208–209
  contaminated 551
  excretion of *254*
  during exercise 333
  exercise in *534–535*
  kidney function and 255, 257
water pollution 679–680
water safety *705*
water-soluble vitamins *204*, 208
weapons 166, 168
Web sites 8, 591. *See also* **Internet**
weight 226–232
  activity level and 227, 316
  bingeing and 93
  body composition and 227
  body mass index (BMI) and **227**
  cardiovascular diseases and 608
  dangerous diet plans 230–231
  heredity and 226
  overweight and obesity **228**–229
  respiratory health and 310
  sensible weight gain *232*
  sensible weight loss *231*
  underweight 229
wellness **4**
West Nile virus *567*
white blood cells *297*, 554
whiteheads 350
whole grains foods 195
win-win negotiation 124–125
wisdom teeth 343
withdrawal **391**, 407, *429*, 440
women
  media portrayal of 165
  in work force 113
  violence against 177
workers, teen 703
workouts 276–277, *328*
World Health Organization (WHO) 163, 589, **657**
worms, intestinal *247*

X-rays 494, 612, 613

yeast 374
yellow fever *567*
yellow marrow 268
young adulthood *35*, 529–530
youth groups 452

zero-tolerance policy 375, 384, 457
zinc *207*
zygote **489**

Acknowledgments

Acknowledgment for pages 16–17: "DECIDE" adapted from the Stanford DECIDE Drug Education Curriculum.

Acknowledgment for page 397: "My Papa's Waltz," Copyright © 1942 by Hearst Magazines, Inc., from *The Collected Poems of Theodore Roethke* by Theodore Roethke. Used by permission of Doubleday, a division of Random House.

Note: Every effort has been made to locate the copyright owner of material reprinted in this book. Omissions brought to our attention will be corrected in subsequent editions.

Staff Credits

The people who made up the **Pearson Health** team—representing design services, editorial, editorial services, education technology, market research, marketing services, planning and budgeting, product planning, production services, publishing processes, and rights and permissions—are listed below. Boldface type denotes the core team members.

Jennifer Angel, Alan Asarch, **Amy C. Austin,** Charlene Barr, **Neil Benjamin,** Peggy Bliss, Stephanie Bradley, **Jim Brady, Diane Braff,** Lisa Brown, Tom Evans, Christian Henry, **Sarah G. Jensen,** Judie Jozokos, Alicia Lankowski, **James Lonergan, Zareh MacPherson Artinian, Dotti Marshall, Lauren McDonough, Maria Milczarek, Natania Mlawer,** Julia F. Osborne, Jennifer Parker, Alice Pihuleac, **Nick Raducanu, Paul M. Ramos, Logan Schmidt,** Malti Sharma, **Aileen Shuman,** Melissa Shustyk, **Nancy Smith,** Cindy Strowman, **Elizabeth Tustian,** Amanda M. Watters, **Berkley Wilson**

Additional Credits AARTPACK, Inc., Dan Breslin, Laura J. Chadwick, Liz Good, Russ Lappa, Ellen Levinger, Brent McKenzie, Laurel Smith, Emily Soltanoff, Linda B. Thornhill.

Illustration

Young Sook Cho: 476; **John Edwards, Inc.:** 61, 243, 267, 268, 269, 273, 279, 280, 293, 294-295, 297, 330, 343, 346, 348, 350, 358, 381, 407, 428, 465, 466, 470, 489, 490, 499, 519, 556, 603, 705; **Phil Guzy:** 307t, 308, 357, 360, 462, 503, 617; **Keith Kasnot:** 255, 256; **Fran Milner:** 245, 307b; **Morgan Cain and Associates:** 282t, 297tr, 555; **Ortelius Design, Inc.:** 566, 588; **Sandra Sevigny:** 283, 294l; **Tyson Smith:** 560-561. All additional art created by AARTPACK, Inc.

Photographs

Every effort has been made to secure permission and provide appropriate credit for photographic material. The publisher deeply regrets any omission and pledges to correct errors called to its attention in subsequent editions. Unless otherwise acknowledged, all photographs are the property of Pearson Education, Inc.

Photo locators denoted as follows: Top (T), Center (C), Bottom (B), Left (L), Right (R), Background (Bkgd)

Photo Research AARTPACK, Inc.

Front Cover–Bkgd Ben Welsh/Corbis; **TL** Yellowj/Shutterstock; **BL** Fuse/Thinkstock

Back Cover–T Tim Pannell/Corbis, **BL** siamionau pavel/Shutterstock

vT SW Productions/Photodisc/Getty Images; **viB** Ariel Skelley/cusp/Corbis; **viiB** David Bishop Inc./FoodPix/Getty Images; **viiiB** Markus Moellenberg/Cusp/Corbis; **ixBL** Michael Goldman/Masterfile; **ixBR** MedioImages/Photodisc/Getty Images; **ixT** Pete Saloutos/Cusp/Corbis; **xB** Jeff Greenberg/PhotoEdit; **xiB** IndexStock Imagery/ThinkStock; **xiiB** JonathanNourok/PhotoEdit; **xiv** J&L Images/Photodisc/Getty Images; **xviT** RubberBall Productions/Imagestate; **xviB** Imagestate-Pictor/PictureQuest; **xviiT** Creatix/Fotolia **xviii** Stockbyte/Thinkstock; **3B** Tetra Images/Corbis; **3L** Roy Morsch/Flirt/Corbis; **3T** FANCY/Image Source; **6** Brian Mueller/Shutterstock; **7B** Ryan McVay/Lifesize/Getty Images; **7C** Jeff Greenberg/The Image Works; **7T** Kaz Chiba/Digital Vision/Getty Images; **8L** Andersen Ross/Photodisc/Getty Images; **8R** Reza Estakhrian/Photographer's Choice/Getty Images; **9L** Keith Brofsky/Photodisc/Getty Images; **9R** Illene MacDonald/PhotoEdit; **10** Stephen Simpson/Taxi/Getty Images; **12** Brand X Pictures/PictureQuest; **13** Robert Rathe/Photographer's Choice/Getty Images; **14** CULTURA RF/Image Source; **15** Peter Hvizdak/The Image Works; **16B** ImageState Royalty Free/Alamy; **16TL** Davis Barber/PhotoEdit; **16TR** Comstock Images/Getty Images; **18** Felicia Martinez Photography/PhotoEdit; **19** Bonnie Kamin/PhotoEdit; **20** Michael N. Paras/Corbis; **22** Calvert Litho Co./Corbis; **23C** Stockbyte/Getty Images; **23T** Aaron Haupt/Science Source/Photo Researchers; **24** Comstock Images/Getty Images; **25** Stephen Simpson/Taxi/Getty Images; **28Bkgd** George Shelley/Masterfile; **30** Brand X Pictures/AGE Fotostock; **31L** BananaStock/PictureQuest; **31R** Fotosearch; **32B** Hinata Haga/HAGA/The Image Works; **32T** Thomas Wanstall/The Image Works; **33** Paul Chesley/Stone/Getty Images; **34CR** Masterfile; **34L** RubberBall Productions/Index Stock Imagery; **34R** Roy Morsch/Corbis; **34TL** Renata Osinska/Fotolia; **35B** Fancy/Image Source; **35L** RubberBall Productions/ImageState; **35TC** Bonninturina/Fotolia; **35TR** Image Source; **37** Timotheos/Shutterstock; **38** Roy Morsch/Flirt/Corbis; **39** Kathy McLaughlin/The Image Works; **40C** Stephen Simpson/The Image Bank/Getty Images; **40L** Masterfile; **40R** Monkey Business/Fotolia; **41C** Ernst Haas/Getty Images; **41L** Larry Kolvoord/The Image Works; **42** PhotoDisc/Getty Images; **44** Matthias Kulka/Corbis; **45BL** Blend Images/Getty Images; **45BR** RubberBall Productions/Index Stock Imagery; **45C** AGE Fotostock/SuperStock; **45T** Cultra RF/Image Source; **46L** Ariel Skelley/Cusp/Corbis; **46R** Rolf Bruderer/Masterfile; **47** Michael S. Yamashita/Terra/Corbis; **48** Exactostock/SuperStock; **49** Rubberball Productions; **50** Comstock RF Images/PictureQuest; **51B** Roy Morsch/Corbis; **51T** Thomas Wanstall/The Image Works; **54** Kaz Mori/The Image Bank/Getty Images; **56** BananaStock/Robertstock; **57** Paul Bradbury/Alamy; **58** Andersen Ross/Photodisc/Getty Images; **59** Jeff Greenberg/PhotoEdit; **61** Rubberball Productions/SuperStock; **62** Viennaphoto/AllOver photography/Alamy; **63** DieKleinert/SuperStock; **64** Tomas del Amo/Stock Connection Blue/Alamy; **65** Rubberball Productions; **66** Comstock RF Images/Getty Images; **67** SW Productions/Photodisc/Getty Images; **68** ImageSource/PictureQuest; **70** Michael Newman/PhotoEdit; **71** Tim Pannell/Corbis; **72** Corbis Super RF/Image Source; **73** Image Source; **74B** Zits Partnership. Reprinted with permission of King Features Syndicate.; **75** Corbis; **76** Blend Images/Alamy; **77B** Blend Images/Alamy; **77T** Paul Bradbury/Alamy; **80** BSIP SA/Alamy; **82** Brandon Sullivan/Masterfile; **83L** Heide Benser/Solus/Corbis; **83R** Nicholas Prior/Stone/Getty Images; **84** Bethlem Art and History Collections Trust; **84L** Josh Westrich/Bridge/Corbis; **84R** Corbis; **85** Shawn Baldwin/AP Images; **86** Bethlem Art and History Collections Trust; **87** Tony French/Alamy; **88** Mark Leibowitz/Masterfile; **89B** Kate Connell/The Image Bank/Getty Images; **89C** Mark Romesser/Alamy; **89T** Christopher A. Record/AP Images; **90B** Tony Freeman/PhotoEdit; **90T** Duncan Smith/Photodisc/Getty Images; **91** Tony Freeman/PhotoEdit; **92** William Sallaz/Duomo/Bridge/Corbis; **93** Donna Day/Stone/Getty Images; **95** SW Productions/Photodisc/Getty Images; **96** Tom Grill/Corbis; **97** Jack Hollingsworth/Corbis; **98** Richard Hutchings/Encyclopedia/Corbis; **99** Dwayne Newton/PhotoEdit; **100** Jim Parkin/Shutterstock; **101** Comstock RF Images/PictureQuest; **102** Comstock RF Images/AGE Fotostock; **103** Lisa F. Young/Fotolia; **104** Zigy Kaluzny/Stone/Getty Images; **105** Dwayne Newton/PhotoEdit; **108B** Simon Punter/Taxi/Getty Images; **108C** Bill Aron/PhotoEdit; **108T** Barros & Barros/The Image Bank/Getty Images; **109B** Courtesy of Kirsten Peterson; **109T** Courtesy of Kirsten Peterson; **110** Chris Robbins/Photodisc/Getty Images; **112** Dasha Petrenko/Shutterstock; **113** Betsie Van der Meer/The Image Bank/Getty Images; **114L** Monkey Business Images/Shutterstock; **114R** George Doyle/Stockbyte/Getty Images; **115L** Eastcott-Momatiuk/The Image Works; **115R** Fancy Collection/SuperStock; **116** Ted Foxx/Alamy; **117** ONOKY/Image Source; **118B** Jeffrey Sylvester/Taxi/Getty Images; **118BL** Maksym Yemelyanov/Alamy; **118CR** Anderson Ross/Photodisc/Getty Images; **118T** Andy Manis/AP Images; **119** Comstock RF Images/PictureQuest; **120** Myrleen Pearson/Alamy; **121** Rachel Epstein/PhotoEdit; **122** Chitose Suzuki/AP Images; **123** Richard Heinzen/SuperStock; **124** Tony Freeman/PhotoEdit; **126** Eastcott/Momatiuk/The Image Works; **127** PhotoDisc/Getty Images; **128** Paul Barton/Cusp/Corbis; **130** Michael Newman/PhotoEdit; **131B** Myrleen Pearson/Alamy; **131T** Monkey Business Images/Shutterstock; **134** Michael Pole/Bridge/Corbis; **136** Big Cheese Photo LLC/Alamy; **137** Ariel Skelley/Cusp/Corbis; **138** Cindy Charles/PhotoEdit; **139** Jeff Greenberg/PhotoEdit; **140** Michael Newman/PhotoEdit; **141** Michael N. Paras/AGE Fotostock; **141** Michael N. Paras/AGE Fotostock; **142** James McLoughlin/AGE Fotostock; **143** Pictorial Press Ltd/Alamy; **144T** Zits Partnership. Reprinted with permission of King Features Syndicate.; **145** Roxana Gonzalez/Shutterstock; **146** Mngostock/Fotolia; **148** Jeff Greenberg/AGE Fotostock; **149** Chuck Savage/Corbis; **150** Brad Wilson/The Image Bank/Getty Images; **153** Jacky Chapman/Janine Wiedel Photolibrary/Alamy; **154** Loretta Ray/Photonica/Getty Images; **155** Claudiu Paizan/Fotolia; **156** SW Productions/PhotoDisc/Getty Images; **157B** Chuck Savage/Flirt/Corbis; **162** Gurinder Osan/AP Images; **162** Comstock RF Images/Alamy; **164** SuperStock; **165** Photononstop/SuperStock; **166** Mario Villafuerte/Stringer/Getty Images; **167** Gilles Mingasson/Liaison/Getty Images; **169** PhotoAlto/Robertstock; **170L** C Squared Studios/Photodisc/Getty Images; **170T** Jim Mahoney/Dallas Morning News/Corbis; **171** Ania Powalowska/Agencja Free/AGE Fotostock; **172** Ariel Skelley/Corbis; **173** Tony Freeman/PhotoEdit; **174** Flying Colours Ltd/Digital Vision/Getty Images; **175** Thinkstock/IndexStock Imagery; **176** Yavuz Arslan/Christoph & Friends/Das Fotoarchiv/Alamy; **177** Bill Aron/PhotoEdit; **178B** Rubberball Productions; **178TL** Rubberball Productions; **178TR** PhotoDisc/Getty Images; **181** Corbis; **182L** Luke Jarvis/Corbis; **182R** BananaStock/Robertstock; **183** SW Productions/Photodisc/Getty Images; **184** Richard Lord/The Image Works; **185** Thinkstock/Comstock Images/Getty Images; **185T** Gilles Mingasson/Liaison/Getty Images; **188** Richard G. Bingham II/Alamy; **189L** Blend Images/Getty Images; **189R** Julia Smith/Taxi/Getty Images; **190Bkgd** G. Biss/Masterfile; **192** SW Productions/Photodisc/Getty Images; **193B** Tom Grill/Corbis; **193C** FoodPix/Jupiter Images; **193TL** Tom Grill/Corbis; **193TR** Comstock Images/Getty Images; **194BL** Photodisc/Getty Images; **194C** John E Kelly/FoodPix/Getty Images; **194R** Judd Pilossof/Getty Images; **195L** Comstock Images/Getty Images; **195R** Pixland/AGE Fotostock; **196BR** Margo555/Fotolia; **196C** Evan Sklar/FoodPix/Getty Images; **196L** Comstock Images/Getty Images; **197** Jiri Hera/Fotolia; **198** Andersen Ross/Photodisc/Getty Images; **199** David Bishop Inc./FoodPix/Getty Images; **202B**

Comstock Images/Getty Images; **202T** Brian Hagiwara/FoodPix/Getty Images; **203B** Burke/Triolo Productions/FoodPix/Getty Images; **203T** Comstock Images/Getty Images; **204B** Africa Studio/Fotolia; **204TL** Comstock Images/Getty Images; **204TR** Clive Streeter/DK Images; **205** Steve Warmowski/Journal-Courier/The Image Works; **206** RubberBall/SuperStock; **207B** Comstock Images/Getty Images; **207C** Jiri Hera/Fotolia; **207TC** Comstock Images/Getty Images; **207TL** Brand X Pictures/Jupiter Images; **207TR** Comstock Images/Getty Images; **208** Matthew Borkoski Photography/Photolibrary/Getty Images; **209** Michael Newman/PhotoEdit; **210** Bob Pardue Signs/Alamy; **211** Pixtal/AGE Fotostock; **212T** U.S. Department of Agriculture; **212BL** Hyrma/Fotolia; **212BR** Cristina Cassinelli/FoodPix/Getty Images; **212CBL** Comstock Images/Getty Images; **212CBR** Elena Schweitzer/Shutterstock; **212CTL** Lew Robertson/FoodPix/Getty Images; **212CTR** Comstock Images/Getty Images; **214** Stockbyte/PictureQuest; **215B** Pixtal/AGE Fotostock; **215T** FoodPix/Jupiter Images; **218** RubberBall/Superstock; **220** Michael Newman/PhotoEdit; **221** Comstock RF Images/PictureQuest; **222BR** Comstock Images/Getty Images; **222C** Jonathan Nourok/PhotoEdit; **222T** Frank Ordo–ez/Syracuse Newspapers/The Image Works; **223** Image100 Food A/Corbis Premium RF/Alamy; **223B** Brand X Pictures/PictureQuest; **224B** John A. Rizzo/Photodisc/Getty Images; **224T** Michael Neelon(misc)/Alamy; **226** Seth Goldfarb/Photonica/Getty Images; **228B** Rubberball Productions; **228L** Michael Pohuski/FoodPix/Getty Images; **228TR** BrandX Pictures/Getty Images; **229** Karan Kapoor/Stone/Getty Images; **230** Peter Dazeley/Photographer's Choice/Getty Images; **231** Mark Harmel/Alamy; **232C** Foodcollection/Getty Images; **232L** Evan Hoffbuhr/Fotolia; **232R** Sergejs Rahunoks/Fotolia; **233** BananaStock/Fotosearch; **234** Foodpix/Jupiter Images; **235B** Comstock Images/Getty Images; **235L** Comstock Images/Getty Images; **235R** Comstock Images/Getty Images; **236** Jeff Greenberg/PhotoEdit; **237B** BananaStock/Fotosearch; **237C** Mark Harmel/Alamy; **237T** Frank Ordo–ez/Syracuse Newspapers/The Image Works; **240** Blend Images/Image Source; **242** Sergey Peterman/Fotolia; **245BR** Prof. P.M. Motta/Dept. of Anatomy/University "La Sapienza", Rome/Science Source/Photo Researchers; **246** CNRI/Science Source/Photo Researchers; **247BL** AJPhoto/Science Source/Photo Researchers; **247BR** David M. Martin, Md/Science Source/Photo Researchers; **247RC** David M. Martin,MD/Science Source/Photo Researchers; **247RT** David M. Martin, Md/Science Source/Photo Researchers; **247T** Andy Crump/Science Source/Photo Researchers; **248** Corbis; **249B** CNRI/Science Source/Photo Researchers; **249C** Comstock Images/Getty Images; **249T** Comstock Images/Getty Images; **250BL** Steve Wisbauer/Getty Images; **250L** Jim Arbogast/Digital Vision/Getty Images; **250TR** Michael Newman/PhotoEdit; **251B** J.L. Carson/Custom Medical Stock Photo; **251T** Jules Frazier/Photodisc/Getty Images; **252** India Images/Dinodia Images/Alamy; **254** Gary Houlder/Bridge/Corbis; **257** Photolibrary/IndexStock Imagery; **258** AJPhoto/Science Source/Photo Researchers; **259** Image Source/Getty Images; **259C** PhotoDisc/Getty Images; **259T** CNRI/Science Source/Photo Researchers; **262B** Tom Carter/PhotoEdit; **262T** Dan Hallman/Photodisc/Getty Images; **263CL** Shioguchi/Taxi/Getty Images; **263R** Inti St. Clair/Photodisc/Getty Images; **264** Aflo Sport/Glow Images; **266** Darrin Henry/Fotolia; **269** RubberBall Productions/Alamy; **270C** BSIP/SuperStock; **270L** David Madison/Getty Images; **270R** BSIP/SuperStock; **271** Ted Horowitz/Cusp/Corbis; **272** Pablo Rivera/SuperStock; **274L** Ron Buskirk/Alamy; **274R** Corbis; **275** Richard Hutchings/PhotoEdit; **281** Stockbyte/SuperStock; **282L** Thomas Del Brase/Stone/Getty Images; **284** Aflo Foto Agency/Alamy; **285L** Steve Krongard/Stone/Getty Images; **285R** Hill Street Studios/Blend Images/Alamy; **286B** Charing Cross Hospital/Science Source; **287B** Steve Krongard/Stone/Getty Images; **287C** Richard Hutchings/PhotoEdit; **287T** BSIP/SuperStock; **290** Richard I'Anson/Lonely Planet Images/Getty Images; **296** Pictor International/ImageState/Alamy; **297B** National Cancer Institute/Science Source/Photo Researchers; **297C** A. Syred/Science Source/Photo Researchers; **297CR** Bill Longcore/Science Source/Photo Researchers; **298** Davies and Starr/Stone/Getty Images; **299** William Whitehurst/Corbis; **300BC** Stewart Cohen/DreamPictures/FoodPix/Getty Images; **300BL** Lew Robertson/Foodpix/Getty Images; **300BR** Repository/Fotolia; **300TL** FoodCollection/SuperStock; **300TR** Mates/Fotolia; **301** Volff/Fotolia; **302** David Stoecklein/Cusp/Corbis; **303** Amber Aiken Photography/Flickr Open/Getty Images; **304** Saxpix/AGE Fotostock; **307L** Daghlian/Phanie/SuperStock; SciMAT/Science Source/Photo Researchers; **309R** Stockbyte/PictureQuest; **310** Andres Rodriguez/Fotolia; **311B** Stewart Cohen/DreamPictures/FoodPix/Getty Images; **314** Nirmalendu Majumdar/AP Images; **316** Rubberball Productions; **317** Howard Grey/Photodisc/Getty Images; **318** Bob Daemmrich/The Image Works; **319B** Alin Dragulin/Alamy; **319BC** Tom Stewart/keepsake RM/Corbis; **319BL** Reed Kaestner/Corbis; **319BR** Michael Newman/PhotoEdit; **319CBL** Scott Markewitz/Taxi/Getty Images; **319CTL** Image Source; **319CTR** Markus Moellenberg/Corbis; **319T** Yoichi Nagata/Getty Images; **320L** Pete Saloutos/Cusp/Corbis; **320R** Alexander Hubrich/Stone/Getty Images; **321C** Tom & Dee Ann McCarthy/Bridge/Corbis; **321L** Inspirestock Inc./Alamy; **321R** Guy Cali/Corbis; **325BL** John Henley/Cusp/Corbis; **325BR** Adam smith/Taxi/Getty Images; **325CR** Andersen Ross/Blend Images/Getty Images; **326** Jeff Greenberg/Alamy; **327B** Bonnie Kamin/PhotoEdit; **330** MichaelSvoboda/E+/Getty Images; **331** PhotoDisc/Getty Images; **332** Peter Cade/Iconica/Getty Images; **333** Belinda Images/SuperStock; **334** Courtesy of The National Institute on Drug Abuse (NIDA); **336B** Jeff Greenberg/PhotoEdit; **336T** Siu Biomed Comm/Custom Medical Stock; **337B** Belinda Images/SuperStock; **337C** John Henley/Cusp/Corbis; **337T** Pete Saloutos/Cusp/Corbis; **340** Ralph A.Clevenger/Bridge/Corbis Images; **342** Sakuoka/Shutterstock; **344BL** Andersen Ross/Stockbyte/Getty images; **344R** Luis Santos/Fotolia; **346** Comstock RF Images/AGE Fotostock; **347** Felicia Martinez Photography/PhotoEdit; **349B** NMSB/Custom Medical Stock; **349T** Jutta Klee/Corbis; **350** Image Source/SuperStock; **351B** Chris Garrett/Stone/Getty Images; **351T** Eye of Science/Science Source/Photo Researchers; **352** Jessie Jean/Taxi/Getty Images; **353** Andreas Kuehn/Stone/Getty Images; **354** Norma Zuniga/Stone+/Getty Images; **356** IndexStock Imagery/ThinkStock; **358** Comstock Images/Fotosearch; **359** Rachel Epstein/The Image Works; **361** EpicStockMedia/Fotolia; **362B** Reed Kaestner/Bridge/Corbis; **362CB** Siede Preis/Photodisc/Getty Images; **362CL** GK Hart/Vicky Hart/The Image Bank/Getty Images; **362CR** DWP/Fotolia; **362TL** Regine Mahaux/The Image Bank/Getty Images; **362TR** Alan Schein/Cusp/CORBIS; **363** Eliseo Fernandez/Reuters/Corbis; **364** MedioImages/Photodisc/Getty Images; **365** Michael Goldman/Masterfile; **366** Zurijeta/Shutterstock; **367** Jessie Jean/Taxi/Getty Images; **370B** Guy Cali/Corbis; **370C** Dynamic Graphics/PIctureQuest; **370T** CULTURA RF/Image Source; **371B** Courtesy of Teodoro Tovar, Jr.; **371T** Courtesy of Teodoro Tovar, Jr; **372** Mike Siluk/The Image Works; **374** Bananastock/Imagestate; **375C** C Squared Studios/Photodisc/Getty Images; **375L** Comstock RF Images/PictureQuest; **375R** David Toase/Stockbyte/Getty Images; **376** Ryan McVay/Photodisc/Getty Images; **377** Ted Foxx/Alamy; **378** Ted Foxx/Alamy; **382** Photos/Index Stock Imagery; **383** Thinkstock/Alamy; **384** Masterfile; **385** Nick Dolding/Stone/Getty Images; **386** Reuters/Corbis; **387B** Martin M. Rotker/Science Source/Photo Researchers; **387C** Southern Illinois University/Science Source/Photo Researchers; **387T** David H. Wells/Corbis; **388L** Dr. Susan Tapert, University of California San Diego and National Institute on Alcohol Abuse and Alcoholism; **388R** Dr. Susan Tapert, University of California San Diego and National Institute on Alcohol Abuse and Alcoholism; **390** Tom & Dee Ann McCarthy/Cusp/Corbis; **391** GARO/PHANIE/AGE Fotostock; **392** WavebreakMediaMicro/Fotolia; **393** SW Productions/Photodisc/Getty Images; **394** Steve Dunwell/Photo Library/Getty Images; **395** Ted Foxx/Alamy; **398** Robert Mora/Staff/Getty Images; **401BL** AGE Fotostock/SuperStock; **401BR** BananaStock/SuperStock; **401TR** Universal/Everett Collection; **402** Photodisc/Fotosearch; **404** Robert Landau/Corbis; **406** PhotoAlto/SuperStock; **408BL** P.Stocklein/Custom Medical Stock Photo; **408BR** 1988 Paul Silverman/Fundamental Photographs, NYC; **408CL** Brand X Pictures/Fotosearch; **408CR** G.DeGrazia/Custom Medical Stock Photo; **408TL** Clayton Sharrard/PhotoEdit; **408TR** Comstock Images/Fotosearch; **409** Courtesy National Institutes of Health; **409** Science Source/Photo Researchers; **410** Luca DiCecco/Alamy; **411** Mel Allen/Imagestate; **413C** Siu Biomed Comm/Custom Medical Stock Photo; **413T** Matt Meadows/Peter Arnold/Getty Images; **414** Sonda Dawes/The Image Works; **415** Scholastic Studio 10 /Photolibrary/Getty Images; **416** Stockbyte Platinum/Alamy; **416B** James Leynse/Corbis News/Corbis; **417** Fotosearch/Corbis; **418B** Rubberball Productions/SuperStock; **418T** Photodisc/Getty Images; **419B** Brian Hagiwara/FoodPix/Getty Images; **419T** RubberBall Productions/IndexStock Imagery; **420B** Martyn Vickery/Alamy; **420T** Doug Martin/Science Source/Photo Researchers; **421B** Photodisc/Fotosearch; **421T** Universal/Everett Collection; **424** Peter Byron/PhotoEdit; **426** Photick/SuperStock; **427** Stephen Mcsweeny/Shutterstock; **429** Mast3r/Fotolia; **430** Brand X Pictures/Getty Images; **431** Brand X Pictures/Imagestate; **432** Steve Warmowski/Journal-Courier/The Image Works; **433B** Science Source/Photo Researchers; **433Bkgd** David De Lossy/Photodisc/Getty Images; **433CB** L. Reneman, J. Habraken, C. Majoie, J. Booij, G. den Heeten, MDMA ("Ecstasy") and Its Association with Cerebrovascular Accidents: Preliminary Findings, American Journal of Nueroradiology, Figure 2, Volume 21, pages 1001-1007, 2000 © by American Journal of Nueroradiology; **433CT** NATIONAL CANCER INSTITUTE/Science Source/Photo Researchers; **433T** Imagestate-Pictor/PictureQuest; **435** Luke Jarvis/Cusp/Corbis; **436** David Grossman/The Image Works; **437** Fotosearch; **438** Thinkstock/Comstock Images/Getty Images; **441** Marga Werner/AGE Fotostock; **442B** Shahn Kermani/Liaison/Getty Images; **442T** Cordelia Molloy/Science Source/Photo Researchers; **443** GeoStock/Photodisc/Getty Images; **444B** Custom Medical Stock Photo; **444C** Bonnie Kamin/PhotoEdit; **444T** Custom Medical Stock Photo; **445** Bartomeu Borrell/AGE Fotostock; **446** Andrew Brookes/Bridge/Corbis; **447** Tony Freeman/PhotoEdit; **448** Michele Cozzolino/Shutterstock; **449** Jeff Greenberg/PhotoEdit; **450L** Michael Newman/PhotoEdit; **450R** Jeff Greenberg/The Image Works; **452** Image Source; **453** Fotosearch; **456B** Banana Stock/Alamy; **456T** Jim Varney/Photo Researchers; **457C** Norma Zuniga/Stone+/Getty Images; **457R** Norma Zuniga/Riser/Getty Images; **458** Stewart Cohen/Taxi/Getty Images; **461C** Stockbyte Silver/Alamy; **461L** Jeremy Maude/Masterfile; **461R** AGE Fotostock/SuperStock; **464** Sartore/Joel/National Geographic/Getty Images; **466B** David M. Phillips/Science Source/Photo Researchers; **467** Suzanne Dunn/Syracuse Newspapers/The Image Works; **468** Aaron Haupt/Science Source/Photo Researchers; **469** Photodisc/Getty Images; **471** RubberBall Productions/Imagestate; **473** Thinkstock/Comstock/JupiterImages; **474** Subbotina Anna/Fotolia; **475B** Robynmac/Fotolia; **475T** Pete Saloutos/Bridge/Corbis; **477** BURGER/PHANIE/AGE Fotostock; **478BL** Tatjana Romanova/Shutterstock; **478BR** Vladimir Voronin/Fotolia; **478TR** Muntz/Getty Images; **479** Thinkstock/Comstock/JupiterImages; **480B** Stockbyte/fotosearch; **480T** Sebastian Kaulitzki/Fotolia; **481** Masterfile; **482** Ted Horowitz/Flirt/Corbis; **483** Stockbyte Silver/Alamy; **486** Martinan/Fotolia; **488** Michael Newman/PhotoEdit; **491B** Petit Format/Science Source/Photo Researchers; **491T** Claude Edelmann/Science Source/Photo Researchers; **492CB** Siede Preis/Photodisc/Getty Images; **493** Brand X Pictures/PictureQuest; **494L** Thinkstock/Getty Images; **494R** BananaStock/PictureQuest; **495R** Gary Bistram/Getty Images; **497CL** ATC Productions/Bridge/CORBIS; **497R** Jeremy Portje/Telegraph Herald/AP Images; **499** Robin Samper/Pearson education; **501** BSIP/Universal Images Group/Getty Images; **502** David J. Green-lifestyle themes/Alamy; **503L** David Schmidt/Masterfile; **503R** Tony Freeman/PhotoEdit; **504** Brand X Pictures/PictureQuest; **506B** Creasource/PictureQuest; **506T** Bananastock/Imagestate; **507C**

Acknowledgments

Fabrizio Cacciatore/Indexstock/PictureQuest; 507L Brand X Pictures/Robertstock; 507R Steve Gravano/AGE Fotostock; 508 Wavebreak Media/Thinkstock; 509B Creasource/PictureQuest; 509T Claude Edelmann/Science Source/Photo Researchers; 512 Spencer Grant/Science Source/Photo Researchers; 514 Egidia Degrassi/Fotolia; 515R Comstock RF Images/PictureQuest; 516L Tim Jones/Digital Vision/Getty Images; 516R Bill Bachmann/Alamy; 517 Bananastock/Imagestate; 519BL Rubberball Productions/AGE Fotostock; 519BR Leland Bobbe/Flirt/Corbis; 519TL Ariel Skelley/Corbis; 519TR Gary Conner/Photolibrary/Getty Images; 520 Michael Keller/Flirt/Corbis; 521 Ron Chapple Stock/Alamy; 522 SW Productions/Photodisc/Getty Images; 524 Don Smetzer/PhotoEdit; 525B Zits Partnership. Reprinted with permission of King Features Syndicate; 526L Philippe Lissac/Godong/Photononstop/Getty Images; 526R Jeff Greenberg/PhotoEdit; 527 Ray Guy/Alamy; 528 Eric Raptosh/Hill Street Studios/Blend Images/Getty Images; 530 Brad Wrobleski/Masterfile; 531 Karen Grigoryan/Shutterstock; 532 Reed Kaestner/Corbis; 533 Nick Dolding/Stone/Getty Images; 534 IndexStock Imagery/ThinkStock; 536 Monkey Business/Fotolia; 537 EPF/Alamy; 538 Spencer Grant/PhotoEdit; 539BR David Samuel Robbins/Encyclopedia/Corbis; 539L Joe Raedle/Staff/Getty Images; 539T Andrew Lichtenstein/Corbis News Premium/Corbis; 540 Dynamic Graphics Group/IT Stock Free/Alamy; 541B Karen Grigoryan/Shutterstock; 541T Egidia Degrassi/Fotolia; 544B Hero/Corbis; 544C Carl Costas/ZUMAPRESS/Newscom; 544T Romilly Lockyer/The Image Bank/Getty Images; 545B John Robertson/Alamy; 545T Rebecca Emery/Digital Vision/Getty Images; 546 Center for Disease Control and Prevention; 548 Brand X Pictures/Getty Images; 549CL Cavallini/Custom Medical Stock Photo; 549CR Eye of Science/Science Source/Photo Researchers; 549L Dr. Gary Gaugler/Science Source/Photo Researchers; 549R Eye of Science/Science Source/Photo Researchers; 550B Doug Menuez/PhotoDisc/Getty Images; 550C Siede Preis/Photodisc/Getty Images; 550T Bartomeu Amengual/AGE Fotostock; 551 Michael Alberstat/Masterfile; 552 Fotosearch; 553L Eye of Science/Science Source/Photo Researchers; 553R Wavebreakmedia/Shutterstock; 554 SPL/Science Source/Photo Researchers; 556R It Stock Free/PictureQuest; 557C Myrleen Pearson/PhotoEdit; 557L Purestock/SuperStock; 557R Randy Faris/Cusp/Corbis; 559L Larry Mulvehill/Science Source/Photo Researchers; 559R K. Kjeldsen/Science Source/Photo Researchers; 560 Aaron Haupt/Science Source/Photo Researchers; 562 B. BOISSONNET/BSIP SA/Alamy; 563 Corbis; 564 Exactostock/SuperStock; 567B CDC/PHIL/CORBIS; 567T Robert Dowling/Terra/Corbis; 568 Pallava Bagla/Corbis News/Corbis; 569B CDC/PHIL/CORBIS; 569T Dr. Gary Gaugler/Science Source/Photo Researchers; 572 Cindy Charles/PhotoEdit; 574 BananaStock/SuperStock; 575 Bob Daemmrich/The Image Works; 576B Brand X Pictures/Fotosearch; 576T Will Hart/PhotoEdit; 577 Roy Morsch/Corbis; 578 Marmaduke St. John/Alamy; 579C NIH/Custom Medical Stock; 579L Eye of Science/Science Source/Photo Researchers; 579R Alfred Pasieka/Science Source/Photo Researchers; 580B Slate River Productions/Alamy; 580L Meredun Animal Health Ltd/Science Source/Photo Researchers; 581B Eye of Science/Science Source/Photo Researchers; 581T David M. Phillips/Science Source/Photo Researchers; 582R Library of Congress; 582TL Martin M. Rotker/Science Source/Photo Researchers; 582TR Dr. Kari Lounatmaa/Science Source/Photo Researchers; 583 ColorBlind Images/Blend Images/Corbis; 584 Hemera Technologies/Alamy; 585T NIBSC/Science Source/Photo Researchers; 587 Lawrence Manning/Corbis; 588 GlowImages/Alamy; 589 Sean Sprague/The Image Works; 590B Center for Disease Control and Prevention; 590T Bartomeu Amengual/Photo Library/Getty Images; 592 E Dygas/Taxi/Getty Images; 593 Guy Cali/Corbis; 594L Klaus Guldbrandsen/Science Source/Photo Researchers; 594R Rachel Frank/Fancy/Alamy; 595 Michael Newman/PhotoEdit; 596 Michael Dwyer/AP Images; 597B Hemera Technologies/Alamy; 597T Marmaduke St. John/Alamy; 600 Jim West/Alamy; 602 Ocean/Corbis; 603L Custom Medical Stock Photo; 603R Custom Medical Stock Photo; 604 Bruce Ayres/Stone/Getty Images; 605 Du Cane Medical Imaging Ltd./Science Source/Photo Researchers; 606BL Mehau Kulyk/Science Source/Photo Researchers; 606BR UHB Trust/Stone/Getty Images; 606TC Bruce Ayres/Stone/Getty Images; 606TL GJLP/Science Source/Photo Researchers; 606TR SPL/Science Source/Photo Researchers; 607 Rob Van Petten/Digital Vision/Getty Images; 608 Tom Carter/PhotoEdit; 610 Via Productions/AGE Fotostock; 611 Miles Ertman/Masterfile; 611B Paul/F1online digitale Bildagentur GmbH/Alamy; 611T Dr. P. Marazzi/Science Source/Photo Researchers; 614 Jason Hetherington/Getty Images; 615 AGE Fotostock/SuperStock; 616BL GK Hart/Vikki Hart/Phototdisc/Getty Images; 616BR Blickwinkel/Alamy; 616TL A. Syred/Science Source/Photo Researchers; 616TR A. Syred/Science Source/Photo Researchers; 617L James Cavallini/Science Source/Photo Researchers; 617R Bill Aron/PhotoEdit; 618 Corbis; 618T Living Art Enterprises/LLC/Science Source/Photo Researchers; 619 Philippe Sellem/Paul Demri/Olivier Voisin/Science Source/Photo Researchers; 620 Kayte Deioma/PhotoEdit; 622BL Jiang Jin/SuperStock; 622C Troels Graugaard/E+/Getty Images; 622CB Masterfile; 622T Royal Philips ElectronicsAP Images; 623 Richard Hutchings/PhotoEdit; 624L Jonathan Nourok/PhotoEdit; 624R Myrleen Pearson/PhotoEdit; 625 Stephen Simpson/Taxi/Getty Images; 626 Steve Dunwell/Photolibrary/Getty Images; 627B Productions/AGE Fotostock; 627T Custom Medical Stock Photo; 630 Tipp Howell/Getty Images; 631C Stephen Derr/The Image Bank/Getty Images; 631R Yellow Dog Productions/The Image Bank/Getty Images; 632 Scott Warren/Aurora Photos; 634 Exactostock/SuperStock; 635BL Bob Daemmrich/The Image Works; 635BR John Henley/Cusp/Corbis; 635CL Keith Brofsky/Photodisc/Getty Images; 635CR Rick Gomez/Corbis; 635TC AJPhoto/Science Source/Photo Researchers; 635TL Peter Beck/keepsake RM/Corbis; 635TR K.Glaser & Associates/Custom Medical Stock Photo; 636BL Jan Kassay/Photo Library/Getty Images; 636BR Tim Sharp/AP Images; 636T Lifesize/Getty Images; 637 Ingram Image/PictureQuest; 638 Edward McCain/Getty Images; 639 Ronnie Kaufman/Bridge/Corbis; 640 Ed Kashi/Corbis; 641 Ragnar Schmuck/zefa/Corbis; 643 Michael A. Keller/AGE Fotostock; 644 William Whitehurst/Corbis; 645 BLEND IMAGES/Image Source; 646 Gary Kazanjian/AP Images; 647B Big Cheese Photo/SuperStock; 647T ThinkStock/AGE Fotostock; 648 L.Steinmark/Custom Medical Stock Photo; 649B Bettmann/Corbis; 649T Bill Bridges/Time & Life Pictures/Getty Images; 650 A. Ramey/PhotoEdit; 651 Richard T. Nowitz/Terra/Corbis; 652 Syracuse Newspapers/The Image Works; 653 Corbis; 654 Holly Harris/Taxi/Getty Images; 655 Yellow Dog Productions/The Image Bank/Getty Images; 657L Paula Bronstein/Staff/Getty Images; 657R Yves Herman/Reuters/Corbis; 658 Super Stock/AGE Fotostock; 659B Syracuse Newspapers/The Image Works; 659T Big Cheese Photo/SuperStock; 662 Phil Schermeister/Encyclopedia/Corbis; 664T Jeff Greenberg/PhotoEdit; 665B Ryan McVay/Photodisc/Getty Images; 665Bkgd Brand X Pictures/Jupiter Images; 665C Donna Day/Imagestate; 665T Jeff Greenberg/The Image Works; 666B Myrleen Pearson/PhotoEdit; 666TL Johnny Crawford/The Image Works; 666TR Bonnie Kamin/PhotoEdit; 667 Imageshop-zefa visual media uk ltd/Alamy; 668 Tibor Bognár/AGE Fotostock; 669 Jeff Greenberg/PhotoEdit; 670 Jim Craigmyle/Corbis; 671B Brand X Pictures/AGE Fotostock; 671T C Squared Studios/Photodisc/Getty Images; 672 StockDisc/PictureQuest; 673 Reed Saxon/AP Images; 674 Brand X Pictures/Alamy; 675 Tomas Abad/Alamy; 676 Photodisc/Getty Images; 677 Somos Images/Alamy; 678L Masterfile; 678R Dana White/PhotoEdit; 679B Jeff Greenberg/PhotoEdit; 680 Philip Wallick/Flirt/Corbis; 681T BrandX Pictures/Getty Images; 682 Tony Freeman/PhotoEdit; 683 Peter Essick/Aurora Photos; 685Bkgd Spencer Grant/PhotoEdit; 685L Jeff Greenberg/PhotoEdit; 685R Jeff Greenberg/PhotoEdit; 686 Michael Newman/PhotoEdit; 687B Ariel Skelley/Comet/Corbis; 687T Tony Freeman/PhotoEdit; 688 Bob Daemmrich/The Image Works; 689B Ariel Skelley/Comet/Corbis; 689T Myrleen Pearson/PhotoEdit; 692 Chase Jarvis/Solus/Corbis; 694 Steve Skjold/Alamy; 695 Jiang Jin/SuperStock; 696 Dana White/PhotoEdit; 697 Eric Fowke/PhotoEdit; 698L NOAA/Handout/ZUMA/Corbis; 698R Mike Theiss/orbis News/Ultimate Chase/Corbis; 699L Rob Carr/AP Images; 699R James Nielsen/Stringer/AFP/Getty Images; 700 Marc Romanelli/Photographer's Choice/Getty Images; 702 Photodisc/Getty Images; 703 Little Blue Wolf Productions/Corbis; 704 Yellow Dog Productions/The Image Bank/Getty Images; 706 Ben Blankenburg/Corbis; 707 Dominic Ebenbichler/Reuters/Corbis; 708B Glyn Jones/Corbis; 708BR Rubberball Productions/Imagestate; 708C Nils-Johan Norenlind/AGE Fotostock; 708TL Mike Powell/Digital Vision/Getty Images; 708TR Brian Sytnyk/Masterfile; 710 J&L Images/Photodisc/Getty Images; 711 Comstock Images/Fotosearch; 713 Robert Llewellyn/Corbis; 714 Exactostock/SuperStock; 715 AGE Fotostock/SuperStock; 716B DK Images; 716T Nicholas Eveleigh/Alamy; 717B Robert Llewellyn/Flirt/Corbis; 717C Nils-Johan Norenlind/AGE Fotostock; 717T NOAA/Handout/ZUMA/Corbis; 720B Tyler Olson/Shutterstock; 720C Zhu Difeng/Fotolia; 720T Dynamic Graphics/LiquidLibrary/PictureQuest; 721B Mischa Keijser/Cultura Creative/Alamy; 721T Will & Deni McIntyre/Science Source/Photo Researchers; 722B DK Images; 722T Tom Stewart/Bridge/Corbis; 723 DK Images; 723B DK Images; 724BC DK Images; 724BL DK Images; 724BR Michael Newman/PhotoEdit; 724T DK Images; 725B DK Images; 725T DK Images; 726C DK Images; 726T Michael Newman/PhotoEdit; 727B DK Images; 727C DK Images; 727TL DK Images; 727TR DK Images; 728B The American National Red Cross; 728C Biophoto Associates/Science Source/Photo Researchers; 728T Bob Daemmrich/The Image Works; 729 Tim Ridley/DK Images; 730B DK Images; 730T DK Images; 731BL The American National Red Cross; 731BR The American National Red Cross; 731T DK Images; 732BL DK Images; 732BR Brian Kuhlmann/Masterfile; 732C It Stock Free Royalty Free Photograph/Fotosearch; 732T J.Patton/Robertstock; 733BL John Millar/Stone/Getty Images; 733BR DK Images; 734B DK Images; 734T DK Images; 735B David H. Collier/Workbook Stock/Getty Images; 735T DK Images; 737 Michelle Del Guercio/Custom Medical Stock Photo/Newscom